The age of the
GALLEY

This edition
is limited to
2000 copies
of which this is
No. 1378.

The age of the
GALLEY

Mediterranean Oared Vessels since pre-classical Times

Editor: Robert Gardiner

Consultant Editor: Professor John Morrison

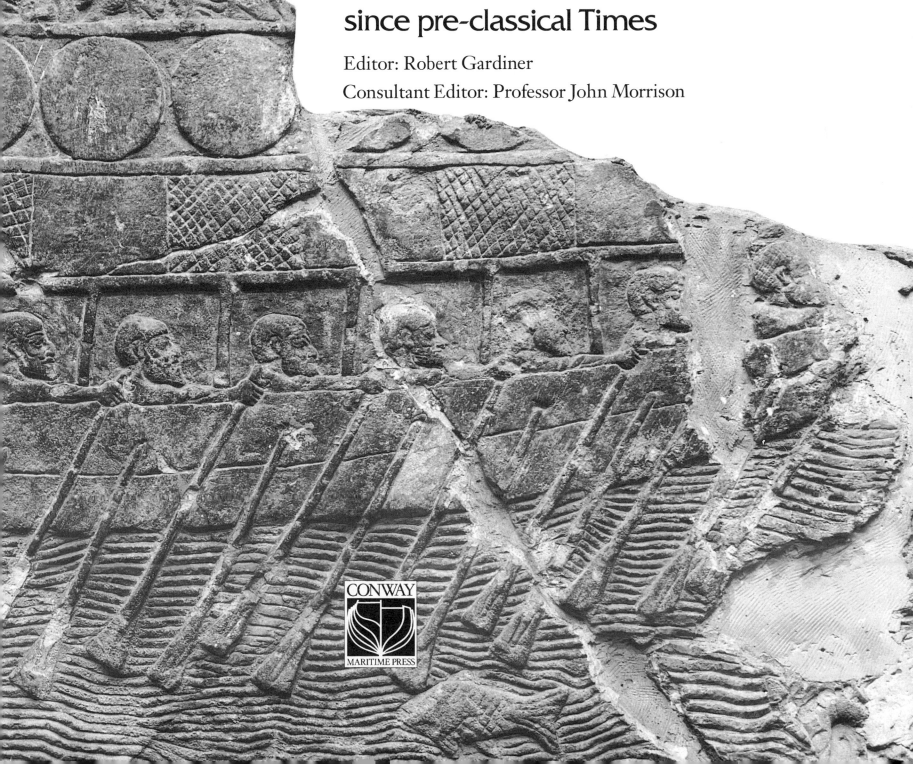

CONWAY
MARITIME PRESS

Series Consultant	DR BASIL GREENHILL CB, CMG, FSA, FRHistS
Series Editor	ROBERT GARDINER
Consultant Editor	PROFESSOR JOHN MORRISON
Contributors	ULRICH ALERTZ DAVID BLACKMAN MAURO BONDIOLI RENÉ BURLET LIONEL CASSON JOHN COATES JOHN E DOTSON VINCENT GABRIELSEN FREDERICK M HOCKER JOHN MORRISON JOHN H PRYOR BORIS RANKOV J TIMOTHY SHAW SHELLEY WACHSMANN HERMAN WALLINGA ANDRÉ ZYSBERG

Frontispiece: One of the earliest depictions of Mediterranean oared vessels, part of the famous frieze from the palace of Sennacherib at Nineveh. The vessels are Phoenician and have been interpreted as the evacuation of the coastal cities by king Lulî in 702 BC, in the face of Assyrian attack, employing both warships and oared merchantmen. (The British Museum)

© Brassey's (UK) Ltd 1995

This limited edition first published in Great Britain 1995 by Conway Maritime Press, an imprint of Brassey's UK Ltd 33 John Street, London WC1N 2AT

ISBN 0 85177 634 5

Translations of Chapter 10 (from German) by Keith Thomas, and of Chapter 12 (from Italian) by Juliet Haydock (and from French) by Christine Wood and Linda Jones

Designed by Tony Hart
Typeset by Dorwyn Ltd, Rowlands Castle, Hants
Printed and bound by The Bath Press, Bath

Contents

Preface

THIS TITLE is the tenth in an ambitious programme of twelve volumes intended to provide the first detailed and comprehensive account of a technology that has shaped human history. It has been conceived as a basic reference work, the essential first stop for anyone seeking information on any aspect of the subject, so it is more concerned to be complete than to be original. However, the series takes full account of all the latest research and in certain areas will be publishing entirely new material. In the matter of interpretation care has been taken to avoid the old myths and to present only the most widely accepted modern viewpoints.

To tell a coherent story, in a more readable form than is usual with encyclopaedias, each volume takes the form of independent chapters, all by recognised authorities in the field. Most chapters are devoted to the ships themselves, but others deal with topics like 'Naval Installations' that are more generally applicable, giving added depth to the reader's understanding of developments. Some degree of generalisation is inevitable when tackling a subject of this breadth, but wherever possible the specific details of ships and their characteristics have been included. With a few historically unavoidable exceptions, the series is confined to seagoing vessels; to have included boats would have increased the scope of an already massive task.

The history of the ship is not a romanticised story of epic battles and heroic voyages but equally it is not simply a matter of technological advances. Ships were built to carry out particular tasks and their design was as much influenced by the experience of that employment – the lessons of war, or the conditions of trade, for example – as purely technical innovation. Throughout this series an attempt has been made to keep this clearly in view, to describe the *what* and *when* of developments without losing sight of the *why*.

The series is aimed at those with some knowledge of, and interest in, ships and the sea. It would have been impossible to make a contribution of any value to the subject if it had been pitched at the level of the complete novice, so while there is an extensive glossary, for example, it assumes an understanding of the most basic nautical terms. Similarly, the bibliography avoids very general works and concentrates on those which will broaden or deepen the reader's understanding beyond the level of the *History of the Ship*. The intention is not to inform genuine experts in their particular area of expertise, but to provide them with the best available single-volume summaries of less familiar fields.

Each volume is chronological in approach, with the periods covered getting shorter as the march of technology quickens, but organised around a dominant theme – represented by the title of the book – that sums up the period in question. In this way each book is fully self-sufficient, although when completed the twelve titles will link up to form a coherent history, chronicling the progress of ship design from its earliest recorded forms to the present day.

This volume is unusual in covering a very extensive period of history – some 4000 years – but one from the shipping point of view unified by the dominance of the oared vessel. This was principally as a weapon of war but from earliest times to the Venetian 'great galleys' oared propulsion was also important for merchant ships carrying especially valuable or perishable cargoes, where the relatively high speed and certainty of progress under oars was prized. This breadth of coverage is reflected in the length of this volume, the longest and probably the most complex in the series so far.

Needless to say, both the quantity and the quality of information varies greatly for different epochs, and it is not a simple case of the later periods being better understood than the earlier. In fact, the combination of classical written sources and modern experimental archaeology makes the Athenian trireme more certain in its characteristics than, say, early medieval galleys. In many areas there is simply insufficient evidence to be more than tentative about overall developments, and what is known is fragmented and very specific to a particular time or place. Archaeologists, historians, naval architects and scientists have all contributed to what knowledge there is, and many of these work in areas where they are first in a field of one. We have been fortunate in obtaining the services of some of the very best of these – and if *The History of the Ship* had no deadlines, we might have had others – so the result is much ground-breaking material.

However, the reverse of this coin is that it is often impossible to present any consensus, because ideas are still developing and the debate still rages. Furthermore, some questions which have always been unanswered, remain so; these gaps we have to acknowledge, but equally there is some apparent chronological overlapping. However since each of the specialists approaches his period from a different perspective this is a strength rather than a weakness.

As with the *Cogs, Caravels and Galleons* volume, it has not proved possible to produce meaningful lists of 'typical ships': there is simply insufficient data. However, true to the spirit of the series, where vessels *are* documented full details of their known characteristics are included in the text.

Robert Gardiner
Series Editor

Introduction

A BOOK on the galley[1] is as important in the history of the ship as it is timely. It is important since the galley dominated the Mediterranean for over two millennia, from the beginning of the Bronze Age to the eighteenth century of the Christian era when warships relying exclusively on sail and their broadside of guns made the galley obsolete in spite of its greater manoeuvrability. Further, the geographical conditions of the area (Chapter 15) were such that in its age communication and the exercise of political power were predominantly by sea, so that the galley in its very varied forms continually played a vital role. The age of the galley in the Mediterranean was far longer than the age of sail, and the role it played more central. Nevertheless, the development of different types in antiquity and again in medieval and modern (ie post medieval) times has until recently been in the case of antiquity an unresolved puzzle and in the later period historically clear but without the necessary additional clarification which naval architecture and ergonomy has been able to bring.

Such a book is timely because in the last decade or so much work has been done in all these unknown or inadequately known fields and the editors have been able to make up their team of contributors from scholars and scientists all of whom have published or are engaged in work which breaks new ground.

The bringing together in a single book of chronologically different departments of work relating to the same problem, the propulsion of an oared ship for roughly the same purposes, warfare and commerce, has given an unprecedented opportunity for comparison and its resultant enlightenment. But the most important association which the book is now able to achieve is between the historical, archaeological, geographical and economic aspects of galley fleets and their aspects from the point of view of the naval architect and ergonomist. The lead in this latter direction was given by so far the most ambitious essay in experimental archaeology, the building of a full-scale trireme, *Olympias*, nearly ten years ago and its successful operation at sea, which has resulted in published scientific reports on its performance under oar and sail. Such expensive, if spectacular, experimentation is unlikely to be possible for other types of galley, but the lead it gave was important in the direction which this book is now able to exemplify by showing in Chapters 9–12 the great advances which can be made in the understanding of this type of ship by attracting the interest of the naval architect and the ergonomist. The book now for the first time enables the reader to assess as a whole, or at any rate see how it may be possible so to assess, the subject of that sophisticated and inscrutable ship, the galley.

This happy situation has not of course meant that the problems have been finally solved. Far from it. At present all that can be shown is the evidence and the arguments about it that have been put forward, the way which is opening up to the solution of problems, which quite recently seemed insoluble, as a result of entirely new approaches. The reader is admitted to the workshop where he will hear the claims and often the loud disagreements of the workforce (of which the present writer is one). He will soon realise that such a book as this can at present only show the way to these ends, not reach them, when, particularly in the earlier periods, the nature of the evidence is seen, in literature, archaeology (terrestrial and underwater), and the various kinds of iconography, every piece of which needs careful interpretation and admits different conclusions. In these matters also, as Myres observed in a very different field of historical and archaeological investigation, 'an increase in knowledge has led only to an increase in ignorance',[2] the more things we know the more things we realise we don't know. Nevertheless, *The Age of the Galley* is itself a move, in which its readers are invited to participate, towards a greater certainty.

Under these circumstances it is the job of the editor to indicate to the reader where the interpretation of the evidence by the contributor has been controversial; and, where the issues are important, to give what alternative interpretations there are or indicate where they may be found.

Chapter 1: Paddled and Oared Ships before the Iron Age

Here the evidence is provided by archaeology enlarged on occasion by relevant inscriptions. The first consists of the diffusion of obsidian flakes from the Aegean island of Melos and it is inferred that they were diffused in reed rafts or skin boats. One such reed craft has recently been proved capable of such use. No representations of seagoing craft are found until the early Bronze Age (third millennium), when Egyptian seafaring to the coasts of Asia is attested, and possibly to the Red Sea. The ships are illustrated on a burial monument.

Aegean galleys of the third millennium are shown on a few of the so-called terracotta 'frying pans' of the Cyclades and from Naxos modelled in lead. The former are taken to be 'cultic' for not very strong reasons. The higher end of the ship shown is taken to be the bow and the lower end the stern with a 'horizontal device'. The interpretation is the opposite of that which later ships suggest with their uniformly high sterns, and low bows, stempost and forefoot. This interpretation rests on the 'horizontal device' taken later as 'cultic' on not very secure grounds when it appears plainly in the sterns of the Thera ships (see below).

The Naxos models are made of three strips of lead, one longer one for the ship's bottom rising at one end and the two shorter ones for its sides. At the lower end the bottom strip is bent upwards at right angles. Interpretation of the model depends on this feature, taken here

---

1. The word 'galley' is derived from the late Latin or (since in Latin *galea* has a different meaning) more likely Byzantine Greek word *galea*. It is used in the title of this book, and elsewhere in it, conveniently if anachronistically, of a type which relied on oar power and used sail only when wind and circumstance were favourable.

2. R G Collingwood and J N L Myres, *Roman Britain* (Oxford 1936 and 1941).

to be a unique 'stern transom' with the consequence that the higher end is the bow. An alternative interpretation is to suppose that the lower end is a forefoot which has been accidentally (and in the case of lead easily) bent upwards, with the result that the higher end becomes, as is usual, the stern.

A third contemporary ship model from Crete is 'tear shaped' with one rounded end and a horizontal projection at the other end. Here the rounded end is taken to be the 'terracotta' equivalent of the 'transom stern' of the Naxos models and the 'horizontal projection' a repetition of the 'horizontal device' of the frying pan ships. The normal interpretation of this model has been that it represents a ship tapering towards the bow and equipped with a forefoot, both for good hydrodynamic reasons.

In the next 500 years the ships of the widely spread Minoan culture are shown on minute seals, but particularly and most clearly on the Thera minature fresco, the interpretation of which has been very much debated. There the naked male bodies in the sea have been variously identified as sponge-divers, battle casualties or 'cultic' human sacrifices (the last in this chapter), according to whether the scene is a peaceful one in a Minoan harbour city, a sea battle or a 'cultic' occasion. The cultic explanation (assumed as correct in the fifth paragraph of this chapter) provides a good explanation of the use of paddles (if they are anachronistic) in the larger ships shown. On the other hand it does not explain why the figures in the sea are behaving more like vigorous sponge-divers than like defunct casualties of battle or of cult. This identification is an important issue since the big paddled craft have 'horizontal stern devices'. If these are explained as gangways properly run out in the stern of a ship about to land her passengers, they do not support the interpretation given above of the frying pan and Naxos model ships as having high bows and low sterns carrying permanent horizontal devices for cultic occasions (?walking the plank by sacrificial humans). Nevertheless the cultic explanation for the scenes of the Thera miniature frescos is attractive, although far from certain.

Since the reader of this book will have plenty of occasions when he must use his own judgment, he may take the opportunity of this enigmatic fresco to sharpen his teeth, since the issue at stake is the interpretation of the earliest type of galley.

The next period (1500–1000 BC) is rich in Egyptian ship portrayal enlarged upon by some very relevant inscriptions: Queen Hatshepsut's ships for the voyage to Punt (Ethiopia: 1479–1457 BC), and the depiction of Ramses III's defeat of the Sea People's fleet about 1176 BC. In both cases the interpretations are informative and convincing.

Mycenaean galleys are mentioned in use in the Rower Tablets (Linear B) and are later shown in numerous vase paintings. The contributor's interpretation of the occasion of the former as the evacuation of a Mycenaean settlement in the face of invaders is not the usual one but most convincing.

Chapter 2: The Ancestry of the Trireme, 1200–525 BC

In this chapter important issues invite the reader's judgment even more urgently than in the last. Evidence for the galley appears in the late eighth century in Homeric poetry and in Athenian Geometric pottery. In the *Iliad* the Catalogue of the fleet Agamemnon takes to Troy shows the pentecontor (fifty-oared ship) predominating. The paintings show a ship, with a forefoot but no ram (bronze sheath), manned by warriors. In the *Odyssey* again the hero's ships at the outset are pentecontors and the (albeit supernatural) ship in which the Phaeacian king Alcinous sends Odysseus home has fifty oars and a hold for cargo 'beneath the thwarts' on which the oarsmen sit. For peaceful missions Homer also knows the twenty-oared 'broad merchantman', and the ship Odysseus builds on Circe's island is 'like a broad merchantman'; but naturally enough no oars are shipped since Odysseus alone is to crew it.

The contributor of this chapter argues that 'broad merchantmen' (and it seems pentecontors as well) were built to carry a loose grain cargo (*ie* not in containers) and so had a watertight deck to keep the grain from spoiling. The reader must be warned that there is no evidence either of grain cargoes in these ships or at this date nor of watertight decks (and a good deal of hard evidence against the latter). The warning is necessary since two important consequences are drawn. The first is that in these ships the oarsmen's seats are on deck rather than on the thwarts as in Homeric galleys and that their oars were rowed (possibly through an outrigger, *parexeiresia*, for which there is no accepted evidence of any kind until the end of the fifth century BC).

The contributor makes the novel claim that the Geometric vases of 760–700 BC show ships with a *parexeiresia*. There are two other interpretations of the 'more or less wide band' which he claims to be such. They are: (i) that it represents an attempt of the vase painter by means of primitive perspective to show the top wale of the far side of the vessel's hull; and (ii) that it represents a canopy deck (far from watertight) or a gangway at a higher level than the open side of the vessel. It is up to the reader to decide from looking at the vase paintings (pages 35–37) which of these three interpretations he thinks most likely, bearing in mind that even if the 'more or less broad band' does represent a *parexeiresia*, a watertight deck does not follow; and that in one of the Geometric vase paintings of a galley cited there is a man standing apparently in mid-air between the top wale and the 'band'. There is the additional improbability attending the contributor's interpretation that the galleys shown on these vases surrounded by fighting men are also decked grain-carriers.

The argument continues that these broad, grain-carrying merchantmen equipped with their necessary watertight decks are also portrayed in a later group of fragments of Geometric vases and in a fragment of one archaic vase, which undoubtedly show parts of ships with two levels of oars. For the contributor the two levels of oars must both be above deck, although in all the representations of ships with two levels of oars (in particular those of the roughly contemporary Nineveh frescos) the lower level of oars is placed in the lower part of the ship and is worked through oarports.

The survey and explanation of the development of fleets of galleys in the Aegean and the eastern Mediterranean during the seventh and sixth centuries BC, which occupy the remaining, and greater, part of Chapter 2 forms an enlightening introduction to the galley fleets of the six and fifth centuries. His rejection of Herodotus's attribution of a trireme fleet to the phil-Hellenic pharaoh Necho is not a view generally accepted. His attribution of the *diekplous* to the battle in 540 BC off Sardinia between the Phoenicians and Carthaginians on the one side and the Phocaeans on the other is controversial, and the statement that the *diekplous* involved 'intricate manoeuvre of fleets *in line abreast*' defies the imagination.

Chapter 3: The Trireme

The suggestion in the second section of this chapter that the warships of the Nineveh fresco were triremes is novel and certainly controversial. It arises from the necessity to provide an adequate explanation (not hitherto given) of one of the two features by which the two types of galley shown in the fresco taking part in the evacuation of Tyre (and Sidon?) in 701 BC differ from one another. Both types are being rowed at two levels like the ships shown on the Geometric and archaic vase fragments mentioned above, and both have a canopy deck on which stand behind bulwarks male and female figures, (some of the former armed). One type has a hull crescent-shaped in profile and hence no forefoot, the other has the normal hull of the galley with stempost, low bow and sharp forefoot sheathed to form a ram, the fixture of the sheath to the forefoot being shown by a vertical broad band at the foot of the stempost. The second feature which distinguishes the second type from the first is that the second, stands higher, having between the edge of the deck and the top of the open side through which the upper file of oarsmen are visible a course (not present in the ships of the first type) of alternate square sidescreens and open spaces which can be recognised as an unmanned oar level by comparison with a contemporary vase painting and later Phoenician ships with three oar levels. The lack of manning at the top oar level is understandable in the warships of a fleet expecting no enemy action and including many two-level auxiliary ships. If the identification proves acceptable, it makes it possible to regard a form of trireme as having been invented in Phoenicia in the latter part of the eighth century BC. The reader is presented with the evidence on which the identification is based.

The evidence of which the conclusions of the rest of the chapter is based is given and discussed in Morrison and Coates, *The Athenian Trireme* (Cambridge 1986).

Chapter 16: The Athenian Navy in the Fourth Century BC

As an example of a galley fleet, this new work, based securely on the inventories of the Athenian naval dockyards at Piraeus, gives the background to Athenian sea power in its final and, in numbers of ships, its greatest period. This background is given in terms of the ships themselves, their crews and gear and the naval organisation behind them. Where interpretation is needed the contributor is uncontroversial. His recently published book *Financing the Athenian Fleet: Public Taxation and Social Relations* (Baltimore and London 1994) sets out his work in this field at length.

Chapter 4: Hellenistic Oared Warships, 399–31 BC
Chapter 9: The Naval Architecture and Oar Systems of Ancient Galleys

These chapters summarise the work of Morrison and Coates on the history and reconstruction of the new types of Mediterranean oared warship developed in the fourth and third centuries BC, and set out in *Greek and Roman Oared Warships* (Oxford 1994). The conclusions embodied in the drawings of Chapter 9 are certainly highly controversial. The reader may be referred to the above book for the evidence and its interpretations on which these conclusions are based.

Chapter 5: Fleets of the Early Roman Empire, 31 BC–AD 324

This chapter gives a comprehensive, succinct and non-controversial account of the Mediterranean fleets and their activities between the battle of Actium in 31 BC and the defeat of Licinius by Constantine in AD 324.

Chapter 15: Naval Installations 5thC BC–2ndC AD
Chapter 11: Oar Mechanics and Oar Power in Ancient Galleys

These chapters add essential detail to the wider subjects of Chapters 1–5.

Chapter 6: Late Roman, Byzantine and Islamic Galleys and Fleets
Chapter 7: From Dromōn to Galea, cAD 500–1300
Chapter 10: Naval Architecture and Oar Systems of Medieval and Later Galleys
Chapter 12: Oar Mechanics and Oar Power in Medieval and Later Galleys

In these four chapters contributors with different approaches deal with the many aspects of the medieval and Renaissance galley. There is some inevitable chronological overlapping in particular between the sixth and seventh chapters but the different interests of the two contributors have produced a result which is only formally repetitious. The tenth chapter is mainly concerned with the ships themselves, the seventh mainly historical, covering the development from the Byzantine dromōn to the medieval galea and the scholarly interpretation of the various available sources and the technical terms employed.

The twelfth chapter is a substantial multi-author contribution taking in the period AD 800–1650 and giving the artefacts, written sources and drawings available for the description of the naval architecture and power systems of the later galleys, but including some historical notes on the French galleys of the period, the last seagoing oared fleet.

The four chapters give a comprehensive and varied account of the nature and employment of the galley in more than a millennium, the pattern in each case following the particular interests of the contributor. The territory is in many areas apparently to a great extent unexplored, so that the conclusions can hardly yet be controversial.

Chapter 8: Merchant Galleys
Chapter 13: The Geographical Conditions of Galley Navigation in the Mediterranean
Chapter 14: Economics and Logistics of Galley Warfare

The Age of the Galley includes three chapters covering three important subjects relating to the period as a whole. Geographical conditions are responsible for the central role of the galley in the history of the Mediterranean for two and half millennia as well as for its nature and the mode of its use. Galley warfare and the rise and fall of sea power cannot be understood without reference to economic and logistic factors. Our account of the galley is incomplete without awareness of its function throughout the period as a fast merchantman. A scene in Rome will stick in our memories, Cato 'contriving to drop a Libyan fig in the Senate, as he shook out the folds of his toga, and then, as the senators admired its size and beauty, saying that the country where it grew was only three days' voyage (by an oared merchantman) from Rome', demonstrating that Carthage was too close to Rome for comfort and that this fact entailed not only her defeat but her destruction.[3]

John Morrison

---

3. Plutarch, *Life of the Elder Cato* 27.

1

Paddled and Oared Ships Before the Iron Age

THE EARLIEST evidence for seafaring in the Mediterranean region are flakes of obsidian from the Aegean island of Melos found in the upper paleolithic and neolithic levels (eleventh–fourth millennia BC) of Francthi Cave in the southern Argolid. As Melos was never connected to the mainland, the obsidian could only have reached Francthi by means of water transport. Perhaps only slightly later in date than the obsidian at Francthi is the kill-site of *Aetokremnos*, located on the Akrotiri peninsula of northeastern Cyprus.[1]

It is not clear how paleolithic seafarers came to know that there was obsidian on Melos. The most reasonable assumption is that considerable seaborne exploration was taking place and that Melos was only one island of many visited by paleolithic and early neolithic seafarers. The lack of established paleolithic living sites on Mediterranean islands, however, apparently had less to do with seafaring capabilities than with the inability of cultures following a hunter/gatherer economy to exist on islands with limited resources.

These prehistoric seafarers left no depictions of their ships. The vessels used for their paleolithic voyages may have resembled *papirella* – primitive reed rafts that are still constructed on Corfu.[2] In the summer of 1988, a 6m (20ft) long experimental *papirella* was successfully paddled by its five-man crew from Lavrion, on the southwest tip of Attica, to Melos, proving that navigation to Melos in a reed raft was theoretically possible.[3] Alternatively, skin craft may have been used. Later, the neolithic toolkit allowed for the felling of trees for monoxylons.

How were these paleolithic vessels propelled? In antiquity, several forms of propulsion were known. Poling (punting) and towing were possible in shallow waters; however, only three options were available to blue-water sailors: paddling, rowing or sailing.

In paddling, the paddle is utilised as a lever to transfer muscular energy to the water. Paddlers normally sit in a kneeling posture, facing the bow, and throw their upper body forward, while using the arm nearest the paddle's blade as a moving fulcrum during each stroke. As paddlers must be situated immediately next to the sides of the vessel to be able to work their paddles, less inboard space is required than in rowing. Due to this consideration, paddling is the typical manner in which narrow vessels traditionally are propelled. Paddling was apparently deeply ingrained among the Aegean seafaring cultures. When images of ships do become available, in the third millennium BC, they primarily depict a long and narrow type of hull which would have been better suited to paddling than to rowing. Furthermore, a tradition of paddling ships during cultic festive races continued in the Aegean as late as the Middle Bronze Age. Paddling was also used for small, canoe-like vessels in the Bronze Age.[4]

A rower faces the vessel's stern and pulls the oar towards the chest while leaning backwards. Rowing is thus a far more energy-efficient mode of propulsion than paddling; it allows the muscles of the lower body to be employed, whereas in paddling only the muscles of the back and arms are utilised. In rowing, energy is transferred to the vessel through the oarlock or grommet against which the oar loom swivels.

The earliest irrefutable evidence for the use of a sail is a painting of a ship on a Gerzean pot from Egypt which dates to the end of the fourth millennium.[5] The square sail is supported on a pole mast stepped well forward in the ship's bow. In Egypt, the innovation of a sail may have resulted from men observing the impact that wind had on shields that are sometimes depicted in the vessels' bows.[6] This evolutionary process might explain why early sails used a boom to stretch their foot; the boom may have replicated the bottom frame of a shield.

The introduction of sail itself, however, may have been a much earlier invention. Broodbank and Strasser have convincingly demonstrated that the neolithic colonisation of Crete in the late eighth or early seventh millennium must have been carried out in an organised manner.[7] To accomplish this feat, a minimum of 15–19 tons of materials – the colonists, their portable belongings, breeding stock and grain – must have been transported in a single season. Moving this amount of cargo would have been exceptionally difficult, if not impossible, were the vessels propelled solely by paddlers. This raises the distinct possibility, but does not prove, that rowing and/or the use of the sail were known forms of propulsion at this time.

The Early Bronze Age (*c*3000–2000 BC)

Egypt

The Egyptians used seagoing galleys on the Mediterranean for the rapid transport of soldiers for attacks on the Asiatic coast, and for transporting the spoils reaped by these razzias back to Egypt. Uni, an officer under Pepi I (VIth Dynasty) describes on his cenotaph at Abydos how he employed ships to land his military contingents:[8]

> When it was said that the *backsliders* because of something were among these foreigners in *Antelope-Nose*,[9] I crossed over in transports

Abbreviations in the footnotes are given in the references at the end of the chapter.

1. Cherry 1990, pp152–154 and there additional bibliography.
2. Tzalas 1989.
3. Tzamatzis 1987.
4. Doumas 1992, pp78–79.
5. Basch 1987, p50, fig 79.
6. Le Baron Bowen 1960, pp119–120.
7. Broodbank and Strasser 1991.
8. *ANET 3*, p228. Uni was sent five times to quell insurrections in the 'Land of the Sand-Dwellers'.
9. The 'Antelope's-Nose' may refer to a mountain range that protrudes into the Mediterranean. This has been tentatively identified by some scholars as referring to the Carmel Mountain range where it comes down to the sea in the vicinity of Haifa.

One of Sahure's seagoing ships. Note the exaggerated sheer and the vertical stem and sternposts. The hogging truss with its tensioning lever can be seen amidships. (From Borchardt 1981)

with these troops. I made a landing at the rear of the heights of the mountain range on the north of the land of the Sand-Dwellers. While a full half of this army was (still) on the road, I arrived, I caught them all, and every *backslider* among them was slain.

One important result of these expeditions was the importation into Egypt of many Asiatics, who were brought to Egypt by the shipload for slave labour.

Another important reason for sailing north was timber. Lacking good indigenous wood, vitally needed for ship construction, building and other purposes, the Egyptians sailed and rowed to the Lebanon for timber. This trade was primarily conducted through the dominant Early Bronze Age port of Byblos. A measure of its importance is that the term 'Byblos-ship' became synonymous in Egypt for any seagoing cargo ship – even if it sailed the Red Sea. There are numerous references to this trade in tim-

Seagoing ships portrayed on a relief from the causeway of Unas at Saqqara; Vth Dynasty. The tripod masts are a notable feature. (From Hassan 1954)

ber, the earliest being by the IVth Dynasty pharaoh Sneferu, who mentions the importation of forty ships filled with cedar logs.[10] An inscribed axehead in the Adonis River may have been left behind by one of the vessels involved in acquiring timber during the reign of Cheops or Sahure.[11]

The earliest known unequivocal illustrations of Egyptian seagoing galleys come from the burial temple of Sahure at Abusir. The ships have an exaggerated sheer, which is an oddly Egyptian characteristic. This sheer may have had some basis in reality, although probably not to the degree shown in the depictions. The ships' stems and sternposts are vertical. The 'Eye of Horus' decorates the stem, an early example of an *oculus*, which in the minds of the ancient mariners enabled a ship to find its path safely.

As Egyptian ships of this period lacked keels they required additional strengthening to permit them to stand up to the rigours of bluewater sailing.[12] For this reason, each ship is depicted carrying a hogging truss connected to the ship's extremities and borne longitudinally over a row of massive crutches. Moreover, a band of rope lashing runs the length of the hull directly below the sheerstake. The ships are shown as rowed and sailed. There are up to seven oars on each side, although this number

may be merely symbolic, the actual number of rowers to a side being greater. Lanyards are attached to the upper rim of each oar blade. Three steering oars, lacking tillers, are placed between the stanchions in the stern castle. Presumably, each ship carried six steering oars; the number is indicative of their inefficiency. Masts are lowered on to a crutch positioned in the stern. The masts' bipodal construction may derive from papyrus raft ancestry.

Two additional Old Kingdom seagoing galleys are carved in relief on an ashlar stone recovered from the causeway of Unas, a Vth Dynasty pharaoh. While similar to Sahure's galleys, they are more telegraphic in execution; much of the detail supplied by Sahure's artists is missing here. One notable difference is that the masts, which are stepped, are *tripodal*. Moreover, Unas ships carry only four oars to a side. Again, this number probably owes more to artistic composition than to reality.

The seagoing ships which Egypt used on the Red Sea must have been of lashed construction. These ships had to be built on the

10. *ANET 3*, p227.

11. Rowe 1936.

12. Greenhill 1976, p62, fig 20; Kennedy 1976, pp159–160.

Three typical Cycladic 'frying pans' with longship motifs. Although highly stylised, the depictions of the ships have a certain consistency. (Shelley Wachsmann)

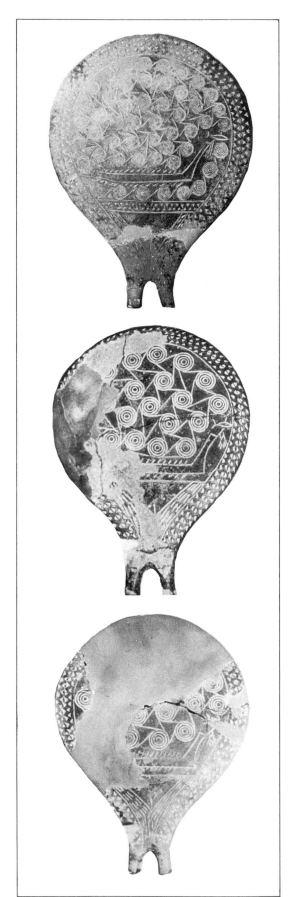

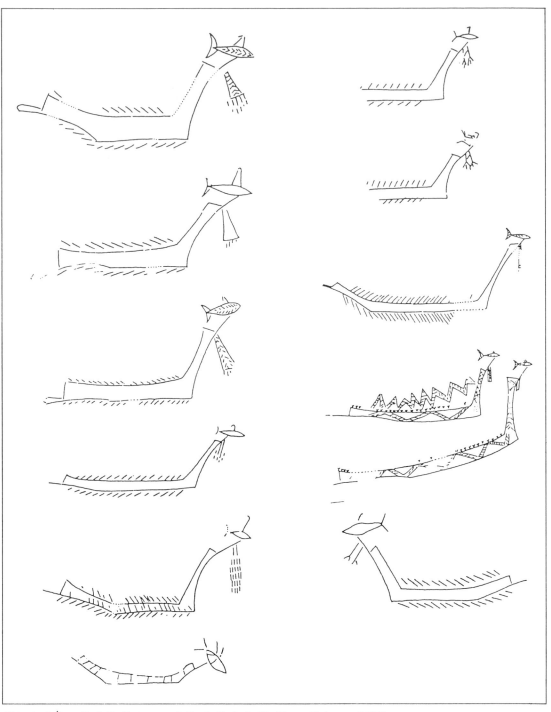

Ships incised on Cycladic 'frying pans'; Early Cycladic II. (From Coleman 1985)

Nile and then disassembled for transport through the East Desert. They were then reassembled on the shores of the Red Sea.[13]

The ships used by the Egyptians for navigating the Mediterranean were also probably of lashed construction. While lashed and sewn construction was used in many cultures, the Egyptians were apparently unique in lashing their ships laterally through mortises that did not penetrate the external sides of the hull planking.[14] Instead they cut V-shaped mortises through which transverse rope lashings secured the strakes and keel-planks. This ex-

plains why there is no evidence for internal lashing on Sahure's ship depictions.

The ships of Sahure and Unas are shown bringing to Egypt Asiatic captives – men, women and children – depicted in subservient postures. It has been proposed that these Asiatics were actually the ships' crews.[15] This interpretation does not give sufficient consideration

13. Kitchen 1971; Wachsmann, forthcoming.

14. For a recent study of ancient Egyptian ship construction see Haldane 1993.

15. Bietak 1988.

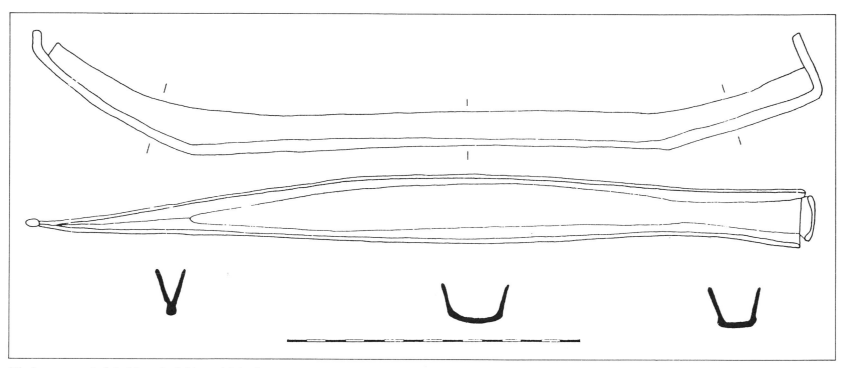

The best preserved of the Naxos lead ship models in the Ashmolean Museum; third millennium. (From Renfrew 1967)

to the fact that in Sahure's relief the Asiatics appear only on ships returning from the Asiatic coast.

The Aegean

Only in the third millennium do images of ships begin to appear in the Aegean. Thus, a greater expanse of time separates the earliest evidence of Aegean seafaring from the first ship depictions there, than from that era to the present day. Two types of vessels are depicted. One appears to be a relatively small vessel with a cutwater at either extremity.[16] The other is a type of seagoing longship.

The latter is perhaps best known from depictions appearing on a group of Cycladic terracotta artifacts that have been termed 'frying pans' due to their unusual shape.[17] Although these enigmatic artifacts are found from Mainland Greece to Anatolia, only those from the Cycladic Keros–Syros culture are decorated with ships. The frying pans may have had a cultic or a ritual function in connection with fertility. This conclusion seems to be supported by the occasional depiction of female genitalia just above the two-pronged handles (legs?).[18] The frying pan ship is narrow in profile. One of its extremities ends in a high post, which is decorated with a fish-shaped de-

The terracotta ship model from Palaikastro; third millennium. (After PM II:240)

vice, from which in most cases hang tassel-like objects. About two-thirds of the length away from the high post, the hull rises at a slight angle from the horizontal. The low extremity finishes off vertically and has a horizontal device extending outboard from it. Rows of numerous short parallel lines depicted on most of these ship images are best interpreted as paddles.

This ship type finds its clearest representation in three metal models from the Cycladic island of Naxos.[19] The models are each constructed from three flat lead strips. One of these, flattened by hammering for two-thirds of its length, forms the bow and lower part of the hull, and two additional strips were used for the sides. The lower extremity is finished off in a vertical transom, indicating that the low end of the ships on the frying pans must be the stern. The somewhat higher bow rises at an angle, although not as steeply as those on the frying pan ships.

Another well-known depiction of this ship

type, made of terracotta, indicates that these ships were also known in Crete. The model has a tear-drop shaped hull with the greatest beam well astern of amidships. The rounded end is presumably the terracotta equivalent of the stern transom of the Naxos models. Like the ships depicted on the frying pans, this model has a horizontal stern projection.

A model made from terracotta normally has a tendency to have more thick-set proportions than the prototype ship which it copies. It is, therefore, likely that the Naxos models give a more accurate view of what the actual ships looked like. The appearance of ships on Cycladic frying pans may indicate that there was a connection between the ships and the

16. Göttlicher 1978, Taf 24, p313.

17. Coleman 1985.

18. Coleman 1985, p196, ill 4.

19. Renfrew 1967, p5; 1972, pp318, 356–357, fig 17: 7 and pl 28: 3–4; Casson 1971, pp41–42.

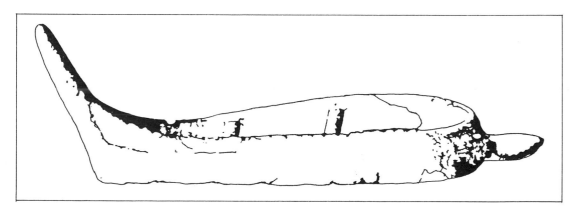

Chinese dragon boat, Yangtze River. (From Bishop 1938)

cult for which the frying pans were created. The large numbers of parallel lines on the frying-pan ships, together with the particularly narrow beam of the Naxos models, indicate that there would have been insufficient inboard space to permit rowing these vessels; *they must have been paddled.*

The 'dragon boats' of southeast Asia constitute a fascinating ethnological parallel to these longships.[20] Dragon boats are long, narrow vessels – their beam/length generally varies between 1:10 and 1:14 – and are propelled by many paddlers. They carry no sail and, although used on the open sea, they tend to hog due to their exaggerated length. Today dragon boats are used only for ceremonial races, but in the past they were employed for war and piracy.

The Middle Bronze Age (2000–1550 BC)

Egypt

The 'Tale of the Shipwrecked Sailor' relates the adventures of an Egyptian mariner who was the sole survivor of his ship, which sank on a voyage to the mines of Sinai.[21] This story relates the earliest recorded shipwreck. And, although phantasmagoric in content, it does contain some valuable information on seagoing galleys during the Middle Kingdom.

The protagonist relates that his ship had a crew of 120 men; even if this number is exaggerated, it must refer to a rowing crew. Moreover, the sailor's ship is 120 cubits long by 40 cubits in beam.[22] The size of the sailor's ship

need not be an exaggeration as Sahure refers to 100-cubit-long ships which he had built.[23] Furthermore, a 1:3 beam/length ratio is credible, although the ship would be beamy and slow.

There are no known depictions of Egyptian seagoing galleys during the Middle Kingdom, nor from the Intermediate periods that preceded and followed it.

---

20. Bishop 1938, pp415–424.

21. *LAE* pp50–56. See most recently Baines 1990.

22. This would make the ship 54m or 63m long and 18m or 21m in beam, depending on whether the regular cubit (0.45m, 1.48ft) or the royal cubit (0.525m, 1.72ft) is intended.

23. *ANET 3*, p227.

Deck and sheer plans of a dragon boat, taken off a boat at Itchang. (From Bishop 1938)

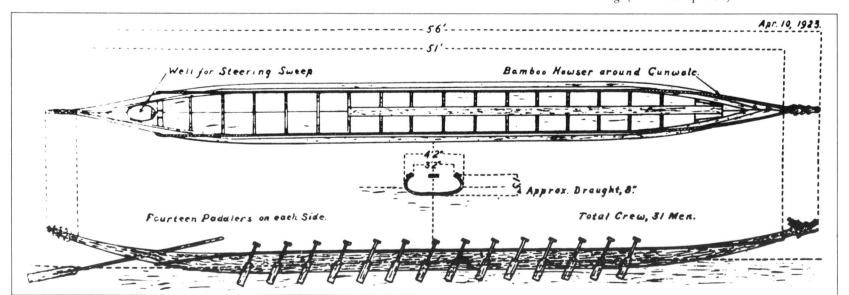

Ship engraved on a Syrian cylinder seal from Tell el Dab^a eighteenth century BC. (After Porada 1984)

The Syro-Cannanite coast

The Phoenicians are considered the seagoing traders of antiquity *par excellence*. In this role, however, they were simply following in the wake of their Syro-Cannanite ancestors, who were undoubtedly major, if not *the* primary, seaborne traders operating in the eastern Mediterranean, at least during the latter part of the Late Bronze Age.[24] Syro-Cannanite seafaring trade was also probably a significant factor in the sudden emergence of maritime city-states situated along the southern Cannanite coast in the Middle Bronze Age IIA c2000 BC.

Syro-Cannanite ships are poorly documented at best. Prior to the Late Bronze Age there is only one depiction, of a (presumably) Syro-Cannanite seagoing ship. The tiny ship is

Line drawing of the best preserved ship in the waterborne procession depicted in the south Miniature Frieze at Thera. (From Marinatos 1974)

engraved on a locally made copy of a Syrian cylinder seal, which dates to c1800 BC, uncovered at Tell el Dab^a the Nile Delta. A Syro-Cannanite smiting god is depicted next to the ship.

The ship has a crescentic hull. One extremity (the bow?) curves gently outboard while the other is vertical. A mast is stepped amidships; stays connect it diagonally to the stem and stern. Two oars are depicted beneath the hull, apparently indicating that this is a galley.

Thera: Minoan and Cycladic ships

Of all the cultures that flourished along the Mediterranean's shores during the Bronze Age, there is none so fascinating, nor so enigmatic, as that of the Minoans. The people of this culture, which evolved in Crete and expanded into the southern Aegean, deserve recognition as the ultimate Bronze Age explorers. They traded for tin in distant Mari and presented their wares to the pharaohs. Artisans schooled in Cretan art forms decorated Asiatic and Egyptian palaces with Minoan motifs. A large corpus of Minoan ship iconography had been known since Evans' discovery of Knossos, but it consisted almost entirely of ships engraved on tiny stone seals, most no larger than a thumbnail. A few rough and fragmentary models completed the repertoire. Minoan ships were as enigmatic as the culture that created them.

Then, in 1972, excavations in the Cyclades at the site of Akrotiri on the volcanic island of Thera (Santorini) revealed a remarkably well-preserved settlement that had been covered by volcanic ash when the island's volcano erupted, c1628 BC.[25] One of the buildings, termed by

its excavator the 'West House', contained a series of polychrome frescoes.[26] The 'Miniature Frieze' in one of its upper rooms shows ships taking part in a nautical race or procession, as well as other naval activities. The Cycladic ships in the scenes are identical, or at least similar in all discernible details, to the vessels known previously from Minoan art. All the vessels in the Miniature Frieze, regardless of their size or the activities in which they are involved, have gently curving crescentic hulls when seen in profile.

The ship procession or race is painted on the south wall of the room. The participating ships are extravagantly decorated. They have struck their sails and some have also unstepped the masts, which lay on a row of crutches. Each ship carries an ornamental stern cabin (*ikria*) and a *stylis*-like pole. Paintings of eight large *ikria* adorn the walls of an adjacent room.

The ships carry a horizontal device, attached to the stern by means of ropes; this device is apparently the same as those carried at the lower extremity of the Early Bronze Age Cycladic longships and is thus an additional indication that the low end of these longships was, indeed, the stern. This device has received numerous nautical interpretations.[27] It is

24. This primary importance of Syro-Cannanite traders in Late Bronze Age trade was first proposed by Bass (1967) on the basis of his study of the Cape Gelidonya shipwreck. Recent studies of the textual evidence, Egyptian tomb paintings, as well as archaeological evidence confirm this conclusion.

25. For a summary of the evidence for this date, see Kuniholm 1990.

26. Marinatos 1974.

27. For example, *PM* II, p240; Hutchinson 1962, p94; Marinatos 1974, p50; Morgan 1988, pp135–136; Casson 1975, pp8–9; 1978; De Cervin 1977; Gillmer 1975, p323; Reynolds 1978; Kennedy 1978; Basch 1987, p128, etc.

The waterborne procession in the south Miniature Frieze at Thera. (From Doumas 1992)

abundantly clear from the Theran material that the horizontal stern device was attached to ships only during cultic ceremonies. Thus, a nautical significance need not be postulated for it.

Perhaps the most surprising aspect of this gay flotilla is that all the ships partaking in the ceremonial race or procession are being *paddled* rather than rowed. The paddlers are depicted bending arduously over the sheerstake to reach the water with their paddle blades, clearly indicating that paddling was not the normal manner by which these vessels were propelled. Furthermore, one of the ships accompanying the flotilla is being rowed.

What are we to make of this intriguing scene? Casson convincingly argues that the

ships are being paddled as an archaic cultic practice, and compares them to the ships in which the classical Athenians sent their em-

Paddlers in the waterborne procession at Thera bend strenuously over the caprail to complete their stroke. (After Marinatos 1974)

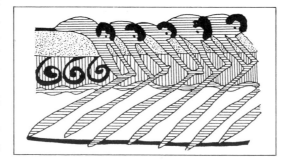

bassy to Delos.[28] The ships used for this purpose were so obsolete that the Athenians could claim that it was the vessel that had carried Theseus to Crete. Indeed, the ships taking part in the race/procession exhibit other clues in addition to their outdated mode of propulsion: the horizontal stern devices, the lowered sails and the profuse decorations. These archaic modifications presumably were meant to make ships then in current use as similar as possible to a specific ship type that was used in earlier times for these cult acts.

By studying the archaisms we can learn something about the older, prototype ships

28. Casson 1975, p7.

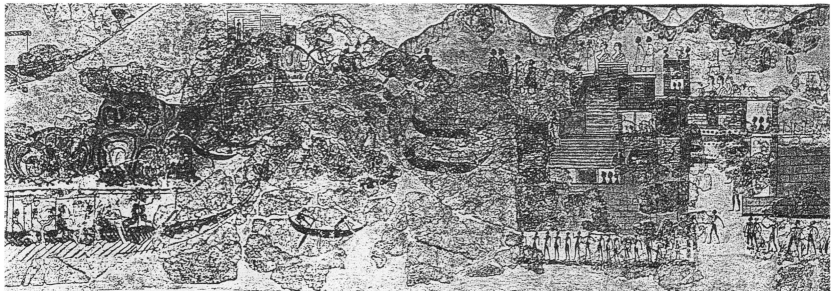

Below: The rowed ship accompanying the procession in the south Miniature Frieze. (After Doumas 1983)

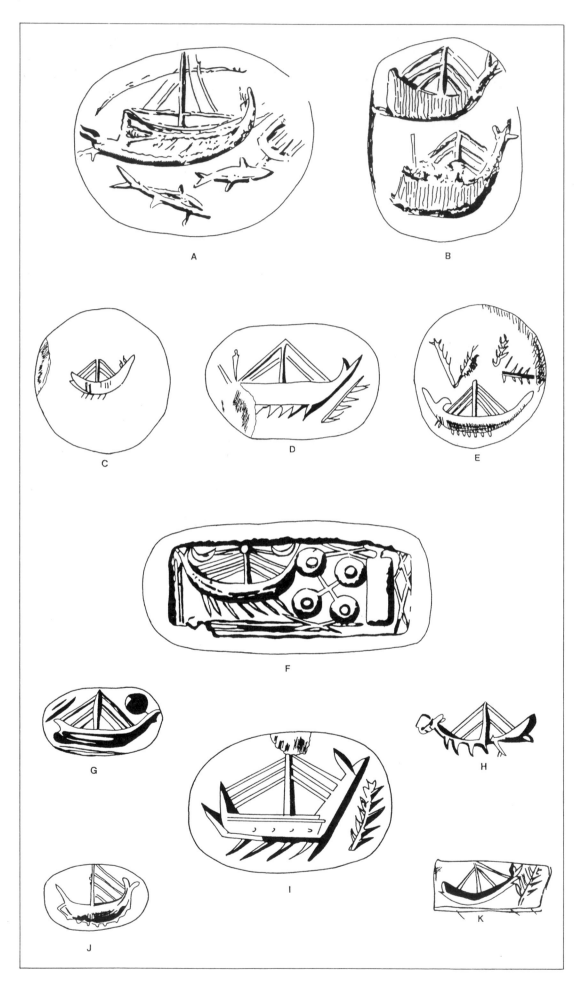

that were being copied.[29] These ships would have: a) been paddled; b) lacked sail; c) at least during festivities been profusely decorated and d) carried a horizontal stern device. These characteristics agree remarkably well with third millennium Aegean longships, discussed above. These ships lacked sail and commonly are portrayed replete with decorations and a horizontal stern device. Furthermore, as we have seen, the narrow dimensions of these ships must have required them to be paddled, not rowed.

Rigging is depicted for the first time in the Aegean towards the end of the Bronze Age, but at that time, as well as in the Middle Minoan period, *ships are always shown with their sails lowered*. Moreover, like the Theran ships, they also carry bow decorations and usually have a horizontal stern device. This curious manner of depicting the ships is best explained if the seals depict ships that are taking part in this typically Aegean nautical festival. It is probable that the vessels depicted on these seals represent a ship type that had recently evolved – or, alternatively, had been introduced into the Aegean.

That the third millennium longships depicted on Cycladic frying pans may have played a role in the cult of fertility has been noted above. Sometimes, leafy branches are incised at either side of the female genitalia that occasionally appear on the frying pans. Interestingly, identical branches appear on later Minoan seals. This connection is completed when the same type of branches appear on seals depicting cultic objects, including horns of consecration.[30] The dragon boat races of southeastern Asia represent an outstanding parallel to this use of highly decorated ships paddled in cultic contexts.

Based on the above considerations, the following hypothetical reconstruction of events in the Aegean seems to explain the evidence best: 1. During the third millennium seagoing longships of extremely long, low and narrow lines were in use. These craft did not use sails and, similar to modern-day dragon boats, were paddled, not rowed. Apart from their functional use, whatever it might have been, these long-

29. Wachsmann 1980.

30. Nilsson 1950, pp171 fig 73, 172 figs 75–76, 264 fig 129, 263 fig 128, 273 fig 137.

Ships with mast and rigging depicted on Early Minoan III (A-B) and Middle Minoan (C-K) seals. In all cases the sails have been lowered. (A-B after PM II; C-E and G-K after Marinatos 1933; F after Casson 1971)

Above: Modern dragon boats line up prior to a race at Aberdeen, Hong Kong. (Hong Kong Tourist Association)

Below: Dragon boats being paddled during a race. These surviving craft bear a remarkable resemblance to the highly decorated vessels of Thera. (Hong Kong Tourist Association)

Minoan seal from Thebes depicting a ship with two paddlers dressed in sheaves of grain and other cultic accoutrements. (After Morgan 1988)

2. Often, the third-millennium longships were depicted in full regalia, perhaps while taking part in the festivities.

3. By the early second millennium, a new type of ship took the place of the longships. The former may have been introduced, although, more likely, it was a natural evolution of the longship.

4. Even though a different type of ship was being used, the waterborne festivities continued, but it now became customary to make the participating ships as similar as possible to the defunct Aegean longships. In their memory, sails were lowered, paddles replaced the oars of daily use and the ships were decorated.

Detail of the ships and dead bodies in the north Miniature Frieze at Thera. The ship at upper left has made land. Note the oars awash in the surf. The ship below it is still approaching the shore; the looms of four oars are preserved, caught at the beginning of their stroke. (From Doumas 1992)

ships served annually in cultic races or processions. Prior to these events the ships were profusely decorated. The ornamentation included the attachment of a horizontal stern device which, even then, probably did not have a functional purpose.

A Minoan seal from Thebes, in Greece, which depicts a cultic ship in full regalia, may be the key to interpreting this cultic custom. The vessel has a double Minoan bird device at the stem. An *ikria* nestles in the stern, and a

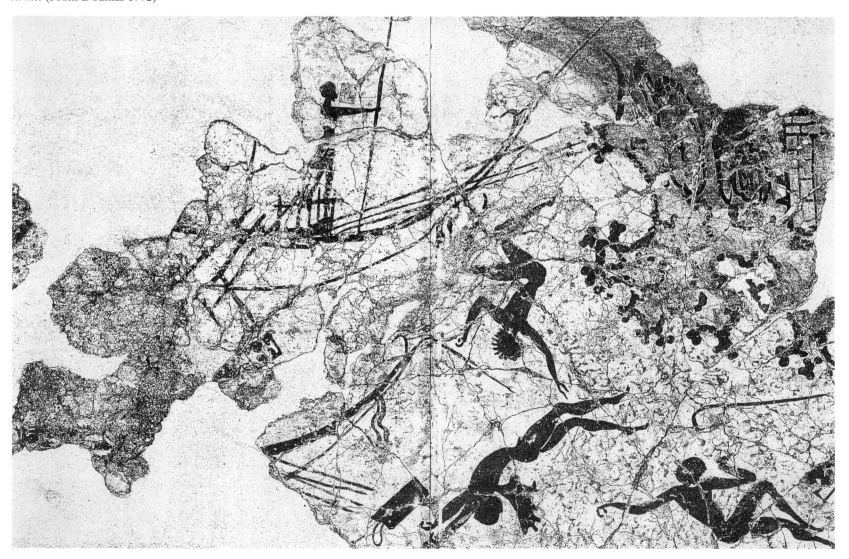

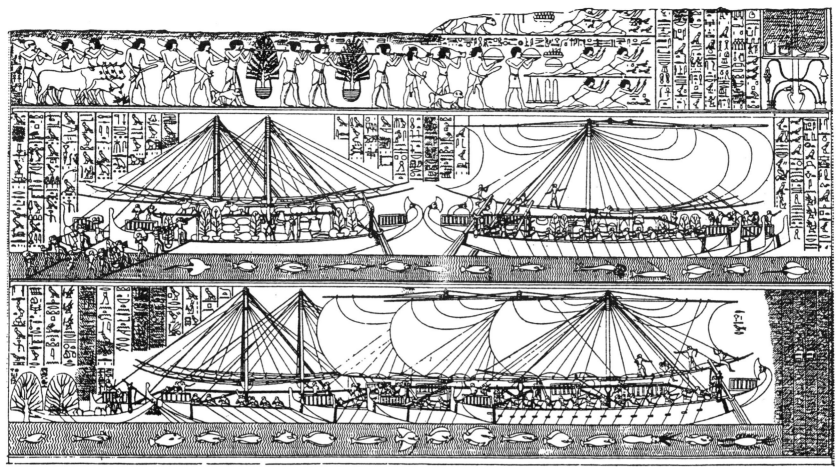

horizontal stern device juts out below it. Two figures stand on the vessel, facing the ship's bow as they paddle. Five diagonal lines beneath the hull represent paddles. Thus, this vessel has elements that, at Thera, are connected solely with the ships taking part in the cultic festivities.

The figures are wearing *sheaves of grain*.[31] These indicate that the waterborne activities were linked to a cultic festival, the main goal of which was engendering fertility. The vegetation cycle was a fundamental aspect of Minoan religion. Apparently, ships played a role in the spiritual striving for abundance.

Portions of four additional ships are depicted on the room's northern wall. A row of soldiers, perhaps the crew of the best preserved ship in this scene, advances inland in single file.[32] The inhabitants of a walled settlement located to the left of the soldiers seem totally oblivious to them.

These vessels lack the decorative elements of the processional craft but are otherwise identical to them. The oars of one ship, attached to the caprail, seem to be awash in the surf as a solitary soldier stands guard in the bow. The bow of the ship below it is crossed by four oars depicted at the beginning of their stroke. This makes it clear that the ships taking part in the

procession or race normally used rowers rather than paddlers.

Three dead nude male bodies float in the water. These have generally been identified as the enemies of the settlement who were killed by the soldiers, or as shipwrecked mariners.[33] An alternative interpretation would see these bodies as evidence of cultic human sacrifice.[34]

The Late Bronze and Early Iron Ages (1550–1000 BC)

Egypt

There are numerous Egyptian references to contact with the land of Punt, located south of Egypt, which was most often reached by the Egyptians via the Red Sea.[35] Only Hatshepsut, *c*1479–1457 BC, saw fit to depict in painted relief the details of an expedition which she sent to that land. This is fortunate, for it is our most valuable source of information on Egyp-

Hatshepsut's expedition to Punt as depicted in her mortuary sanctuary at Deir el Bahri. The details of the hogging truss, with the reinforcing cables at bow and stern, can be seen clearly. (From Säve-Söderbergh 1946)

tian seagoing trading galleys in the Late Bronze Age.

The scene illustrates the voyage to and from Punt of a fleet of possibly five vessels, although the exact number of ships that took part is impossible to determine. The naval part of the expedition is depicted in two registers which contain four temporal movements. The action flows clockwise from bottom right, where the ships leave for Punt, to lower left, where the ships unload their trade goods on to a ship's boat to be ferried ashore. In the upper right, the ships are in the process of being loaded with a variety of commodities of great value to

---

31. For a parallel to this dress worn by a figure in a boat, see du Plat Taylor, Seton Williams and Waechter 1950, p118 fig 29: 7.

32. For the most recent reconstruction of this scene see Televantou 1990.

33. Marinatos 1974, pp45, 54; Marinatos 1984, p40; Morgan 1988, pp150–154.

34. Wachsmann, forthcoming.

35. Säve-Söderbergh 1946, pp8–30; Kitchen 1971.

the Egyptians. Above this scene is the following inscription:[36]

> The loading of the ships very heavily with marvels of the country of Punt; all goodly fragrant woods of God's-land, heaps of myrrh-resin, with fresh myrrh trees, with ebony, and pure ivory, with green gold of Emu (ᶜmw), with cinnamon wood, khesyt wood, with ihmut-incense, sonter-incense, eye-cosmetic, with apes, monkeys, dogs, and with skins of the southern panther, with natives and their children. Never was brought the like of this for any king who had been since the beginning.

Finally, at upper right, the ships depart and return to Egypt.

The ships are depicted with fifteen rowers to a side. As the human figures seem to be drawn to a scale somewhat greater than that of the ships themselves, it is possible that the number of rowers portrayed may be less than the actual number employed.

Beneath the ships, the sea swarms with various types of fishes and other sea creatures, including lobsters, squid and turtles.[37] In fact, it is from these creatures that Hatshepsut's mortuary temple derives its modern name, Deir el Bahri, which in Arabic means 'Monastery of the Sea'. This 3500-year-old diver's guide to the marine life of the Red Sea is the best indication that the ships in Hatshepsut's relief are based on illustrations prepared by one or more artists who accompanied the expedition and recorded the marine life caught by the crew with hook or net, prior to its ending up in the ship's stew.

The hogging truss on each ship is carried over four massive crutches. It is not clear how the truss was attached to the hull, although this may have been accomplished by means of through-beams. Cables were wrapped around the bow and stern where the hogging truss was attached, to prevent the planking from buckling under the enormous strain of the hogging truss.

These ships, shown in profile, appear relatively slender, and indeed the hulls bear a striking likeness to a type of hull that is known from Theban tomb paintings, as well as from models from the tombs of Amenhotep II and Tutankhamun.[38] These models have long, nearly horizontal, stem and sternposts and a beam/length ratio of about 1:5. The models do differ, however, in several details from Hatshepsut's Punt ships: they have a central cabin, their posts are finished in a different manner and they lack hogging trusses.

A terracotta model uncovered at Byblos, apparently patterned after this same type of Egyptian ship, indicates that it was indeed used for blue-water sailing.[39] The Lebanese model clearly shows a massive keel-like structure inside its hull which projects outward at bow and stern, but becomes flush with the hull amidships, in the same manner as in the wooden models from the tombs of Amenhotep II and Tutankhamun. This characteristic has been attributed to the desire to have the models stand upright on a flat surface.[40] That this is not the case is clear because this feature also appears on Hatshepsut's Punt ships – which are painted in relief.

This raises the remarkable likelihood that this feature may indicate that Hatshepsut's ships had a 'developing' form of 'proto-keel'. If so, the Egyptians may have continued using a hogging truss on their seagoing ships because they did not sufficiently understand the keel's use nor appreciate its advantages.[41] Historically, there are numerous cases in which older technologies were used together with technological innovations until confidence was gained in the new system.

Interestingly, this type of keel, one which apparently projected upward into the hull amidships, seems to have been the normative keel form on seagoing Late Bronze Age ships.[42] A keel protruding beneath the hull prevents slippage to leeward, but Bronze Age mariners may not have been concerned with this aspect of the keel if, with their primitive boom-footed rig, they did not set sail unless the wind came from well abaft the beam.

Perhaps for the same reason these ships did not have shrouds to support the mast and sail laterally, but rather depended on tensioned cables which were wound around the bottom of the mast.[43] Thus, the Bronze Age oarsmen were likely to pull at their oars more often, or alternatively, the ships stayed longer at anchor, waiting for following winds, than was the case after the brailed rig came into common use at the beginning of the Iron Age.

Assuming an *interscalmium* of 1m (3.3ft) for each of the fifteen oarsman and an additional 3–4m at either extremity, these ships would have been about 23m (75ft) long. That is, if the number of rowers is not simply a convention.

The rowing of Hatshepsut's Punt ships has been the subject of some scholarly debate. Ballard argues that the vessels were rowed with long sweeps because the oarsmen seem to be standing up to pull their oars.[44] He believes that the men stood near the ships' longitudinal median line, but underwent foreshortening at the hands of the Egyptian artists.

Four rowing positions are depicted at Deir el Bahri in the scenes of the voyage to Punt, a procession on the Nile and the moving of

---

36. *BAR* II: §265.

37. Danelius and Steinitz 1967.

38. Landström 1970, pp107–109; Jones 1990, pp4, 16 Type B, 28–37, pls XVI–XXII, Objects 273, 284, 287, 306, 309–310, 314, 597.

39. Wachsmann, forthcoming.

40. Landström 1970, p107.

41. Hocker, forthcoming.

42. Wachsmann, forthcoming.

43. Wachsmann 1990.

44. Ballard 1920, p165.

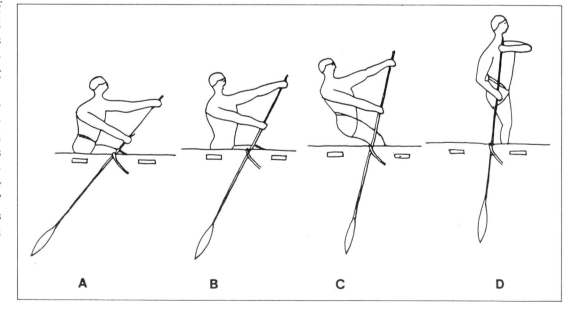

Four positions of rowers in the Deir el Bahri reliefs.
(After Jarrett-Bell 1930)

A   B   C   D

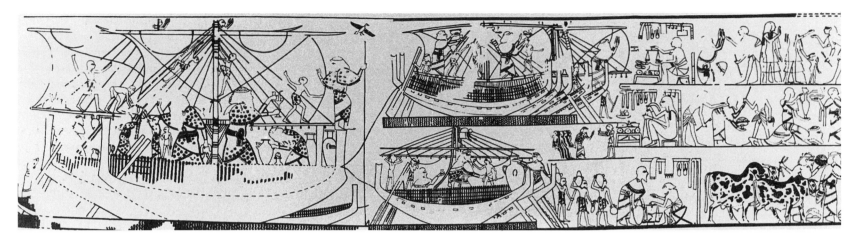

Syro-Canaanite merchant ships depicted arriving at an Egyptian port in the tomb of Kenamum (T 162) at Thebes; Amenhotep III. (From Davies and Faulkner 1947)

Hatshepsut's obelisk barge. Jarrett-Bell used these four positions to reconstruct a single stroke.[45] The rowers lean forward in a sitting position at the beginning of their stroke (A), with their oars at a 40-degree angle from the vertical. For the following stage (B), they continue to sit and lean forward, but their oars are now at an angle of 28 degrees. Then, in the third phase (C), they stand up and lean backwards with the oars at a 15-degree angle. Finally, in the last phase (D) they stand erect, with the inboard arm pressed against the chest and the oar at a 9-degree angle. Jarrett-Bell concludes that the oars must have been turned sideways on the return stroke and never left the water, resulting in a short and choppy stroke. One possible advantage of this type of stroke, however, is that the men would have been positioned near the sides of the hull, giving more room for storing the cargo on deck, as seems to have been the case.

Still, Landström considers the positioning of the oarsmen to be the result of Egyptian artistic conventions.[46] As he points out, Egyptian models complete with rowers depict the oars lifted high above the water, possibly indicating that rowing was carried out in the normal manner. Egyptian rowers used two types of chaffing gear, which had a square patch of leather for a seat, surrounded by a leather net.[47] This garment could be worn by itself, or over a linen garment.

The Syro-Cannanite coast

The most detailed depictions of Syro-Cannanite ships that have come down to us are painted on the walls of the tombs of two Theban notables, Kenamun and Nebamun.[48] In these scenes, the ships are apparently wind-driven sailing ships, pure and simple. There is no evidence for oars or rowers. Information on Syro-Cannanite galleys is limited, and what little there is comes from Ugarit. This major Late Bronze Age sea port and entrepôt is located north of the modern Syrian port of Latakia. Numerous documents dealing with nautical matters, written in Akkadian as well as in the local alphabetic Ugaritic script, have been uncovered here.[49]

One text lists the crews of three different ships. Of these, one, owned or perhaps captained by a man named Abdichor, has a crew of eighteen men who have been called up from three different communities. We do not know the reason for which they are being recruited. The number for the crews of the two other ships are damaged but may be restored also as eighteen men each. These presumably refer to rowing crews. Another text is a list of ship's equipment which includes an entry of 'nine oars'. If the word for 'oars' (*mt tm*) is in the dual form as suggested by Heltzer, then assuming one rower to an oar, the resulting eighteen oars correspond to the crew of Abdichor's ship.[50]

These two documents, taken together, may indicate that there existed at Ugarit a galley type which was manned by eighteen oarsmen. Nine metres (30ft) would have been required for the rowers located on either side of the ship and at least another 7m were needed at the bow and stern to bring the planking in to the posts. Thus, such a vessel would have been at least 16m (52.5ft) long.

A tiny scaraboid seal stamp found at Ugarit bears the images of two galleys. These have box-like hulls, with a second horizontal rectangular feature located above the sheer. This may represent a screen, a feature which appears prominently on the merchant ships in the Theban tomb paintings. Beneath each hull are five parallel diagonal lines, indicating oars. The ships have vertical stem and sternposts. Above the screen, one ship carries a thick mast and a yard with downcurving tips. The other depiction shows an off-centre vertical with an enigmatic, pretzel-like object wound around it.

Mycenaean rowers and galleys

Our information on Mycenaean ships derives primarily from numerous iconographic depictions and to a lesser degree from textual evidence. The Mycenaeans wrote an archaic type of Greek in the 'Linear B' script.[51] The documents are primarily inventories and receipts kept by the palace bureaucracies. Despite their laconic nature, scholars have been able to learn much about Mycenaean life and palace administration from these modest documents, some of which deal with subjects pertinent to seafaring.[52]

One of the two largest groups of Linear B tablets, totalling about 1200 tablets, was uncovered at the palace of Pylos in Messenia. From the beginning of research on the Pylos documents, some scholars felt that the tablets contained allusions to a 'state of emergency'. This impression is derived from several considerations:[53]

45. Jarrett-Bell 1930.

46. Landström 1971, p69.

47. Säve-Söderbergh 1946, pp75–79 figs 13–15.

48. Davies and Faulkner 1947; Säve-Söderbergh 1946, pp54–56; 1957, pp25–27, pl XXIII; Wachsmann, forthcoming.

49. For the most recent collection of the Ugaritic and Akkadian texts dealing with nautical matters, see van Soldt and Hoftijzer, forthcoming.

50. Heltzer 1982, pp188–190.

51. Ventris and Chadwick 1973; Chadwick 1976. On the decipherment of Linear B, see Chadwick 1958; 1987B, pp12–21.

52. Palaima 1991 and additional bibliography there.

53. Ventris and Chadwick 1973, pp183–185, 357–358; Chadwick 1976, pp173–179; Chadwick 1987A; Palmer 1956; 1965, pp143–154; Baumbach 1983.

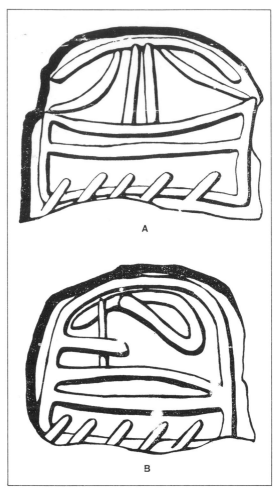

Ships on a seal from Ugarit; thirteenth century BC.
(After Schaeffer 1962)

1. One group of texts, known collectively as the *o-ka* ('Command' or 'Military detachment') tablets, contains lists of men who are assigned guard duty along the coast. The title of one tablet (An 657) reads: 'Thus the watchers are guarding the coast.'[54] It seems reasonable to assume from this that the Pylian high command was aware of an external danger that could come by ship.

2. Bronze, apparently from temple repositories, was being collected for the production of arrowheads and spear points.

3. Linear B tablets were meant for short-term use. No year-dates appear on the tablets, indicating that most, if not all, of the tablets refer to the palace's last year. And Pylos was destroyed by a terrific conflagration. In other words, there is good reason to believe that something was afoot, and that the palace bureaucracy was well aware of it.

4. The possibility that one text, which refers to men and women as *po-re-na* who are given, together with metal vessels, to several gods and goddesses, may refer to human sacrifice, possibly under exceptional circumstances.

5. The most fascinating set of enigmatic clues to this puzzle are three tablets in the Pylos An series, which are known collectively as the 'Rower Tablets' after the word *e-re-ta* (rowers) which appears in the headings of all three. In these documents, more than in any others, there seems to be a sense of urgency.

One tablet (An 1) is a list of thirty rowers raised from settlements. Its title reads: 'Rowers to go to Pleuron'.[55] The five locations from which the men are being mustered are within the palatial domain of the palace at Pylos. The total number of men is interesting, perhaps indicating the crew of a single triaconter (a ship of thirty oars). Homer mentions twenty-oared ships, fifty-oared pentecontors and larger craft, but does not refer to triacontors.[56] Herodotus, however, mentions that triacontors were used in the early colonisation of Thera.

A second tablet, An 610, is badly damaged. It lists 569 men, but it is clear that numbers are missing in the lacunae, and Chadwick reconstructs an original total of about 600 men.[57] Such a group of oarsmen would have been sufficient to man twenty triacontors or twelve pentecontors. Here, the men in An 610 are again identified by their settlements. In two cases, groups of forty and twenty men are brought respectively by two notables, one of whom, *E-ke-ra₂-wo*, may have been the ruler of Pylos.[58] The oarsmen are defined as 'settlers' (*ki-ti-ta*), 'new settlers' (*me-ta-ki-ti-ta*), 'immigrants' (*po-si-ke-te-re*), or by an unidentified term (*po-ku-ta*).

Killen has shown that the call-up in An 1 and An 610 is based on a specific draft system.[59] Four sites are mentioned in the same order in both An 1 and An 610, indicating a close connection between the two documents. The number of rowers taken from the settlements in An 1 are proportional to those taken from the same towns in An 610 at an approximate ratio of 1:5. Thus, it seems that each settlement contributed rowers based on a proportional evaluation of its reserve duty requirements.

The last of the three documents, An 724, deals with rowers who are missing from the muster. This tablet is also badly damaged and there are many erasures at line ends. One of the men missing is identified as a 'settler who is obligated to row' (*ki-ti-ta o-pe-ro-ta e-re-e*).[60] On the tablet's *verso* the scribe drew a graffito of a ship or boat, which has a semicircular object (construction?) located amidships and bough-like items extending from the ship's right extremity (bow?).[61] Interestingly, this is not a typical Mycenaean oared ship. Rather, it finds its closest parallels in Minoan cultic boats and in seven tiny vessels, under paddle or oar,

depicted on a Middle Helladic jug from Argos.[62]

How should we interpret the Pylos 'Rower Tablets'? Unless we accept that raising a fleet that required hundreds of oarsmen was a normal occurrence at Pylos, then these tablets strongly suggest that something out of the ordinary – something exceptional – was taking place at Pylos just prior to its demise. This impression is further strengthened by the other factors, mentioned above.

Assuming that the Rower Tablets *do* indicate a state of emergency at Pylos in anticipation of a danger approaching from the sea, what purpose might the fleet of galleys have served? The large numbers of men mentioned in An 610 immediately bring to mind thoughts of Troy, Salamis and Actium – of naval battles and piracy. The equating of 'oared ships' with 'war ships' seems obvious. A nautical approach to the problem, however, poses two elementary questions: a) What possible reasons are there for massing rowers? and, b) Of these, which best fits the evidence from Pylos?

Of course, the rowers could have belonged to a naval group meant to engage an enemy at sea before it landed. There are, however, other, non-military, contexts which would require amassing large numbers of oarsmen. To judge from her relief at Deir el Bahri, Hatshepsut required about a thousand oarsmen to man the tow-boats that pulled the barge transporting her obelisks from Aswan to Karnak.[63] Such an explanation seems unlikely for Pylos, however. Merchant ships, as we have seen, could be galleys. Thus, fleets of oared merchantmen also would have required the enlistment of many rowers. It seems unlikely, however, given a potentially dangerous situation at home, that valuable ships and men would be sent overseas.

Numerous paddlers, or rowers may be required to take part in ship races. This is a true of the dragon boat races that take place today as it was in Thera in the seventeenth century BC. This explanation is *plausible* for the Pylos

54. Ventris and Chadwick 1973, p189.

55. Ventris and Chadwick 1973, p186.

56. Casson 1971, pp44–45.

57. Chadwick 1987A, p77.

58. Ventris and Chadwick 1973, p265; Chadwick 1976, p71; 1987A, p78.

59. Killen 1983.

60. Palaima 1991, p286.

61. Palaima 1991, fig LXIII: b.

62. Deilaki 1987.

63. Naville 1908, pl CLIII–CLIV; Landström 1971, pp130–131 fig 383.

tablets, particularly as the ship graffito on the *verso* of An 724 appears to be of a cultic type.

Oared ships were also used in expeditions of colonisation, or for mass forced migration, when insurmountable forces threatened. In classical times, pentecontors were used to transport entire populations and their possessions. Undoubtedly, the most informative example of this phenomenon is Herodotus' description of the Phocaean escape from Ionia before the advancing Persian army:[64]

> . . . the Phocaeans launched their fifty-oared ships, placed in them their children and women and all movable goods, besides the statues from the temples and all things therein dedicated save bronze or stonework or painting, and then themselves embarked and set sail for Chios; and the Persians took Phocaea, thus left uninhabited.

The Assyrian king Sennacherib describes a similar 'waterborne flight', this time from the viewpoint of the invader:[65]

> And Lulî, king of Sidon, was afraid to fight me (*literally* feared my battle) and fled to Iadnana (Cyprus), which is in the midst of the sea, and (there) sought a refuge. In that land, in terror of the weapons of Assur, my lord, he died.

In his palace at Nineveh, Sennacherib's artists recorded on stone how Lulî and his retinue escaped to Cyprus. In the Assyrian reliefs, Lulî's fleet contains both warships with waterline rams, as well as round merchant galleys or transports. Heads of men and women passengers peeking from above the bulwarks indicate that both types of ships were used as transports in this waterborne migration.

Which of these explanations fits the Pylos Rower Tablets best? It seems that the last interpretation is to be preferred. An 610 and An 724 may record preparations for a similar waterborne emigration – of at least certain echelons of the Pylian population – to avoid an overwhelming impending attack. One consideration that may support this interpretation is the repeated identification of the rowers in An 610 and An 724 in terms of land owning, *particularly at a new location* ('settlers', 'new settlers', 'immigrants', and a 'settler who is obligated to row'). These terms would seem to make most sense if the documents are concerned with an act of 'migratory colonisation' in which the rowers who man the fleet are also among those migrating to the new location. The consideration that rowers in An 610 and An 724 are differentiated into 'settlers' and 'new settlers' presumes the previous existence of the site being settled. Perhaps the documents refer to the enlargement of a previous Pylian settlement or region, already organised and controlled by the palace at Pylos.

Let us look at this problem from a different perspective. What might we expect to find at Pylos if it had been abandoned and destroyed by its inhabitants rather than being attacked and pillaged by invaders? Presumably, the migrants would have attempted to take their most valuable possessions with them, together with belongings and livestock most needed to begin life in a new location. Due to limitations of space on board the ships, it is likely that less-important items would have been left behind. Furthermore, as the fleeing residents of the palace of Pylos realised that they would never be returning to the home they were now abandoning, they may have destroyed by their own hand as much as possible of what they had to leave behind, to prevent it from falling into enemy hands. There would be no evidence of an armed struggle as no battle would have taken place. The invaders, if and when they arrived, would find the inhabitants gone, with the abandoned palace empty of valuables, and perhaps even burnt to the ground.

How well does the above scenario reflect the archaeological evidence at Pylos? A study of the artifacts found in the palace at Pylos indicates that all the valuable metal vessels listed in the Linear B Ta Series had been removed from the palace prior to its destruction by fire:[66] not a single metal vessel of value was discovered in the palace!

One may argue that such 'housecleaning' is the result of methodical pillagers who stripped the palace of all its valuables prior to torching it. This scenario does not give sufficient weight, however, to the consideration that strata of other sites that have ended in destruction, and presumably have been pillaged in the process, will normally contain some valuables. Pillagers are not infallible.

Metal hoards – at least some of which must have been interred for safekeeping with the intention of later recovery – are a particularly common feature of thirteenth-century BC Mycenaean sites.[67] No hoards, however, were found at Pylos. Indeed, the vast majority of artifacts recovered consisted solely of large quantities of pottery vessels, abandoned in the palace pantries in mint condition. As ceramics could have been easily made from local clay at any given destination, it is highly unlikely that they would have been allotted valuable, and limited, room on board the ships. Furthermore, although Pylos has been excavated ex-

tensively, and many skeletal remains retrieved, not a single human bone was found there. This led Blegen, the site's excavator, to conclude that the inhabitants had escaped Pylos before the palace was destroyed.[68]

Thus, the archaeological evidence can be plausibly interpreted to support a scenario in which the palace at Pylos was abandoned, rather than destroyed by external enemies. Moreover, this interpretation may aid in allowing us to understand the organisational mechanisms that drove the phenomenon of mass seaborne migrations away from the Aegean and into the eastern Mediterranean at the end of the Late Bronze Age.

Clearly, the 'northwesterners' who migrated to Cyprus, Syria and Israel during the upheavals of the twelfth century BC must have come from somewhere, and in doing so must have required some measure of organisation. Thus, the Pylos Rower Tablets may reflect one – palace-orientated, and, therefore, highly organised – form of bureaucratic preparation for a seaborne migration. Considering the estimated size of the kingdom's population, the expedition recorded in An 610 and An 724 probably was only one (and perhaps the last?) of many such expeditions required to transport even a small portion of the estimated population of Pylos, together with their servants, belongings and livestock.

If the above interpretation for the Pylos Rower Tablets is correct, it would have a profound effect on the understanding of the other Linear B documents from Pylos, for it would be highly unlikely that only these three documents, out of all those found at Pylos, refer to preparations for abandonment. Perhaps the most intriguing question that would arise if the people of Pylos abandoned and torched their own palace before sailing off is: where did they go?

For the development of war galleys in later times, the most significant oared ship of the Bronze Age was undoubtedly a type used, and presumably developed by, the Mycenaean culture. This same ship type, as we shall see, was subsequently adopted, apparently with only minor modifications, by the Sea Peoples.

In numerous depictions of Mycenaean ships the single element of ship construction which

64. Herodotus I: 164.

65. *ARAB* II, No 326. See also Nos 239 and 309.

66. Ventris and Chadwick 1973, pp332–348.

67. Knapp, Muhly and Muhly 1988 and additional bibliography there.

68. Blegen and Rawson 1966, p424.

A main element of the architecture of Mycenaean ship depictions looks like a ladder lying horizontally on its side. This is a reserved horizontal space intersected by numerous vertical lines. This aspect of the ship's *construction seems to have been uppermost in the minds of those who portrayed them. Any interpretation of these ships must begin by identifying this element.*

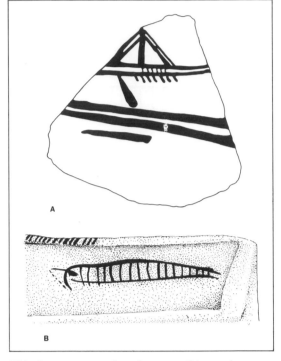

seems to have most caught the eye of the ancient artists was a structure situated directly above the sheerstrake. This appears as a narrow horizontal area, always left *unpainted*, which extends almost the entire length of the ship, and is intersected by numerous vertical lines forming what looks rather like a ladder lying horizontally on its side. This was such a prominent feature on Mycenaean ships that, at times, Mycenaean ship graffiti are literally little more than a 'horizontal ladder design'.

Clearly, to reach a definitive interpretation of the architecture of these ships depicted in Mycenaean iconography it is imperative first to understand the function of this part of the ship's architecture, and particularly how it relates to the rowing of these ships. To do so, it is essential to begin by first studying the most detailed known depiction of a Mycenaean ship. This distinction is currently held by a ship painted on a Late Helladic IIIC krater sherd uncovered at Pyrgos Livonaton in east Lokris.[69] This site, which has revealed a wealth of ship iconography to the archaeologist's trowel, has been equated with Homeric *Kynos*.[70]

Almost all of the ship survives, with the exception of parts of its extremities. Two armed and armoured warriors, one situated in a bow castle, the other abaft the mast, indicate that this ship is engaged in warfare. The vessel faces left and is divided longitudinally into three distinct sections (CB, BX and XA in the figure opposite). The hull, from the keel-line to the sheerstrake (BC) is depicted in dark red paint. Above this is a reserved area (BX) crossed by nineteen vertical lines forming the familiar 'horizontal ladder design'. However, in this case a 'lunette'-like object is situated next to the right (aft) side of each of the vertical lines.

The third and highest area (AX) is embellished with two rows of semi-circles. Elsewhere on Late Helladic pottery this motif also decorates the bodies of bulls and the leather-covered sides of chariots. This leads to the reasonable conclusion that area AX represents

a screen made of leather protecting an open bulwark. Line X continues across the bows, perhaps indicating an element of structural significance. It may be a free-standing wale which would have served as the support for the deck beams and the screen's poles.

As the upper ends of the oars lead straight into the bottoms of the lunettes, these must in some way be related to the ship's oarsmen. The following considerations aid in interpreting the artist's intentions in this matter:

1. The artist perceived of the human body when out of armour as curving and sinuous. This is evident from the ship's helmsmen who, unlike the two warriors, is shown without armour.
2. The rowers are depicted at the end of their stroke, with the oar blades slanting towards the

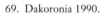

69. Dakoronia 1990.

70. Dakoronia 1993.

This element seems to have been so striking to the observer that some sketches of Mycenaean ships bear little else than this 'horizontal ladder pattern', sometimes with oars and rigging added. For example, ship A is painted on a sherd from Phylakopi on the island of Melos, and ship B is painted (upside-down) inside a Late Minoan larnax (ossuary). (A after Marinatos 1933; B after Gray 1974)

The Kynos ship; Late Helladic IIIC. (From Wachsmann, Seagoing Ships and Seamanship in the Bronze Age Levant, College Station, Texas, in press)

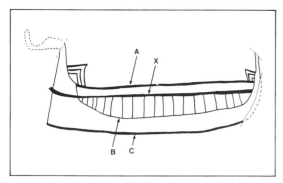

Architectural details of the Kynos ship.

stern. At this moment in the stroke, the rowers' torsos would be thrown back, with their oars drawn up near their bodies. Rowers in this position in Late Geometric art are portrayed leaning strenuously backward on their benches. As the torsos are depicted in frontal view, the far shoulder appears forward.

Thus, it seems reasonable to assume that the lunettes represent the rowers' upper torsos. But if so, where then are their heads? There is general agreement among scholars that later Greek oared ships, which reappear in the ninth century BC, are a direct continuation of the Mycenaean tradition of ship construction.[71] Unfortunately, this scholarly agreement does not extend to the ships that appear on Late Geometric vessels, for which several interpretations have been proposed.[72] It would be imprudent, therefore, to use these later images to explain the Kynos ship. There are, however, three depictions of Greek oared ships, all of which date to the last decade of the Late Geo-

metric period, *c*710–700 BC, on which there is scholarly agreement that they represent two-banked ships (*dieres*). These three images allow us to solve the 'mystery' of the 'headless oarsmen'.

One depiction, painted on a Proto-Attic sherd from the Acropolis of Athens, shows the lower-level oarsmen appearing in an open rowers' gallery partly protected by screens. A second sherd shows part of a *dieres* in which the torsos of the lower-level oarsmen are hidden behind screens. The height where their arms meet their bodies, however, indicates that their heads must be hidden behind the horizontal strip (deck-level wale?) located above them. Were there to be any doubt in the matter, the third *dieres* fragment, painted on a sherd from Phaleron, closes the case. For here the lower-level rowers are depicted *between* the protective screens, and their heads are clearly hidden behind the superstructure.

The above evidence permits the conclusion that the lunettes were indeed intended by their creator to represent the torsos of the ship's rowers. Furthermore, it also allows us to conclude that the 'horizontal ladder motif' on Mycenaean ships represents an open rowers' gallery intersected by a row of stanchions which supported the free-standing wale into which the deck beams were keyed. The Kynos artist, in indicating that the oarsmen's heads were hidden by the screen, has given us a further clue concerning the open rowers' gallery – its height was equivalent to that of a man's torso from the hip to the neck.

Warship with two levels of oars depicted on a sherd from the Acropolis, Athens, c710–700 BC. (Photo from Morrison and Williams 1968)

In an additional ship image uncovered at Kynos, the ship's stanchions are omitted and the oars seem to be attached at deck level. This strongly suggests that Mycenaean galleys, like Late Geometric warships, could be rowed from deck level.[73] The warrior standing abaft the mast on the first Kynos ship indicates that the vessel was at least partly decked. While this deck probably ran the length of the ship from stem to stern, the deck could not have run the entire beam of the ship as this would have left no room for the rowers' heads. Planking must have been left out along the sides. Additionally, this ship bears light castles positioned at the

---

71. The continuation of the Mycenaean ship tradition into Geometric times is the strongest argument for continuation during the Dark Ages. On the problem of cultural continuation during the Dark Ages, see most recently Lenz 1993.

72. Kirk 1949, pp123–131; Morrison and Williams 1968, pp12–17; Casson 1971, pp71–74; Basch 1987, pp161–170. The following interpretation agrees entirely with Casson's reading of late Geometric warship construction.

73. On the Late Geometric evidence, Casson 1971, p55.

A two-level warship depicted on a Proto-Attic sherd from Phaleron. (After Williams 1959)

An oarsman at the end of his stroke; Attic Late Geometric I. (After Basch 1987)

Two-level warship painted on a sherd from the Acropolis; Athens c710–700 BC. (Photo from Morrison and Williams 1968)

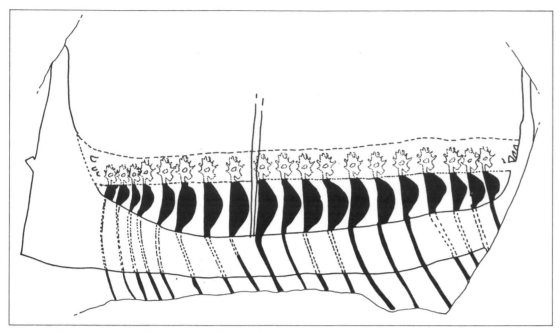

Conceptual reconstruction of the Kynos ship. Torsos of the rowers are depicted as lunettes which are seen through the open rowers' gallery (area XB in architectural drawing above). Area AX was probably a leather screen rising from deck height, which would have hidden the rowers' heads in a manner similar to that seen on images on pottery sherds of late eighth-century BC Greek warships.

Ship depicted on a Late Helladic IIIC sherd from Kynos. (From Wachsmann, Seagoing Ships and Seamanship in the Bronze Age Levant, College Station, Texas, in press)

stem and the stern. The helmsman mans a single quarter rudder which lacks a tiller. Two joined semicircles, however, may represent some form of steering mechanism.

There are numerous depictions of Mycenaean ships. One, painted on a pyxis from a twelfth–eleventh century BC tomb at Tragana, near Pylos, bears a striking similarity to the Kynos ships. Twenty-five rowers' stations in the open rowers' gallery indicate that the artist intended to depict a penteconter, one similar to those perhaps used by the oarsmen in Pylos An 610 and An 724. The ship carries mast and sail, and the recent discovery of missing sherds indicates that the ornament standing atop the forecastle represents a bird, rather than a fish as was previously thought.[74] A contemporaneous ship image painted on a stirrup-jar from the island of Skyros probably depicts a similar type of ship, this time with a more common bird-head stem ornament. Oarsmen remain forever at their oars on a sherd from the island of Cos.

Iconography supplies us with a valuable view of the general appearance of Mycenaean war galleys. We remain woefully ill-informed, however, concerning the manner in which these ships were constructed. Depictions of Mycenaean ships seem to form a cohesive group, but the ships exhibit considerable variety.

The Sea Peoples

In the eighth year of his reign, *c*1176 BC, the Egyptian pharaoh Ramses III defeated a coali-

74. Korrés 1989.

Oarsmen bend to their oars on a fragmentary ship image on a Late Helladic IIIC sherd from the Seraglio on Cos. Note the feather (?) helmets. (After Morricone 1975)

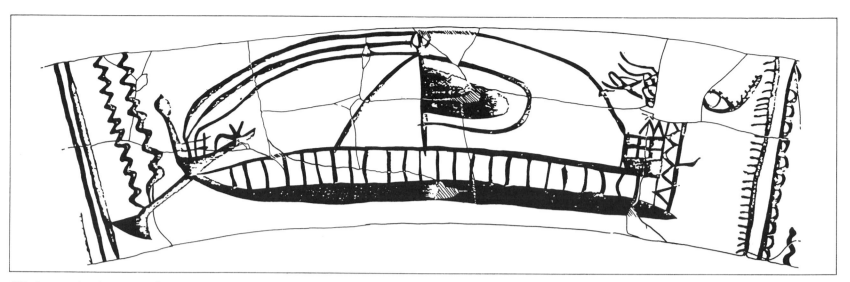

Ship image painted on a pyxis from a Late Helladic IIIC tomb at Tragana, near Pylos. (After Korrés 1989)

Ship image painted on a Late Helladic IIIC stirrup jar from the island of Skyros. Note the bird-head image topping the stem. (After Hencken 1968)

Ramses III's naval engagement against the coalition fleet of the Sea Peoples. (From Nelson et al 1930)

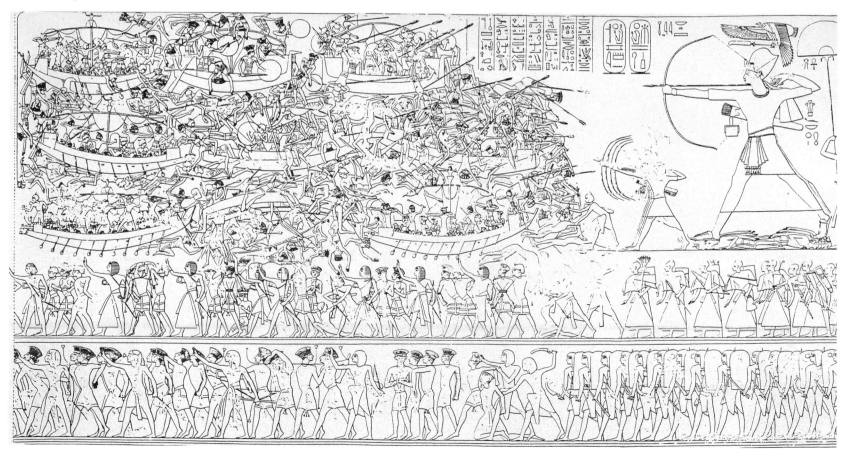

tion of migrating invaders who were known to the Late Bronze Age cultures collectively as the Sea Peoples. In two battles, one on land and the other on water, Ramses III successfully repulsed their advance. He recorded his victories in remarkably vivid painted reliefs on the walls of his mortuary temple at Medinet Habu.[75]

The scene of the nautical battle at Medinet Habu is illustrative of naval warfare prior to the introduction of the waterline ram as the pre-eminent nautical weapon. The sails of the Sea Peoples' ships are brailed up and no oars are visible. Presumably, the invading fleet was surprised at anchor by the Egyptians; the accompanying text suggests an Egyptian trap into which the invaders fell.[76]

Although the scene has a snapshot-like quality, Nelson has demonstrated that the cohesion of the battle revolves around spatial, ideological and temporal conceptual elements.[77] There is the impression of a vigorous naval battle, but within this construction the artists depicted four phases of the conflict. Egyptian ship E1 and Sea Peoples' ship N1 represent the beginning, ships E2 and N2 the middle phase, and ships E3 and N3 the conclusion of the battle in which the invaders are defeated and their ships capsized. Ship E4 signifies the aftermath of the battle, in which the shackled prisoners are carried off to the victory celebration. Two other Sea Peoples' ships, N4

Detail of Ramses III's naval battle. (B Brandle)

and N5, which are juxtaposed to Ramses III, indicate the pharaoh's ideological unstoppable power to utterly destroy and vanquish his enemies.

All five northerner ships illustrate a single type of ship, even though the invaders in them belong to two distinct groups, one of which wears a horned helmet, and the other a helmet

with feather-like protrusions. Clearly the invaders' vessels have been stereotyped into only one form. Similarly, only one type of Egyptian

---

75. Wachsmann 1981; 1982.

76. BAR IV, § 77.

77. Nelson 1943.

The scene of the naval battle with the bodies removed. (From Nelson 1943)

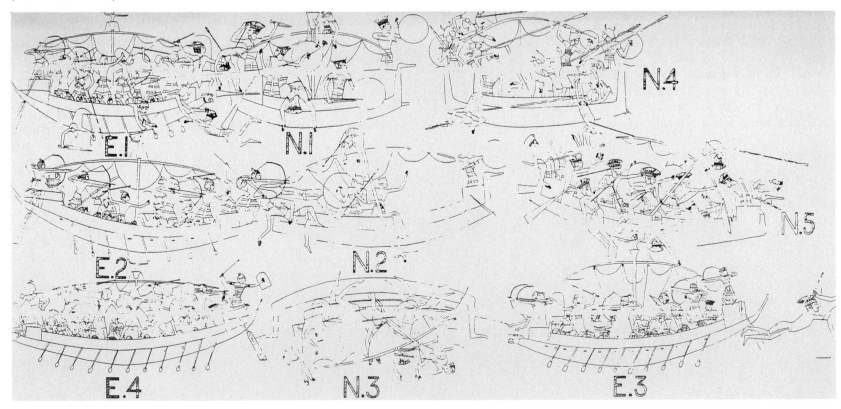

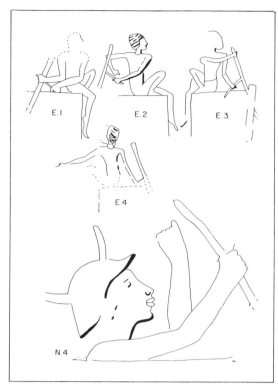

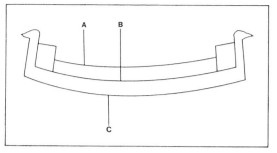

The three horizontal lines on ships N1-2, 4 and 5.

The helmsmen of ships E1-E4 and N4 (After Nelson et al 1930)

vessel is portrayed, even though an accompanying text indicates that at least three different types took part in the engagement. Thus, it is important to remember that the scene depicts five illustrations of a single ship. These images of an invading ship were probably based on field sketches prepared by an Egyptian army artist after the battle.

The scene of the waterborne engagement contains the most detailed known depictions of a type of ship used by the Sea Peoples. Although the engagement was originally a painted relief, the paint has long since disappeared. As the Egyptian artists in this art form did not specifically differentiate between relief and paint, a certain amount of detail has been lost with the paint. There is some indication to suggest that in this particular Egyptian art form, painting dominated the carved relief. Now, only by comparing portions of the temple where the paint has been preserved does it become clear how much detail has probably been lost together with the paint.[78]

This phenomenon is clearly seen in the manner that the helmsman in ship N4 grasps the loom of the oar with his right hand while his left holds a now non-existent tiller which must have been originally applied in paint

An Egyptian ship taking part in the naval battle that Ramses III fought against the Sea Peoples. (Detail from Nelson et al 1930)

alone. This manner of handling the quarter rudder may be compared with that used by the helmsmen of the four Egyptian vessels, all of whom hold the tiller in their left hands, while two hold the oar's loom with their right hands.

The loss of paint may partly explain the differences among the various renditions of what is undoubtedly a single Sea Peoples' ship. It also may explain why some elements are inconsistent, even on the same ship. The bird-head capping the stern of ship N2, for example, is eyeless, while the head atop the stem has a carved eye. Furthermore, the brails are depicted on only one side of the mast. Detail may have been applied in some areas in relief and paint, while in others solely in paint. Furthermore, corrections were made on plaster that was applied to the relief. In some cases we apparently have only the original draft, while the final rendition that had been carved into the plaster has long since crumbled away.

It is possible to determine the construction of the invaders' ships by a careful study of the manner in which the bodies of the dead and dying warriors are draped over the ships' archi-

tecture. The ships are being depicted in sheer view. Four of the hulls – ships N1, N2, N4 and N5 – are defined by three horizontal lines. Dead bodies bent over the near side of the ships cross lines A, B and C, indicate that the ships themselves are seen in sheer view.

Initially these seem to delineate the hull and a screen, as on the attacking Egyptian ships. Arguing against this interpretation, however, is line B, which sometimes serves as a base-line, directly above which the bodies of warriors appear:

1. One warrior, in the process of being speared, lies on line B in ship N2. This is not accidental as his left leg also rests on the same line. Next to him, another warrior falls head first, his left arm seemingly disappearing behind line B.

2. In ship N4 the helmsman and a second

<hr />

78. See Nelson's (1929, p22) description of another war scene at Medinet Habu where the paint has been preserved.

<hr />

The four horizontal lines on ship N3.

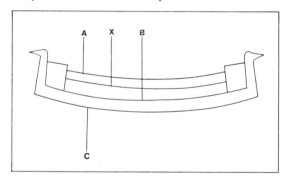

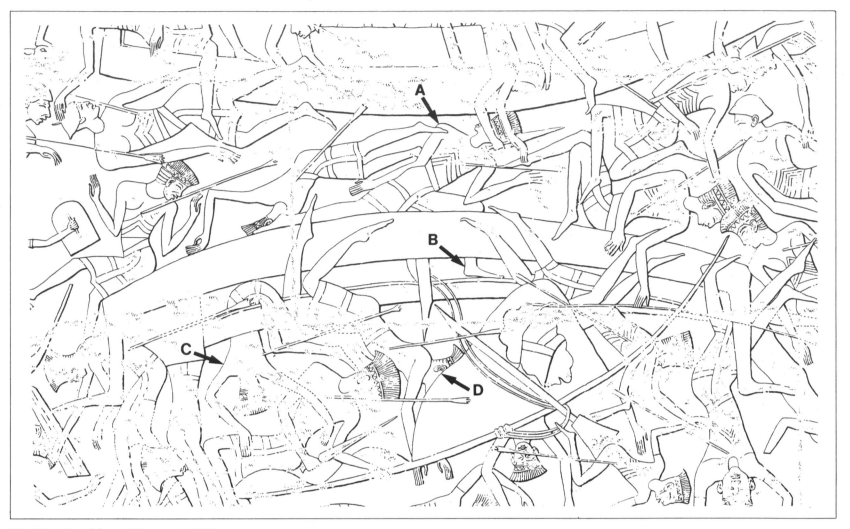

Ship N3. (Detail from Nelson *et al* 1930)

fallen comrade appear directly above line B. The latter is succoured by a warrior standing at a higher level, who bends over line A. This indicates that the Egyptian artist wished to portray these ships as having two levels. That is, the vessel must have been at least partially decked amidships.

These considerations argue that something is lacking in these depictions. And indeed, the 'missing link', a fourth horizontal line (X), appears on ship N3 between lines A and B. The ship's principal architectural characteristics may be determined by studying how three of the warriors are positioned in relation to the three resultant horizontal areas (AX, XB and BC):

1. One warrior lies astride the ship's capsized hull (A). His right leg is stretched out behind him. His left leg disappears behind the hull

Tentative isometric reconstruction of a Sea Peoples' ship portraying the primary elements of the ship's architecture as indicated by the bodies of the dead warriors. (Drawing by F M Hocker)

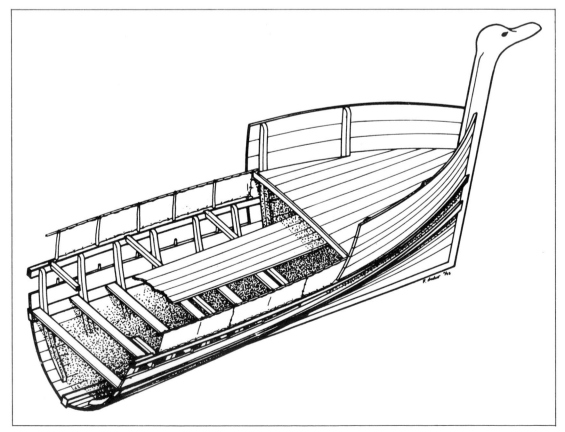

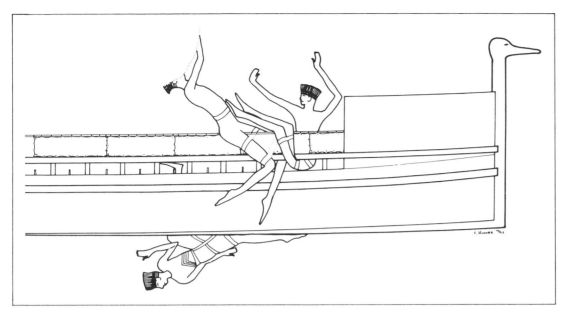

Top: Tentative sheer view of a Sea Peoples ship with the three bodies of warriors in ship N3 added to better illustrate the constructional elements. Note that the bodies are depicted in a scale larger than that of the ship. (Drawing by F M Hocker)

Centre: Standing amidships in ship E1, an Egyptian sailor casts a four-toothed grapnel into the rigging of Sea Peoples ship N1. (Detail from Nelson et al 1930)

Bottom: Sea Peoples ship N3 is capsized by means of the grapnel attached to the bow of Egyptian ship E3. (Detail from Nelson et al 1930)

such an exposed space is that this ship type must have had an open rowers' gallery, through which the oarsmen worked their oars. Above this was a screen (area AX) and below it the hull from caprail to keel (area BC). By adding line X to the ships N2 and N4, the positioning of the figures is made clear. Although no stanchions are depicted, the prototype ship must have carried them, for otherwise there would have been nothing to support the screen and deck beams. Perhaps the stanchions had been depicted in paint only. Alternatively, the Egyptian artists may have left them out to prevent the scene from becoming too burdened with detail.

The single most important conclusion from this evaluation of the Sea Peoples' ship depictions at Medinet Habu is that they seem to be virtually identical in composition to the Helladic galley type typified by the Kynos ship discussed above. In other words, the Sea Peoples seem to have adopted the use of a Mycenaean ship type. There is, however, one difference between the two ship types: the bird-head devices. Mycenaean ships have bird or bird-head devices commonly placed atop the stem. The Sea Peoples' ship images have bird-head devices atop their sternpost facing astern. In this, the latter resemble most closely the 'bird-boats' of the Central European Bronze and Iron Age cultures.[79]

Naval warfare in the Late Bronze Age

The waterline ram did not come into use until well after the Bronze Age had run its course. This being the case, how were galleys employed in naval battles prior to the introduction of the ram? We know of several battles that took place during the Late Bronze Age. Our main source of information for how battles were fought, however, is derived from

(area BC), but his foot reappears in area XB (B).

2. A second warrior (C) is 'wrapped around' area AX; his torso disappears behind line X but his lower abdomen and legs reappear in area XB.

3. The left leg of a third figure (D) reappears from behind line X and crosses lines B and C. This warrior seems to be straddling area AX.

Here, then, are three independent clues that point to a single conclusion: *area XB represents an open space.* The only rational explanation for

79. Wachsmann, forthcoming B.

Ramses III's Medinet Habu reliefs. This conflict was not totally a sea battle, as it appears that some of the forces that took part were contingents of archers on the shore. Egyptian archers, armed with composite bows, were used to good advantage. The bowmen, and slingers, were able to pick off the invading warriors while staying beyond range of the latters' javelins. Once the enemy had been neutralised, the ships closed in. Interestingly, the only specifically nautical weapon depicted in the relief is a four-armed grapnel.

The ships are depicted in a typically Egyptian manner, from two different points of view: the hulls in profile, but the mast and rigging frontally.[80] Although the profiles of the Sea Peoples' ships seem to be upright in the water, actually, by tilting the ships' masts, the Egyptian artists indicated that these ships were in the process of being capsized.

Ships E1 and N1, which signify the beginning of the battle, are portrayed next to each other. Ship N1's mast is still upright. As the Egyptian ship comes abeam the anchored (?) Sea Peoples' ship, a sailor located amidships tosses a grapnel into the enemy's rigging. There then follow three depictions of a Sea

Peoples' ship – N2, N4 and N5 – with the masts askew at varying angles. These represent the slanting deck as the ships are capsized. To add further emphasis to the pandemonium inherent in the progressive capsizing of a ship, the artists depicted the invaders in a variety of unusual positions, falling backwards and forwards, grabbing on to the mast for dear life, and lying on the side of the hull.

In the final phase, illustrated by N3, the ship has capsized and the mast has broken off. Once again the grapnel's rope is depicted, although the grapnel itself is lost in the rigging. Now, however, the rope is attached to the bow of the opposing Egyptian ship (E3). This may indicate that once the grapnel had caught in the

enemy's rigging, the Egyptians moved their ships perpendicular to the enemy and backed water.[81] The final figure illustrates the varying lists on the basis of the angles of the masts to the horizon.

Shelley Wachsmann

Acknowledgements

I wish to thank Professor Morrison for inviting me to contribute to this book. Thanks also to my colleague, Dr Frederick M Hocker for preparing the drawings of a Sea Peoples' ship that appear on pages 32–33.

80. Strictly speaking, they are seen from astern.

81. On backing water see Tilley 1992.

By showing the ships' progressively tilting masts en face, as well as by indicating the chaos onboard the ships as they were overturned, the Egyptian artists were able to illustrate the worsening list of the invader's ships in the process of being capsized by the Egyptian forces. The mast of N4 is reversed left to right. The angle of N3 is based on the upper part of the broken mast. The angle is based on that between the mast and the horizon.

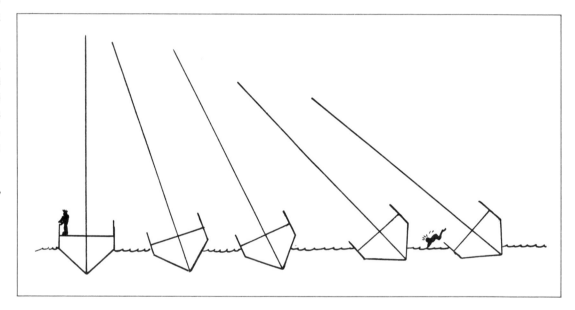

References and abbreviations used in the footnotes

ABSA = *Annual of the British School at Athens*

AJA = *American Journal of Archaeology*

ANET[3] = *Ancient Near Eastern Texts Relating to the Old Testament* (Third edition with Supplement), ed J B Pritchard (Princeton 1969).

ARAB = D D Luckenbill *Ancient Records of Assyria and Babylonia* I–II (New York; reprint 1968).

BAR = *Ancient Records of Egypt*, I–V, ed J H Breasted (Chicago 1906–1907; 1988 reprint).

BCH = *Bulletin de correspondance hellénique*

IJNA = *International Journal of Nautical Archaeology*

JEA = *Journal of Egyptian Archaeology*

JHS = *Journal of Hellenic Studies*

JMA = *Journal of Mediterranean Archaeology*

JNES = *Journal of Near Eastern Studies*

LAE = *The Literature of Ancient Egypt: An Anthology of Stories, Instructions, and Poetry*, ed W K Simpson,

translated by R O Faulkner, E F Wente, Jr and W K Simpson (New Haven 1972).

MM = *The Mariner's Mirror*

PM = A Evans, *The Palace of Minos* I–IV (London. 1921–1964).

RDAC = *Report of the Department of Antiquities, Cyprus*

Thera III/3 = *Thera and the Aegean World*, III Vol 3: *Chronology* (Proceedings of the Third International Congress, Santorini, Greece, 3–9 September 1989), ed D A Hardy (London 1990).

UC,OIC = *The University of Chicago, Oriental Institute Communications*

ZÄSA = *Zeitschrift für Ägyptische Sprachen und Altertumskund*

J Baines (1990), 'Interpreting the Story of the Shipwrecked Sailor', *JEA* 76, pp55–76.

G A Ballard (1920), 'The Sculptures of Deir el-Bahri', *MM* 6, pp149–155, 162–174, 212–217.

R D Barnett (1969), 'Ezekiel and Tyre', *Eretz Israel* 9, pp6–13, pls I–IV.

L Basch (1987), *Le musée imaginaire de la marine antique* (Athens).

G F Bass (1967), *Cape Gelidonya: A Bronze Age Shipwreck*, Transactions of the American Philosophical Society, NS, LVII: 8 (Philadelphia).

L Baumbach (1983), 'An Examination of the Evidence for a State of Emergency at Pylos c1200 BC from the Linear B Tablets', *Res Mycenaeae*, pp28–40.

M Bietak (1988), 'Zur Marine des Alten Reiches', in *Pyramid Studies and other Essays Presented to IES Edwards* eds J Baines, T G H James, A Leahy and A F Shore (London), pp35–40, pls 5–9.

C W Bishop (1938), 'Long Houses and Dragon Boats', *Antiquity* 12, pp411–424, pls I–IV.

C W Blegen and M Rawson (1966), *The Palace of Nestor at Pylos in Western Messenia*, I: *The Buildings and their Contents*, Part 1: *Text* (Princeton).

L Borchardt (1981), *Das Grabdenkmal Des Königs Saȝhu-Reˁ: Band II: Die Wandbilder*, Text. (Osnabrück; reprint 1913).

C Broodbank and T F Strasser (1991), 'Migrant Farmers and the Neolithic Colonization of Crete', *Antiquity* 65, pp233–245.

L Casson (1971), *Ships and Seamanship in the Ancient World* (Princeton).

L Casson (1975), 'Bronze Age Ships. The Evidence of the Thera Wall Paintings' *IJNA* 4, pp3–10.

L Casson (1978), 'The Thera Ships' IJNA 7; pp232–233.

J Chadwick (1958), *The Decipherment of Linear B* (Cambridge).

J Chadwick (1976), *The Mycenaean World* (London).

J Chadwick (1987A), 'The Muster of the Pylian Fleet', in *Tractata Mycenaea*, Proceedings of the Eighth International Colloquium on Mycenaean Studies, Ohrid, 15–20 September 1985, eds P H Iliévski and L Crepajac (Skopje), pp75–84.

J Chadwick (1987B), *Linear B and Related Scripts* (Berkeley).

J F Cherry (1990), 'The First Colonization of the Mediterranean Islands: A review of Recent Research', *JMA* 3, pp145–221.

J E Coleman (1985), "Frying Pans" of the Early Bronze Age Aegean', *AJA* 89, pp191–219, pls 33–37.

F Dakoronia (1990), 'War-Ships on Sherds of LH III C Kraters from Kynos', *Tropis* II, pp117–122.

F Dakoronia (1993), 'Homeric Towns in East Lokris: Problems of Identification', *Hesperia* 62, pp115–127.

F. Danelius and H Steinitz (1967), 'The Fishes and Other Aquatic Animals on the Punt-Reliefs at Deir El-Bahri', *JEA* 53, pp15–24.

N de G Davies and R O Faulkner (1947), 'A Syrian Trading Venture to Egypt', *JEA* 33, pp40–46, pl 8.

G B R De Cervin (1977), 'The Thera Ships – Other Suggestions', *MM* 63, pp150–152.,

F. Deilaki (1987), 'Ship Representations from Prehistoric Argolis (MH Period)', *Tropis* II, pp123–126.

C G Doumas (1983), *Thera: Pompeii of the Ancient Aegean* (London).

C G Doumas (1992), *The Wall Paintings of Thera*, translated A Doumas (Athens).

J du Plat Taylor, M V Seton Williams and J Waechter (1950), 'The Excavations at Sacke Gözü', *Iraq* 12, pp53–138.

T C Gillmer (1975), 'The Thera Ship', *MM* 61, pp321–329.

A Göttlicher (1978), *Materialien für ein Corpus der Schiffsmodele im Altertum* (Mainz am Rhein).

D Gray (1974), 'Seewesen', in *Archaeologia Homerica*, Band I Kapital G.

B Greenhill (1976), *Archaeology of the Boat* (London).

C W Haldane (1993), 'Ancient Egyptian Hull Construction', unpublished PhD dissertation, Texas A&M University.

S Hassan (1954), 'The Causeway of Wnis at Sakkara', *ZÄSA* 80, pp136–139, Tafs XII–XIII.

M Heltzer (1982), *The Internal Organization of the Kingdom of Ugarit: Royal Service System, Taxes, Royal Economy, Army and Administration* (Wiesbaden).

H Hencken (1968), *Tarquinia, Villanovans and Early Etruscans* I–II, *BASPR* XXIII (Cambridge).

Herodotus = *Herodotus* I, translated A D Godley, Loeb Classical Library (London 1975).

F M Hocker, forthcoming, 'Did Hatshepsut's Punt Ships Have Keels?' in S Wachsmann, *Seagoing Ships and Seamanship in the Bronze Age Levant* (College Station, Texas).

R W Hutchinson (1962), *Prehistoric Crete* (Harmondsworth).,

C D Jarrett-Bell (1930), 'Rowing in the XVIIIth Dynasty', *Ancient Egypt*, pp11–19.

D Jones (1990), *Model Boats From the Tomb of Tut'ankhamun*, Tut'ankhamun's Tomb Series IX, general ed J R Harris (Oxford).

D H Kennedy (1976) 'Cable Reinforcement of the Anthenian Trireme', *MM* 62, pp159–168.

D H Kennedy (1978), 'A Further Note on the Thera Ships', *MM* 64, pp135–137.

J T Killen (1983), 'PY An 1', *Minos* 18, pp71–79.

G S Kirk (1949), 'Ships on Geometric Vases', *ABSA* 44, pp93–153, pls 38–40.

K A Kitchen (1971), 'Punt and How to Get There', *Orientalia* 40, pp184–207.

A B Knapp, J D Muhly and P M Muhly (1988), 'To Hoard is Human: Late Bronze Age Metal Deposits in Cyprus and the Aegean', *RDAC*, pp233–262.

G S Korrés (1989), 'Representation of a Late Mycenaean Ship on the Pyxis from Tragana, Pylos', *Tropis* I, pp177–202.

P I Kuniholm (1990), 'Overview and Assessment of the Evidence for the Date of the Eruption of Thera', in *Thera* III/3, pp13–18.

B Landström (1970), *Ships of the Pharaohs* (Garden City).

C Laviosa (1972), 'La Marina Micenea', *Annuario della Scuola Archeologica di Atene* 47–48 (1969–1970; NS 31–32) (Rome), pp7–40.

R Le Baron Bowen (1960), 'Egypt's Earliest Sailing Ships', *Antiquity* 34, pp117–131.

J R Lenz (1993), 'Kings and the Ideology of Kingship in Early Greece (c1200–700 BC): Epic, Archaeology and History', unpublished PhD dissertation (Columbia University).

A Lucas (1962), *Ancient Egyptian Materials and Industries*, revised by J R Harris (London).

N Marinatos (1984), *Art and Religion in Thera: Reconstructing a Bronze Age Society* (Athens).

S Marinatos (1933), 'La marine créto-mycénienne', *BCH* 57, pp170–235.

S Marinatos (1974), *Excavations at Thera VI (1972 Season)*, Text and plates (Athens).

L Morgan (1988), *The Miniature Wall Paintings of Thera: A Study in Aegean Culture and Iconography* (Cambridge).

L Morricone (1975), 'Coo-Scavi e scoperte nel "Serraglio" in località minori (1935–43)', *Annuario della Scuola Archeologica di Atene* 50–51 (1972–73; NS 34–35), pp139–396.

J S Morrison and R T Williams (1968), *Greek Oared Ships: 900–322 BC* (Cambridge).

E Naville (1898), *The Temple of Deir el Bahri*, III: *End of the Northern Half and Southern Half of the Middle Platform* (London).

E Naville (1908), *The Temple of Deir el Bahri VI: The Lower Terrace, Additions and Plans* (London).

H H Nelson (1929), 'The Epigraphic Survey of the Great Temple of Medinet Habu (Seasons 1924–1925 to 1927–

1928)', in *Medinet Habu 1924–28*, (UC, OIC 5), (Chicago), pp1–36.

H H Nelson (1943), 'The Naval Battle Pictured at Medinet Habu', *JNES* 2, pp40–45.

H H Nelson et al (1930), *Medinet Habu*, I: *Earlier Historical Records of Ramses III*, (UC, IOP VIII) (Chicago).

M P Nilsson (1950), *The Minoan-Mycenaean Religion and its Survival in Greek Religion* (Lund).

T G Palaima (1991), 'Maritime Matters in the Linear B Tablets', *Aegeaum (Annals d'archéologie égéene de l'Université de Liège)* 7, pp273–310, pl LXIII.

L R Palmer (1956), 'Military Arrangements for the Defense of Pylos', *Minos* 4, pp120–145.

L R Palmer (1965), *Mycenaeans and Minoans: Aegean Prehistory in the Light of the Linear B Tablets* (New York).

E Porada (1984), 'The Cylinder Seal from Tell el-Dabˁa', *AJA* 88, pp485–488, pl 65: 1–3.

C Renfrew (1967), 'Cycladic Metallurgy and the Aegean Early Bronze Age', *AJA* 71, pp1–20, pls 1–10.

C G Reynolds (1978), 'The Thera Ships', *MM* 64, p124.

A Rowe (1936), 'Addendum A: Axe-Head of the Royal Boat-Crew of Cheops or Sahew-Rā(?)', in A Rowe, *A Catalogue of Egyptian Scarabs, Scaraboids, Seals and Amulets in the Palestine Archaeological Museum* (Cairo), pp283–288.

T Säve-Söderbergh (1946), *The Navy of the Eighteenth Egyptian Dynasty* (Uppsala).

T Säve-Söderbergh (1957), *Four Eighteenth Dynasty Tombs* (Oxford).

C F A Schaeffer (1962), 'Fouilles et découvertes des XVIIIᵉ et XIXᵉ campagnes, 1954–1955', *Ugaritica* 4, pp1–150.

C A Televantou (1990), 'New Light on the West House Wall-Paintings', in *Thera* III/1, pp309–326.

A Tilley (1992), 'Rowing Astern', *IJNA* 21, pp55–60.

H Tzalas (1989), 'On the Obsidian Trail with a Papyrus Craft in the Cyclades', in *Third Symposium on Ship Construction in Antiquity* [Summaries of lectures] (Athens).

A I Tzamtzis (1987), '"Papyrella": Remote Descendant of a Middle Stone Age Craft?' in *Second Symposium on Ship Construction in Antiquity* [Summaries of lectures] (Delphi).

W H Van Soldt and J Hoftijzer, forthcoming 'Texts from Ugarit Pertaining to Seafaring', in S Wachsmann, *Seagoing Ships and Seamanship in the Bronze Age Levant* (College Station, Texas).

M Ventris and J Chadwick (1973), *Documents in Mycenaean Greek* (Cambridge).

S Wachsmann (1980), 'The Thera Waterborne Procession Reconsidered', *IJNA* 9, pp287–295.

S Wachsmann (1981), 'The Ships of the Sea Peoples', *IJNA* 10, pp187–200.

S Wachsmann (1982), 'The Ships of the Sea Peoples: Additional Notes' *IJNA* 11, pp297–304.

S Wachsmann (1990), 'On Sea-Going Vessels Depicted in Egyptian Art', *Qadmoniot* 23 (1989–90), pp2–20, back cover (in Hebrew).

S Wachsmann (forthcoming), Seagoing Ships and Seamanship in the Bronze Age Levant (College Station, Texas).

S Wachsmann, forthcoming B, 'Bird-Head Devices on Mediterranean Ships', in *Tropis* IV, (Fourth International Symposium on Ship Construction in Antiquity), Athens 28th–31st August 1991. ed H Tzalas.

R T Williams (1959), Addenda to 'Early Greek Ships of Two Levels', *JHS* 79, pp159–160.

D Woolner (1957), 'Graffiti of Ships at Tarxien, Malta', *Antiquity* 31, pp60–67.

The Ancestry of the Trireme 1200–525 BC

THE LONG PERIOD between the collapse in the twelfth century BC of what has been called the Near East regional system of civilisations and the creation by the Persian king Cambyses of a 'royal navy' of triremes just before 525 BC witnessed at least four important developments regarding the sea-going galley.

In the first place, ways were found to increase the number of oarsmen without lengthening the ship, *ie* seating capacity was created by 750 BC for a second and, much later, a third rower in the longitudinal space originally taken up by one only (the technical term used for this space is *interscalmium*, 'between-the-tholes'). In Greek terminology these developments made the original *monokrotos* galley first *dikrotos* and then *trikrotos*. They have been the subject of much learned controversy.

In the second place, two specialisations evolved, both resulting in a standardised type of ship, one a merchantman with twenty oars (*eikosoros*) which is mentioned in the *Odyssey* as a 'broad freighter' (IX, 322–23) and therefore was in existence by the second half of the eighth century BC; the other a fifty-oared type (*pentekontoros*). As Thucydides implies, this type was used from later in the same century by the authorities of the nascent Greek city states for various tasks, including conveyance of ambassadors, suppression of piracy and, exceptionally, warfare.

Thirdly, the important double invention was made of outrigger frame and rowing bench (*parexeiresia* and *thranos* in Greek), which made it possible for shipwrights to increase the number of oarsmen in each *interscalmium* without widening the ship, but which originally had the different rationale of enabling them to equip the ship with a deck. It is not inconceivable that this invention, which is represented in Greek vase pictures of around 750 BC, already belonged to the Bronze Age, but had to be re-

Poop section of two-level galley with parexeiresia, *both banks manned, no tholes shown; Athens c760-735 BC.* (Musée du Louvre)

discovered after it had passed into disuse following the disasters of the twelfth century.

The same chronographical reservation is in order concerning the fourth development, the provision of an effective defence in the form of a forward extension of the keel, known as the ram. This fixture is manifest in the pictures just mentioned, and here again a Bronze Age predecessor is not improbable, but re-invention at a later date is not to be excluded.

The situation in which these developments had their origin was one of dire adversity. Indeed, apart from narrowly local craft, the extent and depth of the collapse of twelfth-century shipping can hardly be exaggerated. The far-flung network of Mycenean trade routes (which stretched from Syria and Palestine to Campania and Malta, with Troy at its northern and Egypt at its southern limit) broke down completely. No doubt this meant the disappearance of the bigger and more technically advanced ships it may be assumed that the Myceneans and their contemporaries used on these routes. They could not be operated by the small communities that remained after the

ruin of the Mycenean (and other) palace economies.

In Greece the disintegration of these economies led to widespread emigration. Larger groups of such migrants who found favourable conditions in their new homes may soon have been able to resume something like their former lifestyle. This probably happened in Cyprus, where the establishment of a considerable group of Mycenean immigrants at a number of sites inaugurated a period of great cultural activity. If, as is not improbable, these people travelled from Greece (the Argolid) to Cyprus in the sophisticated ships just mentioned, Cyprus could have become the centre where Mycenean nautical skills were preserved and passed on to others like the Phoenicians in the Lebanon (Mycenean refugees are taken to have settled in Phoenicia also). Since nearby Ugarit, in northern Syria, had been an important centre of seaborne trade in the later Bronze Age, and since part of its population moved southwards after the city was destroyed, the Phoenicians are indeed very likely to have absorbed all the nautical traditions and expertise

Single-level galley, similar to that of previous illustration: fifteen thranite tholes, four 'manned' by oversize oarsmen; Athens c760-735 BC. (Musée du Louvre)

Second, we have references to ships and shipping in works of literature, the most important of which are the Homeric poems; and in the writings of the Greek historians, above all Herodotus (*c*480–420 BC) and Thucydides (*c*460–400 BC). Because the latter collected the data for their histories long after our period ended, their testimony concerning its shipping is at best indirect and may be based to an important degree on conclusions of their informants, as well as their own. This makes their assertions problematic, however reasonable they may seem to be. Where the *Iliad* and *Odyssey* are concerned the situation is even more delicate: not only may elements in the (mostly fictional) worlds of these poems belong to periods as distant from each other as the twelfth and the eighth centuries; they may also be entirely fictitious, either because they are entirely the creation of the poet, or because they were afterwards inserted (interpolated) by others for private reasons, for example, to please local patriots.

A relatively large and important part of this evidence, both iconographic and literary, immediately relates to the eighth century, and in particular its second half (assuming with many Homeric scholars that the poet lived then). Also, important elements in Thucydides' short sketch of early Greek naval developments (I, 13–14) refer to the quarter-century ending in 700 BC. This period is therefore the first that can be discussed fruitfully, and Homer's very varied and lively testimony is the best possible starting point. What can be learned from the contemporaneous pictures will be shown to accord very well with what Homer tells us, and this is also true for Thucydides' *aperçu* just mentioned.

available in this neighbourhood at the end of the second millennium BC. However, the miserable state of information concerning Phoenician shipping makes it impossible to determine if and how they made use of this knowledge, and whether this in its turn could have influenced developments in other maritime centres, such as Greece. This is why there is no really decisive argument in favour of the hypothesis that there was continuity in nautical techniques and skills between the Late Bronze Age and the period covered in this chapter. Only the correspondences between some pictures, which have been noticed above, give some support to the idea. Therefore, this chapter will not address the problem of continuity again; indeed nautical developments in general will be restricted in practice to the Greek world: virtually all surviving evidence originates there.

The evidence

This evidence is of two kinds. It consists, first, of representations of ships painted on Greek pottery (pots and plaques), or engraved on fibulae and coins; of models made of earthenware and other materials; and of reliefs in stone (a single one originating from the Near East) and ivory. In this category we may include the

Late Mycenaean galley with parexeiresia *and ram (?)* (Drawing by W Dodds)

hand platforms for two complete galleys, dedicated before 650 BC to the goddess Hera in her great sanctuary on the island of Samos. The oval plan of these rows of stone slabs must be more or less identical in shape with the deck plan of the votive ships. Most of the ancient representations may be assumed to be pretty well contemporaneous with the craft they picture, and to represent real-life ships, just as the hand platforms did and modern plans do. Only in rare cases is there reason to suspect that an artist pictured an imaginary ship or at any rate one he had not actually seen himself. Omission or accentuation of details to produce an artistic effect is of course another matter. In any case, none of these representations can be taken as technically adequate renderings.

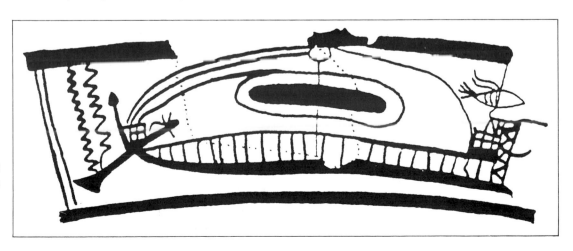

Shipping in the late eighth century

Homer

Homer's galleys are of four kinds. In the second book of the *Iliad* a catalogue is presented of the contingents in the Greek forces besieging Troy, including the fleets that brought them there (II, 484–759). In most cases the ships are simply enumerated (*eg* 'the men from Mycenae . . . of their hundred ships the commander was powerful Agamemnon': 569, 576), but there are two exceptions: aboard each of Philoctetes' seven ships were fifty oarsmen (719–20) – as are elsewhere specified for Achilles' and perhaps implied for Odysseus' ships[1] – who were all archers like their commander; and at the head of the catalogue the fifty ships of the Boeotian fleet have each 120 men on board (509–10). Thucydides' interpretation of these numbers will be considered later, but it is worth noting here that these fleets have no further interest for the poet and do not figure as such in any episode of the *Iliad* – not even the two exceptions just mentioned, and therefore the reader does not learn why these two fleets were particularised in this way, nor whether the others conformed to either of these types.

The next kind of galley is described in the *Odyssey* as belonging to the Phaeacians. One is made ready for Odysseus' final journey home: fifty-two young men are mobilised, and nowadays they are mostly regarded as fifty oarsmen and two officers (VIII, 35). This would make their ship (and its sisters) similar to those of Philoctetes and Achilles. But note that this ship is very different in another respect: it does not need a steersman and finds its way all by itself, *ie* it belongs to the sphere of the *märchen*, the fairy tale. Its conforming to real-world specifications in other respects such as the number of oarsmen is for that reason not to be taken for granted (although Thucydides for instance may have done so, like many modern commentators).

Third, there are several passages in Homer's poems where ships are used in what could be called real-life situations, ranging from the purely private to the public occasion. An aristocratic shipowner from Ithaca wants to use his ship to fetch a mule from distant pastures in the Peloponnese;[2] the same ship is lent out to Odysseus' son Telemachus to enable him to

make the voyage to Pylos and Sparta to get news about his father;[3] a similar ship is used by the suitors of Telemachus' mother Penelope to waylay her son on his journey home (IV, 778–79); Odysseus himself uses such a ship when travelling as an ambassador for the Greeks at Troy, bringing with him all the animals for an expiatory hecatomb.[4] In all these cases the number of oarsmen rowing the ship is specified as twenty and the line 'come, give me a fast ship and twenty comrades', which is twice used[5], suggests by its resemblance to a Homeric 'formula' that for the poet this was the ordinary ship of daily practice. Such a galley would have measured between 15m and 20m in length and something over 3m in width (50–65ft by 10ft): the length taken up by ten *interscalmia* or 9m plus bow and poop (both perhaps variable in length, but not less than 3m each and often probably more, for example to make space for defenders), and the width determined by the looms of the oars and pulling space for the rowers. Its cargo space may be assessed at 30–50 cubic metres at least, on the assumption that the hold (as yet open) had a depth below the beams of 1–1½m.

If Homer's usual galley was of this kind, his fourth type, the broad freighter called *eikosoros* ('twenty-oared'),[6] sets a problem. The question is what made it sufficiently specialised to make this term, which should have applied to all twenty-oared ships, its specific type-name (this, incidentally, it remained for merchant galleys of ever-increasing size up to at least the third century BC). In the absence of any direct information concerning the history of this type only speculation is possible, but a clue to the genesis of such a merchant galley can be reliably inferred from the tradition about Greek emigration to southern Italy and Sicily. The foundation there (after *c*735 BC) of a great many permanent settlements of farmers by Greek communities such as Corinth must have led to the regular exchange of 'colonial' grain

Bow section of two-level galley similar to that of first illustration, tholes of both banks shown; Athens c760–735 BC. (Musée du Louvre)

for more specialised products of the mother cities, such as oil, wine and manufactures. And this long-distance overseas transport of grain called for decked ships to prevent the cargo becoming wet and spoilt.

However, decking an open galley, the beams of which doubled as rowing benches, had far-reaching consequences. It involved the seating of the oarsmen above the deck and away from

---

1. *Iliad* XVI, 169; *Odyssey* IX, 60–1, 289–344; X, 116, 203–09.
2. *Odyssey* IV, 634–37.
3. *Odyssey* II, 386–87.
4. *Iliad* I, 308–11.
5. *Odyssey* II, 212, IV, 669.
6. *Odyssey* IX, 322.

Hypothetical cross-section of decked galley (eikosoros) *with and without* parexeiresia.

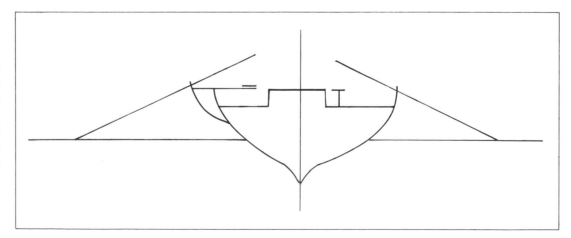

Galley with 39 (meant as 40?) oars, oarage exaggerated at the cost of decks fore and aft; Athens c735-710 BC. (British Museum)

the middle of the ship where hatches now had to be installed to give access to the closed hold. The latter change, moreover, entailed widening the ship to give the rowers sufficient purchase for their stroke, if the tholes were to remain fixed in the (now raised) gunwale. Alternatively, the tholes could be moved outside the gunwale by fixing them in a secondary 'gunwale', a horizontal timber that was fastened 'alongside and outside' (in Greek *parex*) the ship's side by means of stanchions. The Greek term *parexeiresia* is generally, and no doubt rightly, taken to denote such an outrigger construction. At the same time the oarsman was seated close to the gunwale on a bench (Greek *thranos*).

It is impossible to establish which of these alternatives was chosen for the first decked galleys. As the second could be adopted for *existing* ships it may have been the initial response, but as soon as new and bigger ships were laid down for the new bulk transport, the first became at least a possibility. Homer's evidence makes certain that galleys were widened, but if this development followed the invention of the *parexeiresia*, it seems extremely improbable that the builder of the broad freighter would have dispensed with this facility. Its great advantage over merely raising the gunwale was to leave maximum deck space clear for useful load, passengers for instance, who must have been an important consideration during the first generation of a colony's existence, both as new colonists and remigrants.

The difference between the new category of the *eikosoros* and that of the ordinary 'twenty-oared' Homeric galley was thus twofold: examples of the first must have been comparatively few in number, consisting as they did of specialised (and more expensive) ships; and because of that speciality they must have been more uniform, more a definite type. Indeed it seems probable that Homer's ordinary galleys, despite the seeming uniformity of their oarage, were not a standard category and as often had sixteen or eighteen oars as twenty (or even more, aristocratic shipowners no doubt tending to show off). At any rate, they must often have been used with fewer than twenty oars manned if the men were not available or if the circumstances of the voyage favoured the use of the sail in both directions. Such flexibility was hardly possible for the heavier *eikosoros*, which would also have needed all its crew for the defence of its costly cargo.

The pictures

As mentioned above, in the main the Greek pictorial record is in harmony with the Homeric descriptions. Pictures on vases of geometric style (of between 760 and 700 BC) show galleys with the *parexeiresia* represented as a more or less wide band, in some cases simply as a line, mostly with recognisable tholes, which occasionally are not drawn while the rowers are shown in action. The number of oarsmen, or of the tholes, ranges from five a side via ten or eleven to nineteen or even twenty, but the largest numbers are dubious: to suggest speed they emphasise the oarage to the point of making bow and poop of the ship almost nonexistent. They throw suspicion on pictures of eighth-century galleys with thirty-eight or forty rowers at one level, which may well be no more than painters' fantasies.

An early (c760–735 BC) group of pictures in the Louvre is particularly interesting. Together they illustrate a development not mentioned or alluded to by Homer (or any other writer), namely the seating of two rowers per *interscalmium*. This probably was done by reintroducing in an undecked galley furnished with *parexeiresia/thranoi* the original rower's seats on the beams and the corresponding tholes on the gunwale. The implications of these pictures, above all the one complete one among them, have been incorporated by the author into an illustration which is reproduced overleaf. This represents the pentecontor, a ship with twenty-five oarsmen to a side at two

levels, or in two banks, fourteen on the *thranoi* and eleven on the beams, called *zyga* in Greek (the proportion may also have been fifteen to ten, or thirteen to twelve: in fifth-century Athenian triremes with crews of up to 170 oarsmen it was thirty-one to twenty-seven in cases where the banks were fully manned). On the analogy of the nomenclature later used in the Athenian navy one may plausibly assume that the two categories of oarsmen were called thranites and zygians (*thranitai* 'the men of the benches', *zygioi* 'the men of the beams') soon after they were instituted.

Curiously, the author's hypothetical drawing has no complete counterpart in the Greek pictures. Although the painters, as already noted, are not averse to emphasising, even exaggerating, the oarage of their galleys to suggest power and speed, they rarely depict the complete two-level rowing complement; and as the few pictures in question are preserved only as fragments, it is impossible to determine whether they ever tried to paint a fully-manned pentecontor. Perhaps this is because they wanted to avoid cluttering up their composition, but there may be a more serious reason. Galleys provided with two levels of oars remained essentially the ships they had been when only one level had been present. They could therefore be easily rowed with only one level manned. This is already to be seen in one of the Louvre pictures, which shows the zygian rowers in action and has no place for the thranites, although the *parexeiresia* is present. This should cause no surprise or suspicion. As

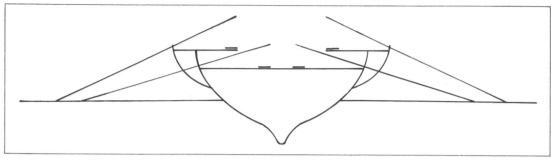

Hypothetical cross-section of open two-level galley.

free men rowers had to be paid, normally the number hired must have been the minimum able to do the job; that is to say that when maximum speed was not required, the principal (in the case of two-level galleys nearly always the state) usually manned one bank only. This must have been the case very often, as the pictures suggest.

Until recently, the pentecontor was generally assumed to be not *dikrotos*, as just presumed, but *monokrotos*, ie a galley with one bank of twenty-five oarsmen a side and an overall length of more than 30m (98ft). This *monokrotos* galley was, moreover, taken as the immediate precursor of the trireme, a three-level (*trikrotos*) ship of comparable dimensions. A very strong argument against this assumption has long been available, but has only recently been recognised as such by the archaeologist A M Snodgrass. The basis of this argument is the presence in the sanctuary of Hera in Samos of the stereobates already mentioned. These stoneworks are *c*23m and 24m long, 3.2m and upwards of 4m wide: the votive ships must have had about the same dimensions. Their prominent position in the sanctuary makes it probable that the dedication was a state affair and this implies that the votive ships were pentecontors: a lesser type would not have been placed in such a striking position (one may compare the triremes which Herodotus says were officially dedicated to commemorate the battle of Salamis: VIII, 121). Pentecontors of so short a length, however, cannot have been rowed at one level.

Thucydides (and Herodotus)

In the introductory chapters of his *History of the Peloponnesian War* Thucydides gives a short survey of the development of what he calls *nautika*, 'naval forces' or 'sea power'. This *aperçu*, by the way, covers much more than the histor-

ical period of this chapter: it goes back as far as King Minos of Crete. In so far as our period is concerned, it summarises Thucydides' reading of the Homeric epic and perhaps other poetry, and of the work of his precursor Herodotus, but also the fruits of his own research, which was chiefly directed at Corinth.

Thucydides asserts (I, 13.2–5) that the polis of the Corinthians was the first of the Greek city states to fit out a navy, and that they succeeded at one go in making it almost like the navies of his own time. He then gives three reasons for his assertion in ascending order of validity: the Corinthians were said to be the first in Greece to build triremes; there was evidence that three hundred years before Thucydides' own times (last quarter of the eighth century) a Corinthian shipwright named Ameinokles was invited by the city state of the Samians to build four ships for them (no doubt after the Corinthian model); it was a fact that forty years later a naval battle (the first known in Greek tradition) was fought between Corinth and its 'colony' Corcyra (modern Kérkira/Corfu) (surely in Corcyraean waters and not a Corinthian defeat). Thucydides explains the Corinthian lead by drawing attention to the city's *emporion* on the Isthmus where the Peloponnesian and extra-Peloponnesian Greeks met overland for trade (we are to understand that this fortunate position enabled Corinth to levy taxes more successfully

than other city states). The Corinthians invested the tax income from this market place in ships and used this navy to eliminate piracy. In this way their *emporion* became the centre of both land and maritime trade and the increased revenues now made the city powerful. Thucydides goes on to relate (13.6) that very much later (during the reigns of the Persian kings Cyrus and Cambyses, *c*550–523 BC) there were also great sea powers in Ionia: the Samian tyrant Polycrates, who thanks to his naval strength could subdue a number of Aegean islands (and according to Herodotus even cities on the Persian-controlled mainland: III, 39.4); and the city of the Phocaeans, who at the time of the foundation of their 'colony' Massalia (modern Marseilles) defeated Carthage in sea battles.

Thucydides then makes a most important statement concerning the galleys used by these powers (14.1ff). However powerful they were, they had few triremes, but used pentecontors and *ploia makra* ('ordinary longships'), like the powers of the times of the Trojan war. Only thereafter, a short time before the Persian wars, that is to say before the death of King Darius of Persia (486 BC), triremes came to be used in great numbers in the Greek world, first in the Sicily of the tyrants and in Corcyra, then – only just before Xerxes' expedition – in Aegina and Athens and other states, powers that until then had had insignificant navies, mostly consisting of pentecontors. Thucydides, in other words, here divides his period (beginning *c*1200 BC and somewhat longer than ours at the end) into three: first the age of the Trojan war or of Homer, which for him clearly continued up to the last quarter of the eighth century; second the era of the first powerful *nautika* (Corinth, Polycrates and Phocaea) which lasted until *c*485; and third the most recent times, when the trireme all but superseded the older naval types.

Now the most striking element in this state-

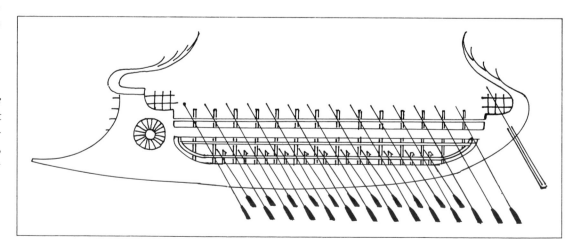

Reconstruction drawing of pentecontor based on the data furnished by the Athenian pottery sherds of c760-710 BC.

Poop section of two-level galley with parexeiresia, *manned by zygian oarsmen, no tholes shown, heroic dead laid down on thranite bench; Athens c760–735 BC.* (Deutsches Archäologisches Institut, Athens)

ment is Thucydides' insistence that the sort of ships used in his second period by and large remained what it had been in the first, triremes being used in small numbers (and obviously not from the beginning of the period) and that only after 486 a radical change occurred in this respect. Only then did the dominance of the trireme really begin. This assessment, which dates any technical innovation that might have been material to the naval developments of the second period to the years before *c*725 BC (if not to the Mycenaean period), implies that the innovation which made the Corinthian *nautika* 'almost modern' was not of a technical nature. This implication is of course borne out by the list of innovations and their dates drawn up at the beginning of this chapter. So there is no good reason to repudiate Thucydides on this point, as has been done all too often.

Moreover, as to the real nature of the Corinthian break with the past, Thucydides gives a vital clue in his remark, already referred to, that the *nautika* of Aegina and Athens (and others) of his second period were insignificant. This assessment seems to contradict figures preserved by Herodotus for the naval forces of these two cities in the years around 490 BC (50 to 70 ships each: VI, 89, 92) which are of the same order of magnitude as Herodotus' figures for the (to Thucydides) powerful fleets of Polycrates and Phocaea (100 and 60: III, 39.3 and I, 166.2 respectively) and therefore cannot be considered insignificant, though weaker. However, since Thucydides no doubt knew all these figures very well (and does not display any disapproval of his great precursor in this context), the contradiction must be considered

deceptive. And for Athens we have indeed evidence to underpin this conclusion.

Late sources (entries in lexica) have preserved the tradition that in earlier times ships were made available to the Athenian state by shipowners entitled *naukraroi* who were the heads of institutions called *naukrariai*. These institutions numbered forty-eight in our period[7] and were incorporated in the civic organisation of the polis (the so-called tribes and the phratries). In Athenian fleets of fifty ships these naukraric, privately owned, ships were clearly reinforced by two others, which have been convincingly identified as the predecessors of the well-known sacred (or state) triremes *Paralos* and *Salaminia*. So it appears that as long as the naukraric system was in use the Athenian state had a navy of two ships only and that most Greek states of the time – except Corinth, Polycrates and Phocaea – had comparable naval establishments (if they had any) which were supplemented by analogues of the Athenian naukraric ships (of which there are traces in Corinth, Eretria and Miletus, but not elsewhere). This surely explains Thucydides' 'insignificant' as a description of such state navies.

At the moment Thucydides was writing (in the late fifth century) his Athenian public was no longer familiar with the difference between state-owned and naukraric galleys, the latter having fallen from use more than two generations earlier. This may be the reason why he gives a second clue to the character of the naval forces of the first period and to the radical innovation brought about in Corinth. This is the remark that 'Homeric' ships were not *ka-*

taphrakta, *ie* had no facilities for defence (screens and their supporting construction) apart from the ram, but were still 'equipped in the ancient fashion rather like pirate craft' (I, 10.4). Here Thucydides stresses the difference between these privately-owned galleys and the naval units of his own time which had such defences, which indeed were fully-fledged warships and the property of the state. A simpler equipment of this sort will have distinguished the state-owned galleys of his second period. In other words, though the naval modernisation in Corinth principally related to the organisation of the state navy, the creation of this new arm did lead to technical improvements (but no radical innovations) in the galleys employed by the state. Furthermore, the states also preferred the pentecontor (when this type is mentioned in the sources, the ships appear almost always to be state property).

It is therefore reasonable to assume that from the outset the first state navy created by the Corinthians consisted of pentecontors, fitted out and probably built according to specifications drawn up by the state authorities. This explains why the Samians preferred to borrow a Corinthian shipwright to build their ships, rather than take an indigenous galley of comparable size and perfect that – though they could have done that just as well, for it appears certain that ships of such size were in existence before Corinth built its first navy. Thucydides' informants said so and they are confirmed by the Louvre pictures, which are earlier than the Corinthian reform. Aristocratic love of parade seems sufficient explanation for such showpieces in the private sphere and the 'fifties' of *Iliad* and *Odyssey* will have this background. But Homer's Boeotian galleys with complements of 120 are another matter. Not only do they not have equivalents in the pictures, but Thucydides also practically disavows them in his remark that the 'Trojan' (Homeric) *nautika* consisted of pentecontors and ordinary longships. His other evidence clearly was so unanimous that Homer's solitary testimony could not bring him to include the 120s in his summing up. They will indeed be fantasy, inserted (as perhaps the whole Boeotian entry in the ships' catalogue) by some rhapsode to flatter a Boeotian audience.

7. Later, *ie* after the reforms of Clisthenes (508 BC), they numbered fifty; they had disappeared by 480 BC.

Two-level galley with parexeiresia, *manned by thranite oarsmen, tholes of both banks shown, oarage exaggerated at the cost of the decks fore and aft; Corinth c735-710 BC.* (Royal Ontario Museum)

and descriptions of smaller galleys, which often come in several sizes, *eg* one *kelēs* of ten and another of four oars (in papyri of the third century BC *kelētes* are mentioned which brought mixed cargoes of foodstuffs from the Aegean to Egypt). At any rate there can be no doubt that in the non-aristocratic farmers' perspective Homer's twenty-oared galleys were big ships: their cargo capacity of *c*30 cubic metres, *ie* about 600 *medimnoi* (the common grain measure of *c*50 litres), surpassed by far the average annual produce (500 of such measures) of Athens' rich *pentakosiomedimnoi*, the highest of the four census classes instituted in 594/593 BC by the law-giver Solon.

The use of these galleys by farmers and landowners has an important implication, namely the owner's dependence on others to man the oars. Even aristocratic landowners can rarely have been in a position to man their 'twenties' with their own 'staff', slaves or free men from their households. They must very often have

8. J S Morrison and R T Williams, *Greek Oared Ships 900–322 BC* (Cambridge 1968), Arch 85.

Shipping in the eighth century

The eighth-century evidence leads to the conclusion that in this period the oared ship completely dominated all shipping. There is indeed no ship picture or model originating from the Aegean area or the Greek continent that cannot be interpreted as representing an oared ship, and no text manifestly referring to a ship without oars. The first unmistakable picture of such a (pure sailing) ship is dated *c*515 BC.[8] Contrary to later western European usage, the Greek terms for sailing ship – 'round ship' and '*holkas*'/'towed ship' – suggest that the sail was not felt to be the distinguishing feature of this type. The *holkas* at any rate will have started out as a pure barge which was towed by galleys and even when fitted out with sails may have continued being accompanied by largish ship's boats to assist manoeuvring. This is not to deny that elsewhere in the eastern Mediterranean pure sailing ships could have been used earlier than the Greek evidence implies. On a route like that between Phoenicia and Egypt it was possible in the summer to sail both ways with the prevailing northwesterlies abeam, and there may have been more such areas.

Otherwise it is a safe assumption that galleys were used for all categories of transport and that practices varied even more than is suggested by Homer. The poet Hesiod's advice on seafaring to his fellow-farmers implies that the

latter – at any rate some of them – had their own sea-going galleys, with which they traded their surpluses to remedy shortages. It is reasonable to assume that these ships were a mixed bag, but generally smaller than Homer's twenty-oared galleys. However, there is no specific evidence to confirm this assumption. It is only for later centuries that there are names

Part of wall relief from the palace of Sargon II at Khorsabad, timber being carried off in Phoenician hippoi; *Dur-Sharrukin between 722 and 705 BC.* (Musée du Louvre)

Drawing of wall relief from the palace of Sennacherib, Phoenician galleys engaged in the evacuation of Lulî, king of Tyre and Sidon, from Tyre; Nineveh 702 BC. (From A H Layard, The Monuments of Nineveh I, 1853)

been dependent on friends and neighbours, who then of course could eventually bring their own merchandise on board and try to make their bit out of the undertaking. This would indeed seem to be the situation that generated the *emporos*, the Greek passenger-trader that was soon to become a vital factor in Greek commerce. It is a pity that there is no illustration in Greek literature of such farmers on their way to markets, but Telemachus' voyage already mentioned may be considered an analogous case. The rather 'carefree manner in which this voyage is proposed and undertaken' suggests that its organiser made use of an existing pool of rowers; and the Athenian *naukrariai* certainly look like a special case of such an organisation.

Such pools must have been insufficient for voyages with the *eikosoros* because they took more time. As already suggested, this type will have been developed with a view to long-distance transport of grain and may be assumed to have served on routes to and from the colonies in Sicily and the Black Sea area (it may not be by chance that the biggest *eikosoros* of antiquity (and also the biggest ancient freighter known) was built in Syracuse in the middle of the third century BC.[9] For such long voyages the crews will have been recruited from a wider labour market from among those who could be spared from the farms for a longer time; these were then given the chance to become professional sailors. That the type survived for so long is proof that it was very serviceable. From the perspective of ship development, the *eikosoros* will have been especially useful as a training vessel to acquaint sailors with the possibilities of the sailing rig for such a heavy craft. In the long run its oars (in the very big specimens of later date no doubt sweeps) will have served solely as manoeuvring and mooring aids. By then – possibly early in the sixth century – the ship was essentially operated under sail and the difference from a fully-fledged sailing vessel had become very slight indeed.

Phoenician shipping in the late eighth century

To the Greek documentation can be added a number of representations of Phoenician galleys on Assyrian reliefs, which commemorate Assyrian war triumphs. These reliefs were dis-

covered in the palaces of the kings Sargon (722–705) and Sennacherib (705–681). A few of these representations are preserved in the original, the rest only in drawings and photographs made at the time they were discovered. The interpretation of all of them, but especially the modern ones, is extremely hazardous, as the Assyrian artists may not themselves have seen the ships, but worked on the basis of descriptions, possibly by word of mouth. Therefore, the modern drawings are at

several removes from the ships themselves. One photograph indeed reveals that the modern draughtsmen were not always accurate. For this reason the technical accuracy of these representations is even less reliable than their Greek counterparts. They must be interpreted in the aggregate, and this approach tends to

9. See Lionel Casson, *Ships and Seamanship in the Ancient World* (Princeton 1971), pp191–199, for details of 'Hiero's Superfreighter'.

support the evidence already analysed from the Greek world.

Three types of ship can be distinguished: one is analogous to the *dikrotos* Louvre galleys, being provided with a pronounced ram and rowed by up to seventeen rowers a side at two levels, but different from its Greek counterparts in that it has a deck over the rowers' heads, where passengers are seated;[10] the second type also has two levels of oars, but appears to be rather wide (round) and conspicuously differs from the first in that it has no ram, prow and stem being of similar form; the third type is like the second in this respect, but otherwise smaller and less rounded. The first two types are represented as serving in the evacuation of Tyre in 701 BC by King Lulî under the threat of Sennacherib, the third type in the carrying off of timber by the Assyrians.

Assuming that the Assyrian artists, like their Greek compeers, were not meticulous where correctness in numbers of oars is concerned, it is tempting to read into this modest range of ships the Greek categories of pentecontor, *eikosoros* and ordinary longships (*ploia makra*). This correspondence presupposes a fundamental similarity between Phoenician and Greek shipping in general, which indeed is probable, though in the absence of any historical evidence about the Phoenicians impossible to substantiate. However, the fact that the Greek tradition does not record any systematic differences and uses the term pentecontor for Phoenician ships (*Periplus Hannonis* 1) is significant. In consideration, moreover, of the overlapping of the Phoenician and Greek economical and cultural orbits, both in the metropolitan and in the colonial areas, there is no reason to play down the resemblances, nor to emphasise differences, for which there is no clear and undisputed evidence.

The resemblances may be taken as contributing to filling a total and hitherto unrecognised blank in the Phoenician record for our period, which concerns the galleys in the ownership of the state, *ie* those mostly described as war galleys. On this point modern scholars all agree that the Phoenician cities possessed numerous fleets of such ships, which they put at the disposal of the king of Persia as soon as they had surrendered their independence to him somewhere between 539 and 525 BC. This really incongruous notion is inferred from Herodotus' description of mobilisations of Persian naval armaments, such as Xerxes'

Two-level galleys under sail, no oars shown, screens under parexeiresia, *half-circular openings for zygian oars; Athens c530-480 BC. (Musée du Louvre)*

armada of 480 BC. This description is phrased in the following terms: 'The number of triremes was 1207; they were furnished by the following: Phoenicians and Palestinian Syrians 300 . . . Egyptians 200 . . . Cyprians 150 . . . Ionians 100 . . .' etc. It may well be that Herodotus himself shared the modern view, because in his own experience the 'Delian' alliance under Athens knew such a system of provision (though far more restricted than is imputed to the Persian organisation).

The most important reason (and decisive in the author's view) for rejecting this notion is that the Persian ruler cannot have allowed his maritime subjects any navies, let alone such large ones, because they obviously could (and would) be used as a means for rebellion. Furthermore, there is evidence pointing in a different direction, a remark concerning the Greek contribution to Xerxes' fleet, which goes back to the historian Ephorus of Cyme (c405–330; Cyme was the great naval base of the Persians in Asia Minor, so good information is likely to have been preserved there). The remark says that the king furnished the ships and the Greeks the oar crews.[11] This is to say that the Persians had a *royal* navy (*basilikos stolos*, the term used by Ephorus for later fifth-century fleets said to consist of Phoenician, Cilician, etc squadrons) which was manned by the maritime subjects, just as the Roman republic from 260 BC on had its own navy which was manned by naval allies (*socii navales*). This is a much more probable arrangement, for which indeed there is subsidiary evidence.

This conclusion clears the way for a more realistic approach to the original naval organisation of the Phoenicians and to pose the

question whether it was similar to the Athenian or the Corinthian organisation; in other words whether it had a small or a large nucleus of state-owned units apart from fleets of 'naukraric' ships. As soon as the problem is stated in these terms, the answer – for all its fundamental uncertainty – suggests itself, for the Phoenician cities with their lively trade were far more like Corinth than like Athens. Some thirty or forty pentecontors may therefore be assumed to have made up the navies of the Phoenician cities. It is not of course to be excluded that in this respect there were considerable and changing differences between the cities, which may be reflected in traditions about the periodical dominance of one or the other of these small states.

The seventh and sixth centuries

The pictures and Thucydides

Greek memories of nautical developments, as collected by Thucydides, did not include recollections of material changes in shipping after the great leap forward of the Corinthians, except for the introduction of the trireme. Re-

10. An authoritative study considers this type as provided with *parexeiresia*, rightly, in the author's view: see A Salonen, *Die Wasserfahrzeuge in Babylonien* (Helsinki 1939), p40.

11. Diodorus Siculus XI, 3.7.

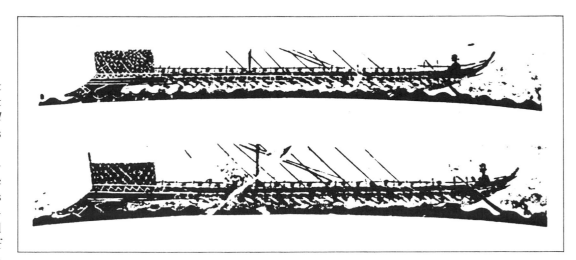

garding the trireme Thucydides suggests that the type was a foreign import by stressing that the Corinthians were the first *in Greece* to *build* the type (I, 13.3); he does not speak of its invention.

On the whole the iconographic record endorses Thucydides' negative judgement on the evolution of the ship in the period *c*700–525 as far as Greece is concerned. Although the representations change in character and style and become more detailed, there is no evidence of new developments. One famous Attic cup in the Louvre, painted around 530 BC, beautifully depicts four practically identical galleys under sail; no oarsmen are in view, but there are positions for fourteen or fifteen a side at two levels; the *parexeiresia* is constructed of two horizontal rails, held parallel to each other and connected with the ship's side by stanchions, the tops of which serve as tholes for the thranite oars; a narrow band below the rails is painted in contrasting red and shows a row of half-circles, each precisely halfway between the thranite tholes; together the band and half-circles clearly represent a screen, protection against spray, with openings for the zygian oars. Apart from this screen, which is paralleled in other pictures of the period, these galleys do not differ much from the early 'pentecontor' of the Louvre pictures of *c*760–735 BC: the painter may well have restricted the (potential) oarage of the ships to enhance the elegance of his tableau.

Other pictures of around 550–530 BC have been taken as signifying that 'biremes with about 100 oars were in use by the middle of the sixth century'. There is perhaps reason to take these pictures in this sense (though it depends on a dubious regard for the meticulousness of the painter), but not as representations of *Greek* galleys of such size, which do not fit into Thucydides' tripartite scheme of *ploia makra/* pentecontors/triremes, as his own implied denial of such a technical innovation also suggests. There is to be sure another context for large galleys, which Thucydides has deliberately left out of account as non-Greek, namely the Egypt of the XXVIth or Saïte dynasty (672–525 BC), which will be considered shortly.

Thucydides is also very laconic regarding Samos and Phocaea, the two Ionian naval powers of his second period, which he recognises as the equals of Corinth and as controlling their home waters during their war with the Persian king Cyrus. Herodotus discusses both these Ionian powers far more extensively, and the Saïte navy at least in outline, discussions which surely were the basis of Thucydides' remarks. The reason why Thucydides chose to be so brief no doubt was that he restricted his observations to Greece and that in contrast to Corinth the raison d'être of these three sea powers had little to do with his 'Greece' and the capacities of the Greek states. This was of course self-evident to him in the case of the Saïte kings; it is implied by Herodotus himself in that of the Phocaeans, whose naval arm he does not even mention when describing the subjection of their city, the first in Ionia, by the Persians; and the greatness (in Greek eyes 'grandiosity', *megaloprepeia*) of Polycrates' career in Herodotus' account, though nowadays almost always taken as an autonomous Samian affair, must have seemed incompatible with a purely Samian basis.

The Egyptian naval armament

The emergence of all three new sea powers of the sixth century is best explained as effected by of the strategic developments in the Levant which were occasioned by Egypt's throwing off the Assyrian yoke (*c*655 BC) and the concomitant organisation of its defence by the kings of the new (Saïte) dynasty. Two momentous steps were taken: in the first place the large-scale recruitment of mercenaries of Greek and Carian extraction, which began under the second of these kings, Psammetichus (664–610), in collaboration with Lydia and with a number of Aegean cities; in the second the creation by Psammetichus' successor Necho (610–595) of two navies, one stationed in the Mediterranean, the other in the Red Sea and said to have consisted of triremes.[12] Even the first of these steps had consequences in the maritime sphere, for the mercenaries are said to have started out as pirates – *ie* in ships – and once hired were settled near one of the mouths of the Nile where they had their own ships to keep contact with their homelands (the slipways of these ships were seen by Herodotus himself: II, 152–154). There is, however, no sign that these mercenaries (with or without their ships) were part of the naval arm of the Saïte kings.

The navies built by Necho were an essential element in the new strategical concept he (and his successors) developed when another traditional policy had failed. This was the attempt to renew the occupation of the Syro-Palestinian coastal area, which had been the Egyptian answer to threats of invasion from the Asiatic continent under the great kings of the New Kingdom (*c* 1580–1085 BC). Necho's new strategy, for which the fleets were built, aimed at keeping out invaders (now especially the Babylonian king Nebuchadrezzar) by fomenting and supporting the resistance and insurgence of the small kingdoms in the previous Egyptian protectorate, such as Judah and the Phoenician cities. Egyptian support in such undertakings now consisted of the supply of troops and above all provisions, and for this a naval arm was indispensable.

However, if Necho's navies were intended for such work, and if it is considered that his adversary had no navy of his own and could not expect to obtain the naval support of more than one or two of the Phoenician cities (support for which there is no sign whatever), it is very improbable that the Egyptian king really needed such a specialised warship as the trireme. His need was for capacious transports, and though in later times the trireme was often used as a troop transport in Persian and Athenian hands, it was less than serviceable as a carrier of foodstuffs and other provisions, its hold being

---

12. Herodotus II, 159.

Hypothetical cross-section of samaina. (Drawing by H
T Wallings)

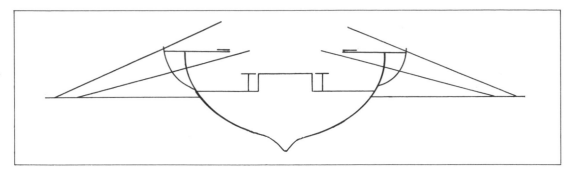

occupied by rowing benches and their supports. This is already reason enough to doubt
Necho's triremes, and there are more grounds
for scepticism. In the Egypt of Herodotus' days
the trireme was called *kbn(w)t*-ship, *ie* Byblos
ship (from Egyptian *Kpn* = Byblos). This was
not a specific type designation, but a generic
term for sea-going ship, more or less
equivalent to Greek *naus*: in the Hellenistic
period it was used for the ship of the line in the
Ptolemaic navy, the *pentērēs*/quinquereme, and
in the early period of the Old Kingdom for the
'long, many-oared craft' then used on the Byblos run. So if Herodotus' informants told him
that Necho had triremes, they most probably –
and quite forgivably, for they were not historians bent on terminological correctness – used
the equivalent of their own day (when squadrons of Persian triremes were manned by
Egyptian oar crews) as a translation of *kbnt*-
ship in the Egyptian traditions concerning
Necho's navies. It follows from Herodotus' account of a naval conflict in the western Mediterranean of two generations after Necho,
which was fought out without triremes being
used on either side, that they thereby introduced an anachronism into these traditions.

Nevertheless, it is in Egypt that we hear of
cargo-carrying galleys (*kerkouroi*) of comparable, and even larger, tonnage than that of the
trireme:[13] in the tradition they figure both as
river ships and as sea-going ships, the latter in
Xerxes' expedition.[14] This makes the assumption entirely plausible that Necho's naval galleys were comparable in size, though not in
oarage, to the trireme. It may even be the case
that knowledge of the measurement of the slipways built for these ships[15] strengthened Herodotus' informants in their naive opinion that
the ships were triremes.

Now some of these big galleys may have
been provided with *dikrotos* oarage after the example of Greek or Phoenician pentecontors,
and a larger number of oarsmen in proportion
to their greater length. They may also have
been intermittent visitors in Greek ports, for
Necho and his successors, in particular
Amasis,[16] fostered diplomatic contacts with the
Greek world where they hired the mercenaries
who were an essential part of their army
(Amasis, for instance, made a generous dona-
tion to the rebuilding fund of the great temple
in Delphi). Visits of such unusual ships may
well have attracted the attention and exercised
the fantasy of painters, inspiring them to such
efforts as that reproduced on p45.

The *samaina*

The maritime policy of the Egyptian kings was
also influential in the creation of a new type of
galley, the *samaina*, by the Samian tyrant Polycrates, who ruled the island from *c*540 to 522.
In discussing Polycrates' career both Herodotus and Thucydides fail to record this detail,
although the first discourses upon Polycrates at
some length (III, 39–56, 120–25). Thucydides'
silence on this point is again to be explained by
his strictly Greek purview. As a result only late
to very late sources of information on this ship
now survive, among them Plutarch (*Life of
Pericles*, 26.4). Plutarch's account is as follows:

> The *samaina* is on the one hand ?-shaped
> [*hupoprōros*] in the upturned part [*simōma*] of its
> prow, on the other it has a relatively large,
> paunchlike hold: as a result it can be used on
> deep-sea routes [as a sailing ship] and for fast
> sprints under oar [as a galley]. It acquired its
> name by reason of its first appearing in Samos.
> Polycrates the tyrant was its builder.

Other sources add that the ship was *dikrotos*
and that it had an overall deck. Plutarch's (or
Plutarch's sources) treating it as still in use
is most probably due to misunderstanding,
because *samaina* is not a specific term (it
translates as 'the Samian girl/ship, etc'). His
hupoprōros is incomprehensible, but since the
word is clearly used to explain why the *samaina*
remained a fast galley notwithstanding its great
cargo capacity, the universally accepted 'emendation' *hupoprōros*/'with boar-shaped prow'
cannot be right. Leaving this minor problem
aside, it is the author's contention that the *samaina* was a cross between pentecontor and
eikosoros. The question remains for what pur-
pose(s) the type was developed.

From an early moment in his career as a
tyrant Polycrates was in alliance with Egypt. In
his account of Polycrates' tyranny Herodotus
suggests that the conclusion of this pact was
followed by an explosive growth of Polycrates'
power, exemplified in a fleet of 100 pentecontors and (? a bodyguard of) 1000 archers and in

conquests of, among others, cities on the continent, then under Persian rule. Herodotus does
not further enlarge upon Polycrates' actions
and is silent about the benefits to Amasis. Nevertheless, it can be argued that his short report
and the tradition about the *samaina* together
contain the essentials of their agreement.

When Polycrates became tyrant in about
540, Amasis could consider himself to be under
a new and acute menace from the direction of
the new superpower Persia. The Persian king
Cyrus had just conquered Egypt's old ally
Lydia (546 BC). A clash with Babylonia (now
also Amasis' ally) appeared foredoomed and
threatened to involve the coastal area Egypt
had depended on for its safety for half a century. In 539 Babylonia was indeed over-
whelmed and this made 'all the kings of the
West land' (including the Phoenicians) bring
'their heavy tributes and kiss the feet' of Cyrus
in Babylon. Such wholesale submission was
more than Nebuchadrezzar had ever managed
to accomplish, so Amasis was in dire need of
new power bases and allies. His alliance with
Polycrates belongs in this context, as does his
conquest of Cyprus.[17] Polycrates' operations
against Persian continental positions and his
creation of the *samaina* provide the clue to its
purport. His operations had the same objective
as the Egyptian support for the resistance and
insurgence of the Levantine cities against
Nebuchadrezzar, namely to tie down the maximum Persian forces in that area so that they
could not be used for attacking Egypt. The fact
that the effectives of Oroetes, the Persian governor of western Asia Minor, were reinforced
and that he was clearly directed against Polycrates[18] confirms that Amasis' policy strongly
affected the Persians.

Naturally Amasis had to pay for his success

13. See below, p123 and Casson, *Ships and Seamanship in
the Ancient World*, pp163–66.

14. Herodotus VII, 97.

15. Herodotus II, 159.1.

16. 569–526 BC: see Herodotus II, 159.3, 180–182.

17. Herodotus II, 182.2.

18. Herodotus III, 120–125.

and the *samaina* is a clear indication of the mode of payment. At the time the Egyptian economy was not yet money-based (it became so only in Hellenistic times), so payment or subsidy was in kind, *ie* in grain, the staple product of Egypt. For the transport of this grain to Samos the *samaina*'s cargo capacity was needed and its full deck, in other words the *eikosoros* potential of the ship. In theory, the allies could have chosen the sailing ship, which was probably being widely used by 540 BC, but their relative geographical positions made such a choice unattractive. Sailing voyages from Egypt to the Aegean have to be slow, since the dominant wind on this route is northwesterly, especially in summer.[19] For grain transport this may not be a fatal handicap, and under the Roman empire the city of Rome was provisioned in large measure with Egyptian grain transported in sailing ships, but now grain transport was not the only function of the ships. Amasis obviously had to be prepared to support Polycrates' offensives like he had supported his Levantine allies. Such support would naturally consist in carrying back to the Aegean the Carian and Greek mercenaries that had been hired there. For this galleys were indispensable since speed was of the essence. As most of these soldiers of fortune were of the type called *auteretai* ('self-rowing') in Greek, it was not necessary – as it normally was in transport galleys – to reduce the oar crew to make space for them: they themselves could man the oars. This explains the *dikrotos* oarage of the *samaina*, which certainly was superfluous on the comfortable voyage from the Aegean to Egypt.[20]

Though Plutarch may have thought otherwise, there is no reason to consider the *samaina* a real novelty. It is clear that the line of conduct of the Egyptian king vis-à-vis Polycrates was but a special application of his time-honoured policy of military and logistic support of potential allies against Asiatic aggressors. Ships like the Egyptian *kerkouroi* were therefore needed in this new theatre of war. What was different in this case was above all the distance between the allies and the less simple navigation on the routes between Egypt and Samos. Sturdier and more seaworthy ships were required here than for the far shorter trips to Judah and Phoenicia. Especially to Greek captains the Egyptian *kerkouroi* may well have seemed too long and therefore too frail for this new assignment, which might require operations in all weathers. And if the *samaina* was to be built in Samos, as Plutarch implies, conservatism of the shipbuilders (and the rational wish on the part of Polycrates not to

overtax their capacities) will have led to their building a Samian variant of the *kerkouros*, or in their own terms an *eikosoros* with *dikrotos* oarage or a widened pentecontor with a full deck.

That the *samaina* was a pentecontor of this sort may well be the explanation of Herodotus' silence on this aspect of Polycrates' achievement, for since all Samian ships could in a sense be called *samainai*, he can easily have missed casual references to the type. From this perspective, his statement that Polycrates obtained a hundred pentecontors after he had concluded the alliance with Amasis could mean that he actually built that number of *samainai*. If he did, this would be a very important indication that the scale of the operations envisaged by the allies was huge indeed. But then so were the dangers that threatened Egypt, which was eliminated as a sovereign power at one stroke by the Persians in 525 BC.

The Phocaean naval surprise and its aftermath

The naval arm of Phocaea, which is so conspicuous by its absence at the time of the Persian offensive against the Ionian cities, loomed large in the West, most emphatically after the fall of Phocaea itself and the emigration of half its population to Corsica, but also for a time before that exodus. According to Thucydides they gained victories over the Carthaginians when establishing their 'colony' of Massalia (Marseilles) and this may date back to *c*600 BC (when Massalia was founded). However there is reason to put a later date on the peculiar impact of the Phocaeans in the West, and especially in far away Tartessos (southern Spain near Huelva), and to place it in the same strategical perspective as Polycrates' in the southern Aegean and as roughly contemporaneous with the first decades of the reign of Polycrates' ally Amasis.

Phocaea was among the Greek states that were most involved in the contacts with Saïte Egypt,[21] and will have played a part in the traffic with the Carian and Greek mercenaries. Now this traffic was most probably interrupted for a time after the coup by Amasis, who came to power on a tide of xenophobia that allowed him to eliminate the legitimate king, Apries, and set up as his successor. For years afterwards Amasis must have been obliged to restrict, if not wholly to forego, the employment of foreign mercenaries, only to return to the traditional Saïte policy when the political situation in Asia became explosive some time before 546 BC as a result of the replacement of Media by the Persians. During the twenty or so years

before that reversal, prospective mercenaries must have been in sore need of other employers.

One of these will have been Arganthonios, the king of Tartessos, with whom the Phocaeans had a very special relationship. According to Herodotus (I, 163), in *c*546 BC this man even invited them to migrate to his country, which proves that their persons were more important to him than the commodities they are generally assumed to have supplied. It is indeed a striking trait in other traditions regarding Phocaean contacts with overseas tribes that their personal (*ie* military) qualities were a decisive factor in their being accepted as settlers. In the case of Tartessos immigration had not yet taken place, probably because the trade in Tartessian metals brought the Phocaeans much profit, but here it may be surmised that the Phocaeans satisfied the Tartessian demand for Greek military men (which will have been caused by the Carthaginian expansion in this area) in another way. Their use of pentecontors for their voyages to Tartessos, which is emphasised by Herodotus, strongly suggests that they supplied mercenaries to its king, for this type of ship with its large oar crew cannot have been used as a merchantman except as a special transporter of personnel.

Herodotus indeed felt obliged to stipulate that the Phocaean pentecontors were used as merchantmen by stressing that they were employed on these long trips in the same way as the 'round' (*ie* sailing) ships of his own days (I, 163.2). This is to say that the Phocaeans' pentecontors were on a par with Polycrates' *samaina*. In the latter's case the possibility that troops would have to be brought from Egypt to Samos made the use of fast galleys (*ie* with oars at two levels) a necessity and a complete deck desirable so that grain could be taken along for their sustenance. For the Phocaeans, on the other hand, oars at two levels were necessary because their ships were threatened by the Carthaginian naval arm all the way from Sicily to Spain. In this case the big crews and the speed which they made possible did not so much serve to expedite the crossing, as to strengthen the fighting potential of the merchant galleys, the mercenaries not only manning the additional oars but also serving as marines. The non-perishable and non-bulky cargo bound for the Aegean did not require an

19. The first part of St Paul's voyage to Rome well illustrates this: see *Acts* 27.

20. See *Odyssey* XIV, 252–57.

21. Herodotus II, 178.

extra-large cargo space nor the protection of a deck. As a result the ships became practically identical with the pentecontors of the Greek state navies: hence Herodotus' use of the term.

With these 'pentecontors' the Phocaeans must have maintained their connection with Tartessos for at least some decades. During these years they appear to have successfully fought a number of battles with the Carthaginians and their maritime allies, fights epitomised in Thucydides' reference to their greatness at sea (I, 13.6). These successes culminated in the great battle 'in the Sardinian sea' of *c*540 BC.[22] On that occasion sixty Phocaean pentecontors vanquished an allied Etruscan and Carthaginian fleet of twice the numerical strength thanks to their mastery of an adequate tactical concept in which the ships themselves were used as a weapon. These 'ramming' or *diekplous* tactics, which involved intricate manoeuvring of whole fleets in line abreast, must have been developed by the Phocaeans in the succession of earlier clashes just mentioned. And in the end their success and the ensuing strategic crisis triggered off developments that resulted in the creation of the trireme, a ship of a format wholly different from that of its predecessors and involving an enormous scaling up of the naval organisations that made use of it.

The extent to which the ability of the Phocaeans to bring their tactical concept to perfection depended on the exceptional character of their connection with Spain is made evident by the sequel. In spite of their brilliant success it is manifest that in the application of their tactical concept they were followed only by powers that were in their way as exceptional as they themselves (in particular imperial Athens and Carthage). On the eve of the battle of Lade (494 BC) that decided the Ionian revolt against the Persian empire most Ionian commanders had no notion of this tactical concept. A last-minute attempt by the Phocaean commander to give the crews the appropriate training was frustrated by their unwillingness: this was one of the causes of the Ionian defeat. Even much later the same was still true for the Corinthians, one of Thucydides' great archaic sea powers. In the battle of Sybota (432 BC), the greatest of Greek sea battles before the Peloponnesian war, there was no question of *diekplous* tactics.[23]

This is no wonder. *Diekplous* tactics required very intensive training by whole fleets of fully or nearly fully manned ships and for that reason were a most expensive business. Corinth, for all its proverbial wealth, clearly had not been able to finance adequate training in

432. The unwillingness of the Ionian crews at Lade no doubt was caused by their being underpaid. That the Phocaeans in contrast with this could afford this training is easily explained: half their rowers were prospective mercenaries who paid for their passage rather than being paid as oarsmen, while the other half – the permanent crew – probably participated in the proceeds of the venture, if they were not *emporoi* who traded (and rowed) on their own account. On the long voyages to the West the crews had time enough to train in the *diekplous*. Hence the Phocaean superiority.

The sudden migration of half the inhabitants of Phocaea to Corsica after the Persian conquest of their city and their turning to piracy for a living (using their pentecontors as a permanent 'navy' for that purpose) created a desperate situation for their neighbours, the Etruscans and the Carthaginians from Sardinia, and gave them a strong motive to search for a means to counterbalance the tactical superiority of their opponents. The aftermath of their defeat is very unexpected: the victorious Phocaeans had to evacuate their Corsican settlement and withdraw to southern Italy. This appears to signify that the Etruscans or the Carthaginians did indeed manage to find a countermeasure. What this was, our earlier Greek sources do not tell us, but the Christian scholar Clement of Alexandria (*c*AD 190) has preserved a tradition, probably going back to the Hellenistic scholar Philostephanus of Cyrene, which may be relevant. Clement records[24] that the *trikrotos naus* – ie a galley with three-level oar system (like that of the trireme) – was first built by the Sidonians. This probably means that this feat was located somewhere in the Phoenician world, including Carthage (even in Homer's time 'Sidonians' could be used for Phoenicians in general) and, also, that Philostephanus' informant came from Sidon, a possession of the then kings of Egypt, Philostephanus' patrons.

It stands to reason that, in a world where the pentecontor was the ship of the line, developing a *trikrotos naus* must have meant the addition of a third level of oars to the two of the pentecontor. The result was a ship with some 50 + 20–22 = 70–72 oarsmen. Because of the building into the ship of the third rowing bench and its supporting construction and the perforation of its sides to let the additional thalamian (after *thalamos*, 'hold') oars pass through, such a galley lost much of its usefulness as a merchantman, but no doubt was easily the equal of the best pentecontors, even the Phocaean ones. The withdrawal of the Phocaeans from their pirates' nest suggests

that a strategic effect of this sort made itself felt, though there is no clear evidence that this was actually the result of the genesis of the *trikrotos naus*.

Nevertheless it is attractive, indeed almost unavoidable, to view things in this perspective, for Clement's testimony makes excellent sense in this context (and hardly in any other). The fifteen years between the 'battle of Alalia' and the participation of the Persian trireme fleet in the conquest of Egypt in 525 BC must in any case be the period of the creation of the *trikrotos* oar system. And precisely in this period the further development – the creation of the trireme through the installation of *trikrotos* oarage on galleys of the class of the Egyptian *kerkouroi* – is very natural.

Once there was a threat of a the third level of oars being mounted on the pentecontors of the Phoenician cities of the Levant, the strategical position of Egypt was in jeopardy. The 'battle of Alalia' had proved pentecontors of superior quality to be a most effective weapon, the equal of far more numerous average galleys and surely also of the Egyptian *kerkouroi*. Phoenician state navies consisting of such tuned-up pentecontors would become a strategical factor of great weight, enabling their possessors to pursue policies of much greater independence vis-à-vis Egypt and gaining them a strong bargaining position in relation to the new masters of the Asiatic hinterland, the Persians. The final outcome of this threatening situation is certain. By 525 Persia had itself put together a navy of triremes, chiefly manned by Phoenicians.[25] Shortly before this an Egyptian trireme is mentioned by Herodotus (III, 4.2), who also ascribes forty triremes to Polycrates at the same juncture (III, 44.2). A form of arms race seems to have taken place, but regrettably the very summary evidence does not allow a clear view of the progress of this race, nor of which was the first of these states to have the new dreadnought. However, in consideration of Egypt's long dependence on naval strength and the necessity for its kings to compensate for the ever growing power of Persia and in particular to eliminate all possible naval rivals, Egyptian priority seems probable. And surely, once the *trikrotos* oarage had been invented, the last step – that of mounting it on big galleys – was a small one here.

H T Wallinga

22. Misnamed the 'battle of Alalia': see Herodotus I, 166.
23. Thucydides I, 49ff.
24. *Stromateis* I, 16.76.
25. Herodotus III, 19.

The Trireme

THE BEST-KNOWN of all classical ship types, the trireme has been the subject of scholarly debate for centuries. Practical knowledge of the structure and characteristics of the type was greatly advanced by the building in 1985–87 of a reconstruction of a trireme, the *Olympias*, which is now operated by the Hellenic Navy. This chapter concentrates on the documentary evidence that formed a basis for the reconstruction, summarising what is known about the seagoing capabilities and performance in action of the trireme, prefaced by a short survey of the naval history of the trireme era.

Sea power in the Eastern Mediterranean, 500–338 BC

By the beginning of the last quarter of the sixth century BC, first Cyrus and then his son Cambyses had subjected to Persia the main sea powers of the eastern Mediterranean, Ionia in 550, Cilicia and Phoenicia in 540 and Egypt in 525. In 500 Darius's unsuccessful attempt to use the Ionian fleet to reduce Naxos led to the beginnings of a revolt which was joined by

Cyprus, but by 497 Cyprus was reconquered and the important maritime province of Caria secured. When in 495 the Ionian and Aeolian rebels mustered a fleet at Lade, a small island off Miletus which was under siege by a Persian

The bow of the reconstructed trireme Olympias, *showing the bronze-sheathed ram and the box-like* epotis, *or ear timber, that protected the outrigger. This reconstruction has given historians and naval architects profound insight into the design and construction of classical Greek warships and suggests that in its way the trireme was as impressive a technical achievement as the surviving architecture of ancient Greece.* (Paul Lipke, by courtesy of the Trireme Trust)

Building the trireme 1 : *December 1985, finishing the rebates in the keel. The keel was supported during construction by a steel mould and the shape of the hull was defined for building up the planked shell by moulds placed at the twenty-one displacement stations marked on the sheer draught. The moulds were taken away when the transverse timbers were fitted and secured.* (John Coates, by courtesy of the Hellenic Navy)

army, their line of battle was composed[1] of 80 Milesian, 100 Chian, 70 Lesbian, 60 Samian ships and small detachments of 17 from Teos, 12 from Priene, 3 from Myous, 8 from Erythraea and 3 from Phocaea, 353 in all. The rebel fleet was defeated by 600 ships from Phoenicia, Cyprus, Cilicia and Egypt, of which the Phoenician contingent, Herodotus says, was the keenest.

Five years later command of the sea and of the sources of naval power thus achieved gave Darius the confidence to launch a raid across the Aegean, which was defeated on land by the Athenians at Marathon. Ten years later Xerxes

assembled in Cilicia for the invasion of mainland Greece a great army, joined there by a great fleet.

After crossing the Hellespont on a bridge of pentecontors and triremes roped together, the army moved to the mouth of the Hebrus and the trireme fleet was there given maintenance ('dried out') and reviewed. It consisted of 307 ships from Asiatic Greece, 300 from Phoenicia, 200 from Egypt and 150 from Cyprus. Further ships came in later from the islands. To oppose them the mainland Greeks had a fleet formed of 200 Athenian triremes (20 of them manned by their allies), 40 Corinthian, 30 Aeginetan,

20 Megarian and 16 Spartan ships. Gelon, the ruler of Syracuse, offered, Herodotus says, 200 ships, but only on the condition, which was refused, that he should take supreme command. Corcyra, a colony of Corinth, sent 60 triremes which were prevented by contrary winds from rounding Cape Malea, and took no part in the campaign.

These numbers give a clear picture of the relative naval strength on the one hand of Persia, whose resources and political dominance enabled her to subsidise the building and manning of triremes in an area already rich in the skills which made them formidable, and of Sicily, which enjoyed the same advantages to a lesser degree; and on the other of the mainland Greeks, who without the 200 triremes built at Themistocles' instance from the fortuitous surplus of her silver mines at Laurium, would have been weak indeed, the 40 ships of 'wealthy Corinth' being only two-thirds the size of the fleet of her richer western colony, Corcyra. The picture emphasises the costliness of a substantial trireme fleet, a point which Thucydides also makes.

In the year after their defeat of the Persian fleet at Salamis the Greek ships under the command of the Spartan Leotychidas sought out and defeated what remained of the Persian fleet at Mycale on the southeastern coast of Asia Minor. When the Delian confederacy was formed to liberate the Greek cities of Asia Minor, Athens saw that under her leadership the confederacy was the means by which she could ultimately acquire the resources necessary for sea power. But while the lesser cities of Ionia supported the Greek cause with contri-

Abbreviations in the footnotes are given in the references at the end of the chapter.
1. Herodotus 8.8.1–2.

Building the trireme 2: *April 1986, bottom planking before the points of the tenon pegs were sawn off. Triremes were built of a shell-first construction with the strakes of planking secured to each other by mortise-and-tenon joints in the thickness of the planking. Note scarfed and tenoned plank butts, and the heads of such frame fastenings (one per plank) as had by then been fitted. The thick strake is a rubbing strake, provided in case the ship should lie over on a beach.* (John Coates, by courtesy of the Hellenic Navy)

Building the trireme 3: *September 1986, internal view from bow. Floors and alternate frame timbers have been fitted and all hull moulds removed. Note mortises for tenons in the edge of top planks.* (John Coates, by courtesy of the Hellenic Navy)

butions instead of ships, the greater islands, Samos, Chios and Lesbos, continued to maintain their own large fleets. In 440 Samos nearly set herself up as an independent sea power. Lesbos at the outset of the Peloponnesian war a decade later still had her own fleet, and in 413 Chios manned 60 ships.

Nothing is heard of the Egyptian fleet in these years. Athens invaded Egypt in 460; and after six years in which she may have lost as many as 250 ships she was forced to withdraw, but there is no record of naval engagement. In the third decade of the fourth century Egypt revolted from Persia and sent a fleet of fifty ships to support Evagoras of Cyprus, who was also in revolt. Throughout the Hellenistic centuries Egypt continued to be a great maritime power.

A Phoenician fleet in Persian pay remained in being after the engagement at Mycale, and was defeated by Cimon, commanding a structurally modified confederate fleet, at the river Eurymedon (in southeastern Asia Minor) probably in 466 and again in 451. For forty years no Phoenician fleet came west into what were thereafter regarded as Greek waters until 411, when the Persian Tissaphernes brought 147 Phoenician ships to Aspendus in Pamphylia; but there was no engagement. After Athens' defeat in the Peloponnesian war Persian policy used the Phoenician fleet to play off Sparta and Athens against each other. Under Alexander and his successors, Phoenicians as mercenaries, with their triremes, then with the new types of warship and abundant naval resources, played a continuing part in the struggle for sea power.

In western Greece, Gelon at Syracuse, threatened by Carthage as the eastern Greeks were by Persia, developed the Great Harbour as a naval base. Yet the naval strength suggested by his offer of 200 triremes in 480 is perhaps belied by his failure to challenge at sea the Carthaginian invasion in 480, defeating it instead on land at the siege of Himera. It must however be remembered that at the beginning of the Peloponnesian war fifty years later Sparta was said to have hoped to raise a naval force of 500 ships, mostly to be built in Sicily and Italy,[2] and that Sicily was then said to have had 'many triereis and men to crew them'.[3] With Corinthian advice and Spartan leadership Syracusan naval power increased under the stimulus of the Athenian attack of 415 BC, and after Athens' defeat she sent a contingent to support the Peloponnesian fleet operating against Athens in the Aegean. Dionysius I, who ruled Syracuse from 405 to 367 BC, was a firm ally of Sparta until her defeat at Leuctra by Boeotia in 371 BC. Athens had made unsuccessful approaches to him as early as 393 BC; and in the end as an ally of Sparta secured his alliance.

Corcyra, situated at the point where the mainly coastal route from mainland Greece stood out across the Adriatic to Italy and Sicily, had a substantial navy in 480 BC. At the beginning of the Peloponnesian war Thucydides gives her envoys to Athens the words: 'the Greeks have only three fleets worth naming, yours, ours and the fleet of the Corinthians'.

Against this background is to be set Athens' naval power, effectively acquired in a mood of patriotic opportunism. Thucydides[4] describes vividly the attitude of her allies to Athens after Salamis. They feared 'the size of her navy which was not previously in existence, and the aggressive spirit she had shown in the face of the Persian attack'. Elsewhere[5] he remarks that immediately after the Persian wars 'she had begun to practice the art of seamanship'. Themistocles was the mainspring both of the Athenians' aggressive spirit and of their naval ambitions.[6]

He persuaded them also to finish the building of Piraeus. A beginning of it had been made previously during his tenure of the office which he had held on an annual basis at Athens. He thought that Piraeus with its three natural harbours was ideal for the purpose, and that if the Athenians became seamen they would take great strides towards the acquisition of power. It was Themistocles indeed who had the courage to say that the Athenians must cleave to the sea.

It is often forgotten that Athens, like Rome later, a novice in maritime affairs, 'took to the sea' as a step in pursuit of power, and thereby, perhaps more consciously, as a means of safeguarding the food supply of her growing population. In Athens, unlike Rome, the common people who crewed the triremes were behind this move. In Aristophanes's play the *Knights* (424 BC), the character Demos (personifying the Athenian people now politically dominant) speaks of *his seamen*.

Aristides[7] shared Themistocles' views and 'urged the people to take the leadership [of the Delian confederacy], quit the country and live in the city'. Themistocles, Aristides, and, later, Pericles were leaders of the *demos*, who as crews (of 200) of the trireme fleet, 'give the city its power'. Those are the words of an anonymous writer, who was no supporter of the democracy, at about the beginning of the

2. Thucydides 2.7.2.

3. Thucydides 6.20.4.

4. Thucydides 1.90.1.

5. Thucydides 1.142.7.

6. Thucydides 1.93.3.

7. Aristotle *Constitution of Athens* 22.39.

Building the trireme 4 : *March 1987, a lower oarport with thole carling being fitted. Note the clenched-over points of the copper frame fastenings.*(John Coates, by courtesy of the Hellenic Navy)

Peloponnesian war.[8] He also puts very succinctly the theoretical basis of Athenian sea power, manifested in her fortified Piraeus dockyards and 200-strong trireme fleet:

> A land power may be resisted by a united force of small cities, but islanders cannot resist a sea power. . . . No commerce can take place without the permission of the sea power. A sea power can invade the territory of a stronger power, can make a landing where there are none or few to resist them, and move away when a force approaches. Distance means nothing to a sea power. A land power can only pass through friendly territory, or fight their way. If crops fail, a sea power can easily import food from abroad. They can import luxuries, and ideas, from the whole world, and alone can have a high standard of living. By occupying an island or a headland they can inflict damage on their enemies. The sea power, if it is not an island, has that one weakness.

The emergence of Pericles as a popular leader in 462 BC, on the death of the aristocratic Cimon, coincided with the renewal of this policy by the start of the building of the Long Walls to secure Athens' communications with Piraeus in time of war. 'Pericles', Aristotle says, 'turned the policy of the city [again] in the direction of sea power.' The consequence of the return to the Themistoclean policy was the vital importance of safeguarding the grain route

from the Black Sea through the Bosporus and the Hellespont to Piraeus. This became the first priority for the Athenian navy in the inevitable war with the Peloponnesian league that followed, for her the essential expression of her sea power. The many sea battles in that area, including her final naval defeat, are clear testimony that this is so.

The naval strength of Athens at the beginning of the war was great. Her fleet of 300 triremes was more than double the 120 which Corcyra could man. In 434 BC, when Corinth sent a fleet of 75 ships against Corcyra, the latter manned 80 to defeat it; and when in the following year Corinth sent a Peloponnesian fleet of 150 ships, including 90 of her own, the 110 ships which Corcyra was then able to man were saved from defeat in the battle of Sybota by first one of 10 and then a second Athenian squadron of 20 ships. It does not appear that the aim of the Peloponnesian league to build and man substantial naval reinforcement in Sicily and Italy was ever achieved.

Athenian naval operations in the year 428 BC are the subject of comment by Thucydides. While at the same time dealing with the revolt of Lesbos and of Potidaea in Chalcidice and maintaining a patrol with 100 ships of Attica, Euboea and Salamis, she attacked the Peloponnese with a fleet of 100 ships, putting ashore the 1000 deck-soldiers for raids on land. 'The total number of ships in service at the same time in a single summer was 250.' It must be

remembered also that there were, in reserve against an emergency, an additional 100 hulls, and their gear.

Athenian naval superiority gave her the freedom to maintain and practise the skilled operation of triremes which she had achieved in the fifty years since the Persian invasion, and not only that but to prevent her enemies from obtaining it by keeping their ships in harbour, as the Spartan admiral Brasidas complained.

The largest single expedition which Athens mounted in the war was that to Sicily in 415 BC, consisting of 134 triremes and 2 pentecontors. Reinforcements of 73 triremes followed. In the first battle the Syracusans manned 76 triremes. Yet in spite of their advantage in numbers and skill, bad leadership led to the Athenian force being trapped in a harbour where their skill could not be exercised. Total disaster followed, which threatened the basis of Athenian power. The defeat stimulated Sparta to build a navy using the only means open to a resourceless mainland city. She levied 25 ships from the Boeotians to match 25 she was providing herself, 15 each from the Phocians, Locrians and Corinthians and 10 each from seven smaller states. Athens herself set about recouping her losses in ships. When Chios revolted in 412 BC she was forced to draw on her emergency financial reserve.

The area of the Asian coast and the Hellespont was inevitably the theatre of the naval struggle which ensued, with the Athenian force at Samos evenly matched by the Spartan at Miletus. A Phoenician fleet of 147 ships was brought by the Persian satrap Tissaphernes, who had been paymaster of the Spartan fleet, as far as Aspendus but no further, allowing Athens to re-establish her naval superiority in a number of battles in the Hellespont. A new Spartan commander, Lysander, with a reinforced fleet strongly subsidised by Persia, defeated the Athenian fleet weakly led at Notium and then blockaded under Conon in Samos: but the Spartan fleet under another new commander, Callicratidas, was defeated and its commander drowned at the battle of Arginusae off Lesbos. A ship had brought news of Conon's plight to Athens, where a relief force of 100 ships had been manned with everyone available of military age, including slaves, and

dispatched within thirty days. In the following year (405 BC) Lysander returned; and with a large fleet challenged the Athenian fleet of 180 ships for control of the straits. He caught them half ashore at Aegospotami and only Conon with eight ships (and his enemy's sails) escaped. Athens was forced to surrender.

The extraordinary combination of circumstances which led to Athens' recovery illustrates the effectiveness of a fleet of triremes, though still more perhaps the power of Persian gold to acquire and man them.

Conon with his eight ships, and the sails which Lysander had put ashore before the battle, made for Cyprus, where he had a friend in the local autocrat Evagoras. From there the Persian satrap Pharnabazus, instructed to raise a fleet of 100 triremes in southeastern Asia, rich as always in naval resources, recruited him as commander. The Athenian popular party, loyal to the fleet, sent him arms (*ie* deck-soldiers and petty officers[9]). When he raided Cilicia with 40 ships he was caught and blockaded in Caunus by a Spartan fleet of 100 under Pharax, presumably sent to deal with him. He was extricated finally by reinforcements from Cyprus. Pharax went to Rhodes, then ruled by a pro-Spartan party, but was driven out when the Rhodians revolted and received Conon and the 80 ships he now commanded. This fleet had increased to 90 when he met and defeated the Spartan fleet under Peisander in August 394 BC at Cnidos. Crossing the Aegean with Pharnabazus he set up a base on Melos and raided Sparta. Finally he entered Piraeus; and with Persian money and the labour of his seamen he completed the rebuilding of the Long Walls (already put in hand by Athens and her allies) and the fortifications of Piraeus, both of which had been destroyed by Sparta.

Athens was once again a sea power, restoring in 392 BC her colonists to their·farms on Lemnos, Imbros and Chios. In 390 BC she sent out to the northern Aegean a fleet of 40 ships which took control of the Bosporus and moved south to the seaboard of Asia. The Athenian orator Lysias states the truth rather brutally in a speech at the Olympic games of 388 BC:

You know well that power belongs to those who rule the sea, that the king of Persia [Artaxerxes II, 405–362 BC] holds the money and the Greeks as physical agents obey those who dispense it. The king of Persia [supporting Athens] owns many ships, and so does the autocratic ruler of Sicily [Dionysius I of Syracuse, supporting Sparta].[10]

Athens' backer was lost when her friend Evagoras of Cyprus revolted from Persia with 200 ships. She also lost control of the Hellespont to a Spartan fleet which included a Syr-

---

9. *Hellenica Oxyrrhyncia* 2.1.

10. Lysias 33.5.

acusan contingent. A Spartan-sponsored peace with Persia followed in 386 BC, in which Persian title to the Ionian Greek cities and Athens' title to Imbros, Lemnos and Skyros were both recognised. Evagoras captured Tyre but was defeated when Persia invaded Cyprus.

Athens was driven to the only remaining means of Aegean sea power, a second confederacy of Greek states, at first Thebes, Chios and Byzantium, with Athens as the executive authority of a common council. In 376 BC a Peloponnesian fleet of 65 triremes based at Aegina was defeated by a large confederate fleet of 85 ships under the Athenian admiral Chabrias, who took his fleet in the following year to the Thracian coast, while Conon's son Timotheus with 60 ships defeated a Peloponnesian fleet off Acarnania. While Athens and Sparta negotiated for peace, the latter sent a fleet, to be joined by 10 ships from Dionysius, to take Corcyra. Iphicrates, who had been serving with a Persian fleet of 300 triremes sent to invade Egypt, returned in 373 and was put in command of an untrained fleet sent round the Peloponnese. He intercepted the Syracusan squadron and relieved Corcyra.

At the King's Peace of 371 BC Athens became an ally of Sparta, and thus of Dionysius. At this point Boeotia emerged as a power able to defeat Sparta on land at Leuctra in the same year; and challenge Athenian influence in the straits by launching a fleet of 200 triremes and sending it to the Bosporus in 363 BC. There it

encouraged the secession of Byzantium and other cities from the Athenian confederation. Six years later Chios, Rhodes and Cos seceded; and with a fleet of 100 ships raided Lemnos and Imbros. The Athenian fleet of 60 ships under Chares was joined by reinforcements of 60 ships under Timotheus and Iphicrates; but Athens, afraid of provoking the intervention of Persia with her fleet of 300 ships, made peace with the rebels.

From 355 to 351 BC under Eubulus's direction Athens' prosperity returned and there was a surplus with which to rebuild the docks and the fortifications of Piraeus and to construct triremes. In 353 BC Chares took a fleet to the Hellespont and seized Sestos.

Philip V of Macedon at this point emerged as a threat to Athenian shipping and her political influence in the northeastern Aegean. In 343 BC Athens had 300 triremes in service, and sent a large fleet to relieve Byzantium when attacked by Philip, who withdrew. His strength was, however, on land, and in 338 he defeated Thebes and Athens at Chaeronea and compelled Athens to dissolve her confederacy. The League of Corinth, formed the following year by Philip, took the place of the Peloponnesian league and the Athenian confederacy and directed Greece, forcibly united under his leadership, into war with Persia, an objective with which many Greeks were in sympathy and which was taken up with vigour on Philip's death by his son Alexander.

The appearance of the trireme

In 701 BC, under the threat of Sennacherib's invading army, King Lulî ordered the evacuation to Cyprus of the population, or perhaps only the fighting men, of his cities of Tyre and Sidon. The evacuation was recorded in a relief adorning the palace at Nineveh which survives in Layard's drawings and in two fragments in the British Museum.

Two types of oared ship are shown engaged in the operation, both carrying soldiers and important people standing on deck. One type has no ram and is the predecessor of the fleet auxiliaries, *kerkouroi*, which accompanied Darius's fleet in the invasion of Greece in 490 BC and of the *lemboi* and liburnians of later times. They are rowed at two levels, a system said by Damastes of Sigeum, a contemporary of Herodotus, to have been invented by the Erythraeans of Ionia.

The other type has a pointed forefoot sheathed (in metal) as a ram and is thus a warship.[11] Two levels of oars are shown, the lower (i) worked through oarports and the upper (ii) over the topwale, the heads and shoulders of the oarsmen of exaggerated size being visible through the open side which is divided into oarsmen's 'rooms' by pillars. Above the open side there is (iii) a course, absent in the fleet auxiliaries, formed (apparently) of alternate lattice work squares and open space. Above this again there is (iv) a bulwark hung with shields, in the usual Tyrian manner,[12] reaching up to the waist of the figures standing on deck.

The raison d'être of (iii) is far from obvious, but with the other distinguishing mark of this category, the ram, it is likely to be connected with the ship's function as a warship as distinct from an auxiliary. An explanation of its pres-

---

11. The trireme's ram was formed by arming the forefoot with a metal (iron or bronze) sheath. This sheath is shown most clearly in an Attic red-figure stamnos of the beginning of the fifth century BC, and it is indicated in the Nineveh warships by a vertical band at the after end of the forefoot. Where, as in the ships portrayed in the fragments of a Geometric vase (760–735) and even an ivory plaque (650–600), there is no such indication, the ships shown are unarmed and like the oared ships in Homer do not confront an enemy at sea but convey fighting men to the scene of action on land.

12. Ezekiel 27.10.

An Attic red figure stamnos (jar) of about 500–480 BC depicting Odysseus's encounter with the Sirens shows a vessel with a sheathed forefoot ram, clearly delineating her as a warship.

Fragments of three vase paintings depicting multi-level oared ships: the top two are late Geometric (735–710 BC) and the lowest is early Archaic (700–650 BC). They show two-level warships with various forms of open latticed side structure.

ence can be found in fragments of three contemporary vase paintings, two late Geometric (735–710 BC) and one early Archaic (700–650 BC) showing (plainly in one case) in a not very realistic style two-level oared warships with courses of alternate open spaces and wide sup-

ports of different kinds including latticework. They recall (iii) with the difference that in their case oarsmen are shown in the open spaces. They suggest accordingly that (iii) is an upper open side accommodating when required the third file of oarsmen of a trireme. However, the third file's extra power and speed is not required in the operation of evacuating people the distance of 25 miles to Cyprus, with no challenge from Sennacherib at sea. On this occasion then the third file was not manned.

If this explanation stands, the Nineveh relief is of the greatest value in presenting pictures of the earliest two- and three-level ships, built in Tyre and Sidon towards the end of the eighth century BC and used on an occasion of which the date is known. The relief is likely to have been made in the palace of Sennacherib in the first decade of the seventh century by Assyrian or possibly Phoenician craftsmen in a style which presents the important features of the ships concerned while manning them with out-size human figures.

The validity of the conclusion must be assessed in conjunction with Thucydides' much debated statements[13] that 'triremes were built first in Corinth of Greece', and that Ameinocles the Corinthian shipwright, it appears, built four ships, in the context triremes as Pliny assumes,[14] for the Samians; and it is about 300 years to the end of this war (either 421 BC the Peace of Nicias or 404 BC Athens' surrender) when Ameinocles came to the Samians (721 or 704 BC). The fourth-century BC tradition, preserved in Diodorus[15] and Pliny, is that the trireme was *invented* in Corinth; but Clement of Alexandria (second-third century BC), attributes the invention of the trireme to the Sidonians [16] possibly relying on Philostephanos of Cyrene who wrote a book entitled *Inventions* in the third century BC. Since a three-level oared warship might have been 'invented' at both Corinth and Sidon, there is nothing in these statements against the presence of triremes in Luli's evacuation fleet in 701. Salmon (1983: p223) puts the 'naval developments' (including the building of the trireme) at Corinth after the establishment of the tyranny in 650 BC, but this is by no means certain. The date and place or the actual invention of the trireme may then be left an open question, and late eighth-century three-level warships, with the main features of those on the Nineveh relief, be accepted. It may be expected that there will be differences in appearance between the Corinthian and Sidonian types.

The next representation of the warship with three levels of oars occurs in the Vienna frag-

ment of red figure pottery of 450 BC. It shows part of the side of a ship with two levels of oarports between pairs of narrow wales, above them the two parallel timbers of an outrigger and above it an open side. The deck has a post and rail guard and is shown supported by two inward-curving stanchions indicating that it is narrower than the overall beam. Forty years later at Salamis the decks of the Athenian ships did not go right across.

13. Thucydides 1.13.2.

14. Pliny *Natural History* 7.57.

15. Diodorus 14.42.3.

16. Clement of Alexandria *Stromateis* 1.16.36.

The Vienna fragment of red figure pottery of about 450 BC. It shows two levels of oarports between pairs of narrow wales, surmounted by the two lines of the outrigger with open side above that.

A detail of the Lenormant relief; three levels of the oars are shown, the lowest emerging from the hull, the next from under the outrigger, and the uppermost from within the outrigger.

The Apulian rhyton (or stirrup cup), shaped to imitate a trireme's bow.

Depictions of Corinthian type triremes on coins:
a. Kios (340–300 BC);
b. Histiaean (340–338);
c. Phaselis (fourth-third century).

however, give a good idea of the fifth-century Athenian trireme's bow. The Apulian rhyton representing the bow of a similar trireme of the fourth century may be compared. Coins of Kios, Histiaea and Phaselis supplement and corroborate the evidence illustrating the trireme of the Corinthian type in the fourth century BC.

There is nothing in literature to suggest that the Phoenician and Palestinian Syrian triremes which were the largest contingent (300) in Xerxes' invasion fleet were substantially different from those of the mainland Greek allies. Representations of warships on the coins of Sidon and Arados in the second half of the fifth century show no oars or other details or an oar system, but must certainly reflect triremes. The deck is hung with shields above a deep open course divided into rooms by deck stanchions which in turn is above a topwale and two lower wales. The recessed courses between these three wales show short uprights at intervals.

The contemporary Sidonian coins show the same features less crudely and less clearly, also a sharp ram like those of the Nineveh warships. The absence of the two open courses of the Nineveh threes makes these Phoenician coins close to the Corinthian type, although there is no clear outrigger. It may be that by the fifth century the Phoenicians had adopted the Corinthian design with one open side, possibly

The two main pieces of evidence for the Athenian trireme of the fifth century BC, which almost exactly corroborate each other, belong to the end of the century, the Lenormant relief and the Ruvo vase. The former shows the middle section of the starboard side of a trireme under oar, with the lowest (thalamian) oars emerging from oarports through leather sleeves (*askōmata*), the next (zygian) level of oars emerging from under the outrigger and the uppermost (thranite) oars worked through the parallel timbers of the outrigger, the supporting brackets of which butt on to the lower wale. The canopy-deck, on which there are reclining figures, is supported by stanchions butting on to the upper wale. The stanchions divide the open side into 'rooms' in which the thranite oarsmen are visible on the starboard side. The bow section of the same or a similar relief, since disappeared, was drawn in Rome between 1610 and 1635 by an artist who did not understand the oar system. It does,

Depictions of Phoenician and Syrian triremes on coins:
a. Early Sidonian (fifth century);
b. Early Arados (fifth century);
c. Sidonian (fourth century); note the curious convention of the stepped oars set under the keel.

a.   *b.*   *c.*

a.   *b.*   *c.*

Seals from the treasury of the Persian palace at Persepolis (fourth century)

without an outrigger. Herodotus's story[17] of fifteen ships of the Persian fleet on the evening before Artemisium mistaking the Greek ships for their own, indicates that some ships of the Persian fleet, but possibly only those of the Asiatic Greeks, were of the Corinthian pattern.

In the next century Sidonian coinage shows oars placed unrealistically under the keel and 'stepped' to indicate three levels. This stepping also occurs in one (possibly both) of two types of Persian seal from the the treasury of the palace of Persepolis. These seals, dated between 520–515 and 330, the year of the treasury's burning, because of the 'stepping' are likely to belong to the early fourth century. The general appearance of the ships show no other difference, both have sharp rams.

In the second half of the fourth century there is a surprising reappearance of the Phoenician/Nineveh type of three-level oared ship at Arados, at Byblos, on an Amathus gem, on the second Persian seal and, most clearly of all, on the Erment model. In all these there are more or less clearly two open courses, as on the Nineveh warships (in the case of the Erment model equipped with the relics of oars). These

The re-appearance of the Phoenician type three-level ship:

a. Arados coin (350–323);

b. Byblos coin (fourth century);

c. Amathus gem (340–330).

are plainly warships with oars at three levels, but at this date when *penteresis* (quinqueremes, fives), had made their first, short-lived appearance in the Sidonian navy (351), and later as flagships in the Phoenician and Cypriot fleets that came over to Alexander at the siege of Tyre (332), these three-level ships could be either surviving or revived Phoenician type triremes or, perhaps more likely, fives developed from that type, as Dionysius of Syracuse had at the beginning of the century invented a five developed from the Cornithian three.

The capability of the trireme

Since the ability to move anywhere to strike an enemy is claimed for the trireme fleet, the ship's potential in this respect needs attention.

The most precise of the relevant passages (but not as precise as might be wished) is Xenophon's statement[18] that Byzantium (on the northern shore of the Bosphorus) to Heraclea, 129nm (236km) distant along the southern coast of the Black Sea, is 'a long day's voyage for a trireme under oar'. In one manuscript the reading is 'a very long day', possibly a protest by a Byzantine scribe who was thinking of the performance of a contemporary galley, possibly an indication that the hours of twilight should be added. Herodotus[19] speaks of a ship (presumably a merchantman) covering in a day 70,000 *orguiai* (700 stades, about 74nm) 'in the season of long days' (Greek, *makrēmeria*). Between the beginning of April and the beginning of September in the Black Sea the period between sunrise and sunset ranges from about 12 hours 40 minutes to about 15 hours (with the 2½ hours of twilight added about 15 hours 10 minutes to 17½ hours). If the maximum period of daylight is taken and twilight added, and if an hour is deducted for the normal midday meal, two periods of 8 hours 15 minutes remain for the day's rowing at an average speed of 7.37 knots. On the assumption that there was no contrary wind and that the short period of strong adverse current through the straight was balanced by the longer period of favourable easterly current along the Black Sea coast, this is a fast, but not impossible, average speed for a trained crew.

The second well-documented voyage of the trireme under oar is between Piraeus and

17. Herodotus 7.194.1.

18. Xenophon *Anabasis* 6.4.2.

19. Herodotus 4.86.

The Erment terracotta model clearly shows three levels of oars.

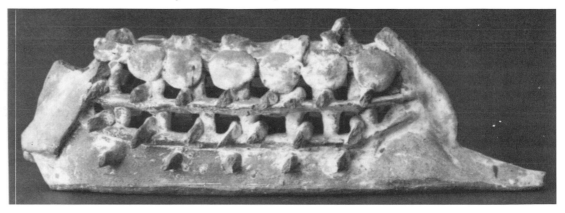

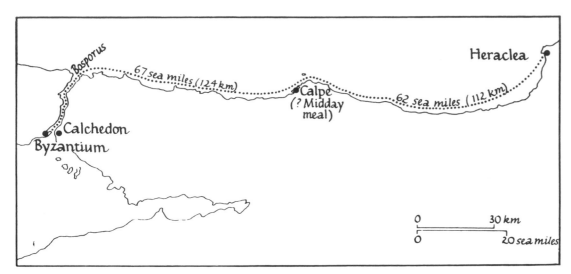

Byzantium to Heraclea.

Mitylene on a famous occasion. In 428 BC Lesbos revolted. An Athenian expedition under Paches besieged Mitylene; and when it fell towards the end of June in the following year the Athenian Assembly decided to put to death all the men taken prisoner, sending a trireme to Paches carrying the decree. At an Assembly on the following day the decision was reversed and another trireme sent at once with the reprieve:

> She had a start of·about a day and a night. The Mitylenian representatives at Athens gave wine and barley bread for the ship and promised

great rewards if she arrived first. The crew [of the second ship] made such haste that they [did not stop for meals but] pulled and ate at the same time, barley bread mixed with wine and olive oil, and [they did not bivouac for the night on shore but] some slept and others pulled, turn and turn about. By good luck they had no contrary winds, and while the one ship did not make haste on such a disagreeable errand, the other hurried in the way described. The first ship did in fact arrive first by enough time to allow Paches to read the decree and start taking steps to carry it out, but the second

ship put in after it and was in time to prevent the actual executions.[20]

The potential of a single trireme moving in normal and in abnormal conditions can be well seen. Normal practice was to go ashore for a meal at midday (where a not unfriendly landfall made it possible), and for an evening meal and sleep in the hours of darkness, but otherwise to row during the hours of daylight. The voyages in question took place some time between the end of June and the middle of July when the northwesterly *melteme* sets in.

In the case of the first ship, since the Assembly began proceedings at daybreak and the fate of the Mytilenian prisoners would have been high on the agenda, departure is likely to have taken place not more than 4 hours after sunrise, leaving 11 hours of a 15-hour midsummer day for the first day of the three-day passage. The unhurried voyage to Mitylene would then have fallen into three stages, the first (11 hours), of about 56nm to the southern tip of Euboea (Geraistos) including a midday break of an hour at Sunium, the second (of 15 hours), after a night bivouacked ashore, across the open sea to Chios, 87nm with no shore break possible, but probably food eaten on board and the oarsmen resting, probably in turn to avoid drift; and the third (of 10 hours) after a night at Chios, of 58.5nm, along the Asiatic coast to Cyme or Carterea, with a midday break of an hour there and then a move across the channel to Mitylene, arriving after a 54-hour voyage at the tenth hour of the day (14.30 in the afternoon).

The total of nautical miles covered is 201.5nm in 34 hours at the oar, an average of 5.9 knots, which can then be taken as a deliberately unhurried speed. Compared with it, the average of 7.37 knots the run from Byzantium to Heraclea looks fast for a voyage of 129nm, but may be normal.

The 34 hours at sea of the first ship are taken to have been at the oar because there is no mention of sailing. There were no contrary winds, but the ship might have taken advantage of a favourable wind to give the oarsmen a rest if a satisfactory speed could be achieved.

The second ship, which set off about a day and a night (*ie* 24 hours) after the first ship, is likely to have started at the same time as the first ship, as soon as possible after the decision had been taken by the Assembly, the fourth hour after sunrise. She was rowed continuously at full pressure but not by a full crew, the men resting and eating in shifts; and she would have

Piraeus to Mytilene.

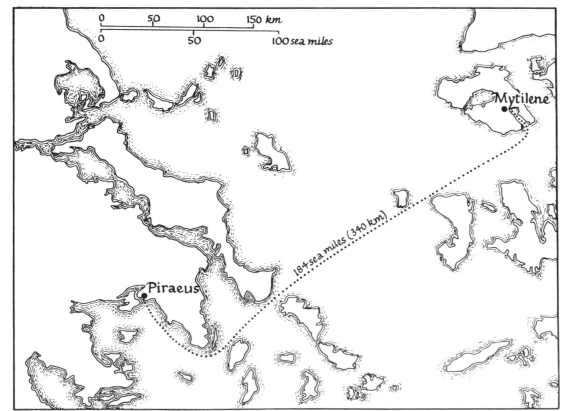

---

20. Thucydides 3.49.

taken the shortest course, 184.5nm. She arrived not more than an hour or two after the first ship (15.30–16.30), having been at sea 31–32 hours, an average of 5.95–5.76 knots. If there had been a wind for sailing that would certainly have been mentioned.

Rowing continuously in shifts at maximum pressure for two or three fewer hours over a shorter course, the crew of the second trireme achieved the average speed of the full oar crew of the first trireme. But the measure of their achievement was not the average speed, but their destination reached in 31–32 hours against the first trireme's 54.

The procedure of an unhurried trireme voyage is confirmed by implication in Thucydides's narrative: a rest period (where possible on shore but otherwise in shifts on board about midday) when food was eaten, and eating and sleeping at night on shore. The narrative is evidence also that, if occasion demanded, rowing in shifts was a normal practice, at any rate for a short period (in this case 31–32 hours), and (the midday and evening) meals were taken on board. The effectiveness of this practice, at any rate again for a short period, is demonstrated by the fact that the second ship could reach the (not very demanding) average speed of the unhurried voyage of a similar ship over a not much greater distance.

The account of the Athenian fleet commander Iphicrates's voyage to Corcyra in 372 BC gives some indication of how a voyage by an Athenian fleet round a hostile Peloponnese was conducted and of how crews were trained in the necessary procedures. Xenophon[21] describes it as an example of good leadership [the paragraphs are here numbered to aid reference]:

[1.] Iphicrates proceeded with his voyage and at the same time made all necessary preparations for action, at the outset leaving his sails behind as if he were expecting an engagement. In addition, even if there was a following wind he used his boatsails (foresails) little but progressed by oar [instead, presumably of using boatsails and mainsails when the wind was favourable]. Thus he both improved the fitness of his men and achieved a higher speed for his ships.

[2.] Often, also, as the fleet [moving in column parallel to the coastline] was on the point of having their midday or evening meal, he would take the column out to sea at those places [where they were to have their meals].

Next he turned the individual triremes and thus formed them into line abreast[22] and would start them off with a signal to race to the shore for a prize . . . Those who came first did everything slowly, and the last had to hurry.

[3.] Again, as to watches, if a midday meal was being taken in enemy country, Iphicrates placed the proper guards on land and besides raised the masts on the ships and kept a lookout from them. . . . Where he had the evening meal or slept he allowed no fire in the camp at night, but kept a light outside to prevent anyone approaching unobserved.

[4.] Often if the weather was fine he put to sea immediately after the evening meal; and if the wind was following, they would take their rest and run before the wind, but if rowing was necessary he would rest the oarsmen turn and turn about.

[5.] When moving by day he ordered them by signal to proceed now in column now in line abreast, with the result that they made progress, and at the same time having practised and learnt all the skills of battle they reached the sea which was commanded, they thought, by their enemies.

[6.] Most frequently they took their midday and evening meals in enemy country; but by restricting himself to the necessary activity [on these occasions] Iphicrates was putting to sea before enemy forces arrived and quickly finishing the incursion.

There are a number of points to be noticed in this description.

In (1) the rather surprising and gratuitous statement is made that by leaving his mainsails behind (the normal practice when going into action), using his foresails little (see paragraph 4 for the occasions when they were used) and making his voyage [solely] under oar, not only did Iphicrates improve his oarsmen's fitness *but also made his ships go faster*. Experience with *Olympias* suggests that the reason for this assertion is not that a trireme moves faster on average under oar than it can on average under sail with a wind astern, but that summer winds in Greek waters are so variable in force and direction that on a long day's voyage triremes consistently under oar and without the extra weight of main yard and mainsail will by and large go faster than those attempting to use their mainsails when the wind is favourable.

Iphicrates' method of exploiting his seamen's hunger to encourage quick manoeuvres of ships and the attendant smart efficiency of individuals is ingenious (2). The

description implies what is stated explicitly in (6), that landings on enemy territory necessary for the operation of Athenian fleets on the often repeated voyage round the Peloponnese had to be done quickly and to be carefully planned.

Masthead lookouts (3) add a further detail to the picture of the midday landings, as the lights burning around the camp do for the night rests. They also provide evidence that, although mainsails were left behind when a fleet expected an engagement, the foresails and both masts were carried. Paragraph (4) describes an apparently frequent practice of proceeding under the foresail at night in fine weather with light and favourable winds, using the oarsmen in shifts when the wind failed. This would be a way of avoiding the dangers incurred by bivouacking in enemy country as well as of making progress.

Fleets in transit either on a voyage or to meet an enemy normally moved in column (5). The Greek phrases *epi kerōs*, *epi keras* for this formation (meaning 'to the wing') are probably derived from military practice. Infantry, and oared warships which like fighting men are vulnerable to attack from the flank, are drawn up in battle (and hence on the parade ground) in line abreast two (or four) deep. To move, infantry, and in imitation of them ships, proceed to the right or left in column with the right or left wing leading. In naval tactics the head of the column is referred to frequently as the right (or occasionally left) wing. This has often led to confusion in the interpretation of accounts of sea battles since it seems to imply line abreast rather than column. Xenophon's phrase for 'in line abreast' is similarly military *epi phalangos*, deriving from the word *phalanx* meaning from Homer onwards a line of battle of men fighting on land.[23]

The trireme in action

Thucydides[24] describes the engagement in late September 433, just before the beginning of the Peloponnesian war, between an invading Corinthian fleet of 150 ships and 110 Corcyraean ships with 10, later 20, more Athenian

21. Xenophon *Hellenica* 6.2.27–30.

22. *cf* Thucydides 2.90.4.

23. *cf* also the hurried voyage of Mindarus's fleet: *AT* Map 11.

24. Thucydides 1.45–54.

ships standing by to prevent the Corinthians landing on Corcyra:

> Both fleets had many hoplites [infantrymen] on deck as well as many archers and javelin men, for the ships were still manned rather unscientifically in the old-fashioned manner . . . The fighting was hard, not so much in terms of matching skill with skill but because it resembled land-fighting more than anything else. For when the ships rammed each other they did not easily separate, because of the numbers and the press of the ships and because success in the battle was seen to depend more on the fighting men on deck. They fought a pitched battle with the ships immobilised. Nor were there any examples of the breakthrough [*diekplous*], but they fought rather with courage and physical strength than with tactical skill.

He makes the contrast between tactical skill in fighting at sea (exhibited in the *diekplous*) and engagements that resembled land-fighting, which is repeatedly echoed by ancient historians. His description also makes the point strongly that the reputation of the few Athenian ships, practising the modern tactic, was able to deter the Corinthian fleet from achieving their objective. Later, the reliance of the Macedonians and Romans, when they took to the sea, on hand-to-hand fighting, resulted in a return to the old-fashioned style. Only the Rhodians continued to rely chiefly on skilled manoeuvre.

The *diekplous* and the defence against it had been evolved in the great trireme fleets of the eastern Mediterranean, the *diekplous* possibly by the Phoenicians, and defence against it by their opponents at sea. The first mention of it (494 BC) was in Herodotus's account of the Ionian revolt. Dionysius of Phocaea was chosen to train the Ionian crews as they waited at Lade for engagement with the Persian fleet.[25] His reputation as a tactician rather than the strength of the Phocaean contingent (three ships) was presumably the reason for the choice: 'He regularly took the ships to sea in column (*epi keras*) with the intention of training the oarsmen in making a *diekplous* with the ships through each other[s' lines] and he turned out the deck-soldiers in full armour.'

The mention of the *diekplous* here is hardly explicit. It does, however, make three points clearly: the manoeuvre necessarily involves ships in column, they pass 'through each other' and the deck-soldiers are fully armed (for close combat). There is no sense in ships in one column passing through other ships also in column. It must be assumed that some ships were

in column and others in line abreast. This assumption is supported by what Herodotus calls a *diekplous*;[26] of the narrow opening (*hupophausin*) left by Xerxes at each end of his bridge of pentecontors and triremes abreast at the Hellespont so that light vessels could pass through one into, and through the other out of, Propontis on the eastern side of the bridge. The manoeuvre is then of contingents of ships in column passing through other contingents of ships in line abreast (*metōpēdon*). This 'breakthrough' was liable to lead to close fighting (with deck-soldiers in armour).

The next mention of the *diekplous* is in Herodotus's description[27] of the preliminary skirmish of some ships on each side at Artemisium in the Salamis campaign: 'since no one put out against them the Greeks waited for the late evening and launched ships against the barbarian with the intention of trying them out in fighting at sea and the *diekplous*' (a hendiadys). From what happened it appears that the Greeks, expecting that a *diekplous* would be tried against them, wished to try out a countermeasure themselves. When the Persian ships approached them (in column) the Greek ships formed a defensive circle, with sterns pointing inwards and bows outwards, around which the enemy column rowed, deprived of an effective

periplous and rashly exposing their sides to the Greek rams. The circle duly exploded[28] and the Persians lost 30 ships.

The defensive circle was also adopted by a Peloponnesian invasion fleet of 47 ships (5 fast) directed at Acarnania at the beginning of the war (430 BC), when threatened by 40 fast ships under Phormio from Naupactus;[29] but the outcome was very different, the Peloponnesian ships being crowded together in confusion.

A papyrus fragment[30] of a work by Sosylus of Sparta on the campaigns of Hannibal describes a tactical defence against the *diekplous* invented, Sosylus says, by Heracleides of Mylasa (a city of Caria between Miletus and Halicarnassus) and practised at Artemisium. A man of that name is mentioned by Hero-

---

25. Herodotus 6.12.1.

26. Herodotus 7.36.2.

27. Herodotus 8.9.

28. In a discussion of this manoeuvre at Westminster School a member of the Sixth Form observed rightly that the Greek ships would have risked losing their rams if they had rammed the Persian ships at right-angles. They must have taken them on the quarter at no more than 45 degrees, moving in the same direction.

29. *AT* 68–71.

30. *F Gr Hist* 176 F 1.

The battle of Salamis.

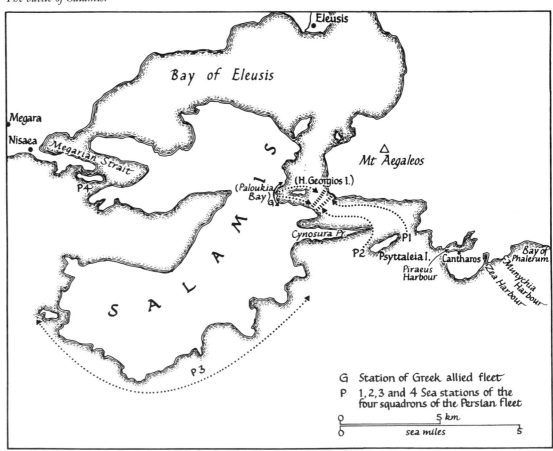

G Station of Greek allied fleet
P 1, 2, 3 and 4 Sea stations of the four squadrons of the Persian fleet

Ivory plaque from the temple of Artemis Orthia, Sparta. The ram suggests a warship but there are no oars visible, although the men behind the row of shields may be oarsmen. Note the open structure beneath the shields.

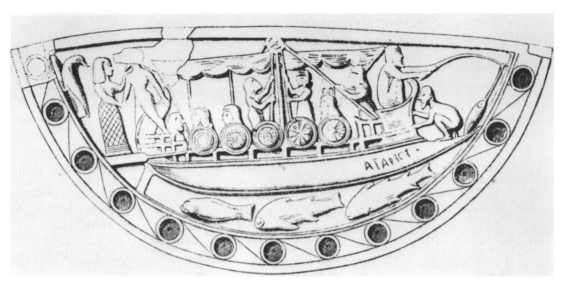

dotus[31] as responsible for the ambush of a Persian army in the Ionian revolt, but Herodotus says nothing about the perfectly possible presence of such a man in the Greek fleet in the Salamis campaign which the fragment implies. Sosylus speaks of the Carthaginians at the battle of the Ebro in 217 (see Chapter 4) being at a double disadvantage because the Massaliots knew of their tactical speciality as Phoenicians (*ie* the *diekplous*):

> For the Phoenicians if they find themselves confronting an enemy prow-to-prow regularly carry on forward as if to engage but do not close at once. After making a *diekplous* (*diekpleusantas*: aorist) they turn and just when the enemy ships are broadside on [as they turn to meet the threat from the rear] smash into them.

This is a particular description of the frame in which the *diekplous* is set which assumes that the reader can fill in the picture itself. It is in fact deducible if his description is taken together with Dionysius's training exercise. The fleets first move towards each other in line abreast. Then the ships planning a *diekplous* turn individually right or left into column and effect a breakthrough, the leading ships in close conflict at the point of breakthrough. After they have moved through the enemy's line and out the other side (the precise meaning of the Greek word *diekpleusantas*) the ships effect a sharp turn and are favourably placed to ram the enemy line as it is in the process of turning [to meet them]. The tradition, of which Sosylus is aware, that the *diekplous* was a particularly Phoenician manoeuvre, may well represent the truth.

The fragment of Sosylus gives also the defensive formation against the *diekplous* which Heracleides of Mylasa, 'superior to his contemporaries in intelligence', practised at Artemisium and whereby he was the cause of the victory. The Massaliots had heard of it and they copied it at the battle of the Ebro:

> They gave orders that when [the commanders] drew up the first ships in line abreast to face the enemy they should leave over other ships to support them at appropriate intervals. As well as alternating with the ships of the first line, these will be in a favourable position to attack the ships of the enemy which were making the

offensive move, themselves staying in the aforesaid position.

Polybius[32] is contemptuous of Sosylus as an historian. The latter, who is said to have been a friend of Hannibal, may however preserve a tradition worth notice relating to the battle on the day following the preliminary skirmish about which Herodotus[33] gives no detail. He states only that the Greeks, after the arrival of a further 53 Athenian ships, put out at the same time as on the previous day and after destroying Cilician ships put back to Artemisium. The main battle on the third day was inconclusive and the Greeks had many ships lost and damaged. It was certainly no victory, whereas the skirmish on the second day could be so described.

The importance of the Sosylus fragment lies in the descriptions of the *diekplous* and of the defence against it. For a further example of a defensive formation against a faster fleet seeking *diekplous* and *periplous*, the battle of Arginusae may be compared.[34]

The *periplous* is an attempt usually made, when there is plenty of sea room, by the more numerous fleet, which can form a longer line abreast to outflank and thus get to the favourable position behind one or both wings of a shorter enemy line abreast. Such a manoeuvre is suggested by the crescent shaped line adopted by the more numerous Persian fleet at the main battle of Artemisium (Day 3), but the most remarkable example is provided by the Athenian fleet at the battle of Cynossema in 411.[35] There, the 76 Athenian ships moving into the Hellespont in column on the north side were met by Mindarus's larger fleet of 86 ships moving in column in the opposite direction on the south side. As the two fleets drew level the ships turned individually into line

abreast. Taking tactical advantage of his longer line, Mindarus sent his fast ships to make a *periplous* of the Athenian right wing, which had been in the rear of the moving column, while he attacked the centre and drove it ashore. In reply the Athenians, temporarily abandoning their centre, did the unexpected and brought off a *periplous* on both wings, routed their opponents and then came to the rescue of their centre. Here, as at the famous second battle of Naupactus[36] in 429 BC, the almost automatic tactical sense of Athenian trireme commanders, matched by the high performance of their crews, brought unexpected victory.

The most spectacular in its effect, and the earliest, of the battle manoeuvres of the trireme was brought off by ships which had not had time to develop the finesse of the later commanders and oarsmen. It was the opening move of the battle in 480 BC between the invading Persian fleet based on Piraeus and the mainland Greek fleet moving out from beaches on the other side of the Salamis strait.[37]

The ships of the Persian fleet, the messenger says[38] in Aeschylus's play the *Persians*, had spent the night patrolling, and at daybreak first heard the Greek seamen singing the paean, then the splash of oars; and then 'quickly they were all plain to see'. This fits a picture of the Greek fleet beached in Paloukia bay (where the modern ferry from Piraeus to Salamis island

31. Herodotus 5.121.

32. Polybius 3.20.5.

33. Herodotus 8.14.2.

34. Xenophon *Hellenica* 1.6.29ff: J S Morrison (1991b).

35. *AT* 80–83, 91.

36. *AT* 72–76.

37. *AT* 55–60.

38. *Persians* 386ff.

arrives), being hidden there from the patrolling enemy ships and only becoming visible when they emerged: 'The right wing first in good order led the array, next the whole fleet came out after it . . . Straightway ship smote her bronze armament on ship. A Greek ship began the attack' shearing off part of a Phoenician ship, and others joined in. 'At first the flow of the Persian fleet kept on.' It had been moving up the channel from its patrolling station, 'but as the mass of [Persian] ships was crowded together and they could not help each other but began ramming each other, they shattered the whole oared fleet.' The Greek ships 'skilfully moving around them in a circle delivered their blows'.

The picture now is of the Greek ships in column by clever tactics surrounding and crowding a disorderly and self-destroying mass of Persian ships as Phormio's ships did later in the first battle of Naupactus;[39] and it is made more vivid a few lines later by the image of the tunny fishers. Tunny are trapped in a large net, and the fishermen place their boats side-by-side around the net in a circle and kill the fish with spears and other weapons.

When Aeschylus says that the Greek right wing led and the rest of the fleet followed, and that a Greek ship began the action with a ramming attack on a Phoenician vessel, it is reasonable to take him at his word, particularly since there must have been many in his audience who had taken part in the battle a few years before. By saying that the right wing led, he implies a column, and when he says that a Greek ship began the action and attacked a Phoenician ship (which Herodotus says[40] was on the Persian left wing) he implies that this Greek ship was at the head of the column. When he says that the rest of the ships followed, the operation can be recognised as a breakthrough, a classical *diekplous* in circumstances where, with the Persian ships crowding up the narrow strait, there was no sea room for a *periplous*. The effect, however, was the same.

The momentum of the Persian ships continued to take them forward, but the breakthrough must have been successful because the next picture which the messenger gives is of Persian ships crowded together and unable to avoid ramming each other (as they attempt to turn) while the Greek ships have them surrounded and are ramming them in a disorderly mass. The comparison with the tunny kill is masterly and leaves no doubt about the Greek manoeuvre and its success.

Fragment of a Geometric vase showing part of the open side structure with pillars defining the oarsmen's 'room'.

Herodotus's account of the opening moves is different:

> Then the Greeks took out all their ships and the Persians attacked them. The other Greeks were backing down and trying to run their ships ashore . . . But Ameinias, an Athenian of Pallene, on the right wing rammed a ship [a Phoenician, see above]. Since his ship was stuck fast and the crew could not get her free, the other ships came to the rescue and joined in.[41]

The moves are in fact the same, though presented as haphazard rather than as part of a deliberate manoeuvre. The point of view is different; and usefully he starts earlier. The Persians moving up the straits appear to be on the offensive. The Greeks have moved offshore first into line abreast and are, as the account begins, starting to back (because the Persian line is advancing on them) and turn to the right into column, the ships appearing to be intent on running ashore prow first (*ie* in panic). Then Herodotus confirms that a Greek (Ameinias, an Athenian) is the first to attack a (Phoenician) ship opposite and that other ships support the Athenian ship (from behind). Herodotus would have had his information about the battle from his elders at Halicarnassus who took part in the battle on the Persian side or watched it ashore from the Attic hillside. Although they do not seem to have understood the Greek manoeuvre, what Herodotus passes on is sufficient to enable us to recognise that he like Aeschylus was describing a *diekplous*, although the word was too technical to find a place in Aeschylus's poetic vocabulary and Herodotus's informant did not recognise the manoeuvre.

Structure and oar system

Direct evidence

Since triremes had positive buoyancy,[42] they did not sink and accordingly no remains recognisable as of a trireme have been found on the sea bed. Nor have any such remains been found ashore. In any case, recognition must rely on such other evidence about the ship, direct or indirect, as can be accumulated. A mark of victory in a sea battle was the ability to tow away the enemy's wrecks.

Shipsheds

An account of the excavation of the Zea shipsheds, built on the limestone rock to house triremes in the fifth, and rebuilt in the fourth, century BC, was published in 1885 by Dragatzes. The sheds provide a secure maximum breadth for the ship of just under 6m (19ft 5in). The length of the slips to the present water level (which may have risen since the fourth century BC) was 37m, but Dragatzes reported continuation below water level. Slips must have extended down to about 0.8m to about 0.9m depth below water, possibly at a greater slope to allow ships to be drawn up from the floating state.

---

39. *AT* 68–71.

40. Herodotus 8.85.1.

41. Herodotus 8.32–84.1.

42. *AT* 128–9, 166.

Language

The word *triērēs* and its synonym, *triskalmos*, are both adjectives of the noun *naus* (ship), which is the case of *triērēs* is usually omitted. *Triērēs* means either 'three-fitted', or, more likely, 'three-rowing'. At any rate as the name of a type of ship it means one which has three of what other ships have a different number. The clue to the thing of which this kind of ship has three is provided by its synonym *triskalmos* used by Aeschylus as an alternative for *triērēs*. This ship has three *skalmoi* (rowlocks) where other oared ships have another number.

The two words may then be considered together with the word which Vitruvius[43] gives as the Greek for the Latin *interscalmium*, meaning the longitudinal distance between one rowlock and the next in a fore-and-aft file of oarsmen, *ie* the oarsman's 'room'. In the manuscripts of Vitruvius, this Greek word is given in Latin characters as *dipheciaca*, which is plainly a corruption either of *dipechuia* nominative feminine of the adjective *dipechus* which appears in Herodotus with the meaning 'of two cubits' or of some nautical variant of that word *dipechiake* or *-ka*, as *thalamax* is nautical slang for *thalamios* in Aristophanes. There can at any rate be no doubt of its meaning 'a space of two cubits'.

The word 'of two cubits', about a yard, indicates a suitable length for the oarsman's 'room'. The words *triskalmos, triērēs* may then be taken to describe a ship in which the number of oars and oarsmen to the room on each side has been increased to from two to three. This time the great leap from a ship with fifty oarsmen at two levels to one with a hundred and seventy seems to have been thought worthy of a new descriptive name, *triskalmos*, or more prosaically *triērēs*.

At the time when Aeschylus wrote the *Persians* the oarsman's room was therefore recognised as the basic structural unit of an oared galley. It appears[44] that the so-called 'Doric' cubit of 0.490m is to be used in calculating the oarsman's room. The number of oarsmen in the longest fore-and-aft file of the trireme is known from inscriptions to be thirty-one (see below). With a cubit of 0.490m the two-cubit 'room' of 0.980m determines the length of the rowing area of the ship at about 30m and hence the length of the whole ship as a little less than 40m, not too long for the Zea slipways if the water level has risen slightly since they were built.

The names for the three categories of oars and oarsmen, *thranites, zygios* and *thalamios*, occur in the naval inventories naming oars: the first and third are also used by the historians naming oarsmen.

The word for the hold of a ship appears to be *thalamos* or *thalame*. The pentecontor with a single level of oars had room for cargo. In the *Odyssey* gifts are stowed under the *zyga* and Herodotus describes the Phocaeans, who preferred exile to Persian rule, sailing away taking their families and possessions with them in their pentecontors. When the second level of oars was introduced, the hold was sacrificed to add power. It is reasonable to assume that in such pentecontors the lower-level oars and oarsmen were called *thalamioi* and that the upper level, being those who before had sat on the thwarts (*zyga*) were called *zygioi*. *Zygitēs* and *thalamitēs* are mistaken Byzantine inventions presumably to match *thranitēs*. The architectural usage, among many, of the noun *thranos* for the top course of masonry is the most likely to be that from which *thranites* derives. In a nautical context the word might transfer to the top wale of a ship's planking. *Thranites* then means the oarsman who, rowing through an outrigger, sat directly above or on what is in modern terminology the gunwale but in reference to ancient hulls may be called the topwale.

The word *parexeiresia* is used by Thucydides for a part of the trireme immediately behind the *epotides* or ear-timbers which are shown in the Apulian rhyton. The two words indicate a structure on each side of the hull above the topwale protected in the bows by timbers projecting like ears. The name *parexeiresia* 'along (para) – outside (ex) – rowing (eiresia)' describes the purpose of the structure. It is (as Assmann and Cartault perceived in the last century) an outrigger, not unlike the Venetian apostis, for the file of oarsmen visible in the Lenormant relief. This outrigger, seen from the side as two continuous horizontal wales between which the oars emerge, appears there in higher relief than the lower horizontal wales on the side of the hull.

Literature

From the first mention of the trireme by the poet Hipponax[45] in the mid sixth century BC, as equipped with a ram and having many thwarts, the ship occurs very frequently. Herodotus[46] speaks of a ship in 525 BC with a crew of 200 which can only be a trireme since that is the number of her crew later and no other type of that size is recorded at that time. However, the information usually given is of her performance as a fast, agile ship rather than of her structure. Perhaps the most important fifth-century text is the account in Thucydides[47] of Corinthian oarsmen being transferred to

Megarian triremes on the other side of the Isthmus and 'carrying each man his oar, his cushion and his oarloop'. This text removes any remaining possibility that trireme oarsmen sat more than one man to an oar, as has frequently been suggested in the past.

The deck (*katastroma*) is well attested. Early in the fifth century it appears to have been built not right across the ship,[48] but was later extended to do so, and thus accommodate more soldiers. The normal complement of armed men on deck in the later fifth century is shown by Thucydides[49] to have been ten hoplites and four archers. But troop-carriers would take up to forty hoplites. Under oar, the armed men on deck were required to be seated.[50]

Another text relating to the trireme's oar system is in Aristotle.[51] Speaking of the fingers of the hand he says that 'the outermost finger is short for good reason and the middle finger long, like the oar amidships'. The author of the fourth-century *Mechanica* attributed to Aristotle[52] gives the reason for the difference in length of the oars of a galley. Answering the question why do the oarsmen amidships move the ship most, he says it is a question of leverage (gearing): amidships the longest part of the oar is inboard (*ie* the loom of the oars amidships is longest) because the ship is broadest there. At bow and stern the convergence of the hull sides made it necessary for the looms to be shorter. Galen[53] makes the same point: 'all the oars extend to the same distance from the ship's side although they are not overall the same length.'

Inscriptions

By far the most important and rich source of direct information about the trireme, and about the Athenian navy in general, lies in fourth-century inscriptions, in particular in those[54] known as the Naval Inventories. They were found in Piraeus and show, in a fragmentary state, the annual records of the outgoing Boards of Dockyard Overseers.

43. Vitruvius 1.2.4.

44. J S Morrison (1991).

45. Hipponax fr 45 Diehl.

46. Herodotus 3.13.1–2.

47. Thucydides 2.93.3.

48. *AT* 160.

49. Thucydides 3.94.9 and 6.43.

50. Thucydides 7.67.

51. Aristotle *Parts of Animals* 687 b 18.

52. [Aristotle] *Mechanica* 4.850 b 10.

53. Galen *De Usu Partium* 24.

54. *IG* 2² 1604–1632: *c*377/6–323/2 BC.

The bronze ram found off Athlit (near Haifa) not only confirms the shape shown in many iconographical sources, but also had sufficient ship timber attached to confirm the mortise-and-tenon shell construction of the hull. This ram is too heavy for a classical trireme and probably came from one of the larger oared warships of the Hellenistic and later periods.

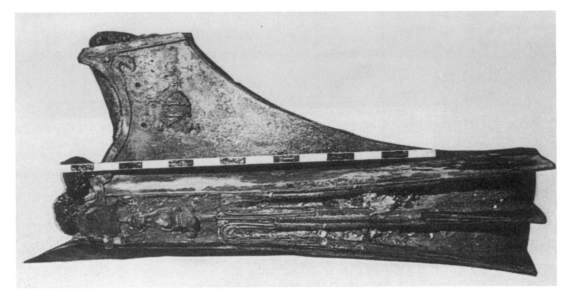

The Naval Inventories give a picture of the organisation and practices of the Athenian navy in the third quarter of the fourth century, and enable us to witness the gradual introduction of the quadrireme (*tetreres*) and quinquereme (*penteres*). They also give valuable information about the trireme itself. When the trireme is in commission she is often described as 'girded', *ie* with the *hypozomata* fitted. An earlier inscription[55] gives a decree prescribing the legal minimum number of men (probably fifty) allowed to rig a *hypozoma*. It is clear that considerable tension was required. In the inventories four are the norm for each ship, while six are taken on a distant mission. *Hypozomata* head the lists of gear. The entries thus show that these ropes were of great importance to the ship's seaworthiness: and this is confirmed by a passage[56] in Apollonius of the maritime city of Rhodes about the fitting of the *hypozoma* to the newly constructed *Argo*. 'First of all' the Argonauts 'girded the ships mightily with a well twisted rope from within, putting a tension on each end so that the planks should fit well with the tenons and should withstand the opposing force of the sea's surge.' Apollonius, being a Rhodian, knew what he was talking about.

Like the *hypozoma*, the *askoma* appears as an important piece of gear. In the earliest naval inventory ships are recorded as either having or not having *askomata* fitted; and if not it is stated where they are. The *Etymologicum Magnum* describes the *askoma* as a leather sleeve through which the thalamian oar emerges from the hull. Since such a sleeve appears to be indicated roughly in the Ruvo vase and is shown clearly in later representations of oared ships, the explanation is acceptable.

The most important items in the Inventories are the entries concerned with the oars. The numbers for each ship are invariably: 62 thranite, 54 zygian and 54 thalamian (31, 27 and 27 on each side), making a total of 170.

A drawing of the Lenormant relief made for the Cavaliero dal Pozzo in Rome between 1610 and 1635. The artist did not understand the oar system, but the drawing does represent the bow section which has since disappeared from the original.

These with the 14 armed men leave a balance of 16 men which form what is termed the *hypēresia*, the body of assistants to the captain (trierarch), composed of two gangs of 5 deckhands (fore and aft) and 6 petty officers of which the most important are the helmsman and the bow officer.

The Inventories[57] also give a fourth category of oars, the *perineō* (spares), and these, 30 in all (to make up the round number of 200), are in two lengths, 9 or 9½ cubits. There has been argument about the significance of this entry; but it could in fact hardly be clearer. Liddell-Scott-Jones quote the inscriptions *kōpai perineō* for the meaning 'supernumerary or to spare in

a ship' and the lexicographers Hesychius and Photius for the word's use to mean a spare mast or other duplicated gear in a ship. The word is used also of persons on board a ship not working their passage at the oar (as opposed to oarsmen – *proskōpoi, auteretai, triēritai* etc) from Thucydides to Procopius. There really cannot be any doubt that the 30 oars are spares very properly carried on board in case of breakages in the 170 'working' oars. Since, then, oars of

55. *IG* 1³ 153 : 440–425 BC.

56. Apollonius of Rhodes I 367–9.

57. *eg IG* 2² 1607.9.19.

The Ruvo vase shows the stern of the Argo *represented as a trireme. The oar system of the original is obscured by figures, but by removing them it is possible to reconstruct the arangement as shown in the right-hand drawing.*

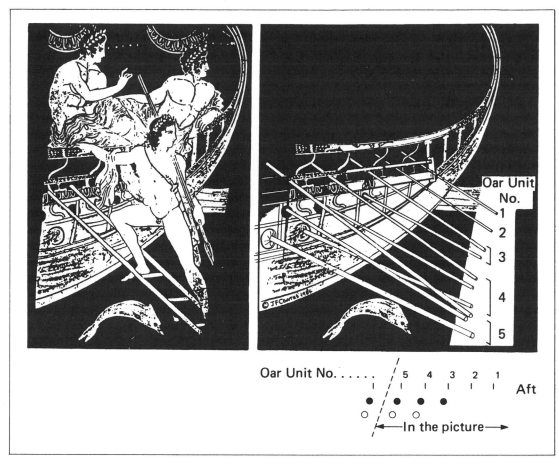

these two lengths are indubitably spares, regularly carried on board a trireme to take the place of unserviceable oars in any of the three named categories, the important conclusion follows that all the oars must have been either 9 or 9½ cubits in length. The reason for the difference has been noted above and seems secure. With a cubit of 0.490m the oars are 4.41m (14ft 5½in) long in bow and stern, or 4.655m (15ft 3in) long amidships.

The Inventories record a big and a small ('boat') mast and yard, and a big and a small sail. Their use as described in the historians suggests that the masts, yards and sails were not alternatively but simultaneously rigged. There is sometimes a set of light sails. The word for the yard, *kerata*, is plural, indicating a practice (visible in some ship pictures on black-figure vases) of making up the yard of two spars fished together. The most notable of the remaining items of gear recorded are rams, the twin rudders, ladders, anchors, sidescreens of canvas, leather and hair.

The indirect evidence

From the 'shell' method of construction revealed by underwater archaeology to have been used in contemporary merchant ships and in the bow timbers, preserved in the Athlit ram,[58] of a late third-century warship, it is reasonable to infer the method employed in building a fifth/fourth-century trireme. There remain the representations of parts of fifth/fourth-century oared warships which may be recognised as showing parts of triremes. The two most important are the Lenormant relief, showing the middle section of the starboard side of an oared ship under oar, and the Ruvo vase, showing the stern of an oared ship which has been beached

(with oars shipped, but not a rudder). Both are dated at the end of the fifth century, before the invention of the quadrireme and quinquereme and long before they appear in the Inventories.

The information gained from the direct evidence gives the trireme a deck, an open side below the deck, a *parexeiresia* through which the thranite oars are rowed, and below that two rows of oarports, the lower fitted with an oar sleeve and big enough to take a man's head.[59] The relief shows a deck with men recumbent on it. It shows also below the deck an open side through which a file of thranite oarsmen are seen with oars at the catch and rowing them through an outrigger. Below, oars emerge at two levels en echelon. There is shown also a bracket supporting the *parexeiresia* and butting

its lower end on a lower wale, while the pillar supporting the deck butts its lower end on an upper wale. The vase shows no oars or oarsmen but an identical deck and (curved) pillars, *parexeiresia* and bracket, and two oarports en echelon of which the lower is larger and shows traces of an oar sleeve. Both representations may be taken to depict triremes with some certainty, particularly because of their common date and since they are in close accord with one another.

John Morrison

---

58. Casson and Steffy (1991).

59. Herodotus 5.33.2.

References and abbreviations used in the footnotes

R C Anderson (1962), *Oared Fighting Ships* (London).

Lucien Basch (1987), *Le musée imaginaire de la marine antique* (Athens).

D J Blackman (1968), 'The Shipsheds', Ch 8 of Morrison and Williams, *Greek Oared Ships*, pp181–192.

C Blinkenberg (1938), 'Lindiaka 7: Triemiolia', *Det Kgl Danske Videnskabernes Selskab Archaeologisk-Kunsthistoriske Meddelelser* II, 3 (Copenhagen).

Lionel Casson (1959), *The Ancient Mariners* (Princeton; reprinted 1981).

—— (1971), *Ships and Seamanship in the Ancient World* (Princeton; reprinted 1986) = *SSAW*.

Lionel Casson and J Richard Steffy (1991), *The Athlit Ram*, Texas A and M University Press (College Station).

I X Dragatzes (1886), 'Report on Excavations at Piraeus' *Praktika of 1885*, pp63–68.

J S Morrison (1991), 'Ancient Greek Measures of Length in Nautical Contexts' *Antiquity* 65, No 247, pp298–305.

—— (1991b), 'The Greek Ships at Salamis and the Diekplous', *Journal of Hellenic Studies* 111.

J S Morrison and R T Williams (1968), *Greek Oared Ships* (Cambridge; reprinted Oxford 1994) = *GOS*.

J S Morrison and J F Coates (1986), *The Athenian Trireme* (Cambridge) = *AT*.

—— (1994), *Greek and Roman Oared Ships: 399–31 BC* (Oxford) = *GROW*.

W W Tarn (1913), *Antigonus Gonatas* (Oxford) = *AG*.

Cecil Torr (1894), *Ancient Ships*, (Cambridge; reprinted Chicago 1984).

4

Hellenistic Oared Warships 399–31 BC

AN ACCOUNT of the oared warships of the Hellenistic centuries, their design and deployment in service, has been given in such detail as the evidence allows by Dr John Coates and the present author in *Greek and Roman Oared Warships: 399–31 BC* (Oxford 1994). Reference will frequently be made to this book for the arguments, details and reconstructions which space does not permit to be included here.

This chapter will attempt to suggest briefly the oar system of the more important of the new types developed in that period and the use to which they were put. The comparative certainty that has now been reached, and in general terms recognised, about the nature of the three[1] in the fifth and fourth centuries BC, has, embodied in the Hellenic Navy's *Olympias* designed by Dr Coates, enabled many, through her series of trials at sea, to understand the working of a sophisticated oared warship of ancient times. This experience has also been helpful for the understanding of those later types, whose oar systems were based on the three.

The method followed will be, after brief reference to the three, to give a summary of the naval history of the period and then to take in turn the various new types and, ranging over the whole period, to give what information about each can be gleaned from the historical sources and iconography.

During the fifth century BC the eastern and western Mediterranean were dominated by trireme fleets joined occasionally (*eg* in Xerxes' invasion fleet of 480) by triacontors and pentecontors. Threes were categorised as either fast (*tachunautousai*) or as troop-carriers (*stratiōtides*), and older threes were converted to take cavalry.[2] Besides being front-line warships they were used, as powerful ships, also to escort (*ie* where necessary to tow) *holkades* containing

A wall painting from the house of the priest Amandus at Pompei, showing a three-level oared warship (probably a five), AD 54–68. The vessel has high bulwarks and a deck full of armed men.

troops, or grain from the Crimea. When in the latter part of the fourth century they ceased to be front-line ships they remained as a large part of a fleet, and were given the task of towing troop- and supply-ships, as well as serving for reconnaissance and communications.

The new types in history

In the fourth and the first half of the third century BC new types of oared warship began to make their appearance in battlefleets. Basing his design on these and introducing double-manning of oars, Dionysius of Syracuse invented the five and probably the six (as well as the catapult, which had a profound effect on warship design when used at sea). His enemies

the Carthaginians later invented the four. Alexander built triacontors, and *hemioliai* (a new species of triacontor), for his Indus fleet (which also contained oared transports, *kerkouroi*, earlier employed in Xerxes' fleet).[3]

Alexander had fours and fives carried overland to his fleet station at Babylon, and just before his death he planned a large fleet of sevens for the conquest of Carthage. At his

Abbreviations in the footnotes are given in the references at the end of the chapter.

1. The ships discussed have Greek names (*trieres, tetreres, penteres*, etc), Latin names (*triremis, quadriremis, quinqueremis*, etc, and English names (trireme, quadrireme and quinquereme); but since the English series stops at quinquereme while the Greek series reaches *tessarakonteres* this chapter will for convenience follow the example of *SSAW* and call the series threes, fours, fives, etc up to the forty.

2. *AT* p227.

3. The *kerkouros* appears to have been an oared vessel employed for various tasks (see *SSAW*), often as a fleet auxiliary.

Roman Republican coins (268–240 BC) depicting the bow of a five.

After the period of naval innovation from Dionysius to Ptolemy III there followed an era of intense naval activity in the eastern and in the western Mediterranean. In the first Punic war (264–241 BC) Rome, a novice at sea, was engaged in a largely naval struggle, by fleets of fives, against the first maritime power of the time for possession of Sicily, while in the eastern Mediterranean first Rhodes, then Syria under Antiochus II, clashed with Egypt over the possession of Coele-Syria and Phoenicia. The second Punic war in the last two decades of the century was mainly conducted on land against the invasion of Italy by Hannibal, but at the outset there was an interesting battle against Hasdrubal in Spain at the mouth of the Ebro;[7] and, at the end, an enlightening encounter between two Carthaginian fours and a Roman five.

While Rome was thus engaged, Macedonian sea power revived under Philip V, finally culminating in the battles off Chios and Lade[8] between the fleet of Philip and the allied fleets of Attalos of Pergamon and Rhodes. Both sides deployed the new types of bigger oared warship now evolved. Roman fleets moved into the eastern Mediterranean after Rome's declaration of war on Philip in 200 BC and with her allies achieved naval supremacy and brought about his surrender after defeat on land at Cynoscephalae in 197 BC.

In the next century and a half before the outbreak of civil war, Roman naval forces, largely fives, were engaged in the eastern Mediterranean against Philip's former ally Antiochus III of Syria, Philip's son Perseus, and Mithridates IV with his allies the pirates.[9] The third Punic war led to invasion of Africa and bitter naval engagements against the desperate Carthaginians. Finally Julius Caesar attempted to match, by the invasion of Britain, Pompey's naval reputation, gained by the suppression of piracy in the east. He found it necessary as a preliminary to destroy the fleet of the Veneti with locally built craft and a squadron of bigger ships from the Mediterranean. These ships eventually took part in the expeditions to Britain (57–55 BC).[10]

death Athens planned, in a surge of 'the Salamis spirit', to regain her lost maritime hegemony with a new Hellenic League and a naval building programme of 40 threes and 200 fours. She was decisively defeated at sea, before that dream could come true, by a Macedonian fleet of 110 threes, sent to Macedon with a cargo of bullion by Alexander before his death, and joined by another fleet of unspecified types under Kleitos.

Of Alexander's Successors Antigonus Monopthalmos (One-eyed), appointed governor of Phrygia, showed[4] 'the firmest grasp of the meaning of sea power and the firmest resolution to win it'. In his way stood Kleitos's fleet, now at the Hellespont, and Ptolemy, another of the Successors and an historian, to whom Egypt had been allocated and who had taken there the Phoenician contingent of the royal fleet.

Antigonus eliminated the threat from Kleitos; but to counter Ptolemy he needed to build a substantial fleet both in size and numbers. If he was to achieve that goal he needed to gain control of the maritime areas of southern Asia Minor, Coele-Syria, and Phoenicia, where were then, as there had been before, sources of manpower and timber. By 315 BC he had built a grand fleet with which, under his son Demetrius in the last two decades of the century, he had conquered Cyprus, invaded Egypt (unsuccessfully) and by the agency of Demetrius laid siege to Rhodes. On the death of Antigonus at the battle of Issus, Demetrius extended and planned to strengthen his power at sea, but a coalition of his rival Successors led to his surrender and death in captivity in 283 BC. Ptolemy succeeded to his maritime empire.

At the end of this period Ptolemy II Philadelphus (283–246 BC)[5] used the great resources of Egypt in money and manpower to build a home fleet which contained small numbers of [experimental] thirties (2), twenties (1), thirteens (4) and twelves (2) while investing more heavily in elevens (14), nines (30), sevens (36), sixes (5), and fives (17), as well as in twice as many (222) of the category of fours, threes and *trihemioliai*. Philadelphus employed in addition 4000 ships of unspecified types in the islands (of the Aegean) and in the cities which he ruled.

An example of such an Egyptian overseas naval squadron is the contingent of 40 ships at Tyre and Ptolemais (Acre) which Ptolemy III Philopator's admiral Theodotos surrendered to Antiochus III of Syria in 219. Polybius[6] says: 'Of these there were 20 cataphracts, very well equipped, none of which was of a lower rating than a four [ie all twenty were fours or above], and the rest were [aphract] threes, *dikrota* [two-level ships of the liburnian/pentecontor type] and *keletes* [one-level scouts].' It is to be noted that, whereas Athenaeus's category of the bigger (and less numerous) ships does not include fours, Polybius's category of cataphract ships (equally balanced with aphract, undecked ships) does include them; and his undecked ships include threes.

4. Tarn *AG* p72.
5. Athenaeus 5. 203 c.
6. Polybius 5.62.3.
7. *GROW* Ch 2.3.
8. *GROW* Ch 2.5.
9. *GROW* Ch 3.4.
10. 57–52 BC: *GROW* Ch 3.4.

The relief from Ostia (second half of the first century BC) showing a large Roman three-level ship, probably a five. Iconography suggests that these vessels had their three tiers of oarports directly above one another, rather than en echeleon as in earlier threes.

The Civil Wars (53–31 BC) between Julius Caesar and the supporters of Pompey in Spain led to a minor sea battle off Massalia which Lucan describes with informative characterisation of the ships involved,[11] to engagements in the Adriatic, then seaborne invasions of Egypt and Africa. After Caesar's murder in 44 BC, his adopted son Octavian with fleets of fives and sixes fought a war at sea off Sicily against Pompey's younger son Sextus, whose ships, apart from his own flagship, a six, were fours.[12] In the final sea battle at Actium, Antony and Cleopatra's fleet was of large ships, fives to tens, while Octavian was content with liburnians, fives and sixes.[13]

The new types of the western mediterranean

The Five

Invention

Under the year 406 BC Diodorus[14] describes the rise to power of Dionysius I of Syracuse in the face of the Carthaginian threat to the Greek colonies in Sicily. In 404 BC he used the temporary peace he had made with Carthage to strengthen his own position in Syracuse by building a secure citadel which could accommodate a fleet of 60 threes; and by 399 BC[15] he was again ready for war with Carthage.

Accordingly he began at once to assemble by decree craftsmen from the cities under his control, and attracted them with high wages from Italy and even from territory controlled by

Carthage. He planned to manufacture a great quantity of arms and missiles of all kinds, and, in addition to them, threes and fives [*naus te triereis kai pentereis*], although a ship of the latter oar system had at that time not yet been built.

In the following chapter Diodorus repeats the same claims with more detail:

In fact the catapult was invented at this moment in Syracuse, when the best craftsmen had been brought together from everywhere to one place. The high wages of course and the number of bonuses offered . . . stimulated their enthusiasm. As a result the craftsmen . . . invented many new missiles . . . Dionysius also began to build threes and fives [*naupegeisthai (naus) te triereis kai penterika skaphe*], being the first to devise that kind of warship. The fact was that Dionysius was aware that a three had been built first in Corinth and was keen to in-

A Carthaginian tomb relief of the third century BC representing a five.

crease the size of warships built in the city which had been colonised from Corinth.[16]

In both the passages above where the Greek is given the texts of Diodorus available to readers (*eg* the Loeb edition) give Wesseling's quite unnecessary emendations[17] of *te triereis* to *tetrereis*, thus attributing the invention of fours as well as fives to Dionysius. Wesseling presumably thought that fours would naturally, and necessarily, have been invented before fives, but it is now clear that fours were developed by double-manning from pentecontors which had two levels of oars, while the five developed from the three, again by double-manning at two levels. The unassailable contemporary authority of Aristotle[18] attributes the invention of fours to Carthage, but the earliest possible mention of them is at the very end of Dionysius's reign, long after his invention of the five. It seems likely, then, that not only did he invent the five but that he was the first to use double-manning, the step which opened the wide field of innovation in the design of oared warships.

The naval forces sent to sea by Dionysius I in the years of his long reign following his early naval building programme do not suggest that the plans so optimistically launched, as described in Diodorus, were carried out at all rapidly or completely. One five at least seems to have been built. In 398 BC Dionysius sent the prototype to bring back from Lokroi to Syracuse the daughter of a distinguished Locrian to whom he had proposed a diplomatic marriage. Eight years later, in 390 BC, Dionysius in a five, his flagship in a fleet of 50

11. *GROW* Ch 4.1.

12. *GROW* Ch 4.4.

13. *GROW* Ch 4.5.

14. Diodorus 13.91.3–36.

15. Diodorus 14.41.2.

16. It is noteworthy that the fourth-century source which Diodorus uses in his *Bibliotheca* (probably his admiral Philistus who was also, like Ptolemy I, an historian) is less ambiguous than Thucydides on the invention of the three (*AT* pp38–40). Thucydides' statement (1.13.2) that 'threes are said to have been built first in Greece at Corinth' has been taken to suggest that their invention took place outside Greece, in Egypt or Phoenicia. The general belief in the fourth century is shown to have been that the three was first built at Corinth.

17. See J S Morrison (1990).

18. Aristotle Frg.600 Rose.

warships attacking Rhegium, is described as escaping shipwreck in a storm in which seven of his ships were lost. The greater oar power of a five would have been useful on a lee shore.

Use

Fives appear with threes (but not with fours) in the fleet of Sidon in 351 BC; and at Alexander's siege of Tyre in 332 as the flagships of the Cypriot kings. There were other fives in Alexander's fleet, all probably derived from Phoenicia. The Tyrian fleet had fives, fours and threes.

In the Athenian naval inventories fives (to the number of seven) appear for the first time in 325/324 BC, fours but no fives having appeared the previous year. Just before his death Alexander assembled a fleet for the circumnavigation of Arabia and Africa, consisting of two fives, three fours, a number of threes and some smaller ships.

In the first Punic war the five was used by both sides to a scale not equalled afterwards. Polybius observes in his summing up of the war[19] that on one occasion[20] the two sides fought each other with more than 500, and on another[21] with very nearly 700 fives.

Oar system

The name *penteres* implies five fore and aft files of oarsmen a side (half room). An arrangement with not more than two men to an oar is implied by Polybius's description[22] of the training of crews for fives on dry land with a long stroke and seated oarsmen. He gives[23] the number of oarsmen in each five of the Roman fleet at Ecnomus as 300. Thus, with two men to an oar at two of the three levels, the five would have 90 oars a side and files with an average of 30 oarsmen in each. With 180 oars she satisfies Lucan's description of one of the Roman ships at the battle of Massalia (not the six) which probably is a five as 'dipping more oars in the water' than the threes (170) and fours (140) he has just mentioned.

A five with an oar crew of 400 is said by Pliny[24] to have carried Caligula. The ship might have been a regulation five with 100 spare crew taken on deck. Alternatively, and it would seem impossibly, if all the oar crew rowed at one time, such a ship would have had an average of forty men to the file and 120 oars a side, 240 in all. A third explanation is that Pliny made a mistake and the ship was a six with 33 men in 8 files and 34 in four and 200 oars.

The fourth-century BC Isola Tiberina monument shows the bow section of what is probably a five or a six.

Design

The Roman five was cataphract and rated as one of the larger ships (*maioris formae*). Diodorus[25] gives the details of Hephaistion's tomb in which 'gilded prows of fives entirely filled up the (outside of the) foundation course (*krepis*) being 240 in number'. The structure was square with sides of 1 stade (196m) on the basis of a cubit of 0.490m. Each prow thus measured 3.26m from presumably epotis to epotis (*cf* 3.30m for *Olympias*). It is not to be supposed of course that 240 fives were sacrificed. If then the prows were specially made, they may have been to a scale rather than full-size models.

It appears that a Roman five stood significantly higher than a Carthaginian four, and this difference in height between the two types is confirmed on two other occasions. That this height, of the deck above the waterline, was 10 Roman feet (2.96m) is indicated by Orosius[26] giving the height of Antony's big ships, fives to tens.

Capability

Polybius[27] regarded it as self-evident that the five was superior to the three as a warship (the four apparently being *hors de concours*). The five serving as Dionysius's flagship[28] did better than the threes accompanying him, seven of which were lost in bad weather in an attack on Rhegium. Livy,[29] giving an account of the engagement in the straits of Gibraltar involving the two types, comes to the conclusion that the Roman five's greater mass enabled her there to respond more slowly and safely to the turbulence of the surface water, whereas the threes were badly affected and fell victims to her. But some fives were better than others: Roman fives on one occasion were said to be heavier and more difficult to turn than the Carthaginian vessels of similar type, which were

better built. There were fives *expediti*, stripped for action and fast movement.

The fives certainly performed better than the fours in Demetrius's fleet when caught by a storm from the north on the voyage to Pelusium. The fours were forced to run for the indifferent mooring facilities at Raphia while the fives were able to press on.[30]

The Six

Invention

There is certainly some reason to believe that towards the end of his life Dionysius made a further invention. Pliny[31] attributes the invention of the six to Syracuse; and Aelian[32] says that Dionysius II 'had his rule well fortified by having in his possession not less than 400 ships, . . . sixes and fives'. The text needs emendation since all 400 ships were most unlikely to have been sixes and fives, and the fleet was inherited

19. Polybius 1.63.5.

20. Hermaia: Polybius 1.36.9–10.

21. Ecnomus: Polybius 1.25.7–9.

22. Polybius 1.21.1–2.

23. Polybius 1.26.7.

24. Pliny the Elder *Natural History* 32.4.

25. Diodorus 17.115.1–5.

26. Orosius 6.19: 'classis Antoni centum triginta navium fuit, quantum numero cedens tantum magnitudine praecellens; nam decem pedum altitudine a mari aberant'. Cecil Torr (p20 n53) says, sensibly as usual, that this definite statement deserves more attention than the grotesque exaggerations of Virgil.

27. Polybius 1.63.8.

28. Diodorus 14.100.4–5.

29. Livy 28.30.3–12, *GROW* Ch 2.4.

30. Diodorus 20.70.4, *GROW* Ch 1.4.

31. Pliny *Natural History* 7.207.

32. Aelian *Various Stories* 6.12.

from Dionysius I. It provides some reason for thinking that Dionysius took the easy step after the invention of the five[33] and built the six before the end of his reign in 367 BC. Whereas the five appears to have developed from the three by double-manning two of the three levels of oars, in the six all three levels would have been double-manned.

It is possible but unlikely[34] that the six was a development of the four by triple-manning oars at two levels. The natural development at this stage is the extension of double-manning to all three levels of the three.

Use

No sixes appear in the Athenian naval inventories. Antigonus had fives, nines and tens in his grand fleet of 315 BC, but no sixes. Demetrius included ten sixes in his battlefleet at Cypriot Salamis in 306 BC. There were sixes also in the fleet which Agathocles collected at Syracuse for an invasion of Africa just before his death in 289 BC. Ptolemy Philadelphus later had five sixes in his fleet.

Rome's invasion fleet in the first Punic war was led at Ecnomus (256 BC) by the two consuls each on board a six. Scipio used a six in the Sicilian fleet on a diplomatic mission to the Locrians. Philip's fleet at Chios contained at least one six which was listed among the casualties. When Antiochus III decided that he needed a fleet of big ships he sent Hannibal to Phoenicia to procure it; and Hannibal came back with four sixes and three sevens with which he fought at Side and (with some of them) at Myonnesus.[35]

Brutus's flagship at Massalia was a six. When Cato sold up the treasure of Ptolemy XII in Cyprus he brought the proceeds back to Rome in 56 BC with a fleet of ships, of which the flagship was Ptolemy's 'royal six'.[36] When Sextus Pompeius came to meet Octavian and Antony in 39 BC near Puteoli it was in a 'splendid six'. At Actium there were sixes on both sides, in Octavian's fleet the largest and in An-

tony's after fives the smallest of the warships. In the early empire one six (the *Ops*) is recorded on a tombstone as belonging to the Misenum fleet, and a six of the same name appears three times with the fleet station unrecorded.[37]

Oar system

Diodorus[38] says that Pleistarchus, sent by Cassander with a fleet to support Lysimachus in 302 BC, lost most of his ships in a storm in the Black Sea. He was himself wrecked in his flagship, a six, carrying not less than 500 men. The nature of his mission meant that he would have had troops on board who with the *hyperesia* might have numbered 140 or more (there were 120 *epibatai* on the Roman invasion ships at Ecnomus). This would leave 360 oarsmen to man the twelve oar files (30 in number) and entail 180 oars.

Design

The height of Brutus's six compared with the other ships of the fleets at Massalia is emphasised by Lucan. But whereas her oar system (a double-manned three) would have entailed greater breadth than a three or a five, it is not likely to have necessitated more than a small additional height. Orosius's statement that at Actium the height of Antony's ships from fives to tens was 10 Roman feet (2.96m) may then cover it. Lucan also speaks of Brutus's ship as having towers alone of the ships in either fleet.[39] Her ample deck was well fitted to accommodate them. This unique feature would have given her the greater height Lucan emphasises.

Capability

There is no positive or precise literary evidence about the performance of the six in battle or about her seaworthiness. In the naval war against Sextus, Octavian's ships under Agrippa which were at least fives and sixes are said by Appian to have been heavy, slow, of deep draught and manned by many deck soldiers, while Sextus's ships under Papias were smaller, light, fast and of shallow draught. The former are not specified by type, except that one which was lost was identified as a six; and of the latter, as will be seen, the flagship itself was a four.

Much, then, of the characterisation of Octavian's ships is likely to apply to the six. She is likely to have had many of the qualities of the five with both the bad and the good qualities magnified. Antony was said to have learnt from Octavian the naval policy which produced the cumbrously large ships of his Actium fleet. The Romans of the Republic who clearly thought of

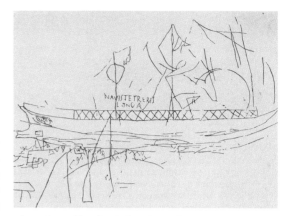

A rough graffito sketch found at Alba Fucentia. It dates from between the first century BC and the first century AD and being marked navis tetreris longa *is clearly a four. Note what appears to be a ventilation course below the weather deck.*

the four and in particular the five as the ships in which they felt happy to fight their kind of naval war, included the six in the preference as a conspicuous type suitable accordingly with its large complement of deck soldiers for a fleet commander in battle and useful to make an impression on prestigious occasions.

The Four

Invention

According to Pliny the Elder,[40] Aristotle said that the Carthaginians constructed the [first] four, and there is no reason to doubt his authority. There is no evidence for the precise date of the invention. There is some rather uncertain evidence for the four's presence in the fleet that Dionysius II inherited from his father in 367 BC. Dionysius I would certainly have been aware of, and would have copied any advance in design made by his naval competitors. He may have become aware of the four in the burst of naval activity in the last years of his life (368 BC), if the four had been invented then. Otherwise, and most probably, the invention was made after the middle of the century.

Use

Aristotle, in the *Constitution of Athens*,[41] speaks of the Athenian Council as responsible for building new threes and fours. That work has accordingly been dated after the archonship of Cephisodoros which is mentioned in it[42] and before 325 BC when fives (not mentioned by Aristotle in the *Constitution*) appear in the inventories for the first time. Fours make their first historical appearance in 332 BC at Alexander's siege of Tyre, both among the Tyrian ships and in his own fleet,[43] largely supplied by

33. J S Morrison (1990) p39.

34. *GROW* Ch 6. 2.

35. *GROW* Ch 3.1.

36. Plutarch *Cato Minor* 39.2.

37. *GROW* Ch 4. Appendix B.

38. Diodorus 20.112.4.

39. *GROW* Ch 4.1.

40. See note 31.

41. Aristotle *Constitution of Athens* 46.3.

42. Aristotle *Constitution of Athens* 54.7.

43. Curtius 4.3.14.

his Phoenician allies. The strong connexion between Carthage and Phoenicia would have made the four known there very soon after its invention.

Two years later (330/329 BC) 18 fours appear for the first time in the Athenian naval inventories, but as there are no lists for the previous three years that may not be the date when fours first formed part of the Athenian fleet. The number of fours in the Athenian navy had by 325/324 BC increased to 50, and when Alexander reached Thapsacus in 324 a fleet of threes, fours and fives which he had ordered, some brought overland from Phoenicia, for the projected circumnavigation of Arabia and Africa, was waiting for him. The growing popularity of fours is shown immediately after Alexander's death when the Athenian Assembly, in a burst of nostalgic patriotism, voted to form a new Hellenic League under Athenian leadership with a fleet which was to include 200 fours. But the dream faded on the defeat of Amorgos.

Naval supremacy in the Aegean was achieved by Antigonus in 315/314 BC with the fleet of 240 warships in which, of the 113 heavier types, 90 were fours. But Demetrius, in 306 BC given command of the fleet in the invasion of Cyprus as a preliminary to the invasion of Egypt, did not share the preferences of Athens or of his father for fours. His fleet contained 53 of the heavier troop-carrying warships which with additions in the final battle consisted of 7 (Phoenician) sevens, 10 sixes, probably 45 fives and only 30 (Athenian) fours, whereas the fleet of his rival Ptolemy was composed of 'nothing larger than a five or smaller than a four'. Since in the description of the battle much emphasis is placed on the disadvantage at which Ptolemy was placed with ships lower in the water than Demetrius's, it is likely that one of his two types of ships was lower than the other and that that was the more numerous.

Oar system

The name *tetreres* ('four'), like the name *trieres* ('three'), indicated the number of oarsmen in each half room or alternatively the number of oar files on each side of the ship. Since four files of oarsmen rowing oars at four different levels is a physical impossibility, a four must have had oars double-manned.

There are two passages, a description of an incident towards the end of the second Punic war (203 BC) and an account of an incident in

the battle of Mylae (36 BC) in the Civil Wars, which show, the latter plainly, that in the four there were two levels of oars. In the first Livy[44] relates that the deck soldiers of two Carthaginian fours were unable to board a higher Roman five. Such a difference in height suggests that the four had two levels of oars to the five's three.

A more precise clue is provided by the second passage.[45] 'Agrippa led the heavy ships at the centre.' Though smaller and lighter, Papias's ships nevertheless, like Agrippa's, had towers at bow and stern. The decks of Papias's ships were lower than the decks of Agrippa's since the latter 'threw missiles from a height to ships of lower level'. When battle was joined, Agrippa, in his flagship, probably a five, attacked Papias's ship and 'smashed into it at the epotis'. 'The ship threw off the men in the towers and began to take in a great deal of water. Of the oarsmen the thalamioi were all trapped, but the others [*hoi heteroi*] broke through the deck and swam away.' The Greek words mean 'the others of *two* categories'; and thus leave no doubt that the ship had two levels of oars only, the *thalamioi*, those in the hold, and an upper level of those who sit on the thwarts, the *zygioi*. There is a clue to the number of oars in an Athenian four. An inscription of 325/324 BC[46] gives a valuation of a four's set of oars (*tarros*, a word which excludes spares) at 665 dr. The number works out as 70, 35 a side.[47]

Design

In one respect the four is unique. There is a rough graffito sketch of a long ship labelled *navis tetreris longa* deriving from the period be-

tween the first century BC and the first century AD. It shows no clues to the oar system, only a long low hull and above the top wale what appears to be a ventilation course surmounted by the deck.[48]

At the battle of Mylae (36 BC),[49] the ships of Octavian's admiral Agrippa, probably fives and above, are described as heavier and standing higher in the water than Sextus Pompeius's under Papias. These latter are said to be shorter (or smaller *brachutera*), lighter and standing lower in the water.

Capability

At the same time the four's beam, broader than that of ships with oars single-manned, would entitle her to the status of a larger ship (*maioris formae*). As the flagship of a Roman fleet commander in 73–71,[50] she seemed like a floating city (*urbis instar*) to the pirates, but under sail she had 'an incredible turn of speed'. This is probably the quality which recommended her to Roman fleets as a reconnaissance vessel.

At the battle of Mylae Papias's fours had the advantage of light draught which enabled them to take refuge in shallow waters where the deeper draught of Agrippa's fives and sixes made pursuit dangerous.

44. Livy 20.25. 2–8.
45. Appian *Civil Wars* 5.106.
46. IG² 1629.
47. *GROW* Ch 6.
48. See *GROW*, General Index under 'Ventilation Courses'.
49. Appian 5 107.
50. Cicero *Verrines* 2.5.33: *urbis instar*.

A tomb relief from about 100 AD showing a Roman two-level oared warship that conforms to the known characteristics of a liburnian.

Liburnian

Invention

Appian says in the introduction to his history of the Illyrian war[51] that the Liburni were a maritime people, an Illyrian tribe who 'practised piracy in the Adriatic sea and islands with fast light ships . . .'. The Liburni then certainly invented this type of *lembos*.[52]

Use

Polybius[53] describes the Roman fleet moving along the coast of Sicily towards Lilybaeum in the first Punic war (249 BC) preceded by *lemboi* 'which are accustomed to move ahead of fleets': and Appian[54] confirms this as the duty of liburnians. Reconnaissance was effected, he says, on land by cavalry and at sea by liburnians. In the same campaign liburnians are described by Appian as used for fleet communication; and Horace[55] expects Maecenas in the coming battle at Actium as an officer of Octavian's staff to move in a liburnian among the towers of the [bigger] ships. When Cleopatra took her ships

A detail from Trajan's column showing ships of his fleet. The centre vessel is his flagship, an aphract trireme, but the foreground vessel is a liburnian.

out of the battle at Actium, followed by Antony, Octavian sent a detachment of liburnians after them under Eurykles. He succeeded in putting out of action one of the two flagships which turned to face him. Under the empire, liburnians are recorded as a part of the Misenum and Ravenna fleets, and as playing a large role in the provincial squadrons, particularly in Egypt.[56] The Moesian squadron on the Danube in Trajan's expedition is shown as composed of liburnians with a three as flagship.

Oar system

When Livy[57] speaks of *lembi biremes* he is concerned with liburnians; and Lucan describes liburnians in the Roman fleet at Massalia[58] as 'content to have grown to two levels'. This type is a simple development of the oared warship with one level of oars, made originally by pirates in the interest of greater oar power.

Since Polybius[59] speaks of thirty *hemiolioi* (*lemboi*) in a fleet of Philip V, it is seen that some *lemboi* (that is to say, Illyrian light ships like Alexander's triacontors on the Indus) had taken the natural step of imitating the one-and-a-half oar system practised in the eastern Mediterranean (see *hemiolia* below).

Design

The passage of Appian quoted under 'Invention' continues: . . . so that even now [early second century BC] the Romans call their light and pointed [*oksea*] ships with two oar-levels [*dikrota*] 'liburnians' [*liburnidas*]. For welcome confirmation that 'pointed' is the right rendering of *oksea* (as against 'swift': Loeb) there is a pertinent passage in Aristotle's *On the movement of animals*:

For birds of prey speed of flight is essential for survival. Accordingly their bodies are built for appropriate movement. They have small heads and slim necks but a breast strong and sharply

51. Appian *Roman History* 10.1.3.

52. *GROW* Ch 6.

53. Polybius 1.53.9.

54. Appian 5.103.

55. Horace *Epodes* 1.1.

56. *GROW* Ch 4, Appendix B.

57. Livy 24.40.2.

58. Lucan 3.534.

59. Polybius 5.101.2.

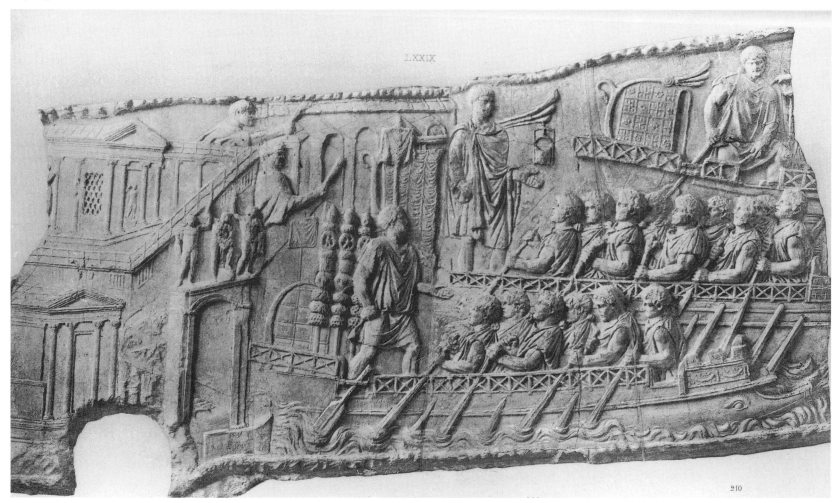

pointed [*oksu*] or streamlined [*to eutonon*] as in the case of the prow of a ship of the lembos kind.[60]

These passages say more about the hull-design of the liburnian than is said anywhere about the hull design of any other ancient oared warship. Her pointed, streamlined, prow was clearly built for speed. It is interesting that ancient authors recognised the streamlining of the bodies of birds and liburnians as analogous and designed for the same end. The ram which the word 'pointed' suggests, and which Propertius's epithet *rostrata*[61] confirms as a regular characteristic of the liburnian, adds an armament to be used as occasion might demand for defence or offence.

In the Suda[62] *liburnika (ploia)* are described as decked, cataphract, ships; and that not very strong evidence is confirmed by Plutarch,[63] who distinguishes them from aphracts. The commander of the detachment of liburnians sent in pursuit of Antony and Cleopatra is described by Plutarch as standing on the deck of his ship, which is confirmation provided that the flagship was not a three (as in the case of Trajan's liburnian squadron). Yet if liburnians took staff officers among the lofty propugnacula of [the bigger] ships, a deck and boxing-in would have been an ordinary precaution.

Capability

In the ship race described in the fifth book of Virgil's *Aeneid*[64] four ships had been chosen to compete: *Pristis* (under Mnesthcus) called fast, *Chimaera* (under Gyas) described as a three, *Centaurus* (under Sergestus) described as big and *Scylla* (under Cloanthus) said to be 'better at the oar [than *Chimaera*] but held back by heavy timber'. *Chimaera* and *Centaurus* suffer misadventures, *Pristis* comes second by hard rowing and *Scylla* wins.

Pristis is the name (meaning 'shark') of *lemboi* equipped with a ram and therefore probably rowed at two levels. *Pristis* the competitor is described by Virgil as fast and her ram is mentioned. It is reasonable to recognise her as a liburnian. *Chimaera* is to be recognised as a [fast] three, *Scylla* as a three built with heavy timber,[65] while the big *Centaurus* may be recognised as a five, an example of the bigger and heavier ships.

The race went according to the book. The odds-on favourite, *Chimaera*, led the field from the start, closely followed by the slow three, *Scylla*. Then come neck and neck *Centaurus*, the powerful but slowly accelerating five, and *Pristis*, rather underpowered; but *Chimaera*'s captain disagrees with his helmsman and

throws him overboard, causing some delay, and *Centaurus* runs on to the rocks. So the slow but strong three, *Scylla*, wins in spite of the magnificent efforts of the liburnian with a much lighter hull but far fewer oarsmen.

The race throws a remarkable light on the individual performances which in the first century BC would be expected by an intelligent Roman observer from the four commonest types of Roman warship, liburnian, fast and slow threes, and five, and on how they would perform in relation to each other.

The liburnian was not a match for the fast three, nearly as fast with a great effort as a slower three, and probably about as fast as a five. Ships from the six upwards were clearly not regarded at Rome as racing material. Rhodians might have entered the *trihemiolia*.

The new warship types of the eastern Mediterranean

Hemiolia [naus], hemiolios [lembos]

Invention

The first references to the light vessel which was usually called *hemiolia* is in Theophrastus[66] in the first quarter of the fourth century, where the nervous passenger at sea is described as seeing a pirate *hemiolia* in every headland. There is also reference to a Carian *hemiolia* in a fragment of a fourth-century Attic orator preserved in the *Etymologicum Magnum*,[67] and in Longus's *Daphnis and Chloe*[68] pirates from Tyre employ a Carian *hemiolia*. Since Carians were notorious pirates the connection with piracy in the eastern Mediterranean is the same. The *hemiolia* then naturally comes in Appian's progressive list[69] of pirate vessels illustrating the growth of their sea power with Mithridates' encouragement: *muoparones* (ships with a single level of oars), *hemioliai* (ships with one and a half files of oars a side), *dikrotoi* (craft with two files of oars) and threes (ships with three files).

The evidence seems strong that the type, like the liburnian, was invented by pirates, probably in the eastern Mediterranean, probably also in Caria. The alternative *hemiolioi lemboi*, used once[70] of thirty ships (distinguishing them from cataphracts and aphracts) in Philip V's fleet against Scerdelaidas in 217 BC, sug-

The famous Nike (Victory) of Samothrace is supported by the prow of a large warship with en echelon oarports at two levels in the prominent oarbox. It probably represents a trihemiolia *, whose midships half-tier would not be present at the bow.*

gests that the eastern type was introduced also to the Adriatic, probably under Macedonian influence.

Use

The *hemiolia* as a respectable naval vessel is attested in 346/345 BC (Diodorus[71]: Phalaikos of Phocis), in 324 BC (Arrian[72]: Alexander on the Hydaspes) and 315 BC (Diodorus[73]: Agathocles). But when Arrian[74] mentions

60. Aristotle 10.701a 31.

61. Propertius 4.11.44.

62. The Suda Lexicon: under *liburnika (ploia)*.

63. Plutarch *Cato Minor* 54.3.

64. Virgil *Aeneid* 5. 114–285.

65. *AT* pp180–181.

66. Theophrastus *Characters* 25.5.

67. *Etymologicum Magnum* 450.38.

68. Longus *Daphnis and Chloe* 1.28.

69. Appian *Roman History* 12.92.

70. Polybius 5.101.2.

71. Diodorus 16.61.4.

72. Arrian 6.1.

73. Diodorus 16.61.4.

74. Arrian *Anabasis* 3.2.3.

Aristonikos of Methymna sailing into the harbour of Chios in 332/331 BC he calls his squadron 'five pirate *hemioliai*'. Later Polyaenus[75] speaks of Demetrius using them in 301 BC; and at the battle of Chios in 201 BC[76] Philip employs a force of four fives, three *hemioliai* and other lighter ships to cut off Attalos's flagship and drive it ashore. In the casualty list of the battle there are three *hemioliai* lost by Philip and one by Attalos. The most surprising mention of them is when, at the outbreak of the third Punic War in 149 BC, a Roman invasion fleet destined for Africa is said to contain 100 *hemioliai* listed together with the capital ships. Since the only function they can have had is as troop transports it seems that *hemioliai* is a general term which includes *trihemioliai*.

---

75. Polyaenus 4.7.4.

76. Polybius 16.6.4.

77. In the first of these oar systems, developed in Italy in the late Middle Ages, groups of 3–5 men sitting on benches placed on the galley's deck in herring-bone pattern each pulled his own oar. In the second each group pulled a single great oar.

Oar system

Following the established type-naming principle, a *hemiolia* has one and a half files of oarsmen on each side of the ship as the trireme has three. The half-file, placed on each side of the gangway amidships, makes economical use of the broader beam amidships, adding power without a corresponding increase in weight of hull.

Design

There is no evidence for the design of the regular naval *hemioliai* since the number of oarsmen in each ship is not known. However, there is a clue to the size of Alexander's *hemioliai* on the Indus in the fact that Ptolemy, whom Arrian quotes as one of his sources, seems to have included them in the overall category of triacontors, that is to say, oared warships with fifteen oarsmen a side. The oar system of these particular *hemioliai* could then have consisted of two full files of ten oarsmen and two half-files of five oarsmen seated amidships. There would then be on both sides three single-manned oars forward and two single-manned oars aft, while amidships there would be five pairs of oarsmen on each side rowing either *alla sensile* or *a scaloccio*,[77] in both cases at one level.

Capability

Alexander in 336 BC built locally on the Hydaspes many triacontors and *hemioliai* as well as transports and supply ships. When the fleet began its voyage down river, Arrian quotes Ptolemy as saying that it consisted of 80 triacontors, together with horse transports, *kerkouroi*, and river boats. Ptolemy seems to have included the *hemioliai* among the 80 triacontors and Aristoboulos, Arrian's main source, to have differentiated the *hemioliai*. At the meeting of the Hydaspes and Acerines the

Detail of the first-century BC mosaic in the Palazzo Barberini at Palestrina. Since the scene is the Nile the ship is thought to be an Egyptian trihemiolia , *the half-tier being invisible amidships beneath the two complete levels of oars.*

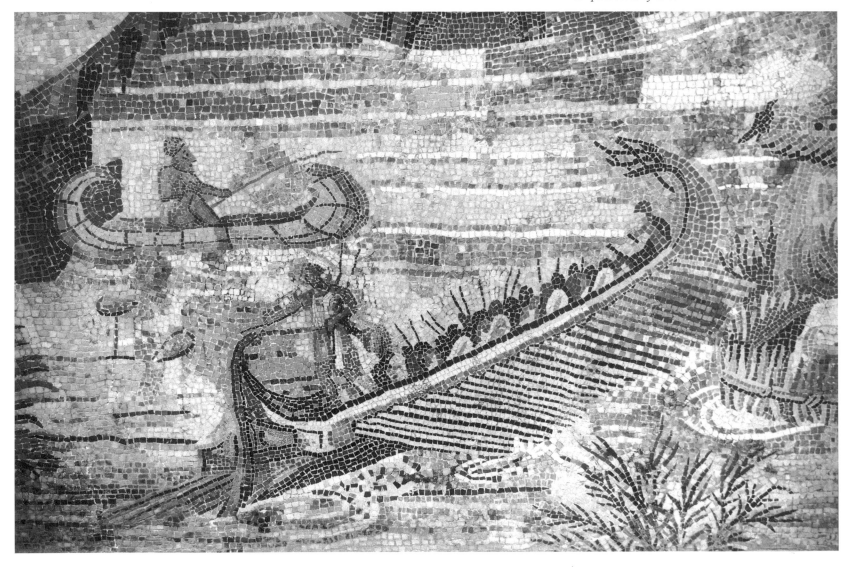

supply boats came through the rapids safely; but the oared warships, that is the triacontors, *hemioliai* and *kerkouroi*, were in difficulties since they were lower in the water. 'All those that were *dikrotoi* having their lower oars not far above the waterline' and two triacontors were in fact lost. Later[78] Alexander took the fastest of the ships (the fastest of the *hemioliai*, all the triacontors and some *kerkouroi*) and continued the voyage.

If the half of the *hemiolia* oar system which occupied the middle half of the ship was rowed *a scaloccio*, the *hemioliai* were certainly not *dikrotoi*, nor if that half was rowed *alla sensile* were they such in the sense of the word *dikrotoi* as it applies to liburnians and fours. The conclusion to be drawn is that some of the triacontors, as might be expected, were in that sense *dikrotoi*, had their lower oarports close to the waterline so that two were flooded and lost. It was accordingly one of the virtues of the *hemiolia* to achieve a more favourable power/weight ratio than the ships with a single oar-level, without incurring the danger of flooding incurred by thalamian oarports.

It should be noted that in the list of the fastest ships the fastest of the *hemioliai* come first, then all the triacontors, followed by some of the remaining *kerkouroi*.

Trieremiolia, Trihemiolia

Invention

In 304 BC, the year following the unsuccessful invasion of Egypt, Demetrius attacked Rhodes to punish her for her lack of support in the invasion of Cyprus. The account of the siege is interesting in introducing the *trihemiolia*. During the siege Rhodes sent out commerce raiders,[79] one squadron under Menedemos consisting of three *trihemioliai*. It went eastwards to Patara in Lycia and destroyed or captured some ships. One of those captured was a four en route from Cilicia to Rhodes containing 'purple robes fit for a king to wear' sent to Demetrius by his wife Phila.

At the approach to the acropolis of Lindos in Rhodes a number of blocks of stone have been found which form part of a large monument in the form of a ship's prow once surmounted by a statue (265–260 BC). It shows the terminal bow section of an oarbox with a boxed-in superstructure consisting of a blank vertical panel between the edge of the foredeck. The list of the fleet of Ptolemy II Philadelphus (283–246 BC) preserved in Athenaios[80] gives the number of 111 big oared warships from thirties to fives 'while the ships from fours to

The remains of a monument representing the prow of an oared warship at Lindos in Rhodes (c265–260 BC). The vessel is probably a trihemiolia, *of which the Rhodians may have been the inventors; they certainly used a number, including some in the role of commerce raider.*

trieremioliai were double these' that is to say 222. This suggests that in Egypt in the first half of the third century BC the *trihemiolia* ranked with the four and the three as a fast, light, naval unit in contrast to the bigger and heavier ships of the line. The *trihemiolia* also appears as an Egyptian naval unit in an inscription of 259 BC.[81] There is no direct evidence of the city or country responsible for the invention of the *trihemiolia*. Rhodes is the most likely, but Egypt is a possible candidate.

Use

There are a considerable number of Rhodian inscriptions of the third, second and first centuries BC mentioning *trihemioliai*,[82] and at the end of the third century BC the *trihemiolia* is recorded in an inscription[83] as a unit in the Athenian navy. *Trihemioliai* appear in papyri[84] and in the list of Ptolemy Philadelphos's fleet in Athenaios.[85] In the account of the battle of Chios (201 BC) nine *trihemioliai* are listed by Polybius as ships of Philip's opponents[86] separately from 65 cataphract vessels on the one hand and 3 threes on the other. In the course of the battle a *trihemiolia* of Attalos's fleet was rammed (accidentally) by Philip's ten. In the list of casualties[87] Polybius gives three *trihemioliai* of Philip's fleet lost against Attalos and one of Attalos's fleet lost against Philip. At this point in history they appear to be regular first-line warships.

Oar system

The name *trieremiolia*, as it appears once, or *trihemiolia* in the usual form, implies two characteristics: three files of oarsmen on each side of the ship and at the same time the *hemiolia*

arrangement. The combination of these two characteristics produces a simple development of the *hemiolia*, a ship with two and a half instead of one and a half files of oarsmen on each side.[88]

Design

For the *trihemiolia*, a unit of Attalos's fleet, to be rammed beneath the thranite thole, there are two implications. The first is that the *trihemiolia* floated fairly low in the water and the second that she had a thranite oarport. Attalos's flagship, being a ten, would have had a high ram (a characteristic described by the Greek word *anasteiros*).

On the lateral face of the oarbox of the monument described earlier, where the oarports might be expected, there is an inscription of which a good deal remains. It can be seen to have contained the names of 288 men who served in *trihemioliai* together with the commander of the two ships and two trierarchs. In view of this inscription the ship represented is almost certainly a *trihemiolia*, and it is possible that the 288 men formed the crews of the two ships of that type (144 each) whose trierarchs are named. If that is so, the inference can be drawn that the two full files consisted of 24 men each and the half file of 12, giving 60 oarsmen a side and 120 all told. A *hyperesia* of 24 men added (compared with 30 of the three and 45 of the four) brings the total up to the 144 of the inscription.

The external aspect of the reconstructed *trihemiolia* matches that of the Samothrace prow which also shows the pairs of upper oarports which the oar system requires, en echelon on the lateral face of the oarbox. The oarports of the lowest, half, file would not appear in a prow. Another ship picture, the Palazzo Spada relief, shows the stern of an oared warship with pairs of oars emerging en echelon from on the lateral face of an oarbox. The lowest, half, file again would not be visible. The relief shows as well, above the oarbox and below the deck, the row of latticework louvres, which are necessary

78. Arrian *Anabasis* 6.18.3.

79. Diodorus 20.93.3

80. Athenaeus 5.203 d.

81. *SSAW* p324.

82. Blinkenberg (1938) 14–15.

83. *Hesperia* 11 (1942) No.57 p293.

84. Wilcken *UPZ* II 251 2–4.

85. Athenaeus 5. 203 c.

86. Polybius 16.2.10.

87. Polybius 16.7.1.

88. *GROW* Ch 6. 2.

A relief carving from Lindos, Rhodes (190–180 BC) of the stern of a warship, again probably a trihemiolia. *Because of earthquake damage the surface of this relief has deteriorated since this photograph was taken before 1914.*

but were not shown on the solid masonry of the Lindos or Samothrace prows.

The Egyptian warship in the Palazzo Berberini mosaic may also be recognised as a *trihemiolia*, the lowest, half, file of oars being again necessarily invisible, obscured here by the upper pair which are complete (2 × 26). With two files of 26 oars and one of 13 on each side, the oar crew of this ship would have numbered 130.

Capability

The use of a detachment of three *trihemioliai* as commerce raiders by the Rhodians, and their capture of a Macedonian four, during the siege of the city by Demetrius in 304 BC, indicate that the ship was a fast and formidable warship. If the identification of the Lindos prow and stern, and the Samothrace prow, as representing *trihemioliai* is correct, the Rhodians were proud of her and found her a useful as well as economical warship with the performance of a three but with a lighter build and smaller crew.

The Seven

Invention

Alexander's ambitious naval plans after his return from India are said by Arrian[89] to have included the circumnavigation of Arabia and then Africa, culminating in the return through the pillars of Hercules and the reduction of Carthage. Curtius[90] gives the practical aspect: 'For this purpose Alexander ordered the rulers of Mesopotamia to cut timber in the mountains of Lebanon and bring it down to the Syrian city of Thapsacus on the Euphrates. Their orders were then to lay down the keels of 700 ships, all sevens', to be taken down to the fleet station at Babylon. Pliny[91] attributes the invention of the seven (and also the ten) to Alexander. There seems no reason to doubt that this was Alexander's plan corroborated by a number of reconnaissance voyages ordered by him.

Use

Alexander did not live to see his naval plans effected. Antigonus, building his fleet less than ten years later, went from fours and fives straight to 3 nines and 10 tens. His son Demetrius included 7 Phoenician sevens in the

Cyprus invasion fleet, omitting the bigger ships either because they were thought unnecessary or because Antigonus wished them to be kept in Piraeus. Later Ptolemy Philadelphus built 36 sevens. In 280 BC the flagship of Demetrius's protégé Pyrrhus when he crossed to Tarentum was probably a seven, since 20 years later at the first battle of Mylae the Carthaginian flagship was a seven which had belonged to Pyrrhus. At the battle of Chios Philip had at least one seven. Antiochos later had 3 sevens built for him in Syria. No ships above the rating of six appear in the Roman imperial fleets.

Oar system, design and capability

The seven would have been a practical modification of the six by the addition of a seventh, standing, oarsman to the lowest pair of oarsmen pulling a single oar.

The design would have followed that of the six with some additional beam.

The seven seems to have been a useful ship. At the crossing to Tarentum Pyrrhus's fleet ran into strong northerly winds. His flagship proved more seaworthy than the smaller ships.

89. Arrian *Anabasis* 7.1.2.

90. Curtius 10.1.19.

91. Pliny *Natural History* 7.206.

92. See *GROW* Ch 6 2.2.2.6.

The Eight

Invention and Use

Two eights appear in Philip V's fleet at the battle of Chios. Much later Antony is said by Plutarch to have had many eights in the fleet he assembled at Ephesus. There is no evidence as to their invention.

Oar system, design and capability

There is no evidence for the eight's oar system or performance. The fact that on two occasions in the battle of Chios eights were rammed prow to prow and holed below the waterline suggests that they were *anasteiroi*, with high rams which would make their hulls in the prow vulnerable to ramming below the waterline by ships with low rams. High rams are characteristic of the bigger ships which used ramming as a preliminary to boarding by their larger complement of deck soldiers.

One eight of unusual dimensions named *Leontophoros* was invented at Heraclea on the Black Sea and belonged to one of Alexander's Successors, Lysimachos. A fragment of Memnon's history of Herakleia describes the ship, which was famous for its size and beauty. There were 100 oarsmen in each fore and aft file, so 800 a side and 1600 all told. Her performance was remarkably good.[92]

The Praeneste relief from Palestrina, dated to the second half of the first century AD, depicts a large warship that is probably Egyptian given the crocodile form of the proembolion or secondary ram. The ship is two-level but the size of the oars suggest multiple manning.

The Nine

There were three nines in Antigonus's Grand Fleet in 315. Agathocles must have built one at Syracuse, since Pyrrhus took over a 'royal nine' there in 278 BC. Ptolemy Philadelphus's fleet contained 30 nines. Philip V had at least one at Chios. Florus says that Antony's fleet at Actium ranged from sixes to nines (Dio from fives to tens). Both these imply nines, but Plutarch speaks of Antony earlier at Ephesus as having only eights and tens. No details of nines are known. The oar system is likely to have been an extension of the oar system of the four with two gangs of four and five oarsmen each pulling single oars at two levels.

The ship depicted in the Praeneste relief may be a nine. She is probably Egyptian (be-cause of the crocodile forming her proem-bolion or secondary ram), with massive oars at two levels en echelon, one set worked through the oarbox and the other through an oarport beneath it, 25 a side, 50 oars and 150 oarsmen if triple-manned. Above the oarbox is a course of what Casson[93] recognised as louvres and on the upper surface of it a *parodos* (side gangway) on which two men are standing. The main deck has a tower forward and a bulwark in-board of which stand armed men. Her prow is, unusually, without a foredeck.

The massive size of the oars is explained if they are triple manned, but the number is sus-pect and also the proportion of the ship's di-mensions, twice as long as the height of the deck above water. It seems that the sculptor, exaggerating in the usual fashion the size of the human figures and hence the oars, has been unable to give enough room for the whole oar system. The number of oars should not there-fore be taken as realistic.

The Ten

Pliny's attribution of the invention of the ten to Alexander is not corroborated. It is not im-possible, since 10 tens formed an important part of Antigonus's fleet eight years later, and it is an innovation of the same pattern as his in-vention of the seven. In the seven a third oars-man is added at one level to a six, in the ten a fourth at one level to a nine.

The 10 tens in Antigonus's fleet like the nines were not taken by Demetrius to Cyprus; and the list of ships in Ptolemy Philadelphus's fleet does not contain them. But Philip's flag-ship at Chios was a ten and Antony is said by Plutarch to have had many of them at Ephesus. At Actium Dio gives Antony tens which in view of Plutarch's statement is likely to be right, although Florus gives him nines as the largest ships.

As in the case of the nines there is no evi-dence for their oar system or for their perfor-mance, but the comments of the historical sources on the clumsiness and immobility of Antony's ships at Actium applies *a fortiori* to the nines and tens. Orosius's statement that [the decks of] Antony's ships at Actium stood 10 Roman feet (2.957m) above water applies to both.

The Eleven to the Forty

As Tarn observed, no ships of a higher rating than tens are known to have been taken into action. Demetrius's acquisition of Cyprus gave him access to the long timbers needed to build an eleven, and in 301 BC after the death of his father the Athenians allowed him to remove from Piraeus the fleet which included a thir-teen. In this or a sister ship Demetrius later entertained Seleucus on a diplomatic mission.

Plutarch also speaks of Demetrius building a great fleet of 500 ships which included four-teens, fifteens and sixteens, and showing them off to his enemy Lysimachus. These types ap-parently were practical and efficient, although no record survives of their use in battle. Ptolemy Philadelphus's fleet included 14 elevens, 2 twelves, 4 thirteens, 1 twenty and 2 thirties. The forty of his successor Ptolemy Philopator (221–204) is described in detail by a contemporary historian, Callixeinus.[94] Plu-tarch observed that it moved laboriously. The warships bigger than eights, with the possible exception of the forty, are likely to have been rowed by gangs of men at oars of two levels.[95]

Philip V had a sixteen which he was allowed to retain by the terms of his peace treaty with Rome. It was described by Livy as 'of almost unmanageable size'; and was later brought to Rome after the defeat of Philip's son Perseus to grace the triumph of the victorious consul. He was rowed up the Tiber in her, 'the populace keeping up with the splashing oars as they [the oars] slowly took the ship along'. The scene makes a fitting finale to the drama, at times the melodrama, of the great oared ships of the Hellenistic centuries.

John Morrison

---

93. *SSAW* Ch 7 n17.

94. See *GROW* Ch 6 2.2.2.10.

95. See *GROW* Ch 7.

References and abbreviations used in the footnotes

R C Anderson (1962), *Oared Fighting Ships* (London).

Lucien Basch (1987), *Le musée imaginaire de la marine antique* (Athens).

D J Blackman (1968), 'The Shipsheds', Ch 8 of Morrison and Williams, *Greek Oared Ships*, pp181–192.

C Blinkenberg (1938), 'Lindiaka 7: Triemiolia', *Det Kgl. Danske Videnskabernes Selskab Archaeologisk-Kunsthistoriske Meddelelser* II, 3 (Copenhagen).

Lionel Casson (1959), *The Ancient Mariners* (Princeton; reprinted 1981).

—— (1971), *Ships and Seamanship in the Ancient World* (Princeton; reprinted 1986) = *SSAW*.

Lionel Casson and J Richard Steffy (1991), *The Athlit Ram*, Texas A and M University Press (College Station).

I X Dragatzes (1886), 'Report on Excavations at Piraeus', *Praktika of 1885*, pp63–68.

J S Morrison, 'Tetrerseis in the fleets of Dionysius I of Syracuse', *Classica et Mediaevalia* 41 (1990), pp33–41.

—— (1991), 'Ancient Greek Measures of Length in Nautical Contexts', *Antiquity* 65, No 247, pp298–305.

J S Morrison and R T Williams (1968), *Greek Oared Ships* Cambridge; reprinted Oxford 1994) = *GOS*.

J S Morrison and J F Coates (1986), *The Athenian Trireme* (Cambridge) = *AT*.

—— (1994), *Greek and Roman Oared Ships: 399–31 BC* (Oxford) = *GROW*.

W W Tarn (1913, *Antigonus Gonatas* (Oxford) = *AG*.

Cecil Torr (1894), *Ancient Ships* (Cambridge; reprinted Chicago 1984).

Fleets of the Early Roman Empire, 31 BC–AD 324

THE BATTLE of Actium in 31 BC and the final defeat and suicide of Mark Antony the following year left Octavian to dominate the Roman political stage alone. No one could say for certain whether or not some new challenger for power would emerge to plunge the empire back into armed turmoil, or exactly what form of government would finally be imposed on a war-weary world. In the event, it took Octavian a decade and much political manoeuvring to establish his own control beyond challenge. His rule was based in part on senatorial and popular willingness to defer to his authority (*auctoritas*) as victor in the civil wars and restorer and best guarantor of peace and stability, and this was reflected in the new name, Augustus, granted him by the senate in 27 BC. His status and political support also ensured that he was given command of the major portion of the empire's armed forces, which became the real basis of his power. Although his legal powers were set within a Republican framework and he was referred to only as the 'first citizen' (*princeps*), few people can have doubted that they were now subject to a monarchy.

If Augustus was to maintain his position and pass it on to a successor when he died, it was essential for him to ensure the continuing loyalty of the armed forces. This meant the creation of a standing, professional army which he himself controlled and which ultimately owed its pay and conditions to him. The huge partisan armies of the civil wars were dismantled. The sixty or more legions left under his control after the defeat of Antony were reduced eventually to twenty-eight permanent units, some from Antony's army, some from his own, and some newly raised. They were stationed in the frontier provinces and by the end of Augustus' reign all but one were under the command of his own deputies. In addition, Augustus kept a bodyguard of nine Praetorian cohorts, three of which were billeted around Rome and the rest in various cities around Italy.

Large numbers of men were discharged from the legions in 30 BC and replaced by volunteer recruits as well as conscripts, who were kept on for the maximum term of sixteen years and received grants of land in Italy on their retirement. Their replacements in 13 BC were mostly recruits, signed up for the full term from the beginning, who received cash rather than land at the end of their service. In AD 5 the standard term was extended to twenty years with a bonus of 12,000 sesterces given on discharge, and in the following year, in order to pay for this, Augustus set up a military treasury (*aerarium militare*) with a grant from his own purse and permanently funded by new inheritance and sales taxes. A fully professionalised army had come into being.

The Italian fleets

It is in the context of these broader developments that Augustus' arrangements for the Roman fleets must be understood. The struggle against Sextus Pompeius and the climactic sea battle at Actium had given the navy a greater political importance than at any time in Roman history, with the possible exception of the first Punic war, and it was impossible for Augustus to overlook it. The victory over Antony had left him with 700 ships under his control, which, as with the legions, were far more than he needed or than it was politically safe to leave in commission. After Actium, one part of Antony's fleet was burned and the rest of the ships were sent off with their crews to Forum Iulii (Fréjus) on the southern coast of Gaul,[1] where a permanent squadron was maintained until the reign of Nero. His main fleets, however, were the *classis Ravennatium*, established on the Adriatic at Ravenna, which was linked to the river Po by a new canal, and the *classis Misenatium*, based at the northern end of the Bay of Naples at Misenum,[2] probably relatively early in his reign. The choice of these locations perhaps had more to do with the availability of large, safe harbours and with good land communications than with what we might regard as purely 'strategic' considerations. The idea of 'patrolling' in the western Mediterranean and Adriatic from these ports, which is often encountered in the modern scholarship, is anachronistic and impracticable for oared warships, although the Misenum fleet was certainly well-placed to intercept any seaborne attack on Rome from Africa or the East, and inscriptions suggest that a number of outposts were maintained, for instance at Ostia, the port of Rome.

In fact, the day of major fleet actions in the Mediterranean was over, at least until the early fourth century. The entire Mediterranean

---

1. Tacitus, *Annals*, IV. 5.

2. Suetonius, *Life of Augustus*, 49.

The Romans were not a natural sea power in the way the Greek states had been and this was reflected in their attitude to naval warfare, which sought to capitalise on the discipline and power of their soldiery at sea. 'Marines' and boarding tactics became important, as depicted in the crowded decks of these ships in a wall painting from the first-century AD temple of Isis at Pompeii.

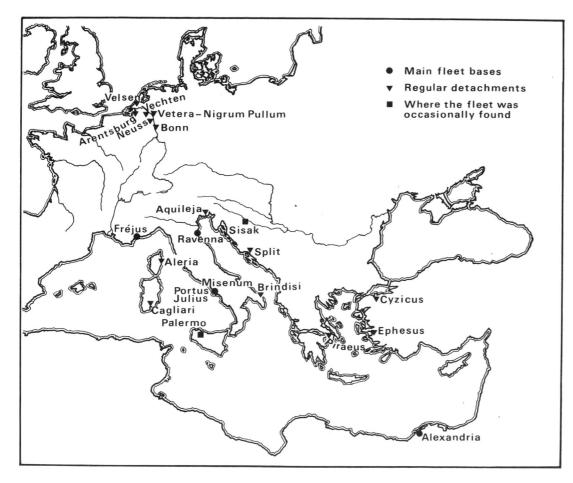

Naval bases and fleet stations at the time of Augustus. (Drawn by Denys Baker after Reddé)

19.[4] Nero even attempted to murder his mother Agrippina in AD 59 by persuading her to travel home from a dinner party on a special collapsing galley of the Misenum fleet.[5] Rather more properly, in AD 68 Nero's successor Galba gave the new governor of Galatia and Pamphylia two triremes from the Misenum fleet to transport him to the East.[6] Nero had also used the fleet to carry out specific missions in a hurry, such as the investigation of a report of the discovery of Dido's treasure in Africa in AD 65 or the transport to Rome of the informer Antistius Sosianus in the following year.[7]

The underemployment of the Italian fleets as a naval force is reflected in the presence of permanent detachments of men of the two fleets in their own camps in Rome, where they helped to stage mock naval battles from time to time in specially constructed arenas,[8] and worked the canvas awnings which shaded the spectators at the Colosseum.[9]

It was also possible for Nero to reorganise men of the Misenum fleet into a new land-based legion, *I Adiutrix*, when he needed to do so in AD 68.[10] Vitellius raised a supplementary, if short-lived, legion from Misenum in the following year,[11] and Vespasian's generals created more permanently the *II Adiutrix* from the Ravenna fleet during their advance on Rome.[12] The number of men required for these transfers would, incidentally, be enough to crew 50 and 25 triremes respectively, although it is difficult to gauge what proportion of the two fleets this represents. We do, however, know from inscriptions the names of 88 ships of the Misenum fleet, including 1 six, 1 five, 10 fours, 52 triremes and 15 liburnians, and of 36 of the Ravenna fleet, including 2 fives, 6 fours, 23 triremes and 4 liburnians.

The relative unimportance of the fleets in the scheme of things is also indicated by the status of their personnel and commanders. Inscriptions show that the ordinary seamen were

coastline was already Roman by the time Augustus had consolidated his position, and civil wars were thereafter infrequent and fought for the most part on land. Despite the occasional outbreak, piracy had been reduced to a relatively minor problem by the late first century BC, as much because the earlier pirate bases on the coasts of Illyricum, Cilicia and elsewhere were now included within Rome's land empire as because of the power of Rome's fleets. The latter were maintained in the Mediterranean partly as a political insurance against the reemergence of such threats, but also, it must be said, partly through inertia, and this is reflected both by changes in their composition and by the new and somewhat peripheral duties which they acquired.

The monster polyremes disappeared. Inscriptional evidence records a six, the *Ops*, at Misenum and one or two fives in both the Italian fleets, but otherwise the latter appear to have consisted of a limited number of fours and light liburnians, but mostly of triremes. This suggests that the possibility of major sea battles in the old style was not entirely discounted, but that the fleets were equipped mainly for duties which required speed and agility rather than maximum fighting power. These duties would no doubt have included the suppression of pi-

racy whenever necessary, but tended in general to be more mundane. In particular, the fleets often, though not exclusively, provided official transport for members of the imperial family and other high dignitaries, for instance Agrippa on his way to the East in 14 BC[3] or Germanicus on his way to Egypt in AD 18 and

The harbour of Misenum in the Bay of Naples, a major Roman fleet base for most of the period of the Empire. (Drawn by Denys Baker after Reddé)

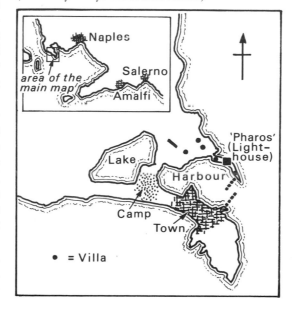

---

3. Josephus, *Jewish Antiquities*, XVI. 21.

4. Tacitus, *Annals*, II. 53–9; III. 1.

5. Tacitus, *Annals*, XIV. 3–5.

6. Tacitus, *Histories*, II. 9.

7. Tacitus, *Annals*, XVI. 2; 14.

8. Tacitus, *Annals*, XII. 56; Suetonius, *Life of Claudius*, 12.6.

9. Historia Augusta, *Life of Commodus*, 15.6.

10. Tacitus, *Histories*, I. 6; Suetonius, *Life of Galba*, 12.2.

11. Tacitus, *Histories*, III. 55.

12. Tacitus, *Histories*, IV. 68; Dio LV, 24.3.

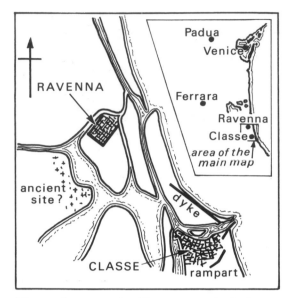

The complex topography of Ravenna reveals why it became a secure naval base during the later centuries of the Empire. (Drawn by Denys Baker after Reddé)

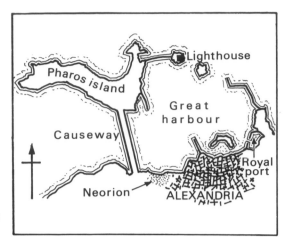

Alexandria, the main fleet base of Ptolemaic Egypt, was an elaborate facility, naturally protected by Pharos Island, which was joined to the mainland by a substantial causeway called the Heptastadion. It was inherited by the Roman Empire, where a fleet was usually based, but it was less important in relative terms than in the Hellenistic era. (Drawn by Denys Baker after Reddé)

and the helmsmen (*gubernatores*). Individual ships of all types were under the command of a *trierarchus*, and squadrons were under a *nauarchus*, the most senior of whom was entitled *nauarchus princeps*. All of these commanders were of a rank equivalent to an auxiliary centurion and may even be referred to in a few of our sources as fleet centurions (*centuriones classiarii*), although some scholars think that the latter were separate commanders of marines. Such men would normally have started out as seamen and would have come up through the ranks. There would therefore have been considerable professionalism throughout the fleet, as there was in the Roman armed forces as a whole.

Fleet commanders, however, were Roman knights pursuing a career in the service of the emperors (although a few imperial freedmen are known to have been appointed to these posts under Claudius and Nero). They bore the title of Prefect (*praefectus classis*), and under the Julio-Claudians they ranked just above the commanders of auxiliary units from whose number they had been promoted. They were assisted by a *subpraefectus* of similar background. Following on from the significant involvement of the Italian fleets in the civil war of AD 68–9, Vespasian gave the latter the honorific title *praetoria* and their commands were subsequently entrusted to the highest grade of equestrian officer, men earning 200,000 sesterces per year and ranking just below the four senior Prefects of the Night Watch, the Corn Supply, Egypt, and the Praetorian Guard. One such was the encyclopaedist and author Pliny the Elder. He was Prefect of the Misenum fleet when Mount Vesuvius erupted in AD 79 and he suffocated when he took his ships across the Bay of Naples to get a closer look and to rescue some of the local inhabitants.[13] Though men like Pliny had usually had considerable experience of military command earlier in their careers, their knowledge of the sea would normally have been minimal. However, Roman senior officers in all branches of the services must have been accustomed to leaning heavily on their more professional subordinates, and in any case very few Prefects of the Italian fleets would actually have seen action whilst in office.

The provincial fleets

The provincial fleets, raised to meet local needs, were smaller than the Italian and appear to have consisted mostly of two-level liburnians with a trireme as flagship. The earliest of these fleets may have been the *classis Alexandrina*, based in the great harbour of Alex-

andria at the mouth of the Nile, whose title *Augusta* indicates that it was a creation of the first emperor. A papyrus fragment found at Oxyrhynchus in Egypt even suggests that it may have been formed after Actium with the ships which escaped with Cleopatra.[14] It was manned entirely by Egyptians, but unlike the Italian fleets which recruited from all classes in this province, it would take only men with Roman or Alexandrian citizenship. Its role was probably no more than that of a fleet-in-being to prevent seizure of the mouth of the Nile from which was shipped a major portion of the corn supply which fed the city of Rome, and for dealing with minor problems along the coasts of Cyrene, Egypt and Judaea. In the Jewish revolt of 115–117 it even operated up the Nile, although peacekeeping there was normally in the hands of a separate river police force, the *potamophylacia*. The fleet also appears to have kept a detachment of ships alongside others of the Syrian fleet far to the west at Cherchel (Caesarea), the capital of Mauretania Caesariensis after the annexation of that province in AD 40. These ships, under their own acting commander (*praepositus*), were charged with the checking of piracy and occasional Moorish raids along the African coast at the western end of the Mediterranean.

The Prefect of the Alexandrine fleet was of relatively junior rank, earning 60,000 sesterces per year. So little was there for him to do that he acquired as one of his main functions the

normally neither Italians nor Roman citizens, but provincials, like the soldiers of Rome's auxiliary forces. The Misenum fleet was recruited mostly from the Eastern provinces, including a large proportion from Egypt, whilst the Ravenna fleet drew its personnel from the Danube provinces. Indeed, a number of the seamen were former slaves, who, like Egyptians, were barred from serving in any other branch of the armed forces. They signed up for twenty-six years (raised to twenty-eight in the third century), compared with the twenty-five expected of auxiliary soldiers, but they did receive the Roman citizenship in the same way at the end of their service.

The fleets were also organised in a manner similar to auxiliary units. Inscriptions show that the seamen called themselves 'soldiers' (*milites*) rather than 'sailors' (*nautae*), and no distinction appears to have been made between rowers and marines as there had been in Greek navies. There were specialist and junior officer ranks, earning pay-and-a-half or double pay, who mostly paralleled those of the auxiliaries: doctors (*medici*), armourers (*armorum custodes*) trumpeters (*cornicines, tubicines* and *bucinatores*), tactical officers (*tesserarii, suboptiones* and *optiones*), standard-bearers (*signiferi* and *vexillarii*), and secretarial and headquarters staff (*adiutores, scribae, librarii* and *beneficiarii*). Alongside these, however, there were specialist ranks derived from the Greek and Hellenistic navies who were concerned with the rowing and sailing of the ships. These were the craftsmen (*fabri*), the sail-trimmers (*velarii*), the supply officers (*nauphylaces*), the rowing masters (*celeustae* or *pausarii*), the bow-officers (*proretae*)

13. Pliny the Younger, *Letters*, VI. 16.
14. *P. Oxy.* 2820.

carrying out of the *epikrisis*, a census which established who in Egypt held the status of Roman or Alexandrian citizen and was therefore entitled to serve in the fleet, but it was also of great importance for the purpose of taxation in the province.

There was another fleet in the eastern Mediterranean, the *classis Syriaca*, but its origins are obscure to us. It may have been a creation of Augustus, although it is equally possible that its role of discouraging piracy along the Syrian and Judaean coastline in the early years of his reign and again in the Julio-Claudian period was fulfilled by a detachment from the Alexandrine fleet. The evidence is lacking, since the earliest firm attestation of the Syrian fleet is by an inscription of the reign of Hadrian.[15] Its main base is presumed to have been Seleuceia at the mouth of the river Orontes, the port for the capital of Syria at Antioch.

Rome's other fleets all guarded its northern frontiers and were, on the whole, much more heavily engaged in actual fighting than those in the Mediterranean. Augustus' moves to conquer Germany after 12 BC involved not only crossings of the Rhine and advances up the rivers Lippe and Main, but also the cutting of a canal, the *fossa Drusiana*, to provide shorter access from the lower reaches of the river to the North Sea. From there, operations could be conducted along the coast as far as the mouth of the river Elbe and even into the Baltic. This entailed the creation of a German fleet (*classis Augusta Germanica*) which was involved in combined operations with Roman land forces over an extended period from 12 BC to AD 16. However, the destruction of three legions in the Teutoburger forest in AD 9 persuaded Augustus and his successor Tiberius that Germany should be left alone. Despite attempts by the heir-apparent Germanicus to convert punitive expeditions, which involved the construction of 1000 transports, into a reconquest, he was firmly recalled in AD 16.

The German fleet then became a mainly riverine force, operating on a Rhine which was divided into more channels and flowed rather more sluggishly than it does today. By the mid first century it was being recruited locally, especially from amongst the Batavians of the Lower Rhine. In AD 47 it consisted both of triremes and smaller ships which were used by the governor Corbulo to destroy the naval power of the Chauci on the lower reaches of the river.[16] Later, there appears to have been a relatively small number of single- and two-level oared ships dispersed along the river frontier, since during the revolt of Civilis in AD 70 we hear of the entire squadron of twenty-four ships from the forts of the Lower Rhine as having been concentrated at the upstream end of the so-called Island of the Batavians. This squadron and another coming downstream from Novaesium (Neuss) were destroyed in the revolt, and an indecisive naval battle was subsequently fought in the vicinity of the Island. The Roman commander's flagship was a trireme (*praetoria triremis*).[17] Apart from this, fleet actions are unknown.

The principal roles of the fleet were presum-

15. *Corpus Inscriptionum Latinarum*, VIII. 8934.
16. Tacitus, *Annals*, XI. 18.
17. Tacitus, *Histories*, IV. 15–16; V. 21–3.

Reliefs discovered at Pozzuoli show vessels that appear to have three levels of oars. Although the proportions are clearly exaggerated, details like the rams and steering oars are convincing and it is notable that one ship has an outrigger, or parados, *while the other does not. Dated anywhere between the first centuries BC and AD, the reliefs are surely based on Roman warships of the time. (Superintendenze alle Antichità delle Province di Napoli e Caserta)*

ably to patrol the river, to watch for unauthorised crossings, to ferry Roman troops when required (Rome maintained no permanent bridges across either of Europe's two great rivers), and to protect army supply. It also appears from the evidence of inscriptions that men of the fleet took part, alongside soldiers of the German armies, in the quarrying of building stone in the Brohltal and of the famous volcanic rock (which was used for quernstones) at Andernach. The commander was a Prefect of intermediate rank with an annual salary of 100,000 sesterces. Since the frontier in Upper Germany lay east of the Rhine, the fleet's main base was at Köln-Alteburg just upstream of Cologne, the capital of Lower Germany. Here a large camp dating from the reign of Claudius (AD 41–54) has been excavated and identified from inscribed tombstones and stamped tiles. These tiles, which were produced by the fleet's own tileries, have been found at several other locations along the Rhine. It is not clear, however, that such tiles were only ever used in fleet buildings, and by themselves they are inconclusive evidence for the presence of fleet detachments. Indeed, it is more likely that ships were distributed in ones and twos at forts all along the river, as appears to have been the case on the Lower Rhine before the revolt of Civilis, and certainly there were quay constructions in the vicinity of most of these forts.

It was probably Augustus who created another riverine fleet on the middle Danube, the *classis Pannonica*. From 15 BC his forces were moving into the territory north of the river Sava to the Drava and the Danube. Although this area, known as Pannonia, was thought to have been pacified by 9 BC, the natives re-

Plan of the excavated camp of the classis Germanica *at Köln-Altenburg.* (Drawn by Denys Baker after Reddé)

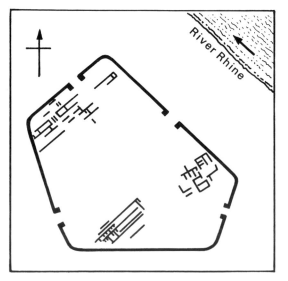

volted in AD 6 and were only subdued by three years of hard campaigning by the future emperor Tiberius. The three rivers must have played some part in the campaigning, but it is unclear precisely when the fleet was formally constituted or how it was deployed. Its role must have been similar to that of the *classis Germanica*, although in its early years it probably operated on the two tributary rivers, helping to consolidate Roman control in the area, more than on the Danube itself. Moreover, the Danube here was wider and presented a more formidable stream than did the Rhine along most of its course, and it must often have been difficult to make headway upstream. During the civil war of AD 68–69, the fleet, together with the Danubian legions, supported Vespasian against Vitellius and was rewarded with the dynastic title *Flavia*, suggesting that it was reformed by the new emperor. The main base may have lain at Taurunum near to where the Sava ran into the Danube and to the legionary fortress at Singidunum (Belgrade) which overlooked the confluence, but inscriptions at Poetovio (Ptuj) and Emona (Ljubljana) suggest that some ships continued to be stationed on the tributaries.

Further downstream from Singidunum, below the narrows known as the Iron Gates, was the section of the Danube patrolled by the *classis Moesiaca* outside the winter months, when regular freezing of the river made navigation impossible. Once again, the precise date of the fleet's formation is unknown. Roman troops were operating on the river bank by the very end of the first century BC, but there was no network of forts along the Lower Danube until the reign of Vespasian (AD 69–79). Nevertheless, the Marcomannic prince Vannius gave himself up to a fleet on the Danube in AD 50,[18] and it was certainly in existence by the time of the civil war, since, like the Pannonian fleet, it received the title *Flavia* to mark its adherence to the victors. The emperor Trajan constructed a towpath and a canal to allow navigation through the Iron Gates, and probably both the Pannonian and Moesian fleets took part in his two Dacian wars of 99–101 and 105–6. Trajan's Column shows the emperor and his army travelling down the Danube on oared warships, including a trireme and several two-level liburnians. Tile-stamps suggest that the main base of the fleet lay at Noviodunum. Possibly because they controlled shorter lengths of river than the Prefect of the *classis Germanica*, the commanders of the Danubian fleets were both of junior rank and were paid 60,000 sesterces annually.

Between them the German, Pannonian and

Moesian fleets played an essential role in maintaining frontier systems based on the lines of forts laid out behind the two great rivers of Europe. At each end of these rivers lay seas, the North Sea and the Black Sea, where Rome acquired territorial interests in the course of the first century AD, and where she therefore needed further fleets. In AD 40, Gaius Caligula made preparations for the invasion of Britain, including the construction of a lighthouse at the invasion port of Gesoriacum (Boulogne) and of a fleet of transports and warships, including triremes.[19] Gaius sent some of these ships back to Rome by land for his victory celebrations (despite his abandonment of the projected invasion), but the bulk of the fleet is likely to have remained on the Channel coast to form the core of the fleet used by Claudius for his successful invasion three years later. This fleet in turn became the permanent *classis Britannica*, consisting of liburnians[20] and at least one trireme.[21] It was based initially at Rutupiae (Richborough) and then at Dubrae (Dover) in Kent, where there was an early second-century fort and two lighthouses situated above each side of the harbour. One of these survives in a good state of preservation within the precincts of the medieval castle. Stamped tiles of the fleet were used in a luxury villa of the same period on the cliffs at Folkestone, and it has been suggested that this was the official residence of the Prefect, a senior equestrian with a salary of 100,000 sesterces per year. Apart from its regular task of protecting communications between Britain and Gaul, the fleet took an important part in the campaigns of Agricola, the governor of Britain from AD 77 to 83, which are known to us from the biography written by his son-in-law, the historian Tacitus. Agricola led Roman forces for the first time into the Highlands of Scotland, advancing by the eastern coastal route with logistical support from the fleet. Ships were then sent north to make the first circumnavigation of Britain and so prove it to be an island.[22] Archaeological evidence suggests that in peacetime it performed a subsidiary role in the large-scale production of iron in Kent.

At the other end of the empire, a Black Sea fleet, the *classis Pontica*, was created by Nero when he annexed the kingdom of Pontus, encompassing both the northern coast of Asia

18. Tacitus, *Annals*, XII. 29–30.

19. Suetonius, *Life of Gaius*, 46–7; Dio, LIX, 25.2.

20. Tacitus, *Agricola*, 28.

21. *Corpus Inscriptionum Latinarum*, XIII. 3564.

22. Tacitus, *Agricola*, 18; 24–5; 28–9; 38.

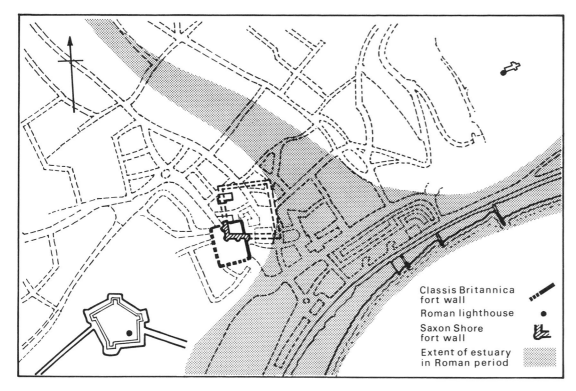

Classis Britannica fort wall
Roman lighthouse
Saxon Shore fort wall
Extent of estuary in Roman period

Minor and the Crimea, in AD 64. Like other nominally independent states within Rome's sphere of influence in the first century AD, this kingdom had kept local piracy in check with its own fleet. As Rome gradually took direct control of such client states, she reorganised their fleets on Roman lines. Attested are a *classis Sicula* based in Sicily (presumably originating from the civil-war forces of Sextus Pompeius) and a *classis Rhodia* maintained by the island of Rhodes,[23] a Jewish fleet operated by Herod the Great,[24] and a *classis Perinthia* based in Thrace.[25] None of these fleets was maintained beyond the end of the first century AD, but the Pontic royal fleet was an exception. After reorganisation, it became the *classis Pontica* and was kept in commission at least until the middle of the third century. Based at Trapezus and under the command of a Prefect earning 100,000 sesterces, it was 40 ships strong and consisted of liburnians and at least one trireme. Hadrian's

governor of Cappadocia, the historian Arrian, describes how he used the fleet to inspect the northern coast of his province in the 130s, and this was presumably one of its regular functions.[26]

The second to fourth centuries

The northern fleets were undoubtedly kept busier than those of the Mediterranean in the first two centuries of the imperial period, but, as with the frontier defences in general, it cannot be said that they were overstretched. It is a tribute to the professionalism of Roman fleets and the efficiency of their training and discipline that they were normally able to cope with any crises which did arise. From the later second century, however, the growth of pressure on the Roman frontiers and the re-emergence of piracy in the more unstable conditions which ensued, meant that the fleets became much more active than before. Unfortunately, the drying up of the historical sources at about the same period means that it is difficult to chart this change in any great detail.

In the 160s and 170s the German frontier was breached by the Chauci and Chatti and the Pannonian and Moesian provinces were ravaged by the Marcomanni, Costoboci and other northern tribes. These incursions across the Rhine and Danube involved the respective fleets in serious fighting. Ships of what must be the Pannonian fleet are depicted taking part in the campaigns of Marcus Aurelius against the Marcomanni on that emperor's Column in

Rome. A famous inscription from Diana Veteranorum (Zana) in Numidia records the career of Marcus Valerius Maximianus, who, amongst many other outstanding exploits in this conflict, was sent to bring provisions down the Danube, probably through enemy lines, to feed the Pannonian armies. He subsequently commanded detachments of troops from the two Italian and the British fleets in reconnoitring the two Pannonian provinces which had been overrun by the Marcomanni.[27] Marcus eventually signed a treaty which forbade the Germanic tribes to cross the Danube,[28] but even after a final peace had been made in 180 by Marcus' son Commodus, a whole series of inscriptions shows that it was necessary to construct a line of watchtowers to the south of Aquincum (Budapest) 'to block clandestine crossings of the river at convenient places by bandits'. The Pannonian fleet must have been instrumental in trying to enforce this policy.

In the Black Sea, the Crimea came under the control of the governor of Lower Moesia and an inscription records the stationing of a trierach of the *classis Moesiaca* at Chersonesus in 185,[29] while pressure on Lower Moesia itself in the 170s seems to have forced the *classis Pontica* to move its main base from Trapezus in the east to Cyzicus at the entrance to the channel to the Hellespont and the Mediterranean. Nor was the Mediterranean untouched by troubles in this period. A resurgence of Moorish raids on the African and Spanish coasts in the 170s is likely to have required the attentions of the Italian fleets, and by the 180s an inscription records the existence of a new African fleet (*classis nova Libyca*).[30]

The assassination of Commodus on the last day of 192 plunged the empire back into civil war. One of the claimants to the throne, Didius Iulianus, who had 'bought' the empire from the Praetorian Guard in a mock auction, summoned the men of the Misenum fleet to aid his cause, but, according to the historian Dio who was a contemporary witness, they did not even know how to drill.[31] The Ravenna fleet declared for Septimius Severus, the governor of Upper Pannonia, who used both Italian fleets to transport his army to the East to campaign against his main rival, Pescennius Niger.[32]

23. Suetonius, *Life of Claudius*, 21.6.

24. Josephus, *Jewish Antiquities*, XVI. 16–21.

25. *Inscriptiones Graecae ad Res Romanas Pertinentes*, I. 781.

26. Josephus, *Jewish War*, II. 366–7; Tacitus, *Histories*, III. 47; Arrian, *Circumnavigation of the Black Sea*, 4.4.

27. *L'Année Épigraphique* (1956), n124.

28. Dio, LXXII. 19.2.

29. *Corpus Inscriptionum Latinarum*, III. 14214[3,4].

30. *Corpus Inscriptionum Latinarum*, VIII. 7030; *cf* Historia Augusta, *Life of Commodus*, 17.7.

31. Dio, LXXIV. 16.3.

32. Herodian, II. 14.7; III. 1.1.

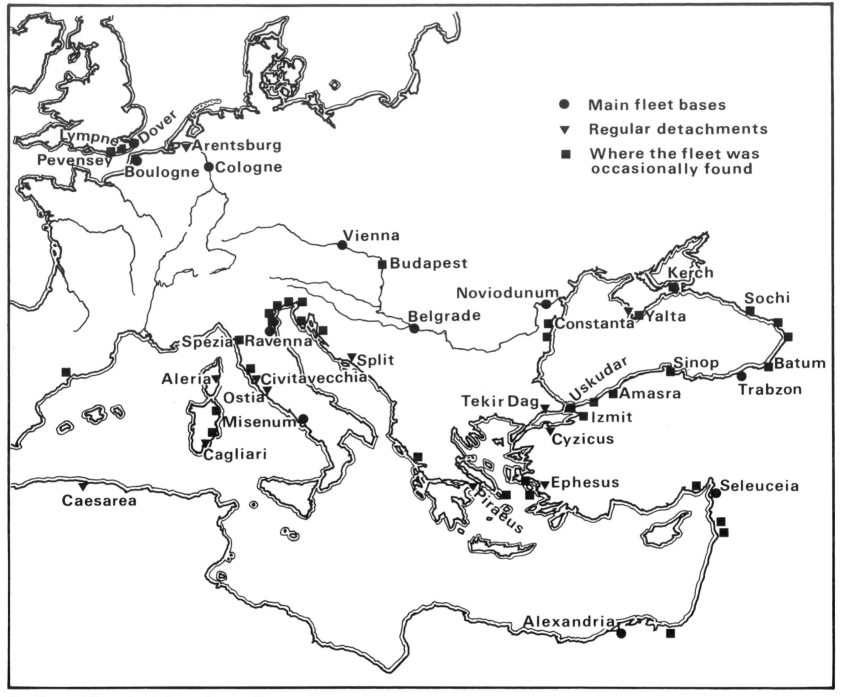

Naval bases and fleet stations in the second century AD.
(Drawn by Denys Baker after Reddé)

From 193 to 196 they conducted the siege of Byzantium on his behalf before returning to Italy.[33]

In the third century, wars in the Orient required the movement of troops and supplies from Italy, and this was effected in part by sea. Severus' son Caracalla took the Italian fleets eastward in 214, himself surviving a shipwreck en route, and a Prefect of the Misenum fleet was involved in his assassination there in 217.[34] The fleets returned to Italy for a while, but, with the emergence of an aggressive new Persian dynasty in the 220s, were again transport-

ing troops to the East under Severus Alexander in 231–233 and Gordian III in 243–244. Inscriptions reveal, however, that the Misenum fleet also had to help suppress rebellion in the western Mediterranean from time to time, for instance in North Africa in 258–260.[35] The frequent absence of the bulk of the fleets together with their Prefects resulted in the appointment of acting commanders at Misenum and Ravenna with the title of *praepositi reliqua-tionis*, literally 'those in charge of the remainder'. These men were usually appointed from the ranks of senior legionary centurions.

Continued pressure on the northern and eastern frontiers resulted both in hostile incur-

sions from without and instability and a resurgence of piracy within the empire. In the 230s inscriptions record the appointment of individual Roman knights to combat piracy in the region of the Crimea and in the Mediterranean,[36] and another records the activity of a similar officer, Valerius Statilius Castus, off the coast of Lycia in 256–258.[37] From the 250s to

33. Dio, LXXV. 10–13.

34. Historia Augusta, *Life of Caracalla*, 6.7.

35. *Corpus Inscriptionum Latinarum*, VIII. 12296 and 21000; *L'Année Épigraphique* (1907), n4.

36. *L'Année Épigraphique* (1948), n201; *Corpus Inscriptionum Graecarum*, 2509a.

37. *Inscriptiones Latinae Selectae*, 8870.

the 270s Gothic and other invaders appeared on the Black Sea, ravaging its coasts and forcing the inhabitants to build them a fleet, before bursting through to the Aegean and both ends of the Mediterranean.

The sources indicate that Roman fleets did offer resistance to these attacks, although it is not always clear which of them were involved. The *classis Pontica* must have suffered badly from the Gothic devastations in the Black Sea and may even have been annihilated, since the fleet which tried to prevent the passage of the Heruli from the Black Sea through to the Mediterranean in 267–268 appears to have been specially constituted either from ships provided by local cities or from ships of the Italian fleets brought to Byzantium by the emperor Gallienus.[38] We may guess, but cannot be certain, that Valerius Statilius Castus was given elements of the *classis Syriaca* with which to protect the coast of Lycia. In 270 it was presumably with the *classis Alexandrina* that a Prefect of Egypt, Tenagino Probus, drove the Heruli away from Cyprus and Cilicia,[39] and an inscription suggests that a squadron of that fleet was also used against the Blemmyes on the Nile in 273. The extent of the survival of these fleets is nevertheless unclear.

On the other hand, we can be fairly sure that the northern riverine fleets did not survive as a significant force. The fact that they do not appear in inscriptions after the middle of the third century is not conclusive, since we have very few inscriptions of any kind from that period. We do know, however, that the Goths had overrun the Middle and Lower Danube frontiers by the 250s and that the *classes Pannonica* and *Moesiaca* can no longer have been fully operational. By 260 the Franks had occupied the estuaries of the Rhine, and later incursions upriver must have reduced the *classis Germanica* to impotence by 280 at the latest.

In the North it is only the *classis Britannica* which is known to have been maintained intact as an effective fighting unit. Britain may have been suffering from Saxon raids across the North Sea from as early as the late second century, but, surprisingly, both Boulogne and Dover appear to have been given up as fleet bases at this period. By about 230, however, new forts had been established at Brancaster in East Anglia and at Reculver in Kent, and several more were added in this area in the 270s and after to form the defensive system which was later known as the Saxon Shore (*litus Saxonicum*).[40]

In 285, the new emperor Diocletian put a Gaul named Carausius in charge of the British fleet, and probably of these forts as well, in order to check coastal raiding. Carausius, however, allowed the raiders to sail through the Channel to loot the southern coast and attacked them only as they sailed back laden with booty. He then set himself up as a rival emperor based in Britain and repulsed all attempts by Diocletian's partner Maximian to regain control. Carausius was murdered by his own deputy, Allectus, in 293 and Maximian's junior emperor Constantius Chlorus was eventually able to carry out a successful invasion of the island in 296.[41]

The Saxon Shore system survived at least until the later fourth century, but the history of the *classis Britannica* after 296 is obscure. It is possible, however, that it was divided into a number of smaller squadrons, like those recorded for the rivers and lakes of Gaul in the fourth century by an administrative document of the early fifth century known as the *Notitia Dignitatum*.[42] A laudatory speech delivered before the emperor Constantine in 310 tells us that he had been able to sail down the Rhone with an army in that year, and the same work seems to show a fleet in operation against German invaders on the Upper and Lower Rhine a few years before.[43] The *Notitia Dignitatum* also indicates that a number of small squadrons were distributed along the Danube in the fourth century, some of them independent, some representing the remnants of the *classis Pannonica*, and others attached to a new Danube fleet, the *classis Histrica*.

The only major fleets in the empire in the early fourth century were therefore still the two in Italy. These now came back into prominence as a multitude of rival emperors vied to achieve sole rule. In 310 or 311, the emperor Maxentius, who controlled Italy, made use of the Misenum fleet to recapture Africa from the usurper L Domitius Alexander.[44] He did not enjoy his victory for long, because in 312 he was defeated and killed by his rival Constantine after the latter had constructed his own fleet in Gaul, with which he blockaded Rome and the west coast of Italy.[45]

The large naval forces which Constantine had thus acquired in the Mediterranean were also instrumental in the elimination of his last rival, Licinius. In 324 these forces, consisting of 200 relatively small ships described as triacontors, were concentrated in the Aegean. Licinius gathered together 350 larger ships, triremes, from the Aegean, the Eastern Mediterranean and Africa. These were presumably drawn from remnants of the earlier fleets or from new squadrons which had been created by Diocletian. When Licinius was forced to retreat to Byzantium after a land battle, 80 of

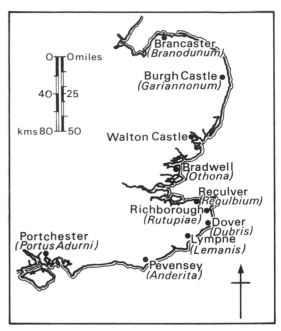

A map of the system of forts (with their Roman identities where known) that made up the landward defences of the Saxon Shore in south-east Britain. Designed to stave off the attacks of raiders from across the North Sea, the forts supported squadrons of ships and all were under the unified command of a Comes , *or* Count.(*Drawn by Denys Baker after V Maxfield, ed*)

Constantine's triacontors defeated 200 of Licinius' triremes in the approaches to the Hellespont. Byzantium was besieged and Licinius fled to Asia Minor, but Constantine used the fleet to follow him across and win a final victory on land.[46]

After 324 triremes are never heard of again. Zosimus, writing in the fifth century, says that the secret of their construction has long since been forgotten.[47] Much more importantly, the defeat of Licinius, following the first major fleet engagement in the Mediterranean for some 350 years, brought the restoration of political stability to the Roman world after a century of civil wars. It was a victory, in its way, as significant as Actium.

Boris Rankov

38. Historia Augusta, *Life of Gallienus*, 6.8; 7.2; 13.6–10; *Life of Claudius*, 9.7.

39. Zosimus, *New History*, I. 44.

40. *Notitia Dignitatum*, Occ. 28.

41. *Panegyrici Latini*, X (II). 11–13; VIII (V). 6–7; 12–20; Eutropius, *Survey of Roman History*, IX. 13–4 (21–2); Aurelius Victor, *Book on the Caesars*, 39.19–21, 39–42.

42. Occ. XLII. 14–15, 21, 23; XXXV. 32.

43. *Panegyrici Latini*, VII. 6.6; 13.1; 18–20.

44. Zosimus, *New History*, II. 12.

45. *Panegyrici Latini*, IX. 25.2.

46. Zosimus, *New History*, II. 22–8.

47. *New History*, V. 20.

Late Roman, Byzantine, and Islamic Galleys and Fleets

OCTAVIAN'S defeat of Antony and Cleopatra at the battle of Actium in 31 BC marked the effective end of classical naval warfare, in which massed fleets of heavy, multi-banked warships faced each other in set-piece battles determined by the success or failure of ramming attacks. Octavian built a monument to his victory at nearby Nicopolis,[1] where he mounted the rams sawn off the largest ships of the vanquished fleet. This wall of trophies might be seen not only as a testament to youthful boasting, but also as a tombstone for a naval way of life. For more than half a millennium, warships had grown steadily larger and heavier, from the *diēreis* and *triēreis* of Archaic and Classical Athens through quadriremes and quinqueremes upward to tens and sixteens, even the grand folly of a forty, built by competing Hellenistic kingdoms locked in an arms race for prestige and political dominance in the eastern Mediterranean. Rome, once stirred to naval effort by the Punic threat, assembled comparable fleets to support its wars of conquest against those same kingdoms.

But the victor of Actium, as Augustus Caesar, eliminated the last organised challenge to Roman rule in the Mediterranean and consolidated Roman administration over the shores of the great sea. As the sole naval power in the Mediterranean, Rome had no need of great fleets or heavy warships manned by large numbers of men. A few larger ships were kept as flagships for the commanders of a peacetime navy, but standing battlefleets were largely retired, not to be seen on Mediterranean waters for almost half a millennium. Instead, Rome concentrated on smaller ships and squadrons to patrol the sea lanes and keep an effective lid on piracy or to guard the frontiers. These duties required swift, manoeuvrable ships to chase the equally swift ships of pirates and raiders, or light boats that could be rowed up and down the rivers that formed the German border. While these ships were more than adequate to deal with small, poorly organised raids or sporadic pirate attacks, they were incapable of responding forcefully to larger fleets; when the decline of political order led to civil war in the third and fourth centuries, naval fleets had to be cobbled together and were quickly dispersed.

With the collapse of western Roman administration in the fifth century AD, competing naval powers were free to emerge, and for a brief period in the fifth century, one of the invading peoples, the Vandals, was able to establish a sizeable naval presence in the Mediterranean. Their piratical raids under the energetic king Gaeseric became such a nuisance to trade that two naval expeditions – the first organised Roman fleet operations in nearly five centuries – were sent out to put down the barbarians, but without great success. It was not until the early sixth century that the Byzantine emperor Anasthasius began the slow process of fleet organisation that led to the large standing navy of the Byzantine Empire, with its Imperial Fleet guarding Constantinople and regional (Thematic) fleets drawn from the principal administrative districts (Themes) of the rest of the Empire. This navy was to become essential in the seventh century with the appearance of Islam on the Mediterranean shores of Syria and Palestine. The Moslems wasted little time in assembling their own naval fleets to challenge Byzantine dominance of the Mediterranean, and the stage was set for the return of fleet actions featuring large, heavily armed ships as Byzantium and a succession of Islamic dynasties struggled for nearly four centuries for the naval supremacy essential to Mediterranean hegemony.

A note on the sources

The primary sources for later Roman and Byzantine naval history are almost all documentary. In addition to histories by late Roman and

---

1. Murray and Petsas 1988 provides a thorough description of the site; Murray and Petsas 1989 provides a more general overview.

View of Octavian's Camp Monument at Nicopolis, commemorating his victory over the forces of Anthony and Cleopatra at Actium in 31 BC. The monument was originally surrounded by the rams sawn off the vanquished ships of the enemy, the sockets for which can still be seen in the lowest levels of masonry. (By courtesy of William M Murray)

The classic shell-first shipbuilding technique of the ancient Mediterranean demonstrated by this tombstone relief showing a Roman shipwright at work (late second or early third century AD). The original is in the Archaeological Museum, Ravenna.

medieval writers, and a few eyewitness accounts of particular events, we are fortunate to have a series of specifically naval texts.[2] Most of our detailed information comes from tenth-century sources, primarily the tactical manuals of Leo the Wise[3] and Nicephoros Ouranos,[4] a shorter descriptive document known as *Anon PBPP* or *PBPP*,[5] and a number of inventories[6] of men, ships, and equipment sent on several tenth-century naval expeditions. There is virtually no iconographic or archaeological evidence to confirm the impressions given by the written sources, and our understanding of ships and naval combat in the early years of the Byzantine–Moslem struggle is somewhat less complete. On the other hand, the step from Roman liburnian to Byzantine *dromōn* or Arab *koumbarion* is not such a long one, and the *Naumachiae* of Syrianos Magistros,[7] written in the seventh century or earlier, indicates that tactics did not change drastically between then and Leo's time.

These documents provide not only detailed accounts of the types of ships and weapons used by both Byzantine and Islamic navies, but also insight into strategic and tactical thinking and medieval ideas of the management of soldiers and sailors, including how much they should be paid and fed. A problem with some of these texts is a conscious attempt on the part of the tactical writers to demonstrate their knowledge of ancient military writers and their familiarity with archaic terms. In most cases, the writer will note that the ancient name for a thing is different from the modern, or that in the 'old days' certain tactics were considered preferable, but it is not always possible to tell with certainty when a writer is describing current tactics and equipment with which he is personally familiar and when he is reporting something he has read in an older source. This problem has contributed, for example, to some confusion over whether ramming was still practised by Byzantine warships.[8]

In the realm of archaeology, we do not even have the opportunity for confusion; except for a few late Roman river patrol boats from the Rhine and Danube, there are no known, identifiable remains of warships from this period. This is not unexpected, as warship remains from the ancient world are also extremely rare. Without large quantities of ballast or cargo to press them down into the bottom and protect them, the timbers of sunken triremes and dromōns were certainly destroyed quite rapidly by boring organisms such as shipworm (*teredo navalis*). Fortunately, the archaeological record for the period does include some examples of merchant ships, and these provide us with some general clues to early medieval shipbuilding which may be applicable to warships as well.

Late Roman navies

The Romans were not a great seafaring people. Despite the Mediterranean Sea that connected many of the provinces of the Empire, provincial administration and outlook were largely land-based. By controlling all of the shore, Rome removed the need to control the water. As one writer has pointed out, there are no famous Roman seafarers known to history;[9] however, the Romans were adept at exploiting the abilities of the peoples they conquered, and the crews of Mediterranean merchant vessels were largely made up of Greeks and Syrians. Even in Ostia, the port of Rome, many of the ancient inscriptions and graffiti are in Greek rather than Latin. In this climate it should come as no surprise that after Actium, the Roman navy withered away. With no organised opposition, there was no need for fleets of expensive, multi-banked warships and their large crews.

This is not to say that there was no need for a naval force. Convoys of merchant ships, especially the grain ships coming from Egypt, Sicily, and North Africa to Rome, needed to be protected. Piracy remained a problem, especially in such places as the Adriatic Sea, where rugged coasts and barrier islands provided shelter and hiding places for small bands of outlaws, or along the North African coast, where population and garrisons were thinly spread. Pirates often hid behind islands and promontories and attacked in small, swift vessels that could be propelled by sail or oars.

2. The Greek texts have been collected in Dain 1943.

3. The text of interest is Book XIX (*Naumachica* or Περὶ ναυμαχίας) of a larger work, the *Tactica*, which deals with military tactics of all sorts; see Dain 1943, pp19–33 and commentary pp14–18. Leo reigned from 886 to 912, and the *Tactica* has been dated to 907.

4. Also an excerpt of a larger *Tactica*, based on or drawing heavily from the work of Leo, this is made up of Chapters 54 and 119–123, generally referred to as Περὶ Θαλασσομαχίας: see Dain 1943, pp71–104. Nicephoros Ouranos was a well-known Byzantine general of the later tenth century.

5. *PBPP* is actually the abbreviation of the name and title (Παρὰ Βασιλείου Πατρικίου καὶ Παρακοιμωμένου, 'Basil, Patrician and Guardian of the Bedchamber') of the patron to whom the anonymous writer dedicated the work. This is the same Basil who was so influential during the reigns of Nicephoros Phocas and the emperor Basil II in the middle and later tenth century. The title of the work is Ναυμαχικὰ Συνταχθέντα; see Dain 1943, pp61–68.

6. Preserved by Constantine Porphyrogenitus in *De Caeremoniis aulae Byzantinae* II, 44–45.

7. The beginning of the text is lost; Dain 1943, pp45–55.

8. Van Doorninck 1993, n17.

9. Lewis 1951, p18.

A third-century AD mosaic of Ulysses and the Sirens from a villa in Dougga, Tunisia. Although highly stylised it shows the main features of the Roman warships of the time, including a decorative representation of the oarbox amidships – it is noteworthy that the oars protrude from below the box and not from within it. (Bardo Museum, Tunis)

Regular patrols by vessels capable of catching these ships had to be coupled with occasional punitive expeditions to keep piracy in check.

The bulk of the Roman Imperial navy seems to have been made up of relatively small ships. In the main fleets, based at Misenum in the Bay of Naples and Ravenna, there were a few quadriremes and quinqueremes, as well as at least one six at Misenum, probably the flagship, but the vast majority of recorded ships are triremes, which were concentrated in the main fleets based in Italy, but were also used as flagships in provincial fleets, and liburnians, a new type.[10] These new ships were small, fast, open vessels propelled by two levels of oars, ideal patrol and pursuit vessels. The type was named for a people of the Dalmatian coast who used similar vessels, probably developed from a local type of light galley called *lembos* in Hellenistic times, in their pirate raids on local commerce. Liburnians are first reliably reported at the battle of Naulochos in 36 BC,[11] and in the Imperial Period formed the backbone of provincial fleets in the Mediterranean.[12]

Imperial warships differed substantially from their Hellenistic predecessors, most notably in the abandonment of the outrigger (*apostis* or *parexereisia*) as a support for the tholes. The large number of surviving representations indicate that the vast majority of later Roman galleys were rowed on no more than two levels, and that the tholes for both levels were mounted in oarports cut directly in the sides of the ship. In some cases, only a single level of oars is shown, and it is likely that even larger ships, such as quinqueremes, could be rowed this way, with larger numbers of men assigned to each oar. This simplification of the rowing system reduced the amount and complexity of superstructure needed to house and support the rowers. Many of these representations show a long, box-like structure strongly resembling an outrigger on the side of the ship, but in most cases, the oars do not pass through this structure, but through oarports in the hull below the box. The function of the box is not clear, but it may have served to protect the oars from being sheared off in a raking attack, a tactic popular since the Peloponnesian war.

At the same time that Roman shipwrights were reducing the rowing superstructure, they were adding heavier forecastles, a cabin or shelter in the stern for the commander, and other deck constructions. Some galleys carried open bulwarks around the deck. Tactics were changing, returning to the land-style warfare initially favoured by the Roman navy in the Punic wars. Ships carried marines and missile weapons with which to attack the crews of opposing ships, and there seems to have been less emphasis placed on ramming. Pirates certainly had no incentive to ram, as capture of a working ship was often their goal. The ram itself was simplified, the older three-bladed design seen in the Athlit ram giving way to a cleaner, pointed casing.

There is evidence that the Roman conquerors attempted to import Mediterranean ship types and construction methods into northern Gaul, Germany, and Britain, but without much success. To the south, shipwrights had the benefit of more than a millennium of experience building ships from the abundant softwoods of the Mediterranean shore, fastening the planks to each other with thousands of mortise-and-tenon joints in a strong, integrated structure. Remains of vessels built in a similar fashion have been found in England,[13] Germany,[14] and the Netherlands,[15] but these vessels are peculiar in that they are generally not built in pine or fir, the traditional woods of the Mediterranean, but in the ubiquitous oak of northern Europe, a wood poorly suited to the carving of so much complex joinery. These vessels also date to relatively early in the Roman occupation of northern Europe, rarely much later than the end of the first century AD. These few vessels, two of which are small patrol boats on the Danube, stand in contrast to over twenty other vessels of the Roman period from the same region, vessels built in a distinctly non-Mediterranean style, without edge fastenings between planks. The majority of these vessels are merchant ships and barges, but a group of patrol boats found in Mainz in 1981 deserve our attention.

River fleets in the northern provinces

The remains of five vessels were found, lying on what would have been the foreshore of the Rhine just outside the city wall of Mogontiacum (Roman Mainz).[16] All of the vessels had been abandoned and partially dismantled in what must have been a breaker's yard. All but one of these vessels seem to be of the same type, a narrow, open boat designed to be propelled by either oars or sail. Vessel 9, the best preserved of this class, was originally approximately 21m long and 2.7m in beam (69ft by 9ft). The stern is conventional, but the bow does not have a stem; instead, the sides are

10. On the liburnian as a type, see Panciera 1956.

11. Appian, *Bel Civ* 5, 111.

12. Casson 1971, p356, n57.

13. The County Hall ship was found at the turn of the century in London: Marsden 1974.

14. Two boats found at Oberstimm on the Danube in 1986 have only been investigated in a preliminary way, but it is clear that they are fastened with pegged mortise-and-tenon joints; Höckmann 1990.

15. The remains of a boat found at Vechten in 1893 included planking fastened with mortise-and-tenon joints, but the remains have never been convincingly reconstructed; Muller 1895 and de Weerd 1988.

16. An overall introduction to the excavation and finds is provided by Rupprecht 1982, while later interpretations of the hull remains can be found in Höckmann 1993.

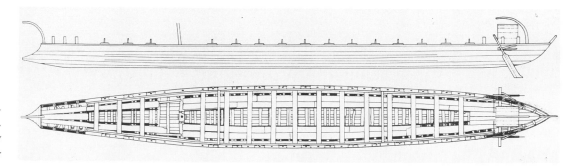

A reconstruction of the Mainz type A patrol boat, provisionally identified as a Roman navis lusoria. Note the low sides, minimal structure, and the unusual manner of closing the bow. (By courtesy of O Höckmann)

connected by a transverse panel that rakes aft. From the side, it gives the appearance of a ram. The vessel carried a mast stepped in a heavy frame relatively far forward, and was rowed by up to fifteen pairs of oarsmen. The construction is relatively heavy for an oared ship, with large, closely spaced frames, but has a keelplank rather than a heavy keel. In addition, the type seems to be distinguished by an internal trunk fastened into the bottom of the hull and running most of the length of the vessel. This may have provided minimal cargo or storage space (a quantity of charcoal was found in one of the trunks), or it may be a structural feature designed to increase the longitudinal stiffness of the long, narrow hull. The absence of mortise-and-tenon joints strongly suggests that either local boatbuilders working in the tradition of Germano-Celtic construction were employed, or that Roman shipwrights had adopted local methods, which were cheaper and less labour-intensive. The type represented by vessel 9, called in the specialist literature Mainz type A, has been provisionally identified as the *navis lusoria*, a small, rowed

A general view of the excavations of the late Roman patrol boats along the ancient waterfront in Mainz (Roman Mogontiacum): the remains of vessel 1 are prepared for removal in December 1981. (By courtesy of O Höckmann)

vessel quite common in later Roman sources, especially the descriptions of Rhine warships by Ammianus Marcellinus,[17] but the identification is disputed by at least one scholar, on the grounds that the term is often applied in a very general way to a wide variety of boats.[18] Whether or not it is a *lusoria*, these long, narrow boats are quite similar to some contemporary representations of warships from the Rhine.[19]

A second type, represented by vessel 3, was a beamier – approximately 17m long and 3.5m in beam (56ft by 11½ft) – transport vessel, possibly a *navis cubiculata* (which refers to a cabin provided for passengers) or *navis iudiciaria* for ferrying VIPs. It is not known how it was propelled, as preservation was relatively poor except at the stern, but it did not have conventional thwarts for oarsmen. Steering was accomplished by quarter rudders mounted in a complex protective structure attached to a throughbeam. The stern also preserved the heads of several frames, which extended above the gunwale to become bitts, probably for belaying running rigging.

Two of the vessels were dated dendrochronologically, with an initial construction date for both vessels falling around AD 375/376. Vessel 1 had also been repaired twice, once in 385, and again in 394.[20] The excavators believe the Mainz vessels were abandoned on the foreshore not long thereafter, possibly in the general abandonment of Mogontiacum before the German occupation of 406.[21]

These boats represent the last developments in Roman frontier defence on the Rhine, and were almost certainly attached to one of the legions stationed at Mogontiacum;[22] the German naval fleet, the *Classis Germanica*, was based farther down river, at Cologne. At Mainz they probably served to guard the confluence with the Main and to patrol the river, looking for signs of German activity on the east bank. The enemy travelled in large canoes, either dugout or plank-built, and these vessels may have influenced the development of the Mainz type, just as pirate *lemboi* and liburnians had influenced the development of Roman naval

vessels in the Mediterranean. The proportions of the type A boats suggest that they were built for speed or ease of rowing, and were probably not intended to engage in waterborne combat (although they would have been adequate for attacks on German canoes), but to scout the bank and transport small detachments of men to trouble spots. The river was divided into relatively short segments by a large number of fortresses and camps on the west bank, and a few smaller blockhouse-like structures on the east bank, and individual vessels may only have been responsible for one segment at a time, rowing or sailing easily down stream, then working their way back against the current. A similar system was in use on the Danube; two narrow, shallow boats built in Mediterranean fashion and discovered at Oberstimm[23] may have served a similar function, although they are much earlier in date and may predate the establishment of co-ordinated defences on the Danube.

Temporary measures

The river boats of the Rhine and the liburnians of the Mediterranean were perfectly adequate to the task of suppressing piracy and guarding the frontier, but were neither large nor numerous enough to oppose an organised fleet or engage in a protracted naval campaign. When a large Gothic fleet from the Black Sea forced a passage through the Bosporus in 267, they were able to plunder the rich coasts of the Aegean and down into the Adriatic almost at

---

17. Höckmann 1993, p131, citing as examples Ammianus Marcellinus XVII, 3.3 and XVIII, 2.12.

18. Haywood 1991: 47, noting that in one of the examples cited by Höckmann (Ammianus Marcellinus XVIII, 2.11–12), the ships described only carry seven or eight men each.

19. Höckmann 1984.

20. Hollstein 1982.

21. Höckmann 1993, p126.

22. The elaborate river defence system on the Rhine and Danube has been described in Höckmann 1986.

23. Höckmann 1990.

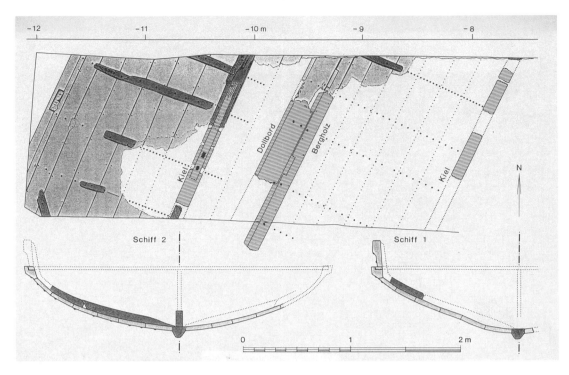

Plan of the extant remains and cross sections of the Roman-period boats found at Oberstimm on the Danube. The construction technique, with mortise-and-tenon edge joints suggests a Mediterranean building tradition rather than the framed structure of the Mainz boats. The planking is pine, with oak keel and frames. (Drawing by H-J Köhler, by courtesy of O Höckmann)

The naval struggle between Byzantine fleets and their opponents

By the early sixth century the Mediterranean world had fragmented sufficiently, and relations between Byzantium and her western neighbours, particularly the Ostrogoths in Italy, had become sufficiently tense that the emperor Anasthasius began to see the need for organised naval power. In 508 he sent an expeditionary force, including a hundred warships, to ravage Italy. In 515 the pretender Vitalian was able to achieve some success with a fleet of 200 ships, as Anasthasius was unable to respond in kind, but the following year a fleet under Marinus, equipped with an inflammable liquid similar to the Greek fire of succeeding centuries, was able to rout the usurper. Marinus's fleet, created as a response to an organised naval threat rather than a motley and temporary conglomeration of ships assembled for a single campaign, is, in many ways, the ancestor of the great standing navy of the later Byzantine Empire.

will. In the fourth century, when Constantine went to war with Licinius, neither could call on a standing fleet and so the early stages of the war were fought entirely on land. By 324 it had become apparent to both commanders that naval power could offer an advantage, and so both assembled fleets to transport and support their armies. Both were able to field sizable fleets, but it appears that many of the warships were quite small, some no bigger than the pentecontors of the Bronze Age. Constantine was victorious, and it was not long after that Licinius was forced to submit.

By the fifth century, Roman authority in the West had declined sufficiently that the Vandals were able to establish a short-lived but widely feared naval empire based in North Africa. Under the ambitious Gaeseric, the Vandals sent out annual plundering expeditions, sometimes numbering hundreds of ships, to raid the western islands and as far east as the Greek mainland. While many of these ships were no doubt sailing ships with holds large enough to carry booty home, some must have been swift galleys, probably not vastly different from the traditional Roman liburnians. Eventually, both Rome and Constantinople were forced to act against Gaeseric, and each sent a fleet in the 460s to try to solve the Vandal problem, but without success. While the sources do not give us much detail about these expeditions, it is hard to imagine that they differed vastly from the fleets scraped together by Constantine and Licinius over a century before. Fortunately, Gaeseric's successors were much less aggressive, and relative calm settled over the Mediterranean in the last decades of the fifth century.

A sketch of a galley based on a coin of Allectus (AD 293-6) minted in Britain. The details are very similar to the ship depicted in a fourth-century mosaic found at Low Ham in Somerset; taken together they give some indication of the type of single-level vessel probably employed by the Classis Britannica, *or British Fleet, in the last centuries of Roman occupation in Britain.*

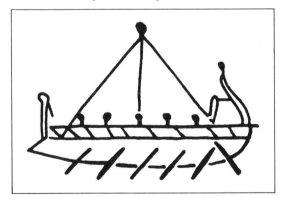

But it is to Anasthasius's successor, Justinian, that the bulk of the credit goes for the re-establishment of standing fleets composed of purpose-built warships. In the wars of reconquest waged by Justinian and his able generals Belisarius and Narses, naval power was an essential component. By controlling the sea lanes and denying the advantages of seaborne transport and communication to his enemies, Justinian was able to project Byzantine military strength over great distances. Consequently, relatively small numbers of troops were required to take and hold large stretches of the Mediterranean shore. Only once was Byzantine naval power seriously challenged, by the Ostrogoths in 551, when a fleet built in Italy and led by Totila successfully supported the invasion and recapture of Sardinia and Corsica. From this position, the Ostrogothic ships were well placed to threaten Byzantine links between the eastern and western Mediterranean, but were defeated in the same year at Sena

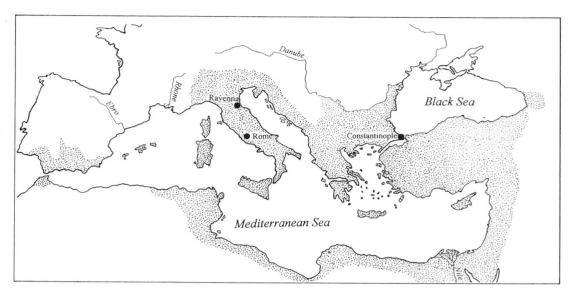

The Byzantine Empire at the close of Justinian's reign, about AD 565. Outside of the Balkans, Asia Minor and Italy, it is little more than a narrow strip of coastline around the Mediterranean. (Map by Frederick M Hocker, INA)

Gallica. With the final defeat of Totila in 553, the threat evaporated, but the lesson was not lost on Justinian.

In contrast to the empire of his Roman predecessors, the Byzantine Empire recreated by Justinian was a decidedly maritime construct, confined largely to coastal regions and ports that could be supplied or reinforced from the sea; it has been referred to traditionally as a 'thalassocracy'. For it to work as effectively as it did, a professional navy was vital. The fleet built by Anasthasius in 516 was expanded into a large, permanent force responsible for supporting invasion forces sent to Africa and the western Mediterranean, and thereafter for patrolling and reinforcing trouble spots. As part of the system of taxation developed by Justinian and his successors, certain towns or regions were expected to build ships for the navy, foreshadowing the system of Themes developed a hundred years later.[24]

This system worked well for a century, and Byzantium was the unchallenged master of the Mediterranean and Black Seas. When disaster came in the seventh century, it came from the long land frontier in the East. First the Sassanian Persians, bought off by Justinian but grown increasingly restive, poured over the borders into the rich lands of Syria, Egypt, and Asia Minor. By 626, the capital itself was threatened by a Persian army, and an Avar invasion of Thrace included a flotilla sent into the Golden Horn. The Empire was saved largely because the Byzantine fleet could still be counted on to dominate the sea lanes. Heraclius's armies could be landed and supplied from the sea, and thus could attack Persian positions in the Levant almost at will. By 628, the territory lost in the first decades of the century had been regained, and in 629 the Persian capital, Ctesiphon, was captured and plundered. The jubilation in Constantinople was short lived, for in 634 the first wave of the Moslem conquest appeared, and by 641 Syria and Egypt had fallen, their economic strength and maritime expertise lost to the invaders from the desert.

Although not a seafaring people, the Arabs were not slow to appreciate the importance of naval power, especially after a Byzantine attempt to retake Alexandria in 645 demonstrated Arab vulnerability to naval attack. Local shipwrights were pressed into service to build warships doubtless quite similar to those they had built for their former Byzantine overlords, and Copts and Syrians were recruited as sailors and oarsmen.[25] The first Arab fleet was assembled by the future caliph Mu'āwiya in 648, when 1700 ships harried Cyprus. Further raids in the early 650s prompted a Byzantine response, and in 655, the Arab and Byzantine fleets met in the Battle of the Masts (or Dhāt Al-Sawārī), off the Syrian coast. The outnumbered Arabs chained their ships together to prevent their line being broken, and the Byzantine navy was dealt its first serious defeat. It may have been partly in response to this defeat, as well as reverses on land, that the Byzantine army and navy were reorganised around a central Imperial fleet and army supplemented by large regional armies and fleets raised from individual administrative districts, called Themes. The Arabs, for their part, did not immediately follow up the victory, but resumed their attacks on a much larger scale in 669. In 670 they landed a large force in North Africa, and in 673 began the first of their two great attacks on Constantinople itself. The siege lasted until 679, when the Imperial fleet, armed with Greek Fire, broke out of the Golden Horn to burn and scatter the Arab ships.

Although initial Arab designs on North Africa in the 670s had been repulsed, a better organised effort, beginning in 695 with the capture of Carthage, succeeded in wresting control of this vital section of the Mediterranean shore from the Byzantines. By 700, central North Africa was firmly in Arab hands, and the caliph 'Abd Al-Malik sent a thousand Coptic shipwrights to Musa, the governor in Carthage, and ordered him to establish a naval base and shipyard in Africa. Musa established his base inland from the old port, at Tunis, which could be more easily defended from By-zantine attack. By 704 Tunis was home to a large fleet that exercised sufficient control over the western Mediterranean that Musa was able to complete the conquest of western North Africa. From there, the Arabs were able to cross the Straits of Gibraltar and begin the conquest of Spain.

In 717, the Arabs besieged Constantinople a second time, both with a fleet of 1800 vessels and an army that advanced from the Asian side of the Bosporus. The European side was simultaneously under attack by the Bulgars. In this dark hour, Leo III (the Isaurian) stretched a chain across the Bosporus, and during the winter of 717–718 persuaded the Bulgars to make war on the Arabs instead. The Imperial fleet, armed with Greek fire, attacked the Arab ships and destroyed many of them. The siege was lifted, and Leo went on the offensive, driving the Arabs back out of the Aegean. The Arabs were unable to mount a major naval offensive again until 747, but from 726 both sides carried out raids against the other until mid-century. Byzantine power was weakened by the destructive revolt of the Aegean Themal fleets in 727, and required assistance from the infant navies of the rising city-states of Italy in 742, but had recovered by 747, when the combined Arab fleets of Syria and Egypt were destroyed by the fleet of the Kibyrrhaeots Theme, based in southern Asia Minor. Ommayid naval power in the eastern Mediterranean was effectively broken, and the Egyptian fleet did not reappear until the tenth century.

24. Lewis 1951, p31.

25. Arab sources specifically note that at the Battle of the Masts in 655 the Copts who formed the ships' crews did not participate in the fighting, which was the responsibility of the Moslem soldiers; see Fahmy 1966b, pp103–106.

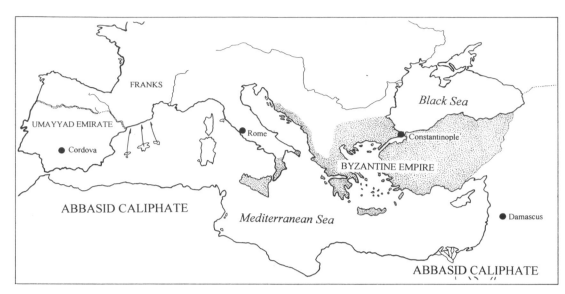

The major powers in the Mediterranean basin about AD 775. (Map by Frederick M Hocker, INA)

During the last half of the eighth century and the first quarter of the ninth, the Mediterranean was primarily a Byzantine lake. There was some resurrection of Syrian naval power, Charlemagne's Franks created a short-lived fleet based in northeastern Spain, and Venice began to exercise effective control in the northern Adriatic, but none of the putative challengers was strong enough to threaten Byzantine hegemony directly. Byzantium was weakened in the early 820s by the revolt of Thomas the Slav, assisted by the Aegean Themal fleet. The revolt was successfully put down, but the destruction of the Aegean fleet by the Imperial fleet cost the Empire ships it badly needed.

When the Arabs returned to the sea in force under the 'Abbassīd caliphs, they did so with deadly effect. In 827, exiled Spanish Arabs in Alexandria raised a fleet and sailed on Crete, which they managed to capture in short order. For a century and a half they were the scourge of Aegean commerce and a perpetual threat to Byzantine power, despite numerous attempts to dislodge them. In an even more disastrous development for Byzantium, 827 also marked the beginning of the Aghlabid Moslem conquest of Sicily, the key to control of the Western Mediterranean and the gateway to Byzantine possessions in Italy. The process was slow (the last pockets of resistance did not fall until 902), as Byzantine armies and fleets forced the conquerors to pay heavily for each port, but initial gains were helped by the defection of the Sicilian Themal fleet under Euphemios. By 831 the port of Palermo was in use as an advance base for further Moslem attacks on

Sicily; by 841 the Moslems were raiding the Italian mainland and into the Adriatic. It is in this period that the first mention of Arab vessels equipped with Greek Fire or a similar weapon occurs;[26] due partly to its use, Byzantine fleets sent to relieve Sicily were badly defeated in 840 and 859. Byzantine naval supremacy in the Mediterranean was broken, never to be fully restored, and Moslem ships, many of them independent pirates, controlled most of the Mediterranean outside of the Aegean and northern Adriatic Seas. Arab attacks on the Italian mainland led to the establishment of pirate bases in Calabria and Apulia. Added to the misery for the Empire in the west was a new threat from the north: ships of the Varangian Rus, Scandinavians working their way to the Black Sea by the rivers of Russia, besieged Constantinople in 860.

Byzantine fortunes revived somewhat under Basil I, assisted by Moslem dynastic turmoil in the Levant. A naval expedition in 879 defeated a large force of Cretan pirates, bringing sta-

The major powers in the Mediterranean basin about AD 923, near the apogee of Islamic naval strength. (Map by Frederick M Hocker, INA)

bility to the Aegean until the end of the century. Cyprus was briefly recovered, and the Empire was able to re-establish control over some of its former Italian Themes with an invasion under Nicephoros Phocas in the 880s. With Venetian assistance the pirates were ejected from Bari and Otranto.

The revival was short, for a large fleet sent from Constantinople in 888 was mauled north of Sicily, and Byzantium ceased to be a naval power west of Italy for more than thirty years. The first quarter of the tenth century was dominated in the East by the raids of Leo of Tripoli, who sacked Salonika in 904 and terrorised the Aegean and eastern Mediterranean from bases in Syria until 923. It was during the siege of Salonika that Leo employed the celebrated stratagem of lashing together the long lateen yards and quarter rudders of paired ships to form mobile siege towers.[27] The North African fleets were less trouble, as they were involved in the Fatimid struggle to conquer Egypt, but in the western Mediterranean the Moslems of Spain had taken to the sea to raid the coast of Provence since the 830s, and by the end of the century had established several bases on the Frankish coast. Fraxinetum was occupied from 888, and for more than ninety years allowed Moslem pirates to raid Provence more or less at will, although there seems to have been little or no development of organised naval forces until the tenth century.

This low point in Byzantine naval power, the high water mark of Moslem naval supremacy in

---

26. In 835, according to Ibn Al0Athîr VI, 289.

27. Described by an eyewitness, John Cameniates, in *De Ex. Thess MGH* CIX, 525–538.

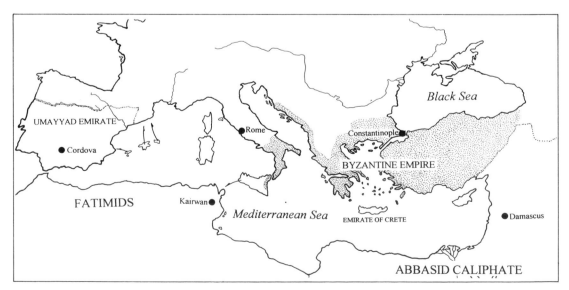

the Mediterranean, came to an end under the reign of Romanus Lecapenus. The destructive career of Leo of Tripoli was ended and the Byzantine fleets were enlarged and strengthened. Raids were sent to Egypt in 928, a large Russian fleet under Prince Igor of Kiev was destroyed in 941, and a strong but unsuccessful attempt was made to throw the Moslem pirates out of Crete in 949. Constantinople even managed to send a fleet to the Tyrrhenian Sea to attack Fraxinetum and, in 956, recaptured Naples. Under Romanus's successor, Nicephoros Phocas, Crete was finally recaptured in a huge assault (over 3300 ships in all) in 960, and Cyprus was taken in 963. The Moslems were driven out of their bases in Cilicia and northern Syria, and the Syrian fleets, for centuries one of the key elements of Moslem naval power in the eastern Mediterranean, ceased to be a threat to Byzantium. Despite the renewal of Byzantine activity in the East, naval activities in the western Mediterranean in the middle of the tenth century were dominated by the struggle between the Fatimids and Ommayids for control of western North Africa, a struggle in which Fatimid power was bolstered by its control of the Sicilian fleet. A Byzantine force did succeed in retaking Taormina and Rametta on Sicily, but in 965 the Fatimid navy defeated a large Byzantine fleet in the Straits of Messina. The Byzantine navy did not return in force to Italy until 1025.

The last third of the tenth century was occupied in the eastern Mediterranean by a Byzantine-Fatimid struggle for dominance in Syria. As Basil II was preoccupied with Bulgar and Russian threats to his north, as well as revolts in 976 and 987, the wars lacked much of a naval component until the very end of the century (998), when a Byzantine fleet was defeated off Tyre. The truce signed in 999 recognised an effective stalemate, and both Basil and his Fatimid counterparts turned their attentions inland for the next twenty years. In the West, Fatimid attacks on the Italian mainland increased, although the corsairs were evicted from Fraxinetum in 972. Naval opposition was led by Venice, foreshadowing one of the major developments of the next century.

While the first quarter of the eleventh century was relatively peaceful at sea, except on the Italian coast, where Sicilian-based Fatimid pirates continued to raid the Tyrrhenian and Adriatic coasts, the years 1025–1043 saw the last major fleet actions by both Byzantium and her Islamic opponents. In 1025, Basil sent a large force, supported by a fleet, to pacify Italy and recapture Sicily. A Moslem fleet, sent by the Ziridite Al-Mu'izz, was destroyed by

storms before it could meet the Byzantine ships in battle. Renewed hostilities in the East included a naval battle in 1035, in which one of the last Moslem fleets to appear in the eastern Mediterranean was defeated, and another Byzantine force, under George Maniaces, descended on Sicily in 1038. The Spanish Moslem navy that had dominated the northwestern Mediterranean for much of the later tenth century largely disappeared in the dynastic struggles following the death of the Ommayid Al-Mansūr, but the corsair fleet of Mugahid of Denia remained a threat to maritime traffic and the Italian coast into the 1040s.

The decline of Byzantine and Moslem naval power in the eleventh century is paralleled by the growth of Italian fleets. The city-states of the Ligurian coast, principally Genoa and Pisa, were able to repel attacks by Mugahid and began raiding Moslem strongholds in Italy and to the west. These small pirate raids were the first wave of maritime expansion that carried these cities and their Adriatic rival, Venice, to a dominant position in Mediterranean naval and economic life in the high Middle Ages.

Byzantine and Islamic fleet organisation

By the second half of the seventh century, Byzantine naval and military organisation was changing in response to the Persian and Arab invasion.[28] The Empire was divided into separate regions, called Themes, for defence and administration. Each Theme was under the civil and military control of a *strategos*, and was responsible for raising its own troops. Several of the maritime Themes were also responsible for building and manning fleets of warships. These armies and fleets supplemented the main Imperial forces based at Constantinople, and were normally subordinate to them. The principal naval Themes of the later seventh century were the Theme of the Kibyrrhaeots, raised on the southern coast of Asia Minor, the Aegean Theme, the Theme of Sicily, a Theme based at Ravenna, and possibly a short-lived African Theme. Each was commanded by an admiral, the *drungarios*, who had a fair amount of regional independence, but answered ultimately to the *strategos* of the Karabisians, who commanded the main Imperial fleet at Constantinople. Other, smaller Themes, such as those of Hellas, the Peloponnese, Pamphlagonia, and Cephallonia, also contributed ships, and some of the original Themes declined or disappeared by the eighth century, but the Kibyrrhaeots and Aegean Themal

fleets in the East and the Sicilian fleet in the West remained the core of regional naval power until the ninth century.

The system was an efficient method of defending the far-flung reaches of the empire, but could be turned on its masters, as the emperor discovered in 698, when the Kibyrrhaeot fleet rebelled and sailed on Constantinople. The rebels were defeated by the Imperial fleet. The problem recurred in 727, when the Themal fleets of Hellas and the Cyclades sailed on the capital, but once again the main Imperial fleet remained loyal and turned the new weapon of Greek Fire on the rebels. By the eighth century, the *drungarios* of the Kibyrrhaeots had been elevated to the rank of *strategos* (although this may also simply be part of the general trend of title inflation that plagued Byzantine administration), and the apparently superior position of the *strategos* of the Karabisians was abolished.

In the ninth century, the losses of Sicily and Crete required some reorganisation of the Themes. The Sicilian Theme continued to exist, at least on paper, until the fall of Taormina, the last Byzantine stronghold in Sicily, in 902, but its strength and usefulness declined noticeably. Byzantine naval operations in the western Mediterranean in the later ninth and tenth centuries usually involved elements of the Imperial fleet or other ships sent directly from Constantinople on specific expeditions. There is some evidence for small numbers of ships occasionally provided by the Themes of southern Italy, but for much of the later Byzantine period this area was in frequent dispute.

In the eastern Mediterranean, the Theme of the Kibyrrhaeots remained the primary bulwark against Syrian naval aggression, but Moslem advances had allowed bases quite far west in Cilicia, with a large force operating out of Tartus. After the recapture of Cyprus in the 960s, a base for the Kibyrrhaeots fleet was set up on the island, so that the fleet could more effectively counter the Syrian fleet. The Moslem capture of Crete in 827 greatly increased the danger to Aegean shipping, and so the Aegean Theme, based on the western side of the sea, was supplemented by a new Theme, that of Samos, on the eastern side. In addition, part of the Imperial fleet was based on the island of Mitylene to guard the approaches to the Hellespont and Constantinople. The supremacy of the commander of the Imperial

---

28. Byzantine fleet organisation is discussed in Lewis 1951, pp73–75 and 155–158, and at greater length in Eickhoff 1966, pp79–105. Moslem naval organisation is discussed in Eickhoff 1966, pp129–134 and above all in Fahmy 1966b.

fleet, now known as the *Drungarios* of the Ploimen, was reasserted by the second half of the ninth century.

The Arab arrangement of forces appears to be essentially similar under the Ommayids, with powerful regional fleets based in Syria, Egypt, and, after 700, North Africa, although the caliphs never seem to have developed a standing force similar to the Byzantine Imperial fleet. Partly, this is the result of geography; the Arab capitals (Damascus, Baghdad, Kairouan, Cairo) were usually inland or well up river, and so did not require a 'home fleet' to guard them, although there was a small flotilla stationed at the mouth of the Nile to protect the approaches. Another factor is the political structure of the caliphates, with strong centrifugal tendencies, both religious and political, encouraging the development of regionally independent sub-dynasties, which maintained their own navies. There are strong indications that in the first two centuries of Moslem naval activity ships and fleets were often more piratical than naval in character, and only after administrative structures grew up and matured was there a definitive move toward more professional standing navies. By the ninth century in some areas, such as Fatimid North Africa, and certainly by the tenth century in many places, Arab fleets were more closely modelled on the Byzantine navy, with ships built and maintained in government arsenals and commanded by professional officers. In Ommayid Spain, the admiral in command of the fleet was one of the great officials of the realm. Still, throughout the period of Islamic expansion, pirates and corsairs, privately sponsored but whose income could be taxed, were numerous, and could be employed to ravage shipping and harass coastlines ahead of more permanent invasions. Newly conquered coastal territories rapidly became forward bases for pirate fleets raiding farther into the economic core of the Byzantine Empire. Both Crete and Sicily became home to large raiding forces that harried shipping and coastal settlements on a regular basis, and the annexation of much of the southern coast of Asia Minor allowed the development of the port of Tartus as a base for the powerful Syrian fleet. After the conquest of

Spain, the ports of that Mediterranean coast became home to the Ommayid fleet and served as a staging point for first the plunder, and later the capture of the Balaeric Isles and coastal Provence.

Ships of the rival fleets

Byzantine galleys evolved from the Imperial Roman ships that preceded them, most probably from the liburnians that formed the backbone of later Roman fleets, and Islamic warships were developed originally by copying Byzantine examples. Later developments largely involved increases in the size of the ship and crew, which seems to be an almost universal tendency in organised navies. Major changes occurred in the specific details of how these ships were constructed during the period under discussion, and the development of incendiary weapons changed the way in which the ships were used, but the basic arrangement of a tenth-century Byzantine or Arab galley would have looked reasonably familiar to a first-century Roman admiral.

The workhorses of the Byzantine fleet, the 'ships of the line' that were intended to play the major part in pitched battles, were known as dromōns.[29] The term is in common use by the sixth century, when it refers to relatively fast, single-banked, decked ships. By the ninth century the term refers to double-banked ships without continuous decks. In the tenth century and after, the term is both a generic word for all galleys large enough to be included in the

line of battle and a specific term for the largest and most heavily-armed ships. The word refers to the speed that the earliest versions no doubt possessed, and hints at a possible relationship to the swift liburnians of Roman times.[30] Three main types of dromōn are reported in the tenth-century sources: the *ousiakos*, the *pamphylion* or *pamphylos*, and the *chelandion*. Each of these ships had two levels of oarsmen, with 25 benches per level the standard arrangement, for a total of 100 oars, working through ports in the side of the hull, without an outrigger. The primary distinction between types seems to be the number of crew assigned to each. The *ousiakos* was manned by a single *ousia* of 108 men, and thus cannot have had more than one man to an oar. As in all of the dromōns, the lower level of oarsmen were usually rowers only, while the men of the upper level were expected to fight, and were thus armed and armoured in some fashion. The *pamphylion* carried more men, up to an *ousia* and a half, so that there were twice as many men on the upper level to row and fight. The extra men were often picked fighters, sometimes foreigners. A *chelandion* was the largest type of dromōn (the term was interchangeable with *dromōn*), carried 200 oarsmen (three per oar on the upper level) and a total crew of up to

---

29. On Byzantine ship types, see Dolley 1948.

30. Early references to the type can be found in Procopius, *Bell Vand* I, 11.15–16, where he describes them as decked, single-banked ships, and Cassiodorus, *Varia* VI, 16. See also Casson 1971, p148.

The use of the square sail on seagoing vessels seems to have died out in late antiquity, but the chronology of its replacement by the lateen is still uncertain.
Unfortunately, this graffito of a lateen rigged craft, found on a roof tile at Thasos, has proved impossible to date precisely, and may be as early as the Hellenistic period or as late as the Byzantine. (From Lionel Casson, Ships and Seamanship in the Ancient World)

The author's hypothetical reconstruction of a tenth-century bireme dromōn, based on the few contemporary documentary sources. An Arab heavy warship would have looked similar in many respects. (Frederick M Hocker, INA)

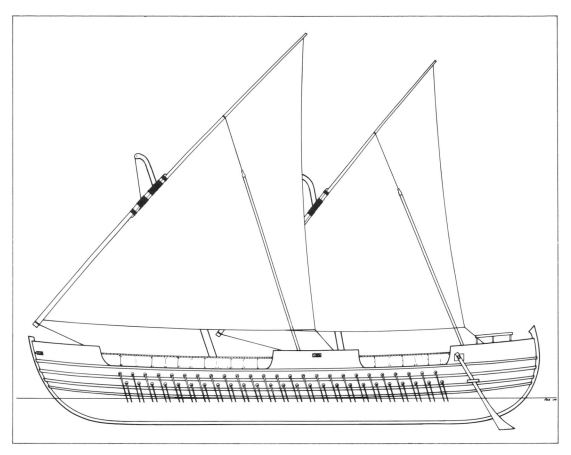

three *ousiai*, many of them heavily armed and armoured. Just to make matters more confusing, the term was also sometimes used in the tenth century as a synonym for *dromōn* in its more generic sense.[31]

In addition to the battleships, the navy made use of lighter galleys. Two terms, *moneres* and *galea*, survive for types of single-level galleys with minimal crew. These vessels were stout enough to be used at the end of the line of battle, but were more commonly used for their speed in a variety of scouting/reconnaissance roles. A diminutive form of *dromōn*, *dromonion* or *dromonarion*, appears in some sources,[32] but it is not clear if this term refers to a distinctive ship type.

Arab ships[33] were similar enough to Byzantine warships that they were often referred to as dromōns as well, in both Greek and Arab sources,[34] and the Greek terms *chelandion*, *galea*, and *dromonarion* also found their way into Arabic naval terminology, with *shalandi* one of the most common Arabic terms for large, dromōn-like ships.[35] Where they are distinguished in the Greek sources, the names most commonly applied are *koumbarion* for the large ships and *satouron* for the small. The main Arab ships were considered to be larger, higher, heavier, and slower than their Byzantine opponents. Generally, the Arabic sources are less definitive, with most of the names applied to warships varying little from generic terms for watercraft. Types that do appear to be more specific, besides *shalandi*, include *shīnī* (or *shīniyya* or *shāni*) and *ghurāb* (possibly derived from the Greek *karabos*) for galleys and *musattah* for a type of large, decked galley common in later periods, especially during the Crusades. Another Arabic type of note is the *harrāqa*, or 'fire ship', which is the type most often equipped with Greek fire.

The dimensions of Byzantine and Arab dromons and other warships are almost entirely unknown to us. The eleventh-century Persian traveller Nasir-i-Khusru observed the remains of a huge ship in Egypt (part of the fleet of al-Mu'izz, abandoned during his attack on Egypt in 969), and noted its dimensions as nearly 85m long and 35m in beam (280ft by 115ft),[36] but these dimensions hardly seem credible for a warship. An estimate of typical length may be derived from the number of rowing benches, as it has been accepted that

the minimum *interscalmium*, or distance from thole to thole, should be in the region of one metre for maximum efficiency (although some Viking longships of the same period managed with an *interscalmium* of as little as 0.78m, 2½ft, or even less).[37] At an *interscalmium* of one metre (3¼ft), which makes sense if the structure to support two levels of oarsmen has to be accommodated as well as the men themselves, the rowing space for a 25-bench ship such as a dromōn requires about 26m, if the two levels of oars are staggered. The ends beyond this are entirely conjectural, but the total overall length probably lay between 35m and 40m (115ft–130ft). The beam is even more difficult to estimate, but the practicalities of propelling ships by human power necessitate a narrow form, and length-to-beam ratios as fine as 10:1 are not unknown for some galley types. Ancient *triēreis* were just under 6m (20ft) in beam at the outrigger,[38] and this is not a bad measurement for a vessel that carries marines and projectile weapons on deck.

Anon PBPP provides an apparently detailed account of the construction of dromōns, but the author says in his introduction that his work is a compilation from existing works, and the text makes it clear that some of these works were quite old.[39] On the other hand, some components, such as the Greek Fire apparatus, are certainly contemporary, and other terms

are still in use in modern Greek. Excavated wrecks of medieval merchant ships, particularly the seventh-century ship at Yassi Ada[40] and the early eleventh-century ship at Serçe Limanı (both in Turkey),[41] also provide some clarification of how shipbuilding in general had changed since Roman times.

As in most Mediterranean sea-going ships since the end of the Bronze Age, the 'foundation' of the ship's structure was the keel (*tropis*), which provided primary longitudinal support

31. See, for example, the inventory from the 949 expedition to Crete; Constantine Porphyrogenitus, *De Caeremoniis* II, 45.

32. For example, Leo, *Tactica* XIX, 82. Dolley 1948, p53 believes they are a distinct type, the 'forgotten ships of the East Roman Navy', but he admits that the term may be a *demotiki* corruption in at least one later tenth-century source.

33. On Arab warships, see Fahmy 1966b, pp125–137.

34. Fahmy 1966b, pp125–126.

35. Fahmy 1966b, pp130–131.

36. Lewis 1951, p191.

37. Olsen and Crumlin-Pedersen 1967, pp115, 141.

38. Based on the width of the remains of the sheds in which they were kept for the winter; see Chapter 3 above.

39. *Anon PBPP* Preamble, 10. See also references to Homer throughout section 1, as well as the references to *triēreis*, a ship type no longer in use, in 1.2 and 2.7.

40. Bass and van Doorninck 1982, pp32–86.

41. Steffy 1982 and 1991.

to the hull and to which the frames (*engkoilia*) were attached. Even in small ships, it was usually necessary to assemble the keel from several pieces, although one might expect the state to have access to superior timber resources. Still, a scarphed keel is a certainty for a ship 35m or more in length. According to *PBPP*, the forward piece of the keel was called *proembolis* (which in ancient times referred to a small, secondary ram mounted on the stem above the waterline) and the aftermost piece *podostema*, although the text is not clear if this refers to a component or an area in the stern.

In contrast to ancient Mediterranean ships, in which the primary structure of the hull was the shell of planking, fastened together with thousands of individually pegged mortise-and-tenon joints, by the tenth century ships relied on the frames for a much larger proportion of their hull strength. The ancient method produced hulls that were tremendously strong and very good at distributing local stress (such as the shock of ramming), but it was expensive in terms of materials and especially labour. Frames had been in use since at least Classical times to strengthen the shell, and the Roman period saw an increase in frame size and greater thoroughness in their fastening to the shell. The use of mortise-and-tenon joints had atrophied late in the Roman period, and by the seventh century they were nearly vestigial. They were no longer pegged, and thus did not hold the planks together in an integrated shell or semi-monocoque, but served only to align the plank edges during construction. By the eleventh century, merchant ships were built without any such joints, and the design and construction process had moved largely, although not completely, away from heavy reliance on the shell. It is significant for warships, although not at all surprising, that even though the author of *PBPP* was familiar with classical literature, and his list of ship terms is reasonably thorough, he includes no terms that can be construed to refer to mortise-and-tenon joints.

Certain heavy planks, called wales (*peritona*),

were still important, especially in a long, narrow ship, and these are given quite a lot of attention in *PBPP*. There are at least two sets of these, one below each row of oarports, and they are responsible for 'holding together the sides from without'.[42] In addition, the strakes (two on each side) through which the oarports (*trēmata*) pass, the 'window planks' (*thyrea*), are specifically mentioned. These may have been noticeably thicker than the other planks in order to handle the stresses imposed by the oars. The oarports themselves were kept reasonably watertight by a piece of leather fastened to the opening in the plank and tied around the oar. The author gives both the ancient term for this gasket (*askoma*) and the Byzantine term (*maniskellion*).

Some ships were decked throughout, like Roman warships, but others were open amidships,[43] with only partial decks (*sanidomata*) down the sides and a central gangway (*sterea*). The upper bank of rowers sat above this deck, so that they could join the fray more easily, but the lower bank sat below. The deck rested on beams (*hermata*), and there were throughbeams (*epotides*) in the stern to support the two quarter rudders (*pēdalia*) with which the ship was steered.

Superstructures included an enclosed and decked over forecastle (*xylokastron*), which housed the main Greek Fire siphon, called the 'raven' (*katakoraks*). The forecastle had a parapet around the upper deck to protect the marines stationed there in battle. Another parapeted castle (*kastellōma*) was built amidships, or around the middle mast, or around the middle of the mast (the texts are not clear),[44] from which marines could bombard the enemy or fire down into his decks. A structure of sorts (*kravatos*) was erected in the stern

to shelter the captain of the ship, but it had to allow him a wide view of the battle, and his men had to be able to see him standing there resolute and courageous.[45] The upper works were further protected by hides and metal sheathing nailed over the wood.

It has been suggested, on the basis of one of the entries in the inventory of equipment sent with the 949 fleet to Crete,[46] that Byzantine warships were sheathed in lead, in the same manner as ancient merchant ships.[47] This is unlikely, as the amount of lead specified, 150 pounds (about 50 kilograms) per ship, is insufficient to sheath even a small hull completely.[48] Instead, the lead must have been carried for patching, a use documented on Mediterranean wrecks since the fifth century BC,[49] although it is possible that it was intended for covering the upperworks to protect against enemy missiles, as described in *PBPP*; the following entry in the list is hides for this purpose. Byzantine galleys were generally well equipped with spares and supplies for repairs, including timber for frames and planks, extra spars, tow, pitch, and plenty of rigging spares.[50] It was also recom-

---

42. *Anon PBPP* 2, 11–12, also 2,1.

43. *Anon PBPP* 2,6.

44. Leo, *Tactica* XIX, 7.

45. Leo, *Tactica* XIX, 8.

46. Constantine Porphyrogenitus, *De Caeremoniis* II, 45 is the passage; see Dolley 1948, p51 for an older, influential interpretation.

47. For an example of lead sheathing on an ancient merchant vessel, see Steffy 1985, pp98–99.

48. The sheathing on the Kyrenia ship, a Hellenistic merchant vessel less than 15m long, weighed over 200kg; J R Steffy personal communication.

49. Eiseman and Ridgway 1987, pp11, 16.

50. Leo, *Tactica* XIX, 5.

Diagram showing evolution of mortise-and-tenon joint. 'A' is typical Graeco-Roman joinery, with large, closely-spaced, tightly fitted joints. 'B' is similar to the smaller, more loosely fitting, more widely spaced joints found on the late fourth-century shipwreck at Yassi Ada, Turkey. 'C', with its small, infrequent, unpegged tenons, is found on late sixth- and seventh-century ships, such as the Byzantine wreck excavated at Yassi Ada. Note that as the mortise-and-tenon joints become less important, the planking becomes thinner as well. (Frederick M Hocker, INA)

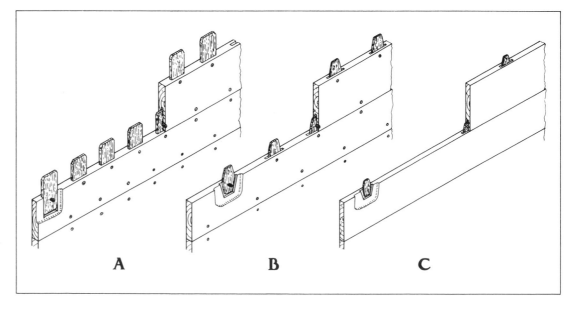

A   **B**   **C**

Underwater archaeology has yet to discover a dromōn wreck, and in the absence of a warship hull assumptions about structure have to be based on what is known about contemporary merchantmen. In 1973 the wreck of a small trading vessel was discovered at Serçe Liman on the Turkish southern coast; the sinking could be dated to 1024 or 1025 but it is not clear if the ship was Byzantine or Muslim. The principal interest in the surviving structure was the absence of mortise-and-tenon edge joints, the hull shape being determined by a partial system of internal frames. The floor timbers are shown here in the process of excavation and recording by a team from the American Institute of Nautical Archaeology. (Photo by Robin C M Piercy, INA; by courtesy of Frederick M Hocker)

mended that one of the rowers be a trained carpenter/shipwright (*naupegos*), and that he have his tools with him.[51]

In addition to the oars, sails were used to propel dromōns. These were almost certainly lateen sails, set on masts (*katartia*) stepped in separate blocks (*trapezai*) fixed to the spine of the ship. *PBPP* suggests that there was only a

The remains of the Serçe Liman vessel displayed on a steel frame at the Bodrum Museum of Underwater Archaeology. The relatively square bilge section would have been impossible to contrive with the traditional edge-jointed construction, but was easy to build with the partial frame-first method used for this ship. There is no firm evidence that dromōns employed similar techniques, but since they were not expected to use ramming tactics they certainly had no need of the light but shock-resistant mortise-and-tenon construction of classical galleys. (Photo by Don Frey, INA; by courtesy of Frederick M Hocker, INA)

single mast and sail, but other texts make it clear that two masts were the order of the day for most medieval Mediterranean ships, both merchant and military.

Crews

In the Byzantine navy, the commander of the fleet is generally addressed in the tactical manuals as *strategos*, as he is presumably the commander of the Imperial fleet. Themal fleet commanders are called either *drungarioi*, *tourmarchai*, or *strategoi*, and Leo informs us that in his day they were supposed to be subordinate to the *strategos* of the Imperial fleet, even though they may also be called *strategoi*. The *strategos* was responsible for the disposition of the fleet, for directing war councils, and formulating strategy and tactics. He was also responsible for seeing that the fleet was properly outfitted and provisioned for the campaign. He did not command the entire fleet directly, but appointed intermediate commanders (*archontes*) who had to be of the rank of *comes* and who commanded not only their own individual ships but small squadrons of three to five ships. The *strategos* was advised to sail on a flagship which was a large, fast *pamphylos*, the pride of the fleet, manned by picked men, and the *archontes* should also choose outstanding ships and superior crews.

The individual ship commander is variously referred to as *navarch* or *kentarch* (leader of a hundred, *ie* the oar crew), and in some of the more classicising sources, even *trierarch* or *keubernetes*. He was assisted by an executive officer, the 'holder of the banner', two helmsmen (*protokaraboi*), and a bow officer (*proreos*). The oar crew included two specialists, the two bow oarsmen on the upper level. One (the *siphonator*) was responsible for the Greek Fire, the other for casting the anchors. Commanders were advised to pick the crew for the upper deck carefully, so that the best and bravest fighters would be in the front lines and the cowardly were relegated to the lower deck as reserves. All of the deck crew exposed to battle were at least lightly armoured and armed, so that all could participate in the battle.

Fleet commanders of Arab navies had varied titles, depending on the duty of the fleet; for example, the admiral of the Spanish convoy fleet was the *Amīr-Al-Rahl* (the title from which the English 'admiral' is derived, although it is possible that the Moslems borrowed the term from medieval Spanish to begin with).[52] A generic term for admiral is *almilland*. One of the 'Abbāsid caliphs of the tenth century outlined the duties of fleet commanders in a set of official instructions, advising his admiral on the selection and treatment of crews, the construction and anchoring of

---

51. Leo, *Tactica* XIX, 5.

52. See Fahmy 1966b, p139.

ships, and the proper measures to be taken to maintain security, while still spying on the enemy.[53] Ship captains (*ra'īs*) were in charge of navigation and anchorage, but direct command of the sailors (*nawātiya*, from the Greek *nauta*) was vested in a warrant officer of sorts, the *qā'id al-nawātiya*, the 'chief of the sailors', who was responsible for maintaining the ship's weaponry and directing the crew in battle.[54] This arrangement may be ultimately derived from the early Arab practice of recruiting the sailing crew from the Coptic and Syrian population, but the soldiers from the Moslem army. It should be noted that Arabic naval terminology in the Mediterranean differs markedly from that in the Indian Ocean and Persian Gulf.

Weapons and tactics

The tactical manuals are full of advice for *strategoi* on managing their fleets, planning campaigns, preparing for combat, and directing the battle, but it is important to remember that the model for these manuals is Leo's *Tactica*, which was written during one of the low points in Byzantine naval fortunes. The outlook favoured by Leo emphasises husbanding resources and avoiding pitched battles, rather than the aggressive strategies that marked the successful campaigns of emperors before and after him. Still, Leo had the benefit of centuries of naval tradition to draw on, and there is probably much in his work that was standard practice in the previous century.

Leo's primary theme is the importance of preparation. Commanders are exhorted to drill their ships so that manoeuvres are executed accurately, efficiently, and consistently. *Strategoi* are expected to acquire accurate intelligence on the size, composition, and disposition of enemy forces before going into battle, and to know the waters in which they will do battle. Councils of war should be held beforehand, so that all ships know their responsibilities, and a complex system of signals, using flags, something similar to modern-day shapes, and lanterns at night, are to be used to communicate changes in orders. Ships are expected to keep station exactly, so that battle plans could be carried out to the letter. Individual initiatives by ship commanders are discouraged in fleet actions, as

success depended on a 'team' effort. In many ways, the general policies advocated by Leo the Wise presage the practices of modern navies.

A secondary theme is prudence and preservation of the fleet. Full-scale battles are to be avoided. If possible, the enemy fleet should be divided or attacked before it can assemble, so that ships can be picked off singly or in small groups. Commanders should take advantage of misfortune, such as shipwreck, storm, or grounding, that befalls the enemy, and do everything to encourage misfortune. Commanders should not go into battle without a decided advantage in numbers and position, the advantage confirmed by thorough intelligence. It is these admonitions more than any others in the *Tactica* that reflect the defensive, demoralised outlook of the Byzantine navy during Leo's reign; however, if war could not be avoided, it should be 'total war', in which no resources were spared, no punches pulled in the effort to attain a decisive victory.

In fleet actions, commanders were advised to choose the site carefully: if fighting off the enemy's coast, fight near the shore, so that his sailors or soldiers will be encouraged to jump ship for the safety of the shore; by the same token, if fighting off your own shore, stay well out to sea to avoid the same problem. If fighting in open water, a crescent formation with the heaviest ships at the ends and the flagship in the middle was often favoured, with the hope of encircling the enemy. Other tactics suggested by Leo included a line abreast formation to take advantage of the power of Greek Fire, ambuscades, and the feigned retreat to draw the enemy into an ambush.

The *Tactica* of Nicephoros Ouranos provides more detailed descriptions of different formations for fleet actions, as well as instructions on how best to execute and counter those formations. For example, the crescent formation

could be countered by splitting the force and outflanking the horns of the crescent, or by sending a small force into the crescent as 'bait', then surrounding the enemy after he had closed around the smaller force. A reverse crescent could also be used, with the heavier ships in the middle and the medium ships behind them. While fighting 'by the book' was encouraged, improvisation and unconventional tactics were not unknown. Leo encouraged commanders to have rowers trained to swim and dive, so that they might sabotage enemy ships. Both Nicephoros Ouranos and Leo acknowledged that once the battle started, plans would have to be changed and it would be up to the *strategos* to evaluate the situation and respond accordingly.

Arab tactics do not seem to have differed significantly from Byzantine models (Leo's *Tactica* was translated into Arabic[55]), although there is less direct evidence for Moslem tactical thinking. It is hard to imagine the Cretan, Syrian or Sicilian fleets, with their pirate heritage and tradition of aggressive attack, settling for the defensive or passive mindset seen in Leo's *Tactica*. On the other hand, Leo indicates that a tactic of which Byzantine commanders had to beware was a willingness to wait and allow the opponent to exhaust himself firing missiles at the high, strong sides of the Arab *koumbaria* before sweeping in for the kill.[56] The looser organisation of Moslem fleets also suggests that there may have been less reliance on the complex signalling advocated by Leo.

53. The source (*Kitāb Al-Kharāj*) is a manuscript in the Kuprili Library, Istanbul; see Fahmy 1966b, pp140–142.

54. Ibn Khaldūn, *Muqaddima* II provides a detailed listing of the titles and responsibilities of different naval ranks in the later Islamic period.

55. Christides 1984.

56. Leo, *Tactica* XIX, 15.

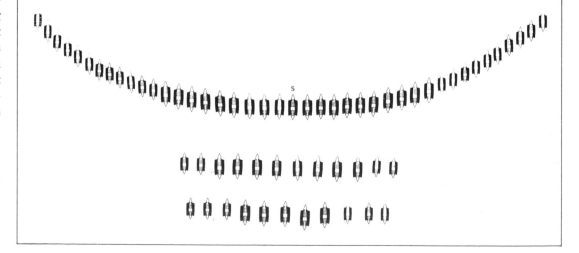

A small fleet arrayed in the crescent tactical formation often used by Byzantine navies, with a reserve kept behind the crescent. The larger ships are kept towards the centre, with smaller, faster ships on the wings to sweep out and surround the opposing force. The 'S' denotes the position of the strategos, *the supreme commander.* (Frederick M Hocker, INA)

An illustration from an eleventh-century manuscript of an amphibious siege. The ships are lashed together in pairs to form platforms for battering rams and assault bridges; these look very precarious but the Venetians are known to have used similar devices in their successful scaling of the sea walls of Constantinople in 1204. Acting as pontoons, the hulls have neither oars nor a sailing rig, but the details of bow and stern shapes have many parallels in the iconography. (Biblioteca Apostolica Vaticana, Rome)

Once the battle was joined, it was up to the individual crews fighting ship-to-ship battles to prevail through superior weaponry, skill, and determination. Of course, the weapon for which the Byzantine fleets are most widely known and for which they were most widely feared was Greek Fire, an inflammable liquid discharged through a metal-sheathed tube (*siphon*). This may have been invented or discovered as early as the sixth century, when a flammable compound was used by Marinus against the usurper Vitalian. The 'official' introduction of Greek Fire, in the form in which it was most commonly used by later Byzantine fleets, is traditionally dated to the first Arab siege of Constantinople in 673–679. The invention is credited to Callinicus, a Syrian living in Constantinople. The exact nature of the mixture is unknown, but it has been recently suggested that the key ingredient was naphtha or a similar petroleum product collected and distilled from natural crude oil seepages.[57] The resulting liquid may have had a similar consistency and effect to modern napalm, and would have been every bit as devastating as the medieval sources suggest. It rarely seems to have failed.

Most ships carried a single large siphon in the bow, but larger vessels sometimes carried up to three, with a pair mounted at the sides. The operation of the siphon required a specialist, the *siphonator*, and the main siphon itself was carefully protected inside the forecastle. There were also small, portable siphons which could be used in boarding actions. There is some evidence that Greek fire was not widely distributed throughout the navy, but was usually limited to the Imperial fleet at Constantinople.[58] This may have been for reasons of security, to prevent the weapon falling into enemy hands, or due to difficulties in supplying large quantities of the unstable materials from which it was made. The Arabs did eventually obtain the secret, or succeeded in developing their own version in the ninth century. The first mention of Arab *harrāqas* equipped with its occurs in 835, and it has been suggested that the Byzantine traitor Euphemios, the *strategos*

of the Sicilian Theme, may have carried the secret with him when he went over to the Arabs in 827.[59]

In addition to their ultimate weapon, Byzantine ships carried a wide variety of 'conventional' projectile weapons, from hand-held bows and crossbows firing small bolts called 'flies' (*muiai*) to small catapults and large, mounted crossbows (*toxoballistrai*). The catapults could launch stones, pots of Greek Fire or quicklime, or containers full of scorpions or other venomous creatures. The last receives a fair amount of comment in histories of the Byzantine navy, but it is difficult to imagine that a bowl full of vipers was a more practical projectile than a good stone or a pot of flaming oil. Caltrops were also thrown on to the enemy's decks, and Leo encouraged ships to carry stones that could be thrown at the enemy.

When ships reached grappling range and the hand-to-hand fighting began, some ships carried cranes that could be used to drop large stones into the hold of the enemy, but the fight was primarily in the hands of heavily armed and armoured troops, called in the manuals *hoplites* (in good classical style) or *kataphractoi*. After softening up the opposition with projectile weapons, and possibly using long spears to stab the enemy rowers through their own oar-ports, the marines would wade into the melée with spear, sword and shield, or if boarding was not desired, they would use long poles to push the enemy ship away before it could grapple

successfully. Leo also advocates the use of a secret pumping device which could be used to fill the enemy ship with water.[60]

One weapon long associated with galleys does not appear to have been commonly used by Byzantine or Arab ships, and that is the ram. Although deliberate ramming and sinking at the battle of Sena Gallica in 551 are reported by Procopius,[61] there is no mention of waterline rams in the texts from the seventh century onward, not even in the detailed listing of ship parts in *Anon PBPP*, which favours archaic terminology. The *proembolis* mentioned in that text might be construed to refer to a projection at the forward end of the keel, but there is no indication that this component was intended as a weapon. The abandonment of mortise-and-tenon joinery may be another indication of the rarity of ramming, as the frame-based construction of the Byzantine period is poorly suited to distributing the shock of delivering a ramming blow. A passage in Leo's *Tactica*,[62] which describes a manoeuvre involving a deliberate collision between ships, has been inter-

57. Haldon and Byrne 1977; Pászthory 1986.

58. Lewis 1951, pp71–72.

59. Lewis 1951, p134.

60. Leo, *Tactica* XIX, 71.

61. Procopius, *Bel Goth* VIII, 23.34.

62. Leo, *Tactica* XIX, 69.

preted as describing ramming,[63] but a careful reading of the original Greek reveals that the purpose of the attack, which requires two ships, was not to puncture the hull of the enemy, but to roll it on to its side and swamp it.[64]

Conclusions

It many ways the Roman Empire marks a definite break in the development of galleys and warships in general. The drastic change in naval policy from massive Hellenistic fleets, technological embodiments of expansionist political ambitions, to a waterborne police force had far-reaching consequences not only in the choice of warship types but also in the role of naval power. The pattern of an established power trying to curtail or suppress pirate activity governed not only later Roman naval his-

tory, but, on a larger scale, the first century or more of the struggle between Byzantium and Islam.

The long centuries of Roman rule meant that, when fleet actions resumed, the vessels employed were smaller, two-banked ships with one man to an oar, modelled after what was originally a pirate raider. Even after the development of large dromōns late in the first millennium, ships were still smaller and more lightly manned than Octavian's sixes. These ships were cheaper to build and man than the big polyremes of the end of the Hellenistic arms race, not only because of their size, but because of their simplified construction. For the same expenditure, more ships could be put into the field and lost vessels could be replaced with less hardship. Large fleets could be built relatively quickly, theoretically giving their owners more flexibility in naval planning and response than their ancient predecessors.

That flexibility was needed in the changed political reality of the later first millennium. Rather than many small powers each maintaining a single fleet in a limited area, or a single power organising regular patrols of an immense area, the seventh through tenth centuries saw two or three major powers struggling for dominance in several theatres. Both the Byzantine and Arab states rapidly set-

tled on a policy of regional fleets with primarily regional responsibilities, although the Byzantines also maintained the Imperial fleet, which could be sent out to reinforce the Themal fleets or in response to specific needs. To a certain degree, this was a logical outgrowth of the organisation of the Roman 'police' navy, but was developed by the Byzantines at their peak in the later eighth century into a financially efficient and militarily effective force on a much more elaborate scale. Meanwhile, the caliphs and their dependents, already unavoidably limited to a regional style of government, combined the efficiency of the Byzantine system with the aggressive, daring military tradition that had carried them out of the desert and into the Middle Sea to produce fleets capable of defeating the might of Byzantium and dominating three-quarters of the Mediterranean in the middle of the tenth century.

Frederick M Hocker

63. Dolley 1948, p49 and 1953, p331. This interpretation was accepted without question by later scholars such as Fahmy (1966a, p168), Eickhoff (1966, p166), and Casson (1971, p152).

64. Van Doorninck 1993 discusses the manoeuvre and Leo's text in detail, and provides a clearer translation of *Tactica* XIX, 69.

Acknowledgements

I would like to thank Professor Morrison; I am deeply honoured to be asked by a scholar of his stature to contribute to this book. I would also like to thank Frederick van Doorninck, Jr, from whose knowledge of Byzantine maritime history I have benefited as both a student and as a colleague.

References used in the footnotes

G F Bass and F H van Doorninck, Jr (1982), *Yassi Ada I: A Seventh-Century Byzantine Shipwreck* (College Station, Texas).

L Casson (1971), *Ships and Seamanship in the Ancient World* (Princeton).

V Christides (1984), 'Naval warfare in the eastern Mediterranean. An Arabic translation of Leo VI's *Naumachica*', *Graeco-Arabica* 3, pp137–148.

A Dain (1943), *Naumachica* (Paris).

R Dolley (1953), 'Naval tactics in the heyday of the Byzantine thalassocracy', in *Atti dell' VIII Congresso di Studi Bizantini*, pp324–339 (Rome).

R Dolley (1948), 'The warships of the later Roman Empire', *Journal of Roman Studies* 38, pp47–53.

F H van Doorninck, Jr (1993), 'Did tenth-century dromons have a waterline ram? Another look at Leo, *Tactica*, XIX, 69', *The Mariner's Mirror* 79, pp387–392.

E Eickhoff (1966), *Seekrieg und Seepolitik zwischen Islam und Abendland* (Berlin).

C J Eiseman and B S Ridgway (1987), *The Porticello Shipwreck: A Mediterranean Merchant Vessel of 415–385 BC* (College Station, Texas).

A M Fahmy (1966a), *Muslim Sea-Power in the Eastern Mediterranean* (2nd ed, Cairo).

A M Fahmy (1966b), *Muslim Naval Organization in the Eastern Mediterranean from the Seventh to the Tenth Century AD* (Cairo).

J Haldon and M Byrne (1977), 'A possible solution to the

problem of Greek Fire', *Byzantinische Zeitschrift* 70, pp91–99.

J Haywood (1991), *Dark Age Naval Power: A Reassessment of Frankish and Anglo-Saxon Seafaring Activity* (London and New York).

O Höckmann (1984) 'Darstellungen von Ruderschiffen auf zwei römischen Ziegelstampen aus Mainz', *Archäologisches Korrespondenzblatt* 14, pp319–324.

O Höckmann (1986), 'Römische Schiffsverbände auf dem Ober- und Mittelrhein und der Verteidigung der Rheingrenze in der Spätantike', *Jahrbuch des römisch-germanischen Zentralmuseums*, pp33, 369–416.

O Höckmann (1990), 'Römische Schiffsfunde westlich des Kastells Oberstimm', *Bericht der römisch-germanischen Kommission* 70, pp321–347.

O Höckmann (1993) 'Late Roman Rhine vessels from Mainz, Germany', *International Journal of Nautical Archaeology* 22, pp125–135.

E Hollstein (1982), 'Dendrochronologie der römerzeitlichen Schiffe von Mainz', in G Rupprecht, *Die Mainzer Römerschiffe: Berichte über Entdeckung, Ausgrabung und Bergung*, pp114–123 (Mainz).

A R Lewis (1951), *Naval Power and Trade in the Mediterranean AD 500–1100* (Princeton).

P Marsden (1974), 'The County Hall ship, London', *International Journal of Nautical Archaeology* 3, pp55–65.

Fz S Muller (1895), 'Verslag van de opgravingen van Romeinsche oudheden te Vechten . . .', in *Verslag van het verhadelde in de Algemeene Vergadering van het Pronviciaal*

Utrechts Genootschap van Kunsten en Wetenschappen, Gehouden den 25 Juni 1895, pp129–142 and 160–161 (Utrecht).

W M Murray and Ph H Petsas (1988), 'Octavian's Campsite Memorial for the Actium War', *Transactions of the American Philosophical Society* 79/4, (Philadelphia).

W M Murray and Ph H Petsas (1989), 'The spoils of Actium', *Archaeology* 41/4, pp27–35.

O Olsen and O Crumlin-Pedersen (1967), 'The Skuldelev ships (II): A report of the final underwater excavation in 1959 and the salvaging operation in 1962', *Acta Archaeologica* 38, pp73–174.

S Panciera (1956), 'Liburna', *Epigraphica* 18, pp130–156.

E Pászthory (1986), 'Über das "Griechische Feuer" ', *Antike Welt* 17, pp27–37.

G Rupprecht (1982), *Die Mainzer Römerschiffe: Berichte über Entdeckung, Ausgrabung und Bergung* (Mainz).

J R Steffy (1982), 'The Reconstruction of the 11th century Serçe Liman vessel. A preliminary report', *International Journal of Nautical Archaeology* 11, pp13–34.

J R Steffy (1985), 'The Kyrenia ship: An interim report on its hull construction', *American Journal of Archaeology* 89, pp71–101.

J R Steffy (1991), 'The Mediterranean shell to skeleton transition: A northwest European parallel?' in *Carvel Construction Technique: Fifth International Symposium on Boat and Ship Archaeology, Amsterdam 1988*, pp1–9, eds H R Reinders and C Paul (Oxford).

M de Weerd (1988), *Schepen voor Zwammerdam* (Amsterdam).

7

From Dromōn to Galea: Mediterranean bireme galleys AD 500–1300

At sea in the Mediterranean, the transition from antiquity to the Middle Ages was marked by the replacement of the classical Greek trireme (*triērēs*) and Roman bireme (*liburna*) by the Byzantine *dromōn*.[1] The earliest specific mention of dromōns is in papyrus charters from Ravenna dated to the late fifth century, but from the sixth century the sources which refer to this ship type proliferate rapidly: John the Lydian in *On the magistracies*, Cassiodorus in his *Letter collection*, John Malalas in his *Encyclicon*, the emperor Justinian in a rescript of AD 534, and the *Strategicon* of Maurice, amongst others. But the first source to give any detail of the ship type is the *History of the Wars* by the great Byzantine courtier and historian Procopius of Caesarea, who accompanied general Belisarios as his secretary on the Byzantine expedition to Vandal Africa in AD 533. He wrote of the fleet that:

> And they had also ships of war prepared as for sea-fighting, to the number of ninety-two, and they were single-banked ships covered by decks, in order that the men rowing them might if possible not be exposed to the bolts of the enemy. Such boats are called *dromōnes* by those of the present time; for they are able to attain a great speed. In these sailed two thousand men of Byzantium, who were all rowers as well as fighting men.[2]

When first developed, the dromōn was a monoreme cataphract galley with a full deck to protect the oarsmen beneath it.[3] Whether it had square sails as had the *triērēs* and *liburna* of antiquity or whether it already had the lateen sails of medieval galleys, Procopius does not make clear. He refers to Belisarios's own ship as a *naus* (generic for ship) rather than as a dromōn but he does write that 'the sails (*histia*) of the three ships (*nēes*) in which he [Belisarios] and his following were carried he painted red from the upper corner for about a third of their length.'[4]

This passage has been widely considered to indicate that the sails of at least part of the

Sixth-century sailing ships on a mosaic from S Apollinare Nuovo, Ravenna show that the square sail survived at least that late in the Mediterranean, although it seems to have disappeared thereafter, being replaced exclusively by fore-and-aft rigs – and in particular the lateen – until the square sail was re-introduced into the area from northern Europe in the fourteenth century.

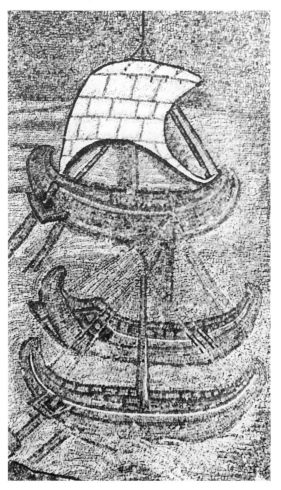

Byzantine fleet, perhaps including the dromōns, were triangular; that is, lateen. Although the square sail survived in the Mediterranean into the sixth century, from that time on it disappeared until re-introduced from Northern Europe in the fourteenth century.

The dromōn was the product of a fourfold evolution: firstly, demonstration of the superiority of faster monoremes over biremes and triremes in the context of changing requirements for naval warfare after the defeat of Licinius by Constantine at the battle of the Hellespont in AD 324; secondly, evolution of the square sail into a lateen by a process of setting the sails more fore-and-aft than square and then tailoring the luff and leech; thirdly, application of the fully decked cataphract concept to a monoreme; and last, replacement of the underwater ram (*embolos* or *rostrum*) by an above-water 'spur' (medieval Latin *calcar* or *speronus*). The purpose of this change in the

---

1. Throughout this chapter I have used the terms 'monoreme', 'bireme', and 'trireme' to refer to galleys rowing one, two, or three files of oars on each side, irrespective of the arrangement of the oarsmen's benches on different levels and of the number of oarsmen on the same bench. So also I have used the word 'galley' generically to apply to oared ships of every kind, except where the specific type of *galea* is discussed.

2. Procopius of Caesarea, *History of the Wars: Book III. The Vandalic War*, xi.15-16, in H B Dewing ed & trans, *Procopius*, vol 2 (London 1916), p105. The 2000 men cannot have been all the oarsmen. Battle dromōns must have had many more than the 22 or so oarsmen each that this figure would give. They must have been marines taken aboard in addition to the other oarsmen.

3. Procopius used the word '*orophas*', literally a 'roof' or 'ceiling', rather than *katastrōma*, the conventional word for the half-deck of a *triērēs*. He was using literary, rather than technical, language, but probably used a word for a complete covering because these were full rather than half decks. Some Roman cataphract triremes had also had full decks, but the important innovation appears to have been to give a monoreme a full deck. See L Casson, *Ships and Seamanship in the Ancient World* (Princeton 1971), pp52–4, 74–6, 123–4, 142–3, 148.

4. *Ibid*, xiii.3.

The earliest known depiction of a dromōn is in this fifth-century 'Roman' manuscript of the Aeneid by Virgil. The original is in the Vatican Library, Rome. (Vatican Library, Cod Lat Vat 3867, fol 77).

have a lateen sail with the slope of the yard towards the bow reversed through artistic ignorance, and that in the foreground has a broken mast.[5] The sail could equally as well be lateen if imagination is used to restore the mast to its unbroken state. Plate XXVII of the *Iliad* manuscript, in the print of the 1819 edition by Angelo Mai, clearly shows lateen sails.[6] This is the only miniature of the codex which shows unfurled lateen sails. In all other cases bar one, the sails are furled and may be either lateen or square. The exception is Miniature VIII.[7] The ship in this miniature clearly has a square sail. At the turn of the sixth century both rigs may have been used on dromōns in the East.

Both the *Aeneid* and *Iliad* manuscripts show above-water spurs rather than underwater rams. The entire configuration of their bows is radically different to that of the Greek *triērēs* and Roman *liburna*. In the case of the dromōn of the *Aeneid* manuscript the spur is supported from the stempost by a coupling or chain, as is found on thirteenth-century galleys of the Latin West.[8]

Although dromōns are mentioned in Byzantine sources after the age of Procopius (died AD 562), there are no detailed descriptions of them and no iconographic depictions survive. Only in the age of the emperor Leo VI (reigned AD 886–912) does information about the construction of the dromōn and its cognate warships recur. A series of treatises on naval warfare dating from this period provides the most detailed information about ships and naval warfare between antiquity and the thirteenth century: especially, the *Concerning naval warfare* of Leo VI himself, dated to 905–6; the anonymous treatise *Commissioned by the Patrikios and Parakoimomenos Basil*, dated to c960; and the excerpt *From the Tactica* of admiral Nikephoros Ouranos, dated to the late tenth

Byzantine dromōn in a graffito, possibly of the ninth-twelfth centuries, from the Theseion/Hephaistion, Athens. (From M Goudas, Byzantis 2 [1910], fig 2, p339)

century, which in parts is a close paraphrase of the *Concerning naval warfare* of Leo VI.[9]

By the tenth century 'dromōn' had become a generic term for a 'battle ship' as well as retaining the specific meaning it had had in the sixth. A new term for a warship, *chelandion*, first appears in the chronicle of Theophanes (died AD 818), probably derived from *kelēs*, a fast-sailing merchant galley in classical Greek. Dromōn and *chelandion* became interchangeable words, although the latter appears to have the specific meaning of an oared horse transport in some sources. Dromōn also lost its specific reference to a monoreme. The tenth-century treatises are very clear that by then the dromōn par excellence was a bireme galley with two levels of oars, and that some large trireme dromōns existed, as also did monoreme dromōns, equated to galleys (*galeai*), which had a single level of oars.

main offensive weapon is revealed by the etymology of '*calcar*'. Latin '*calcare*' meant 'to tread under foot, to ride over, to trample'. The spur was designed to ride up and over the oars and/or gunwale of an enemy ship, smashing the oars and/or rolling the enemy ship over by the weight of the bows so that it shipped water and sank.

The earliest surviving depiction of a dromōn is an illustration from the fifth-century 'Roman' manuscript of the *Aeneid* of Vergil, whose provenance was some metropolitan centre in the West. It is followed shortly thereafter by miniatures of many dromōns in the Ambrosiana manuscript illustrations of the *Iliad* of Homer, dated to the early sixth century with a provenance in Constantinople. The *Aeneid* manuscript appears to show square sails. However, the dromōn in the background may

5. The illustration is of *Aeneid*, I.84-101: the storm at sea. A broken mast fits the context.

6. R B Bandinelli, *Hellenistic-Byzantine Miniatures of the Iliad (Ilias Ambrosiana)* (Olten 1955), Fig 63 (p67). Cf the now mutilated original in Fig 190 (Plate 34).

7. *Ibid*, Fig 44 (p56) and Fig 96 (Plate 9).

8. See below, p111.

9. Edited by A Dain, *Naumachica partim adhuc inedita* (Paris 1943).

Dromōns in a sixth-century manuscript of miniatures illustrating the Iliad of Homer, probably originating from Constantinople. The original is in the Ambrosiana Library, Milan. (Ambrosian Library, Cod Ambros, fol 205 inf)

The only treatise which at face value describes the actual construction of dromōns is that commissioned by the *Patrikios* and *Parakoimomenos* (Grand Chamberlain) Basil, an illegitimate son of emperor Romanos I Lekapenos (919–944). He rose to great power from AD 963 under Nikephoros II Phokas, John I Tzimiskes, and Basil II until his overthrow in 985. The treatise he commissioned was executed by an anonymous client (hereafter 'the Anonymous') and is an unashamed attempt to flatter a patron by displaying knowledge of classical sources. The Anonymous derived much of his information on ships from the *Onomasticon* of Julius Pollux, professor of rhetoric at Athens from *c* AD 178. Pollux himself used classical Greek sources such as Plato, Thucydides, Herodotus, and Homer and what he said about the construction of ships reflected a *triērēs* of Themistoclean Athens more

than a Roman *liburna* of the second century AD, let alone a tenth-century dromōn. Moreover, the manuscript of the *Onomasticon* used by the Anonymous was not classical. Rather, it was compiled in the ninth century in literary circles in Constantinople.[10] Either the compiler of this manuscript or Pollux himself misunderstood some of the classical Greek terminology, and the Anonymous then misunderstood parts of the Pollux manuscript. Rather than describing the construction of a tenth-century dromōn, he essentially describes a classical *triērēs*, but with numerous errors. Some terminology used is so common to ships of all kinds that it can be presumed to be relevant to tenth-century dromōns also. A few characteristics ascribed to them can be definitely accepted because they are confirmed by other sources, and a few can be discarded because they are clearly anachronisms misunderstood.

However, most lie in the realms of probability and possibility.

The standard bireme dromōn had two levels of oars, each with 25 oarsmen per side, for a total complement of 100 oarsmen plus officers, specialists, and marines. According to the Anonymous, it was raised on a keel (*tropis*) laid down on stocks (*dryocha*). It had a keelson (*tropidion*), stempost (*proembolis*), sternpost (*podostēma*), floor timbers (*enkoilia*), futtocks (*stamines* or *stēmonaria*), and planks (*sanidas*). The prow (*prōra*) housed the ship's main offensive weapon, a flamethrower for Greek Fire (*siphōn*), above which was a fortified foredeck (*pseudopation apo sanidōn, kai auto periteteichismenon sanisin*). The prow also had a spur, referred to by the Anonymous by the classical Greek *embolos*, which was either made of iron or iron-clad.[11] The poop (*prymnē*) had a tent or awning (*skēnē*) or at least a berth (*krabatos*),[12] for the commander set on stanchions (*trochantēres*). Right aft was a recurved stern

10. The manuscript was owned and interpolated by Arethas, archbishop of Caesarea, *c*AD 900. This is now lost, and of the surviving manuscripts, all of which are incomplete, interpolated, and abridged, the earliest is dated to the tenth century. How much Pollux's original work may have been altered in the ninth century, or in earlier transitional manuscripts, is impossible to say.

11. Anonymous, §6.2: *Eti de kai pros tas embolas tōn enantiōn byrsai tautais prosēlousthōsan, opōs ho sidēros periolisthainē pros to antitypon antilabēn ouk echōn, . . .* ('Moreover, hides should be fastened to them (the dromōns) against the ram (spur) of the enemy, so that the iron glances off in reaction and does not take hold, . . . '). Neither Leo VI nor Nikephoros Ouranos mention the spurs. However, see Frederick H van Doorninck, jr, 'Did tenth-century dromōns have a waterline ram? Another look at Leo *Tactica* XIX,69', *The Mariner's Mirror* 79 (1993), pp387–92 for further evidence that dromōns had spurs rather than rams.
   The passage indicates clearly that the hides were attached to the upper hull to take the impact of a spur and cause it to glance off. Hides thrown around the hull below water would have no such effect on an underwater ram.

12. Leo VI and Nikephoros Ouranos use the term 'couch' (*krabatos*), which almost certainly means a 'berth', or even 'cabin', much as we would say 'bed and breakfast' for 'room and breakfast' . Only the Anonymous refers to the commander's 'tent' (*skēnē*) or 'berth' (' . . . , *entha dē kai skēnē pēgnytai tō stratēgō ē triērarchō, ēgoun krabatos.*'). This reference to a *skēnē* is almost certainly taken from Pollux, I.89: 'The timbers projecting around the poop are called the *peritonaia*. The part which is called 'the tent' is constructed thereabouts for the strategos or trierarch' . (*'ta de peri tēn prymnan prouchonta xyla peritonaia kaleitai. ekei pou kai skēnē onomazetai to pēgnymenon stratēgō ē triērarchō'.*).

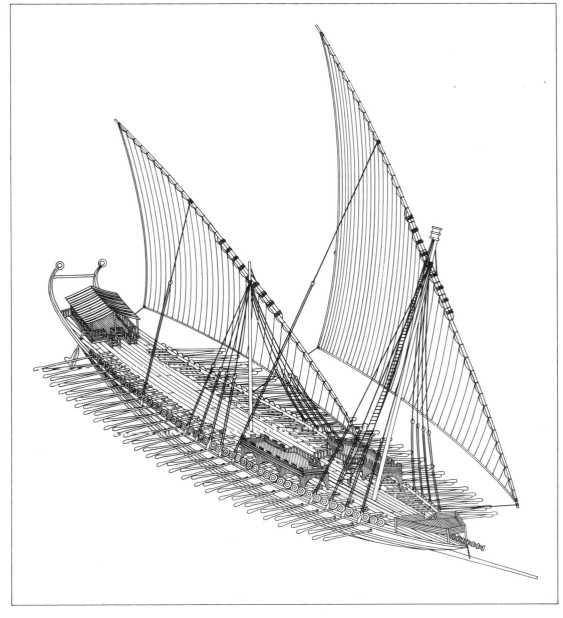

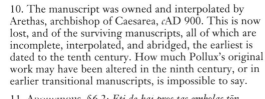

The author's reconstruction of a Byzantine bireme dromōn of the tenth century. Noteworthy are the fully decked hull, with no outrigger, and the various 'military' features: the siphon for Greek Fire under the fortified foredeck, the 'spur', and the castles amidships — all of which are supported by documentary evidence.

ornament known as an *aphlaston* in classical Greek but, according to the Anonymous, as *bardōnes* in the tenth century.[13]

This much can be accepted but, according to the Anonymous, on either side of the poop were 'side wings' (*paraptera*), composed of 'spreaders' (*petasoi*), 'splits' (*schista*), and 'ear timbers' (*epōtides*),[14] and which formed the housing (*parexeiresia*) for the steering oars (*pēdalia*). The latter were composed of loom (*auchēn*), tiller (*oiax*), and blade (*hyperyption*).[15] Where the helmsmen stood were the *enklimata*.[16] There are problems here. In classical Greek the *parexeiresia* was the outrigger for the upper level of oars, and the *epōtides* were the timbers at the bow of this outrigger which took the shock of any head-on collision.[17] This misunderstanding is clear evidence that tenth-century dromōns did not have outriggers. The Anonymous misunderstood his sources because he had no familiarity with galleys with outriggers. These had been discontinued since the days of the Roman *liburna*.

Again according to the Anonymous, from poop to prow at the centre line, dromōns were undecked (*asanidon*) and along this line, above the floor (*amphimētrion*) and hold (*kytos*) ran a 'stiffener keel' (*tropis sterea*) which also held crutches (*kathormeis*) in which the yards rested when lowered. This may be a misreading of Pollux,[18] but, alternatively, such a stiffener may have performed the same function of preventing hogging as the *hypozōma* of Greek triremes,[19] and the *cursia* of medieval galleys.

Given that the Anonymous was deliberately aping classical texts, it is unlikely that tenth-century dromōns were undecked at the centre line as he says. This was the design of the Greek *triērēs*. Dromons were almost certainly still fully-decked, just as they had been in the days of Procopius.

An otherwise incomprehensible passage in the *Concerning naval warfare* of Leo VI suggests that this was the case. It says that: 'Constructions known as wooden castles (*xylokastra*) fortified with planks, should be put around the middle of the mast on the largest dromōns'.[20] As it stands this is meaningless. No galley would go into battle with a wooden 'castle' slung halfway up a mast. Any shock of impact would bring it crashing down, and the men in it would have been sitting ducks for an enemy with rigging cutters, which were a normal part of the equipment of warships. In any case, masts were invariably lowered before going into battle to avoid damage and loss of life if they came crashing down.[21] A falling mast would almost certainly smash the fragile hull of a galley and sink it. That was why galleys had crutches to take the masts when lowered. On Byzantine dromōns, each mast (*histos* or *katartion*) was set in a mast step (*trapeza*) on the keel and could be lowered on to a crutch (*histodokē*) before combat. A 'castle' halfway up a mast could have no conceivable purpose. But the critical phrase 'around the middle of the mast' in the text (*peri to meson tou katartiou*) stands easy amendment to 'around the middle [*ie* halfway between] of the masts' (*peri to meson ton katartiōn*). According to the late-Roman writer on military tactics, Vegetius, such castles had existed on larger Roman *liburnae*.[22] They are also seen clearly on bas-reliefs and other iconographic depictions of Roman galleys. Bireme dromōns, therefore, almost certainly had two masts, one towards the prow and the other amidships.

Castles between the masts must have been raised on full decks. Pollux wrote that 'if the ship is fully decked, they build platforms for towers, and on these are two towers, left and right, between which [is] the deck'.[23] This

makes sense. Towers were built on both sides, presumably on scaffolding to raise them clear of the oarsmen, with a gangway on the deck between them. It accords with the construction of cataphract Roman *liburnae* of the age of Vegetius and, if the text of Pollux as we have it reflects Byzantine dromōns of the ninth century, it indicates that they were fully decked at that time and in the tenth century also.

Finally, when Leo VI, and Nikephoros Ouranos following him in paraphrase, writes that: 'If you (the admiral) realise that any of the soldiers are cowardly, send them to the lower bank of oars, and if any soldier should be wounded or fall, you should fill his place from those below only out of necessity',[24] it again suggests that the dromōns were fully decked. Cowardly and wounded soldiers were dismissed to the oar benches 'below', to below the deck implies the text, where they would be safe. The calibre of men found there were brought into combat above the deck only when the need was dire.

The evidence that at least some Muslim and Western galleys of the tenth to twelfth centuries, all of which were ultimately descended from Byzantine dromōns, were fully decked,[25] adds to the supposition that the prototype on which they were based was as well.

On either side were the rowing benches. These were arranged on two levels, one 'above' (*anō*) and the other 'below' (*katō*). Above and below what, none of the texts says; although the deck must surely be meant. According to the Anonymous, the deck (*katastrōma* or *sanidōmata*) ran on beams (*xyla diatona*) from hull (*toichos*) to hull. Below the deck were thwarts (*zygoi*) for the lower oarsmen (*zygioi*). Their oars rowed against tholes (*skalmoi*) set on a beam (*episkalmis*) and were held to the *skalmoi* by leather thongs (*tropōtyres*). They came

13. Anonymous, §2.5: 'The parts on which the berth [of the commander] is supported (are) the *trochantēres* and *aphlasta*, which are known as the *bardōnes*' ('*en hois de ho krabatos epereidetai, trochantēres kai aphlasta, hoi legomenoi bardōnes.*'). *Bardōnes* is an otherwise unknown word. The usage is unique to this text. See also below, p111.

14. These terms are used only by the Anonymous. They are not mentioned by Leo VI, Nikephoros Ouranos, or Pollux. The Anonymous probably got them from classical sources.

15. An unknown word, probably a misreading of *pterygion* (Pollux, I.90) for the classical *pteryx* for the blade of an oar.

16. Cf Pollux, I.90: 'Where the helmsman lies down is called the *anklima*' ('*hina de kataklinetai ho kybernētēs, anklima kaleitai*'). Why helmsmen should be 'lying down' is very unclear.

17. Thucydides, *History of the Peloponnesian War*, 7.34.5, in C Forster Smith, trans, *Thucydides*, Vol 4 (London 1935), pp64–5. Corinthian ships at the battle of Naupactus (413

BC) rammed the Athenian ships prow to prow and smashed their outriggers (*parexeiresiai*) because they had 'reinforced outrigger cheeks (*epōtides*) for this very purpose' ('*ep' auto touto pachyteras tas epōtidas echousōn*').

18. The Anonymous, §2.10 has '*Kai hoi legomenoi kathormeis epi tēs tropios stereas, prosēlountai kata stoichon treis ontes, eph' hōn hē keraia katagomenē epikeitai.*' ('And what are known as the *kathormeis* (crutches), three in number, are nailed in a row to the 'stiffener keel', and the yard rests on these when lowered.' Pollux, I.85 has '. . . *steira*, [*tropoi*]. *to de steira prosēloumenon phalkēs*, . . . ' ('. . . stempost, [beams]. That nailed to the *steira* (stempost) is called a *phalkēs* (rib), . . . ').

19. The *hypozōma* is not mentioned in the tenth-century Byzantine treatises and is misunderstood in Pollux, I.89, where the word is applied to the loom of an oar. This must mean that Roman *liburnae* no longer had a *hypozōma*.

20. Leo VI, *Peri Thalassomachias*, §7: *alla kai ta legomena*

xylokastra peri to meson tou katartiou en tois megistois dromōsin epistēsousi periteteichismena sanisin, . . .

21. At Ayas/Lajazzo (Yumurtalik, Turkey) in 1294 a superior Venetian fleet of 68 galleys made the cardinal mistake of going into battle against a much smaller Genoese fleet with masts still raised and sails unfurled. The result was a catastrophe. The Venetian admiral Marco Basegio was killed and 25 galleys were lost.

22. Vegetius, *Epitoma rei militaris* (Stuttgart 1967), IV.44 (p162).

23. Pollux, *Onomasticon*, 1.92: '*Ean d' ē kataphrakton to ploin, epinaupēgountai pyrgouchoi, kai ep' autōn pyrgia dyo, dexion kai euōnymon, hōn meson to katastrōma*' .

24. Leo VI, *Peri Thalassomachias*, §20: *Ei de tinas tōn stratiōtōn anandrous epignōs, toutous eis tēn katō elasian parapempe, kai ei pote tis plēgē ē pesē tōn stratiōtōn, ton ekeinou topon ek tōn katō ex anankēs anaplērōseis.* Cf Nikephoros Ouranos, §18.

25. See below, p107 and 110.

Battle between two Byzantine dromōns of the eleventh century in a MS of the Cynegetica *of Pseudo-Oppian. Note the pavesade with a row of shields.* (Biblioteca Marciana, Venice, Cod Gr 479, fol 23r)

through ports (*trēmata*) in one of the hull strakes known as the 'shield' (*thyreon*). These were sealed against water by leather sleeves around the oars (*askōmata* in classical Greek, but *manikellia* in tenth-century Byzantium). Above this level of *zygioi* was a wale (*peritonon*), then another shield strake for the upper level. The upper oarsmen rowed from benches (*thranoi*) and were called *thranitai*. The hull was topped by a gunwale (*epēnkenis* in classical Greek, but known as a *katapatēton* in the tenth century). This had a pavesade (*kastellōma*) to which marines could attach their shields, as seen in the eleventh-century Biblioteca Marciana manuscript of Pseudo Oppian's *Cynegetica*.

Dromōns had an array of weapons, including the great flamethrower (*siphōn*) at the prow, a bronze tube from which a flame could be projected. According to the Anonymous this was called a 'raven' (*katakorax*), but this is an anachronism derived from classical sources for the grapnels (*korax*) used on *triēreis* and *liburnae*. The emperor Leo VI had himself, he says, invented a hand-held flamethrower (*cheirosiphōn*), two of which could be used along the sides when engaged broadside. As well as these, normal weapons included crossbows at the prow,

stern, and along the sides called *toxobalistrai*, which could fire quarrels known as 'flies' (*myiai*). Other projectiles familiar from Latin and Arabic sources also appear: pots of quicklime or Greek Fire hurled by catapult which smashed on impact, small iron caltrops to impede enemies' movement on their decks, large caltrops wrapped in combustibles and hurled aflame on to enemy ships, and cranes (*mangana*) which could drop heavy weights or combustibles on to enemy ships alongside to smash their hulls or set them alight.

The dimensions of such dromōns are unknown, but an estimate can be based on the *interscalmium*, the space between any two tholes or oar ports. On the one hand, a *triērēs* such as *Olympias*, in which the oarsmen were fully seated during the stroke, had *interscalmia* of only 0.888m or 0.98m.[26] On the other, thirteenth-century South Italian galleys, in which the oarsmen used a 'stand-and-sit' stroke, had *interscalmia* of approximately 1.20m.[27] But, without a moveable seat, it is virtually impossible for a fully-seated man to pull an oar handle more than a metre. A metre for the *interscalmia* should be right for fully-seated oarsmen.[28] Since dromōns had one level of oars below deck, these oarsmen cannot pos-

sibly have used a stand-and-sit stroke, and in order to synchronise with them effectively, it must have been necessary for the upper oarsmen also to be fully seated. A metre for the twenty-five *interscalmia* of a dromōn makes 25m, and one must then allow for prow and poop to the extremities of the stempost and sternpost. On thirteenth-century galleys this increased the total length by approximately 22.5 per cent,[29] which would give a bireme dromōn an overall length of approximately 30.625m. This is as accurate an estimate of the length of a bireme dromōn as is possible.[30] As for the beam amidships, the ratio of maximum beam at the deck amidships to overall length from stempost to sternpost of *Olympias* is approximately 1:7.53, whereas that of thirteenth-century Sicilian galleys was 1:8.58. Assuming 1:8 for bireme dromōns, a maximum beam amidships of around 3.83m should not be too far from the truth.[31]

However, dromōns did vary in size, and with that must also have come variation in arrangements, if not in fundamental structures. The monoreme dromōn (*monērēs*), also known as a galley (*galea*), apparently had only 50 or so oarsmen. Since it is explicitly said to have been fast and light for scouting purposes, it no doubt

26. *Olympias* was built with *interscalmia* of 0.888m based on the classical Athenian cubit of 0.444m. However, it has proved to cramp the oarsmen's stroke excessively. It is now thought that the earlier archaic cubit of approximately 0.49m. should have been used, which would make the *interscalmia* 0.98m. See B Rankov, 'Reconstructing the past: the operation of the trireme reconstruction *Olympias* in the light of historical sources', *The Mariner's Mirror* 80 (1994), pp131–46.

27. See below, p112.

28. See J Coates, 'The naval architecture of European oared ships', *The Royal Institution of Naval Architects*, Spring Meetings 1993, Paper No 9, p2.

29. See below, Table 7/1.

30. *Olympias*, which has 27 benches per side for the thalamite and zygite oars, and 31 benches for the thranite oars, has an overall length from stempost to sternpost of only around 34m.

31. The estimates of R H Dolley in 'The warships of the later Roman Empire', *Journal of Roman Studies*, 38 (1948), pp47–53, which were based on little but sheer guesswork, were 130ft (39.62m) long by 17–18ft (5.18-5.49m) wide. His estimates were too high, and a dromōn as he reconstructed could not possibly have been capable of any speed.

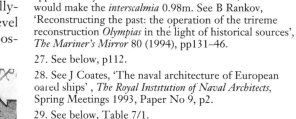

Byzantine dromōn with a siphon for Greek Fire – the best-known weapon of the period – in a twelfth-century Sicilian manuscript of the chronicle of Joannes Skylitzes. (Biblioteca Nacional, Madrid, Vitr 26–2, fol 34v)

had a higher beam:length ratio than the bireme dromōn. Perhaps it was undecked and had only one mast. Trireme dromōns built to accomodate three files of oarsmen may have had a third mast, although there is no concrete evidence for this.[32] Fifty oarsmen served the oars below deck and 150 those above it. According to the Anonymous, the three files of oarsmen were renamed so that the *zygioi* became *thalamioi*, the *thranitai* became *zygioi*, and the additional file became *thranitai*. But here he was following his sources, probably Pollux.[33] Whether this was actually true in the tenth century is impossible to say. This additional file of oars on trireme dromōns was rowed above deck, but how is unknown.

Two terms used from the tenth century for warships, *ousiakos* and *pamphylos*, are very difficult to interpret. An *ousia* was a full ship's company of 108–110 men. *Pamphylos* was used for large dromōns or *chelandia* of a type associated with the province of Pamphylia, usually used for transport purposes rather than in battle. *Ousiakos* and *pamphylos* were initially used as qualifiers for *chelandion* (eg, *chelandion ousiakon*, *chelandion pamphylon*) and then epithetically in themselves. Nomenclature was not consistent, but that is hardly unique to Byzantium. Galleon, barque, frigate, liner, and other terms have varied in meaning over time and from place to place. Slight changes in rigging have resulted in ships being called by different names. Nautical terminology has always been variegated and changeable, and that of the Middle Ages cannot be expected to be rigorously consistent.

The largest dromōn crew known is 230 oarsmen and 70 marines. Crews were tailored to meet specific circumstances and varied from 108 to 120, 130, 150, 160, and 220 oarsmen. The figures do not suggest any simple method

of assigning men to oars, and in some cases the additional men may have been taken aboard as supernumeraries to relieve exhausted oarsmen or, since some oarsmen doubled as marines, when larger fighting crews were needed.

Detailed sources for the dromōn and Byzantine naval warfare disappear after the tenth century. The ships are mentioned in narrative and documentary sources until the end of the Middle Ages, but few details emerge to add to what is known from the tenth century. From the eleventh century more iconographic representations begin to survive, but these are never sufficiently realistic for reconstructions to be based on them. Not one, for example, shows more than a single file of oars or more than one mast.

If the Byzantine sources are frustratingly few, those for Muslim warships after their irruption into the Mediterranean *c* AD 650 are exiguous in the extreme. Few iconographic representations bear any semblance of reality before the thirteenth century, and there are no treatises on ship types or construction. Even discussions of naval warfare are extremely few. The most notable are the 'Form of instructions to the Commander of the Maritime Frontier' in the *Book of revenues* of Qudāma ibn Ja'far (a customs official in tenth-century Baghdad) and some passages from the *Concerning naval warfare* of Leo VI translated at an unknown date by an anonymous author and inserted into the *Royal rules and customary regulations for the art of naval warfare* of ibn al Manqalī (an official in late-thirteenth-century Mamluk Egypt).[34]

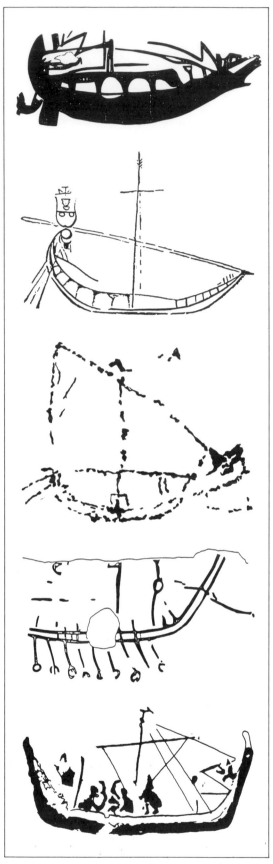

Ships of the fifth to seventh centuries from Byzantino-Muslim Egypt seem to indicate that early Islamic seafaring depended on the adoption of local ship types.
(From L Basch, 'Navires et bateaux coptes: état des questions en 1991', *Graeco-Arabica* 5 [1993], pp23–62)

---

32. Note that the surviving text of Pollux, which, as mentioned above, is derived from a now-lost ninth-century Byzantine manuscript, mentions three masts for ships: the fore mast (*akateios*), the midships mast (*epidromos*), and a smaller one (*dolōn*) (Pollux, I.91). These ships are not, however, specifically dromōns.

33. Pollux, I.87: '*kai to men edaphos tēs neōs . . . kaloito d' an kai thalamos, hou hoi thalamioi erettousi. ta de mesa tē neōs zyga, hou hoi zygioi kathēntai, to de peri to katastrōma thranos, hou hoi thranitai.*' (' and the lower part of the ship . . . might also be called the *thalamos*, where the *thalamioi* row; the middle of the ship the *zyga*, where the *zygioi* are seated, and the part at the deck the *thranos*, where the *thranitai* are.')

34. See V Christides, 'Two parallel naval guides of the tenth century: Qudāma's document and Leo VI's *Naumachica*: a study on Byzantine and Moslem naval preparedness', *Graeco-Arabica*, 1 (1982), pp51–103; *Idem*, 'Naval warfare in the Eastern Mediterranean (6th-14th centuries): an Arabic translation of Leo VI's *Naumachica*' , *Graeco-Arabica*, 3 (1984), pp137–48.
One may add the extracts from an anonymous manuscript, possibly by Muhammad ibn Qasim al-Nuwairī (fourteenth-century Egypt), concerning the attack on Egypt by Peter I of Cyprus in 1365, published by J Gildemeister, 'Ueber arabisches Schiffswesen', *Nachrichten der Königlichen Gesellschaft der Wissenschaften zu Göttingen. Philosophische-Historische Klasse* (1882), pp431–49. However, this post-dates the time frame of this chapter.

A good example of the less than realistic depiction of contemporary ship types is provided by this twelfth-century Byzantine dromōn in a manuscript of the Sermons of St Gregory of Nazianzus in the monastery of the Panteleimon, Mt Athos.
(After S M Pelekanides, *et al*, *Oí Yhsauroi tou agiou orous*, series A, vol 5 [Athens 1975], fig 307, p182)

Most modern scholarship is etymological and philological in nature, with attributions of particular characteristics to Muslim galley types based on fragmentary, and frequently contradictory, references.[35]

When they acquired Mediterranean coasts after their conquest of Syria (AD 638), Egypt (AD 642), and Tunisia (AD 670–698), the Muslims quickly took to the sea, attacking Cyprus in 649 and achieving a major victory with the destruction of the Byzantine fleet under Constans II at the 'Battle of the Masts' near Cape Gelidonya (Cape Taşlik) in 655. In this period they made use of Syrian and Egyptian seamen and took over ship types which had long been used on these coasts under Roman and Byzantine rule. The Muslim sources for the Battle of the Masts refer to the ships as *sufun* (singular *safina*) and *maraqib* (singular *marqib*), both generic terms in Arabic for ships of any kind. One ninth-century source does mention a specific ship type, the *qārib* (plural *qawārib*), but this probably reflects ninth- rather than seventh-century terminology.

Papyri from Umayyad Egypt dated to AD 706–9 mention three Muslim warship types, *dromonarios*, *akation/akatēnarion*, and *karabos/karabion*. These appear in abbreviated Greek forms ('*karabōn [kai] aka[tiōn] [kai] dro[monarion]*', etc).[36] These terms were used by Greek-speaking functionaries in the chanceries of their Muslim rulers writing directives to fellow Greek-speaking functionaries of other Muslim officials. They used terminology with which they were familiar rather than that of their Muslim masters. The ship types are clear enough. *Karabos/karabion* also appears in By-

Lateen rigged galley of the ninth–tenth centuries on a lustre-ware dish from Egypt, Museum of Islamic Art, Cairo (Inv No 7900). Like so many craft in the early history of Islamic seafaring, its exact designation is unknown.

zantine sources for a small oared warship. It gave rise to *qārib* in Arabic. *Dromonarios* was, of course, the dromōn. The word passed into Arabic as *dermin/darmin/adrumūnun*, etc, but did not have particularly wide usage in later times. *Akation/akatēnarion* was derived from Greek *akatos* and Latin *actuaria* for a small merchant galley. The only Muslim ship type possibly derived from the *akation* is the *qit'a* (plural *aqtā'*), which appears in Arabic sources from the twelfth century, but the *katena* which appears in Byzantine sources from the ninth century, and which is not derived from any classical ship, may be a reverse transliteration from Greco-Arabic *akation/akatēnarion*.

These Greek terms were not used by the Muslims themselves. They had their own terminology which was not a mere transliteration of the Greek. For some Greek papyri there exist corresponding Arabic versions which were destined for Muslim officials rather than Greek functionaries. In these, *karabos*, *akation*, and *dromonarios* are translated indiscriminately as *qadis* (plural *qawādis*), *ala(?)n* (an unidentified word), and *safina* (plural *sufun*). Both *qadis* and *safina* were pre-Islamic Arabic words for ships in general. There is no connection between them and the terms used by the Greek-speaking functionaries.

The first independent emir of Egypt, Ahmad ibn Tulun (AD 868–84), built a fleet for defence against both the 'Abbāsid Caliphs and the Byzantines. The names of the ships in it include numbers of small boats and transports: *'ulābi* (plural *'ulābiyyāt*), a small boat; *hamāma* (plural *hamā'im*), probably a transport ship; *'usharī* (plural *'ushāriyyāt*), an oared transport, especially for horses; and *sandal* (plural *sanādil*), a lighter. But the major elements of the fleet were 100 large 'Arabic' ships (*marāqib 'arabiyya*) and 100 warships (*marāqib harbiyya*). *Marqib* was the widest generic for 'ship' in Arabic and *harbī* literally meant 'of war'. What 'Arabic' ships may have been is unknown. These terms reveal nothing of specific ship types.

From this period, terminology in Arabic for ships proliferated rapidly and widely in the Levant. Many names referred to places where a ship type was built or originated. Others were generics applied to specific situations, and characteristics attributed to them by sources in different periods vary widely. Amongst the most common are: *harrāqa* (plural *harrāqāt*), used from the twelfth century to refer to fireships designed to burn enemy ships with Greek Fire; *marqib*, a generic but frequently applied to warships, especially as *marqib harbī*; *musattah* (plural *musattahāt*), used from the twelfth cen-

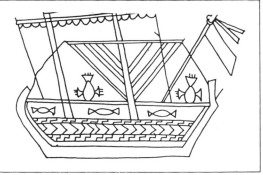

Muslim ship with fire-grenades in a manuscript of the late thirteenth to fourteenth centuries attributed to Hasan al Rammah, Egypt or Syria, Bibliothèque Nationale, Paris (MS Arabe 2825, fol 100r). The Muslim sea powers employed a specialist type of 'fireships', known as the harrāqa, *which was not intended for self-destruction like later Western fireships, but rather as platforms for incendiary weapons. (From D Nicolle, 'Shipping in Islamic art: seventh through sixteenth century AD', American Neptune 49 [1989], fig 29a)*

tury for decked warships in which marines fought on deck while oarsmen rowed beneath; *safina*, a generic but sometimes used to refer to warships or oared transport ships; *shalandī* (plural *shalandiyyāt*), from Greek *chelandion*, used from the tenth century with reference to Byzantine fleets and described as having a deck on which marines fought while oarsmen continued to row below; *tarrīda* (plural *tarā'id*), a transport galley, especially for transporting horses, of which it could carry around 40 in the twelfth century; and *ustūl* (plural *asātīl*), from Greek *stolos* for a war fleet but sometimes used for a warship.

Shīnī (plural *shawānī*), used from the tenth century to refer to both Muslim and Byzantine warships, was said by ibn Mamātī in the twelfth century to be a 140-oared galley and the same as the *ghurāb*, itself perhaps just an alternative for *qārib*. *Qit'a* is used for a warship from the twelfth century, on occasions for transports in a war fleet or for unusually large warships. The *satoura/saktoura* mentioned in Byzantine sources in the fleet of Muslim Crete raiding the Cyclades in the ninth century may possibly have been the Arabic *shakhtūr*: a 'large ship'.

35. See in particular (apart from works in Arabic), A M Fahmy, *Muslim Naval Organisation in the Eastern Mediterranean from the Seventh to the Tenth Century AD* (Cairo 1966); H Kindermann, "*Schiff*" *im Arabischen. Untersuchung über Vorkommen und Bedeutung der Termini* (Zwickau 1934) (a work which is extremely difficult to use).

36. See C H Becker, 'Arabische Papyri des Aphroditofundes', *Zeitschrift für Assyriologie und verwandte Gebiete* 20 (1907), pp68–104.

Galley on a fragment of polychrome ceramic from thirteenth-century Egypt or Syria, Museum of Islamic Art, Cairo (Inv No 5379/25). The sail is almost certainly a lateen.

These terms for galleys in sources from Egypt and Syria are also found in those from Muslim North Africa, Sicily, and Spain.[37] Muslim fleets from Syria to al-Andalus had a variety of galleys, modelled initially on those they had taken over from the Byzantines or had observed them using. Their varying names were either transliterated from Greek or derived from generic Arabic terms for ships. As was the case in Byzantium, and was to be also in the medieval West, there was no consistency in Muslim nautical terminology.

As for specific characteristics of Muslim galleys, little is known. They certainly had spurs and lateen sails rather than rams and square

Galley on a fragment of paper with warriors fighting from the deck, probably from thirteenth-century Egypt, Museum of Islamic Art, Cairo. The steering oar is prominent.(From D Nicolle, 'Shipping in Islamic art: seventh through sixteenth century AD', American Neptune 49 [1989], fig 29a)

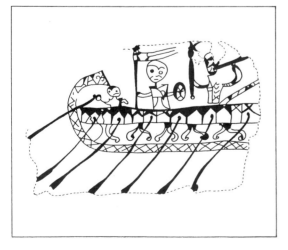

sails, because there is no evidence that Muslims ever used anything but lateen sails in the Mediterranean,[38] and no Arabic sources refer to underwater rams. There are, however, references to two stern-quarter steering oars, and some *qawārib* and *shawānī* are said to have had castles. There were definitely both monoremes and biremes, and some biremes had decks on which marines could fight above the lower bank of oars. The anonymous translator of Leo VI's *Concerning naval warfare* incorporated into ibn al-Manqalī's *Rules*, wrote that: 'And every ship must be well proportioned in length and must have two banks. Moreover, two officers are needed in charge [one for the top and the other for the lower bank]'.[39]

There were at least some triremes. Leo VI says that Muslims used *koumbaria* which were large and slow, and that the Byzantines should build and equip dromōns accordingly.[40] *Koumbarion* may have been derived from Greek *kymbē*/Latin *cumba*, a small skiff, but more probably was a transliteration from Arabic, either of *qunbār*, found in Cairo Geniza documents for a large sailing ship,[41] or of *marqib kabīr*, meaning 'large ship'. Whether they were galleys or sailing ships is debatable, although, since Leo advised building special dromōns to combat them, they were presumably galleys. If they were so unusually large, they were probably triremes. By the twelfth century in Egypt some *aqta'* and *shawānī* were certainly triremes. In his *Historia Hierosolymitana*, Albert of Aachen wrote that in 1108 the Egyptians sent a fleet to the relief of Sidon that included '*triremium octo, quos dicunt cattos*' ('eight triremes, which they call *catti*').[42] The *cattus* is identified with the Muslim *qit'a*. The *shawānī* with 140 oars mentioned by Ibn Mamatī must have been triremes.

When Latin Western sources for maritime history become prolific from the eleventh century, terms familiar from Greek and Arabic appear in Latin transliterations. As *germundus/dermundus/dromundus*, *dromōn* became applied to any large warship, and sometimes even to sailing ships, by landlubber literati. They learnt the word from the *Etymologiae* of Isidore of Seville, who wrote;

there are long ships which we call dromōnes, called that because they are longer than others, the opposite of which is a musculus [little mouse], a short ship. A dromo is so called from decurrendo [overtaking]; for the Greeks call cursum [running] dromōn.

Amongst other common terms were: *cattus/gattus* (from *akatos/akation* and *qit'a*), *chelandra/chelandium* (from *chelandion*), *galea* (it is not possible to prove whether the Latin or the Byzantine *galea* was the primogenitor), *golafrus/gulafrus/gulabus/garabus* (from *karabos* and *qārib* or *ghurāb*), and *sagena*. The Pisan fleet which attacked the Balearics in 1115 was composed of: '*Gatti, drumones, garabi*, and swift *galee, barce, currabii, lintres*, and large *sagene*, and many other ships of various names.'[43]

Sagene appear in many Western sources from the ninth to early twelfth centuries, after which the word disappears. In Byzantine sources they appear in the *Strategicon* of Maurice and in the *De administrando imperii* of Constantine VII Porphyrogenitus (*c*950) as a term for fast raiding vessels of Muslim and Croatian 'pirates' rather than for ships of Byzantine fleets. This galley type was not Byzantine and was developed amongst the Slavs of the east coast of the Adriatic.[44]

The *sagitta*, which appears in Latin sources from the eleventh century, was a specifically Western galley. As its name ('arrow') implies, it was fast and appears frequently as a corsair ship. It was smaller than the normal 100/108-oared galleys. Thirteenth-century Genoese sources mention *sagittae* with 48, 58, 64, and 80 oars.[45] The type continued through to the sixteenth century as *sagetia* and *saetia*, but its specific characteristics are unknown other than that it remained smaller and faster than standard bireme and (from the fourteenth century) trireme war galleys.

37. M A Ageil, *Naval Policy and the Use of the Fleet of Ifriqiyyah from the First to Third centuries A H (seventh to ninth centuries AD)* (PhD thesis, University of Michigan 1985); F Morales Belda, *La marina de Al-Andalus* (Barcelona 1970).

38. I know of no Muslim illustration of seagoing ships with square sails from anywhere in the Mediterranean between the seventh and sixteenth centuries; although, some depictions of Nile river boats do have a type of lug sail.

39. Christides, 'Naval Warfare', p143: The translation is of Leo VI, *Peri Thalassomachias*, §7, last sentence.

40. *Peri Thalassomachias*, §78: '*Hoi men gar koumbariois chrōntai meizosi kai argoterois, hoi barbaroi, . . .*'

41. A collection of documents of the tenth to thirteenth centuries in Arabic written in Hebrew script found in the Geniza, 'storehouse', of the Old Synagogue of the Jewish community in Cairo.

42. See also note 46 below.

43. C Calisse (ed), *Liber Maiolichinus de gestis Pisanorum* (Rome 1904), p105: *Gatti, drumones, garabi, celeresque galee, barce, currabii, lintres, grandesque sagene, et plures alie variantes nomina naves.*

44. See K M Woody, 'Sagena piscatoris: Peter Damiani and the Papal election decree of 1059', *Viator* 1 (1970), pp33–54.

45. See E H Byrne, *Genoese Shipping in the Twelfth and Thirteenth Centuries* (Cambridge, Mass 1930)

The *cattus* or *gattus* is consistently described in the late eleventh and twelfth centuries as being large, very strong, a trireme, and having castles.[46] William of Tyre says they had 100 oars, each rowed by two oarsmen, but this is almost certainly a mistake.[47] There is no other evidence before the fourteenth century for oars rowed by multiple oarsmen. Moreover, with only 100 oars, it is difficult to imagine how they could be triremes because, irrespective of how many men pulled each oar, the oars must have been rowed from only 16–17 benches per side. But, from classical antiquity to the Renaissance, the norm was around 25–27 benches. The 140 oarsmen, presumably rowing from 23–24 benches, cited for twelfth-century Egyptian *shawanī*, would fit the bill much better. At the least, *catti* were certainly larger than other monoreme and bireme galleys of the eleventh to thirteenth centuries. In all probability, contemporary sources mentioned some of their characteristics simply because they were unusually large and attracted attention.

An anonymous chronicle of the Third Crusade, the *Itinerary of King Richard*, describes a battle off Acre between galleys of the besieging Crusaders and those of the Muslim defenders of the city in AD 1190. One passage suggests that some galleys had two levels of oars, one below and the other above, a full deck:

> Indeed by now the enemy had boarded another vessel (and), having dislodged the marines, (was) master of the upper deck; while those to whom the lower post had been assigned tried to escape by the help of the oars. Extraordinary and pitiful was the struggle; for the oars being pulled in opposite ways, the galley was driven sometimes this way by our (men), and sometimes that way as the Turks rowed. At length our (men) prevailed and, being dislodged by

Genoese galley redrawn from a twelfth-century manuscript of the Genoese Annals (Bibliothèque National, Paris, MS Suppl Lat, 773, c 105 B). It is highly stylised but clearly shows the single level of oars, the spur, and the fore fighting deck.

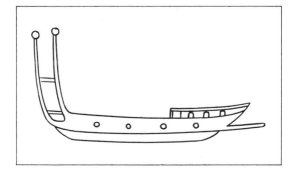

46. See Albert of Aachen, *Historia Hierosolymitana*, in *Recueil des Historiens des Croisades. Historiens Occidentaux*, Vol 4 (Paris 1879), XI.xxvii (p675): 'Dehinc, post dies aliquot, incomparabilis navilis exercitus a regno Babyloniae in galidis, in biremibus et triremibus, dictis vulgariter cattis, turritis et bello compositis, advectus est ad civitatem Baruch vel Baurim, . . . '. Cf X.xlix (p654) & XII.xvii (p699). Here the description is of Muslim *catti* from Egypt, but the shiptype also appears amongst contemporary lists of ships used by maritime powers in the Latin West.

47. It is significant that the early-thirteenth-century French translation of William of Tyre alters his 100 oars with two oarsmen per oar to 100 oarsmen. The translator is known to have been familiar with the sea and probably went on the Third Crusade.

A comparison between Byzantine dromons (top) in a twelfth-century Sicilian manuscript of the chronicle of Joannes Skylitzes, Biblioteca Nacional, Madrid (Vitr 26–2, fol 34v), with Sicilian galleys of the late twelfth to early thirteenth centuries in a manuscript of the Carmen ad honorem Augusti of Peter of Eboli, Burgerbibliothek, Berne. They both feature two levels of oars, an above-water spur, and twin 'wings' at the stern. (From A Grabar and M Manoussacas, L'illustration du manuscrit de Skylitzes de la Bibliothèque Nationale de Madrid (Venice 1979), fig 183; and from Peter of Eboli, De rebus Siculis carmen, ed E Rota [Città di Castello 1905], p100)

the onset of the Christians, the enemy rowing above was overcome.[48]

If this tale is true,[49] and the Muslims who had captured the deck were unable to get at the oarsmen rowing below, this galley must have had a complete deck and two levels of oars.

Although huge numbers of Western galleys were involved in naval expeditions between 1050 and 1250, and although Crusaders both leased them and had them built, no detailed information about them survives before the 1270s. Of all the galleys of the many Genoese, Venetian, Pisan, and other fleets, little more is known than the name: *galee*. It is not even known whether early galleys were monoremes or biremes. As for Crusader fleets, Richard Coeur de Lion leased galleys in Marseille for the Third Crusade, the Venetians supplied a battle fleet of fifty galleys for the Fourth Crusade, and Frederick II sent war galleys (*galee*) and transport galleys (*chelandre*) to the East between 1220 and 1228, but no construction details survive. Although these were specified for the transport galleys (*taride*) that Louis IX obtained from Genoa for his Crusade of 1248, those for the war galleys (*galee*) he ordered from Marseille were not.

The explanations for this dearth of information about Western war galleys appear to be simply that they were so invariable in characteristics that observers felt no need to describe them in any detail and that no contracts for their construction survive.

The earliest depictions which are more than stylised 'banana boats', are miniatures in the *Genoese annals*, commenced in 1099 under the authorship of Caffaro. The miniatures, however, date from the later twelfth century. They show monoreme galleys with high curved 'wings' at the stern, foredecks for fighting, and pronounced spurs.

More detailed than these is an illustration of a bireme galley in a South Italian/Sicilian manuscript of the *Song of Sicilian affairs* of Peter of Eboli (*c*1300).[50] This galley is similar to others in the manuscript of the Byzantine chronicle of

Table 7/1: Galleys of Charles I of Anjou, primary specifications

	Dimensions or Quantity (to two decimal places)	Number
Overall length from stempost to sternpost	39.55m.	
Length on keel	28.21m	
Height of sternpost	3.60m	
Height of stempost	2.99m	
Depth in hold from floor to deck at centre line amidships	2.04m	
Height of ceiling above floor amidships	.09m	
Number of frames on the keel		95
Dimensions of frames	.13m x .13m	
Distance between frames	.17m	
Number of *furcata* frames on stem and sternpost		38
Dimensions of *furcata* frames	.13m x .13m	
Distance between *furcata* frames	.16m	
Scantlings of hull planks (estimated)	0.02m	
Distance between tholes; *ie*, rowing 'room' or *interscalmium*	1.195m	
Number of stringers per side		4
Number of wales (*cinta*) per side		1
Height of wales above the floor amidships	1.32m	
Height of deck above the wales amidships	0.455m	
Beam amidships at the wales (*cinte*)	3.69m	
Beam at the *delfinum* of the bow at the wales	1.67m	
Beam at the *delfinum* of the stern at the wales	1.58m	
Beam amidships at the floor	2.97m	
Number of deck beams		55
Beam of deck beams	4.61m	
Camber of deck (estimated)	.27m	
Length of poop from transom (*drigantus*) to aftermost rowing bench	2.90m	
Length of foredeck from rowing platform to stempost	4.35m	
Length of beak or spur	6.59m	
Height and breadth of centre gangway (*cursia*)	.40m x .66m	
Number of oars		108
Length of oars	6.86m	
Length of fore mast	15.82m	
Circumference of fore mast	.92m	
Length of fore mast yard	26.89m	
Length of midships mast	11.07m	
Circumference of midships mast	.79m	
Length of midships mast yard	20.57m	
Length of fore mast sail on yard and in leech	26.89m	
Length of midships mast sail on yard and in leech	20.57m	
Length of stormsail (*tertiarolium*) on yard	14.24m	
Length of top ladder	14.77m	
Length of auxiliary steering sweeps (*spati*)	16.875m	
Length of primary steering oars (*temones*)	6.06m	

Joannes Skylitzes made in Norman Sicily earlier in the twelfth century. They represent the same artistic and maritime traditions. The Peter of Eboli galley has a high curving stempost and pronounced spur, two files of oars, one rowed against tholes above the outrigger and the other through oar ports set below it, two steering oars, and a poop crowned by two curving 'wings'. These stern ornaments may have become known as *ale* ('wings') in South Italy and Sicily in the twelfth and thirteenth centuries. This word, which is otherwise unknown as part of a galley, appears in two documents in the chancery registers of the Kingdom of Sicily from the reign of Charles I of Anjou (1266–1284), dated 1273 and 1274.[51] However, South

48. W Stubbs, (ed), *Chronicles and Memorials of the Reign of Richard I. Vol I: Itinerarium peregrinorum et gesta regis Ricardi* (Rerum Britannicarum medii aevi scriptores, 38) (London, 1864), I.xxxiv (p82): Aliam [ratem] vero jam hostis, victor superius tabulati, bellatoribus depulsis invaserat, at illi quibus inferior statio fuerat deputata, remorum auxilio elabi contendunt. Mirum quidem et miserandum certamen: nam remis in diversa tendentibus, nunc huc nostris, nunc illuc Turcis agitantibus galea depellitur. Nostri tamen praevalent, et hostis superius remigans, Christicolarum superventu detrusus succumbit.

49. This is the only Western text which suggests that a Western galley might have two superimposed levels of

oars. The text is, however, very questionable. It is a reworking of a now-lost original, possibly written in French, which was also the original for the closely-related poem, the *Estoire de la guerre sainte* by Ambroise. See G Paris (ed), *L'estoire de la guerre sainte: histoire en vers de la troisième croisade (1990–1192) par Ambroise* (Paris 1897), ll. 3315–7 (col 89).

In describing this same incident Ambroise writes:

As estoires iert la huee:
             On the fleets was the din of battle,
Chascone iert sovent remuee
             Each was often driven back,
Sovent ensemble s'ajostouent
             Often together did they come.

Ambroise's version is far shorter but still has the essential idea of the ships being driven first one way, then another. What the lost original had is unknown, but it is possible that the author of the *Itinerarium* either failed to understand his source or else embroidered it with this tale of two levels of oars being rowed in opposite directions.

50. Peter of Eboli, *De rebus Siculis carmen*, ed E Rota (Muratori, *Rerum Italicarum scriptores*, nuova serie, t XXXI, pt 1, fasc 36–7) (Città di Castello 1905), p100.

51. R Filangieri, *et al*, eds, *I registri della cancelleria angioina*, 33 vols (Naples 1950–81), vol X, pp220–21 (Reg 49, no 32), vol XII, pp159–60 (Reg 66, no 11).

	Dimensions or Quantity (to two decimal places)	Number
Number of anchors		4
Weight of anchors	111.37kg	
Crew:		
oarsmen (*marinarii*)		108
masters (*comiti*)		2
helmsmen (*nauclerii*)		4
marines (*supersalientes*)		36
ship's boys (*pueri*)		2
Armaments		
wooden, one-footed crossbows		15
wooden, two-footed crossbows		13 or 15
crossbow baldrics		26
boxes of crossbow quarrels		8
shields		40
lances		200
halbards		10
axes		47
darts		400
helmets		108
padded jackets		108
pots of Greek Fire		2
iron rockets for shooting fire		25
glass bottles of Greek Fire		40
pots of powdered quick lime		100
iron grapnels		2
rigging cutters		?
Other equipment		
silk and buckram banners and flags		4
silk penons		34
silk poop canopy		1
awning		1
shields with Angevin coat of arms at bow and stern		2
hides for making thole straps		5
leather sleeves for sealing oar ports		32
Provisions (per crew member)		
Ship's biscuit	22kg per month	
salt meat	1.485kg per month	
cheese	1.185kg per month	
legumes	.60kg per month	
wine	69.90 litres per month	

might have been translated into Latin as *ala* in south Italy.

The earliest specifications for bireme war galleys to survive from the West occur in the Angevin chancery registers. Throughout the reign of Charles I, the chancery ordered construction of galleys conforming to a model derived from a 'Red Galley of Provence', apparently considered to be a particularly fine design. This standard war galley used in Angevin fleets, together with data from the registers concerning costs, crews, armaments, other equipment, and provisions, have been studied and reconstructed.[53] The data vary a little in different documents; however, they are sufficiently consistent to allow tabulation of a standard as in Table 7/1.

These galleys were raised on a keel (*carina*), stempost (*rota de prora*), sternpost (*rota de poppa*), floor timbers (*matere*), kelson (*paramessale*), and futtocks (*stamenaria*). Deck beams (*latte*), four stringers (*fila*) per side, a single wale (*cinta*) per side, and one or two stringers mortised to the deck beams completed the essential shell before planking. On the stempost and sternpost, the frames were not composed of floor timbers and futtocks but rather consisted of 'forked' frames (*furcate*), single timbers curved to form the frame.

At the bow there was a foredeck (*palmentella de prora*) and a spur (*calcar* or *sperone*). This was not an integral part of the hull, but rather a long spar or beam attached to the stempost[54] and sustained by a chain or metal coupling from its head, as can be seen clearly in a late thirteenth-century painting of a Catalan galley.

At the stern there was a poop deck, raised on a transom (*drigantus*) set on the head of the sternpost, which almost certainly overhung the sternpost.

The rowing platform was bounded by two fore-and-aft beams (*aposticii*) with yokes at bow and stern (*iugum proris* and *iugum puppis*). The

Italy and Sicily had a long tradition of Byzantine influence in matters maritime, and it is curious that the Byzantine Anonymous referred to the housing for the steering oars on either side of the poop as 'side wings' (*paraptera*). The Anonymous said that the *aphlaston* had become known as *bardōnes* in his time;[52] however, since this word is otherwise unknown and has no offshoots in medieval Latin or Italian, he may have been confused. With the demise of the traditional *aphlaston* and its replacement by the new style of stern ornament, the latter may have become known in Byzantium as *paraptera* or simply *ptera* ('wings') and

Aragonese galley of the late thirteenth century on a painted beam from a church near Teruel, Museo del Arte de Cataluña. Note the spur supported by a chain or metal coupling. (From F Foerster, 'The warships of the kings of Aragón and their fighting tactics during the 13th and 14th centuries AD', International Journal of Nautical Archaeology and Underwater Exploration, 16 (1987), 19–29; Figure 6.)

52. See note 13 above.

53. See J H Pryor, 'The galleys of Charles I of Anjou, King of Sicily: c1269–84', *Studies in Medieval and Renaissance History*, ns 14 (1993), pp34–103.

54. A contract for the sale of two oak spurs, each 10.42m. long and .25m wide, survives from Genoa in 1267. See Pryor, 'Galleys of Charles I of Anjou', p52.

Sicilian galley of the late twelfth to early thirteenth centuries showing shields hung on the gunwales in a manuscript of the Carmen ad honorem Augusti *of Peter of Eboli, Burgerbibliothek, Berne.*

aposticii were carried on thrusting knees (*braccioli*) from the heads of the frames. The tholes (*scalmi*) for the outer oars and a series of stanchions (*bande*), which formed a railing from which shields could be hung, were set into them. The tholes were set corresponding to alternate deck beams, which were themselves set on alternate hull frames. Thus an *interscalmium* corresponded to every fourth frame. The inner oarsmen rowed through ports (*columbaria*) in the planking covering the *braccioli*, and the rowing benches were angled towards the bow to make this possible. Both inner and outer oarsmen rowed oars 6.86m long from benches on the deck, except for a few at bow and stern who had oars of 7.91m.[55]

Down the middle from poop to prow ran the gangway (*cursia*), which also helped to prevent the hull hogging and sagging. Together with the *fila* mortised to the deck beams, it performed the same function as the *hypozōma* of classical *triēreis* and possibly the *tropis sterea* of Byzantine dromōns.

The shrouds (*candele*) for the two masts were composed of pendants (*corone*) from the mast head and tackles at the deck to tighten them. Each mast had its own lateen sail, that of the fore mast being larger than that of the midships mast, and there was also a smaller storm sail (*tertiarolium*) for the fore mast. These sails were very large, the fore mast artemon sail containing approximately 240m² of canvas, and required much manpower and extensive rigging systems to handle them. The yards were held to the masts by a parrel (*troccia*). They were raised by two ties (*amanti*), rove through sheaves (*polegie*) in the block mast (*calzensis*) at their heads, made fast to the yard by a strap (*paroma*), and taken up by two tie tackles (*collaturi*). These were complex tackles with two multi-sheaved blocks and at least six falls of rope. The yards were managed by tackles (*orsie*) running fore and aft at their feet, which controlled their angle to the vertical, and by vangs (*seste*) on the upper yards which braced them against the wind.

The specifications are just sufficient to permit for the first time in history a defensible reconstruction of the midships section and oarage system of a galley based on surviving data.[56] Limitations of space make it impossible to reproduce here the detailed argument which has led to the elimination of all other possible reconstructions, and what is presented is merely the conclusions drawn and the most salient criteria which have determined them.

The lines of the hull are unknown, but are determined to a degree by the known positions of the deck beams (B) and wales (A) at the hull. The line of the *braccioli* to the *aposticii* is also unknown, but cannot be closer to the vertical than a straight line through the wales and deck beams because outriggers of all kinds, from the *parexeiresia* of Greek *triēreis* to the *aposticii* of Renaissance galleys, were always flared outboard from the hull. In fact, since there is considerable flare in the hull between the wales and deck beams in any case, the *braccioli* must flare outboard even more than this if the line of the hull is continued into that of the *braccioli*. The flare can be modified a little because the beam at the wales was internal inside the hull, whereas that at the deck beams was external. Nevertheless, the flare from wale to deck is very pronounced and therefore that of the *braccioli* must be kept as shallow as possible to prevent the flare to the *aposticii* becoming excessive, destabilising the galley and reducing its ability to heel under sail.

For the oarsmen, there are two possibilities. Either they used the 'stand-and-sit' stroke of fourteenth-century trireme galleys, or they used the fully-seated stroke of Byzantine dromōns and ancient *triēreis* and *liburnae*. But the length of 1.195m for the *interscalmia* of these galleys is unnecessarily great for a seated stroke and seated oarsmen could not make full use of it.[57] A stand-and-sit stroke must have been used on these galleys and, this being the case, the height above the deck of the oarsmen's grip on the handle during the pull of the stroke must be around the lower chest level of an average man; say, 1.25m.[58]

As for the oars themselves, from antiquity to the advent of multiple-oarsmen oars, they had a gearing ratio, that is the ratio of the inboard to outboard lengths (grip-on-the-loom to thole: thole to centre-of-pressure-on-the-blade) in the order of 1:2.8 to 1:3.4. Gearings of this order allowed oarsmen to drive galleys fast, and with oars as short as the 6.86m of the Angevin galleys they should have been able to handle them quite easily. Their angle to the horizontal was around 15° when the blades were dipped in the water.[59] The angle might

be greater than this, but should be kept as low as possible because the greater it is, the lesser is the mechanical advantage of the oarsmen.

The level of the loaded waterline is unknown. However, it must have been somewhere below the wale, which was 0.455m below the deck at the hull. Even moderate breezes of Beaufort Force 4 raise waves of around 3.5ft (1.07m). Since galleys were not designed to ride waves, and since there must have been scuppers on the deck in the planking covering the *braccioli*, the crests of waves even as small as these would wash over the deck amidships if the freeboard was less than this. A loaded waterline of anything from 0.45m to 0.75m below the deck agrees with the evidence for the freeboard of light galleys of the later Middle Ages and Renaissance.[60]

In traditional ship design everything was a question of give and take. Shipwrights could achieve one thing only at the expense of another. For a galley, the need to minimise submerged hull surface in order to reduce water resistance and maximise speed had to compete with that of maximising the mechanical advantage of the oars by keeping the angle to the waterline as low as possible. Freeboard should be as great as is reasonable.

Both inboard and outboard oars were only 6.86m long. Geometry shows quickly that the major problem with the midships section of these Angevin galleys is how to achieve a reasonable freeboard and at the same time to minimise the angle of the oars to the water. With a grip on the oar handle at 1.25m above the deck, an angle of 15° would mean that the waterline

55. The reason for these longer oars was that new galleys were built with a concave keel so that, as hogging took place over time, the keels would eventually straighten out. See Coates, 'The naval architecture of European oared ships', p4. Because the forward and after ends of the *aposticii* were higher above the waterline than amidships in any case, longer oars were needed.

56. For reconstruction of the longitudinal section and other aspects of these galleys, see 'Galleys of Charles I of Anjou'. The midships section and oarage system is discussed here because the reconstruction now differs markedly from that presented in the earlier study. Although published in 1993, that study was in fact completed in 1989, and further research since then has forced radical reconsideration of the midships section and oarage system.

57. See above, p105.

58. Cf Coates, 'The naval architecture of European oared ships', Fig 3 (p4).

59. Coates, 'The naval architecture of European oared ships', p4. Coates believes that 15° was the norm.

60. Coates, 'The naval architecture of European oared ships', p4. See also F C Lane, 'Cotton cargoes and regulations against overloading', in his *Venice and History* (Baltimore 1966), 253–68, here pp253–4.

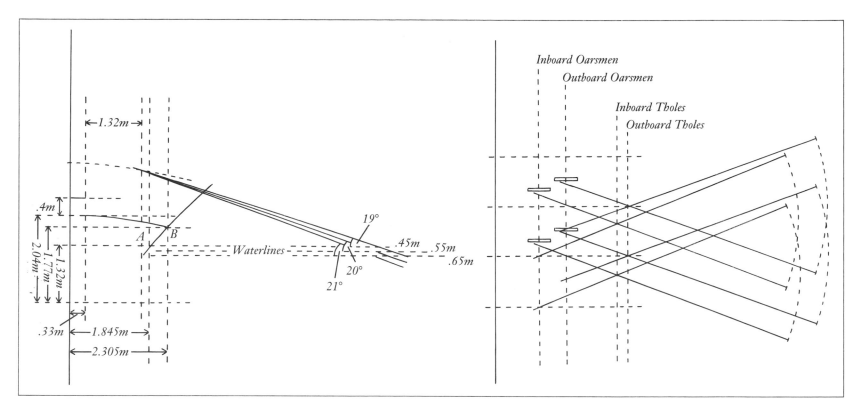

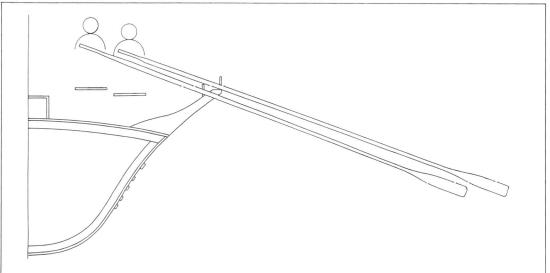

Midships section of the galleys of Charles I of Anjou, as reconstructed by the author from contemporary sources.

counterweights by analogy to those designed for *Olympias* after practical experiment. The oar must be balanced at a point outboard of the thole which gives a 'weight in hand' (*ie* the downward force needed to lift the blade from the water for the return stroke) of no more than approximately 3.5kg. The latest oars designed for *Olympias*, made of spruce with a specific gravity when dry of approximately 0.50, have a weight in hand of 3.60kg.[62] The oars of medieval galleys were also made of fir or spruce. An oar of spruce proportional in dimensions to those of *Olympias*, 6.86m long and with a gearing of 1:3.0, is 8.88cm in diameter at the loom,[63] has a weight in hand of 3.71kg, and has the following dimensions and weights:

Overall length	6.86m
Thole to butt of handle	1.815m
Thole to blade tip	5.045m
Shaft	4.2545m
Loom	1.33m
Neck of loom to handle	0.085m
Handle	0.400m
Mid-handle to butt	0.200m
Centre of pressure of blade to tip	0.200m
Blade	0.7905m
Neck of blade (section)	0.071 x
	0.044m
Loom (section)	0.0888 x
	0.088m

61. F Foerster, 'The warships of the kings of Aragón and their fighting tactics during the thirteenth and fourteenth centuries AD', *International Journal of Nautical Archaeology and Underwater Exploration* 16 (1987), pp19–29. The weights measure 46cm long by 8cm wide by 3–3.6cm thick, and weigh 14.5kg. This is at least two or three times heavier than would have been necessary to balance single-oarsman oars. See the data given below on the weight of the oars of the Angevin galleys designed by analogy to those of *Olympias*. It is possible that they are from the much longer and heavier multiple-oarsmen oars of a later galley of the Renaissance.

62. Information supplied by Mr John Coates.

63. To have a stiffness and strength the same as the oars of *Olympias*, the formula:

$$\frac{(\text{diameter at thole})^4}{(\text{length from thole to mid-handle})^3}$$

must be the same for both oars (information supplied by Mr John Coates). This makes the diameter of the medieval oar 8.88cm.

would be only 17.5cm below the deck, which is obviously impossible.

The design of the oars themselves is unknown. Foerster suggested that some oars used on late-thirteenth-century galleys were counterbalanced by lead weights set in the looms. What he believed were such lead weights were found near the site of the battle of Las Hormigas (AD 1285) off the coast of Catalonia. However, these are too heavy to be counterweights for single-oarsman oars.[61] Moreover, there is no mention in any of the extensive historical sources for the Angevin navy of lead counterweights for oars.

An acceptable gearing and balance for medieval oars can be derived without the use of

Handle (section)	0.044 x 0.044m
Gearing	1:3.0
Weight of oar	c15kg
Weight in hand	3.71kg

With any higher gearing the weight in hand becomes unacceptable. With a lower gearing, the weight in hand decreases.[64] However, a gearing of 1:3.0 gives the most reasonable combination of weight in hand and gearing.

Given this oarage system, the oars can be set at only one position for any freeboard. With the thole set on the arc of the *braccioli* and the mid-handle 1.25m above the deck, approximate angles to the water range from 19° with a freeboard of 0.455m at the wale to 21° with a freeboard of 0.65m The most probable reconstruction is an angle to the water of 20°, with a freeboard of 0.55m and with the file of outboard oarsmen approximately 1.32m from the *cursia*.

The angle to the waterline can be lowered in only three ways. First, by increasing the gearing. But even increasing the gearing to 1:3.4 makes minimal difference to the angles, and the weight in hand becomes unacceptably high.[65] Secondly, by making the flare of the *braccioli* more pronounced in order to lower the position of the thole. However, this would decrease stability, and reducing the angle by a mere 1° in this way would put the outboard benches off the deck. Thirdly, by decreasing the freeboard. But decreasing the freeboard to less than 0.55m would mean that the midships decks really were awash except in a millpond. Although Western bireme galleys were hardly designed for rough weather, there is no evidence to suggest that their decks were continuously awash when at sea.

Although medieval artists no doubt did not intend to portray a precise geometrical relationship, the iconography does show the two files of oars parallel to each other. Although it is, in fact, not possible for them to be exactly parallel, no matter what the freeboard is and where the oarsmen are positioned, nevertheless, the iconography obviously did reflect an approximate relativity. The inboard oars must, therefore, have a gearing and angle to the water as close to those of the outboard oars as possible.

The inboard tholes must have been set on a stringer on the *braccioli*, and unless they were close to the planking over the *braccioli*, the *columbaria* would have to be very elongated. However, the iconography invariably shows these as round circles. Even if they were not necessarily geometrically circular, they cannot

have been as elongated as would be necessary if the tholes were very much inboard of the *columbaria*. The two files of oarsmen must also, therefore, have been close together. The shoulder width of an average man is around 55cm and, allowing for 20cm freedom of movement between the two files, the inboard oars have a grip on the handle approximately 0.68m from the *cursia*, an angle of 21° to the waterline, and *columbaria* at 2.72m from the *cursia*. With *braccioli* equivalent in scantlings to the frames (*ie*, 0.13m), the inboard *scalmi* are 2.54m from the *cursia* and the gearing of the oars is 1:2.25, as opposed to the 1:3.0 of the outboard oars. The height of the benches is around 0.60m for a stand-and-sit stroke, and the height of an oarsman during the pull is around 1.5m The midships section during the pull should, therefore, have approximated that shown in the reconstruction drawing.

The Angevin registers do not distinguish between inboard and outboard oars, but, with a gearing as low as 1:2.25, the inboard oars must have been designed differently. To have the same stiffness at the thole as the outboard oars they would need looms 10.39cm in diameter. Beyond that, they would need a different configuration to reduce the weight of the looms or they would have a negative weight in hand and be unusable. With looms the same length as those of the outboard oars and the shoulder of the handles increased by the same length as the shafts are decreased, then the weight in hand is 2.03kg, which is low but acceptable.

The draught from keel to waterline is 1.33m and the submerged cross-section approximately 3.44m². The length and plane area at the waterline are approximately 33.25m and 90m² respectively. If the lines of the hull are similar to those of Venetian light galleys of the late Middle Ages, then an estimated loaded displacement tonnage would be 90 tonnes.[66] Of this, at least 6.9 tonnes would be the weight of water supplies,[67] 12.16 tonnes the weight of a full complement of 152 crew at an average of 80kg per man, and another 20 tonnes or so the weight of food, armaments, and miscellaneous equipment. The light displacement tonnage of the galley, fully rigged and equipped but unloaded, would be around 50 tonnes, perhaps a little less.

Under sail, galleys normally shipped their oars 'a-wing', with handles on the deck and blades raised as high as possible.[68] This would allow an angle of heel for these galleys of only 10° in moderate breezes (Beaufort scale Force 4 with waves of around 3.5ft or 1.07m). At that point wave crests would lap the *aposticii* and the leeward oars would be parallel to the wave

crests and only centimetres above them. Even allowing for the ability to counteract heeling by transferring the weight of 54 oarsmen and all other 44 crew to windward, a safe angle of heel of only 10° is very low. Tacking would be virtually impossible and sailing close-hauled difficult. In winds above Force 4 such galleys must have had to lower sail and/or run before the wind. They were designed to be rowed rather than sailed and to operate in calm conditions. Their sails were normally used only when the wind was moderate and astern.

Crews varied somewhat according to mission, but normally there were 108 oarsmen, 2 masters, 4 helmsmen, 36 marines, and 2 ship's boys. When senior fleet officers were aboard there were also attendants, notaries, and other officials. Angevin fleets were always commanded by members of the knightly nobility, and large numbers of armoured knights also sailed into battle on the galleys. The masters were not 'captains' since they shared command and surrendered it to senior fleet officers, admirals, vice-admirals, and *prothontini* (port commanders), when the last-named were aboard. The four helmsmen stood watches in turn on the two steering oars. Oarsmen doubled as deck hands when the sails were in use, and some had specific offices: stroke oarsmen, prow hands, and mooring hands. On occasions supernumerary oarsmen (*marinarii subtani* or *tercillerii*) were enlisted to take over from exhausted oarsmen. The marines were men-at-arms who did not serve at the oars. They handled the rockets and catapults for

64. With a gearing of 1:3.1, the weight in hand becomes 3.925kg, and at 1:3.2 it becomes 4.11kg. With a gearing of 1:2.8, the weight in hand reduces to 3.19kg, which is unnecessarily low.

65. Increasing the gearing to 1:3.4 reduces the angles to the waterline at the three waterlines by only 0.3, 0.5, and 0.7°. At the same time it raises the weight in hand to 4.43kg.

66. See Coates, 'The naval architecture of European oared ships' , p6, Fig 7.

67. This is based on a ration of 4 pints per man per day for a cruise of 20 days. See 'Geographical Conditions of Galley Navigation', below pp206–216, and J H Pryor, *Geography, Technology, and War: studies in the maritime history of the Mediterranean 649–1571* (Cambridge 1988), pp75ff. However, this is now regarded as a very conservative estimate. Note that in sea trials of *Olympias* the rowers sweated profusely and needed a litre of water per person per hour. See Rankov, 'Reconstructing the past', p138. If an allowance for the oarsmen of one litre per hour for eight hours per day is made and the rest of the crew are allowed only four pints (2.27 litres) per day, then the crew of an Angevin galley would need not 6.9 tonnes but rather 19.3 tonnes of water for a 20-day cruise.

68. 'Normally' , because this obviously cannot have been possible in storms and very heavy weather. In such conditions oars must have been brought inboard and stowed away.

Greek Fire and other projectiles and also used the crossbows, except when specialist cross-bowmen were enlisted.

Galley fleets were expensive. Across the period *c*1269–86 the cost to the Angevin court of provisions and salaries was approximately 50 ounces of gold tarins per galley per month. The price paid to building contractors for basic hulls, oars, masts, yards, rigging, sails, steering oars, anchors, and cables remained around 100 ounces per galley during the 1270s and then rose to 120 in the 1280s. This did not include further costs of armaments, fitting out, water barrels, carpenter's stores, and the hundred-and-one other necessary items. Excluding these, to build and put to sea a squadron of six galleys for six months with full crews and provisions would cost around 2400 ounces. Perhaps 3500 ounces would be closer to the real cost. This was a huge amount of money at a time when the total revenues of the Kingdom of Sicily were only around 220,000 ounces per annum. On occasions the Angevins put fleets of over eighty galleys to sea. The drain on the treasury, even if many galleys were leased and campaigns were often shorter than six months, was enormous.

By good fortune, two sets of documents survive for thirteenth-century transport galleys. In the twelfth and early thirteenth centuries these were most commonly referred to as *thelandra/chelandium*, but by the mid thirteenth century these terms were replaced by *tarida*, derived from the Arabic *ṭarrīda*. Why the change was made is unknown. No evidence suggests that a design change was involved. Indeed, on occasions the same galleys in the same fleet were described in different sources as either *chelandre* or *taride*.[69]

In March 1246 Louis IX of France contracted with Genoa to provide ships for his forthcoming Crusade, amongst which were 20 *taride*.[70] Then in the 1270s and 1280s the Angevin chancery ordered large numbers of *taride* for various squadrons.[71] In both cases, detailed specifications for the construction and equipping of these transport galleys were recorded in the contracts. They permit reconstruction of *taride* of the later thirteenth century as in Table 7/2. In the case of the Angevins, specifications vary a little from contract to contract.

Taride were designed especially to carry horses, but their capacity varied. In 1224 Frederick II ordered the construction of horse-carrying *usserii* (a generic for a horse-carrier, not a ship type), which were either *chelandre* or *taride*, each capable of carrying 40 knights and their horses. The Genoese *taride* ordered by St Louis in 1246 carried only 20 horses each, but

Table 7/2: Taride of Louis IX (1246) and Charles I of Anjou (1274–81) Primary Specifications

	Louis IX Dimensions or Quantity (to two decimal places)	Number	Charles I of Anjou Dimensions or Quantity (to two decimal places)	Number
Overall length	35.71m.		37.97m	
Depth in hold amidships	2.23m		2.11m	
Headroom from ceiling to deck			1.98m	
Height of sternpost			3.82 or 3.96m	
Height of stempost			3.43m	
Camber of the deck	.125m			
Beam on the floor	3.35m		3.56 or 3.69m	
Beam at the wale (*cinta*)	4.09m		3.96 or 4.09m	
Beam of the deck beams			4.88 or 5.01m	
Sternposts		3		
Ports at the stern for embarking and disembarking horses		2		1 or 2
Dimensions of the port			2.24m high x 1.45m wide	
Length of fore mast	19.34m		17.40m	
Circumference of fore mast	1.24m		.99m	
Length of fore mast yard			28.48m	
Length of midships mast	14.88m		13.45m	
Circumference of midships mast	.99m		.86m	
Length of midships mast yard			23.73m	
Sails		4		3
Length of first sail on yard	29.76m		28.48m	
Length of second sail on yard	27.53m		23.73m	
Length of third sail on yard	25.30m		18.98m	
Length of fourth sail on yard	23.06m			
Anchors	166.78kg	6	133.65kg	3 or 4
Steering oars		2	7.38m	2
Oars			half 7.38m , half 7.65m	108 or 112
Stern loading ramp			3.69m x 1.45m	
Water butts	total capacity 39,750 litres	150		
Water barrels	?	25		
Crew				
Oarsmen (*marinarii*)		19		
helmsman		1		
Stalls for horses		20		30
Length of horse stalls			1.98m	

by the 1270s those of the Angevins carried 30. They were shorter, broader in the beam, and deeper in the hold than war galleys. Nevertheless, they were oared warships proper, designed to be rowed rather than sailed, and their depth in hold was only a few centimetres greater than that of war galleys. As opposed to the 1:10.72 of Angevin war galleys of the 1270s, their ratio of beam-at-the-wales to overall length was 1:8.73 for the Genoese *taride* of 1246 and either 1:9.28 or 1:9.59 for those of Angevin Italy.

At the stern, *taride* had either one or two ports: doors which could be sealed at sea but let down when backed on to a beach to load and unload horses. As the *Annals of Cologne* said, knights could mount their horses inside the *taride* and ride directly on to land across bridges thrown from the port sills to the beach:

For each *usserius* [horse carrier, *ie chelandra* or *tarida*] there was a landing ramp so that if there

should be need, the knights, armed and having mounted their horses on board ship, could easily and without danger of injury disembark via those ramps as if already drawn up in ranks to give battle.[72]

This required unusually designed sterns, described as 'round' (*rotunda*). Some *taride* had only one such port, set between two sternposts

69. See J H Pryor, 'The Crusade of Emperor Frederick II, 1220–29: the implications of the maritime evidence', *American Neptune* 52 (1992), pp113–32; here pp125–7.

70. L T Belgrano, *Documenti inediti riguardanti le due Crociate di San Ludovico IX, re di Francia* (Genoa 1859), pp19–25.

71. Filangieri, *I registri della cancelleria angioina*, 33 vols (Naples 1950–81), esp vol 12, pp175–6; vol 12, pp242–5; vol 13, pp242–3; vol 14, pp161–3; vol 18, pp302–5; vol 24, pp33–7.

72. *Annales Colonienses maximi*, ed K Pertz in *Monumenta Germaniae historica. Scriptores*, Vol XVII (Hanover, 1861), p837. See also Robert of Clari, *The Conquest of Constantinople*, trans E H McNeal (New York 1936), p68.

Ottoman horse transport of the sixteenth century. The specialist horse carrier, or taride, *often had twin or divided sternposts to allow the fitting of a ramp, rather like a primitive version of the Second World War landing craft.* (Topkapi Sarayi Müzesi Müdürlügü, Istanbul, A 3595, fol 102v)

taken off the keel in a 'Y'-shaped fashion. Others had two ports and three sternposts. There was a central sternpost on the keel and one on both sides branching off in a 'Ψ'-shaped fashion, thus allowing for two ports.

On the Angevin *taride*,[73] for which much more detail survives than for those of Louis IX, the horses were stabled in threes fore and aft across the beam. Each trio was allotted a length of 1.98m, and between each trio another 0.13m was allowed for a '*catena mortua*'.[74] A total of 2.11m for the length of a horse is just about right as a minimum. As was the practice everywhere, the horses were suspended by canvas slings under their bellies while at sea. These acted as gimbals to keep the animals vertical when the ships rolled and thus minimise seasickness and prevent them being injured if thrown around. Medieval warhorses were around 75cm wide and Angevin *taride* were 3.56m or 3.69m wide on the floor. Three horses side-by-side, even allowing for some space between them, would still allow access to them by their grooms via gangways along the hulls.

The displacement problems caused by thirty horses and their provisions must have been considerable. A medieval warhorse weighed around 650kg and horses consume large amounts of water, anything from five to ten gallons a day depending upon their size and activities. Even if the animals were inactive while at sea, the holds of *taride* must have been extremely hot in Mediterranean summers, and these were large animals which would have needed considerable water. Allowing 7.5 gallons (34.09 litres) per horse per day, a cruise of 20 days would require 20.45 tonnes of water and the weight of the horses would add another 19.50 tonnes. Then there is the weight of the crews and their water, at least equivalent to that of war galleys. This explains why Louis IX specified that each *tarida* to be supplied by Genoa for his Crusade should have 150 water butts with a total capacity of 39,750 litres, weighing well over 40 tonnes when the weight of the butts themselves is taken into account.

By the 1280s the age of the bireme galley was drawing to a close. Writing early in the fourteenth century, the Venetian Crusade promoter Marino Sanudo Torsello wrote:

> It should be known that in the year of the Lord 1290, two oarsmen used to row on a bench on almost all galleys which sailed the sea. Later more perceptive men realised that three oarsmen could row on each of the aforesaid [benches]. Almost everyone uses this nowadays.[75]

Exactly how this transition from bireme to trireme galleys took place is not known. However, the most probable hypothesis seems to be that around 1280 some naval powers realised that greater speed and endurance could be obtained by taking aboard additional oarsmen. These were known as *tersols* in Catalan, *tercilerii* in Latin, or alternatively simply as 'supernumeraries' (*marinarii subtani*). They may possibly have pulled on oars together with some oarsmen, but more probably simply relieved them when exhausted. Even when they were aboard, Angevin galleys of the 1270s and 1280s never shipped more than the standard 108 oars, so on these galleys at least they did not pull their own oars. But at some point between then and *c*1290 it must have been realised that by rearranging the benches three oars could actually be used. This probably occurred during the protracted War of the Sicilian Vespers between the Angevins and the Sicilians and Aragonese. In 1308 a definite trireme galley with 150 oars, the *Sancta Kathalina*, left Genoa on a voyage to Aigues Mortes. The additional power generated by this change then led to a gradual increase in the size of galleys, eventually producing the 'great galleys' of Genoa and Venice in the fourteenth century.[76]

From the fourteenth century even light war galleys became triremes. The age of the monoreme and bireme was over, except for smaller galleys used for scouting purposes and by corsairs.

John H Pryor

Acknowledgements

The author wishes to acknowledge his debt to Mrs Elizabeth Jeffreys for her unfailing generous and expert assistance with the Byzantine Greek sources used in this chapter.

73. These ships will be the object of a future study in depth by the author.

74. This term (literally, 'dead beam') appears only in these contracts. It has been much discussed without producing any consensus as to its meaning. I believe it is a Latinization by chancery scribes of some South Italian-Greek term for a manger or horse trough. In classical Greek this was *phatnē*. It is not difficult to see how *phatnē* could have been corrupted into some vernacular form which became *catena* in a chancery Latinization. But what '*mortua*' represented is still unknown.

75. Marino Sanudo Torsello, *Liber secretorum fidelium crucis super Terrae Sanctae recuperatione et conservatione* (Hanover 1611), II.iv.5 (p57).

76. J E Dotson, 'Merchant and naval influences on galley design at Venice and Genoa in the fourteenth century', in C L Symonds (ed), *New Aspects of Naval History: selected papers presented at the Fourth Naval History Symposium* (Annapolis 1981), pp20–32.

8

Merchant Galleys

FROM the earliest days of the oared ship down to the ninth century BC, more or less the same sort of galley served for war and for the transport of goods and passengers. There were, to be sure, some differences between the two, but these were not basic. The war galley tended to be slenderer to permit greater speed, the merchant galley beamier to permit greater capacity for cargo, but often the same ship was used for both purposes. When Homer's heroes left Greece to attack Troy they sped over the water in the sleek galleys the poet describes so lovingly, and when they returned these same galleys were loaded down with the women and children taken as captives and the massive amounts of booty plundered from the stricken city.

Then, in the ninth century BC, that distinguishing characteristic of the war galley, the ram, made its appearance and this created a clean split between the two types of vessel, much in the way the introduction of cannon on shipboard some two and a half millennia later created a clean split between the sailing man-of-war and the sailing freighter. From now on war galleys were built in a very special way to enable them to withstand the brutal shocks of ramming, and their prows were encased in the heavy and expensive bronze casting that formed the ram. Merchant galleys had no need of these costly features.

The standard vessel in antiquity for hauling cargo was the sailing ship, and, when the destination involved a long voyage over open water, it was the carrier par excellence. But the merchant galley had its own special and essential role in maritime commerce, for, with its shallower draught and propulsion by oars, it performed services that the sailing vessel, with deeper hull and moved by wind alone, could not. It was able to guarantee delivery of

Phoenician war galleys and transport galleys. Drawn from a relief in the palace of Sennacherib (705-681 BC). (After A H Layard, The Monuments of Nineveh, *1849)*

urgently needed goods or transport of passengers in urgent haste when the wind was either contrary or non-existent. If a port lay in the teeth of a wind, it could still make its way in by running out the oars. On short hops along the coast it could, thanks to its shallow draught, stay comfortably close to shore.

Egyptian galleys

The earliest representations of galleys that we have are in reliefs and paintings from Old Kingdom Egypt (c2700–2200 BC), which portray what are strictly river boats, the various types used on the Nile. It is the New Kingdom to which we owe our first representations of sea-going merchant galleys. These are the vessels pictured on the mortuary temple of Queen Hatshepsut (c1479–1457 BC), which have been discussed in detail in Chapter 1; we see them both under way with their vast mainsails billowing and at the quay with sail lowered. We know they are sea-going, for, as an inscription in hieroglyphs makes clear, they are on an expedition that took them from some Egyptian port on the Red Sea to the land of Punt, either the Ethiopian shore of the Red Sea or the coast of Somalia beyond; the queen had ordered it, since the region of Punt offered a range of products desired by the Egyptians, notably frankincense and myrrh, which they burned on their altars and used for their embalming. And, though the ships are long and slender enough to be war craft, in this expedition they are serving as cargo vessels pure and simple: we see several of them fully loaded as well as one in the process of being loaded, with stevedores swarming up its gangplanks and depositing their burdens on its deck. There was such scant hold space in these shallow hulls that, as the portrayal of the fully loaded ships reveals, not all of the cargo could be stowed below and much was carried on deck. A narrow register on top shows a line of stevedores hauling more things to go on board: one leads a monkey on a leash (the picture of a departing ship shows another monkey running free along a cable above the deck); a group of men carry myrrh trees for transplanting in Egypt, the roots bagged as tidily as any gardener would do it today; other men lead cattle. The inscription just mentioned lists the contents of the cargo. Other inscriptions provide vivid detail about the activities going on: 'Hard to port,' is carved over the pilot of one of the ships in motion; 'Watch your step,' is carved over the stevedores in the loading scene.

Thanks to the Egyptian artists' care in rendering detail and to the Egyptian practice of

Roman merchant galley with common convex prow; end of the first century BC. Wall painting from a villa near Sirmione. (Fototeca Unione, Rome)

including explanatory inscriptions, we know these merchant galleys of Hatshepsut's reliefs better than any other of the ancient world; never again will we enjoy such a fullness of information. And, though they are ships of a distinctive Egyptian type, they illustrate certain features that we will find throughout the centuries: a full sailing rig in order to use the wind whenever possible and thereby save the rowers' energy for when it was needed; the carrying of cargo on the deck since a galley's hull, necessarily shallow, provided a hold of limited capacity.

Greek and Phoenician craft

In the *Odyssey* Homer likens the mighty staff the Cyclops carried to 'the mast of a broad-beamed, black-hulled, 20-oared merchantman that sails the great sea'. Although the poet has in mind the ships of his own day, his description neatly hits the key characteristics of all ancient seagoing merchant galleys. The mast was thick and powerful – as thick and powerful as a giant's staff, no less – because it had to support a rig that saw more and harder use than any war galley's rig. The beam was broad to provide adequate space for cargo. The ship in his simile, presumably a very common size, has 10 rowers to a side; this is much fewer than the 25 of the standard contemporary war gal-

leys, but quite enough for merchant galleys, since they had no particular need for speed.

From the beginning of the first millennium BC on, two maritime peoples dominated the waters of the eastern Mediterranean, the Greeks and the Phoenicians. The earliest clear representations that we have of the merchant galleys of the age are of Phoenician craft – craft that, it so happens, are unlike the general run of merchant galleys, their hulls being stubby and deep rather than long and shallow. They appear in a relief from the palace of the Assyrian king Sennacherib (705–681 BC) that illustrates an episode in Sennacherib's capture of the Phoenician port of Tyre in 701: we see the king of Tyre along with men and women of his court fleeing from the city in the fastest craft available, merchant galleys as well as war galleys. The war galleys are easily distinguished by their greater length and prominent rams. The merchant galleys are almost bowl-shaped and are propelled by 8, sometimes 9, oarsmen a side; the hull is too short for all these to row in one level but deep enough to put them in two, as in the men-of-war. The Phoenicians had certain sailing ships that were so round they were called *gauloi*, the Greek form of a Phoenician word meaning 'bowls'; obviously they had merchant galleys that were bowl-shaped as well.

We also owe to the Phoenicians – or, more exactly, to their descendants, the Carthaginians – the only detailed evidence we have for the construction of ancient merchant galleys. It is provided by two Carthaginian wrecks that were discovered off the western coast of Sicily between Trapani and Marsala. Although divers have come upon the remains of over a thousand sailing freighters, these are the sole examples they have found to date of merchant galleys. This is chiefly due to what the two types of vessel generally carried. Sailing ships took aboard cargoes of the heavy clay jars in which wine and oil, among the ancient world's principal commodities, were shipped, as well as massive loads of building stone, which went from various quarries to sites all around the Mediterranean. When a vessel with its hold full of such materials went down and landed on the bottom, the action of wind, water, and sand soon destroyed the topsides, laying bare the cargo; this, being well-nigh impervious to destruction, lies on the sea floor, not only signalling the presence of a wreck but preserving from decay the part of the hull under it. On the other hand, merchant galleys that sank tended to vanish without trace, since they were carrying passengers or miscellaneous light goods or other perishable cargoes.

vertical stempost and a curious projecting cut-water; we will deal with this sort of shape in a moment.

What Phoenician or Carthaginian sources have to tell about ancient merchant galleys is invaluable but limited. Most of our knowledge comes from the Greeks, who were the key figures in the trade of the Mediterranean from about the eighth century BC on, and whose maritime technology was taken over by the Romans. From this time until the end of the ancient world the representations we have of merchant galleys are from Greek and Roman sources – paintings, mosaics, sculptures. One mosaic, found at the Roman town of Althiburus in Tunisia, is particularly helpful because it pictures and identifies by name twenty-one different types of vessel, including a number that are merchant galleys. In addition, much useful information is supplied by Greek and Roman writers: they frequently relate incidents in which merchant galleys figure, and in so doing sometimes give the names of the types and indications of their size, shape, or use.

The Greek word for merchant galley is *histiokōpos*, 'sail-oar-er'. The Latin word is *actuaria navis* or just *actuaria*, 'ship that moves'. Apparently, for the Greeks the prime feature of a merchant galley was that, unlike its relative, the sailing freighter, it used oars as well as sail, while what struck the Romans was that it could keep moving, even when there was no wind to fill the sail.

The pictures of Greek and Roman merchant

Exceptional circumstances somehow saved the remains of the two Carthaginian ships, which are of the late third or early second century BC, to judge from the datable remains – fragments of jars and other pottery – found in them. We know they are Carthaginian because the shipwrights who built them, as was not uncommon ancient practice, painted words or letters at certain spots to indicate where nails were to go, mortises were to be cut or frames were to be set, and in both of these hulls the letters are in the Punic (*ie* Carthaginian) alphabet. The shape of the vessels, long and narrow and shallow, shows unmistakably that they are galleys.

One of the hulls was excavated fully and, though the forward area is missing, enough of the ship is preserved to make possible an estimate of its dimensions; 5m (16ft) in beam and 30m (98ft) in length, a ratio of 6:1. This is just what we would expect: ancient sailing vessels tend to run 3 or 4:1, war galleys 10:1. The hull was put together in standard ancient fashion: first a shell of planking was created by pinning the planks to each other with closely set mortise and tenon joints, and then frames were inserted into the shell. As a protection against marine borers, the underwater surface was covered with lead sheathing laid over fabric impregnated with resin. Ancient sailing vessels were commonly so sheathed, and it is no surprise to find it on this hull: like sailing ships,

merchant galleys when not under way were tied up to buoys or docks and hence needed such protection (war galleys, which were drawn up on land when not in use, neither needed it nor could afford to have their speed handicapped by the weight it added to the hull). In the wreck were found not only fragments of jars, which may have held provisions for the crew, but also a variety of bones of animals: a small dog (a crewman's pet?), ox, sheep or goat, deer, pig, horse. Some of the bones show signs of butchering; the others presumably came from animals carried as cargo.

Although the second hull was not excavated, examination of the surface remains revealed that the prow was preserved. It consists of a

Greek merchant galley of the late sixth century BC. Painting on a Greek jug in the Meermanno-Westreenianum Museum, The Hague.

River galley with 21 oars a side transporting barrels of wine; c300 AD. The six figures, since they face forward, should not be rowers, perhaps they are the deck crew. Funerary monument from Neumagen now in the Landesmuseum, Trier.

galleys, together with what can be gleaned from remarks dropped by ancient writers, enable us to divide the ships roughly into three groups according to the shape of the prow. One group, no doubt the largest, has the common convex prow. A second has straight-line prows; the line sometimes descends vertically to the waterline, sometimes it descends at an angle slanting aft, more rarely forward; the forward slant, it so happens, appears in the earliest picture we have of a Greek merchant galley, dating to the sixth century BC. A third group has prows that are concave and end in a forefoot jutting out so prominently at the waterline that it strongly resembles a warship's ram. Although this might seem an unusual shape for non-combatant craft, it is found on sailing freighters as well as merchant galleys, and on all sizes of both, from mere dories to big seagoing carriers. The prow of the Carthaginian galley described above seems to be a hybrid, combining the straight stempost of the second group with the jutting cutwater of the third.

(a) Remains of a broad shallow galley used for harbour work found in the mud of what was once the harbour of Rome at the mouth of the Tiber; Roman Imperial period. (b) Drawing of the remains and possible reconstruction.

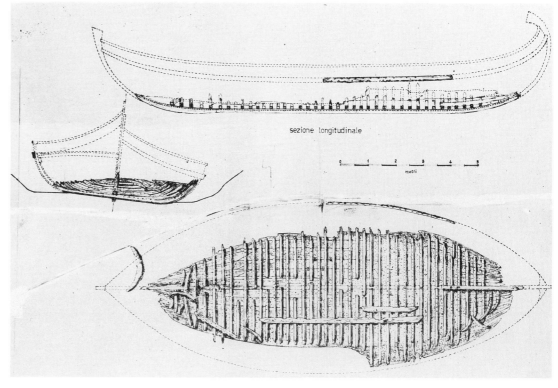

sezione longitudinale

metri

Galleys for transport of beasts for the gladiatorial games; fourth century AD. The artist has taken the liberty of depicting both the loading (at the stern) and the unloading (at the prow). Mosaic from a villa at Piazza Armerina, Sicily.

A single broad square sail, like the mainsail of sailing ships, was the standard rig. The largest galleys might also have an *artemon*, as the ancient version of the foresail was called, a smaller square sail set on a mast that slanted over the bows. The main – and perhaps the *artemon* – was fitted with the standard ancient system for shortening sail, a set of brails. These were a series of equally spaced lines that ran from the foot up the forward surface to the yard and then over the yard to the deck aft; pulling on them bunched the sail up toward the yard, much in the way a venetian blind is raised. They were a splendid device, for they permitted quick and total control over the sail expanse: by pulling given brails a given distance it was possible to present to the wind the precise portion and amount of sail that was desirable.

As noted briefly earlier, merchant galleys supplied the services that sailing craft were unable to do or did less efficiently. Greek and Roman travellers found them the best means for getting to a nearby destination, because arrival was assured even if there was no wind or if it was foul. Cicero, for example, used a merchant galley when he went from Puteoli, just west of Naples, across the Bay of Naples to Pompeii, a trip of some eighteen miles. One could even cover long distances in merchant galleys by a series of short hops from port to port along the coast, but it was a wearisome business. Prince Agrippa, who in AD 38 had to get from Rome to Palestine, thought of doing it this way until Emperor Caligula talked him out of it (Caligula told him to take one of the 'crack sailing freighters . . . [whose] skippers . . . drive their vessels like race horses on an unswerving course that goes straight as a die'). Gladiatorial games, the Romans' national pastime, required a steady supply of wild animals for some of the events; they were caught in Africa and were shipped from ports on the north coast across the Mediterranean in merchant galleys. The voyage must have been hard on the beasts, and the merchant galley offered the fastest way of doing it. Similarly it was the carrier favoured for perishable cargoes, at least when the distance involved was not overly great. This is indicated by a business document drawn up in Egypt that has come down to us. (Relatively few routine everyday non-literary writings have survived from antiquity, and of those that have, the vast majority, written mostly in Greek, come from Egypt when it was under Greek or Roman rule. In Egypt, a well-nigh rainless land, discarded papers, instead of being destroyed by dampness and vanishing as everywhere else, got covered by dry sand and many survived under this protective blanket.) The document in question is a customs listing dated 259 BC that gives the details of a shipment from Syria of table and dessert wines and miscellaneous foodstuffs – honey, cheese, various kinds of meats – destined for the table of a high official at Alexandria. The shipment must have taken place some time between May and September, since voyaging over open water was confined almost exclusively to these months, and it went not in a sailing vessel but in two merchant galleys, no doubt to limit the amount of time a cargo of this nature had to spend in a damp, overheated hold. A famous anecdote about Cato the Elder tells how, during his campaign to convince his countrymen that 'Carthage must be destroyed!', he dramatised the nearness to Rome of the putative hostile city by holding up a ripe fig in the Senate and assuring the members that it had been plucked in North Africa just three days earlier; it must have been brought to him by a fast merchant galley. Even cargo that nearly always went by sailing ship was on occasion put aboard merchant galleys, as a picture of one with a load of shipping jars filling every inch of its deck shows; presumably the need for speed determined the choice.

Merchant galley types

There are a number of types of ancient merchant galley that can be identified by name.

One of the biggest and most versatile types was what the Greeks called an *akatos* and the Romans an *actuaria*. Though the term *akatos* in a general sense could refer to any kind of oared ship, and though *actuaria*, as noted earlier, was the Romans' term for merchant galleys in general, both also had a specific sense, namely a particular type of big merchant galley of the group with concave prow and projecting forefoot. We know it was big because Roman authors mention *actuariae* with crews of 30 or even 50 oarsmen. We know it had the concave prow with projecting forefoot because a galley pictured on the Althiburus mosaic and identified as an *actuaria* has such a prow. And confirmation is provided by an incident related in Caesar's *Alexandrian War*. In 47 BC Vatinius, Caesar's general stationed at Brindisi, in answer to appeals from Caesar's forces across the Adriatic, went to their aid. Desperately needing war craft for the venture and having few at his disposal, he improvised: 'he fitted *actuariae* with rams, even though their size was not at all right for battle'. To put a ram on a galley with the common convex prow would require total rebuilding, and Vatinius was in a hurry. But putting it on a galley with a projecting forefoot would require merely the strengthening of the timbers and the addition of a bronze casing. The craft he refitted are characterised as 'not at

Galley loaded with amphoras; second or third century AD. Mosaic found at Tebessa, Algeria.

all right for battle' because they no doubt had to fight against triremes, and even if they were the biggest size attested, with 50 rowers, they would hardly be a match for such opponents. They would, however, stand a chance against war galleys lighter than a trireme. The picture in the Althiburus mosaic shows that the rig was the usual merchant galley rig, a single broad square sail.

Akatoi/actuariae were to be found throughout the eastern Mediterranean, from the Adriatic where Vatinius commandeered his *actuariae*

An actuaria. *Drawing of a detail of the Althiburus mosaic; third or fourth century AD. The figure in the prow is the time-beater who pounds on a drum with a* portisculus *'mallet'. (After École française de Rome,* Mélanges d'archéologie et d'histoire *61, 1949)*

to the southeasternmost corner, where an *akatos* is recorded as carrying cargo between Alexandria and Ascalon. And they had a long career: they were still being used in the seventh century AD, in the fleet of the Arab conquerors of Egypt.

The *lembos* (Latinised by the Romans to *lembus*) shares several of the characteristics of the *akatos/actuaria*. The term has both a wide and narrow sense. In the first it can refer to oared craft of many types – harbour craft, fishing dories and riverboats. In the second it means specifically a large galley that had a concave prow with projecting forefoot, as can be deduced from the fact that *lemboi* were frequently fitted with rams for use as naval auxiliaries; such adaptation, as noted a moment ago, was most easily done on a prow with projecting forefoot. That they were given rams indicates they were used in combat and hence must have been fairly big. When, in 195 BC, the Romans defeated a despot of Sparta, the treaty they made him sign included a stipulation that 'he could have no ships except two *lembi* driven by no more than 16 rowers'. These vessels, clearly of a minimal size too small to be of use for fighting, still accommodated 8 oarsmen on each side. Those used for combat had as many as 25 a side, and the mention of 'bireme *lembi*' reveals that some of the ships were made shorter and deeper in order to put the rowers on two levels. A key virtue of *lemboi* was their speed: descriptions of battles in which they saw

service reveal they were fast enough to dart about and harry triremes.

And speed was one of the advantages the *lembos* offered as a cargo carrier, as we can deduce from another of the business documents preserved by Egypt's sands. Dated 259–258 BC, it is a listing of a cargo, some 54 tons of olive oil, that was shipped from ports in Asia Minor and Syria to Alexandria in three merchant galleys, two *lemboi* and a *keles*. Any sailing freighter of average size could alone have carried four times that much and more. The only possible reason for sending the oil in so seemingly inefficient a way must have been an urgent need for it, and the *lemboi* and a *keles* – particularly noted for its speed, as we shall see shortly – could assure quick delivery. Fast merchant galleys must have been narrower and shallower than their slower sisters in order to move swiftly through the water; inevitably they would be less commodious. As a consequence, even this modest quantity of oil required three such craft: the biggest, one of the *lemboi*, had aboard about 25 tons, the other *lembos* 15, and the *keles* 14.

The *lembos* seems to have had a short life. Its heyday as a naval auxiliary was in the third and second centuries BC and there are no references to it after the first century BC.

The very name of the *keles* refers to speed, for the basic meaning of the word is 'racehorse'. Similarly, the Roman term for the vessel was *celox*, meaning 'fast' (the *cel-* is akin to the first syllable in 'celerity'). It may well have been the fastest of the non-combatant galleys afloat, so fast that pirates favoured it for overtaking their victims, and navies for carrying dispatches. The news, for example, that the Spartan fleet had been defeated by the Athenian in the battle of Arginusae in 406 BC was rushed to Sparta in a *keles*. Herodotus reports a story he was told that, at the crucial battle of Salamis in 480 BC between the Persian aggregation and the combined contingents of the various Greek cities, the squadron from Cor-

A celox. *Drawing of a detail of the Althiburus mosaic; third or fourth century AD.*

inth deserted in fright but was summoned back to do its duty by a mysterious group of men who gave chase and caught up with it; the ship they were in was a *keles*. The fig that Cato showed to the Roman Senate may well have come to him from Carthage in a *keles*.

The *keles* was smaller than the *lembos*. A picture in the Althiburus mosaic shows it had a straight prow. As in the case of the *lembos*, there are no references to it after the first century BC.

The *phaselos* (Latinised to *phaselus*) was yet another fast merchant galley, chiefly used for carrying passengers. It ran the gamut of size, from small private yachts to vessels able to accommodate hundreds and make voyages of considerable length. It was a *phaselus*, for example, that brought the Roman poet Catullus safely home to Italy from Bithynia on the southern shore of the Black Sea in 56 BC, and a poem he wrote in its honour enables us to reconstruct the route: the ship followed the coast from 'the savage Pontus [Black Sea]', through the 'rough Propontis [Sea of Marmora]', along the west coast of Asia Minor to 'famous Rhodes', then through the 'isles of the Cyclades' into the 'menacing Adriatic'.

Phaselos means 'bean-pod'; the vessel presumably was long and narrow. Like the *akatos* and *lembos*, it could be fitted for naval combat and this would indicate it had the same form of prow as they, concave with projecting forefoot. And it was fast: Catullus, with pardonable licence, boasts that his *phaselus*

> was able to outstrip the drive
> of any other craft afloat,
> whether to fly with flashing blades
> was called for, or with linen sail.

Alongside the sleek *lembos*, *keles*, and *phaselos* there were beamier types, merchant galleys designed for capacity rather than speed, and of these the best known are the *kybaia* (*cybaca* in Latin) and the *kerkuros* (*cercurus* in Latin). The name *kybaia* means 'cubic'; presumably vessels of this class had a boxlike shape. And, indeed, a business document from Egypt mentions a *kybaia* that was about 18.3m (60ft) long with a beam of just under 3.5m (11½ft), a truly boxy ratio of *c*5:1, almost equal to the 4:1 ratio common in sailing ships. This was a small *kybaia*, for Cicero in one of his orations speaks of 'a ship truly big as the biggest *cybaea*, the likes of a trireme', which implies a length of double 18.3m.

Kerkuros derives from the Assyrian term *qurqurru*, the name of a type of Mesopotamian riverboat, and the *kerkuros* certainly saw con-

siderable use on rivers. When Alexander the Great crossed the Hydaspes in India in 327 BC, he used *kerkuroi* to ferry over his heavy gear, and it was the standard carrier of grain on the Nile under the Ptolemies, *ie* the third to the first centuries BC. For example, a business document gives the details of the fleet that gathered at Ptolemais, a Nile port in the Fayum, to haul the annual revenues in wheat – the year involved was about 171 BC – downriver to Alexandria; it consisted of *kerkuroi*, of which the smallest had aboard 225 tons and the largest double that. The cargoes, as great as those carried by sea-going sailing freighters, show how big *kerkuroi* were; they could well have been the biggest merchant galleys afloat.

There are no references to either the *kybaia* or *kerkuros* after the first century BC.

It may seem curious that so many of the craft described above receive no mention after the first century BC. This does not mean that they, or merchant galleys in general, were no longer to be found on the water. It simply reflects the capriciousness and haphazardness of our information, notably the fact that writers, in dealing with the ships that carried passengers or goods, more often than not saw no need to be specific. When the word *navis* occurs in a Latin text, the context often indicates that the 'boat' in question was a merchant galley, but, since the author was content to use the general term, we have no way of being certain. A business document from Egypt dating in the third century AD describes a fleet of *ploia* loaded with grain for shipment down the Nile; these 'boats' could well have been *kerkuroi* or craft very like them – but we cannot be sure.

Thus, because of the fragmentary nature of what we know about merchant galleys, we cannot follow their history in an unbroken line from the end of the ancient world into the Middle Ages. The best we can do is pick it up at times and places for which information happens to be available.

In the Mediterranean, we can assume, *lemboi* and *phaseloi* and the other types, or their descendants, continued to ply the waters. Although outside the scope of this volume, it is worth remembering that merchant galleys were also employed in northern Europe. From the ninth to the eleventh century, the lords of its seas were the Vikings; the combination of a body of writings describing their exploits and some fortunate archaeological discoveries gives a fair idea of the ships that were the key to their success. We think of Viking galleys as men-of-war, and, no question, they were that, but recent archaeological finds of the highest import-

ance have revealed that the Vikings also had galleys designed for the transport of passengers and goods as well as rower/warriors. At Roskilde in Denmark were uncovered the remains of a series of boats that, about AD 1000, had been loaded with stones and sunk to block a narrow channel; two of these turned out to have been merchant galleys. (These are detailed in the first chapter of *Cogs, Caravels and Galleons* in this series.)

Medieval merchant galleys

The final episode in the history of the merchant galley is the most glorious, for it is a time when the merchant galley no longer played its customary subordinate role in maritime commerce but shared the lead. The setting is Venice. From the Middle Ages on, the city became rich and powerful through a far-flung trade that took its ships not only the length and breadth of the Mediterranean but out into the Atlantic and on to northern Europe.

Until the end of the thirteenth century the merchants of Venice had shipped their goods in sailing craft, mostly of small size. Since the city was often at war, especially with Genoa, and since marauders of all sorts were loose on the waters, the ships went out in convoys escorted by a powerful force of war galleys to protect them. In 1294 the Venetian state instituted a crucial change that ushered in the merchant galley's new role: it built the first of the so-called 'great galleys', vessels that had the lines of a galley and a full complement of oarsmen but were longer, wider and deeper, enabling them to spread more canvas and, most important, have room for a sizable amount of cargo. The oarsmen were arranged just as on Venice's men-of war, three men alongside each other on the same bench, each pulling his own oar. In such a system, known as *alla sensile*, the oars were necessarily very long, some 10m (33ft); they pivoted on an outrigger with fully a third of their length inboard and were heavily weighted with lead at the inboard end so that they would balance and relieve the rowers of their weight. On the earlier 'great galleys', which were relatively small, there were some 25 three-man clusters on each side. The rig consisted of an enormous lateen sail on a mast stepped forward of amidships and a smaller lateen aft of amidships. Steering was done by the centreline stern rudder, which by this time had come into universal use. Though so much of the ship was given over to the elaborate rowing arrangement and the housing of multitudinous oarsmen, the 'great galleys', like all merchant galleys, travelled under sail as much

A Venetian 'great galley' of the late fifteenth century.
Woodcut from Bernhard von Breydenbach's
Peregrinatio in Terram Sanctam, *published in 1486.*

this reduction in rowers freed space for more passengers, and of the passengers there were sure to be enough able to bear arms to fill the requirements of defence.

Among the pilgrims who sailed on these galleys were a few who have left accounts of their voyages – and their words provide us with what is for ancient and medieval times a rare and precious form of evidence, that of an eye-witness. Here, for example, is what Brother Felix Fabri tells about the ship that in 1483 brought him to the Holy Land. As his report makes clear, he was aboard one of the bigger types equipped with three masts:

> Venetian galleys are as like to one another as the nests of swallows. They are built of the stoutest timbers, and fastened together with many bolts, chains, and irons. The first and foremost part of the galley, which is called the prow, is sharp where it meets the sea, and has a strong beak, shaped to look like a dragon's head with open mouth, all of iron, with which it can strike any ship advancing against it. On either side of the beak are two holes, through which a man can put his head, through which are passed the cables of the anchors, and through which the anchors are let out and pulled up; nor can the sea run in through these holes except in great storms. . . . The prow also has its own sail . . . and it has a small chamber below, in which ropes and sails are stored, and in it sleeps the officer in charge of the prow, who has a staff of his own who stay only in that chamber and carry out whatever has to be done there. . . .
>
> The stern, which is the other and aftermost end of the galley, is not sharp where it meets the sea, like the prow, nor does it have a beak, but it is wide and curves from above downwards to the water, and is much higher than the prow, having upon it a tall structure which they call the castle. From the stern there hangs down into the sea the rudderpost, or rudder, above which, in a latticed chamber, is the steersman, holding the tiller in his hands. The castle has three storeys: the first, in which are the helmsman and the compass, the man who tells the helmsman how the compass points, those who watch the stars and winds, and those who point out the routes across the sea; the middle one in which is the chamber of the lord and captain of the ship, and of his noble comrades and messmates; and the lowest one in which noble ladies are housed at night, and

as possible and turned to their oars only when entering or leaving port, rounding a headland in the teeth of a foul wind, drifting in a calm toward danger, and so on. The key reason for having all those rowers aboard was defence: they were there to wield not only oars but, when the occasion required, weapons; indeed, a certain number of them were bowmen selected by public contest from among the best shots in Venice. The whole point of this new type of galley was to eliminate the expense and planning involved in providing warship escorts; even if sailing alone it was able to repel attack.

The first 'great galleys' launched measured c40.3m by 5.3m by 2.5m (132ft × 17ft × 8ft) and could stow below the deck some 140 tons of cargo. They grew steadily: by the end of their career, in the early sixteenth century, they were c46m by 8m by 3m (151ft × 26ft × 10ft), could stow 250 tons below the deck, had 30 clusters of rowers on each side, and carried three lateen sails. Shipments of cheap and bulky goods, such as cotton, alum, wine and grain, continued to go in sailing craft; the 'great galleys', well defended and expensive to man, were reserved for the costly cargoes of spices, silks, gems, and the like.

In the course of time a special kind of 'great galley' came into being, one fitted to handle a special kind of cargo – pilgrims to the Holy Land. Venice had been the leading port of embarcation for these travellers ever since the Crusades. In the fourteenth century, despite

the fact that the fare was higher, galleys began to be their preferred mode of transport. Sailing ships took them straight across the water without a stop; the galleys followed the coasts and frequently put into port, which provided a welcome chance to those aboard not only to stretch their legs and buy in some fresh food, but also to see the sights. The pilgrim galleys were just like their cargo-carrying sisters save that usually there were but two rowers to each bench; the rationale could well have been that

Detail, showing the arrangement of the rowers, of a
model of a Venetian galley of the fifteenth century.

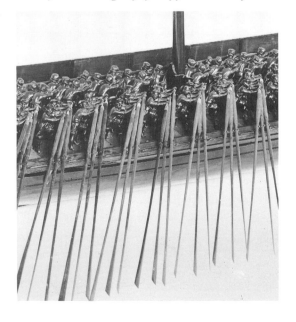

where the captain's treasure is stored. This chamber receives no light except from the hatchways in the floor above. On either side of the poop hang the skiffs, or boats, one large and one small, which in harbours are lowered into the water, and people are taken off in them. On the righthand side are the steps down which one goes to, or comes up from, the boats in the water. The poop also has its own sail, bigger than the sail at the prow. . . . Also on the poop a pennant is kept raised at all times to indicate the varying direction of the winds.

Two benches beyond the cabin on the poop [ie, two rowers' benches forward of the sterncastle], on the righthand side is the kitchen, which is not covered over: beneath the kitchen is the cellar, and beside the kitchen is the stable for the animals that are to be slaughtered; sheep, goats, calves, oxen, cows, and pigs all stand there together. Further on, on the same side are benches with oars right up to the prow. On the lefthand side are rowers' benches all the way from the poop to the prow, and on every bench are three rowers and an archer. Between two benches on the edge of the ship on either side there hangs a *bombarda* in a mov-

able iron swivel, and on either side there is a *bombardana*; from these, in case of necessity, stones are fired. In the middle of the ship is the main mast, a tall, thick, and strong mast made of many timbers fastened together, which supports the yard. . . . On deck next to the main mast there is an open space where men gather to talk as in a forum; and it is called the forum of the galley. . . . Now on this upper deck of the galley live the ship's company of the galley, and the rowers, each man upon his own bench, and there they sleep, eat, and work. Between the benches on either side in the middle is a fairly wide space, in which stand great chests full of merchandise, and above these chests there is a walkway from the prow to the poop; the rowing masters also run along here when the oars are being worked.

Close to the main mast is the main hatchway, through which one descends by seven steps into the hold which is the place where the pilgrims live, or where the cargo is put in cargo-carrying galleys. Now in length this hold reaches from the cellar in the stern to the small chamber in the prow, and in width from one side of the ship to the other, and it is like a

great and spacious chamber. It receives no light except for what comes through the four hatchways by which it is entered. In this hold every pilgrim has his own berth or space. Furthermore, the berths of the pilgrims are so arranged that, for the length of the ship, or rather of the hold, one berth is alongside the next without any space in between, and one pilgrim lies by the side of the other, along both sides of the ship, having their heads towards the sides of the ship and their feet stretching out towards each other. Since the hold is wide, there stand along the middle of it, between the berths, chests and pilgrims' trunks, reaching from the cellar to the chamber in the prow, in which the pilgrims keep their own private property, and, when they sleep, on both sides, to the left and to the right, they stretch out their feet up to these trunks. Beneath the pilgrims is a large cavity reaching in depth down to the bottom of the vessel. . . . This . . . is filled with sand right up to the planks on which the pilgrims lie; and the pilgrims lift up the

Plan of the 'great galley' described by Felix Fabri (After J Sottas, *Les messageries maritimes de Venise aux XIVe & XVe siècles*, Paris 1938)

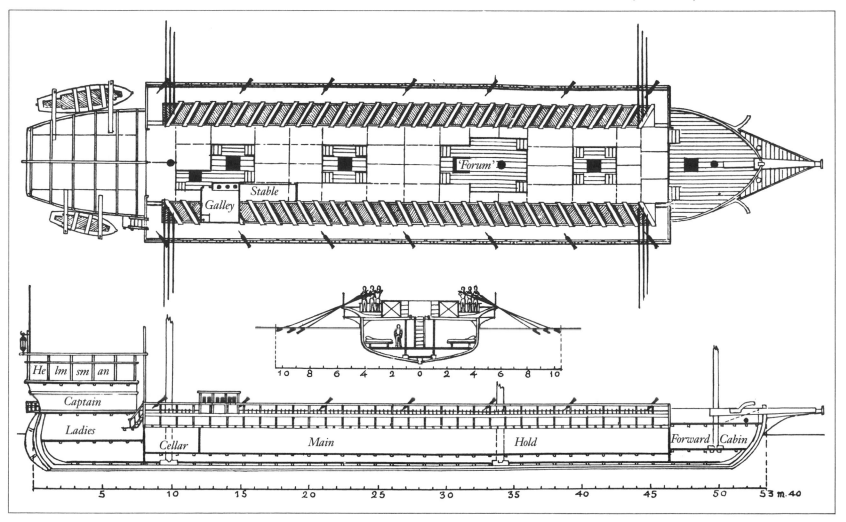

planks and bury in that sand the little jugs in which they keep their wine, and eggs, and other things which need to be kept cool. Also below, in the pilgrims' quarters, next to the middle of the main mast is the well for bilge water, and this well does not collect human filth, but all the moisture and water that visibly and invisibly gets into the galley drips and flows into that well, and it gives off the foulest possible stench, worse than that from any latrine for human excrement. This well has to be pumped out once every day, but in rough weather all the water has to be drawn up out of it with no let-up. Along the outer sides of the galley are places for emptying the bowels.

On all the 'great galleys', even those with three masts like Fabri's, most of the drive, as on ancient vessels, was produced by the mainsail. One of the shortcomings of the lateen rig is that the only way to take in sail is by hauling down whatever is being carried and replacing it with something smaller. On an ordinary lateener this is hard enough; on a 'great galley', whose mainsail was huge, it must have been

tremendously difficult: the crew not only had to handle a vast spread of canvas but also lower and then raise a massive yard almost as long as the vessel itself; with only muscle for power, the procedure must have been long as well as laborious.

There could not have been many such time-consuming changes of sail during Fabri's voyage because it was relatively quick: he spent 18 days at sea and 11 at various stops en route for a total of 29; usually it took 40 or 50. The ship stayed as close to land as possible: the route followed the east coast of the Adriatic to Corfu, then on to Modon on the southwestern corner of the Peloponnese, then through the channel between Cerigo and Cape Malea and over open water to Candia in Crete, then again over open water to Rhodes, from Rhodes along the coast of Asia Minor until the mouth of the Gulf of Adalia and from there over open water to Paphos on Cyprus, from Paphos to Larnaca, and – the welcome last leg – from Larnaca to Jaffa. We must look behind Fabri's matter-of-fact words to perceive how grim an experience even his quick passage must have been. The

pilgrims, probably close to a hundred of them, were packed in at night like sardines, breathing fetid stale air; their closeness – pates against the bulkhead and feet against their chests – probably kept them wedged in place when the ship tossed in rough seas but could only have exacerbated the effects of seasickness, creating without doubt a smell that overpowered even the bilge. The sanitary facilities for everybody aboard, perhaps up to 300 in all, were a few outhouses at the stern hanging over the water.

The pilgrim galleys were far outnumbered by those 'great galleys' that carried cargo. A Venetian historian of the fifteenth century reports that each year

four brought from Syria, and an equal number from Egypt, perfumes, silk, precious stones, and pearls. Three others picked up in Libya gold, gems, slaves. Three brought from France's Mediterranean coast a very precious wool, and, from Spain, the most beautiful silks of all. Four go to pick up at the Palus Maeotis [Sea of Azov] salt fish, carpets, emeralds, and, besides these, four others collect in French ports on the ocean wool, gold, tapestries, and a considerable amount of Flemish cloth.

Actually, Flemish cloth was picked up where it was made by the so-called 'galleys of Flanders'. These, four or five in number, carried out the most difficult voyage of all, from Venice through the Straits of Gibraltar, along the Atlantic coast to London and Bruges.

About the middle of the sixteenth century, this last and greatest age of the merchant galley came to an end. Improvement in the design and especially in the rig of sailing vessels not only made them a more efficient mode of transport than they had been, but also made them harder to attack and easier to defend; pilgrims now chose them in preference to the galleys. The discovery of an all-water route to India and the Far East and the other major shifts in the commercial picture took away the geographical advantage Venice once enjoyed, and what was left of her declining trade could no longer afford to go in the costly galleys and went in full rigged sailing ships instead.

The 'great galleys' themselves still had more than a century of active life ahead of them, for the Venetians ingeniously converted them into men-of-war – but that is another's story.

Lionel Casson

Map showing the routes taken by the 'great galleys' from Venice to to the Holy Land. (Adapted from Sottas, Les messageries *by Denis Baker)*

9

The Naval Architecture and Oar Systems of Ancient Galleys

THIS chapter is about the material characteristics and architecture of the warships with which extensive naval wars were fought in the Mediterranean in the course of about a thousand years leading up to the relative peace of the Roman empire. The evidence is scanty, consisting of a number of statements scattered through the surviving historical literature; a number of representations of ships or parts of ships ranging from quite small stylised images on coins to a few nearly full-sized but mutilated stone monuments; remains of slipways for warships and one wreck only, to date, of an oared ship which was probably a fleet auxiliary. About one type of warship, the Athenian trireme, there also survive inscriptions from the ancient naval dockyard at Piraeus, which give the numbers of oarsmen and classes of oarsmen in those ships as well as mentioning various items of gear and equipment, thus making the type the best documented of all. The numbers of other ships' complements, or parts of their crews, appear in the literature, as do some references to passages at sea under oar from which average speeds can be deduced. These sources have been studied by a few classical scholars upon whom the writer, a naval architect, has relied for historical evidence. His reconstructions, some of which are shown in this chapter, but necessarily only in summary, would not have been possible without the active collaboration of John Morrison and the use of his detailed studies.[1]

During the pre-Christian millennium, warships in the Mediterranean grew from 20- and 30-oared open boats, some possibly with hulls whose planks were sewn together, to huge ships with complements of 500 and more and weighing up to 200 tonnes. There were also a few even larger vessels built but not apparently ever taken into battle. Fleets were often numbered in hundreds of combatant ships, in one case over a thousand. Hundreds of thousands of men could be engaged in a single battle. It is clear that the broad equivalents of the cruisers and destroyers of those fleets were relatively fast for oared vessels, and that the ships of the line, apart from the larger polyremes, were not much slower. Our understanding of these large events, of this long period of naval history, and particularly of most of its remarkable ships nevertheless remains sketchy.

One method of enlarging our understanding has been by the collaboration already mentioned between classicist and naval architect, creating a two-way exchange by which the knowledge and experience of each can inform the other. Thus the demands of the laws of physics and human ergonomics can be brought to bear on the evidence to reduce the room for choice in recreating practicable designs of ships which accord with evidence and would be likely to approximate to their attested performance. These are, however, no more than a start towards more thorough design studies of these ships and their oar systems. In this chapter some general characteristics of oared ships are discussed before summarising reconstructions of the principal types of warship in this period.

Characteristics of oared ships

Speed under oar

Men sitting on fixed seats, or standing, cannot move water past a boat or ship with oars of workable dimensions and proportions much faster than about 10kts, which is therefore the upper limit of speed at which they can propel a vessel. That limit has only been exceeded, by about 1½kts, in rowing as a sport in recent times by oarsmen sitting on sliding seats which enable oarstrokes to be longer and bring a larger mass of muscles into play. To be capable

1. [with R T Williams], *Greek Oared Ships, 900–322 BC* (Cambridge 1968); [with J F Coates], *The Athenian Trireme* (Cambridge 1986); [with J F Coates], *Greek and Roman Oared Warships, 399–31 BC* (Oxford 1994).

The Olympias, *the reconstructed Greek trireme, under oars at Poros in 1992.* (Alexandra Guest)

of more than about two-thirds of the upper limit of speed for fixed-seat rowing, oared ships must be proportioned so as to minimise the wetted area of their hulls and avoid as far as possible making waves in the water, while providing room for the largest possible number of oars to be worked effectively and at the necessary speed. These requirements become more imperative, to the progressive exclusion of other attributes needing weight or space in the ship, or causing its centre of gravity to rise, as the maximum speed to be achieved under oar rises towards the 10kt limit.

The design of oared ships is dominated by the demands of their oar systems. Accommodation of oars and avoiding wavemaking call for hulls to be long relative to their displacement. In fast ships, breadth on the waterline (BWL) has to be minimised to reduce wetted area, and the surface of the hull underwater should be kept as smooth as possible to reduce frictional resistance with the water. Lateral stability, however, and useful capacity for carrying sail or troops both call for greater beam than performance under oar by itself, so in oared ships, all of which have used sail extensively for making longer passages at sea, a compromise has had to be struck between these conflicting requirements. Satisfactory working of oars also restricts freeboard and hull depth, which in turn limit seaworthiness and the strength of hulls to withstand bending among waves. Oared ships, particularly if intended to be fast under oar, therefore demanded the utmost skill of their builders as well as long development to achieve the most useful but practicable balance to provide the required combat capability, per-

formance under oar and under sail, acceptable seaworthiness, and a service life with an acceptable degree of watertightness.

Oar systems have very low densities, weighing when fully manned only about 0.045 tonnes/m³, or 1/20 of the density of water. The power produced in an oar system relative to its total volume is also low, about 0.05 kilowatts per cubic metre, reckoned at 70 watts per man, the general level of power sustainable for some hours. That power density is of the order of 1/5000th of that of a modestly-sized outboard motor today. It follows that the space required by the oarsmen in a fast oared ship has ensured that there has never been much to spare for much other gear or people unless they were on top of the ship, making a greater BWL necessary for stability.

Hull forms

With the possible exceptions of the larger polyremes of the Hellenistic period, performance under oar has been an important characteristic of oared warships. Their hulls have therefore been slender, long and of shallow draught relative to their displacement volumes. The slenderness of a hull form is measured by the non-dimensional ratio

$$\text{Ⓜ} = \frac{\text{Length on the waterline}}{(\text{Displacement Volume})^{1/3}}$$

The fastest of all oared ships, the trireme, has the most slender hull form whose Ⓜ is 9.0. For comparison, a modern rowing 'four' has an Ⓜ value of about 15, a modern naval frigate about

8 and the medieval and later war galleys between 8 and 6.5.

Relative to their total volume, oared warships were light in weight so their BWLs were large relative to their draughts, BWL being between 6 and 8 times the depth below water of the main part of the bottom, neglecting the protruding keel and garboards. Such proportions prevented both the wetted area of the hull and so frictional resistance from the water, and wavemaking resistance from being minimised for propulsion alone. There was therefore some penalty in speed incurred as a consequence of their high centres of gravity. Those heights were unavoidable, but they would surely have been minimised by the ancients to get the best out of their ships under oar. On the other hand, the length of an oared ship of about 30 'rooms', about 40m (130ft), kept wavemaking resistance to very low levels except at sprint speeds of 7kts and more.

It may be thought that ballast might have helped by lowering centres of gravity, but this would not have been the case because it would have brought with it penalties in displacement and hence wavemaking and wetted area, in hull bending moments, and in agility of manoeuvre large enough to outweigh any advantages. It is virtually certain that the faster oared warships carried no ballast, as has been made clear by Thucydides (1.45–54) and Creuze,[2] and probable that none did. Oared auxiliaries, carrying stores and other supplies for a fleet, on the other hand, would have had to be ballasted when light to keep their waterlines within the quite narrow range in which oars could be worked in commonly-met sea conditions (the third-century BC oared ship excavated near Marsala in Sicily by Honor Frost[3] and which sank while in ballast is likely to have been such an auxiliary).

Oar power and the human engine

The power with which a given oar system can propel a given ship depends upon many factors, the chief among which are the number of the oar crew and their physical strength, condition and training, the time over which the power is

2. A F B Creuze, *A Treatise on Naval Architecture* (Edinburgh 1841), p4.

3. H Frost, 'First Season of Excavation on the Punic Wreck in Sicily', *International Journal of Nautical Archaeology* 2/1 (1973), pp33–49.

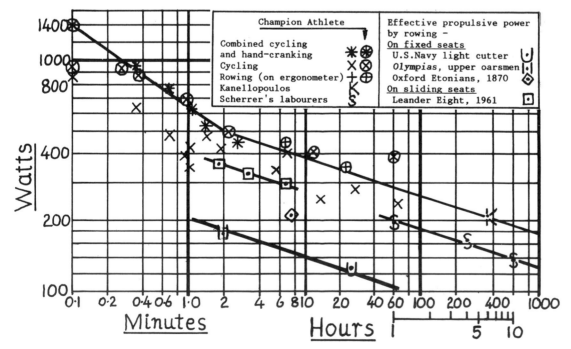

Curve of sustainable human power v time, showing various recorded outputs (in watts) over particular periods (in minutes; hours are shown by separate scale). (Graph by J T Shaw)

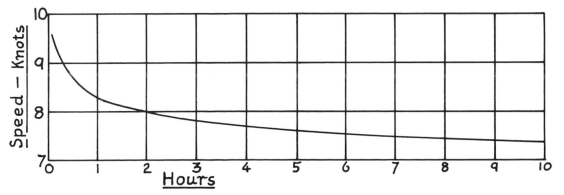

A reconstruction of a five of the Greek type, based on the Isola Tiberina monument in Rome. The raised forecastle, which offerred numerous tactical and seakeeping advantages, is not a feature universally accepted by scholars in the field. (Garth Denning)

sustained, the ventilation if the ship is enclosed, the state of the sea, and, by no means the least, the design of the oars and the oar rig, which are discussed in Chapter 11.

For short periods of up to a minute, a man can produce more than 500 watts, but to sustain effort for more than a minute or two the muscles have to be resupplied with oxygen by the blood and the sustainable power falls progressively with time, being determined to a great extent by the capacity of the heart and lungs as well as by the volume of muscles being employed. Some data about this important aspect of human mechanical power are shown in the power v time diagram on the previous page, where the lower line is drawn through the only points so far found for fixed-seat oarsmen in seaboats, namely for a US Navy light cutter[4] and the trireme reconstruction *Olympias*,[5] and above that is a single point calculated by Shaw for a fixed-seat river racing 'eight' in 1870.

Approximate speeds sustainable in a trireme (as in the speed v time diagram) for various periods of time accord with the lower line in the power diagram and with the scanty surviving literary records of passages (probably notable ones) made by ancient triremes under oar. It will be seen that in these curves speed varies much less than power over the various periods of time because power varies roughly as the cube of the speed.

Ventilation

Comfort and therefore sustainable power in an enclosed ship full of sweating oarsmen would have been affected by the physical atmosphere within and therefore by its ventilation. In the earlier fast types of ramming ships in which oar

crews had to be protected only from relatively light missiles, that consideration could have encouraged the continued use of screens able normally to be stowed to give the oar crew in ordinary circumstances as much ventilation as possible. That amenity could have been judged worth the greater risk of injuries in battle owing to the more flimsy protection from hair or leather screens. Battles between ramming ships would, however, have been generally fought in more open formations and melées than later, when boarding became the principal tactic. Such battles also predated exchanges of heavier catapulted missiles between fleets before they clashed in close engagements.

The need to protect oar crews more heavily but also to ventilate them must have interacted in determining tactics, battle formations and ship design after the introduction of heavier missiles and catapults on warships. It could have been the main reason for the consequent disappearance of triremes ('threes') from the line of battle: their speed capability simply could not be combined with the extra weight needed to provide the protection sufficient to enable them to remain mobile long enough to perform their ramming function in a battle. The emergence of the *trihemiolia* is particularly

interesting in this light. How was the balance between protection and ventilation struck in such a way that that type could be effective in ramming heavier ships in battle? The *trihemiolia* is unique in appearing to be the only type of ship that was fast, boxed-in and armed principally with the ram at a time when the principal ships in most main fleets were heavy troop-carrying vessels.

The importance of ventilation, first pointed out by Casson[6] in connection with oared warships, lies in its necessity for the evaporation of sweat to remove waste heat from the body. That necessity is proved by the inability of men working in still air on a cycling ergometer to maintain more than 150 watts for periods greater than half an hour, or 400 watts for more than a few minutes, whereas if working in air moving past them at 12m/second they can maintain 400 watts for a hour or longer (Whitt and Wilson). The reason is that in an ordinary room a man can lose heat at the rate of only about 600 watts, corresponding to an ability to produce only 150 watts of mechanical work (at a thermal efficiency of 0.20) for any appreciable time, that is of hours rather than minutes.

To ventilate the oar crew of a quinquereme (a 'five'), containing about 300 men, each working at about 150 watts on their oar handles and breathing out 4–4½ per cent car-

4. W L Rodgers, *Greek and Roman Naval Warfare* (Annapolis, Maryland 1937), p32.

5. J T Shaw (ed), *The Trireme Project*, Oxbow Monograph No 31 (Oxford 1993), p65.

6. L Casson, *Ships and Seamanship in the Ancient World* (Princeton, New Jersey 1986), p145.

Curve of sustainable speed v time for a trireme, showing speed (in knots) against time (in hours). (Graph by John Coates)

An impression of the interior of a five of the Greek type, showing the disposition of the rowers. (Garth Denning)

crew of 300 at a speed of about 6.7kts, making 80 sea miles in a day under oar only, with a water mileage of 40 sea miles per tonne.

With nearly 400 men on board, the seventeenth-century scale would have called for an allowed average consumption per day of 2.8 tonnes, so in a five a storage capacity of 10 to 15 tonnes of water may be expected to have been usual, for water would not have been available at every landing.

That sweat is salty and that salt so lost from the body has to be replaced has been known for centuries, so it is possible that salt was carried by oared ships for that purpose. The amount of water needed to prevent dehydration caused by sustained exertion can be reduced for some hours if it contains a food that can be absorbed quickly, and sodium as in the *Daedalus* flight. Glucose, however, was not known until modern times and the only known reference to food taken during a prolonged passage under oar is by Thucydides who wrote (3.49), 'they pulled and ate at the same time, barley bread mixed with wine and olive oil'. That food would not have been so quickly absorbed as glucose, to which the bread would have been converted in time by the body. There is no record of ancient routine practices to prevent dehydration, which must always have been a major factor in operating oared ships.

bon dioxide, 30m³/minute of fresh air would have to be drawn into and exhausted from the ship to keep the concentration down to the practicable upper limit of 2 per cent. But the men would also be breathing out water vapour and evaporating sweat to dispose of their waste heat. About 150m³/minute would be needed to carry away that water vapour in the humid conditions often obtaining near water, providing ample reason for interpreting the patterned panels seen in many representations of boxed-in ships as panels of protective louvres. They are also shown in the reconstruction drawing of a five reproduced above. To ventilate the interior by convection a low entry for air would have been essential, so the undersides of oar-boxes must have been open. In boxed-in ships, the necessary fore-and-aft gangway would also

have been protected by louvres overhead which would probably have been put in place only when the ship was preparing for action or exercising in the action condition. Such louvres are shown in place over the gangway in a reconstructed six reproduced below left.

Fresh water

The ability of oarsmen to maintain high speeds for long periods or for a succession of periods is also limited by the amount of water on board. The *Daedalus* Project,[7] culminating in the man-powered flight of four hours from Crete to Santorini, established that 1 litre per hour had to be drunk by a man producing 210 watts for that length of time if he were not to become dehydrated. For that flight the water contained 10 per cent glucose and 0.4 gramme/litre of sodium and the pilot (in this case the engine also) showed no signs of incipient fatigue in the course of the flight and little loss of body weight afterwards. The rate of consuming water was in that case 0.02 litre/watt-hour, which indicates that the allowance of 7 litres/man-day in seventeenth-century AD French galleys would suffice for an average daily expenditure of oar crew energy of 1200 watt-hours per man, allowing 2 litres/man per day for the other bodily needs for water. That amount of energy could, for example, allow the crew to be used at the rate of 100 watts/man for 12 hours, which would drive a five with an effective power of 18 kilowatts from an oar

Hygiene

The entirely practical consequences of lack of hygienic discipline by oar crews working within hulls would have been so severe that it must be assumed until proved otherwise (despite Aristophanes's joke, in *The Frogs*, about an oarsman excreting from his seat) that in fact

7. E R Nadel and S R Bussolari, 'The *Daedalus* Project', *American Scientist* 76 (July–August 1988), pp351–360.

A half-section of a Punic five, showing the single rower on the outrigger for the lowest level of oars, and two men per oar for the other two levels. (Drawing by John Coates)

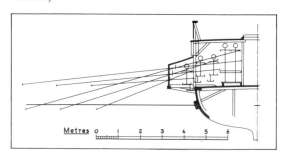

A half-section of a six, showing the six rowers handling three oars, each oar at a different level. (Drawing by John Coates)

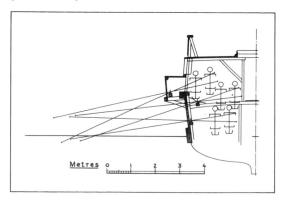

excretion and urination inside hulls would have been strictly forbidden. It was, moreover, very likely that bilges would have been periodically swabbed down with fresh water and then baled out to wash away dried sweat, as has been done in *Olympias*. The later decked galleys were an altogether different case because their oar system was entirely above a heavily cambered watertight open deck, freely draining overboard. Nevertheless it was said that the odour of a galley could be perceived a mile or more to leeward.[8] In those ships much may have depended upon whether the oar crews were free and paid, or chained captives. Ancient ships were rowed with very few exceptions by free men. Hygiene may have been a factor in the development of the only type of ancient warship likely to have had a decked main hull, the Carthaginian five, which was widely adopted in the third century BC by Rome and other naval powers.

Hull strength and construction

In very early times plank-built ships in the ancient Mediterranean, as elsewhere in the world, were sewn together. Bronze tools made more extensive joinery practicable and until the slow change to frame-first building from the fifth to the eighth century AD, ships in the Mediterranean were built shell-first. By this method adjacent planks were strongly joined together edge-to-edge by large numbers of closely spaced tenons fitted tightly into individual mortices sunk into the plank edges and then, when the close-fitting seam had been made, the tenons were pegged in place. The result could be called a shell in the modern engineering sense, because if the tenons were fitted

tightly in the fore-and-aft direction they would prevent planks from sliding upon each other and enable them to carry shear forces acting in the plane of the shell, particularly where it forms the side of the hull. The superiority of the tenon over stitching could have enabled warships to be lengthened from 15 oars to 25 oars a side, and hulls to withstand the shocks of ramming after the introduction of that weapon.

This method of building a ship, however, required considerable skill. Shear stiffness between planks would have depended upon achieving a simultaneous fit of the tenons in their mortices and therefore great accuracy in marking and cutting. In the 40m-long hulls of oared ships, tenons can be calculated to have been heavily loaded, crushing them across the grain, the direction in which timber is weakest. Tenons, however, were made of a selected hardwood, usually Turkey Oak (*quercus cerris*) which can carry a particularly high stress in that direction without being crushed. Tenons were also thicker in long ships, to judge from the only one so far found, near Marsala, in which they were 10mm thick, compared with 5mm commonly found in shorter, rounder merchant ships. When set very closely along a seam, tenons were often placed alternately nearer one side of the plank and then the other.

The pegs, through each plank and transfixing each end of a tenon, were usually of a commoner oak. They also take a part in the action, doing more than just locking the tenons in place. The taper of both mortice and tenon, as shown in the accompanying figure, would have helped in achieving a simultaneous crush-fit as the top plank is driven down over the tenons to close the seam. The quality of this work, totally hidden when complete, would have largely determined the strength, tightness and useful life of a ship.

The bottoms of ancient Mediterranean hulls were not flat but rose sharply on each side of the keel where the first planks, the garboards, were laid at a steep angle. What an ancient shipwright would have given as the reason for this will probably never be known, but it did enable the lower tenon pegs of the garboard seam, which had to be driven into the keel, to be short and accessible, which could have been important because they were necessarily in blind holes. Keels were of deep section, not connected to the floors, nor were keelsons fitted, until the first or second centuries AD when in merchant ships, if not in warships, floors were flatter so that the keel and its associated planking would not have formed such a stiff middle-line girder for the bottom of the

hull. In those later ships the garboard seam became perforce more complicated. A keelson would have compensated for loss of stiffness previously provided by the rising garboards and the nearby planking on each side. Apart from providing local strength, rising garboards would have improved performance under sail on a wind and protected the shell from damage on grounding in the nearly tideless Mediterranean, where extra draught and rise of floor carry fewer penalties than in the tidal and commonly shoal waters round the coasts of northwest Europe, as Julius Caesar found out on the shores of Kent in 55 BC, when some of his beached warships filled as the tide rose.

Transverse framing was fitted as the shell was built up. Individual timbers were placed in tiers which overlapped but were not joined to each other. Spacing of timbers in each tier was usually about one cubit (0.49m), but there was little need for them to be finely wrought, except on their outer faces faying with the shell, nor to be accurately laid. Framing was secured to shell planking by copper and later iron spikes, generally having tapered square shanks and large shallow domed heads. These spikes were usually driven up pine dowels previously driven up holes bored through plank and framing. The points of the spikes were clenched over and driven back into the face of the framing, forming a herring-bone pattern. This technique would have resulted in a fastening more pliant to movements along the framing. The dowel, of a timber relatively impermeable to water, would also have to some degree insulated the metal of the spike from the timbers round it, protecting them from developing 'nail sickness' through alkaline attack by electrolytic action.

Slender timber hulls, relying on mechanical joints between their components, cannot give satisfactory service if longer than certain limits.

8. W L Rodgers, *Naval Warfare under Oars* (Annapolis, Maryland 1940), p234.

The necessarily light structure of the classical galley depended on a form of shell construction in which the plank seams were attached by tenons that fitted into mortises and were then secured with dowels. (Drawing by John Coates)

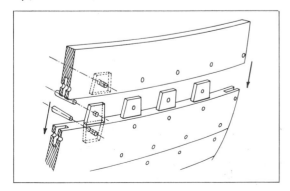

The hull structure of a classical galley, as reconstructed for the Olympias, *showing the strengthening wales and the internal stiffening.(Drawing by John Coates)*

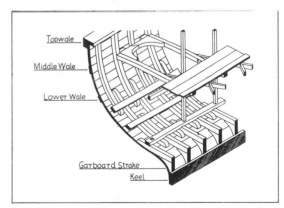

The similarity, with very few exceptions, between the lengths of oared warships from the single-level pentecontors right up to the big polyremes (apart from the monstrous but apparently useless forty), indicates that they were at the practical structural limit in length when combined with the shallowness of their main hulls (which were, moreover, in most types undecked) relative to their length. Ratios of length on the waterline (LWL) to the structural depth of hull were large, between 12 and 14 or so for the three, for the open-hulled five and for the six. In the later decked hulls of galleys, it was similar, about 13, if the 0.9m high heavily timbered *corsia* running down the middle line on deck is included. This ratio affects the strength of timber hulls quite critically, and to show how extreme oared ships were in this respect, Lloyd's Register of Shipping, of London, in the nineteenth century, demanded that all timber hulls (at that time invariably built frame-first and decked) if more than only 8 depths long were to have iron diagonal straps, fitted between frames and planking, to resist the mainly vertical shear forces acting upon the hull and tending to cause its ends to drop, *ie* to 'hog'. It must follow that hulls 12 to 14 depths long but with no such reinforcement either had brief lives indeed or were built most conscientiously and with excellent workmanship, necessary to achieve the shell strength and stiffness obtainable by means of the tenoned construction.

Hypozomata and hull bending stresses

Longitudinal stresses caused by hull bending are also high in long and shallow hulls. White,[9] an eminent naval architect writing when wooden ships were still in general use, gave 4.6

9. W H White, *A Manual of Naval Architecture* (London 1901), p403.
10. Shaw (ed), *The Trireme Project*, Ch 15.
11. Morrison and Coates, *The Athenian Trireme*, p153.

Newtons/mm² as the maximum permissible stress in hull members if clear of scarfed joints (but otherwise only 2.9 N/mm²). In *Olympias* the maximum hogging stress in the topwale amidships when the ship was balanced on the crest of a wave of length equal to the LWL of the ship and LWL/40 (1m) high from trough to crest could only be reduced to that former figure if the *hypozoma*, the undergirding, composed of two loops of 40mm diameter ropes stretched from bow to stern, was tensioned to 13.5 tonnes. Its height caused the *hypozoma*, just under the hull beams, to impose longitudinal compressive stresses on hull cross-sections varying from nearly zero at the keel (already carrying a compressive stress owing to hull bending) to 1.1 N/mm² at the topwale, relieving the hogging tensile stress there by that amount. How *hypozomata* were rigged, tightened and subsequently kept tight as the natural fibres, of which the ropes were made, relaxed as they do under a sustained tension, is not known. The problem is the same as in the hemp standing rigging of sailing ships, which was stretched before being made up into mast stays and shrouds and then tightened in place by means of well-greased deadeyes and lanyards. It is possible that the same method was used in the ancient warships.[10]

Unless, however, a *hypozoma* is rigged so that it arches up over crutches like a hogging truss, as shown, for example, in the well-known Egyptian relief of Queen Hatshepshut's ships for the expedition to the Land of Punt, it cannot contribute towards reducing hogging shear forces in a hull. There is no evidence that *hypozomata* were so rigged, their name, 'undergirding', would deny it and in a warship a tightly-tensioned rope arching high amidships would have been very vulnerable to the enemy as well as to accidental damage. It seems therefore virtually certain that *hypozomata* stretched in a straight line close under the beams and gangway between strong points at each end of the ship.

Watertightness

Nothing useful has been recorded about whether, when and how plank seams were stopped to make them watertight. There are references to a number of materials used for that purpose and for coating the bottom planking, but no specific details of recipes or methods survive. Plank seams must have been merely stopped as necessary: many may have been made so well and so close as to be watertight without the need for any stopping to be pushed into them during the ship's life, except when, despite being held together by tenons, the dry and therefore open seams of ships long stored on slipways would have needed at least some composition brushed into them to prevent water from coming through them, until they were closed by the swelling of the planks. Seams are not likely to have been caulked as in frame-built ships because first the tenons would have got in the way, and could have been damaged by the action of caulking iron and mallet, and second plank thicknesses, except possibly in the heavier ships, would have been too small: in no ancient wreck in the Mediterranean have seams been found with the gap at the outer edges of the planking, necessary to receive caulking. However, there must have been a direct connection between 'drying out' and stopping seams as well as recoating the bottom planking.[11] No material or composition then available would have adhered to planking unless the bottom of the ship was dry. 'Drying out', therefore, almost certainly had much to do with stopping leaks, if only for a while after tenons had worked loose, and with smoothing and recoating the bottoms of ships, not only to preserve them but to reduce frictional resistance, which could often have been of more immediate operational importance. That wax was one of the ingredients mentioned for bottom compositions suggests that the ancients understood the importance of smoothing the underwater surfaces of hulls to reduce their resistance.

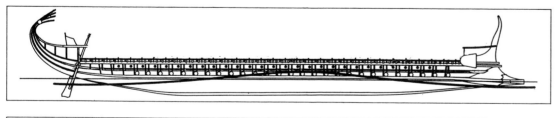

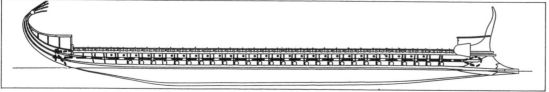

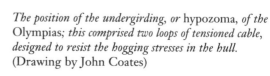

The starboard elevation of Olympias, *showing a typical wave profile. In such a situation the ends of the hull received less support than the midships, tending to make the hull arch upwards, a condition known as 'hogging'.* (Drawing by John Coates)

The position of the undergirding, or hypozoma, *of the* Olympias; *this comprised two loops of tensioned cable, designed to resist the hogging stresses in the hull.* (Drawing by John Coates)

Attack and defence

Ramming

A preliminary study by J H Haywood[12] of the structural mechanics by which a ram of the type found at Athlit, near Haifa,[13] could penetrate a hull has shown that, in the case of a three like *Olympias* attacking an identical ship:

> . . . the speed of the attacking ship need be only 3 to 4 knots at angles of attack (*ie* the angle between the middle lines of the two ships in plan view) between 20° and 70° if the target is either stationary or moving towards the attacker. As might be expected, somewhat smaller speeds, 2 to 3 knots, are sufficient when the target ship is struck amidships. In attacks on the quarter of a pursued ship, on the other hand, greater attacking speeds are necessary and these increase rapidly at finer angles of attack, as indicated below:

Angle of attack (degrees)	Factor increasing required speed	Approximate upper limit of speed required (knots)
60	1.2	4
45	1.6	5
30	2.4	8

As mentioned above, the right-hand column gives the speed of the attacking ship only. The speed of the target ship is not given. It could be even higher than that of the attacker, if the target were unfortunate enough to cross the bows of the attacker at the critical moment. Nevertheless it appears that attacks on the quarter (following, for example, a *diekplous* or *periplous*) were tactics for fast ships only. If that point were to be firmly established, it would have a great bearing on our understanding of tactics.

These results suggest that resistance to penetration could be appreciably increased by thickening the waterline wale and increasing the flexural stiffness or the numbers of the side frame timbers supporting the wale in resisting the ram force. Roman representations of the heavier ships developed from the three during the Hellenistic period show much heavier wales and there are literary references pointing to the ability of later, heavy, ships to resist ramming attacks on the waterline, at least by lighter ships.

Steering a three to ram another has also been considered by Shaw, particularly one pur-

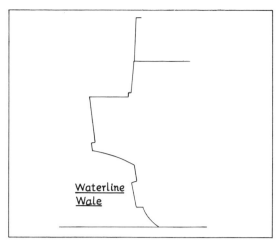

A section of a galley, based on the Isola Tiberina monument in Rome, demonstrating the heavy waterline wale often found in large warships of the Hellenistic and early Roman periods. (Drawing by John Coates)

suing the other to ram on the quarter, a manoeuvre often used by threes. He shows, based on Haywood's findings, that the difference in speed between pursuer and pursued need not be very great, on account of the closing speed with which the pursuer would collide after turning towards his victim to ram. Shaw writes: 'Were this not so, the attested tactic of ramming from astern would have been successful only against grossly inferior crews, and against ships that for some other reason were stationary or nearly so'.[14]

Heavy waterline wales are shown in Hellenistic representations, and such a wale is very marked in the Isola Tiberina monument in Rome. Heavy Roman ships were sometimes if not always built with rams well above the waterline, it is said, to lock them to their victim for boarding, not to cause him to swamp. It may be thought that so raising rams reflected the success of heavy protective belts at the waterline. The alternative use for rams implied acceptance of the longer time required by boarding compared with ramming to cause swamping, a time during which the attacker would be a stationary target for attack by another enemy ship. The recorded tactic by the Rhodians of ramming heavier ships underwater, below the waterline belt, presumably by trimming down by the bow, also indicates the effectiveness of heavy protection at the waterline in defeating ramming at that level. The necessary bow trim in a *trihemiolia* could have been obtained by moving, for example, about 30 men 30m forward in the ship, and larger but practicable numbers of men similarly in a four. It was a good tactic in that a hole of a given size below water level would cause quicker flooding than one of the same size at the waterline.

After being holed by a ram, a ship would not necessarily be immobilised immediately (unless also locked to its attacker). Flooding would take some time. The amount of water entering the ship through an idealised rectangular hole b metre wide and h metre deep below the waterline would be about

$$100 \; b \; (h^{3/2}) \text{ tonnes per minute.}$$

For example, if the hole were 0.33m both wide and in depth below the waterline, water would flow into the ship at the rate of about 5 tonnes per minute. In the case of a three, that would cause the ship to settle by about 6cm after one minute, and after 3 minutes about 18 tonnes would have been taken on board and the ship would be 0.2m lower in the water, making the oars much less effective, and the ship less manoeuvrable and more crank, heeling over noticeably if people moved athwartships. Eventually, when completely bilged and lying waterlogged in the water, she may be expected to have floated with the hull beams awash inside the ship and have little lateral stability. In such a state ships are likely to have lolled on to one outrigger or the other, quite immobilised and so *hors de combat*. Movements of men on board would cause exaggerated changes of trim and heel, and if many men were to climb on to the canopy or deck the ship might roll over far enough to tip them into the water and then she might either recover or capsize, though the weight of the bottom structure when above the water would probably have prevented that.

A swamped hull would be exposed to severe straining if in any appreciable swell, owing to its much increased weight which would include that of the water inside the hull. That hazard would have had to be avoided by victors towing hulks away from the scene of a battle. A warship of the types presented in this chapter would sink to the bottom of the sea after being holed only if she had on board sufficient dense stores, cargo or other material to weigh in water enough to overcome the buoyancy of the hull structure and its furniture, roughly 40 per cent of the weight of the complete hull in air, assuming that its density is 0.6 tonnes per cubic metre. The weight of a man in water is negligible. If a ship were burnt to near the waterline without losing much from her hold, she might then well sink. A swamped ship on the verge of sinking would in practice usually sink by the bow or the stern owing to lack of longitudinal

---

12. In Shaw (ed), *The Trireme Project.*

13. L Casson and J R Steffy, *The Athlit Ram* (College Station, Texas, 1991).

14. *The Trireme Project*, Ch 19.

balance between weight and buoyancy. The Punic ship excavated near Marsala would seem to have been a case in point.[15]

In penetrating their targets, ram castings were analogous in action to the heads of arrows or spears, but on a larger scale and with much lower velocities. The timber structure behind the cutting edges of the casting was quite as important as the casting itself, and to refer to the casting alone as 'the ram' is misleading. Upon impact, that structure had not only to sustain a large compressive force, of the order of the ship's mass, between the casting and the main mass of the ship, but also lateral and vertical forces, both of which could be appreciable.

The impact of a successful ramming felt in an attacking ship could have been of the order experienced in a motor car when efficient brakes are applied hard on a dry road. In a light type of ship trying to ram a heavy one, and failing to penetrate, however, the shock would be more severe and could well have been damaging to the attacker. There were orders and a drill for oarsmen to hold water and back-down, and probably for others (eg to sit down) just before impact so that all should be ready for action immediately afterwards (Livy 26.39.6 and Lucan 3.544).

Finned rams like that found at Athlit, a pattern in use for five centuries or so, were designed to cut into planking and longitudinal timbers along their grain, and to do so at large angles from the athwartships direction so that penetration could be achieved over a wide range of angles of attack. The more glancing impacts, however, would generate large lateral forces and so call the ram wale timbers into play in resisting them. To be effective in supporting the whole ram sideways, the wale timbers must be assumed to have been scarfed strongly and tangentially on to the waterline wales of the hull, which, next to the keel and topwales, were the most substantial longitudinal timbers of the ship. There is evidence[16] that the ram was a structure wholly external to the hull proper, as may be expected, in view of the real risk of a ram being wrenched off sideways in battle. In the event of the ram being torn off (for instance, by attacking a moving target), the attacker would not then necessarily be holed forward and flooded.

Rams would also have been subjected to appreciable vertical forces after impact with a tar-

The supporting structure for the ram, shown during construction of the Olympias; *it can be seen clearly that the ram was separate from the hull proper, which finished in a straight stem.* (John Coates)

get. As the target ship would have been struck well below its centre of gravity, it would immediately start to roll towards the attacker and therefore press down on the ram with the structure just above the breach in its hull. The target would also be accelerated bodily sideways by the main ramming force and as its velocity increased so would the water resistance. That resistance force would act at a level below the waterline, so the target would soon be subjected to a moment rolling it the other way, away from the attacker and reversing the direction of the vertical force imposed on the ram. Those vertical forces would have had to be carried by the heavy bracing timber, found in the Athlit ram and also to be seen in *Olympias*. The vertical forces can be expected to have been large enough, if fracture of the ram timbers were to be avoided, to prevent the ram extending very far forward of this brace.

The ram structure of *Olympias*, while following the design of the Athlit ram, was external to the hull which ended with a vertical stem. It is believed that rams were generally external to ships and built on to the bows of the hulls themselves. It is not unlikely that, at the larger naval building centres, rams were built by specialist tradesmen, who might have made the castings too. The moulds for making such castings would normally have been made individually, probably by means of the 'lost wax' process used for casting bronze statues, a very similar operation. It would in that case have

been easiest to form the wax 'positive' on the ram structure itself because in that way the necessarily slow process of fitting those timbers to the inside shape of the casting would be much reduced.

The weight of ram castings would not have been excessive relative to that of their ships. The Athlit casting weight 0.465 tonnes and probably belonged to a four of about 65 tonnes. The numerous sockets excavated by Murray[17] from Augustus's memorial of the battle of Actium in 31 BC suggest that the weights of the rams of the larger polyremes up to tens, which took part in that battle, went up to about 2 tonnes. Ram castings, though impressive in themselves, accounted for only about 1 per cent of the displacement of a ten, decreasing to ½ per cent in the case of a three.

Breaking the oars of an enemy ship

It may be estimated that in a combat between threes, one ship, initially going at 5kts, would have enough kinetic energy, before coming to rest, to break about 50 oars by sweeping close

15. H Frost, 'The Punic Wreck in Sicily', *International Journal of Nautical Archaeology* 3/1 (1974), pp35–54.

16. Morrison and Coates, *Greek and Roman Oared Warships*, p500.

17. W M Murray and P M Petsas, 'Octavian's Campsite Memorial for the Actium Wars', *American Philosophical Society* 79 (1989), Part 4.

alongside the other, having stopped rowing and also shipped oars on the engaged side before breaking the first oar. However, a more likely method of carrying out this disabling manoeuvre would have relied less on initial speed and ship's kinetic energy: this method was to approach the victim at about 20 to 40 degrees off his bow or stern, ship the oars on the engaged side and drive ahead hard with the others when the *epotis* is nearly in contact with the victim's outrigger. The oar thrust generated should be more than sufficient successively to break, by bending, the victim's oars not shipped in time on the stem of the attacker. Before being broken, oars would have been pushed aft, or forward as the case may be, 50 to 60 degrees from athwartships before jamming in oarports or against stanchions. The attacker therefore needed to keep his *epotis* against the victim's outrigger. The unbalanced oar thrust from the oars on one side of the ship only would provide a turning moment which would just about balance that from the oar-breaking force acting on the stem. In the manoeuvre described, the *epotis* performs the important function of keeping the stem about a metre away from tholes and oarports to give it enough leverage to bend and break the victim's oars easily. This manoeuvre would seem to be more difficult with ships without *epotides* and outriggers because oars would be harder to break if the stem pushes on them near their tholes or oarports: they would then have to be sheared off, not bent, and larger forces would be needed to break them.

Boarding

Troops assembled towards one side of the bows for boarding another ship would cause the attacking ship to heel by as much as 3 degrees and thus risk hindering the oar crew at a crucial time. The practice may therefore have been for troops to stay centred on the middle line of the ship before boarding and springing towards the victim at the last moment just before contact was made. Making fast by grappling irons on short lengths of chain (to prevent grappling ropes from being cut immediately) must have called for much skill not only to grapple successfully but also to prevent those doing it (obvious targets in trying to defeat the action) from being shot by archers defending the other ship. Downward fire from towers would have added to the casualties on

18. V Foley and W Soedel, 'Ancient Oared Warships', *Scientific American* (April 1982), pp116–129.

19. Foley and Soedel, 'Ancient Oared Warships'.

A first-century BC graffito representation of a warship equipped with a firepot over the bow.

the other side and given shelter to troops as ships approached bow to bow. The manner of the approach, however, details of weapons, protection, numbers of troops and how formed up for boarding, timing, and tactics used in capturing the other ship are all unknown. This could be a rich field for research by operational analysts, likely to cast light upon the layout of the forward decks of ships.

Missiles

The use of missiles in naval warfare of this period has not been much studied, but it would certainly have influenced ship design.[18] The main response to the use of missiles at sea would have been to protect oar crews, to maintain sufficient mobility in battle. Against hand-thrown javelins vertical sidescreens and light wooden canopies seem to have been sufficient, but with the advent of heavier missiles boxing-in and protective ventilation louvres became necessary. The accuracy and therefore the lethal effect of missiles shot from one moving (and possibly rolling or listing) ship at another is easily overestimated. There are references to the first exchanges between approaching fleets being a hail of missiles and arrows. It was presumably a worthwhile preliminary to close engagement in spite of the difficulty in achieving accuracy from moving platforms. To improve it and to reduce the pulsating motion of a ship at speed under oar, speeds would probably have been deliberately kept low, but sufficient for steerage. In earlier ramming battles, threes would have generally moved faster and troops on board were trained to throw javelins from the sitting position (Thucydides VII, 67.2), probably on account of their consequent pulsating motion.

The accuracy of shooting would have been greater in direction (*ie* in training) than in range, so a target ship which is head-on to a thrower or archer is more likely to be hit somewhere along its length than a target lying at an

angle to the line of flight. Ships approaching in line abreast would be good targets. On the other hand, missiles and arrows would be coming mainly from one direction only, which would make use of shields or other protective devices more effective, except against the heavier ones such as those thrown by catapults. An arrow with a pyramidal head of a type developed in about 500 BC and thrown by the smallest sinew-powered catapult could penetrate 50mm of limewood.[19]

Missiles from more powerful catapults could penetrate timber of a greater thickness than could easily be provided in decks, except in the heavier ships, which could carry the additional topweight without undue further loss from their already relatively modest performance under oar. The need for what amounted to armoured decks could have been a significant factor encouraging the development of heavier ships. Equally, the effectiveness of heavier missiles in penetrating ships' decks must have been a spur to their use at sea. The disruption caused to the working of an oar crew by an intruding missile needs no explanation and it could have been to minimise that, as suggested by Foley and Soedel, that two-level oar systems were adopted in the larger polyremes, sevens and larger.

The effective range of catapults and bows operated on board ships was probably about 200m to 300m and it would have been much affected by sea conditions and the consequent motion of ships. The time taken to rewind and reload would have been short enough to allow several shots to be made at the likely approach speeds of fleets. Judging range, however, must have been a matter of great skill. Ranging shots by catapults of known performance would presumably have been used to ascertain when a more general release of missiles would be effective. The range of catapults may be surmised to have been continually tested relatively to each other with missiles of various weights, the heavier ones for use as the range closed. Practice would have made for such greater effectiveness in the opening phase of a battle that it must be presumed to have been a frequent part of fleets' exercises, though no record of such, or of other details about shipborne artillery, has survived. Any means of causing smoke within a ship would have been particularly effective in incapacitating its oar crew, and missiles aimed at doing so were probably in use before the advent of Greek fire during the late Roman Empire. There is, indeed, one representation of a ship with a firepot hung over her bow, presumably to be emptied into an enemy ship.

Comparative profiles to the same scale of a single-level pentecontor (top), a two-level pentecontor and a trireme. (Drawing by John Coates)

Types of ships

Early oared craft

Warships of the Bronze Age appear to have been open boats with a single file of oarsmen on each side. Vessels with 20 and 30 oars are mentioned in literature and they seem to have been broadly of two types, one designed to be fast and therefore light and slim, the other beamier for carrying goods and people, including troops when required, without being totally dependent upon the wind. Both had mast and sail for use whenever the wind served. Transport, piracy, blockades, raiding and warfare, all were uses for such ships. Any conflicts between ships or fleets were fought by arrow, spear and sword, hand-to-hand.

Any reconstruction of the early craft can only be conjectural. Representations from the centuries around the start of the first millennium BC are stylised and indicate a variety of forms over the extent of the eastern Mediterranean. It is likely that some of the faster types were given what could be taken as rams but were at first more likely extended forefoots, of ram shape, made to reduce wavemaking by sharpening the entry of the hull. If sewn, such craft could have been built very lightly for speed, but even with a ram-shaped entry their fairly small length would have limited sprint speeds. A generally serviceable 20-oared vessel would have been about 16m (52ft) in length on the waterline (LWL) and would have been limited to about 4kts maximum speed sustainable for hours, unless very fine and light, when 5kts might have been possible. A ram entry might add about a ¼kt to short sprint speeds of about 7kts in lightly-built vessels in calm conditions. With 30 oars, LWL would increase to about 20m (65ft) without a ram entry, adding about ½kt to possible speeds.

Pentecontors

Representations of vessels identifiable as pentecontors always show them with an extended forefoot or ram-shaped bow. With a single file of oarsmen on each side, such ships must have been at least 30m (98ft) in LWL and if they could have been simply lengthened versions of light 20-oared craft more than 6kts sustained speed might have been possible, but their length would have made such a propor-

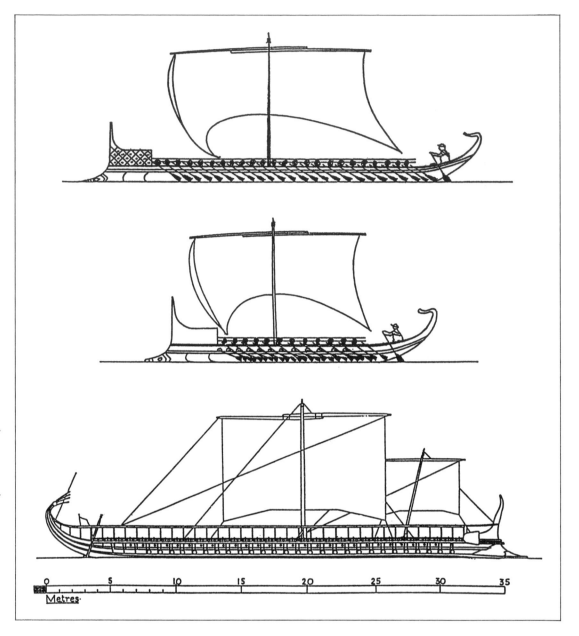

tionately very long hull too weak when bending among waves to be seaworthy. Single-level pentecontors, therefore, must be expected to have been built with enlarged, deeper, more capacious but heavier hulls, which is borne out by their use for carrying colonies of people overseas. Their hulls must have been fastened by tenons, for they could not have been strong enough if sewn. Representations on vases show these ships with oarsmen working their oars over the topwales of hulls with considerable freeboard. Sustained speeds would probably have been about 5 to 5½kts. Such long single-level ships would also have been rather slow to turn and manoeuvre, a handicap in a ramming battle. To increase agility in battle and make the most effective use of the ram, 50-oared two-level ships soon appeared, certainly by the eighth century BC.

The two-level pentecontor may be claimed

to have been the first true warship, designed to wield the ram, a purely anti-ship weapon. The hull could have been a shortened, lightened, and cheaper version of the single-level pentecontor, with the second file of oarsmen sitting in the hold, so there would have been little or no space in a two-level ship for cargo or any number of passengers. This type would have eclipsed the single-level ship in battle because it would have manoeuvred at least twice as quickly and therefore would usually have got its blow in first. There is a later, sixth-century, representation, and both types of pentecontor are reconstructed in profile in the drawing above. The shorter vessel, though necessarily subject to increased wavemaking on that account, would have had only about half the wetted area of hull and, having the same oarpower, would on balance have had the edge in sustained speed but a much greater acceleration,

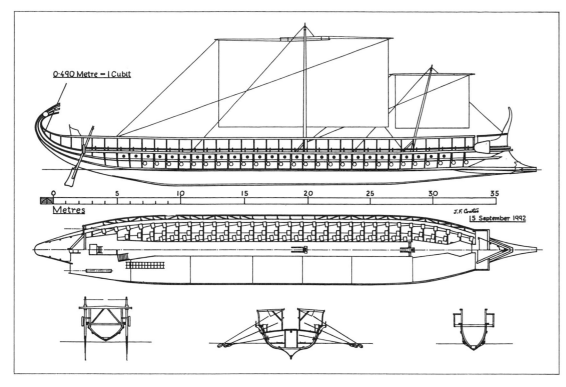

being lighter, having a manned displacement of about 15 tonnes. Sprint speed would probably have been about 7½kts.

The two-level pentecontor was evidently a most successful type of ship because there are references to it in fleets over many centuries. There were other names for two-level ships, such as *lembos*, and later derivatives such as the liburnian, which was a common type of warship during the Roman empire.

The trireme

The trireme, or three, was the first fully-developed ship of the line and represented a very remarkable development from either form of pentecontor, but the relatively numerous and quantitative pieces of evidence about it allow no lesser vessel than one with three levels of oarsmen on each side of the ship in files of up to 31 men in each file, 170 in all, each working one oar generally 9½ cubits (4.66m or 15ft 3in) long. Technical considerations confirm such a conclusion. Manned, a three would have displaced about 48 tonnes, three times as much as the shorter two-level pentecontor and it would have been about three times as expensive.

Speed was the aspect of performance in

which the three particularly excelled. There can be little doubt that it was the fastest oared ship of all time. In view of its high cost, such speed must indeed have been of great value at that time (the sixth century), when the eastern Mediterranean was becoming more prosperous. There could therefore have been greater need for the more powerful city states to protect trade and project naval power over greater distances.

A passage in Xenophon (6.4.2) shows that the three could keep up 7 to 7½kts 'for a long day'. That implies a short sprint speed of 9½ kts, which is not far short of the maximum possible on fixed seats. An advance of 2kts on say 5½kts may not seem much nowadays but it

is an increase of over a third, cutting a day off a previous passage time of three days. A three could also catch any pirate ship, sometimes pentecontors. It remained in service, latterly in the equivalent role of the frigate of the sailing navies, for nearly a millennium.

The three was the archetype for the numerous polyremes developed from it, and like those successors it exploited the strength and lightness of tenoned hull-building to the limit. In view of its historical and technical importance in naval history, and because the evidence about it had relatively recently become so definitive when combined with the technical constraints arising from its high performance, it became worthwhile as well as possible to make a reconstruction of an Athenian three (named *Olympias*) with a claim to authenticity. This project, the ship and the lessons thus rediscovered about this type and oared ships generally have been fully reported.[20]

In Phoenicia there may have been other kinds of three. The evidence from coins[21] shows that the Phoenician three throughout the fifth and the first half of the fourth century BC could have been similar to the Greek and was not obviously without an outrigger. When the five began to be used in Phoenicia, there is evidence, in the Arados and Byblos coins (as well as from the Erment model), of a quite different type which could be reconstructed as

20. Morrison and Coates, *The Athenian Trireme*; Shaw, *The Trireme Project*.

21. Morrison and Coates, *Greek and Roman Oared Warships*, pp271–276.

A close-up of Olympias *at speed (about 7kts), seen from the port quarter. The efficient disposition of 170 oarsmen made the trireme the fastest oared warship of all time.* (Photograph by Mary Pridgen, by courtesy of the Trireme Trust)

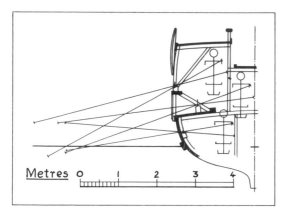

A half-section of the Phoenician form of trireme without outrigger, leading to a different disposition of oarsmen from the Greek model.(Drawing by John Coates)

a three without outriggers, in which the oar crew must consequently have been arranged differently. A practicable reconstruction calls for the middle level of oarsmen to be well inboard, together with their tholes, because, if this type was fast, it must have had oars of about the same length and gearing as the Greek three. The large hull openings needed for those middle oars, however, would have reduced the effectiveness of the hull sides between and above the openings in contributing to the bending strength of the hull as a whole. The remaining effective depth of hull, about 1.9m, is only 1/19th of LWL, very shallow indeed for a timber hull. The hull could nevertheless have been strong enough if there had been substantial planking over the beam-ends forming side decks (for which the inboard position of the middle oarsmen makes room), as indicated in the reconstruction, together with a *hypozoma*. In threes and fives without outriggers, for structural reasons it is hard to see how such side decks or equivalents could have been avoided.

It is possible that these side decks were to be developed within the next century into complete decks in later Carthaginian fives, to become an important type of warship in Roman and other navies also. The basis of this suggestion is entirely structural: there is no literary evidence for it and, as this feature is not visible externally, there can be no iconographical evidence for it either. However, it does make structurally practicable the reconstruction of both Punic types otherwise based solely on the iconographical evidence.

The later warships of the Mediterranean

While the three was the practicable ultimate in the fast, ram-armed oared warship, accounts of

later battles and the evident later growth in the weight of protective wales on the waterlines of ships indicate that ramming attacks could be resisted to at least a useful degree by such measures. The three, being virtually a one-weapon ship, relied for its agility and therefore its effectiveness upon the quality and training of its oar crews, the maintenance of which at a high pitch could have been less than easy in many social and economic circumstances in both war and peace. The attraction of a less technically demanding mode of fighting, if ram attacks by threes could be adequately countered, could have brought about the later heavier types.

The five

Whether for that reason or not, a five was developed at Syracuse in around 400 BC. The changes to the three necessary to turn it into a ship able to carry a main armament of 70 to 120 troops, a moving topweight on what had been a relatively light protective canopy over the oar crew, while remaining stable enough to be a useful fighting platform, would have been considerable. Displacement would double to about 100 tonnes, breadth on the waterline (BWL) would increase from 3.6m to over 5m, the ship would become slower but there would be room and buoyancy to accommodate two extra files of oarsmen on each side of the ship to make up some of that loss by adding oarpower. It would become necessary for the two upper levels of oars to be double-manned, for the hull side structure to be strengthened to resist some, if not all, ram attacks by more agile ships, and for protection of the oar crew from missiles and boarding troops to be strengthened, because in battles fought by boarding troops ships would be closer than when manoeuvring to ram.

The five was thus a very appreciable development from the three, and more than six times greater in displacement than the little

A half-section of a five based on the ship of the Isola Tiberina monument. The lowest level of oars are manned by single rowers, with the upper two tiers being double-manned.(Drawing by John Coates)

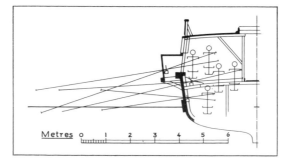

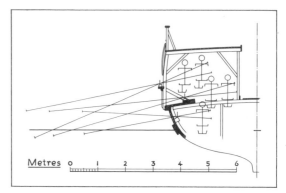

A half-section of a ship based on the Erment model reconstructed as a Phoenician five, without outrigger. (Drawing by John Coates)

pentecontor. A five would have stood, to its fighting deck, about 3m above the water fully manned, would have been about 45m long overall, and would have carried a total complement of about 400, of whom about 300 would have been oar crew. The accompanying reconstructions depict the general appearance of a five, the scene within its oar system, and the section of the ship, showing its derivation from the Greek three, the outrigger for the top level of oars having been boxed in. This type of ship would probably have been able to reach 8kts and sustain 7kts for long periods.

The Phoenician and Carthaginian types of five

There are strong arguments to indicate that the Phoenicians had fives in the latter half of the fourth century BC similar in appearance to their threes, without outriggers, as suggested by the so-called Erment model. Such a five is represented in the reconstruction (top right) with the necessary heavy side deck. From the middle of the next century representations of large ships show oarboxes from which all three levels of oars protrude, requiring a quite different oar system. This type was evidently widely used, well established and of a different derivation from the previous type of five. It is known that the Romans captured and copied a Carthaginian five in the middle of the third century. They adopted it for their navy and it appears in later Roman representations.

All of this suggests that Carthage, originally a Phoenician colony, had developed this type from the earlier Phoenician five, with which it has the important similarity of decked-over hull beams. A practicable reconstruction is shown in section on p130, and exhibits some interesting changes. The oar system is entirely above the hull proper, which is fully decked, and the oar crew are more or less on one level instead of being superimposed. Separation of the oar system from the hull could have had advantages in the organisation of trades during building, in ventilation and hygiene of the oar crew, and in stowage of water and stores in the hold. This type of five may look as if it could have been the ancestor of the medieval galley, but there is nothing to support such an idea.

The six

Roman flagships were often sixes and the large-scale monument in Rome, on the Isola Tiberina, can be identified as a six. Its interior space can be reconstructed as a six as well as a Greek type of five. Its reconstruction as a six in section is shown on p130. It would have been very similar in appearance to the Greek type of five, but about 0.4m higher.

General arrangement and oar system of a trihemiolia, *based on the Lindos relief and the Victory of Samothrace monument. Note the 'half' row of thalamian oarports amidships.(Drawing by John Coates)*

The four

Invented, according to Pliny, in Carthage, the four was slim enough to fit into shipsheds built for threes with outriggers. They were therefore about 5.6m (18ft) in breadth overall. Their fighting decks were lower than in fives and they had only about 90 oars, which must therefore have been on two levels and double-manned. Reconstruction indicates a likely displacement of about 60 tonnes but a capacity to carry about 75 troops, making the four into an economical yet well-armed ship, capable also of much the same speeds as a five. It is not surprising that large numbers were built and that they were in service for four or five centuries.

The hemioliai

The *hemioliai*, with up to about 50 oarsmen, though small, were notably fast for their size. They must therefore have had fine, lightly-

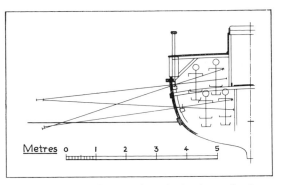

A half-section of a four, a relatively simple two-level layout with both tiers of oars double-manned.(Drawing by John Coates)

built hulls. Reconstruction indicates that the half-length files would have been amidships, where there would have been room for them in addition to the full-length files outboard of them but necessarily within the topwales of the hull. In such a layout the oar crew would vir-

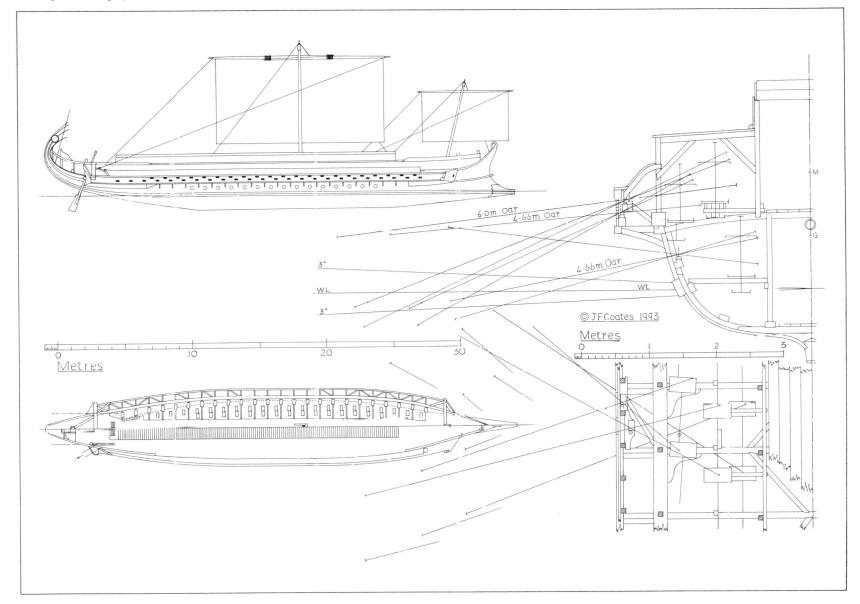

tually be on one level and, as the BWL need be no more than 2.7m, outriggers would have been necessary to provide fast-working oars about 4.7m long with the right gearing of about 2.7 to suit a sprint speed of 7½kts or more in the case of a 50-oared boat. Their greater length (21m LWL) and slightly smaller displacement compared with two-file pentecontors or liburnians, combined with slimmer lines, would have given *hemioliai* the edge over them in a sprint.

Trihemioliai, with oar crews numbering around 120, were much bigger ships classed with threes. Photius states, 'the *trihemiolia* is not three times a *hemiolia* but a *trieres* [*ie* a three]'. He indicates clearly how the principle of the *hemiolia* was applied to a larger and longer ship, which would have needed a deeper hull for strength, by using the space in the fine

General arrangement and oar system of a Liburnian. (Drawing by John Coates)

hull to accommodate a short file of thalamian oarsmen on each side. The ship's prow of the Victory of Samothrace monument in the Louvre can be worked out[22] to be about two-thirds full scale, and can be identified as that of a *trihemiolia*, as can the prow and the relief at Lindos. The general arrangement of a reconstruction shows a low, boxed-in ship of about 40 tonnes and capable of speeds only ½kt or less short of those of a three. It may be noticed that in this reconstruction the oarports *en echelon* have not been made actually to overlap as they do in the Samothrace monument: they could do so, but at what seems greater risk of damage to the knuckles of the outboard upper oarsmen in rough water, by fouling the looms of the other upper oars.

The larger polyremes

There is little evidence upon which the larger ships can be reconstructed with any useful de-

gree of certainty. Orosius tells us that the ships of Antony's fleet at Actium, many of which were big polyremes, stood about 3m out of the water, so the big ships, up to their fighting decks, were about as high as fives, in spite of the huge numbers of oarsmen inside them. It follows from making scaled drawings of possible sections of such ships that their oar systems were on two levels and that, as there were so many at each oar, oarsmen worked standing. The ships would have been relatively slow.

Eights and above may be seen to have been attempts to create fortress-like ships, immune to ramming, difficult to capture by boarding, and carrying a powerful armament of catapults and missiles as well as large numbers of troops. They would have carried high towers from

22. A W Sleeswyk, 'The Prow of the "Nike of Samothrace" reconsidered', *International Journal of Nautical Archaeology* 11/3 (1982), pp233–243.

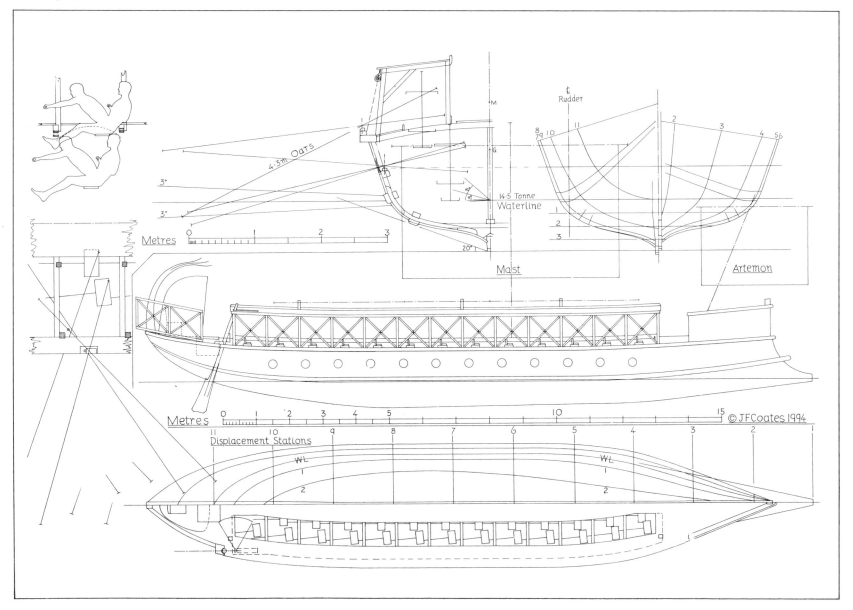

Silhouettes of some the commoner types of ancient Mediterranean warships drawn to the same scale for comparison.(Drawing by John Coates)

which downward fire could be directed. They could also have been a logical response, for those who could afford it, to the arming of warships with heavy missiles of considerable penetrating power[23] requiring a great weight of protective deck to prevent injury and disruption of oar crews.

The liburnian

Literature suggests that liburnians, after being adopted by the Roman navy, were developed into a number of variants not only for different roles but also to suit different conditions in various parts of the Roman empire. Unlike the *hemiolia*, the liburnian's oar system, being on two levels, would not have required outriggers any more than the two-level pentecontor before it. For naval use some form of protection for oar crew would have been provided as is apparent in the more informative representations, particularly the Lindos relief where sidescreens are shown lowered, obscuring oar crew. A reconstruction of a typical 15-tonne 50-oared liburnian based on that relief and the ships on Trajan's column in Rome is given here. Such a ship would probably have been capable of up to 7½kts for a short sprint and 5kts or more for a long period in favourable sea conditions.

Conclusion

The warships of the ancient Mediterranean were as impressive in their own way as any of the much admired surviving buildings and sculptures which are the more visible legacy of the Greek and Roman world today. In performance the ships reached the then practical limits of both oar propulsion and structural strength. The relative sizes of the most used types are shown in silhouette, to scale for comparison, in the accompanying illustration. They ranged from boats no larger than launches up to ships displacing about 200 tonnes and as long as the larger galleys and Third Rate 60-gun ships two millennia later in history.

John Coates

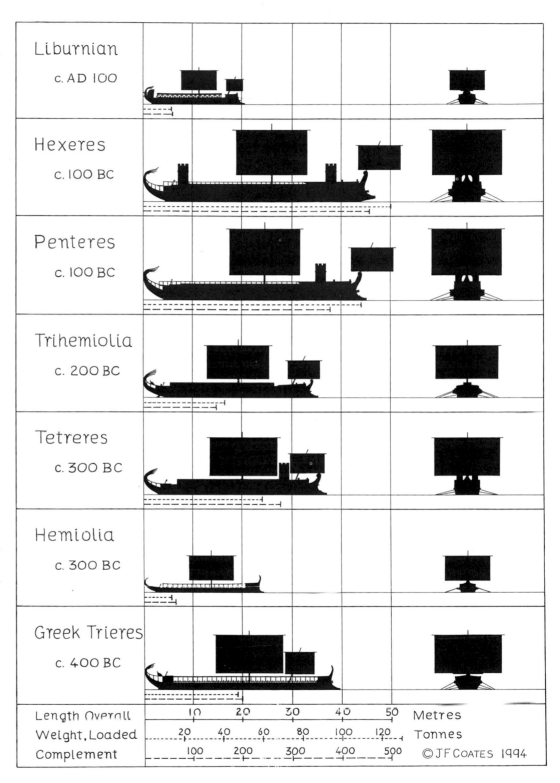

Acknowledgements

Besides his debt to John Morrison, already acknowledged, the writer has been helped greatly by collaboration with Timothy Shaw, research scientist and life-long rowing coach, and René Burlet, engineer and ergonomist, on oar systems. For the building and testing of the Greek trireme reconstruction *Olympias*, without which any realistic investigation of other types of ancient oared warships would not have been possible, the support and labours of hundreds of people in Greece, other parts of Europe and in the USA are gratefully acknowledged, in particular the Hellenic Navy and other national authorities in Greece for funding the ship, her builders, Dimitri Tzakakos and his willing shipwrights, and not least the thousand or so who organised several periods of sea trials, manned *Olympias* and rowed her so willingly and energetically to rediscover how a large and fast oared ship worked.

23. Foley and Soedel, 'Ancient Oared Warships'.

10

The Naval Architecture and Oar Systems of Medieval and Later Galleys

Surviving documents and artefacts

In terms of archaeological finds, the extant remains of Mediterranean galleys from the period between 800 and 1650 are sparse indeed.[1] For this reason what follows is based on written sources and drawings. In these documents the image of the galley and of the oared warship is vague and undetailed until close to the end of the fourteenth century. The Byzantine Emperor Leo VI, 'The Philosopher' (886–912), included in his surviving *Naumachica* information on the building and fitting out of

Galleys depicted in a mosaic at San Marco, Venice, from the thirteenth or fourteenth century. (From E Concina, L'Arsenale della Repubblica di Venezia, p25)

warships, even though the document was written with the emphasis on naval fleet tactics rather than from the point of view of the shipwright. According to Leo, the dromon was now used in wartime for the same tasks that the triremes had fulfilled in earlier times. The following paragraphs are also directly relevant to the design of the dromon, the characteristic oared warship of the Byzantine Empire:

4. However, the dromon should neither be too broad, as this makes the vessel difficult and awkward to row, nor so narrow, light and weak that it can be wrecked by an enemy ship's ram attack. Ideally it should be of moderate design, so that it is fast and mobile, but can also fight off the enemy strongly and reliably.

6. The prow is always fitted with a Siphon, clad in the usual way with bronze, which is used to hurl fire at the enemy. And above the Siphon an enclosed, planked platform should be erected, on which warriors stand . . .

7. The largest dromons are also fitted with what is termed the timber castle, enclosed by planks . . . these dromons should be long enough to accommodate the two rows of oars already mentioned: the one above and the other below.

9. A further type of dromon is built to a very large size, with room for 200 men – sometimes more, sometimes less, the number varying to suit the particular task in hand. Of this number 50 are oarsmen at the lower level, while 150 armed men are stationed above, ready to do battle with the enemy.

10. Small dromons are also built, known as a *galea* or *monērēs*. These are fast and light, and are very useful as guard-ships and for all other tasks where high speed is required.[2]

William of Tyre (*c*1130–1185) mentions '. . . *naves longae, rostratae, geminis remorum instructae ordinibus, bellicis usibus habiliores, quae vulgo*

galeae dicuntur . . .'.[3] This type of galley with oars arranged in pairs on one level, on a single gunwale, is shown in Spinello Aretino's painting (pre-1400) in the Palazzo Pubblico in Siena, and in a mosaic of the thirteenth or fourteenth century from San Marco, Venice. It appears that larger galleys gradually took over the tasks of the dromons in naval warfare. In any case the term 'galea' eventually came to be used for all larger oared warships in surviving Latin documents.

By the thirteenth and fourteenth century the authorities in northern Italy had begun to regulate 'state' shipbuilding by means of 'decretti' [decrees] – which applied primarily to galley building.[4] These documents laid down prescribed basic methods from which shipwrights developed specific building directions, and developed them further to form constructional procedures. It is on these decretti that the oldest surviving shipbuilding manu-

1. Keel, bottom timbers and lower planking strakes of a small sixteenth-century Venetian galley were discovered by Enrico Scandurra in Lake Garda. Enrico Scandurra 'Die Seerepubliken: Schiffe des Mittelalters und der Rennaissance in Italien' ['The Marine Republics: Ships of the Middle Ages and the Renaissance in Italy'], in George F Bass (ed), *Taucher in die Vergangenheit* [German ed of *A History of Seafaring*] (Lucern and Frankfurt am Main 1972), pp208–210, 220–221.

2. Leo VI, *Peri Naumachias*, 19, 4–10 – J P Migne (ed), Patrologia Graeca, Vol 109, pp991–994; Alphonse Dain, *Naumachica – partim adhuc inedita, in unum nunc primum congessit et indice auxit* (Paris 1943), pp19–20.

3. William of Tyre, *Historia rerum in partibus transmarinis gestarum*, lib XX, caput XIV; J P Migne (ed), Patrologia Latina, Vol 201, p790.

4. These *decretti* [decrees] are the first documents to provide dimensional information. See Adolfo Sacerdoti and Riccardo Predelli, 'Gli statuti marittimi veneziani fino al 1255', *Nuovo Archivio Veneto*, new series, IV (1902), pp113–161 and V (1903), pp161–251; Auguste Jal, *Archéologie Navale*, 2 vol (Paris 1840), Vol 1, pp252–253, 272, prints a Genoan edict of 1333 regarding the dimensions of galleys '*de Romania et de Syria*', and a corresponding Venetian ordinance of 1320.

scripts are based, dating from the early fifteenth century. They provide an overall impression of Mediterranean shipbuilding as it took the first steps along the path which led from pure craft skills to engineering drawings. Today it is difficult to imagine how a large and complex ocean-going vessel such as a naval or merchant galley could be built without any form of plans. And yet these ships were seaworthy. The apparent chaos reigning at the shipyard was no worse than is expected today. Every worker knew what his own task was in the construction process. Just as the carpenters of the day mastered every stroke and procedure by practising them so long that they could eventually be carried out automatically, without instruction, the budding shipwright simply learned his teacher's instructions by rote. The following verse was an introduction to a set of rules for the construction of sailing ships:

Al nome de dio questo sie lo amaistrameto de
  far una nave /
cose grada come pichola e da la raxon ch pro-
  cede infina che /
la possa andar a vello come vederai qui de soto
  per singula.[5]

Spoken as an anapaest (two unstressed syllables followed by one stressed one), each of the three lines amounts to seven groups of three syllables and one trailing syllable. The master shipwrights, or so we can assume, recited aloud or sang the essential constructional rules and details of their projects to their pupils and assistants while the work progressed. Such instructional verses were later written down and collected to form the earliest written building instructions, lyrical in form and based fundamentally on word and number. The 'Fabrica di galere'[6] – from which the above verse is taken – passes these design methods down to us. The early Italian shipbuilding manuscripts give no visual images of ship design; instead they give what amounts to an acoustic idea of the teachings of the master shipwrights. Their highly detailed descriptions give a profound insight into the art of Italian galley building in the early fifteenth century, but they also allow us to make soundly based deductions on its origins and earlier patterns.

The roots of the art of galley building lay in the East. The technical terms *schermo, paraschuxula, parascena, panixelo* and several other expressions mentioned in the 'Fabrica' refer to

Main frame and stem/stern of a 'galia grosa'. (After British Library, Cott. Mss, Titus, A.26, G Trombetta, f29v, 40r)

Greek predecessors.[7] Of course, we should not underestimate the importance of later, independent developments, but the use of Greek technical terms does show clearly that Venice – in particular – was able to exploit the uninterrupted development of Roman-Byzantine shipbuilding traditions. Just at the time when the 'Fabrica' was written, some of the finest Venetian master shipwrights, such as Theodoro Baxon, his nephew Nicolo Palopano and his son Giorgio il Greco, were of Greek stock.[8] Thus the Venetian galleys in particular, and the Mediterranean galleys of the fifteenth century in general, must also be counted in terms of shipbuilding technology as the direct successors of Leo VI's dromons.

In time, shipwrights also began to use drawings to define their designs, possibly under the pressure of more and more detailed official 'decretti' relating to the dimensions of individual ship types, and also under the influence of architectural drawings based on central perspective; a highly regarded technique developed at this time. The first examples of sketches of individual ship components showing the deliberate use of parallel perspective projections are found in Giorgio Trombetta's notes[9] dating from the years 1441–1449. His sketches are very small and drawn freehand, but such 'plans' were further developed in the course of the next hundred years until they had reached the level of large-format line drawings of engineering standards.[10] Pre Theodoro, a Venetian master shipwright of the mid-sixteenth century, used his drawings expressly as building plans, so that he could define the form of the frames and the rounded stem and stern. His manuscript also represents the oldest extant true-scale side elevations.[11]

These early Venetian shipbuilding manu-

5. 'In the name of God, these are the instructions for building a sailing ship / large or small, and in such detail that – if the procedures are followed – / it can run under sail, as will be shown in detail below.'

6. The original is lost. Two copies exist: Biblioteca Nazionale Centrale di Firenze, col Mag, cl XIX, 7, 'Fabrica di galere' (probably from the fifteenth century) and Austrian National Library, Marco Foscarini collection, cod 6391, 'Arte di far galee e navi' (perhaps from the sixteenth century). A Jal, *Archéologie Navale*, Vol 2, pp6–30, has published parts of the text from the Florentine version, with a French translation.

7. See Ulrich Alertz, *Vom Schiffbauhandwerk zur Schiffbautechnik* [From Shipwrighting to Shipbuilding Technology] (Hamburg 1991), pp45–47.

8. See ASV, Arsenale, busta 566, 'Quaderno dei salariadi'.

9. London, British Library, Cottonian Mss, Titus, A 26, Giorgio Trombetta da Modon; in part published and translated by Roger Charles Anderson, 'Italian Naval Architecture about 1445', *The Mariner's Mirror* 11 (1925), pp135–163.

10. Greenwich, National Maritime Museum, NVT 19, 'Ragione antique spettanti all'arte del mare et fabriche de vasselli'; published in full with explanations, Giorgetta Bonfiglio Dosio *et al*, *Ragioni antique spettanti all'arte del mare et fabriche de vasselli – manoscritto nautico del sec XV* (Venice 1987).

11. Two copies have survived: Biblioteca Nazionale Marciana, Ms Ital, cl IV, 26 Pre Theodoro de Nicolo, 'Instructione sul modo di fabricare galere'; and Archivio di Stato di Venezia, Archivio Proprio Contarini, 19, Theodoro de Nicolo, 'Arte di far vaselli'.

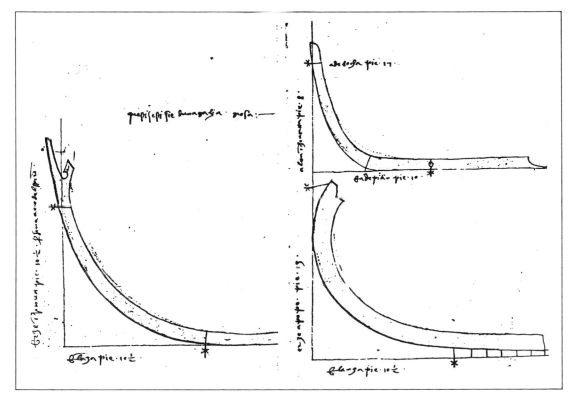

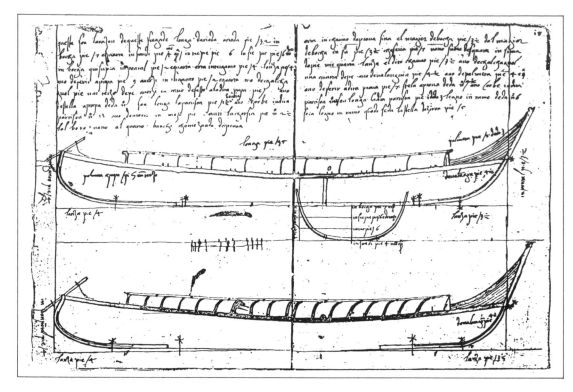

Two small oared ships of the 'fregada' type. (After Biblioteca Nazionale Marciana, Ms Ital, cl.IV, 26, Pre Theodoro, f18)

scripts, written for the initiated and the expert, are very difficult to interpret from today's standpoint. However, in the seventeenth century handbooks which are easier to understand were written by two men: Joseph Furttenbach,[12] a substantial Genoa-based international merchant who operated between 1609 and 1617, and who necessarily had virtually daily contact with ships; and Steffano de Zuanne,[13] a Venetian master shipwright. At the climax of centuries of development, Furttenbach and de Zuanne described from their own experience the achievements and successes of an epoch drawing to its close. It was ending in the sense that the separation which today exists between ship design and ship construction was already becoming distinct in the seventeenth century – for example in the works of Anthony Deane and Edmund Bushnell.[14] The image of the master shipwright was fated to become divided into the twin profiles of the designing engineer on the one hand and the implementing carpenter on the other. The art of drawing would eventually differentiate between the naval architect of the future and the shipwright of the past: the ability to design a ship, to draw an image of it on paper with ruler, compasses, adjustable batten and ink so clearly and completely that any ship's carpenter could determine the form and shape of the parts, and fabricate them, without additional rules and without referring back to the draughtsman.

But these shipbuilding manuscripts do more than simply describe; since they were intended

for practical usage, they in fact contributed to ship development itself. As early as the beginning of the fifteenth century, at the time the 'Fabrica' was written, the rules and dimensional information required to build a large ship were so extensive that rote-learning and instructional verses alone were no longer sufficiently reliable to provide all the instructions required. The shipbuilding manuscripts were considered to be the most important means of expressing a new technology, for the purpose of noting dimensions, determining rules of construction and not least for describing components and interrelated structures by means of plans and drawings.

The naval architecture of the galley

The shipwright of the Middle Ages and the early modern period was not able to discover experimentally the most efficient, streamlined shape for a stable and commodious waterborne vessel. Data gathered from tests with models could not have been evaluated, and any findings could not have been applied to the hydrodynamic conditions affecting a full-size vessel. Complex calculations regarding stability and optimisation would have degenerated into a lifelong task using the few aids available at the time. It was essential to reduce to a minimum

the life-threatening risks to the crew of a seriously flawed vessel, but different means had to be found. Experience with earlier ships and comparisons with proven vessels helped the shipwright to improve his skills of estimating the qualities of his own new design. The shipwright based his ideas on his successful predecessors, and aimed at laying down simple rules which would govern the main dimensions and form of the hull.

Great importance was attached to certain crucial individual components. In addition to keel, stem and stern the *corba maistra* – the main frame – proved to be a vital component for defining the hull shape. Once the main frame was defined, a series of carefully selected variations – known as *partisoni* in Venice[15] – could be used to derive the shape of all the other frames. The Venetian master shipwrights developed a purely mathematical/geometrical procedure for designing ships, which, viewed from the point of view of the present-day shipbuilder, looks absolutely ideal for Computer Aided Design.[16] The ship's

12. Joseph Furttenbach, *Architectura Navalis* (Ulm 1629; reprint Hildesheim and New York 1975). Furttenbach published a dozen more books on the subjects of the art of building, architecture and various areas of art and science.

13. British Library, Add Mss 38655, Steffano de Zuanne de Michel, 'L'Architettura Navale'.

14. Edmund Bushnell, *The Compleat Ship-Wright* (London 1664); Brian Lavery (ed), *Deane's Doctrine of Naval Architecture 1670* (London 1981).

15. According to B Drachio, in ASV, Arsenale, busta 1, Visione, f6; published and translated by L Th Lehmann, *Baldissera Drachio Quinto, Visione del Drachio* (Amsterdam 1992).

16. This technology was used in preparing the reconstructions.

Small galley under sail from a Catalan Atlas of about 1375. (From Monique de la Roncière and Michel Mollat du Jourdin, *Portulane*, fig 8)

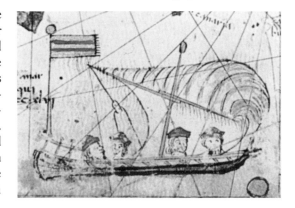

shape was recorded digitally. Dimensional data using a two-dimensional co-ordinate system on a series of planes defined the shape and position of all the critical components. Although constructional drawings were not deemed essential, they were useful in giving the shipwright an idea of the appearance of individual components. The master shipwright only had to provide the input values for the appropriate ship type and draw the diagrams, and then he could leave the construction of the hull to the routine manual labour of the carpenters.

Leo VI provides very vaguely formulated instructions for building the dromon, eschewing accurate dimensional information. He does not prescribe the size, the exact beam or the height of the hull to the shipbuilder, as the 'shell' form of construction makes this impossible. The hull was built over 'false' frames – this is clear from Leo's description – to which the strakes were not permanently connected. These formers dictated only the minimum dimensions. The curvature of the strakes corresponded to that of the flexible batten and, to a certain extent, defined itself automatically. The structural frames, fixed permanently to the outer hull skin, were not installed until later, so their purpose was not to determine the hull shape, as became standard later. This method of construction is based on the premise that the strakes are connected permanently to each other to form the outer shell of the vessel. This is true, for example, of clinker construction, where the strakes overlap, but in Mediterranean carvel construction the outer skin planks can be joined to each other by rebates [rabbets] or by mortice and tenon joints. The dromon shipwright was therefore restricted in what he could determine beforehand to the dimensions of the keel, the shape of the stem and stern, and perhaps the overall length of the vessel. The exact dimensions of beam, side height and displacement set themselves during construction, and could at best be taken off the completed ship.

The earliest accurate dimensional information on the construction of galleys dates from 18 February 1275. Charles I of Anjou, King of Sicily, commissioned the construction of a new series of galleys based on a proven ship.[17] The shipbuilders could only adhere to the prescribed beam and hull height dimensions if they completed at least a substantial part of the frame structure before building the hull shell. As described in the 'Fabrica di galere' of 1410, the Venetian shipbuilder of the fourteenth and fifteenth centuries was already using a frame skeleton, which was held together by parts of the old hull shell known as the *maistre* (special

ribbands installed before the actual strakes, whose purpose was to determine the hull curvature). Presumably the majority of the frames were only installed subsequently, until the vacant gaps between the *maistre* could be sealed by fitting the strakes. This can be seen as a transitional phase between the old shell construction and the new frame construction. In the course of time the detailed constructional information was expanded until it formed an increasingly comprehensive system of *partisoni*.[18]

'Other nations do not follow the same procedure, but instead rely on experience and a good eye rather than on rules, when building both sailing ships and galleys. For this reason their vessels are not of the same high standard which is expected of the Venetians.'[19] Steffano de Zuanne, convinced of the superior quality of his own shipbuilding methods, sees the essential difference between his and other countries' practice in the precise rules which provided the means for Venetian shipbuilders to design and build a complex ship's hull *di tal perfezione* [of such perfection].

> 255 uniquely different wooden parts – the bottom and frame timbers – are required for a galeasse, and I say that only two frames – varied as described above – are required to prepare all those parts. Moreover only two different frames are needed for the 240 wooden parts of a light galley. This works so perfectly that all you need to do is set them at the prescribed position, and they form a perfect hull.[20]

The first step was to determine the shape and size of the main frame. Calipers were used to determine the frame width at different heights. The points determined in this way were linked by a faired (kink-free and bulge-free) line. The author of the 'Fabrica' measured the frame at set intervals of 1 *pie* with extra values at the ½ and ⅓ *pie* points, but according to Pre Theodoro and Alessandro Picheroni four caliper measurements were sufficient for the same purpose regardless of the absolute height of the frame. Using this less complicated but still effective procedure, which was based more on the shape of the frame than on its absolute height, a single value determined the width of the hull bottom (*in fondi*) and the spacing of the frame ends (*in bocha*). Between them two caliper measurements were made at ⅓ and ⅔ of the frame height *in tre pie* and *in sie pie*.[21]

This process produced the shape of the widest frame at the centre of the hull. The next step was to determine the shape and size of the

two *cavi di sesto*, the reference, or aligning frames at the hull ends. The main frame served as pattern for these two frames. Later Venetian building regulations laid down three or four steps by which the *cao di sesto* was to be developed from the shape of the main frame. The *cavi di sesto* formed the forward and after ends of the *chorbe in sesti* (frames determined by the *partison* process). The first step, *partison de fondo*,[22] gave its name to the whole procedure. It shortened the *fondo*, the flat section of the hull, and allowed the bottom of the galley to taper inward at the ends. The second step, the *ramo*[23] or *legno in ramo*, increased the frame side angle. Compared with the U-shaped midship frames the front and rear frames were more V-shaped.

Pre Theodoro, Baldisera Drachio and Steffano de Zuanne also mention a third step, the *scorer delli forcami* or *scorer del seste*, which presumably concerned the curvature of the *forcami* (frame top timbers). 'The first is used on the bottom, the second on the ends of the frames, near to the mark for the topmost timber at the sheer strake, right at the top of the galley's hull, and the third on the centre part, between the two others.'[24] Etymologically based on *scorrere* (to flow) and *escoriazione* (abrading), the *scorer* showed the carpenter where he had to apply his tools in order to chamfer the angled part which was a result of the three other steps between *corba* (bottom frame timber) and *forcame* (frame top timber). This process restored the flowing curvature. Alternatively it determined by how much the ends of the *corba* of the *cao di sesto* had to be shortened compared with those of the *corba* of the main frame, and by how much the lower part of the *forcami* had to be extended (or vice

17. See R Filangieri, *I regestri della cancellerina angioina*, Vol 12 (Naples 1959), pp126–129; John H Pryor, *Geography, Technology and War* (Cambridge 1988), pp64–66.

18. On this matter in particular, see A Chiggato, 'Le "ragioni antique" dell'architettura navale, ppLVII–LXIV', in Giorgetta Bonfiglio Dosio *et al*, *Ragioni antique spettanti all'arte del mare et fabriche de vasselli*.

19. BM, Add Mss 38655, Steffano de Zuanne, f18v.

20. BM, Add Mss 38655, Steffano de Zuanne, f18v.

21. Pre Theodoro (BNM, Ms Ital, cl IV, 26, Pre Theodoro, f36v; ASV, Archivio Proprio Contarini, 19. Theodoro de Nicolo, f38v) names a rule of thumb for measuring *tre pie* and *sie pie* based on the width of the floor.

22. BM, Add Mss 38655, Steffano de Zuanne, f18r–23r.

23. See R C Anderson, 'Jal's "Memoire No 5" and the manuscript "Fabrica di Galere"', *The Mariner's Mirror* 31 (1945), pp166–167.

24. ASV, Arsenale, busta 1, Visione, f7v; L Th Lehmann, *Baldissera Drachio Quinto*, 7v.

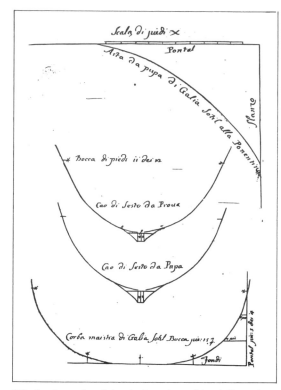

The 'corba maistra' (main frame), and 'cavi di sesto' (aligning frames) derived from them of a 'galia sotil'. (After BM, Add Mss 38655, Steffano de Zuanne, f8r)

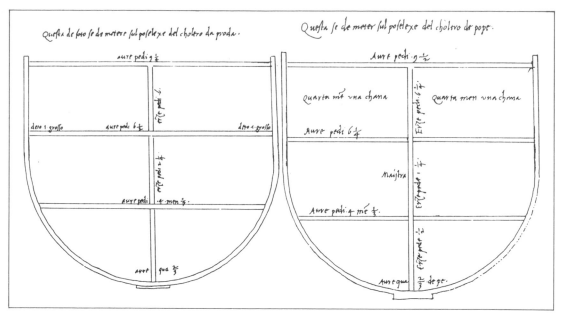

Two 'sesti' for describing the contours of the hull ends. (After BNCF, col Mag cl XIX, 7, 'Fabrica di galere,' f4)

versa). This process has the same effect. At the final stage the main frame components were set on a plinth (*stella*), so that the deck rose slightly towards the ends, and the waterlines ran at a more pronounced angle fore and aft at the bottom.

The numerical values for the separate steps of the *partison* procedure are only stated by the shipwright for the two *cavi di sesto*. The values for all the intermediate frames had to be determined by the carpenter using a geometric process. Steffano de Zuanne explains his version using the example of the *particion del fondo*: The short side of a right-angle triangle with sides of 3/3, 4/3 and 5/3 (relative to the length of the *particion del fondo*) is divided into exactly the

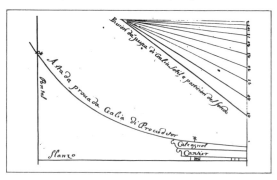

Galley stem and 'Partison' diagram. (After BM Add Mss 38655, Steffano de Zuanne, f8v)

number of unequal parts as the shipbuilder wants to calculate frames between main frame and aligning frame. These accurately calculated frames – in the case of the *galia di Mercanzia* every fourth frame – were called *onze*. The points thus established are connected by straight lines to the opposite angle. Starting from the 4/3 length side, the values for the *particion del fondo* of each individual *onza* can now be found using compasses.[25] According to Steffano de Zuanne, a similar procedure was also used to determine the *stella, ramo and scorer*. Presumably the same diagram was used for this, but the values were read off at different positions.

One severe fault of the *partison* procedure cannot be overlooked: it could only be applied at the central part of the hull, at the *corbe in sesti, ie* the frames between the aligning frames. The hull ends were outside its scope. Perhaps the formation of these critical areas was guarded by shipbuilders as a professional secret, because it was assumed – not without justification – that the key to a successful design lay in the bow and stern sections of the vessel, which were difficult to design and construct. Naturally the shipbuilders did not want to disclose their solution to these problems. It is also possible that there was nothing to disclose, because there was no method of incorporating the complex shapes of the fore and after hull frames into a system of *partisoni*, and for this reason it had to be left to the shipbuilder to find the best solution. It appears that even the rib method of construction did not extend to these two areas, and that the planks were curved in to stem and stern in the ancient way, and frames were only added later to reinforce the structure. The curvature of the stem and

stern would have been produced automatically using this method. Presumably the *sesti* (templates) as shown in the 'Fabrica' would be used to check and adjust the curvature. These two templates were positioned half-way between *chodera chorba* (= *cao di sesto*?) and hull end at the point marked *poselexe del choltro*, the joint areas between keel and stem/stern, instead of the frames.[26]

According to Furttenbach, the Genoan shipbuilders used a procedure similar to the Venetian *partison del fondo*, to shorten the length of the *matere* (floor timbers) towards the hull ends. A plumb line is dropped over a reference line, and compasses are used to draw a semicircle of radius ⅛th the width at the inside edge of the main frame. Furttenbach divides the two quarter-circles into 60 equal angles, and connects the points determined in this way to each other by straight lines parallel to the reference line. These straight lines cut the perpendicular into 60 points and thereby determine the amount by which the floor timbers of the first 60 frames abaft the main frame have to be shortened compared with the main frame floor timbers. If a conversion factor of 1.054 is applied, the same diagram can also be used for the 55 frames forward of the main frame (place frame 55 on line 58, and so on with the other

25. The example drawn using n = 9 applies to the *pavion da prova*, the forward floor of the *galia di mercanzia*.

26. See BNM Ms Ital, cl IV, 26, Pre Theodoro, f17, 18; ASV, Archivio Proprio Contarini, 19, Theodoro de Nicolo, f19, 21.

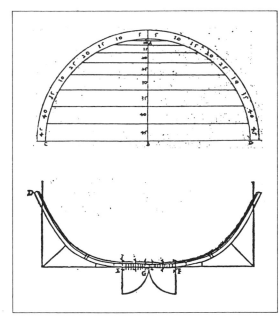

'Brusca' for determining the flat (width of the bottom) and application of the 'brusca' on the 'matera' (flat) of the main frame. (From B Crescentio, pp 17, 18)

frames).[27] Because the galley was built taller at the stern than at the bow, the after frames had to be placed on a higher plinth than the forward ones. This produced waterlines which were less acute at the bow and more acute at the stern.

Because the aftership is higher than the foreship, the whole of the 'stella' must be used at the aftership, but at the foreship ¼ less . . . the Venetian galleys also have less of it [rise at bow and stern?], in order to make the galley less conspicuous, and less of a target. The same applies to the Turkish galleys, on which the gangway gun is set up aft of the prow, where it can be aimed more easily; it is possible to depress the gun virtually to the horizontal without recourse to tackles. To achieve this end the first ten frames behind the main frame and the first ten frames in front of the main frame are not set on a plinth at all, so that all 20 form the flat bottom of the galley.[28]

The *meza luna*-shaped *brusca* also existed as part of the older Venetian shipbuilding tradition of the fifteenth century. The exact function of these diagrams is not clear from the manuscript texts. In Anderson's opinion[29] Giorgio Trombetta would have used the *meza luna* and a further diagram based on an extended triangle, divided into unequal parts, to determine the frame widths. Judging by the technical expressions *parttiso* and *chorba* which were used, this is presumably a simple *partison* procedure based on only two variation steps:

the *stella* and the *partison del fondo*.[30] In contrast, the two similar diagrams in the 'Fabrica'[31] seem to have been intended as an aid to constructing the rigging and cutting the sails.

Partison procedures were also known in Portugal, in southern France and presumably in the entire shipbuilding areas of southern and western Europe. Although in principle the same procedure was used everywhere, it seems that each arsenal, and perhaps each master shipwright, would have had its own ideas of the best method of 'regulated' shipbuilding; including highly specific details.

I have already seen how a simple line on paper, drawn freehand, can produce a very good and serviceable partizion, both for round [sailing] vessels and for oared ones. Skilled mathematicians and others have developed many methods for drawing the lines, but the simplest and most reliable is the freehand method with a sheet of paper. The desired oval lines may simply be drawn based on a circle produced using compasses, others use only a circular arc; I prefer the oval.[32]

When comparing the *partison* procedure of Pre Theodoro and Steffano de Zuanne with the *meza luna* procedure used by Bartolomeo Crescentio and Joseph Furttenbach a difference in the quality of the results is evident. For this reason the *meza luna* was not highly regarded at the Naples arsenal: 'Nevertheless this procedure is not so highly regarded at the Naples arsenal, where it is believed that the hull curvature is neither smooth nor pleasing to the eye. For this reason the shipbuilders there use a

A 'Partiso' procedure for 'navi' and 'galie'. (After BM, Cott Mss, Titus, A.26, G Trombetta, f45r)

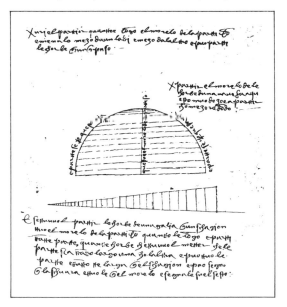

different procedure: more appropriate and correct.'[33]

According to Furttenbach only the height of the frame plinth and the length of the bottom timbers were varied over the ship's length, but it was Venetian practice to vary the frame side angle, which resulted in disproportionately more elegant waterlines, as the reconstructions show. 'Such slight refinements in design may have had much to do with the high reputation of the Venetian galley builders.'[34]

The following characteristics are common to all procedures: design and 'as built' dimensions could be varied or chosen at will, as could the rules and the types of diagram; for the resultant curves – mostly sinusoidal – defined the floor line and the deck line, the side angle of the frames, the height of the frame plinth and even the shape of the sails. The shipbuilder always avoided designing 'from scratch'. If he was called upon to design an unusual vessel, or meet new and unusual requirements, then the rules were of little assistance, and he could have no confidence in its likely success. The rules gave no idea at all of the hull form. The rules were devoid of any scientific or mathematical foundation, and their existence was due solely to the simple fact that common ship shapes could be reproduced easily by their means. If the shipbuilder mastered the rules, the vessel could hardly go wrong. However, only very small variations on the prescribed scheme were safe, larger alterations being very risky. The ships built to them – especially the galleys – were therefore much the same: 'All galleys of the same size are so similar in all respects that a man who moves from his own galley to another would hardly notice that he was on a different

27. See J Furttenbach, *Architectura Navalis*, p37.

28. Bartolomeo Crescentio, *Nautica mediterranea* (Rome 1602; 2nd ed Rome 1607), p19.

29. R C Anderson, 'Italian Naval Architecture about 1445', *The Mariner's Mirror* 11 (1925), pp153–155.

30. John Patrick Sarsfield, 'Mediterranean Whole Moulding', *The Mariner's Mirror* 70 (1984), pp86–88 and L Th Lehmann, 'Mediterranean Whole Moulding', *The Mariner's Mirror* 70 (1984), p88, attempt to explain Crescentio's and Trombetta's procedures.

31. BNCF, col Mag, cl XIX, 7, 'Fabrica di galere', f120v, 121r; OeN, Foscarini, Cod 6391, 'Arte de far vasselli', f120v, 121r. The way in which these diagrams were used cannot be determined clearly. It is also clear that the copyists of the 'Fabrica' did not have accurate knowledge on how these aids were used: the rectangular diagram in the Florentine manuscript shows 20 vertical lines, that in the Viennese version only 19.

32. BM, Add Mss 38655, Steffano de Zuanne, f21r.

33. B Crescentio, p21.

34. Frederic Chapin Lane, *Venice and History* (Baltimore 1966), p172.

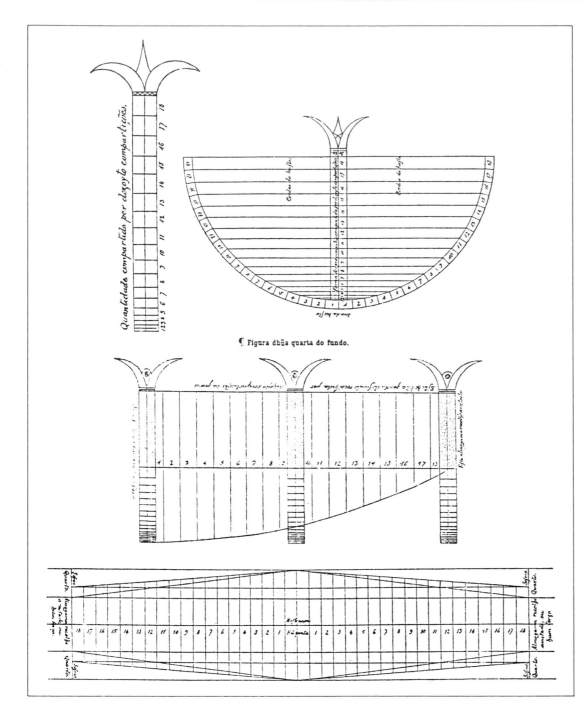

¶ Figura dhũa quarta do fundo.

Portuguese 'Partison' diagrams. (From Lopes de Mendonca, Fernando Oliveira, pp 189, 191, 195, 196)

a unique vessel, like the dromons, the Viking ships and the Hanseatic cogs. It would have been possible to imitate individual successful vessels and copy them plank for plank, but continuous development would not have occurred, and vessels could not have been optimised for particular tasks. Systematic improvements are only possible when regulations and plans define a ship accurately. The hydrostatic and hydrodynamic characteristics of the ship, which in earlier times could only be attributed to the experience and skills of the master shipwright, could now be described, compared and to a certain extent explained by rules, dimensional relationships and drawings. The great galleys built exclusively in accordance with the prescribed *sesti* and building rules could be designed and commissioned with a level of confidence previously unknown. For example, as far as is known not one of the pilgrim galleys was lost through faulty construction or effect of wind and sea. Italian merchant galleys linked the most important ports of the Mediterranean, England and the Netherlands by regular service. Contemporaries considered the great galleys to be the safest, most reliable, fastest and relatively most comfortable means of transport.[36]

The power systems

The oars

8. Each [dromon] should have at least 25 thwarts on which the oarsmen sit. Thus there are 25 thwarts below and a further 25 above, making 50 in total. And each thwart should support two oarsmen: one on the right, one on the left. The vessel therefore holds 100 men, oarsmen and warriors, all together, top and bottom.[37]

vessel, . . . and Venetian galleys are as similar to each other as one swallow's nest to the next.'[35]

To the modern engineer's eye these qualities appear primarily as weaknesses. His aim is to define in advance the detail characteristics of his design and to optimise them. However, at that time it was not possible or expected to predict accurately the characteristics of the planned vessel. The simple question 'will the ship be good?' – far too vague a question for the modern engineer – could be given a positive answer from the outset, since it was built into this 'regulated' form of ship design. With no great effort the *partison* system guaranteed the success of a project; success which the

modern draught can only offer once many additional calculations have been completed.

At first sight the implementation of this building method was only of advantage to the master shipwright and the internal workings of the shipyard. However, the regulatory procedure also fulfilled indirectly the most important prerequisite for the expansion of Mediterranean sea traffic. It was particularly successful when large series of the same type of vessel were to be built. To a great extent it excluded the risk of a failure in ship design, and supplied a secure base on which to develop steady, systematic improvements. Without the new procedure with its exact dimensional statements and rules, every galley would have been

35. Based on Cunradus Dietericus Hassler, *Fratis Felicis Fabri Evagatorium in Terrae Sanctae, Arabiae et Egypti peregrinationem*, Vol 1 (Stuttgart 1843), p118.

36. See C D Hassler, *Felicis Fabri Evagatorium*, Vol 1, pp114–152, Vol 3, pp174–380; M Margaret Newett (ed), *Canon Pietro Casola's Pilgrimage to Jerusalem in the Year 1494* (Manchester 1907), pp155–220 and pp292–336; F C Lane, 'Venetian Shipping during the Commercial Revolution', *American Historical Review* 38 (1933), pp219–239. Until the sixteenth century it was considered superfluous to insure goods shipped on galleys, in contrast to goods on the 'navi,' or large sailing ships.

37. Leo VI, *Peri Naumachias*, 19, 4–10, J P Migne (ed), Patrologia Graeca, Vol 109, pp991–994; A Dain, *Naumachica*, pp19–20.

Midship section of the 'galea de Fiandra' (Flanders galley). (reconstruction by the author)

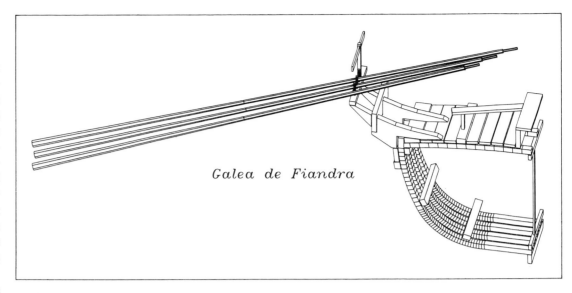

Galea de Fiandra

It is clear that the oarsmen of the dromon sat on two levels, each with his own oar. The centre part of the hull was undecked (Greek *asanidon*), and the only fore-and-aft gangways ran along the sides. The lower oarsmen were seated below the gangway level, while the upper oarsmen were at the height of the gangways, together with the armoured warriors and the archers.[38] This makes the dromon similar to the Attic *triērēs*, whose oarsmen also sat at different levels without being separated by a closed deck.[39] On the other hand the dromon's two half-decks were already part-way to the completely covered galley of later times.

All the oars of the galley which Leo VI terms the *monērēs* were located at one level on a single gunwale. Around 1170 William of Tyre mentioned galleys with a twin oar arrangement. Probably two oarsmen worked one oar each, but shared a bench. In the early fourteenth century Marino Sanuto the elder[40] wrote that by the year 1290 this oar system had been expanded to a triple arrangement. From that time until the time of Pre Theodoro (around 1550) the Venetian galleys were usually fitted with three *schermi* (thole pins) per *banco* (thwart) on the *postiza* (gunwale). Three oarsmen per bench worked one oar each:

> . . . the oar known as the *pianer* is larger than the two others at 32 feet in length, and is the one which is worked by the oarsman who sits directly adjacent to the gangway. The second, known as the *postizzio*, is 30½ feet long and is worked by the second oarsman on the thwart. And the third, which we call *terzicchio* and those in the West call *terzarolo* – the same name is used for the oarsman who pulls it – is 29½ feet long, . . .[41]

The thole pins of the *pianer* with his 32ft long (11.13m) oar was located furthest aft. At inter-

vals of 1 *palmo* forward followed the thole pins of the *postizzio* and the *terzicchio*, who had the shortest oar at 29.5ft (10.26m). The distance from one *postizo* to the next varied between 3⁷⁄₁₆ft (1.2m)[42] and 3½ft (1.22m).[43] On merchant galleys the space between the *zovo a prova* (the forward transverse outrigger beam) and the first *postizzo* was the same as the distance between the *postizi*. To avoid the problem of oarsmen on one thwart obstructing each other with their long, heavy oars, the thwarts were angled forward and outward.[44]

The warships of the Middle Ages, the Byzantine dromons and the Italian galleys were, as Leo VI emphasised,[45] different from Athenian *triērēs* and more recent galleys rowed by armed soldiers.[46] The *galeotti* of the merchant galleys were paid professional seamen,[47] and worked the oars together with the archers and crossbowmen.[48] They were also minor entrepreneurs, carrying their own goods for trade.[49] During their long voyages through the Mediterranean, into the North Sea or into the Black Sea, this powerful crew formed the protection for ship and cargo.

After the end of the fifteenth century the position of the *galeotti* worsened. Professional oarsmen and – in wartime – enlisted members of the guilds were increasingly replaced by convicts, prisoners of war and slaves. In Venice this development began relatively late, and the change affected the merchant galleys, if at all, much less than the warships. But in Genoa at Furttenbach's time (around 1610) the larger warships, galleys and galeasses were already rowed exclusively by men who were forced to work in one way or another:

> It should be known, that there are three species of oarsmen, first the . . . *bonavoglia* or volunteers, . . . those are the sons of Christ with a

disastrous passion for gambling . . . Because they have embarked on the galley in a carefree manner, or have pledged themselves . . . they

38. Basileios Patrikios Parakoimomenos, 5, 2, 6–7, in A Dain, *Naumachica*, p65; ancient biremes are discussed in Jürgen Hansen, *Schiffbau in der Antike* [*Shipbuilding in Ancient Times*] (Herford 1979), pp125–129.

39. See in particular the reconstruction by John S Morrison and John F Coates, *Die athenische Triere* [The Athenian Trireme] (Mainz 1990); and John F Coates, 'The Greek Trireme of the 5th Century BC', in *Sailing into the Past* (Roskilde 1986).

40. Marino Sanuto, *Liber Secretorum Fideliorum Crucis*, pp57, 65, 77.

41. BBM, cl IV, L Ms, Cristoforo da Canale, quoted by Luigi Fincati, *Le Triremi* (2nd ed Rome 1881), p19.

42. BNCF, col Mag, cl XIX, 7 'Fabrica di galere', f2v; OeN, Foscarini, Cod 6391, 'Arte de far vasselli', f5v.

43. ASV, Arsenale, busta 1, 'Visione'.

44. See BM, Add Mss 38655, Steffano de Zuanne, f10, 11, 27; BNM, Ms Ital, cl VII, cod 379, A Picheroni, f3r and f18.

45. Leo VI, *Peri Naumachias* 19, 9.

46. They are wearing helmet and chainmail in the galleys portrayed in mosaics in San Marco, Venice.

47. See Rawdon Brown (ed), *Calendar of State Papers and Manuscripts, relating to English affairs, existing in the Archives and Collections of Venice, and other Libraries of Northern Italy*, Vol I, 1202–1509 (London 1864), Nos 230, 264.

48. See Alberto Sacerdoti, 'Note sulle galere da mercato veneziane nel XV secolo', *Bollettino dell'Istituto di Storia della Societa e dello Stato Veneziano* IV, (1962), pp81–82 and F C Lane, *Venice and History*, pp189–192.

49. See Rawdon Brown (ed), *Calendar of State Papers and Manuscripts, relating to English affairs, existing in the Archives and Collections of Venice, and other Libraries of Northern Italy*, Vol I, 1202–1509, No 130; H G Rawlinson, 'The Flanders Galleys', *The Mariner's Mirror* 12 (1926), pp148–149 quotes the 1485 instructions of the Doges to Bartolomeo Minio, the Captain of the Flanders galleys, with detailed conditions regarding goods which could be handled by the captain and the *galeotti*, and where they could not be stowed. A Sacerdoti, 'Galere da mercato', p93, lists the weights of goods which individual crew members were allowed to have on board.

Diagrammatic functions of the simple 'palamento' ('a sensile'). (After BNM, Ms Ital, cl. VII, cod 379, A Picheroni, f3)

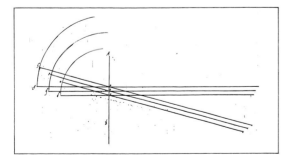

are handled leniently and receive the best treatment. The second species is that of the *sforzati*, or enforced sons of Christ, who for their sins are condemned to the galleys often for two, three, ten or as much as twenty years, and sometimes for life. The third group is the slaves: captured Turks, who are essentially slaves in perpetuity.[50]

The change from professional oarsmen to galley slaves occurred at a time when galley building – especially that of the *palamento* – was also entering a crisis. Classically trained laymen with technical shipbuilding knowledge produced new designs in an attempt to push the galleys to higher speeds and superior fighting power. Examples of highly imaginative ideas, inspired by ancient multi-oar vessels, have survived in the manuscript of Alessandro Picheroni.[51] At the time one vessel in particular caused great excitement: the 'quinquereme', or five-oared galley, which Vettor Fausto tried to introduce, based on the work of shipbuilders in the early fourth century before Christ.[52]

Vettor Fausto, who teaches Greek in this country, is returning from the Doges, to whom he has presented a wonderful model of a galley with five oars per thwart, compared with only three on our light galleys. His presentation was so successful that, before the assembly, he was instructed to carry out his plan.[53]

Fausto convinced the Doges and the Council, and was given leave to build his galley and compare its performance in a spectacular race.

. . . Now at the hour fixed, when the signal was given, the said galleys came rowing, racing one with the other, and in front rowed the [trireme] *Cornera*, but when they had almost arrived at the castles the quinquereme was on the outside, and the *Cornera* hugged the land so close that the quinquereme passed it in front of His Serenity [the Doge] and so came ahead rowing as far as San Marco, with so many boats in the canal, and sails of large barks and fishing boats that it seemed like an armada. It was most beautiful to see. This quinquereme has a very suitable oar system, which is [positioned] closer to the bow than on the other light galleys, so that Vettor Fausto the author who gave the design for it will be immortal.[54]

A light galley with five oarsmen per bench in-

stead of the usual three would not have aroused such attention if other innovations had not marked it out as different from the usual *galia sotil*. Details of these improvements are not mentioned in our sources. Around 160 years later Steffano de Zuanne referred to old-style stem, stern and oar shapes as *alla Faustina*.[55]

The five-oared galley '. . . is 28 paces long, and thus more than three paces longer than the light ones.'[56] The technical complexity and financial outlay for Fausto's design proved to be excessive, and the improvement too small.[57] That is the reason why a new type of galley was introduced which also used five or more oarsmen per bench, depending on size, but which only used a single oar for each thwart worked by all the *galeotti* on the one bench. This was a system which demanded no extra rowing skills, and was perfect for slave work.

The outrigger which supported the oars consisted of the *postiza* (gunwale) and the *lattoni*[58] or *baccalari*, whose number varied according to the number of *latte*, or deck beams, which on many galleys were nailed to every second frame,[59] on others to every frame.[60] The *baccalari*, in addition to bearing the gunwale, also supported the *banda* and in some cases one or two additional fore-and-aft stringers. On the *postiza* stood the *forcate*, the stanchions of the *pavesate* (rails). According to the illustrations[61] the outrigger was not planked on the underside, and its only stabilising buoyancy effect was due to the volume and upthrust of its timbers and its long moment arm, since it was a considerable distance from the midship plane.

The *voga*, the *banchi*, the oars and the outrigger took up almost the entire deck of the gal-

50. J Furttenbach, *Architectura Navalis*, pp16–17; see also: L Fincati, *Le Triremi*, pp34–41; F C Lane, *Seerepublik Venedig* [*Marine Republic of Venice*] (Munich 1980), pp556–563; G B Rubin de Cervin, *La Flotta di Venezia* (Milan 1985), pp31–32.

51. BNM, Ms Ital, cl VII, cod 379, A Picheroni, f8, 11–21.

52. See A Jal, *Archéologie Navale*, Vol I, pp377–384; F C Lane, *Navires et Constructeurs a Venise pendant la Renaissance* (Paris 1965), pp59–65; E Concino, *L'Arsenale della Repubblica di Venezia* (Milan 1988), pp108–134.

53. Marino Sanuto, *I diarii di Marino Sanuto 1496–1533*, Rinaldo Fulin, Federigo Stefani, Nicolo Barozzi, Guglielmo Berchet, and Marco Allegri (eds), 58 vols (Venice 1879–1903, Vol 39, p322; see also Fausto's letter to the Doges and his counsellors, Vol 42, pp766–768.

54. M Sanuto, *I diarii*, Vol 50, p363; F C Lane's translation.

55. See for example: BM, Add Mss 38655 Steffano de Zuanne, f27, 67v; see also the chapter on the rudder.

56. M Sanuto, *I diarii*, Vol 50, p364 (28 *passa* = 140 *pie* = 48.7m). Fausto's light galley therefore exceeded the length of Pre Theodoro's large galleys, built about twenty years later, by around 2 *pie* (0.7m).

57. E Concina, *L'Arsenale della Repubblica di Venezia*, pp108–134 discusses in detail Fausto's influence on the shipbuilding tradition of the Arsenal, but gives a much more positive assessment of its effect than F C Lane, *Navires et Constructeurs*, pp59–65.

58. J Furttenbach, *Architectura Navalis*, p54.

59. Deduced from BNCF, col Mag, cl XIX, 7, 'Fabrica di galere', f2r, OeN, Foscarini, Cod 6391, 'Arte de far vasselli', f5r (spacing of the *latte* 1¾ *pie*); see also E Paris, *Die grosse Zeit der Galeeren und Galeassen* [*The Great Period of the Galleys and Galeasses*] (Bielefeld and Berlin 1973), p33.

60. J Furttenbach, *Architectura Navalis*, p23, gives a contrasting view: '. . . that in the galley the same number of battens is used for the deck as there are *stamenali*, *marere* and *forchaze*.'

61. BNCF, col Mag, cl XIX, 7, 'Fabrica di galere', f3, 7, 11, 18, 24, 30; OeN, Foscarini, Cod 6391, 'Arte de far vasselli', f6, 10, 14, 21, 27, 33; J Furttenbach, *Architectura Navalis*, engraving Nos 4–6; B Crescentio, p38, 119; BM, Add Mss 38655, Steffano de Zuanne, f10, 27.

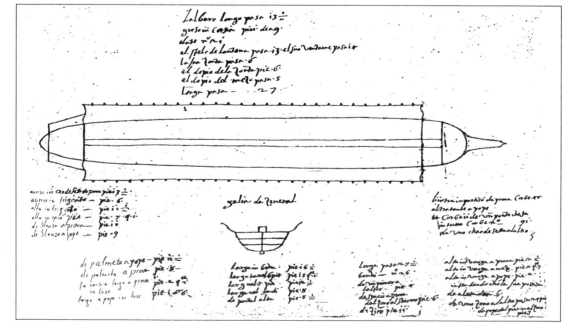

Deck plan and main frame cross-section of a 'galia da Zeneral'. (After BNM, Ms Ital, cl. VII, cod 379, A Picheroni, f6)

After section of a light galley from Vittore Carpaccio's painting The Lion of St Mark.

ley. The only vacant topside area comprised two short decks, fore and aft, known as the *palmete*. On merchant galleys up to the sixteenth century the open forward *palmeta* was surrounded by a bulwark. After the sixteenth century galeasses were fitted with an enclosed forward superstructure, the *castello da prova*, and this was also a feature of later merchant galleys. On merchant and war galleys the after *palmeta* bore a light open poop structure, while galeasses were fitted with a heavy *castello da pupa*. The forward and after sections of the ship were linked by the *corsia*, or gangway. On merchant galleys the *corsia* was narrow and low, just wide enough for two seamen to pass each other and at the height of the *banchi*. Presumably spare masts and yards were sometimes stored in the *corsia*. After the fifteenth century, war galleys carried a heavy gun on the gangway. The gun was mounted on a carriage, and recoiled as far back as the main mast. The gangway of the Lepanto galeasse was '. . . 8 *palmi* wide, and 8 *palmi* high, designed in such a way that above this wide and high *corsia* many warriors could stand, and use their hand guns to defend themselves stoutly against the enemy, without hindering the slaves . . .'[62]

The rudder

The side rudders (*timoni Latini*) of Mediterranean ships, a standard feature since Greek and Roman times, were gradually replaced in the thirteenth and fourteenth centuries by the stern rudder, following the pattern of the northern European cogs.[63] The Mediterranean shipbuilders developed a special form of stern rudder (*timon bavonescho*) to suit the curved sternpost of the galleys.[64] However, it seems likely that they did not entirely trust the new technology, and kept the two side rudders in reserve for safety's sake – as shown in the 'Fabrica'. The two side rudders can also be seen folded up in Erhard Reuwich's woodcuts of 1486, which also show the rudder mountings on both sides at the level of the *centa* (wale). This mounting possibly consisted of a beam (*timonera*?)[65] running through the after ship with two curved timbers which held the rudders. As late as 1571 the galeasses at Lepanto still carried the two antiquated side rudders in addition to the stern rudder. However, these slow, heavy ships did not keep the side rudders in reserve, but used them to support the effect of the stern rudder. Because of the low speed of the water flowing over the rudder, additional rudder area was needed to steer their excessive

mass. 'There are also two oars on either side of the rudder which help the vessel to turn more quickly, as shown in the illustration.'[66]

Judging from the drawings in the manuscripts, the stern rudders on Venetian galleys were not fitted with a tiller – in contrast to the Genoan '*Capitanea Galea*'. Pictures of completely fitted-out galleys show the rudder shaft ending simply in a circular or spherical knob. It is easy to imagine that the rounded form of the leading edge of the *timon alla Faustina*[67] would balance the rudder, making a tiller superfluous, provided that the pintle axes were fitted at a favourable angle. In his reconstruction of a tiller-less rudder, Alberto Sacerdoti suggests a block-and-tackle mechanism,[68] as indicated by Tintoretto (see the accompanying illustration). The straight stern and rudder form *alla ponentina*, introduced in the seventeenth century, with the rudder hinges on a single axis, ruled out such a lever effect. Nevertheless, Steffano de Zuanne also draws this type of rudder without a tiller.[69] If we assume that this is not an oversight, then it is possible that even the older Venetian galleys *alla Faustina* had rudder tillers which were removed when not needed.

The helmsmen of the merchant galleys and galeasses could have been protected below the poop house or on a small gallery above the rudder, where they would have been relatively safe. However, Andrea Vicentino's painting of the Battle of Lepanto (1571) shows the helmsmen on some Venetian and Turkish galleys balancing precariously on the *triganto* (stern beam), outside the *castello da pupa*. 'And indeed our helmsman, who sits outside the after house, is the target for every attack, in contrast

to the Western and Turkish helmsmen, who are safe under the after house.'[70] In the seventeenth century this design was corrected, and the helmsman was protected by an extended poop house projecting out over the stern. The new protective roof also gave the galley an even more elegant appearance.

62. J Furttenbach, *Architectura Navalis*, p79.

63. BNCF, col Mag, cl XIX, 7, 'Fabrica di galere', f12, 19, 31, OeN, Foscarini, Cod 6391, 'Arte de far vasselli', f16, 23, 33.

64. Termed *bavonescho* after the Bayonne ships which are said to have introduced the stern rudder into the Mediterranean (see August Jal, *Glossaire Nautique* (Paris 1848), p1500; and Christiane Villain-Gandossi, 'Navires du Moyen-Age', *Archeologia* 114 (1978), pp14–16).

65. See BNCF, col Mag, cl XIX, 7 'Fabrica di galere', f2; OeN, Foscarini, Cod 6391, 'Arte de far vasselli', f5; BM, Cott Mss, Titus, A26, G Trombetta, f42r; BNM, Ms Ital, cl IV, 26, Pre Theodoro, f1; ASV, Archivio Proprio Contarini, 19. Theodoro de Nicolo, f3. R C Anderson, 'Italian Naval Architecture', p140, believes that he can explain the term with '. . . the gallery overhanging the stern abaft the rudder'. However, *timonera* seems more likely to be a mounting for the *timon* than a gallery aft of the poop house, the more so since in Trombetta's view the galley did not have a gallery, just as in the drawings in the 'Fabrica', while Steffano de Zuanne draws a gallery, but does not use the term *timonera*. See also Christiane Villain-Gandossi, 'Terminologie de l'appareil de gouverne (IXe–XVIIIe siecles)', *Archaeonautica* 2 (1978), pp284, 294, 300 and figs 32, 33; A Jal, *Glossaire Nautique*, p1453, Jan Fennis, *La Stolonomie 1547–1550 et son vocabulaire maritime Marseillais* (Amsterdam 1978), pp514–516; Jan Ferris, *Un manuel de construction des galeres* (Amsterdam and Maarssen 1983), pp92–95, 126, 152, 286.

66. B Crescentio, p62.

67. So named by Steffano de Zuanne.

68. A Sacerdoti, 'Galere da mercato', Fig 3.

69. BM, Add Mss 38655, Steffano de Zuanne, f67v.

70. L Fincati, *Le Triremi*, p16.

Galleys lying off the Piazza San Marco, Venice, in the famous woodcut by E Reuwichs (1486) from von Breydenbach's Peregrinatio.

turies the galley's rig was very simple. With the exception of the number of masts, the galley's rig remained practically unchanged from the fourteenth century right into the nineteenth century. This in turn may have corresponded to the state of development at the time of the crusades.[73] One to three masts were fitted with long yards, often consisting of two overlapping spars lashed together, each of them carrying a triangular lateen sail. A square sail with the same effect as the spinnaker on a modern yacht served to improve thrust and directional stability with a following wind.

According to the Flanders dimensions the above-named galley has a mast length of 14 paces and a circumference of 7 spans, and a *cholzexe* 12 feet in length. The *cholzexe* is ⅕th as wide as it is long. The galley has a yard 19 paces long with a circumference of 4¾ spans, increasing to 3¾ feet at the 'rider' [probably in the centre of the two-part yard, where the timbers were lashed together]. And it has a medium-sized mast which is — feet long and — feet in circumference, and a *cholzexe* — paces and — feet in length, which is — feet wide. And the medium-sized mast has a yard of paces —; and a doubling of — feet. This galley also carries a yard of 14 paces, which has a

71. J Furttenbach, *Architectura Navalis*, p9.

72. ASV, Achivio Proprio Pinelli, 2, 'Misure di Vascelli', flv; see Ugo Tucci, 'Architettura navale Veneziana', *Bollettino dell'Atlante Linguistico Mediterraneo* 5/6 (1963/64), pp277–293, here p283.

73. See John H Pryor, 'The Naval Architecture of Crusader Transport Ships', *The Mariner's Mirror* 70 (1984), pp363–372, 378–486.

Old and new rudder forms. (After BM, Add Mss 38655, Steffano de Zuanne, f67v)

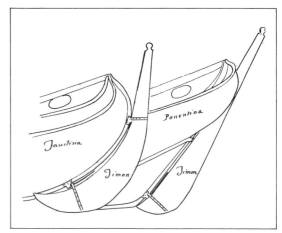

The rig

Mediterranean oared ships carried up to three masts, but only as a form of auxiliary propulsion '. . . for additional advantage and assistance . . . designed so that a good wind in a helpful direction might be enjoyed and captured, and the vessel driven forward thereby . . .'[71] – at least in theory. In practice, this was not what occurred: the light war galleys were usually under sail, the large galleys almost always *'a vela'*. 'The great galley has only twenty-five benches per side, because the oar arrangement is seldom used. The vessel is almost always under sail, and in any case it is impossible to row if the deck is under water.'[72]

Compared with the square rigged sailing ships of the sixteenth and seventeenth cen-

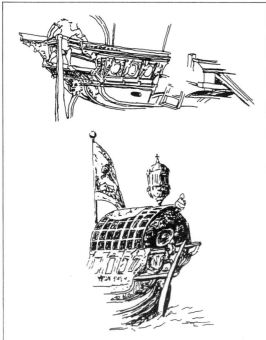

Helmsmen balancing on the 'triganto'. Based on paintings by Tintoretto (top) and Vicentino (bottom), Palazzo Ducale, Venice.

The 'Castello da pupa' of the 'Galia sottil'. The point at which the actual poop house meets the protective roof over the helmsman can be seen at the separation line on the roof. (After BM, Add Mss 38655, Steffano de Zuanne, f10)

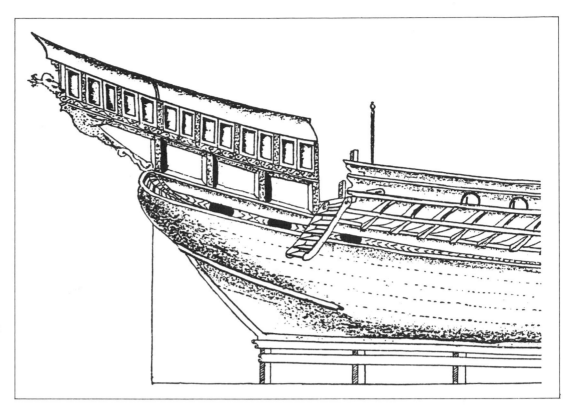

[circumference?] of 3½ paces, as can be seen in the drawing below.[74]

The *galea de Fiandra* of 1410 carried two masts, three yards and four sails: '*artimon, terzaruolo, papafico et cochina*'.[75] However, the drawings in the 'Fabrica' show only a single mast and a single yard. The text also mentions only a single mast step, a *schaza a late 18*'.[76] The *galea de Fiandra* usually had only one mast, one yard and one sail set at any one time. The sail could not be reefed, and the main sail and yard had to be replaced by a smaller set if the wind freshened; in some cases even the mast had to be changed. As described by more recent sources, development led towards the two-master and finally the three-master. We cannot exclude the possibility that the great galleys around 1400 already carried their *arboro de mezo* – the half or small mast – forward or aft, and occasionally set it in addition to the *arboro*, the main mast. Trombetta's unique method of calculating also gives an indication of this.

In 1546, around the time of Pre Theodoro, an anonymous *proto* (senior master shipwright) at the Arsenal wrote '*La galia grosse ha tre alberi: mezana, artimon e trinchetto da prova*'.[77] In the late fifteenth century, reports of the pilgrims' voyages mention two sails, which were set on two small masts fore and aft in addition to the main sail: '. . . the Captain ordered that the

rear and front sails, which were both set, should be furled.'[78] Erhard Reuwich's woodcuts also show one medium-sized mast bearing sail abaft the main mast, and a remarkably small mast without sail – perhaps a flagstaff – forward, in front of the gangway. A large galley behind St George's lance in a Carpaccio painting[79] carries a *mezana* aft. The larger galleys must have been fitted with at least two masts from the late fifteenth century, and often three masts, which presumably were erected simultaneously.

Around twenty years after Pre Theodoro the

Lepanto galeasses carried three masts and, in so far as the paintings of the battle allow us to see, had no means of changing or shortening the masts during a voyage. 'The rig of the galeass is the same as that of the galley, except that it has two small masts, both lateen rigged. However, the Spanish vessels have square sails and a rudder like a sailing ship, because this provides better control in those seas.'[80] '. . . 8 feet forward of the after transverse beam stands the medium-sized mast. The fore mast is located as far forward as possible so that the mast step can be fixed on the deck. Between the two

74. BNCF, col Mag, cl XIX, 7, 'Fabrica di galere', f8v (see OeN, Foscarini, Cod 6391, 'Arte de far vasselli', f11). Both versions of the 'Fabrica' occasionally lack dimensional information. For the meaning of *cholzexe* see the reconstructions and J H Pryor, 'Naval Architecture of Crusader Transport Ships', pp286–287.

75. Assumed from the chapter on the similar *Galea de Romania* (BNCF, col Mag, cl XIX, 7, 'Fabrica di galere', f20, 23; OeN, Foscarini, Cod 6391, 'Arte de far vasselli', f23, 26); with the exception of the *cochina*, a square sail after the pattern of the *cocha* (or 'cog') these are all lateen sails of different sizes.

76. BNCF, col Mag, cl XIX, 7, 'Fabrica di galere', f2r; OeN, Foscarini, Cod 6391, 'Arte de far vasselli', f5r.

77. ASV, Achivio Privato Pinelli, 2flr.

78. Based on M Newett, *Casola's Pilgrimage*, p183.

79. See Vittore Carpaccio, *Saint George and the Dragon*, Scuola dei SS Giorgio e Trifone, Venice.

80. B Crescentio, p62.

Large galley in the background of a painting by Vittore Carpaccio in the Scuola dei SS Giorgi e Trifone, Venice.

The rig of the 'Capitanea Galea'. (From J Furttenbach, Architectura navalis, engraving No 1)

to the wind (lee side). If the galley wanted to go about or tack (turn through the wind) the yard had to be reversed. Bartolomeo Crescentio describes how the yard and sail were hauled upright, then both were swung forward past the mast and on to the new lee side.

Every time the wind is unfavourable relative to the direction of sailing, the sail has to be reversed. It must always be set on the side opposed to the wind, so that it can drive the vessel forward. To this end, every time the wind shifts, it is necessary to set the yard carrying the sail, first on the righthand side, then on the lefthand side, in such a way that the *carro* – that is the large end of the yard – comes forward, and the *penna* – that is the small part – to the rear.[84]

The *spiron* or prow, a component which must be considered as an integral part of the hull, was actually part of the rigging as far as its function was concerned, since it served as a belaying point for the tack of the fore lateen. The long beak projecting forward was not intended just to make the galley look elegant. Equally it is hardly likely to have developed from the ancient *rostrum*, the bow ram,[85] but more from the need to gain favourable leverage for the braces of the long lateen yard of the fore mast,[86] projecting beyond the stem.[87]

Reconstructing typical galleys

To a Venetian master shipwright it cannot have been difficult to design a hull according to the building rules of a shipbuilding manuscript; a hull which fulfilled the requirements of the

stands the main mast.'[81] Joseph Furttenbach provides accurate dimensions of the masts and yards of a Genoan light galley. An impression of the types of mast, how the masts were rigged, how they were fixed to each other and to the hull, can be gained from another Car-

paccio painting,[82] although the overall views of the galleys in the 'Fabrica' and *Architectura Navalis* are also helpful. The 'Fabrica' also lists the ropes required for rigging the *galea de Fiandra*, their lengths and their weights.[83]

The lateen sail was set on the side opposed

81. BM, Add Mss 38655, Steffano de Zuanne, f22r.

82. For example, *Arrival of the Ambassadors*, St Ursula Cycle, Gallerie dell' Accademia, Venice.

83. BNCF, col Mag, cl XIX, 7, Fabrica di galere, f9, 10; OeN, Foscarini, Cod 6391, 'Arte de far vasselli', f11–13.

84. B Crescentio, p122.

85. See Arvid Goettlicher, *Die Schiffe der Antike* [*Ships of Ancient Times*] (Berlin 1985), p41, fig 21, pp95–100. The 'main weapon' of the galleys, located 'curiously high above the waterline' (E Heyck, *Genua und Seine Marine*, p67), could not possibly have served as a ram.

86. See BNCF, col Mag, cl XIX, 7, 'Fabrica di galere', f9v; OeN, Foscarini, Cod 6391, 'Arte de far vasselli', f12v

87. Clearly visible on Furttenbach's engravings, Nos 1, 4.

Going about with a lateen yard. (Based on a watercolour by Raphael)

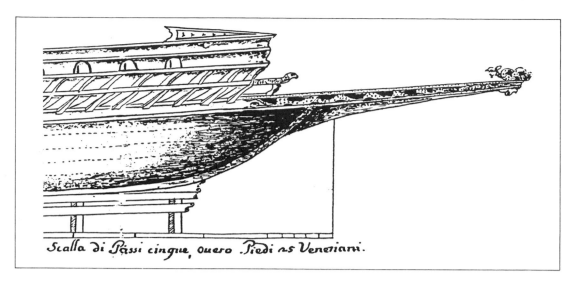

Scalla di Passi cinque, ouero Piedi 25 Venetiani.

The 'spiron' (prow) of the 'Galia sottil'. (After BM, Add Mss 38655, Steffano de Zuanne, f10)

commissioning agent. The main dimensions of length, beam, height and the connecting points for the *triganto* (stern beam) and *spiron* (beak) were laid down. Stem, stern and main frame were clearly defined in shape and size by offsets and drawings, as were the position of one aligning frame forward and one aft. The frames' shape could be found using calipers or using the input values of the *partison* procedure, which were also pre-defined.[88] The shipbuilder drew the standard *partison* diagrams and then derived the caliper dimensions of all the remaining frames between main frame and aligning frames using compasses. Only the shape of the frames at the hull ends, *ie* between stem, stern and aligning frames, had to be determined individually.

Even though our knowledge of the galley builders' manual tasks and technology has come down to us incompletely, the descriptions included in the surviving shipbuilding manuscripts are adequate to allow all the essential parts to be reconstructed reliably. Galleys and galeasses were more complex and technically more demanding than sailing ships, and they represented the peak of technology within the Italian art of shipbuilding. As a result they are often given first place in the shipbuilding manuscripts, and are described in considerable detail. The following text presents reconstructions of a Venetian 'Flanders galley' (*galea de Fiandra*) of 1410,[89] a great galley (*galea grossa*) of 1550 and a Lepanto galeasse, as these vessels are also representative of other ship types from the epoch when building rules applied. In contrast, the line drawing of the dromon from the time of Leo VI is unfortunately based on very incomplete information, and therefore represents no more than a suggestion for a possible reconstruction of this ship type, which remains very mysterious to this day.

The line drawings are drawn at the outside edge of the frames (*ie* moulded – they do not include the thickness of the planking). Technical expressions in the manuscripts which could be assigned to the components shown, are – as far as possible – included on the drawings. The dimensional unit of the galleys is the *piede*, which is made up of 16 *dedi*; 5 *piedi* = 1 *passo*. According to Giorgio Trombetta[90] 5 *pie* was the same length as 7 *palmi*. This is the overall relationship:

1 *passo* = 5 *piedi* = 7 *palmi* = 80 *dedi*
(1 pace = 5 feet = 7 spans = 80 inches)

In his *Architectura Navalis* Joseph Furttenbach defines the length of a *palmo* by a line 0.244m long or 9.6 imperial inches (in today's units), and offers this statement: 'one palmo is a measurement/or a small Werckschuch [?= working shoe]/whose length amounts to 10 inches of a Nuremberg Werckschuch.'[91] I have worked on the following assumption for converting values into SI (and imperial) units:

1 *piede* = 0.348m (13.70in)
1 *palmo* = 0.248m (9.76in)

We are hardly in a position to assess the accuracy of measurements now several hundreds of years old. In comparison with modern-day practice we can presume that planning and construction were carried out to extremely coarse tolerances. The Venetian shipbuilding manuscripts use 1 *dedo* as the smallest unit, *ie* around 0.02m. Neither is it possible to know whether the *piede* of 1400 was exactly the same length as the *piede* of 1700. As a result the metric dimensions should only be considered as an approximate guide. It is impossible to define accurately the relationship of the size of the plan to the size of the ship.

The dromon of 890

Reconstructing a dromon is bound to be very difficult, if not impossible, with the present state of knowledge. Some authors seem to have

found the missing link in the direct line of development from the trireme of the Peloponnesian War to the armoured cruiser of the First World War, but they are unable to provide a credible representation of the predecessor of the Mediterranean galley.[92] No single illustration exists of which we could say today that it definitely represents a Byzantine dromon. Leo VI only provides very general recommendations: that the dromon should neither be built too wide nor too narrow, and offer space for at least 25 thwarts below and 25 above. Accurate dimensions and plans were not possible because the vessels were built using the shell method. Dromons were – like the contemporary ships of the Vikings – all built in the same way to the same overall design, but differed considerably in size, especially in beam and height. Leo writes that all dromons carried their main weapon, a large bow-mounted 'siphon' to project Greek Fire, and a wooden platform above.

The illustration shown here of a dromon with siphon[93] and a platform above agrees amazingly well with Leo's description. The

88. See Ulrich Alertz, *Vom Schiffbauhandwerk zur Schiffbautechnik* [*From shipwrighting to Shipbuilding Technology*], pp110–129.

89. This ship may have been very similar to the great galleys of the period around 1310, according to the main dimensions which have survived – see F C Lane, *Ships and Shipbuilders of the Renaissance* (Baltimore 1934, p236).

90. British Library, Cott Mss, Titus, A26, G Trombetta, f16r.

91. J Furttenbach, *Architectura Navalis*, p19 and engraving No 2, Joseph Schmitz, *Vollstaendiges nach einer ganz neuen Lehrart bearbeitetes Rechenbuch* [*Complete Reckoner based on an Entirely New Method*], second part (Aachen 1821), pp205, 314, measures: 1 Genoan *Palmo* = 0.249830m, 1 Venetian *pie* = 0.347397m.

92. Numerous treatises have been based on the highly detailed perspective reconstruction (suspiciously reminiscent of an auxiliary cruiser) by Rudolf Eickhoff in Ekkehard Eickhoff, *Seekrieg und Seepolitik zwischen Islam und Abendland bis zum Aufstiege Pisas und Genuas 650–1040*, [*Naval War and Marine Politics between Islam and the West until the rise of Pisa and Genoa, 650–1040*] (Saarbrücken 1955). His illustration then became promoted to a 'Zeichnung aus einem byzantinischen Kodex' [drawing from a Byzantine codex] in Paul Laechler and Hans Wirz, *die Schiffe der Völker*, [*Ships of the Nations*] (Olten, Freiburg 1962), p311; Alfred Dudszus, Ernest Henriot and Friedrich Krumrey, *Das grosse Buch der Schiffstypen – Berühmte Segelschiffe* [*The Great Book of Ship Types – Famous Sailing Ships*] (Stuttgart 1990, p91).

93. A 'pole-like ram prow' as H D L Viereck writes in *Die römische Flotte* [*The Roman Fleet*] (Herford 1975), p287, would be a functionally absurd solution, and can hardly have been intended here.

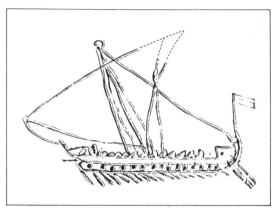

Byzantine warship; a graffito from Malaga, now in the Museo Naval, Madrid. (Drawing from Olaf Höckmann, Antike Seefahrt [Ancient Seafaring], fig 109)

lively but somewhat crude graffito from Malaga shows the shape of an oared warship of the type which Leo describes, but lacks any artistic ambition. The sketch shows no detail at all. It does not appear to be based on a picture by a third party, and it is assumed that it was drawn by an eye-witness.

The dark circles in the lower half of the hull seem to indicate the ports for the lower row of oars. The lower edge of the upper half of the hull overlaps the ports below, and may represent a projecting outrigger for an upper row of oars, although a second row is not shown. This could be a small dromon, *monērēs* or *galaia*, or alternatively perhaps a particularly large dromon. The bulwark projecting over the lower hull side could then represent the wooden castle mentioned above, the *xylokastron*, which was located in the centre (between forward and after superstructure) on the largest dromons. The *xylokastron* would then correspond to the *kastelloma*, as mentioned by Leo, which was used by the 150 armed men standing above to fix their shields.[94] The mast is raked strongly forward and is supported by shrouds, in contrast to its classical Greek predecessors, and carries a triangular lateen sail. The rig is similar to that of the later Italian galleys, right up to the archaic ring at the masthead.[95] The curved stern and the two side rudders could even date from Roman predecessors. The ship has neither a waterline ram like ancient warships nor a projecting prow in the manner of later galleys.

For good reasons H D L Viereck and Olaf Höckmann judge the sketch cautiously as dat-

ing from the sixth century,[96] when for several decades the area around Malaga belonged to the Byzantine Empire. According to the above considerations, however, the graffito could not pre-date the time of the Greek Fire, which according to tradition, had been introduced as principal weapon on the dromons by the Syrian Callinicus around AD 672.

The reconstructed line drawing of the dromon from the time of Leo VI is thus based on two very paltry sources, each completely independent of the other, but agreeing in certain characteristic areas. Moreover, the line and curvature of the sheer timbers and the form of the stern are not dissimilar to an illustration of a twelfth-century Byzantine warship. The frames are likely to have had a pronounced U-shape – as on the Byzantine Yassi Ada ship dating from the seventh century[97] – which may have continued from the main frame to the hull ends. In this respect the dromon was similar to the *Galea de Fiandra* of 1410, the oldest galley which can be recon-

structed reliably. Details such as the curvature of the keel, of the deck edge and of the outrigger, and also the shape and proportion of the underwater hull, have therefore been drawn in the style of this ship.

94. Basileios Patrikios Parakoimomenos, 5, 2, 13, in A Dain, *Naumachica*, p65; Lionel Casson, *Ships and Seamanship in the Ancient World* (Princeton 1971), p152, makes the very original claim that Leo's wooden castle was a platform erected around the mast (at half mast height?).

95. A sleeve, probably made of metal, with two annular pendants for the square yards is shown on Odysseus' ship in its encounter with the Sirens (around 500 BC), J S Morrison and R T Williams, *Greek Oared Ships 900–322 BC* (Cambridge 1968), Plate 21.

96. H D L Viereck, *Die römische Flotte* [*The Roman Fleet*], p287; Olaf Höckmann, *Antike Seefahrt* [*Ancient Seafaring*] (Munich 1985, p120, fig 109).

97. See G F Bass and F H van Doorninck (eds), *Yassi Ada, Volume I: A seventh century Byzantine shipwreck* (College Station 1982); Frederick van Doorninck, 'Byzanz, Herrin der Meere', [Byzantium, Mistress of the Seas], in George F Bass (ed), *Taucher in die Vergangenheit* [*A History of Seafaring*], pp133–158.

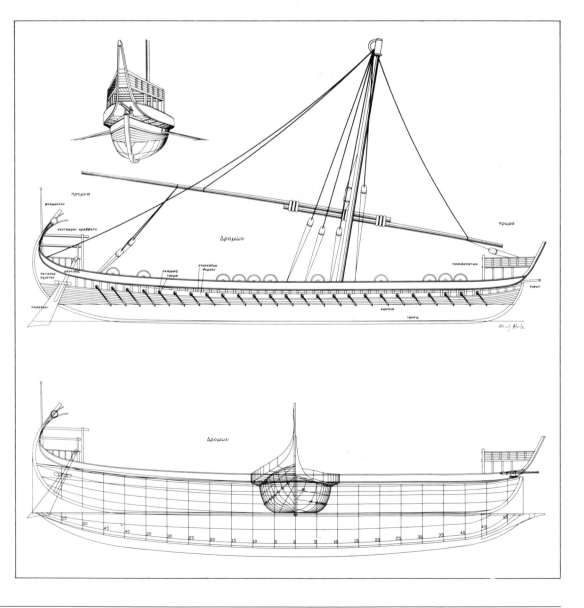

Top: Sheer elevation of the dromon and perspective views of the foreship with the siphon and above it the platform. Bottom: Hypothetical lines and body plan, reconstructed by the author.

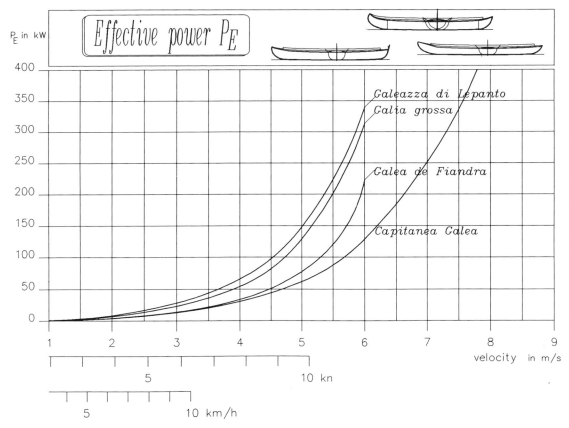

Rowing performance and speed diagram. The left-hand scale shows the power in kW, the scale at bottom the speed.

Presumably the measurement was made amidships from the water's surface to the top edge of the *catena*.[101] If the galley was to sail 'armed' – with a strong crew – it was permissible to reduce the minimum freeboard. At the same time the centre of gravity would have shifted higher. A high level of security against pirates had to be bought at the price of reduced seaworthiness.

Under such circumstances it was not possible to preclude a dangerously low range of stability. For example, if the centre of gravity of the loaded ship was 7 *pie* (2.43m) above the top edge of the keel at the waterline,[102] then 12 degrees of heel were sufficient to capsize the ship. An extremely dangerous aspect of the vessels was that the short righting arm might well have been very difficult to deduce at first, since the vessel's initial stability would have felt adequate. If the centre of gravity was just 1 *pie* (0.3477m) lower – keeping the draught the same – then the vessel's stability would be several times better. If the draught is reduced also by 1 *pie* to 6 *pie* (2.09m) – corresponding to a freeboard of slightly more than 2 *pie*, according to the definition above – *ie* if 63 tons of loading is removed – the length of the righting arm increases to 13cm and the zero point of the graph shifts to 55 degrees. The stability envelope – the area below the righting arm curve – then reaches values which correspond approximately to today's requirements for dry

The 'Galea de Fiandra' of 1410

The dimensions of the *galea de Fiandra* in the 'Fabrica di galere' and of the *galia grosa* as described in Trombetta's records agree almost exactly, with one exception[98] – evidently a writing or copying mistake. The caliper dimensions of the 'Fabrica' main frame coincide with the outer frame line drawn by Trombetta, within the tolerances dictated by the thickness of the pen nib. A single plan was therefore drawn up, based on both manuscripts.[99]

The *chorbe* (frames) are spaced very close together, with a spacing of only about 1 *pie*. Every second *chorba* lacks a *lata* (deck beam). The fore-and-aft timbers, especially the *columba* (keel) and the *paramezal* (kelson), look rather weak. The midship section is tall and full for a galley, and its pronounced U-shape indicates a strong hull without excessive structural problems as a result of bending tension. The extended waterlines with their pointed entry and exit angles leave an impression of elegance. This shape results in high frictional resistance, but keeps wavemaking resistance low. The outcome was a ship which, in favourable weather and moderate winds, offered a clear advantage in speed compared with contemporary and also more recent sailing ships.

However, U-shaped frames have a powerful influence on the hydrodynamic efficiency of the underwater hull if the ship heels (inclines

to one side), and therefore the shape has a negative influence on the vessel's handling characteristics under sail. The sharp, low foreship of the Flanders galley dipped low in heavy weather and high seas, and was easily awash. Reserve buoyancy was slight, and even at normal draught the foreship displaced too little water. The *galea* could therefore not carry a heavy *canone di corsia* (gangway gun) forward on the *zovo de prova* (forward outrigger transverse beam).

The manuscript authors give no information on the ship's design waterline. Presumably the shipbuilder of the time also knew of no such line, by which he might have predicted, right at the design stage, how low the ship was to float in the water. The ship was probably loaded gradually, with careful eyes checking that it floated upright, perhaps that it trimmed lower aft for better rudder response, and that the freeboard was not less than prescribed. Laws laid down by the Serenissima, the Venetian Republic, dictated that a freeboard of 2 *pie* (0.7m) was required for galleys fitted out by the State. Privately equipped galleys had to keep to 2½ *pie* (0.87m): 'similarly every galley must measure two feet and a half from the underwater part of the hull as far as the *Catena*, or *Lata* . . . measured from the top edge of the *Catena*, or *Lata*, to the water . . .'.[100]

The freeboard must have been measured from the outer *catena*, or the edge of the deck.

98. Trombetta's dimension for the keel length '*loga i choloba pasa 23 pie 3*' requires an overall length of almost 140 *pie*. The resultant aspect ratio of the hull of more than 8:1 would exceed even the 7.5:1 length:beam ratio of a seventeenth-century light galley, and would result in a hull which was far too narrow for a merchant galley. However, Trombetta's dimension agrees remarkably well with the '*longa da alto passa 23 et piedi 3*' of the 'Fabrica' for the *galea de Romania*. Instead of '*i choloba*' it should be probably read '*i choverta*'.

99. See also Ulrich Alertz, 'Venezianischer Schiffbau – die Flandern-Galeere von 1410' ['Venetian shipbuilding – the Flanders galley of 1410'], *Das Logbuch* 27 4 (1991), pp140–147.

100. Archivio di Stato di Venezia, Capitolare Ufficiali del Levante, Secreta Capitolari, f56v.

101. Genoan merchant galleys had three 'irons' which served as freeboard markers.

102. This very unfavourable assumption rests on Chapman's recommendation for the position of the centre of gravity on privateers – see Fredrik Henrik af Chapman, *Tractat om Skepps-Byggeriet* (Stockholm 1775). It might have been somewhat lower with the shallower galleys, in which case this critical value can be considered as an extreme case which, in practice, probably did not occur.

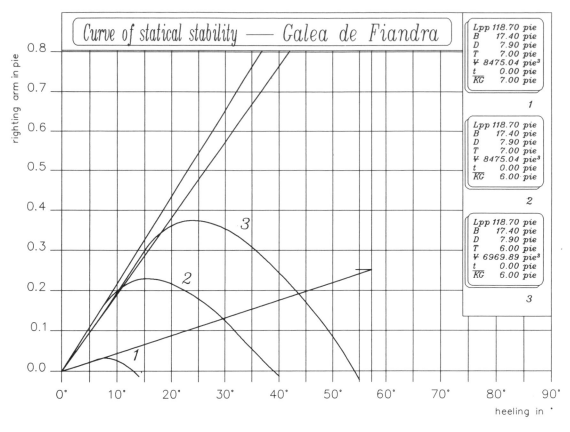

Lpp	118.70 pie
B	17.40 pie
D	7.90 pie
T	7.00 pie
∀	8475.04 pie³
t	0.00 pie
K̄C̄	7.00 pie

1

Lpp	118.70 pie
B	17.40 pie
D	7.90 pie
T	7.00 pie
∀	8475.04 pie³
t	0.00 pie
K̄C̄	6.00 pie

2

Lpp	118.70 pie
B	17.40 pie
D	7.90 pie
T	6.00 pie
∀	6969.89 pie³
t	0.00 pie
K̄C̄	6.00 pie

3

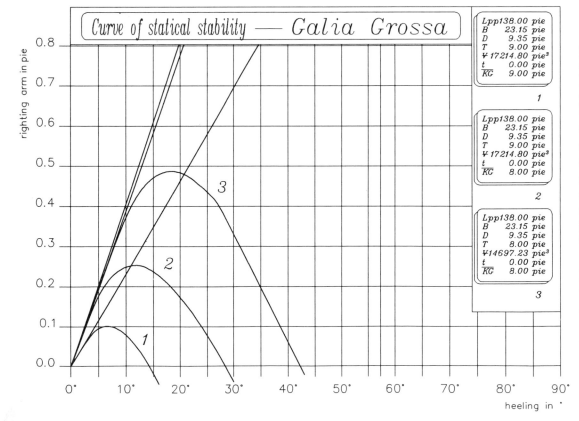

Lpp	138.00 pie
B	23.15 pie
D	9.35 pie
T	9.00 pie
∀	17214.80 pie³
t	0.00 pie
K̄C̄	9.00 pie

1

Lpp	138.00 pie
B	23.15 pie
D	9.35 pie
T	9.00 pie
∀	17214.80 pie³
t	0.00 pie
K̄C̄	8.00 pie

2

Lpp	138.00 pie
B	23.15 pie
D	9.35 pie
T	8.00 pie
∀	14697.23 pie³
t	0.00 pie
K̄C̄	8.00 pie

3

Stability of the 'galea de Fiandra' and of the 'galia grossa'. The moment arm curves show the horizontal interval between weight and displacement centres of gravity with increasing angles of heel. The product of the moment arm and the ship's weight gives the righting moment. When divided by the ship's weight to form a standardised stability moment curve, the moment arm curve provides an idea of the magnitude of the righting moment. The graph shows the calculated values for three hypothetical loads.

and 356 cubic metres, depending on draught. Unfortunately the shipbuilding manuscripts lack any information on the weight of the hull, so that the load-bearing capability of the ship, which is important for economic purposes, can only be calculated approximately. A Senate's decree of 1440[105] complains of the excessive size of the merchant galleys of 500 to 600 *milliaria* and limits the additional loading of future vessels to 400 to 440 *milliaria*. The *milliarium* was a unit of mass and weight. It is likely that it is the same as the *milliarium ad pondus subtile* which equates to about 301kg. This means that the galleys before 1440 would have been able to carry a load of around 170 tons, and those after 1440 only about 130 tons. With an average load capability of 150 tons the merchant galleys of the time certainly did not count as particularly large ships for Mediterranean conditions. In the Hanseatic region of northern Europe, however, they would have cut an impressive figure in the ports of Bruges or Antwerp, for example. The *galea de Fiandra* was twice the size of the Bremen Hanseatic cog in terms of displacement, carrying capacity and also length. The cog weighed around 60 tons and could carry a load of 40 'Last', that is around 80 tons.[106] It should be mentioned that the cog achieved a much better, more economical ratio of load to ship's weight, thanks to its broad, tall hull.

The author of the 'Fabrica' calculates the labour required to build a *galea de Fiandra* as follows: '... in mathematical terms 500 sawyers are required to work to produce such a galley, plus 1000 ships' carpenters and 1300 caulkers, to caulk, seal and paint the galley

---

103. 0.20m righting moment arm, zero point of curve 60 degrees, angle of maximum moment arm 30 degrees – see Herbert Schneekluth, *Entwerfen von Schiffen* [*Ship Design*] (Herford 1980), p60.

104. See Archivio di Stato di Venezia, Senato Mar, reg 3, f112 (decree dated 28 April 1449).

105. Archivio di Stato di Venezia, Senato Misti, reg 60, f249.

106. See Paul Heinsius, *Das Schiff der hansischen Fruehzeit* [*Ships of the early Hanseatic period*] (second ed, Cologne and Vienna 1986), pp256–257.

freighters laid down by modern shipping agencies.[103] At this point the ships can be considered to be more or less safe. As can be expected then, the *galea de Fiandra* was sensitive to overloading (excessive draught, too little freeboard) and to deck loading (centre of gravity too high). For this reason the Senate expressly forbade stowing cargo and the crew's effects on deck,[104] but the rules were not always followed, as Erhard Reuwich's woodcuts show.

The moulded displacement is between 292

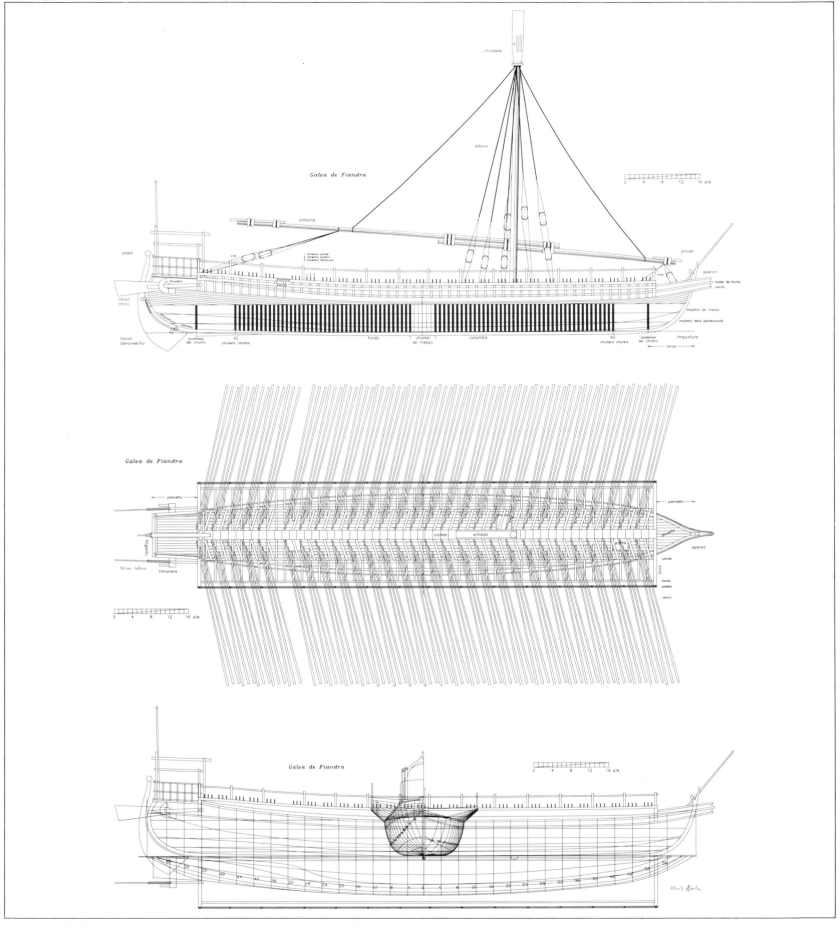

Lines and body plan, sheer elevation and deck view of the 'galea de Fiandra' as reconstructed by the author.

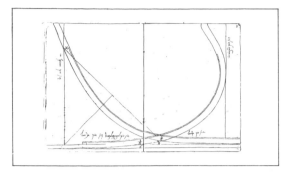

Above: Stem and stern of the 'galia grossa'. (After BNM, Ms Ital, cl. IV, 26, Pre Theodoro, f3)

Below: Comparison of main frame areas of a 'galia grossa' and a 'galia sotil'. (after BNM, Ms Ital, cl. VII, cod 379, A Picheroni, f9)

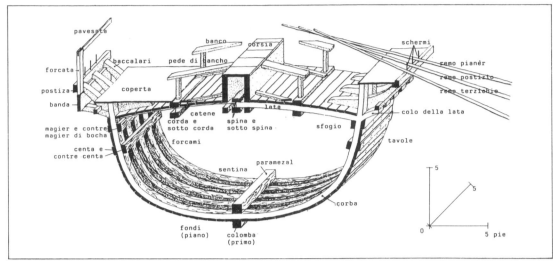

Isometric reconstruction of the midship section of a large galley with variants in the design layout. (Drawn from BNM, Ms Ital, cl. IV, 26, Pre Theodoro, ff1-3, 5, 9, 36 and ASV, Archivio Proprio Contarini, 19. Theodoro de Nicolo, ff 3-5, 7, 11, 38)

. . .'.[107] These figures are difficult to interpret, and are presumably statistical values which the Arsenal used to calculate labour requirements and costs. Based on 250 working days per year, the figures mean that the Arsenal had to employ 10 *segadori*, 20 *marangoni* and 26 *chalafadi* to complete every *galea de Fiandra* ready to sail.

The 'Galia Grossa' of 1550

Pre Theodoro describes three types of great galley, differing only slightly from each other. With one exception – the distance between the forward aligning frame and the forward perpendicular[108] – the following reconstruction is based on the second model. In many respects the constructional information is difficult to understand from today's viewpoint, and as a result it proved to be difficult to obtain a clear image of this galley. No overall views are provided. A *chastello*, evidently the after superstructure, is mentioned, but not described. The *chastello* and the *speron* (beak) as drawn here are based on the paintings of Carpaccio.[109]

With an assumed draught of around 10 *pie*[110] the ship displaced more than 720 cubic metres moulded, and as such was not only twice the size of the *galea de Fiandra*, it was even larger than the average English sailing West Indiaman of the eighteenth century.[111] The waterlines are fuller than those of the *galea* de Fiandra and run into stem and stern at a rather blunt angle, particularly at the bow. Rounded frames in midships – offering favourable resistance values – blend into a V-shape forward and aft. The bluff foreship forces the current flow down under the hull in an inefficient, energy-sapping way. As indicated by the hull form, the ship was probably run under sail almost exclusively, and perhaps only propelled by oars inside harbour.

The lines of this ship make it clear that the vessel's primary purpose was no longer peaceful, *ie* merchant and pilgrim voyages. The demand for such journeys had fallen off greatly in the first half of the sixteenth century. At the same time the number of large galleys in the Arsenal had dropped from thirty-two in the year 1504 to six in the year 1560.[112] The majority of the merchant galleys had presumably been laid up or scrapped during this crisis.[113] New potential applications arose for the remaining ships.[114] In fact the *galia grossa* could also be designed as, or converted into, a warship, in which guise it was termed a *galeazza*. The extra upthrust below the *proda* made it

107. Biblioteca Nazionale Centrale di Firenze, col Mag, cl XIX, 7, 'Fabrica di galere,' f73v.

108. '. . . *ano deferir aprova pie* 12½ . . .' (BNM, Mx Ital, cl IV, 26, Pre Theodoro, f1; in the National Library version the ½ is written between the lines and was evidently added later); see ASV, Archivio Proprio Contarini, 19, Theodoro de Nicolo, f3. Pre Theodoro might have allowed a writing error to slip in here, for the corresponding dimensions of the two other – otherwise very similar – *galie grosse* are 20 *pie* and 20½ *pie*. Otherwise the aligning frame would be located close to the rounded stem.

109. See Vittore Carpaccio's painting *Saint George and the Dragon*, Scuola dei SS Giorgio e Trifone and *The Lion of Saint Mark*, Palazzo Ducale, Venice.

110. '*Una Galia grossa over Galiaza, armada, pesca pie 10*', ASV, Archivio Proprio Pinelli, 2, (earlier: Miscellanea codici, no 125), f 1r, *cf* U Tucci, *Architettura navale veneziana*, p282.

111. See F H af Chapman, *Architectura Navalis Mercatoria*, Plate LII.

112. See F C Lane, *Navires et Constructeurs*, pp25–26, 230; by 1581 their number had risen again to 18.

113. Economic and political difficulties were followed by technical problems: '*Le developement du "trois mats carré" et de l'artillerie navale avaient ôté à la galère la plupart de ses avantages . . .*' (F C Lane, *Navires et Constructeurs*, pp25–26); see also F C Lane, *Seerepublik*, pp456–459, 531–539, 542–550; L Fincati, *Le Triremi*, pp18–20; G B Rubin de Cervin, *Flotta di Venezia*, pp30–39; F C Lane, *Ships and Shipbuilders*, pp26–34; F C Lane, *Venice and History*, pp12–16.

114. Pre Theodoro's type designation, *galia grossa* ['great galley'], instead of 'Flanders galley' or 'Merchant galley' already indicates a multi-purpose ship.

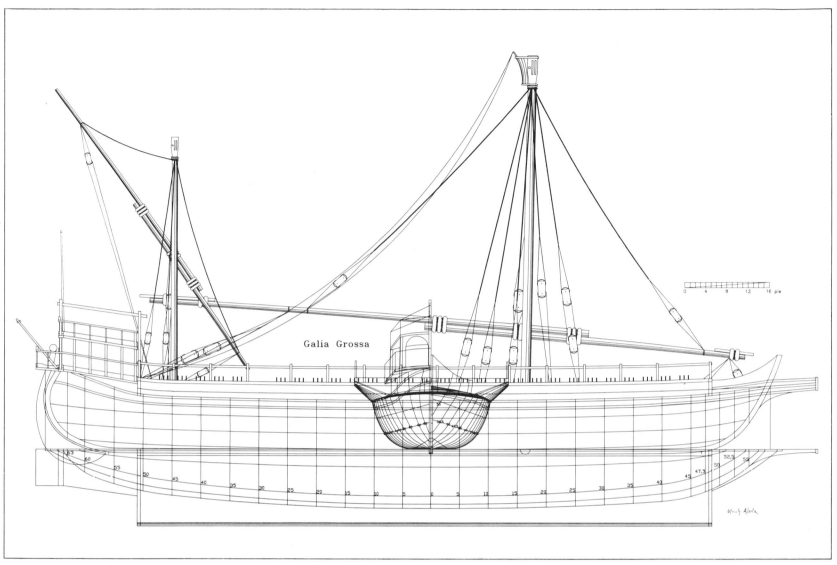

Galia Grossa

Lines plan of the 'galia grossa' as reconstructed by the author.

Right: Lepanto galeasse based on an engraving by Fernado Bertelli (1573).

Below: Galeasse at the battle of Lepanto, 1571. (Based on Andrea Vicentino's painting in the Palazzo Ducale in Venice)

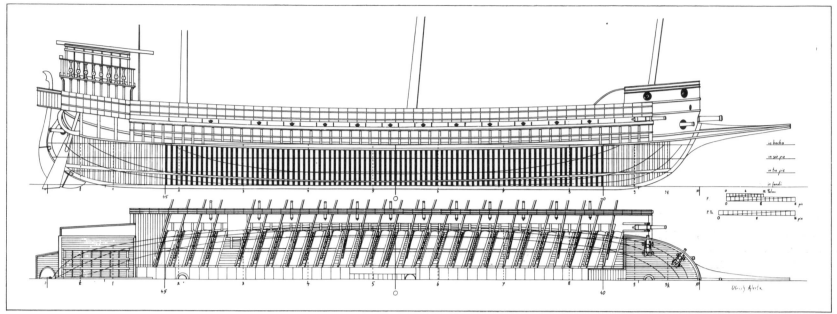

Sheer and plan elevations of the Lepanto galeasse as reconstructed by the author.

possible to accommodate numerous heavy guns forward in a turret-shaped superstructure.

The *galeazza* is no more and no less than a very large *galea*, designed not for general use but exclusively for sea battles. Five large and five small guns are set up at the *proda* and the *giogo di proda*. On each side between the oars 12 small guns are mounted on strong iron yokes, fixed on the other topmost *drapera* in such a way that they cannot recoil.[115]

Two further heavy cannon were located aft, below the *dragante* (stern beam). 'In all, this *galeazza* can carry up to 35 guns.'[116]

Hydrostatic curves of the 'galea de Fiandra' of 1410 and the 'galia grossa' of 1550.

During his sojourn in Venice Furttenbach had seen two galeasses set up as a memorial to their victory at Lepanto (1571), and he took the opportunity to take approximate measurements of them. Since the Lepanto galeasses had been converted from *sei vecchie galeazze di mercanzia che da anni giacevano inoperosa sui loro scali di alaggio*,[117] and since Furttenbach's dimensions produce a ship of identical proportions to the *galia grossa*, side and deck line drawings of a Lepanto galeass are shown here on the lines of the *galia grossa*. Other details have been reconstructed based on three sources: Fernando Bertelli's engraving dating from 1573, now housed in the Museo Storico Navale and also shown here; Vicentino's fresco of the Battle of Lepanto in the Palazzo Ducale; and Steffano de Zuanne's *galeazza alla Faustina*.[119]

Ulrich Alertz

115. J Furttenbach, *Architectura Navalis*, pp78–79.

116. J Furttenbach, *Architectura Navalis*, p79; see also Furttenbach, *Itinerarium Italiae*, pp249–250.

117. Rubin de Cervin, *Flotta di Venezia*, p49; see also Cayetano Rosell, *Combate Naval de Lepanto* (Madrid 1853); Luis Carrero Blanco, *Lepanto* (Barcelona 1971); J Furttenbach, *Architectura Navalis*, pp115–134.

118. However, Furttenbach's absolute dimensions do not agree with Pre Theodoro's. In the reconstruction drawing this changes nothing, of course: only the scale. The shorter scale refers to Furttenbach's dimensions converted into *piede* (enlargement factor compared with the *galia grossa*: 1.116).

119. BM, Add Mss 38655, Steffano de Zuanne, f27.

120. BNM Ms Ital, cl VII, cod 379, A Picheroni, f9. 'Frame of a great galley of 27 paces length/beam in the frame opening 22½ feet/in fathoms 22 feet/in yards 15 feet/at the bottom 12 feet/side height 9 feet/The surface comprises 172 square feet/and the length is greater by 2 paces and 3 feet' . . . 'Frame of the light galley *Corana* of 24 paces and 2 feet length/beam at the frame opening 15 feet/in fathoms 14 feet/in yards 11¾ feet/at the bottom 7 ½ feet/side height 5 feet 2 inches/the area comprises 62 square feet.'

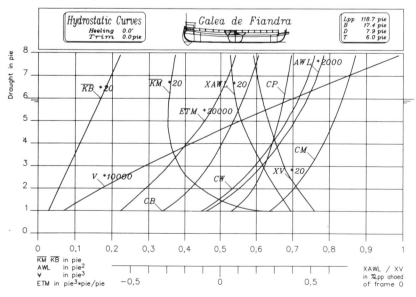

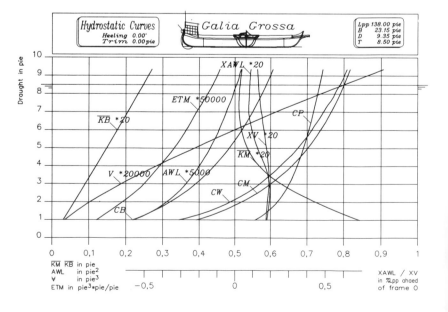

11

Oar Mechanics and Oar Power in Ancient Galleys

IT MAY be no coincidence that ancient Greece, so famous for its progress in abstract thought, was also the earliest recorded home of that remarkable exercise in kinetic geometry, the trireme.[1] One hundred and seventy men with one hundred and seventy oars, all moving back and forth, occupied interlocking spaces at three levels in such a way that they all had enough room to row effectively.[2] Yet the total space they occupied must have been the very minimum, otherwise the attested high performance could not have been achieved; and somewhere, without interfering with the movement, space was ingeniously found for the essential cross-beams of the hull and for the other necessary furniture therein.[3]

Since the speed of the fastest of the ancient triremes has probably never been equalled, let alone surpassed by any other type of oared ship, their oars must have been so good that even today it would be hard to improve on them given the same tools and materials. Even without help from their mathematical contemporaries the oarmakers would have arrived, after many generations of trial and error, at designs of solid wooden oars similar to those that modern calculations and experience would suggest.

The information concerning oars that ancient Greek writers, painters and sculptors have left us is summarised in the next section. Scanty indeed, it refers mainly to triremes of the type used by the Athenians, their allies and their enemies of the fifth century BC and the succeeding couple of centuries. However, much can be inferred from experiments with modern oars, such as those made for the reconstructed trireme *Olympias*,[4] by reference to the sciences of physics, engineering and physiology, and to the properties of wood and water.

Ancient oars probably had blades of a relatively short and wide shape, as in this single-level pentecontor depicted on an Athenian bowl of the second half of the sixth century BC; the original is now in the Louvre. (Williams and Morrison, Greek Oared Ships, Arch 55)

The conclusions are provisional of course, as they are liable to be revised in the light of further experiment and scholarship.

Information on oars from ancient sources

The information is given first, and is commented on below.

There is a description of the making of oars by stripping coaxial layers from saplings of *elate*, the silver fir *abies cephalonica* (Loudon).[5] In the *Odyssey* 'shaved *elatai*' is a synonym for oars. Various shapes of oar blades are shown in vase paintings and reliefs but no depictions of trireme oar blades are known. Mostly the shapes are indicated in a rather impressionistic way, as in one example dated to about 540 BC. There are two apparent exceptions to this which date from about 500 BC and about 300 BC respectively.[6] The unshipped oar shown in the last of these has a pommel.

A great deal of information is given in the Naval Inventories, a fragmented series of inscriptions excavated in the Piraeus.[7] They show that the spare oars of a trireme numbered 30 and were of two lengths, 9 and 9½ cubits. Other texts show that all the oars extended to the same distance from the ship's side although they were not overall the same length[8] and that those used towards the ends of the ship were shorter than those towards the middle;[9] and that each oarsman had an oar, an oarloop (for attaching the oar to its thole pin) and a cushion.[10] Apart from the spares, the 170 other oars of a trireme were divided into three classes, named thranite, zygian and thalamian. Nearly all the ancient inventories giving the numbers of these show that the classes contained 62, 54 and 54 oars respectively, but it has been argued that the iconography of the ships, such as it is, suggests 60, 58 and 52.[11]

1. This chapter deals with what is known and what can be plausibly inferred about the oar mechanics and oar power of the galleys of classical antiquity: the oars of later galleys are dealt with in the following chapter. Explanation of the necessary technical terms is given in the Glossary at the end of the book.

2. Thucydides, *History of the Peloponnesian War*, I, 13.2; J S Morrison and R T Williams, *Greek Oared Ships* (Cambridge 1968), pp158–159.

3. J S Morrison and J F Coates, *The Athenian Trireme* (Cambridge 1986), figs 57, 62, 64, 65–66 (pp199, 209, 211, 215); J F Coates, S K Platis and J T Shaw, *The Trireme Trials 1988* (Oxford 1990), figs 2, 5, 6, 8 (pp4–8); J T Shaw (ed), *The Trireme Project* (Oxford 1993), figs F3, F4, 9.1.

4. Coates, Platis and Shaw, *The Trireme Trials*, pp49–55; Shaw, *The Trireme Project*, pp58–60.

5. Theophrastus, *Enquiry into Plants*, 5.1.6–7.

6. Morrison and Coates, *The Athenian Trireme*, figs 20a, 47, 27 respectively.

7. IG2² 1604–1632 (see Bibliography for an explanation of IG).

8. Galen, *On the Use of the Parts of the Body*, 1.24.

9. Aristotle, *On the parts of Animals*, 4.10, 687b18.

10. Thucydides, *History of the Peloponnesian War*, II, 93.2.

11. Morrison and Coates, *The Athenian Trireme*, pp139–151.

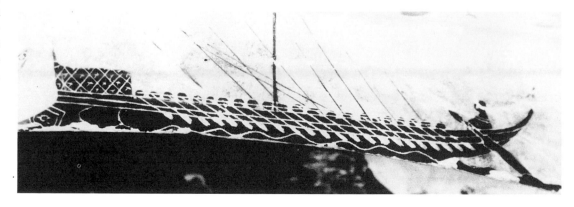

For economy in wood and ease of manufacture the blades were probably flat rather than spoon-shaped. As to the handgrip at the butt, this was (and is) limited to a diameter of about 5cm by the size of a man's hand. It was probably long enough, about 40cm, for a man's hands to be kept about two hands' breadths apart. If the oars were balanced well enough to eliminate unnecessary waste of energy, their blades would have been kept off the water during the return by the mere weight of the men's hands and forearms resting on the handles.

It is clear that in triremes each oar was pulled by one man only, and that he rowed whilst sitting down. This was surely true of the earlier ships too, the pentecontors and triacontors. There is no firm evidence as to whether the oar was placed aft or forward of the thole pin, but certain vase paintings showing thole pins with hooks on the aft side suggest that the oar was on the forward side,[21] and this is supported by usage in the Mediterranean going back at least four centuries as shown by a fifteenth-century AD painting of a *triremi* by Carpaccio.[22] The oarloop would then have had to take the whole strain of the pull and it would have had to be much stronger than would have been needed had the oar pressed directly against the thole pin. Homer refers to oarloops of leather,[23] but experience in *Olympias*, a ship

The thalamian oarports were closed against the ingress of water by leather sleeves called *askomata*.[12] The earliest naval inventory, that dated 377–376 BC, gives the money held for these as 43 drachmae 2 obols per trireme.[13] Since there were 6 obols per drachma, this sum is divisible by 52, not 54. An inventory states that 'of these thranite oars, four are zygian'.[14]

For the oars of fours, fives and polyremes generally, we have to rely mostly on inference, as little information has survived from antiquity. Anderson (following Tarn) has stated that 'one of our few scraps of real knowledge is that the oars of an Athenian trireme could be transferred to a "four" and those of a "four" to a "five"',[15] but Morrison has argued cogently that this is not a justifiable deduction from the ancient text that Tarn relied on.[16] However, calculations referred to in the section on 'Multi-manned oars' below show that oars very like those of a trireme could have been rowed by two men apiece (as would certainly be required in a four) and so Anderson's statement might be true at least in part. If so, it would have implications for the design of a four.

In describing Ptolemy Philopater's monster forty of the third century BC, Callixenus, a contemporary historian generally regarded as reliable, stated that its uppermost level of oars were 38 cubits in length, *ie* nearly 19m if the cubit was 0.49m.[17] This is twice the length of a standard telegraph pole. (According to Athenaeus, in the course of a test more than 4000 oarsmen were put on board along with 3250 others! The ship is thought to have had twin hulls.)

Comment

The design and manufacture of an oar for use at the highest power and speed requires much time and skill, but naval warfare in antiquity would have required oars in their tens of thousands. Mass-produced oars would have varied in quality, the best being reserved no doubt for the 'fast ships' which formed only a small fraction of each fleet (as at Salamis in 480 BC[18]).

The method of making oars by stripping coaxial layers from saplings ensured that the grain of the wood was aligned along the shaft, making the oars strong for their weight. These were probably the best oars. Presumably the thicker end was used for the loom of the oar, for reasons of strength, balance and economy. Recent maritime tradition argues for blades that are flat, and very long in relation to their width; oars having these characteristics can be made in one piece without wasting much wood and they are economical of storage space. However, experiments in *Olympias* have shown that a shorter but wider oar blade is preferable (in her) to a long narrow one at all three levels.[19] For this there is also a theoretical justification.[20]

A vase painting of about 500 BC in the British Museum provides evidence that some ancient oar blades were indeed fairly short and wide, probably consisting of a separate piece spliced and riveted on to the shaft, as was virtually unavoidable if the blades were at the thin ends of the saplings. As water-resistant glues were unknown at the time, rivets or dowels would have been needed instead.

12. Morrison and Williams, *Greek Oared Ships*, pp283–284.

13. IG2² 1604.

14. IG2² 1604.56.

15. R C Anderson, *Oared Fighting Ships* (Hemel Hempstead 1962), p22; W W Tarn, *Classical Review* 55, (1941), p89.

16. J S Morrison, *Classical Quarterly* 41 (1947), pp122–135.

17. Callixenus, quoted by Athenaeus, *The Deipnosophists*, 5.37.203e–204d, and by Plutarch, *Demetrius*, 43.4.

18. Aeschylus, *Persae*, 338–343.

19. Coates, Platis and Shaw, *The Trireme Trials*; Shaw, *The Trireme Project*.

20. J T Shaw, *Transactions of the Royal Institution of Naval Architects*, Part B 135 (1993) pp211–224.

21. J F Coates, in Shaw, *The Trireme Project*, pp48–49.

22. Vittore Carpaccio *c*1465–*c*1522. Painting 'The Return of the Ambassadors', from the Saint Ursula cycle, Gallerie dell'Accademia, Venice.

23. Homer, *Odyssey*, 4.782.

in which the oars are rigged forward of the thole pins, which are not fitted with hooks, has been that leather oarloops stretch and break. Rope grommets are better. They would have to be especially strong to withstand the pull of a multi-manned oar.

The oars in active use in a trireme were probably of the same two lengths as the known lengths of the spares, namely 9 and 9½ cubits. The appropriate cubit is now believed to have equalled about 0.49m; if it was that long the oars of a trireme were 4.41m and 4.66m in length overall. As explained in the following section, the oars of triremes would require a 'gearing' (the ratio of outboard to inboard length) of about 2.7. Galen's statement that all the oars reached the same distance from the ship's side was made some 500 years after the heyday of the Athenian trireme. It seems to have been an approximation, as it is not quite compatible with other requirements of the design of the ship and oars.[24] It was possible to make it roughly true in *Olympias*.

The names of the three classes of oars of a trireme that are not spares are taken to refer to the three levels at which they were used: the thranites highest, the zygians midway, and the thalamians underneath.

The ancient stocktaker's remarks have been held to show that at least two of the three classes of oars of a trireme could be distinguished,[25] but it is uncertain how. In *Olympias* it has been found that there is no 'rowing' reason why the oars of a given length should differ in design according to their level. The stocktaker may simply have counted four too many oars in the thranite pile, four too few in the zygian pile. The reason for keeping them apart may be that the thranites, who were paid best, claimed the newest and best oars, and the thalamians had to put up with the oldest and worst. The underwater form of the hull could be made slightly finer or shorter if there were 52 thalamians rather than 54.

It is about as certain as anything can be in this field that the oars of a *tetrērēs* or four (a ship having four files of oarsmen on each side) were double-manned and were at two levels. Whilst no ancient text states this directly, several lines of argument lead to that conclusion. Only one need be mentioned here: the deck of

a four was considerably lower than that of a five,[26] and so its oars cannot have been arranged at more than two levels. If they were all at one level, implying four men per oar, the ship would have been too wide for the slipways and sheds. A mixture of single-manned and triple-manned oars being impractical, all the oars must have been double-manned.

As regards the oars of Ptolemy Philopater's double-hulled forty, it may be speculated that there were three levels of oars, with 14 men per oar at one level and 13 at the other two (making 40); of whom perhaps about half pulled and the rest pushed.[27] If there were 7 pullers and 7 or 6 pushers on each oar and these men were separated laterally by 0.65m as discussed below, and the No 7 was not very near the thole, the inboard length of an oar cannot have been less than about 6½m nor more than about 8½m (the width of each hull) – unless there was a deck between the hulls – giving a gearing of less than 2 and arguing for a low maximum speed. Like the various thirties, twenties and tens, none of which are recorded as seeing action, this ship was evidently too unwieldy for naval warfare, and her impractical and very expensive oars receive no further discussion here.

General remarks on oars and their use

The first principle is that an oar cannot be designed in isolation: the designer must take into account the type of ship in which the oar is to be used, and the seas likely to be met.

How an oar works

Rowing coaches can sometimes be heard telling their crews that an oar should be used to lever the boat past the blade which is locked in

the water. In reality the water yields to the blade: this is called slip. The blade must move through the water if work is done on the oar. At the catch, when rowing hard, the man tries to drive his whole weight from the stretcher and hang it on the oar handle: if the blade creates enough resistance he lifts his weight almost completely off the seat. Through the oar he necessarily imparts to the water a sternwards momentum or impulse, equal and opposite to that which is imparted to the boat and its contents. Despite the slip, a successful catch gives the oarsman a feeling that the blade is temporarily fixed. It is a paradox that the harder the man pulls, the more the water yields, but the stronger the feeling that it does not.

If the speed of the boat is the same at the beginning of one stroke as it is at the beginning of the next one, then the momentum gained by the boat and its contents during the pull is exactly balanced by the momentum they lose by skin friction, eddies, wavemaking and air resistance during the return.

Inefficiency of oars, avoidable and unavoidable

Notwithstanding what has been said about the inevitability of bladeslip, slip velocity should be minimised as it is a source of inefficiency. Since momentum is the product of mass and velocity, one way of reducing slip velocity is to increase the mass of water involved. With a given oar

24. Shaw, *The Trireme Project*, p19 note 6.

25. Morrison and Coates, *The Athenian Trireme*, pp172–173.

26. Livy, *History of Rome*, XXX, 26.6.

27. J S Morrison, *Long Ships and Round Ships* (London 1980), p46.

The Olympias *under way, seen from the port quarter. The oars are relatively short and, contrary to theoretically-based expectations, oar blades of the same shape for each level have proved effective in practice. The short, wide blade shown here follows the rather sparse evidence of iconography. (Mary Pridgeon, by courtesy of the Trireme Trust)*

that can be done by increasing blade area, but it must not be overdone or it will overload the oarsman and possibly cause backwatering by the inner end of the blade with obvious waste of power. When a boat is rowed under a bridge, it should seem to a spectator leaning over the parapet that during the pull an oar rotates about a point a few centimetres up the shaft from the neck of the blade. To achieve this, good oars and good oarsmanship are both needed.

Another source of inefficiency in an oar is its moment of inertia about the thole, abbreviated here as MIT. This manifests itself as the resistance the oar offers at the handle to having the blade manipulated up and down and back and forth, irrespective of the balance of the oar and of the resistance of air and water. The greater the MIT and the higher the stroke rate, the more power these movements absorb. The MIT can be kept low by keeping the oar short and by paring the wood down, particularly near the ends of the oar, but the latter step may cause too great a loss of stiffness. Some flexibility of oars has to be accepted and allowed for by users of wooden oars. Whilst high rigidity in an oar would minimise lost motion during the pull, it is not attainable in wood except at high cost in weight and MIT. A skilful oarsman can exploit the flexibility of an oar to help him obtain a clean finish, as his hands will reach the deadpoint of the horizontal component of their motion while the blade is still working.

Gearing

The gearing of an oar with a given area and shape of blade can be thought of most simply as the ratio of the outboard length to the inboard length. Modern racing eights with sliding seats have oars with a high gearing of about 2.4, but high speed in fixed-seat craft calls for an even higher gearing because the oarsmen's strokes are shorter. Triremes were no exception, but they needed a high oar gearing for other reasons too. These are discussed below.

In a trireme, the depth of hull needed to accommodate oarsmen at three levels prescribed the height above the waterline of the sills of the topmost tholes. Also, if the oars were to be pulled hard, they could not be too steep. When expressed numerically these two requirements dictated the minimum outboard length of the topmost oars as about 3.4m. For reasons of weight, balance, moment of inertia and economics this was probably also their maximum outboard length. Thus the inboard length was fixed as well, about 1.26m, since the overall length was 9½ cubits, or 4.66m. (There would have been no reason to include any of

the 9-cubit oars in the topmost level.) The gearing of the 9½-cubit oars was thus about 2.7, which would have been fully adequate for high speed. The same gearing probably applied to the 9-cubit oars.

The scope for vertical movement of the oar butts of seated oarsmen is not great, but a gearing of 2.7 would have multiplied it at the blades by enough to allow the two upper levels of oarsmen to cope with waves that were just high enough to oblige the lowest level to draw their oars in; waves higher than this would have been dangerous to a trireme.

It can be seen that the design is self-consistent and well-balanced.

It should not be overlooked that the definition of gearing as outboard:inboard length ratio applies to oars with a given shape and area of blade. A more refined concept, which takes some account of variations in these, has the gearing of a one-man oar as the ratio the distance between the centre of pressure of the blade and the thole bears to that between the effective point of application of the pull and the thole. These distances, however, are not known exactly. In a 9½-cubit trireme oar they would have been about 3.2m and 1.06m, giving a 'refined' gearing of about 3.0.

There are various ways of making sure that a modern oarsman rows with a particular gearing, but this is not always done. The opportunity of varying the gearing by drawing the oar a little inboard or pushing it a little outboard without stopping rowing could have been a valuable resource in an ancient ship since a low gear is desirable for initial acceleration or for rowing against a headwind, whereas a high one is needed at top speed. The *dal Pozzo* drawing now in the British Museum shows a galley in which the oar handles extend for some distance inboard of the men's hands: although some details of the drawing are clearly unreliable, this one could suggest that a variable gearing was available. The oarsman could have made the gearing higher by sliding the oar further outboard, or lower by moving himself further inboard in order to pull opposite the extension of the handle.

Balance of oars

The balance of an oar has two aspects: static balance and dynamic balance. An oar that is well balanced statically is one whose blade can be kept off the water effortlessly, by the mere weight of the oarsman's or oarsmen's hands and forearms on the handle, yet whose blade floats at the right depth in the water when that weight is removed.

An oar that is well balanced dynamically will

seem to catch the water of its own accord. It will give no impulse to the thole at the inception of the catch if the oarsman or men at that instant let go of the handle. This requires that the centre of percussion of the oar should be a few inches inboard of the tip of the blade, *ie* it should coincide with the momentary position of the centre of pressure of water on the forward face of the blade as it enters the water with a backsplash. An explanation of this concept can be found in the section on the compound pendulum in any good textbook of dynamics.

It is not at all easy to design a wooden oar that is well balanced both statically and dynamically, as it requires most careful attention to the distribution of mass along the oar (*ie* the taper of the shaft and loom, and the buoyancy of the blade), and is hard to reconcile with needed stiffness, blade area and lengths inboard and outboard. If the gearing is altered it is bound to alter the balance. The best oars will need individual attention because the density of the wood will not be uniform. They can be roughed out to a standard design which is rather too heavy and then each one should be pared down very carefully by a skilled man.

The sitting stroke in calm water and in waves

For the simple reason that a person can develop more power with an oar when seated than in any other position, there can be little doubt that, like the oarsmen in triremes, those in *tetrērēs* (fours) and (probably) *pentērēs* (fives) rowed whilst seated.

In calm water the most effective stroke from a sitting position is rapid and long. It has the oar blade just fully immersed whilst the handle is about level with the oarsman's shoulders when he has swung fully forward. With a given oar and a given gearing this fixes the height of the man's seat in relation to the sill of his thole. Because this gives little scope for lowering the handle at the end of the pull, the blade cannot be lifted far enough during the return to clear the tops of even moderate waves, but that is no handicap when the sea is calm. A rapid stroke entails the use of short, handy oars which commit the designer to a low freeboard incompatible with a ship's ability to survive rough weather: this is referred to again below. Other aspects of hull design conducive to speed also militate against survival in rough water.

If nevertheless the ship encounters rising seas, if the gearing is about 2.7 and the blade is to clear even moderate waves no more than one metre in amplitude, the oarsman's seat must be lowered, but then the man must change his style of rowing, reaching up to pull,

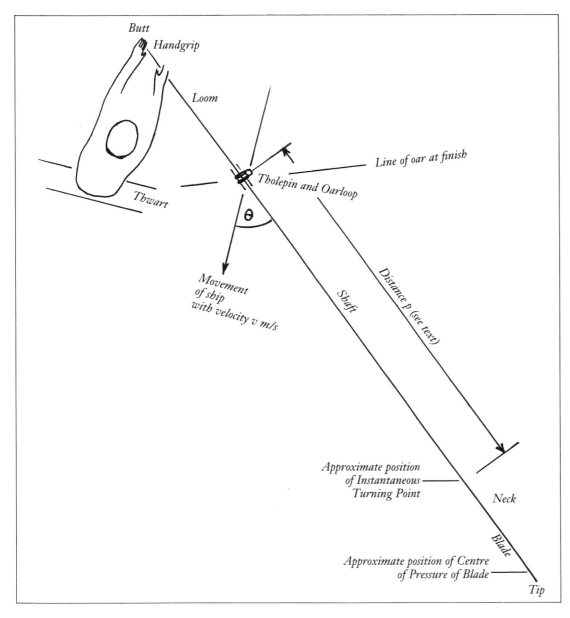

Butt

Handgrip

Loom

Thwart

Line of oar at finish

Tholepin and Oarloop

θ

Movement of ship with velocity v m/s

Shaft

Distance p (see text)

Approximate position of Instantaneous Turning Point

Neck

Blade

Approximate position of Centre of Pressure of Blade

Tip

Diagram of a trireme oar seen in plan (oarsman seen at the catch). (J T Shaw)

probably have kept an ancient trireme in harbour. Vitruvius pointed out that naval battles are fought when the sea is calm (*pugna navalis tranquillo committitur mari*).[28]

Other things affecting this question of adaptability to different sea conditions are the man's own dimensions, those of the oar, the height of the man's seat above the water, and the lateral displacement between the seat and the thole.

Other aspects of ship design bearing on the use of oars

Because it is awkward to row hard with an oar that makes a steepest angle of more than about 30 degrees to the horizontal, there is a limiting relationship between the outboard length of an oar, short of the blade, and the height above water of the sill of the thole. The former should be at least twice the latter. If a ship must have a high freeboard in order to cope with rough seas, her oars must be long outboard. However, as already discussed, Athenian triremes of the fifth and fourth centuries BC used what were by later standards short oars: they were 9 and 9½ cubits long. Because they were short and light, trireme oars had a low mass moment of inertia about the thole (MIT), a property that has enabled similar oars in *Olympias* to be worked by one man apiece at very high rates of up to 47 strokes per minute.[29]

Other aspects of ship design that are highly relevant to oar performance by seated men are the height of the seat above the heels and the slope of the foot stretchers. Few men can swing far forward for the catch without bending their knees and it is therefore necessary, if seats are fixed, to mount the stretchers at such a height that the men's knees are bent to an angle of about 150 degrees. Furthermore, the thighs must be either horizontal or sloping gently down from hip to knee, in order to provide clearance for the return of the oar. But if the stretchers are too low or their slope is incorrect the men's pull will be impaired. In *Olympias* each stretcher is placed so that the oarsman's toes come underneath the seat of the man next aft, with a small clearance. They are adjustable fore-and-aft, and their slope is 45 degrees from the horizontal. This arrangement of heights and angles has proved satisfactory, but the steepness of the stretchers could be increased to about 60 degrees with advantage, particularly if the oarsmen wear shoes with heels. Here it is worth noting that if the stretcher is

particularly in the troughs: this shortens and weakens his stroke, unavoidably reducing oar power just when more power may well be needed to avoid trouble. No oarsman could maintain the high rate of striking or the length of stroke required for high power and speed if he had to impart to his oar blade the large, energy-using vertical movements required in rougher water.

An oarsman can partially re-adapt a rough water rig to one suited to calm water by raising his seat by means of a thick cushion, but if they were thick enough to make much difference, cushions would correspondingly increase the vertical clearance needed between levels of oarsmen, increasing the ship's weight and so impairing performance. A probably less practical adaptation would make use of a removable

wooden block to adjust the sill of the thole; it would call for taller oarports than seem to have been used in triremes.

In short, the ability to make progress in a seaway, or indeed to survive in one, is gained at the expense of high performance in calm water, and the converse is also true.

The designer of an ancient oared ship had therefore to consider how far he could or should allow for the difference between these conditions. Ancient accounts show that triremes were not able to make progress in rough water, nor could their hulls survive it, and it may therefore be assumed that their oar system was not well adapted to it but was designed for optimum performance in calmer seas. An illustration of this has been given by *Olympias*, which has been rowed in waves of up to one metre, but they prevented the use of the lowest oars, which were drawn in, and progress was laboured. Waves higher than a metre would

28. Vitruvius, *On Architecture*, IV, 43.

29. Shaw, *The Trireme Project*, p43.

correctly angled for fixed-seat rowing it is too steep for effective sliding back and forth on the seat, but there are simple ways of reducing the steepness of the feet which could have been used in antiquity.

It should be pointed out that if an oarsman swings forward correctly on a fixed seat for the catch (*ie* if he swings from the hips), anatomy dictates that his knees must rise a little even though he does not slide on the seat.

Seen in plan, the angle of attack of an oar at the catch and the angle swept by the oar are other features in which ship design interacts with that of oars.

An oar blade must be moved through the water if it is to create useful resistance. If in the oar diagram the speed of the ship is v m/s and the distance between the thole and the instantaneous turning point of the oar with respect to undisturbed water is p metres, the needed angular velocity of the oar is v (sin theta)/p, where theta is the angle between the oar and the line of advance of the ship, seen in plan. The angle theta is affected by the spatial relationship between the thole pin and the seat, and by the cant, if any, of the rig. (For an example of a canted rig see p173, showing the herringbone pattern of the benches in a Renaissance galley.) If theta at the catch is reduced, the required angular velocity is also reduced, other things being equal, and this could be used to ease to some extent the problem of obtaining an effective catch with a long and clumsy oar; the cost is that the effective propulsive force is a lower proportion of the blade reaction than it would be if theta were larger.

A compromise has to be made. In Renaissance galleys having oars 8m to 10m long, the horizontal angle swept by them was unavoidably small, so that if the angle theta at the catch (the angle of attack) was to be kept small in order to ease the acceleration of the oars the rig had to be canted; the whole of the stroke was completed before the oar made a right angle with the line of advance of the ship. We do not know whether anything like this was done in antiquity, though it is not unlikely. A possible advantage of the Renaissance compromise was that it may have drawn more water into the slipstream, thus reducing its velocity and thereby slightly improving the efficiency of propulsion.

The interior of the Olympias *showing the three levels of rowers. The very confined nature of the rowing positions is apparent, and it is interesting that some of the oarsmen prefer an underhand grip for the hand at the outer end of the handle. All oars are single-manned and rowers use a fully seated stroke.* (John Coates)

How the oars were used

The oars of triremes and probably those of triacontors and pentecontors were single-manned, whereas those of *tetrērēs* were double-manned as already argued. Probably all the oars of a *hexērēs* ('six') were double-manned. The *pentērēs* may have had, in each section or 'room', one single-manned oar and two double-manned ones. If it is accepted that no ship had oars at more than three levels, denominations above *hexērēs* must have had three or more men per oar on at least some of their oars. In the trireme it is certain, and in ships with single- and/or double-manned oars probable, that all the men rowed a sitting stroke and that their seats were fixed. The wheeled seats incorrectly called sliding seats of some modern racing craft can be ruled out from all the ancient ships, as can moving tholes and moving foot stretchers, on the dual grounds that the attested speeds of the ships do not require

them, and that they would have been impractical at sea. However, men may sometimes have lengthened their stroke by sliding back and forth on fixed seats, for example when a sprint was ordered. Geometry indicates that unless oars with more than three men were made very long inboard, it is likely that the man or men nearest the butt had to row a stand-and-sit stroke, or to walk back and forth, otherwise the man nearest the thole would have had too little work to do.

Effect of seated oarsmen's stature on their length of stroke and their power, and on the required interscalmium

The average height of the natives of Greece in antiquity seems to have been about the same as that of Greeks in 1944; namely about 1.67m.[30] This limited the length of stroke that was possible from a fixed seat to about 1.1m at the butt of an oar, measured along the chord of the arc. In comparison, the best English amateur oarsmen in fixed-seat eights of the late nineteenth century are credited with a stroke of 1.2m,[31] but they were probably up to 15cm taller. (In 1994, first class oarsmen using sliding seats achieve a stroke of 1.6m,[32] but these men are very tall.) It is suggested that in antiquity, in ships in which all the oarsmen were seated, the fore-and-aft separation between oarsmen of the same file was no more than just enough to permit the men to row their oar butts through 1.1m with a safety margin of perhaps 10–15cm. In this way high oar power could be obtained without unduly lengthening the ship.

Power available

Olympias was built to a cubit of 0.444m, giving an interscalmium of 0.888m, which turned out to be too short, restricting the length of stroke. A man as short as 1.67m required more room. It now appears that a cubit of 0.49m should have been employed.[33] A carefully selected and trained modern crew of height 1.67m rowing at 48 strokes per minute (spm) within an interscalmium of 0.98m (cubit of 0.49m) would have enough room, and they could be expected to deliver an effective propulsive power of about 200 watts per oar at 48 to 50spm for a few minutes. This would require each oarsman to apply some 330 watts to his oar handle. (The

30. J H Musgrave, quoted by S McGrail, in Shaw, *The Trireme Project*, p10; Angel, Musgrave, Hasluck and Morant, quoted by Shaw, *ibid*, p64.

31. T A Cook, *Rowing at Henley* (Oxford 1919), pp63–64.

32. Bill Sayer, *Rowing and Sculling: The Complete Manual* (London 1991), pp110, 114.

33. J S Morrison, in Shaw, *The Trireme Project*, pp12–13.

difference comprises first the dissipation in the water of about 50 watts; secondly about 70 watts required to reciprocate the oar itself in the vertical sense and horizontally during the return, and thirdly about 10 watts to accelerate the oar itself during the pull. All these powers are averaged over the cycle of pull plus return, which occupies 1.25 seconds at 48spm.)

It has been shown that a likely length inboard for a 9½-cubit trireme oar was about 1.26m. The effective point of application of the pull is the midpoint between the oarsman's hands, and this may be taken to be 0.2m from the butt. Thus the leverage was 1.06m. If the man can move the butt 1.1m, he moves the midpoint between his hands $1.1 \times 1.06/1.26 = 0.925$m. The effective length is further reduced by the loss involved in obtaining even a clean catch and finish; skilful oarsmen with well-balanced trireme oars of low MIT would lose no more than 10 per cent, and then the effective length of the triremer's pull would be 0.83m.

The work done on the handle during the pull is the relevant fraction of the total power multiplied by the duration, *ie* 260×1.25 or 325 newton metres. Taking the *effective* length of a triremer's stroke measured along the chord as about 0.83m, the mean pull is 325/0.83 or about 390 newtons, or say 88 lbf, 57 per cent of the weight of a man weighing 11 stone or 70kg. Tests of modern oarsmen suggest that this was feasible in antiquity for a carefully selected, well fed and well trained crew. If so, and if ancient triremes had the same resistance to motion as that of *Olympias*, it would seem that an ancient trireme in good order could attain a speed of very nearly 10kts in a sprint lasting about 5 minutes. Cruising speed would have been 7½–8kts and could be maintained all day. It would call for 70 to 90 effective watts per oar, and 135–160 watts applied to the oarhandle. This large reduction in power for what may seem a small reduction in speed accounts for the large increase in endurance. It arises because the power required varies roughly as the cube of the speed. If the stroke rate was 30spm, the mean cruising pull would have been 220 to 280 n, 49 to 63 lbf.

Multi-manned oars

Although no modern experiments on multi-manned oars have come to the writer's notice, some facts about them are indisputable and are stated in the following paragraphs, along with some more-or-less plausible conjectures. The man pulling at the butt-end will be called No 1, the others, if all pulling, Nos 2, 3 etc. Pushers,

Oarport of a Hellenistic galley as represented on the base of the Victory of Samothrace, second-first century BC. It suggests that for some larger vessels oarports were oblong and bisected by a thole pin, from which the oar probably pivoted, secured by an oarloop. The after end of the oarport is chamfered, presumably to allow the oar to be pulled nearer the hull and avoid damage in action, when shearing off the enemy's oars was a common tactic. (From L Casson, Ships and Seamanship in the Ancient World)

if any, would have sat or stood on the opposite side of the loom from the pullers, facing them. Compared with pulling, pushing is a very weak action for a seated man, and for that reason it seems unlikely that seated pushers were used unless it was to help with the return of a very heavy oar, when they would, of course, have been pulling. The pushing stroke, the walking stroke and the stand-and-sit stroke receive only brief mention in this chapter.

As Nos 2, 3, etc necessarily row a shorter stroke than No 1 they exert less power, but their endurance is correspondingly great. This has the consequence for crew management that it would pay to interchange No 1 and No 2, etc from time to time.

Oarloops

What these were made of remains in doubt. It is probable but not certain that they had to take the strain of the pull.

Thole pins

Thole pins for use with multi-manned oars would have had to be correspondingly strong.

Handgrips

The handgrip at the butt may have resembled that of a trireme oar, but for reasons of strength and balance the loom opposite the next man or men will probably have had too large a diameter to be grasped in the hand, and if so, an auxiliary handle must have been provided. In order not to weaken the loom by inserts this may, in the smaller varieties, have been a simple affair like the rung of a rope ladder linked to the loom by grommets.

Lateral spacing of the men

Unless the men worked in tandem after the manner of a tug-o'-war team, which seems most unlikely, they must have been spaced far enough apart laterally to give them enough room to pull without getting in each other's way, particularly towards the finish of a pull when a man's elbows tend to move outwards from his trunk. The adjacent hands of the men on a multi-manned oar must not be so close together that their elbows would clash: accordingly, the centres of the seats must be separated laterally by about 65cm measured parallel to the oar in mid-stroke.

Whilst the men's lateral separation should be no less than about 65cm, it should be no larger either, in order to minimise their differences in leverage without unduly increasing the inboard length of the oar since that, given the need to maintain a fairly high gearing, would entail a severe increase in MIT. Moreover, a greater separation would require the ship to be wider, which would make it slower.

Use of three or more men per oar

When three men rowed an oar, they may all have used a sitting stroke, but the stand-and-sit stroke or a walking stroke may also have been employed by the No 1. With more than three men the use of stand-and-sit and/or walking strokes (in which the men would lean heavily backwards during the pull as they pressed against foot-pieces) becomes more likely and it might extend to most, if not all, of the men.

In an interscalmium or 'room' of 0.98m a stand-and-sit stroke of 1.3m by the No 1 is possible. Any longer stroke at the butt would have needed a longer 'room', lessening the number of oars in a given length of ship: the gains and losses would have had to be carefully investigated. Standing or walking men would have required more headroom, or a sunken gangway, again affecting the design. They would have had to be provided with somewhere to sit at times, and possibly this was immediately behind them, as in galleys using a stand-and-sit stroke. If the oars were so hard to return that pushers had to be added, the interscalmium would have had to be increased still further, using up space to an extent that would have been counter-productive.

When the number of men per oar compelled increases in the oar's overall length, it seems inescapable that the stroke rate, so high in triremes, was considerably lowered. These long oars must have had such high inertia in relation to the available leverage and pull that they could not be moved so quickly. Also the stand-and-sit stroke that may have been used in some ancient ships was very exhausting, as is known from studies of seventeenth-century galleys. A walking stroke (ie without sitting) was perhaps less taxing but it could not have been performed effectively at anything like the high rates believed to have been characteristic of triremes. A sitting stroke was surely preferable from that point of view.

How is the oarsmen's pull related to their stroke rate?

The design and use of multi-manned oars depend on the answer to this question. If a crew is asked to lower the 'pressure' it normally does so by reducing the work done in such a way that the mean pull and the stroke rate are both lowered. However, they need not be linked thus. It is a common experience among oarsmen rowing a sitting stroke that if they lower the rate of striking they can, if required, pull harder, although not normally so much harder as would maintain their original power. (Power = mean pull × effective length × frequency.) Individuals vary, but in order to facilitate the comparison of different hypothetical oars the writer proposes the following easy-to-use, albeit rough approximation to cover a wide range of oarsmen, namely that if men are rowing a sitting stroke of given length, and the stroke rate varies by a factor A, the strongest available pull varies by the reciprocal of the square root of A, and hence the power the crew can exert on their oar handles varies by the square root of A. The writer hopes to arrange for some experiments to test this formula.

Merits of various different oars rowed by seated men

The writer has carried out a series of calculations on the leverage, MIT and so on of various hypothetical designs of one-man, two-man and three-man oars, all men seated, in order to investigate their merits and to see whether they would rule out, for example, the possibility that trireme oars could have been used in a tetrērēs. The conclusions depend very much on the assumptions that have to be made, but the following ones seem to be reasonably securely founded.

In what follows the midpoint between an oarsman's hands is taken to be the point of application of his pull, and the distance between this point and the thole is the man's leverage. Leverages of adjacent men differ by 0.65m. The effect of varying the leverage of the man nearest the thole was studied; the leverages of the others of course follow suit.

It turned out that by a careful choice of leverages it was possible to devise hypothetical two-man oars of the same length and handiness as trireme oars: the two versions, separated by level, could be employed together in a ship designed for that purpose. Furthermore, a set could be used in an appropriately designed tetrērēs. Thus a trireme oar could have been

A rather crude representation of a two-level galley of the second-first century on a frieze originally probably part of a tomb. The long tapered oar blades have many parallels in ancient iconography and in terms of manufacture would make the best use of natural timber shapes. (From L Casson, Ships and Seamanship in the Ancient World*)*

The stern of a Roman galley from a relief of the second-century AD date. This vessel also shows the tapered blades of earlier representations, but may depict the longer oars that were probably associated with multi-manning. (From L Casson, Ships and Seamanship in the Ancient World)

adapted for use by two men if it had a slightly larger blade spliced on and were rowed with a little more of its length inboard to give a little more leverage and a little lower gearing. Because of its short length outboard it could be used, like a trireme oar, only in a ship with a low freeboard or through oarports fairly near the waterline, *ie* a ship much like a trireme. This oar transmits about one-third more power than a trireme oar rowed by one man. The main reason why the power is not doubled is that the stroke of No 2 is very short.

By lengthening the two-man oar outboard by 50 per cent, a 50 per cent higher freeboard can be obtained. If the gearing remains more or less unchanged, the increased length inboard gives more leverage for both men and a longer stroke for No 2, but the MIT increases substantially and so the highest useful stroke rate falls by at least a fifth. However, the men can pull harder if they are so minded, whilst the angular acceleration required of the oar is less. The power this longer oar transmits, at best, is about the same as that from the shorter two-man oar at its best, but as the optimum stroke rates differ appreciably, the two types cannot both be worked at their best together. If the two kinds were used together in one ship the stroke rate could not usefully exceed the best stroke rate of the longer oar, restricting the power of the shorter oar, and the same is true of the use of the longer two-man oar with a one-man trireme oar.

A three-man oar could not be usefully rowed at such a high rate of striking as a trireme oar. Even with a fairly short leverage of the No 3, its highest useful stroke rate is limited to about four-fifths of that of the trireme oar. As this is about the same as that of the longer of the two-man oars just considered, they could well be used in combination. At best the power transmitted by this three-man oar is about half as much again as that of a one-man trireme oar. If the three-man oar were lengthened to give more leverage without altering its gearing, its highest useful stroke rate would be lowered further and it would become difficult to use it in combination with two-man oars without sacrificing some of the latter's potential power. It is most unlikely that a three-man oar would make a successful combination with a one-man oar, *eg* in a *tetrērēs* (as already stated).

It has been noted that multi-manned oars make poor use of the men's potential power. There are three main reasons: the necessarily short stroke of the men who are not nearest the butt, the reduced stroke rate associated with the longer oars, and the higher MIT of the longer oars, which absorbs a higher proportion of the men's power. In partial compensation for these failings the men, in particular Nos 2, 3 etc, of these oars should have greater endurance. This suggests that by interchanging the No 2s, 3s etc routinely with the No 1s the cruising speed in calm seas could be prevented from falling as much below that of a trireme as would otherwise be probable.

In rough seas the higher freeboard that could be given to ships with long oars should have made them less easily swamped than triremes, and if the scope for vertical movement of the oar butts was great enough, enabling the blades and shafts to be raised high enough to clear the waves, they may have made better progress into the wind under oar, provided that the air resistance of the taller hulls was not too great.

Need for experimental testing of the foregoing conclusions

It is obvious that conclusions of the kind mentioned throughout this chapter ought to be tested by a comprehensive programme of calculation informed and followed by experiment. The discussion has done no more than bring out the more likely possibilities.

J T Shaw

Acknowledgements

The writer, who is a scientist and not a classical scholar, wishes to make it clear that he has relied on translations of the ancient Greek or Latin texts, relevant to oars, referred to throughout the chapter. He gladly acknowledges his debt to J F Coates, J S Morrison and R T Williams, whose writings have been his main source of these translations. He also wishes to thank I Whitehead and N B Rankov for help with the bibliography.

12

Oar Mechanics and Oar Power in Medieval and Later Galleys

GALLEYS ARE propelled by oars; indeed, the words 'galley' and 'oar' are inextricably interlinked. In reality, however, these vessels used the wind as much as they could because the human engine is not very powerful and tires quickly. Yet the oar remained the *raison d'être* of the galley: it was under oar that they fought, and in some circumstances to such effect that it was to be a long time – the nineteenth century – before the last naval oared craft disappeared from the Baltic.

Therefore there was great incentive to improve the mode of rowing by every means possible. Designers in medieval times followed the natural engineering route: to increase the power and (if possible) improve the efficiency of the 'engine'. Given that the unit power in galleys was the power of a man, their way of thinking was to multiply the number of oarsmen, and since a hull could not be lengthened *ad infinitum* they doubled the oar arrangement and then tripled it. As outlined in the previous chapter, the shipbuilders of Ancient Greece had been faced with the same problem and had come up against the same constraints a thousand years earlier.

Because the restrictions of this route quickly became apparent, they tried to improve efficiency, and this produced a number of innovations. The outrigger or oarbox was already a familiar piece of equipment. It was used to increase the leverage of the oarsmen without the disadvantage of having to increase the size of

the midship beam at the waterline. The oarsmen were grouped together in twos and threes and were positioned on the same bench. This reduced the top hamper and really made the galley a low-freeboard ship. This arrangement did improve things, but because each man had his own oar – a very ancient practice – the benches had to be angled so that each oarsman could row properly. This system was known as *alla zenzile* (or *alla sensile*) rowing, which was very popular with the Venetians. However, it is a matter of debate whether they invented it, whether it was inherited from Byzantium, or

whether its origins lie even further back in time. Medieval galleys were biremes (two men per bench), then triremes (three men per bench), and even quadriremes. But development was slow, and the system which was first noted in the twelfth century was to last until the sixteenth century.

Nevertheless, an arrangement of this type had its limits. In 1530 the brilliant Venetian humanist Vettor Fausto tested a quinquereme, but the trial was not conclusive. With any more than three oarsmen to each bench, the outside positions were difficult to maintain and be-

A French manuscript illustration of a galley of the late fifteenth or early sixteenth century, certainly rowed alla zenzile *and probably with more than three oars per bench. The flags suggest Genoese nationality, and the three lanterns on the poop indicate a special vessel. Genoa had no equivalent of the French* Réale, *or galley-fleet flagship, but it may represent a* capitane, *or squadron flagship. The rig, with its tiny square fore sail, is unusual, although it may well have been useful in manoeuvring. There is the usual forward-firing gun battery on the forecastle, one large and two smaller barrels being visible.* (Bibliothèque Nationale)

cause the oars were very close together clashes were inevitable. This meant that oars were used up at a most alarming rate.

Because of all these problems, another system was then tried, although derived from the previous one. The idea was to make all the men on one bench use a single oar, but one which was longer and stronger. This was called *a scaloccio* rowing, which undeniably made life a little easier for the outside oarsmen without obstructing the cycle of the man at the end of the oar. He – called the *pianero* or 'lead rower' depending upon region – led his group and set the stroke. He was to keep this role until the end of the galley era. The transition from *remi piccoli* (small oars) to *remi grandi* (large oars), was slow and lasted more than half of the sixteenth century. By the end of the century there were those who were still not convinced of the suitability of the method. We must not forget that there were other factors which developed at the same time, but it is not intended to describe them in any detail because they have no connection with the subject being dealt with here. Guns made their appearance at sea, changing battle tactics and also the balance of

the galley hulls. Furthermore, sails were improved by increasing their size. The sixteenth century was an era of change, even if guns on ships had made their appearance somewhat earlier. Contrary to a current widely-held belief, passages under oar power were quite simple in the galleys used at the end of the century.

Finally, it is impossible to conclude this introduction without mentioning the human factor which played such a successful role. It is now known beyond any doubt that there were occasions when chained convicts and slaves rowed *alla zenzile*, duty which was once reserved for free men. However, because both feet were chained, the rowing technique had to be adapted to their situation, so short, fast strokes were necessary. Some commanding officers were always to prefer this style of propulsion.

The new *a scaloccio* mode of rowing made the 'tuning' of the oar crew easier because a single man, the *pianero*, controlled the oar, giving the others no alternative but to match the stroke rate. This factor was certainly quite important, because this new mode of rowing also required those oarsmen who were convicts or slaves to be shackled differently, by one foot only.

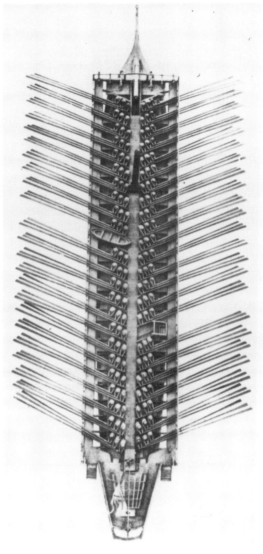

An overhead view of Admiral Fincati's model of the Venetian trireme that was designed to demonstrate his research into the medieval method of alla zenzile *rowing. The main feature to notice is the angled, herringbone pattern of benches from each of which three rowers pull at separate oars working against closely spaced tholes.*

1. The model is currently kept at the naval museum in Venice, together with models of a *fusta* (small galley), a *brigantino* and a *fregata* made for the same occasion.

2. The research of L Fincati, collected in *Le Triremi* [The Triremes] (Rome 1881) was sparked off by an article written by the French Admiral Jurien de la Gravière, who, in the *Revue des Deux Mondes*, 'absolutely denied the possibility of fitting out galleys with three oars and three men per bench, not only in the case of ancient Greeks and Romans, but also for the relatively more modern Venetian and Genoese galleys.' (*Le Triremi*, p3), going on to add, and in doing so striking close to the heart of the Italian Rear Admiral who had already found occasion to criticise the work of A Jal: 'et puisqu'on y croit posseder le secret des trirèmes du moyen âge, qu'on en fasse descendre une toute équipée des chantiers.' (p65).

3. Jurien de la Gravière, p65.

4. Before Fincati, contributions were made by G Gasoni, 'Dei navigli poltremi usati nell marina dagli antichi veneziani' [On polyreme vessels used in the ancient Venetian navy], in *Atti dell'Ateneo veneto* (Venice 1838), and A Jal, *Archéologie Navale* (Paris 1840), Vol I, Mémoire No 4.

5. R Burlet and A Zysberg, 'Le travail de la rame sur les galères de France vers la fin du XVIIe siècle', *Neptunia* 164 (Paris 1986).

6. 'The birth of this science is relatively recent and dates back to the Second World War. It is well known that a war brings only disadvantages apart from in certain scientific respects where it provides an unparalleled stimulus,' in *Analisi tempi e maitodi*, Istituto Callegaris, Treviso, Vol I.

7. The preceding period is less well documented. Apart from certain information taken from notary contracts, the first documents of any importance are those contained in the records of the Angioina Registry in Naples, lost during the last war, the Genoese Statutes, and certain sections of the Venetian Memorials – and none of these permits their certain reconstruction.

Rowing *alla zenzile*: the historical perspective

A wooden model of a sixteenth-century Venetian galley,[1] commissioned by Italian Navy Rear Admiral Luigi Fincati, was presented to the public on the occasion of the International Geographical Exhibition held in Venice in 1881 to demonstrate the possibility of fitting out a galley *ad tres remos ad banchum*[2] (with three oars per bench). For this reason it was complete with an entire crew of remarkable miniature oarsmen, all engaged in the act of rowing. Visitors to the Exhibition were also able to admire a full-scale navy lighter fitted out for the occasion with ten thwarts and thirty oars which was, according to the author 'rowed excellently by thirty men'.[3]

Although more than a century has now gone by, knowledge of the rowing of medieval galleys is still based completely on Fincati's findings, because no-one has undertaken similar research since his day.[4] As with previous studies into *voga a scaloccio* (galleys rowed by stepped tiers of long galley oars),[5] it was realised that ergonomic analysis needed to be applied to the results of historical research in order to

shed new light on this subject.[6] Four years' research in the Venetian archives revealed that the Venetian narrow galley underwent considerable development during the time period considered, in other words from the beginning of the fifteenth to the end of the sixteenth century.[7] This was partly due to an increase in naval artillery, which significantly altered the original layout.

A steady increase in the size of vessels, a shifting of the *corba de mezo* (midship frame) further forward and the raising of the bow and stern ends were some of the innovations that forced builders in that period into a continual empirical quest for new balance in order to adapt the *motore umano* (human engine) to these new requirements and achieve greater propulsive

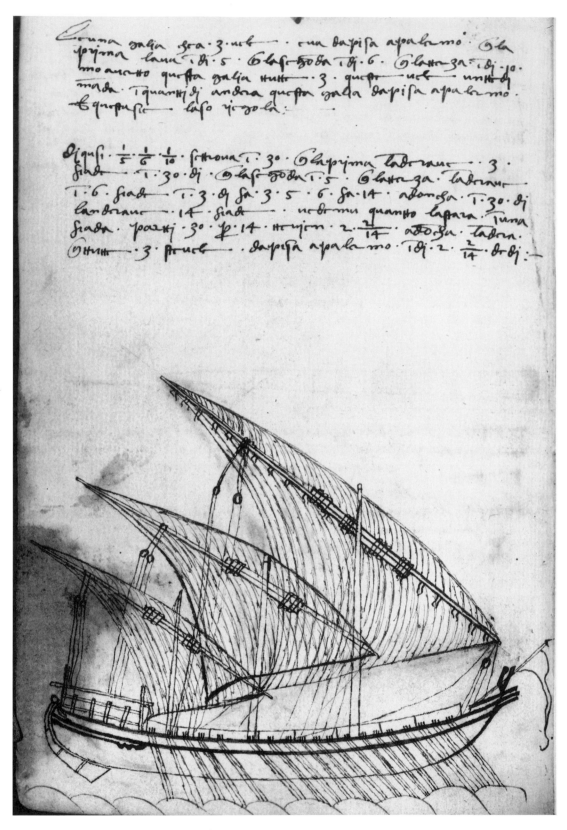

A page from the so-called Timbotta MS by Zorzi da Modone, dating from the middle of the fifteenth century. The vessel depicted is a Venetian galea grossa, or great galley. The largest mercantile galley of the period, this type clearly employed the 'trireme' alla zenzile rowing system, although in practice while at sea it would spend as much time as possible under sail; for this purpose it carried a powerful three-masted lateen rig. The manuscript is in the British Library, Cotton ms, Titus A XXVI, this illustration being f48v. (British Library)

Vettor Fausto in 1529, it marked the high point of galleys outfitted with several oars per bench, but also the beginning of their rapid decline.

The future of galley rowing lay in the use of a single large oar by the men on each bench, *remo a scaloccio*. The development of galley rowing was being further complicated by the increasing difficulty of finding men to work the oars. Mediterranean fleets had always made extensive use of volunteer, paid rowers whose availability, for various reasons, began to fall rapidly between the end of the fifteenth century and the beginning of the sixteenth century. In Venice, the use of slaves was strongly contested, officially for ethical reasons, but then finally introduced in 1545.[10] Volunteer oarsmen from mainland territories were initially used in order to fill gaps owing to recruitment difficulties. Because of the discomfort encountered by these new recruits, unused to a life at sea and unskilled as rowers, various ways of making their contribution more effective were put to the test by Fausto.[11]

The task was therefore to identify as precisely as possible the oldest well-documented rowing model that had not yet been excessively

8. Because we are discussing a galley with several oars per bench, and thus several thole pins, and this could give rise to confusion, we will use the term 'room' to denote the distance between thole pins of the same type, in other words relating to the same type of oar on two successive benches and not between thole pins of different oar types belonging to the same bench.

9. A Genoese, a Turkish and a French respectively (the last was apparently subsequently reduced to a quadrireme): 'and then as you know Your Highness ordered the building of a galley with five oars . . . and this galley was also a success and Prince Doria ordered the construction of a similar vessel with five oars for the Prince of Spain, which was not successful and is moored in Zenna and similarly another was built in Constantinople and did not succeed', ASV, Senato Mar, File 10: Archives Départmentales des Bouches-du-Rhônes, Cour des Comptes, B 1260, c.440-443: 'Inventaire de la galère reale quinquirème', 24 April 1545.

10. Alberto Tenenti, *La marine venitienne avant Lépant* (Paris 1962).

11. Vettor Fausto was one of the authors of these attempts due to having, 'found a way of fitting out these galley so well that they could be rowed easily by mainlanders as by sailors from the Levant', ASV, Senato Mar, reg. 26, c.160v.

thrust. Since it was obviously impossible to alter the physiological limits of the rower, an initial attempt was made to extend rowing movements through an increase, of necessity slight, in the spacing between benches,[8] together with a simultaneous changeover to a larger oar capable of providing greater leverage. Once the possibilities of system refinement were exhausted,

interesting attempts at new solutions were made.

The celebrated quinquereme was one result of this period of experimental transition. Although this exceptional vessel aroused harsh criticism as well as praise from its contemporaries, it prompted at least three attempts at imitation.[9] Built in the Venetian Arsenale by

contaminated by any later changes. With this criterion in mind, a strict ergonomic analysis was carried out on data relating to the rowing equipment of a narrow galley with 29 benches dating from the early part of the fifteenth century, which is accurately described in one of the records from a Venetian shipyard.[12] A sixteenth-century report that had already been brought to the attention of researchers, but had never been looked into, brought to light the general laws that governed oar arrangements.[13] The subsequent discovery of another report, predating the first by about thirty years, which very clearly illustrated rowing movements, confirmed the results of this research by providing incontestable historical evidence.[14] 'They made very small vessels with only one order of oars [ie file of oarsmen on each side of the vessel], called *galeas* which are very light for racing: they are useful for guard duties, reconnaissance, and for all expeditions where speed is a necessity.'[15] Thus stated a section of the *Tactics* concerning galleys included in the *Tema* by the Byzantine emperor Leo VI (AD 866–911).[16] The term *galea* (galley) is actually used in Byzantine sources from the tenth century, whenever the writer wished to describe a small war dromon that was fast, light and always equipped with a single order of oars.[17] Although there is no evidence to suggest that it was on these ancestral vessels that a second oar was introduced on the same bench for the first time, it is interesting to note that the term *galea* outlived the wide variety of other terms used to describe ancient vessels. Many hypotheses may be formulated, but it has to be remembered that medieval sources were often written long after the event and do not help to clarify the origins and development of bireme galleys. The iconography[18] and few surviving texts apparently confirm the presence of long vessels rowed by two rowers per oar,[19] with overlapping oars,[20] throughout the twelfth century and part of the thirteenth.

It is, however, difficult to establish how far this type was similar to the vessel used in the classical Greek or Roman period because no explicit descriptions of ancient rowing systems with more than one oar per bench are known. Nevertheless, the lack of documentary evidence does not necessarily mean that such vessels did not exist.

If it is considered that the third, outboard, rower, who was initially only an auxiliary rower with other duties,[21] was probably introduced about 1290[22] by the Genoese Benedetto Zaccaria,[23] it is dificult to explain how it was poss-

---

12. More specifically, the one described in 'Libro di appunti' by Zorzi Trombetta da Modone, British Library, Cotton ms, Titus A XXVI . See R C Anderson, ' Italian Naval Architecture about 1450', *The Mariner's Mirror* XI (London 1925). Readers may find useful the following full list of other reports in addition to the above manuscript: 'Libro di marineria', Biblioteca Nazionale di Firenze [National Library of Florence, hereafter referred to as BNF], ms Magliobechiano, cl XIX cod. 7 (by convention, since the partial analysis carried out by A Jal in his Mémoire No 5 of the *Archéologie Navale*, this work is always referred to as 'Fabrica al galere', although its actual title given on the title page is 'Libro di marineria'); 'Ragioni antique spettanti allíarte del mare et fabriche de vasselli', National Maritime Museum, Greenwich, NVT 19 – see A Chiggiato, *Le ragioni antique dell'architettura navale in Fonti per la storia di Venezia* (Venice 1987); 'Misure di vascelle etc. di . . . Proto nell'Arsenale di Ven.', ASV, Pinelli Files, Envelope 2, (published in U Tucci, 'Architettura navale veneziana. Misure di vascelli della metà del Cinquecento', in *Bollettino dell'Atlante Linguistico Mediterraneo*, 1963–64) ; 'Disegni di biremi, triremi, quadriremi', by Alessandro Picheroni, Biblioteca Nazionale Marciana, mss it, cl VII cod. 379 (7588) (although the innovative oar arrangements in this manuscript were considered improbable by contemporaries, it nevertheless contains historically accurate information on vessel dimensions and is thus worthy of serious attention), 'Instructione sul modo di fabricare galee', by Maestro Pre Teodoro de Nicoló, BNM, ms. it, cl, IV cod. 26 (5131) – see C F Lane, 'Naval Architecture about 1550', in *The Mariner's Mirror* XX (1934), and *Venice and History* (Baltimore 1969); Italian edition *Le Navi di Venezia*, Turin 1983); 'Navilii soma cioe vele lattine', by Hieronimo and Nicoló di Bernardin Secula, an unpublished manuscript found by Mauro Bondioli [of the two existing versions, one complete version is in ASV: early records which could fill gaps left by the Memorials, I volume, from p186 to p188 and a partial volume in another hand in ASV, Contarini files, envelope 11 (in course of publication)]; 'La Visione di Drachio', by Baldissera Drachio of 1594 in ASV, Contarini Files, envelope 25 (analysed by Fincati in *Le Triremi*). Missing from this list is the oldest known manuscript, compiled by Michele da Rodi and dating from about 1434. This was sold at auction by Sotheby's in London in 1966 and then disappeared without trace.

13. 'A brief essential summary of all the things that had to be done for the defence of the State in the Venetian Republic', by Alessandro Zorzi, formerly Nicoló – see E Concina, *Navis* (Turin 1990): a member of the Zorzi family from Negroponte, born on 17 July 1509, married to Donna Maria Michiel di Nicoló formerly Alise, he became Procurator, Senator, Counsellor reponsible for documents, Censor, Head of the Council of Ten and one of the 41.

14. Account by Nicoló Michiel, formerly Francesco dei Michiel di San Zuanne Novo, Governor of Biave, Galley Captain and ordained one of the Wise in 1554, died 23 April 1558 (ASV, Miscellanea, ms, Higher Council elections, reg. 1).

15. *Institutiones Militaires de L'Empereur Léon le Philosophe traduites en français par M. Joly de Maizeroi* (Paris 1770), quoted by Noël Fourquin, 'Galères du Moyen-Age', in *Quand voguaient les galères*, catalogue of exhibition held at the Musée de la Marine in Paris from October 1990 to January 1991.

16. Hélène Antoniadis-Bibicou, *Études d'histoire maritime de Byzance à propos du Théme des Caravisiens* (Paris 1966).

17. Hélène Ahrweiler, *Byzance et la mer* (Paris 1966), p414.

18. In particular: *Rerum Italicarum Scriptores*, Collection of Italian Historians from the Sixth Century to the Sixteenth century, edited by L A Muratori, Vol XXXI, Pietro da Eboli (Città di Castello 1904); 'Annales Genuenses Cafarii ejusque commuatorum', National Library of Paris, ms lat. 10136 (second half of twelfth century to the end of the thirteenth); 'Cantigas', by Alfonso il Saggio, National Library of Paris (thirteenth century).

19. 'Historia rerum in partibus transmarins gestarum a tempore successorum Mahumeth usque ad annum Domini MCLXXXIV, by the venerable William of Tyre, Archbishop', in *Gesta Dei per Francos* (Hanover 1611), Liber XII, pars XXII, p828 referring to an event of 1122: 'Erant sane in eadem classe quaedam naves rostratae quas gatos vocant, galeis maiores, habentes singulas remos centenos, quibus singulius duo erant remiges necessar.' Compare the theories of L Basch, *Le musée imaginaire de la marine antique* (Athens 1987), p222 and pp361–362.

20. A Anthiaume, *Le navire, sa construction en France et principalement chez les Normands* (Paris 1922), p133 quotes a passage from 'Historia rerum in partibus transmarinis gestarum', *Gesta Dei . . .*, Liber XX, pars XIV, p982 ('Erant sane in praefato exercita, naves longae, rostratae, geminis remorum instructae ordinibus, bellicis usibus habiliores, quae vulgo galae dicuntur, centum

quinquaginta'), interpreting this as evidence of the existence in the twelfth century of ships with two sets of overlapping oars. We also think it likely that Archbishop of Tyre intended to refer to galleys with two oars per bench, *geminis remorum*, considering the high number of such vessels in the above fleet and the fact that the ancient expression 'orders of oars' has never been clearly understood.

21. F C Lane, 'From Biremes to Triremes', *The Mariner's Mirror* XLIX (1963) and then in *Venice and History*; p47 of the Italian edition gives a passage from *The Chronicle of Muntaner* translated by Lady Goodenough (Hanover 1920) in which the author, writing between 1325 and 1328, tells us about a battle that took place in 1286: 'And while the galley slaves rowed, the crossbowmen were occupied with their weapons . . . and therefore the crossbowmen are not required to row as third rowers; they cannot aim their crossbows if they do. Apart from this, the conscripted crossbowmen do one more useful thing: when they see that a sailor in the crow's nest, or a rower on the bench is tired, and wants to refresh himself or drink, a crossbowman arrives to take over their oar until they have done what they need to do and are free again. This does not mean that there should not be ten galleys out of every hundred with third rowers on board able to reach any galley when they are needed.'

22. Marino Sanuto detto Torsello, 'Liber secretorum Fidelium Crucis super Terrae Sanctae recuperatione et conservatione', in *Gesta Dei per Francos* (Hanover 1611), Liber II, cap IV; the author, who was writing at a time between 1306 and 1321, tells us on p57: 'Sciendum quod in MCCXC anno Domini, quasi in omnibus galeis quae transfretabant per mare, duo in banco remiges remigabant: postmodum perspicaciores homines, cognoverunt quod tres possent remigare remiges super quolibet proedictorum, quasi omnes ad praesens hoc utuntur' (with reference to this work, note the finding of a copy of a fifteenth-century manuscript in BMC, Donà delle Rose Archive, ms No 223, which will allow researchers to make a comparison with the printed version). We should not, however, imagine that the entire oarage of the galley suddenly increased by one third, because this is much more likely to have happened gradually. It would be interesting to know whether the third oar was added simply because space was available on the bench, in the hope of a speed advantage, or if this was the result of specific experiments.

23. A famous sailor of the period – see C Manfroni, *Storia della marina Italia* (1902), Vol II, and R S Lopez, *Storia delle colonie genovesi nel Mediterraneo* (Bologna 1938).

Pages relating to the rowing of galleys in the mid sixteenth-century manuscript treatise of Alessandro Zorzi on the defence of the Venetian state. Archivio di Stati di Venezia, Archivio Proprio Contarini, busta 10. (By courtesy of the author)

ible for this new system of rowing to be invented, tested and become generally accepted within such a short space of time. The most probable hypothesis is that its origin, judging by the terms *ante quam* and *post quam*[24] in the documentation must date back to any time between the eleventh and twelfth centuries. It is certain, however, that as the galley gradually came to be considered a valid alternative to the most powerful warships of the period, it began to look more and more like the popular image of a pointed hull with an almost rectangular superstructure[25] known as a *telaro* bordered at either end by two transverse beams known as the *zovi* and at either side by *postizze* in which were mounted the thole pins of the oars.

In galleys with a single order of oars, the galley rowers were lined up near the central *corsia* (gangway) located on the *coverta* (deck) in line with the longitudinal centre line or *colomba*, and could therefore benefit from a much greater *zirone* or leverage of the oar than available on board previous hulls. In previous types of galley, the movements of the rowers were also essentially limited to stretching their arms as far forward as possible and then arching their backs in order to draw the oar towards themselves; they always remained seated on their own rowing bench. When a second rower was introduced, also equipped with his own oar, the bench was angled and much greater leverage was possible. It now became obvious that the rower was able to perform a much wider range of movements to give the *corpo* (hull)[26] of the vessel a much more effective propulsive thrust. The rower was thus at last able to rise from the bench and thrust his arms towards the bench in front of him (*ie* aft) to exploit his body strength and weight to the full.

It is, however, difficult to establish if the new system was the result of a slow evolutionary process or simply the result of combining two different types of rowing that were already known: rowing *seduta* (seated) and rowing *piedi* (standing).[27]

The fourteenth century saw the development of new triremes and trials in using first four and then five rowers on the same bench.[28] These experiments probably disappeared from the collective memory, and the ideas reappeared only much later with the advent of Vettor Fausto's quadriremes and quinqueremes.

As already discussed, the development of oarage was closely connected with a desire to achieve greater propulsive thrust. The Venetian shipbuilders of the fifteenth century lacked ergonomic knowledge and therefore could progress only by experiment and experience. By such methods, change must necessarily have been slow and uncertain. One thing that never

underwent any change and dated back to the period from the fifteenth to the sixteenth century and even later, was the height of the *puntale in coverta* (deck pillar or stanchion) and hence the depth in hold. The pillar always fluctuated between 185cm and 187cm, while the vessel's draught was only 139cm or four Venetian feet.[29] An increase from 133cm to 154cm was nevertheless recorded in the distance between the rest point of the oar on the *postizza* and the waterline. The dimensions of Venetian narrow galleys were not, however, observed by all navies. The navies of the western Mediterranean preferred a higher stanchion that would have improved seaworthiness under both sail and oar, as well as preventing the hull's progress being impeded by the oarage and topside dragging through the water when heeled. The shipwrights could hardly increase the spacing between benches at all, because it depended on the size of the human body.

---

24. Or the tenth century with the *Tactics* of Emperor Leo, and 1290, when biremes changed over to triremes.

25. Slightly trapezoid in fact, because the *zovo* in the bows was shorter than that in the stern.

26. State Archives of Florence, Archivio Mediceo del Principato, file 2131, c.1v: 'By the hull of the galley and the first shell we now mean all the wooden structure that makes this galley whole and perfect in itself: without any mast, lateen or any other addition and exactly what one sees in the shipyard before launch, what is known as "black".'

27. Assuming this latter style was already known. Even today, particularly at the time of the Regatta, one can still see Venetian-style rowing practised by oarsmen standing upright on the deck.

28. 'Liber secretorum Fidelium Crucis', *Gesta Dei per Francos*, Liber II, cap. IV, p57: 'nihilominus sciendum est quod in MCCCXVI anno Domini, probatum fuit per gentem Venetam de faciendo quod in galeis quatuor remiges pro banco remigarent: quaeque experientia visa est utilis, tam pro navigio quod bene regebat eos, quam quia dextre remigabant remiges antedicti: & quia navigium ex quaterna remigatione pro banco, velocius & celerius navigabat, quam ad terzarolos tantummodo deputatum', p65: 'Rerumtamen, ut remiges galearum ad quartarolos melius valeant remigare, & proecipue qui fuerint in maioribus ad quintarolos remos', p77: 'Caeterum si caperetur pro consilio quod galeae armarentur remis ad quatuor pro banco, quod aliquando est probatum, & laudabile potest esse, ut est dictum,

consulendum est, acetiam faciendum quod praedicta gens tota in XL galeis, & praedicto navigio non munito decenter ponentur'.

29. The Venetian foot was about 34.77cm. The units of measure were divided into a long step of 5 feet; a short step of 3 feet; a foot of 12 large finger-breadths or 16 small finger-breadths; each small finger-breadth was further divided into 4 rods (ASV, 'Navilii sottili'). The span also existed and measured exactly the same as the Genoese span: 'And 7 spans make one pace', Libro di Zorzi, c. 16r. According to a paper on the construction of Venetian galleys currently under preparation that has involved more than eight years of research in the archives, it transpires that the span was probably divided into eighty-sevenths, each measuring about 3mm.

A description of the movements of the first rower next to the central gangway,[30] known as the *pianiero*,[31] reveals how these movements must necessarily have an absolute limit. From the beginning of the fifteenth century to its peak size, occurring before 1530–1540, the bench spacing increased by only 6.5cm.[32] The development of the oar inner *zirone*, leverage (or length of the oar loom) was more complicated, however. In order to assess this correctly on the basis of the available documentation, it was necessary to compare the ratio between the *zirone* of the *pianiero* oar and the width of the galley deck. From these data it was established that the ratio increased from 58 per cent dur-ing the first years of the fifteenth century to stop at 64 per cent during the first half of the sixteenth century.[33] In simple terms, this means that the gradual increase in galley length and breadth in time was accompanied by a much greater increase in the *zirone*, and thus in the size of the actual oar. It is extremely inter-esting to note that the maximum dimensions of both bench spacing and *pianiero* oar during the first half of the sixteenth century were the same as those adopted during experiments with long galley oars in Venice, and they remained the same thereafter for more than a century with-out undergoing further change. The extreme limits had been reached.

Owing to the development of artillery and the increasing use of this weapon on board gal-leys, the *corsia* or central gangway was further extended both toward the stern and, more par-ticularly, towards the bows. The first cannon were located directly on a *palmetta* on the bows,[34] but were then installed on the *corsia* with the *palmetta* simultaneously lowered from the top edge of the *zovo* to the lower edge in order to make the aiming of the artillery easier. This left less space available for rowing, however, because the *zirone* was reduced. One reason was because one end of the forward bench rested directly on the *zovo*[35] and a fixed space, a foredeck platform or *coniglia*, had not yet been introduced for the use of the artil-lery.[36] The stern did not escape change either, although those modifications did not directly affect the efficiency of rowing.

One of the first problems faced at the begin-ning of this research arose because information provided by manuscripts did not agree with rowing requirements calculated through ergonomic studies: the breadth between the outer end of the *zovo di popa* and the thole of the *postizzo* oar did not allow enough space for oarsmen on the aftermost bench, although the rowing rhythm was set by the oarsmen on that very bench. Thorough examination of the ico-nography[37] subsequently showed that one ap-

30. From the *Della Milizia Marittima*, p153: 'You must know that the freemen [free rowers], when they begin to pull the oar, brace their foot against a beam they call a *pontapiede*, which is positioned between benches and pull themselves upright until they are over the bench in front and then they throw themselves back toward their own bench with great force. In this way, they stretch and extend their rowing movements as far as possible.'

31. The term *pianieri* denotes both the rower and the oar and its associated *schermo* or thole. The *postizi* and the *terzichi* were the second and third rowers respectively.

32. A study of the two fifteenth-century galleys (the one described in 'Libro di marineria' is incomplete) ie one in 'Libro di Zorzi' and one in 'Ragioni antique', the 'room' was 3 feet, 6½ finger-breadths, while Maestro Nicoló's was 3 feet, 6 finger-breadths; from 'Misure di vascelli', rounded up to 3 feet 9 finger-breadths when specified as 3 feet 8½ finger-breadths or 3 feet 8¾ finger-breadths.

33. Narrow (*sottil*) galley from beginning of fifteenth century (Zorzi Trombetta da Modon, c. 43r and 44r): deck width . . . 13 feet, 7 small finger-breadths

grip of *pianiero* oar . . . 7 feet, 12 small finger-breadths Narrow galley from about 1540 ('Misure di vascelli', c 13v and 14r):

deck width . . . 15 feet, 4 small finger-breadths grip of *pianiero* oar . . . 7 feet, 12½ small finger-breadths.

34. See drawing in *Peregrinatio in Terram Sanctam* by Breydenbach, reproduced on this page.

35. This remains constant in fifteenth-century documents, and is the distance between the outside of the forward zovo and the first postizzo thole pin; 1½ feet in all cases.

36. This had already been introduced at the time *Visione* was produced (1594).

37. See drawings in Raphael's *Quaderno* in the Gallery of the Accademia in Venice: drawing No 12650 recto by Leonardo da Vinci kept in Windsor Castle – see *The Drawings of Leonardo da Vinci in the collection of Her Majesty the Queen at Windsor Castle*, by Kenneth Clark (London 1969), Vol II. This drawing was a draught for a vessel that could be rowed artificially. See also plan by Bartolomeo Crescentio, *Della Nautica Mediterranea* (Rome 1601), p46, and the bas-relief of a galley in the monument to General Ship-Chandler Alessandro Contarini and kept in the Basilica di S Antonio in Padua (Published in *Della Milizia Marittima*, tables VI and VII). The first two drawings do not contain a small step, but it can be seen that the *zovo* is lower than the *postizza*.

A well-known engraving from Breydenbach's Peregrinatio in Terram Sanctam *showing merchant galleys at Venice preparing for a voyage about 1485. The galley reveals an early form of cannon mounted directly over the bow; later developments in galley design were partially dictated by the desire to increase and improve firepower. (Author)*

parently unimportant detail was paradoxically out of place. The aft structure of seventeenth-century galleys, whose form is well known to researchers, has always been characterised by a cross-deck known as a *spalla* located at the aft end of the gangway between the after *zozo* and the aftermost bench that permitted easier access to the galley by a ladder. Because the cross-deck was at the same level as both the *zovo* and the *postizza*, it seems logical that the top of the ladder should also have been at the same height, and this is borne out by numerous illustrations from the period. In other sixteenth-century images, however, the upper edge of the ladder is located lower than the *postizza*. This suggests that because the foremost beam did not exist, the aftermost beam was not present either, and the space necessary for the oarsmen on the aftermost bench was cut out of the poop deck to accommodate the angle of the benches. These forward and after beams were introduced on narrow galleys only during the second half of the sixteenth century.

This short summary of the main stages in the development of rowing *alla zenzile* could not be concluded without discussing the oars themselves. Mainly made out of beech owing to its flexibility and strength, and sometimes made out of maple, birch and larch, *zenzile* oars were narrow, manageable, and could be carried by one man. Venetian *zenzile* oars were greater in diameter than western Mediterranean oars

and had broader blades. Two wooden 'fishes' known as *galaverne* were also applied to oars to protect against wear.[38] Twelve to fourteen kilogrammes of lead[39] were inserted into the *collo* (neck) of *pianieri* oars as a counterweight. This could explain why oars broken during voyages had to be returned to the dockyard.

Captain Pantero Pantera wrote in his *Armata Navale*, published in 1614: 'some say that it would be better to fit out galleys with three oars per bench in the ancient manner, that was termed rowing *alla zenzile* (and is still so-called by sailors today)', and added, 'but because I have not yet seen any galley fitted out in this manner, I do not dare to make judgement and would not be able to select the best manner.'[40] If, even at that time, a memory of rowing *ad tres remos ad banchum* (with three oars per bench), here referred to as *alla zenzile* in the sense of a simple (ordinary) oar as opposed to a long or *scaloccio* oar, was only retained by a few survivors of the era, it is easy to understand how Admiral Jurien de la Gravière found Fincati's theory scarcely credible.

In 1583 the nobleman Nicolò Suriano, returning from his duties as Navy Quartermaster after three years, eight months and twelve days of absence, presented a concluding report to the Venetian Senate before he left office.[41] His report not only recounted the main events that occurred under his command, but also contained certain important notes on improve-

ment of the fleet. In particular, the author remembered a conversation he had had with Gian Andrea Doria on the occasion of his visit to the Venetian Arsenale. Doria was interested to find out Suriano's opinion on the two systems of rowing, and, after agreeing on the reasons that prompted the latter to prefer three oars per bench, then went on to discuss the use of the *galozza* oar widely used by the Genoese. This must have surely left the Venetian perplexed, because Suriano's report actually advanced a proposal for reintroducing the old *zenzile* system abandoned after the Cyprus war (1569–1573).[42] Although his observations must have seemed somewhat anachronistic to many in view of the fact that all contemporary navies had already adopted the large oar some time previously,[43] they nevertheless gave rise to a certain amount of discussion within the Senate, as we may see from two accounts kept in the Venetian archives. This was not really a struggle between two opposing factions, between conservatives and progressives as they would be described today, but rather an important reflection on events occurring within the shipyard and consequently within the fleet. After the Cyprus war, in fact, work within the *Casa*[44] fell off considerably. Quite the opposite was true of shipyards under Turkish control, which restored the Turkish fleet to full strength following the battle of Lepanto. The numbers of *marangoni* (carpenters) employed in the

---

38. 'I would also like the oarage, and by that I mean the oars to be narrower than those we use and with the blade smaller (as Western sailors use them), and with the inner part known as the *zirone* one-third the length of the oar, with their battens (as you know these are the two bands of wood inserted above and below the *zirone*) of varying size in order to adapt the oar's weight,' *Della Milizia Marittima*, pp78 and 79. The item *galaverna* or 'fish' appears constantly in a list of expenses at the shipbuilding yard from 1536 to 1544 (ASV, Contarini Files, envelope 25), apart from the years 1540 and 1541.

39. 'If the oar is properly counterweighted, the rowers need much less lead, which is recovered if the oar is broken, because *pianieri* from other galleys are normally paid XXV to XXX lire', ASV, Contarini Files, envelope 11, Account by Nicoló Michiel. The Venetian navy was the only navy to pay its rowers for the lead.

40. Pantero Pantera, *L'Armata Navale* (Rome 1614), p151.

41. Several copies of this account exist, though we preferred the one kept in the BMC, Donà delle Rose Archive, file 153, because the fact that it contains many corrections in the same hand suggests that it is the original.

42. 'He asked me what I thought of the rowing *alla galozza* and rowing with three oars per bench and I told him that there was no comparison when one wished to make a galley go fast with equal effort and I told him

many reasons, that he was already well aware of, and this confirmed my opinion, so I suggest, so that Your Excellency is aware, do not row your galleys with a single oar but fit them out with small oars. He answered me: for our sins and for one single benefit, when we need to go to Spain, Barbary, Sicily and Levant, where we are always in great danger of Barbary vessels, we take ordinary galleys so that four or five men can row per bench and when necessary we reinforce them with sailors from other galleys. This sole benefit makes us overlook many other inconveniences and expenses because it means we can sail safely.' Report by Nicoló Suriano, BMC.

43. The date of introduction of the long galley oar is uncertain. In Venetian records, the first firm evidence of the dispatch of 60 long oars to the General Sea Captain was on 30 July 1534 (ASV, Masters and Chandlers at the Arsenale, reg. 8, c37v). Once the first experimental stage was over, it was decided to make these new long oars during May 1537, though their application was left to the decision of galley captains (ASV, Sea Senate, reg. 24, c21r). One hundred were listed in a 1559 inventory at the Arsenale (ASV, Miscellaneous papers not belonging to any archive, envelope 2, paragraph 18). A figure of one thousand was mentioned in another copy (BMC, Gradenigo Archive, file 193) for the same date. It certainly seems curious that at this time (1534), the records do not attribute this invention to either Vettor Fausto (who launched his first quadrireme two years earlier and did not neglect his studies of rowing after that date because in 1542 he presented a plan on this subject for mainland galleys), Proto Bressan or other Venetian

masters. This would appear to indicate that the *galozza* oar came from outside the Venetian Arsenale. This is confirmed by the galleys of the Knights of Rhodes back in 1530. A French document (Bibliothèque Nationale de Paris, ms Fr 3174, c.21-26: 'Description au vray de la construction du corps d'une galère neufve, subtile ou bastardelle, qu'on poura armer à la galoche, c'est à dire quatrirame, et l'order qu'il convyent observer en lad. construction', Marseille, 25 June 1521; another copy in the National Archives in Paris (Marine, B-6, c18–23) shows, if the date is correct, not only that long galley oars came in before 1530, but also that the need for a fourth man as reserve was already apparent at that time. Conversely, from the report already quoted ('It is more useful to have three oars per bench than a single oar'), the author states: 'They say that Western sailors row with four men to the oar. When in the Western Mediterranean in 1526, I saw galleys of the King of France and Prince Doria and again in 1532, when Prince Doria was crowned, I spent some ten days with him in the Gulf of Valona and several times rowed with them, I never saw four men per bench. It is true that men taken in friendly or hostile places are immediately put in chains and made to row. If taken for ransom, they are given greater torment so that they are ransomed sooner and for larger sums. If not held to ransom, they make them row to make them accustomed to it and train them until they have enough men to outfit another galley with three men per oar.'

44. This was the name given to the Shipyard in Venice (an abbreviation of Casa dell'Arsenale).

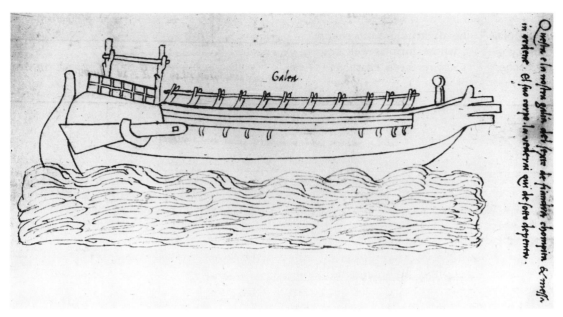

Drawings of the large galea di Fiandra *of about 1400 from the manuscript known as 'Fabrica di Galere' in the Biblioteca Nazionale Firenze, manoscritto Magliabechiano, cl XIX cod 7. These Venetian merchantmen were designed for the long and potentially tempestuous voyage to Flanders, which as the illustrations suggest was carried out under sail wherever possible. A point of interest is the retention of the traditional steering oars as emergency back-up to the curved centreline rudder (referred to in the 'Fabrica' as a* timon bavonescho, *indicating that it was introduced into the Mediterranean from Bayonne or the Biscay ports).* (Author)

shipyard fell from 1022 in 1559[45] to just 250 in 1581.[46]

Galley captains also intervened increasingly to urge master-builders to make changes to the angle of rowing in an attempt to find the optimum arrangement.[47] This situation prompted some to present reports on the re-organisation of the shipyard.[48] One of these memos was drawn up by Alessandro Zorzi, and formed part of an extremely important document in which rowing was at last tackled from a technical viewpoint by comparing it *'alla similitudine de una stagiera'* (to a model) in order to obtain general rules and apply them also to more ancient writings.

Zorzi provides the modern reader with the only contemporary description of the early *scaloccio* rowing carried out by free rowers:

the *pianiero* rower, who is the first towards the central gangway to pull the oar *a strapada*, he makes three movements: one above the bench in front of him, the second above the *pontapiede* and the third above his bench pulling backwards. But the *postizzo* makes only two movements, one above the *pontapiede* and the second above his bench pulling backwards. The *terzichio* actually makes only one movement which is above his bench pulling backwards and for greater strength, he often rests one foot on the *pontapiede*.

Zenzile rowing, usually carried out by rowers who were freemen, was described by Nicolò Michiel:

I say that all galleys have 150 *galiotti* (oarsmen) who all row in different ways, and firstly the *pianiero*, who makes more movements owing to the fact that he determines the speed of the galley by rowing, this man makes three movements: one when he rises on to the *pontapiede*, the second when he climbs on to the bench, the third when he throws himself back on to the bench. These movements provide very great force when rowing[49] . . . the *postizzo*, which is the second oar, makes only two movements,[50] the *terzichio* climbs only onto the *pontapiede* and therefore makes only one and no more.[51]

So far, movements have been described for a type of rowing known as *a strapada*,[52] in other words, the broadest, most powerful form possible. This was performed by free rowers rowing with both *zenzile* and *a scaloccio* oars, although movements were less accentuated using the latter method.[53] As pointed out above, however, another type of rower was also used, the convict, who rowed in yet another way: *la rancata*.

As I have said, *rancata* rowing was short and fast (the only thing governing these two conditions was the chain that prevented *galiotti* from rising high and moving backwards). This is good . . . because it brings two advantages. One of these is the speed of movement that the short, fast rowing action provides because the galley can move very fast without resting or stopping, while the other thing is that, when rowing, the *galeotti* are forced to stand upright

45. ASV, Miscellaneous papers not belonging to any file, envelope 2; BMC, Morosini Archive, file 302; BMC, Gradenigo Archive, file 193.

46. ASV Secret Senate, significant mixed subjects, file 55, 'Writings of Zuan Faher, 1581, 24 October'. Although 250 are noted in the report, 100 of these were actually old carpenters unfit for work. The number of different trades employed at the Arsenale reached abnormal proportions during the period 1569–1570 during the great preparations for the war of Cyprus. See F C Lane, *Navires et Constructeurs à Venise pendant la Renaissance* (Paris 1965), tables J and K on pp231–232, which do not, however, refer to the above document. In 1580, in a memorial to two old and leading carpenters at the Arsenale, it is said that during a test to take on new tradesmen for the *Casa*, 150 carpenters presented themselves, but only 20 or 30 had previous experience in the Arsenale (ASV, Contarini File, envelope 10).

47. Suriano complains that, against all logic, the galley captains themselves, who he defines as 'fanciful intellects', are responsible for these changes.

48. 'Ricordi intorno la Casa dell'Arsenale', by Baldissera Drachio (ASV, Masters and Chandlers to the Arsenale, envelope 533) and report by Taduri (*idem*).

49. Until this time, therefore, *liberi* [free] *pianieri* rowers made the same movements whether rowing with a long oar or *alla zenzile*.

50. As we have already seen, the *libero* [free] *postizzo* at the long oar did not reach the bench from the front but simply mounted the *pontapiede*.

51. In this case too, the *libero* [free] *terzichio* at the long oar made a less expansive movement because he did not mount the *pontapiede* like the *libero*.

52. Cristoforo Da Canale tells us in this regard that; 'this manner of rowing, as we have said, is long and laborious and for two more reasons damaging not only to the men who use it but also to the galley's progress. Rowing slowly in this way makes the men lose momentum and speed. Because the men throw their entire bodies backward, they lose much effort and become dazed by the shaking of their heads.' (*Della Milizia Marittima*, p153)

53. It is, however, interesting that the Senate, when deciding on the construction of long galley oars on 7 May 1537, made the following statement with regard to the experiment carried out on Jacomo Marcello's galley: 'This measure has made what was originally the worst into the best and much faster than all the others in the fleet, despite being such a large galley.' (ASV Senato Mar, reg.24, c.21r)

and brace their foot against a small step in front of them (usually called a *scalettino* by westerners) so that they are working with their entire bodies and with their head and brain more rested and calm.

The description of this *forzata, zenzile* rowing (*ie* by convicts)[54] is surprising because we know that convict *scaloccia* rowers from subsequent periods rowed using much more extensive movements.[55]

Another interesting report[56] completes current knowledge of the differences between rowing *alla zenzile* and *alla galozza* and shows that such differences can essentially be separated into three categories: one strictly technical, one economic and one utilitarian. Although opinions vary over the propulsive thrust obtained by rowers using the two methods and the consequent speed of the galley, it is evident that speed also depends on the lines of the hull and not only on the type of rowing. Although manuscripts describe only theories put forward by supporters of three oars per bench, it is significant that of the three men who handled the big oars,

the *pianiero* alone takes the oar towards the stern yet sometimes occasionally his [two] companions do the pulling, which may be misleading because the captain will not be aware of this, and he soon becomes tired and then the other two become tired, since the rowing cannot be sustained over a long voyage, [and be-

cause the size of the oar makes it more subject to wind action], it is worse with the sea rough and windy because those big oars prevent the galley moving forward and the *galiotti* experience much hardship and become tired more easily and if an oar falls into the sea, the *galiotto* finds it difficult to retrieve because of its size.[57]

If one of these rowers becomes ill, and because all of them are almost indispensable to work an oar of such size, the result was that 'the other two, who could not perform the task of three, ship the oar and that bench becomes useless.'[58] This consideration is fundamental for understanding the reasons why galley captains insisted that they wished their galleys to be crewed *inquartare*[59] (with an extra fourth man). All of these considerations naturally did not apply to *zenzile* rowing because the lighter, more slender oars could each be moved independently of the others. One curious detail is that the fourth man had no space to sleep except upon a board positioned between the benches close to the crossbow stowage. The other rowers were also accommodated with greater discomfort than rowers who rowed with three oars per bench, where one rower rested above the three *zironi*, one on the bench and the other in *balanza*, in other words leaning on the bench.[60]

One basic factor probably taken into consideration by the Venetian treasury was the fact that an extra fourth man for narrow galleys and a fifth for great galleys would have led to a

significant increase in cost.[61] However, because convicts were not paid any money at all, on 24 February 1586 the Senate did permit convict galleys to take on a fourth rower.[62] Although not specifically authorised, the same must have occurred in galleys rowed by free men. The extra man on each bench increased overall vessel weight by more than four tons, owing to the weight of his body, possessions and barrel of water – not to mention the weight of his biscuits, wine, water and wood for cooking.[63] The waterline therefore rose up to the lower edge of the *zenta* (wale) at the *corba de mezo* (midships frame), and reduced the galley's seaworthiness.

Although many more arguments against *galozza* rowing[64] exist in archive documents, only one final and important observation need be made. Cristoforo Da Canale tells us that there were two types of *zenzile* rowing: one which employed all three oars of equal length measured from the outside of the *postizza* to the end of the blade, and another which used oars of three different lengths, but the same problem evidently also applied to *galozza* rowing:

I believe . . . the unequal length better for two reasons: the first is that if each of the oars extends over the sea by its own length, they will all break the surface at three different points at the same time . . . This allows the galley to travel twice as fast as the other type. Since the oars are the same size on the second type, these

54. The fact that convicts could also row *alla zenzile* is easily borne out by a magnificent inventory carried out in 1555 of five Tuscan galleys (Florence State Archives, Medicean Archive of the Principate, file 627. The inventory carried out upon the return of these galleys is in file 2131 of the same archive). After listing all the *armizzi* or equipment on board each one, including 150 or 144 *zenzile* oars 'with their leads and "fishes" ', according to whether the galleys were captains' vessels or ordinary vessels, the document lists all the rowers, almost 800 divided into a starboard gang and a port gang, including both convicts and slaves. Their names, distinguishing marks, ages (usually between 20 and 40) and origins were also indicated. The reason for the sentence, the judicial body, sentence, duration of punishment and roll number were also given in the case of convicts.

55. 'Le travail de la rame sur les galères de France vers la fin du XVIIe siècle'.

56. 'It is more useful to have three oars per bench than one single oar.'

57. *Idem.*

58. *Idem.*

59. The fourth oarsman was not, though, of any advantage during rowing *a scaloccio* or *alla zenzile*: 'Whoever wishes to discuss a galley with four oars per bench will say that the fourth oar only performs half a movement (compared to the single movement performed by the *terzichio*)', report by Nicoló Michiel on the fourth

zenzile oar. Zorzi was of the same opinion; 'whoever wishes to be clear on this point, let them carry out a manual trial in a *sottil* galley in this way: firstly make the *pianiero* stand in his place and work that oar, he will see that he rows it perfectly well, but with all the necessary effort: then let him make the *postizzo* alone row the same oar standing in his place, he will see that he succeeds in rowing but more slowly, with greater difficulty and with greater effort than the *pianiero*; then let him make the *terzichio* alone standing in his place work that oar, he will see that he can barely move it. But if the fourth tries to row standing in his place, he cannot move it at all and neither can the fifth because they are too close . . . to the thole . . . The fourth and fifth are therefore superfluous and do not add any advantage in a *sottil* galley but are a pointless expense, bringing disadvantage to the rest of the galley, with danger of drowning and harming all the others.' It is also interesting to note that when a fourth man was added to *sottil* galleys, the commanders' galleys naturally had to have five men to maintain their extra prestige. This gave rise to a series of extremely dangerous complications, as Suriano reported; 'and because the galley captains clearly see that if they wish to pursue galleys rowed by four or five rowers per oar they will have to increase their crews or be left behind, so they do everything in their power to add a fourth man to their galleys and as a result of this every four galley crews become three.'

60. He also refused to believe that rowing *alla galozza* would allow two soldiers to be carried rather than one,

except for relatively short periods (but it was shown that this occurred with *zenzile* oars as well). The biggest worries were the excess weight on the hull, with so many men on board, and the risk of sickness that immediately arose.

61. The author of 'E' più utile . . . [It is more useful . . .]' considered the Venetian fleet at the time of writing, made up of 10 rowed by free men and 19 by convicts, thus calculating the increased expense due to an extra man per bench at 160,070 ducats per year and 1292 rowers to cover the additional requirement.

62. Also establishing that all convict galleys should have 24 benches per gang. In 1559 it was also decided that these galleys should be standardised and built only under the instructions of the foreman carpenter.

63. 'E' più utile . . . [It is more useful . . .]': 'This multitude of people was the reason why biscuits could be carried for little longer than 40 days and even less when extra soldiers were added. An extra man per bench will weigh 14 *miera* in all, which, with the biscuits, wine and water and wood for cooking will load down the galley so much that the deck is under water, which will make it go very slowly whether rowed or sailed. Experience has shown that any small load over the ordinary causes great damage to any vessel and more to the galleys.'

64. Apart from the debatable possibility of greater speed, points in favour of a single long oar were an improvement in the *sciare* [wake] and the elimination of 'rowing noise on secret missions', 'Brief summary . . .'.

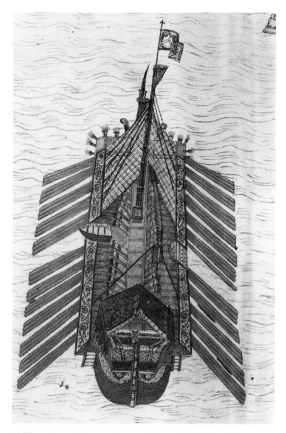

A Venetian galley under oars from Cristoforo da Canale's sixteenth-century published work De Milizia Marittima. *The vessel is being rowed* alla zenzile. *Many of the details of contemporary galleys can be seen in this drawing, including the tent-like canopy that could be rigged over the waist of the vessel. The enhanced forward gun battery of the galleys of this period is marked by stylised explosions from the cannon muzzles.*

are bound to break the water surface in the same place and, because they are positioned only a short distance apart, almost all the breaks occur at the same point . . . The other reason is that the blades of the *postizzio* and *terzichio* oars cannot be drawn to produce a wake in the same way as others of the same size.[65]

65. *Della Milizia Marittima*, p80. Also A Zorzi, 'When the oar is pulled by one and then another, the water is live and resistant instead of dead and broken so that the galley rower pulls harder on the oar and expends much less effort by pushing forward on to the *pontapiede* and throwing himself back.' ASV, Contarini Archive, envelope 25) gives the following lengths and quantities:

33 ft *sottil* galley *pianieri*	No 98
31 ft *sottil* galley *pianieri*	No 442
30½ ft *sottil* galley *pianieri*	No 750
29 ft *sottil* galley *postizi*	No 352
28½ ft *sottil* galley *postizi*	No 596
26½ ft *sottil* galley *terzichi*	No 528
27 ft *sottil* galley *terzichi*	No 132
28 ft *sottil* galley *terzichi*	No 192

Preliminary observations on the problems involved in rowing

The oared propulsion of ancient vessels had little in common with the rowing familiar to-day. It would hardly be a paradox to say that the only common factor is the use of an oar. In those days, rowing was linked to a notion of time rather than distance. Time in galleys was regulated by small, half-hour sandglasses or 'ampoulettes'. Galleys might row one or two ampoulettes, or more if the relay system was adopted, because the effort involved could not be sustained very long without rest, otherwise the rowers risked getting tired rapidly.

Another even greater difference was in the rowing technique itself. As in *alla zenzile* rowing, oarsmen rowing *a scaloccio* made use of the weight of their bodies. They had to rise from their bench and then drop back on to the same bench, applying the maximum weight possible to the oar. This operation was carried out with arms outstretched in both rowing modes. This simple description clearly shows that it is far removed from the type of rowing as now understood.

The benches were made of wood covered in sheepskin or cowhide, and the oars were heavy, though well-balanced (particularly in *a scaloccio* rowing). The large oars used in *a scaloccio* rowing were anything up to 12m long in an ordin-ary galley and weighed around 130kg. They were to go even further, because at the end of the seventeenth century the *Grande Réale* of King Louis XIV – a prestige flagship – used oars 14.6m long; it would seem that this figure was never exceeded. The oars used in *alla zenzile* rowing were 'lighter', weighing 50 to 60kg, but the largest of them measured close on 10m and the mode of rowing was sufficiently complex for oarsmanship to become a real craft. In *a scaloccio* rowing, the size and weight of the oars made them dangerous objects unless handled expertly. It is obvious that they were a world away from sliding seats and lightweight oars.

Any study or analysis of the working methods of oarsmen can only be conducted on the assumption that conditions are favourable: more or less flat calm, vessel horizontal and at its design waterline. Waves, rolling and pitching in fact imply a number of parameters which this chapter glosses over because there are too many to include them all and they are a somewhat difficult proposition. There are campaign accounts, moreover, to remind us that it only needed a slight swell to cause rowing difficulties and that rowing directly into the wind would quickly become an impossible task.

The work of the oar is governed by a number of size parameters such as:
– The height from the base of the thole above the waterline.
– The length of the oar.
– The relative lengths of this oar inside and outside the thole.
– The position of the oarsmen's seat relative to the thole line. In a vertical plane, the position

Schematic section of galley. (René Burlet)

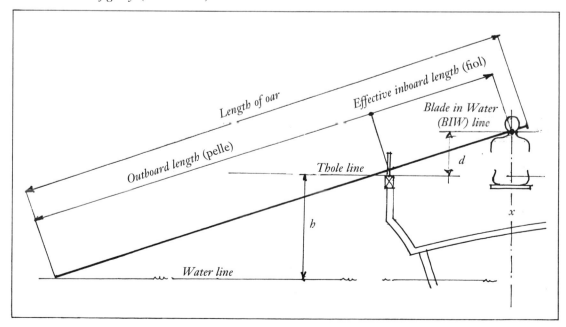

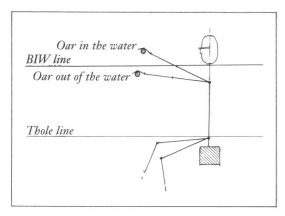

The position of the rower. The relationship between the BIW line and the rower's body was crucial in terms of efficiency. (René Burlet)

of the seat once again has to be calculated relative to that of the thole.

Faced with such a large diversity in the size of the oar blades, the authors always took as reference the axis of the oar and the end of the blade.

When the oarsman is holding the oar, with the latter out of the water, if he slowly lifts his wrists there is a moment when his oar touches the water. This point is very important because it represents the limit of engagement marked by a line parallel to the ship's centre line for a given oarsman (blade in water line or BIW line). If the oarsman lifts his wrists above this line, his oar dips into the water and he starts his work cycle, and if his wrists are below this line his oar is out of the water, corresponding to the non-active part of the cycle.

The position of the oarsman relative to this line is important:

- If this line it very low (for him), he will have to lower his arms to a greater or lesser extent to keep his oar out of the water in the return stroke, and this might impede or restrict his movement.

- If, on the other hand, this line is very high, when the rower comes to engage his oar in the water he may have to raise his arms too high. This is not a very comfortable position, and means that he is unable to put as much effort into the stroke. This is almost instinctively understood, but we must not forget that the exercise could last for hours.

The authors have attempted to find representative models for this study. This has not always been easy because it is vital to know all the parameters of the work station. For *a scaloccio* rowing, which was the first method to be studied in France, there was a lot of good quality and verifiable information. At the end of the seventeenth century the galley had a well defined form and constant dimensions. There

is no question but that we owe this abundance of writings to Colbert, a minister in the time of Louis XIV, because it was a subject in which he had a particular interest.

For *alla zenzile* rowing, the problem was more difficult. This method was used for a much longer period and at a time when galleys underwent considerable change with the advent of artillery. There is plenty of documentary evidence from Venetian times, but few descriptions of the method of rowing – everybody in Venice would know how to do that. Special circumstances were required in order to obtain accurate information, for example a comparison with another method. The major development in hull structures led the authors to adopt two examples: one a vessel from the fifteenth century and the other from the sixteenth century, and it will be seen that there is a considerable difference between the two. In particular, between these two dates, the rowers' work station underwent considerable modification, and the sixteenth-century galley was already equipped to make the transition between the two types of rowing: *alla zenzile* and *a scaloccio*. It might even have been possible without too much difficulty to change over

Zorzi's Principle, which advocated positioning the rowers within half the distance between the outrigger (apostis) *and the edge of the gangway* (coursie) *for maximum leverage. 'Zorzi's limit' was followed down to the end of galley construction for all except* Réales *with seven rowers per bench and* Patronnes *with six.* (René Burlet)

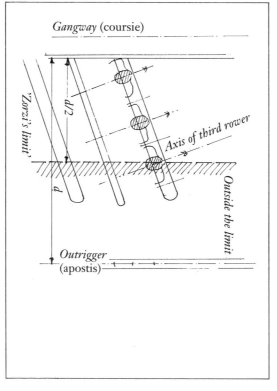

from one type of rowing to the other in the same vessel. In the following pages, Zorzi's Principle will very often be mentioned. To make comprehension of the text easier, it would appear to be essential to say a few words about it.

This text is part of the work 'Archivo Proprio Contarina b.10', and can be dated to the second half of the sixteenth century. It is of such importance in the history of galleys that the subject would normally be developed at length, but this chapter will be restricted to simply giving the conclusions.

Alessandro Zorzi was a member of a large family from Venice's aristocracy, and knew at first hand the problems of galleys, in which he had obviously had to serve. He lived in a key era in the history of this type of vessel, an era in which the two types of rowing, *alla zenzile* and *a scaloccio*, still existed alongside each other, and in which attempts were made to make the galleys faster and more powerful by increasing the number of oarsmen on each bench.

In his writings, he severely criticised *alla zenzile* rowing, which he considered to be 'unstealthy' (the impact of the oars was noisy) and in which it was difficult to back the oars – to row in the opposite direction to enable the vessel to turn more easily. He took an interest in the comfort of the oarsmen because in his opinion this would help them to row better. He explained in great detail that it was of no use to try to squash a fourth rower on to an (extended) 'suttile' galley bench designed for three. Speaking from good experience, he explained shrewdly that the best way of rowing, in whichever of the two modes, was to give the oarsmen the maximum possible leverage. To achieve this, he advocated the principle that all the men should be grouped in a space no larger than half the distance between gangway and apostis, measured to the third rower's 'belt buckle'. As stated earlier, the men were grouped together near the gangway, which explained why it was impossible to fit in a fourth rower on very narrow 'suttile' galleys designed for three. A fourth rower would have nothing but difficulties on such a galley, and zero effect. This was the situation in the example fifteenth-century galley. If they wanted to use four or even five men per bench, particularly in *a scaloccio* rowing, they had to increase the distance between one apostis and another, and this was what happened in the sixteenth-century galley chosen as an example.

The accompanying diagram shows a half midship section of each of these two galleys, and the comparison speaks for itself. Drawn to the same scale is the half beam of an ordinary

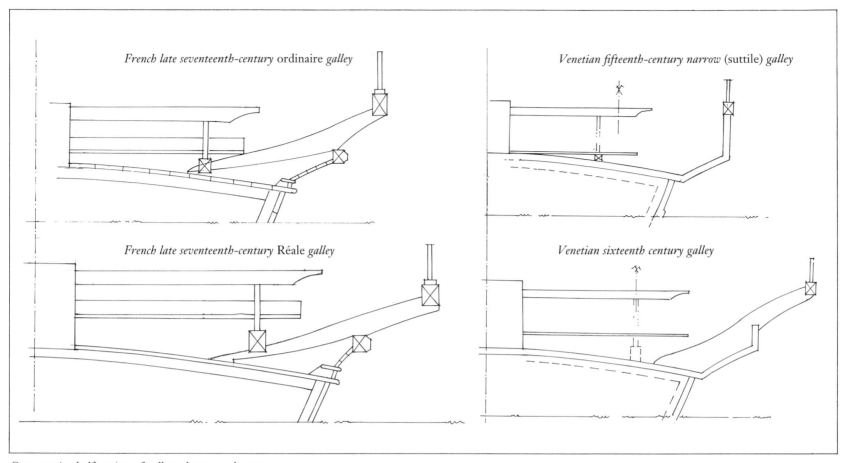

French late seventeenth-century ordinaire *galley*

Venetian fifteenth-century narrow (suttile) *galley*

French late seventeenth-century Réale *galley*

Venetian sixteenth century galley

Comparative half-sections of galleys, drawn to the same scale. If the sixteenth-century Venetian galley is typical, then there was great similarity between it and the comparatively standardised ordinaire *galleys of the later seventeenth and eighteenth centuries which rowed with five men per bench. It is noteworthy that the height of the thole line above water varied little throughout these centuries.* (René Burlet)

galley at the end of the seventeenth century and the same section of a special galley (a *Réale*) of the same period.

The principle formulated by Zorzi must have been around for some time, but to our knowledge was never written down. It was, however, scrupulously observed right up to the eighteenth century, and only special galleys were exempt. Zorzi achieved his aims by comparing '*suttile*' galleys and '*bastarda*' galleys, and this comparison was the beginning of what might be called the 'modern galleys', *ie* those of the seventeenth and eighteenth centuries.

Zorzi was a major trailblazer, and was concerned about the oarsmen, even if it was only to do with the speed of the galleys. However he also demonstrated a genuine knowledge of physical laws, which was something little understood in his day. He was one of the main influences in galley development. Incidentally, he was one of the few people to have given any details about how the oarsmen rowed *a scaloccio*.

Alla zenzile rowing in a fifteenth-century galley

The rowing station

The angle of the benches relative to the athwartship plane of the galley is 20°, and was the standard angle at the time. This was vital for this type of rowing, and without it it would have been impossible to row. The width measured from the bulwark of the gangway (the *corsia*) to the axis of the thole is 2.61m. The useful part – where the men are able to row without unreasonable effort – is half this figure, that is to say 1.305m. This follows Zorzi's principle. However, this figure is not the size of the bench as we have already seen, but represents the distance from the edge of the gangway to the 'belt buckle' (axis) of the third rower. Owing to the angle of the bench, this 1.30m becomes 1.40m in true length. Under these conditions, each of the three men has a space of 0.56m. As the third rower has to have a full seat, the bench will be extended to 1.68m. A few extra centimetres should be added to allow the three men a little extra space, making a bench 1.90m long.

No other specifications are given for this bench. In those days it would certainly have been a standard piece of equipment. Apart from its length, this bench depended solely upon human factors totally extraneous to the ship. Only the build of the oarsmen was taken into account. It was easy enough to find the missing elements on other galleys of the next era because the human body changed little in the intervening years, certainly less than the ships themselves. The oarsmen placed their feet on a form 46cm wide with a foot board 14cm high and 8cm wide around the edge. The bench is 53cm above this form, which more or less aligns the seat with the top of the gangway – quite a normal occurrence in galleys.

This fifteenth-century galley offered its oarsmen little in the way of space for them to carry out their work, both in terms of apostis-to-apostis width and in also in terms of height. The bench/form assembly barely met the required dimensions.

A figure of 1.61m for the stature of the rowers will be used because this is the dimension also adopted in the analysis of *a scaloccio* rowing below. With a seating area of 56cm, the men have no difficulty sitting down, but they are unable to bend their arms at the end of the cycle and therefore have to row with their arms outstretched. This is the major disadvantage of this type of rowing.

The oars

The dimensions of these oars are known:
Pianero: length overall 8.52m; fiol 2.61m; blade 5.91m
Postizzo: length overall 8.35m; fiol 2.44m; blade 5.91m
Terzichio: length overall 7.83m; fiol 2.08m; blade 5.71m
From now on the abbreviated term 'blade' will be applied to all that part of the oar outside the thole, rather than use a more complicated term. The *fiol* is that part of the oar which is inside the thole, and is also called the *giron*. In order to get a proper handhold, the axis of the oarsman must be approximately 30cm from the end of the oar, which leaves him about twelve centimetres clearance. The point 'against the oarsman's belt buckle' will be used as reference for this study into the effective length of the oar. The following lengths of fiol will be used here: 2.31m, 2.14m and 1.78m.

This system was used on an initial diagram, but it only needed a glance to show that this situation was not acceptable.

Experimental diagrams for rowing a fifteenth-century galley alla zenzile. *The first set-up is clearly unacceptable; the second is workable but the rowers follow very different rowing cycles; the enlargement shows the 'effective* fiol*', or lever arm, that forms the basis of subsequent calculations.* (René Burlet)

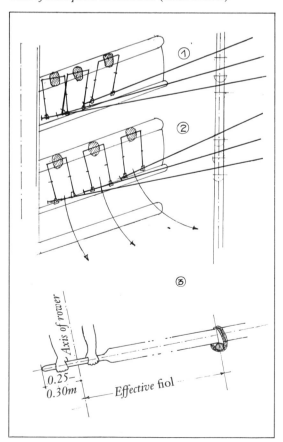

–The *pianero* is much too close to the gangway. Even a not very muscular man would not be able to move.
–The *postizzio* is out of his normal position on the bench, and because his fiol is too long it fouls the *pianero* and his handhold is above the latter's arm. He is completely off-centre relative to his position on the bench.
–The same applies to the *terzichio*, who ends up completely out of his seat.

None of the three can sit normally because all three are squashed into about a 1.20m space, so preventing any movement. Even in the fifteenth century it would have been impossible to have asked these men to work in such conditions. It is clear, therefore, that oars used as the sources suggest they were used are not suitable for this ship. Further research into what would have to be done to allow the system to operate properly, and for the three men to be able to row satisfactorily, was carried out.[66] To achieve this, each of the three would have to have a handhold which would enable them to sit down normally. It is worth remembering that, with this method of rowing, the oarsman stands up, lunges forward and then drops back on to his bench – and not to the side! This would mean that the effective fiol dimensions are as follows:
–*Pianero*: 2.25 rather than 2.31m
–*Postizzo*: 1.75 rather than 2.14m
–*Terzichio*: 1.35 rather than 1.78m.

The differences compared with the earlier figures are significant:
–a 4.3 per cent reduction in fiol size for the *pianero*
–a 17.8 per cent reduction in fiol size for the *postizzo*
–a 24.5 per cent reduction in fiol size for the *terzichio*.

In order to calculate the actual lengths of the oars, keeping the outside section unchanged, 30cm was added. The fiols then measured 2.55m, 2.05m and 1.65m. If the conditions for the first oarsman remained virtually unchanged, the two others were then greatly inconvenienced.

The fact that the distance between one apostis and another is minimal on this galley presents enormous difficulties for the *terzichio*. His lever arm (the fiol) is only 60 per cent of that of the head rower, while the *postizzo* has a better deal, with 78 per cent. The working conditions of this third man will be harsh. This obviously did not escape the notice of the commanding officers because the situation was to improve, if belatedly. The sixteenth-century galley was distinctly better organised.

Allowing for these initial factors, the move-

ment of the rowers will be conditional upon their engagement height (BIW line). Calculated from the base of the thole, these three men have the following limits, starting with the *pianero*: 0.60m, 0.545m, 0.50m. None of these three figures really causes much of a problem for the rowers and they will not be restricted in their movement by this parameter.

The rowing diagrams show the BIW line and also a line marked 2000. This is the limit, for each rower, at which the blade is plunged 2m (or 2000mm) into the water.

The action of rowing

An accurate picture of what the *alla zenzile* mode of rowing entailed survives. In November 1553 a master shipbuilder at the Venetian Arsenale, Francesco Bressan, gave his opinion on a new system of rowing recommended by an Admiral, Francesco Fiandra. The Admiral proposed rowing using only two oars on a quadrireme, each manned by two oarsmen. To make a comparison, Francesco gave the name *alla zenzile* to this method:
–The *pianero* steps on to the foot board; places his other foot on the bench in front; pushes his oar beyond the bench (the text says 'pushes his belt').
– The *postizzo* steps on to the foot board; places his other foot on the bench in front.
– The *terzichio* steps on to the foot board.
It will be shown that this routine was never any different, and an analysis of the reasons why will be offerred.

The Pianero

There is nobody in front of him to obstruct him, so he can row without any particular difficulty.

66. Several assumptions regarding the adjustment of these *fiols* were possible. The one selected was the least disruptive, but there are two others:

– *Pianero* and *postizzo* effectively use identical oars and no change is made to these. With the same *fiol* measurement, it is the axes of rotation which have to be shifted to enable the men to sit down. The tholes and their supports are therefore offset. A bireme has to have two apostis and a trireme three. The theory is an appealing one for a bireme, though it causes constructional problems. It is, however, unrealistic for a galley with three oars per bench, and therefore three apostis.

This type was without doubt never built, but studies were undertaken and these led to the adoption of a single length of oar – a considerable improvement.

– The oars are able to slide along the tholes, maintaining their real length. This operation would reduce the size of the *fiols*, increasing the external part (the blades). This theory was rejected because is it totally disastrous for the oarsmen. This would, in fact, tend to accentuate the difference between them, which is more or less the opposite of what people sought to do over the centuries.

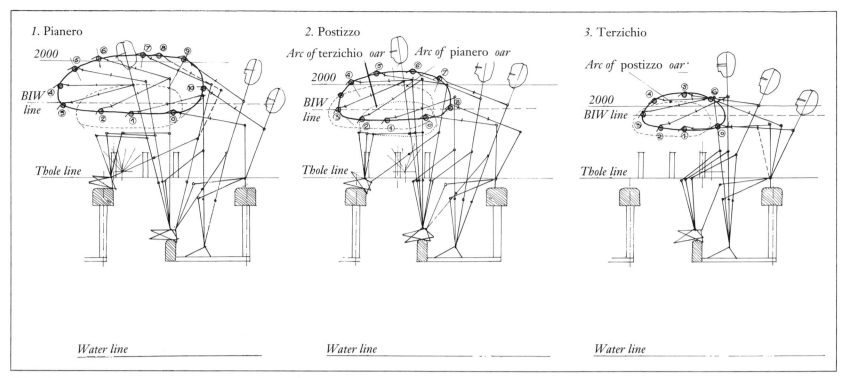

*Fifteenth-century galley: rowing diagrams
(perpendicular to bench).* (René Burlet)

−0. Position of rest or beginning of cycle. The rower is seated on his bench with arms slightly raised, the oar out of the water.

−1. The oarsman stands up, places one foot on the foot board, keeping his oar out of the water.

−2. Taking his weight on the foot board, the rower moves forward and places the foot which has up to this point been resting on the form on to the bench in front of him, lunging forward with his leg bent. He still keeps his oar out of the water (wrists below the BIW line).

−3. The lunge forward becomes more accentuated, the back leg remains tensed and the inboard end of the oar ends up quite a long way beyond the bench facing him, by some 30cm. However, the forward lunge must not be too great because the rower will have to stand back up again by using this leg to support him.

−4. In a quick movement, the rower lowers his oar into the water, raising his wrists. This is the beginning of the active phase.

−5,6,7. The rower will gradually brace his front leg, keeping his back leg in tension and his foot on the foot board. At the same time, his arms are raised and the oar is plunged into the water. His body (and the oar) moves backwards gradually and the movement continues until the front leg is straight (7).

−8. Heaving himself backwards, he prepares for the next movement.

−9 and 10. The rower continues to pull backwards, his front leg leaves the bench and returns to the form, and pulling his oar backwards with all his weight he drops back on to his bench. The cycle can now begin again.

In actual fact, movements 9 and 10 are executed simultaneously. It is almost impossible to illustrate the action in very great detail.

The arc swept by the wrists of the *pianero* is approximately 1.15 to 1.20m. Apart from a few improvements, this cycle was used for both *alla zenzile* and *scaloccio* rowing, and was to remain in use until galleys went out of service in the eighteenth century.

The Postizzo

His cycle should, in theory, be identical, and so it would have been if the rower was on his own and had free movement. The *pianero* has the dominant position and precedes him, making his oar an obstacle. The pattern made by the latter's oar is the broken line on the diagram, showing the *postizzo*'s rowing cycle.

−1. The rower stands up and places his foot on the foot board, his arms outstretched in front of him and lowered slightly to keep his oar out of the water. In this position, his oar is more or less parallel with that of the *pianero*.

−2. He moves forward, still keeping his oar out of the water, and places his foot on the bench in front of him.

−3. He is about to start his lunge forward, but will quickly come to a halt because the *pianero*'s oar is raised in front of him, preventing further movement. The oar only goes about 10 or 15cm beyond the bench, as against 30cm for the *pianero*. His leg will hardly go beyond the bench on which his foot is placed, and these are the conditions under which engagement will take place because the oarsman can go no further forward.

−4. The man raises his arms and carries out his active cycle, lowering the oar in the water by stretching out his front leg as with the *pianero*. At a given moment, due to the position of the two men in relation to one another, his oar will be above that of the *pianero*.

−5,6,7,8. The end of the cycle is the same as that of the preceding oarsman, so need not be described again.

This *postizzo* is therefore restricted in his forward movement by the *pianero*'s oar, and this is the disadvantage of this type of rowing. The arc swept during this cycle is reduced to about 0.90m, or maybe a metre if the oarsmen are well-trained and have the skill to make use of the *pianero*'s oar.

The Terzichio

He too will have an oar which crosses his field of action, but this time it will be the *postizzo*'s oar. The *pianero*'s also crosses it, but so far in front of him that it will not obstruct him.

They always start from the 0 position, where they are seated with their arms outstretched and holding the oar.

−1. The oarsman leans forward and begins his movement by placing one foot on the foot board.

−2. He is standing up, one foot on the foot board and the other on the form. Due to his position, his oar is above his neighbour's.

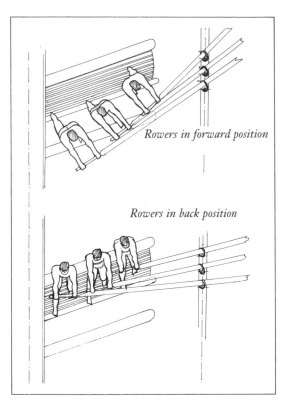

Rowers in forward position

Rowers in back position

Fifteenth-century galley: rowing diagrams (plan view). In the forward position only the first two rowers can use the bench in front for leverage and all three are distinctly separate. In the back position, on the other hand, the rowers are more closed up when seated, but this is the only point in the cycle where the oars are separated from one another. (René Burlet)

–3. He leans forward but is unable to go so far. His lunge will be very quickly halted by the *postizzo*'s oar when he lifts it in front of him, which he will do very soon. Under these conditions he will have to begin the same movement and engage his oar in the water, prematurely from the point of view of efficiency.

–4,5,6. The return is carried out as normal. This is obviously a very short movement, and the arc travelled does not exceed 0.65 to 0.70m. Not very much at all.

It is easy to see that the working conditions deteriorate from one oarsman to another. The *pianero* is able to row freely, the *postizzo* has quite a reasonable position, but the working conditions of the *terzichio* are difficult, throwing into doubt his efficiency. The angles of the various arcs swept are 29°, 29°, and 30°, starting with the *pianero*. The three men describe almost similar arcs.

The effort demanded from these three oarsmen will not vary very much. On a purely energy level the system is not implausible. However, on the physical level – operational as it were – there must be some reservations. Owing to the lack of distance between one apostis and another, the lever arms of the oars

are short, but more particularly the clearance between the oars is extremely tight: a few centimetres at best. The diagrams show the possible movements, but what would happen if there was a slight swell?

It is possible to row in this galley, but it would certainly require a well-trained crew and more particularly a good arrangement of the crew based on their stature. The difficulties faced by the *terzichio* are substantial, to the extent of raising the question whether this man was not 'added' to a bireme – a vessel rowed conventionally. The question remains open.

Alla zenzile rowing in a sixteenth-century galley

On a purely practical level, rowing in this galley was not fundamentally different from the methods employed a century before. There were, however, quite a few changes made in the attempts to push this system of rowing to the limit of its capabilities. The *a scaloccio* system was appearing on the scene.

The hull was lengthened and widened and artillery had to be accommodated on very narrow hulls, causing problems. The breadth of this hull was increased from 12ft to 15ft (Venetian) and though not a great increase was enough to cause difficulties for the rowers. The wider the vessel, the greater the effort required by the rowers. The apostis-to-apostis breadth did, however, increase by 36 per cent, going from 16ft to 22ft. To give these enlarged superstructures some rigidity, the *bacalas* system was adopted, and with it the structure of the modern galley. The galley remained low-freeboard because the technique of rowing demanded that the oarsmen were not too far from the water.

They then realised the need for the oarsmen to have good leverage, and it was in that period that Alessandro Zorzi was to put forward his ideas. The features of the rowing station changed slightly, but the authors' researches were to reveal that there were still similarities with the way things had been.

The angle of the benches remained unchanged at 20° and was subsequently to vary little, but to remain, within one or two degrees, close to this figure.

Because the apostis-to-apostis breadth was greater, it was possible to install a bench 1.85m long while still complying with Zorzi's principle. To all intents and purposes it was a quad-

rireme in which the oarsmen were a little bit squashed together, but it will be treated as a trireme.

The *interscalmium* distance (distance between thole pins) was different, but faced with the large number of possible values the authors settled on the 1.185m which had already been used. This variation was never to be very high, and depended exclusively on the size of the men. By the end of the seventeenth century it would have increased by 6cm altogether.

One vital element was to increase the spacing of the tholes on the same bench. It increased from a hand's breadth (24.8cm) to a foot (34.8cm), corresponding to a 40 per cent increase. This was calculated from the central thole so that the oarsmen furthest away, particularly the *terzichio*, were not penalised in any way. This development was sure to have been introduced for two reasons:

1. With only a hand's width between tholes, and taking into account the space available once the oar and its strop were in place, it was impossible to fit any protection to the oars, which quickly became subject to wear. With a foot, protection can be applied in the form of *galavernes*, which are like small pieces of wood between 2cm and 3cm thick. These prevent wear of the sides of the oar and also prevent direct contact with the apostis.

2. The second reason is undoubtedly a more important one: by spacing out the oars more, it makes rowing easier for the men because their oars do not clash against each other, and it also extends their work cycle a little. This brief overview of sixteenth-century galleys can be concluded by noting that the height of the apostis above the water increased from 1.39m to 1.55m, and was to change little over the following centuries. The same distance could be seen on conventional galleys at the end of the seventeenth century, and even on a *Réale*. All of these factors are interlinked, and it is virtually impossible to change one without having an impact on the others. They all go to make up a system almost in the mathematical meaning of the word because they meet real geometrical criteria. It is not certain whether all that would have been clearly explained in those days, but in the sixteenth century people already knew a lot about rowing.

For the earlier vessel, exact oar sizes could be supplied for the three men. This is no longer the case now: the *pianero*'s oar is given, but the others had to be deduced from it, based on a geometrical code which cannot be derived directly. It can, however, be found in the writings of the day. By taking the drawings of A Picheroni which show the oars, and by establishing a mean from several triads of oars, the following relative sizes are obtained:

Pianero 100; *Postizzo* 93.9; *Terzichio* 86. With a given 11.31m oar using these ratios, the dimensions are: 11.31m – 10.62m – 9.73m.

From these dimensions we are able to obtain, on one plane, 'effective' fiols, that is to say measured from the axis of the rower to the axis of the thole:

Pianero 3.25m, as against 2.25m in the fifteenth century

Postizzo 2.75m, as against 1.75m in the fifteenth century

Terzichio 2.25m, as against 1.35m in the fifteenth century

Each of these oarsmen gained about a metre compared with the dimensions of the previous century, but it corresponds to increases of varying percentages: 44 – 56 – 69. In the sixteenth century the *terzichio* used a fiol the same as that used by the *pianero* the century before.

By allowing 25cm for the rower's handhold, it can be calculated that the parts outside the thole were equal to: 7.84m, 7.62m and 7.23m.

These longer fiols are significant in another respect. The radius of the rotation of each man during his forward movement is appreciably larger and the arc described less curved (larger radius of curvature), giving the oarsmen an almost rectilinear trajectory and making life much easier for them.

In the course of a century the dimensions of engagement developed little and were not to cause any particular difficulties on sixteenth-century galleys. By continuing to take the thole line as reference, we obtain the following

Sixteenth-century galley: rowing diagrams (perpendicular to bench). Although similar to the earlier system, the tholes have been moved apart to ease the rowers' task. (René Burlet)

heights: *Pianero* 69.3cm, *Postizzo* 61cm, *Terzichio* 54.5cm.

The action of rowing

If each rower had unrestricted movement he could perform a complete cycle without any problem. However, as we have already seen, this was not the case for two of them because they were obstructed by the oar in front, *ie* the *postizzio* and the *terzichio*. It will therefore be of interest now to analyse the action of 'the other man's oar'.

The Pianero

Because he is not obstructed by anyone, this oarsman is able to complete his cycle without any particular problem. It is also virtually identical to that of *pianeros* a century before, but with the improvement of the changes in parameters as already described. The arc actually swept is 21° and the distance travelled between about 1.15m and 1.20m. During *a scaloccio* rowing, this cycle would certainly not have been disrupted. We have already looked at an identical cycle in detail, so we will not go over it again.

The Postizzo

The *pianero*'s oar, as anticipated, will limit his forward movement. At some point he will not be able to move any further forward – which he would have been able to do had he been on his own – and he will be forced to begin the active part of the cycle a little prematurely. He has no other alternative unless he wants to risk banging his wrists on the oar in front of him. The arc swept will only be 20°, as against the 24° which could have been attained, and the distance travelled about a metre. Ten centimetres

were gained thanks to the spacing of tholes. He is able to get to the bench sited in front of him, but his lunge forward is very poor and does not go beyond the bench's axis.

The Terzichio

By adopting the same approach and looking into the action of the *postizzo*'s oar on his cycle, it becomes clear that the third man has the most difficult time of it, because he is very much obstructed and therefore his movement will be very limited. On his own and without any restrictions he would be able to cover a 28° arc. The reality, however, is very different and he will be unable to get to the bench in front of him. He is able to place one foot on the foot board and lean forward a moderate amount. To keep his balance, he has to keep one foot on the form. These restrictions mean that the arc swept is reduced to 18–19°, and the distance travelled is about 17 to 80cm. Again, the new spacing of the thole pins increased the cycle by about ten centimetres.

In the course of a century of empirical research and by trial and error, *alla zenzile* rowing reached the limit of its possibilities using this formula. It was obvious that another way had to be found to stop the oarsmen being constantly restricted in their efforts and forced to pay very close attention to their work in order to avoid breakages.

This is the appropriate time to look at *a scaloccio* rowing, which is far from being the sudden change that is sometimes imagined, but a logical extension of what went before. In fact the sixteenth-century galley as it stands and apart from truly minor modifications can be rowed *a scaloccio*, because:

– The oarsmen's work stations were no different.

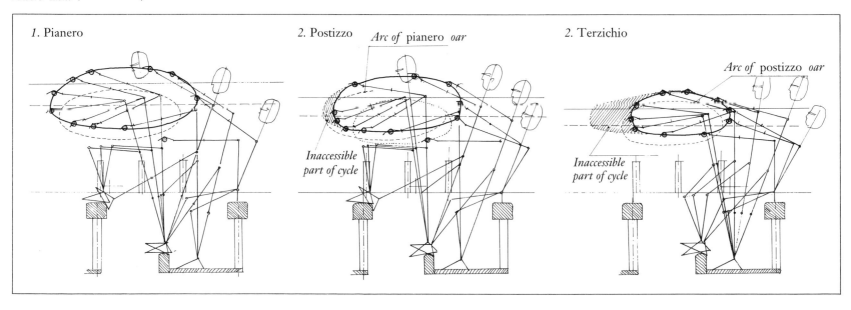

1. Pianero   2. Postizzo   *Arc of* pianero *oar*   2. Terzichio   *Arc of* postizzo *oar*

Inaccessible part of cycle   *Inaccessible part of cycle*

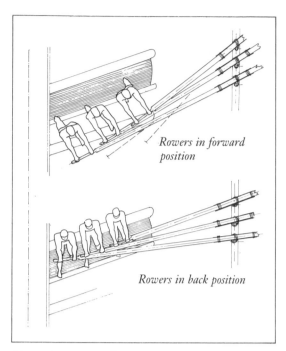

Sixteenth-century galley: rowing diagrams (plan view). (René Burlet)

Sixteenth-century galley: a scaloccio *rowing diagram* (plan view, rowers in the forward position). *It required minimal alteration to existing galleys, and in allowing all three rowers much the same movement was a major step towards equalising their workload.* (René Burlet)

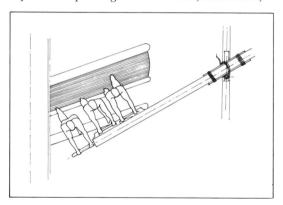

Detail of thole fittings. Both the chock (auterelle) *and the fish* (galavesne) *were designed to save wear on the apostis and oar respectively; they were replaceable and were always made of evergreen oak. The step in the* galaverne *acted like the button on a modern oar, helping to stop the oar sliding along the thole pin.* (René Burlet)

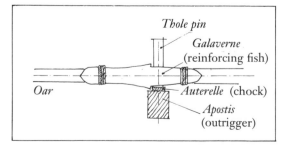

— The *pianero*'s thole was to be the only one used. Later on, the cross-section was to be increased, but it was not a significant change. The two other tholes were removed.

— The single oar had a much larger cross-section fiol which was impossible to grip directly, and so battens (handholds) had to be nailed to it to allow the men to have a conventional grip.

— They were already giving some thought to protecting the apostis by inserting an *auterelle* (a block of timber to prevent wear) between the apostis and the *galavernes* (wooden reinforcing pieces, the equivalent of a modern leather and 'button'), but that brought only a minor benefit.

The next task was to look at how these three men would row using this new method. A *scaloccio* rowing with three men was used on a number of vessels (large galliots, half-galleys, etc).

The results observed were as follows. The large oar was 12m long, but its greater diameter would give it better balance. The lead counterweight on these oars never exceeded 2–3kg, whilst it was as high as 8–10kg on the oars used in *alla zenzile* rowing, in which the proportions of the two parts of the oar were less balanced.

— There was no change in the *pianero*'s work cycle. However, the role of the *pianero* did develop a little. He was already leader of his group of rowers because he was the first to start, but his position was to be strengthened and the other two had no choice but to follow him without any conscious effort being necessary to achieve this.

— For the two other rowers, the situation was different. Until this time, rowing demanded not just power but sustained concentration – vital to the success of operations. Now rowing demanded just their power, and the head rower attended to the rest. Their cycles were those set by the large oar in front of them.

— For the *postizzo*, his cycle was moved slightly downwards compared with his previous position, his hold on the battens causing him to move a little further back by about fifteen centimetres.

— The same happened with the *terzichio*, but because he was less obstructed than before, he would be able to move more easily.

As just pointed out, there was a logical relationship between these two types of rowing. As soon as there is enough apostis-to-apostis breadth in a galley, *a scaloccio* rowing becomes conceivable and possible. Even if on a theoretical level this mode of propulsion gave rise to numerous debates and much posturing, on a

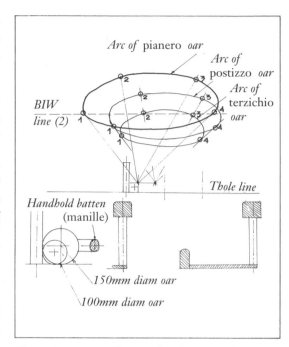

Sixteenth-century galley: a scaloccio *rowing diagram* (perpendicular to bench). (René Burlet)

strictly physical level it was quite easy to achieve.

The authors have therefore reproduced the same sixteenth-century galley with its three men in *a scaloccio* formation on a small drawing beneath the drawings illustrating *alla zenzile* rowing. This trireme could be converted into a quadrireme without major modification and without excessively overstepping Zorzi's limit. This conversion would have been impossible on fifteenth-century triremes.

In the accompanying rowing diagram showing the three oarsmen, only the movement made by their wrists during the cycle is illustrated for each. Had the position of the bodies been shown, the drawing would have become too confused. The oarsmen are shown in four positions during the cycle:

— In 1 and 4, on engagement with and on removal from the water.

— In 2 and 3, two points in the active part of the cycle when the oar is in the water.

In all cases, the gap between the *pianero*'s handhold and his two team members will be noted. This is essentially due to the use of battens which create this gap.

It will also be noted that if the lead rower (or *pianero*) with a larger physique is chosen, the two other oarsmen must follow. This device was to extend the cycle by as much as 15cm or even 20cm, and the two other oarsmen, being unobstructed, are able to follow, the *postizzo* intensifying his lunge forward and the *terzichio* at long last getting to the bench on which he had never been able to place his foot.

This advantage did not escape the captains, and particularly the galley masters with special responsibility for rowing. 'Setting up' the galley slaves was to be one of the major preoccupations on modern galleys, and the utmost care would be given to it.

This brief summary leads smoothly and naturally to the galleys of the later centuries, which would all row *a scaloccio* with all the refinements which it was possible to imagine to avoid exhausting the oarsmen too rapidly. This study, which was chronologically the first to be carried out, will also demonstrate how it was possible for the oar crew to live on this type of vessel.

A scaloccio rowing

French galleys at the end of the seventeenth century

The recreation of a fleet of galleys was one of the first priorities when Louis XIV took power in 1661. The 'Sun King' needed them to help fulfil his military ambitions in the Mediterranean. He could not become a great king without displaying the finest and strongest warships, for, as Colbert wrote, 'there is no more powerful sign of the greatness of a prince than his show of galleys, which guarantee his good reputation abroad'.[67] Like medals that portray a monarch's victories and successes, the eulogies of the historian, and the abundant paintings and scuptures that celebrate an heroic, almost deified sovereign, the galley, too, was a display of king-worship. Groups of ornate carvings decorated the poop of every ship. They depicted the king possessing the terrifying grandeur of Jupiter, the strength of Hercules, the invincibility of Alexander and the magnanimity of Augustus. The Protestant convicts on board the *Heroine* were shackled in a galley whose poop displayed the 'glories' of both the revocation of the edict of Nantes and the devastation of the Palatinate. 'The galley is

a victory chariot' according to Nicolas Arnoul; 'nothing speaks of its king quite like these ships, with their slightly raised poops and three hundred slaves in chains below; even Roman emperors were not so triumphant.'[68]

Apart from the huge sum spent every ten years on decorating and and fitting out a *Réale* (the fleet flagship), galleys were inexpensive ships. For the price of a single first-class ship you could build and fit out twenty standard galleys. Built almost entirely of softwood and fitted with a more than modest range of guns – five cannon installed in the bow – the galleys did not require a great amount of capital. It was the type of fleet favoured by the Mediterranean states, at least those which did not have the financial and technical resources to build a shipyard and stock it with all the equipment necessary for a sailing navy. The king of France, together with Colbert and later Seigneley, his son and successor as the head of maritime affairs, wanted to confirm his supremacy on two levels: with a 'wealthy' navy, with ships of the line and frigates in Brest, Toulon and Rochefort, and a 'poor' navy made up of galleys, set up in Marseilles in 1665.

A century after the fearful slaughter of Lepanto, this arrangement, justified as being part of a plan for political supremacy, was also undeniably a tactical necessity. Indeed, the story of the Sun-King's galleys was rather that of a non-battle. Happily for the *chiourmes* (the oar crews), the 'ladies' who mocked Duquesne were never to find themselves engaged directly in a big naval battle. Only one captain, Charles Davy de la Pailleterie, was promoted Commander, following a brilliant feat of arms – not, significantly, in the Mediterranean but in the North Sea.[69] 'It is nearly eighty years', wrote the town-major of Bombelles, 'since a galley captain was killed in action.'[70] Far away from

the front line of battle and damned by their officers, who still harboured certain prejudices against them, the fighting galleys began to take on a different role. They cashed in on their survival after the 1680s by carrying out various exercises from one end of the Mediterranean to the other, even in the west, becoming to a certain extent ships-of-all-trades in a naval war whose prime action was still taking place around the shore. Acting as cargo carriers, coast guards, escorts, and landing craft, the French galleys pursued the corsairs from Algiers to Flushing, transported troops, arms, hay and money, protected merchant vessels, looted barques in the Dogger Bank area and the Piombino channel, and guarded the entrance to the Gulf of Fos during the Beaucaire fair – not to mention their famous parades along the coast of Italy, from port to

67. National library, NAF 21306 p159, 6 November 1665.

68. National archives, B⁶ 78, p186, 19 June 1669.

69. It should be recalled that a squadron of 15 galleys was built at Rochefort in 1690. They were to join the vessels commanded by Tourville, but missed the rendezvous: the galleys of the bailiff of Noailles were in the Aber Wrac'h when the battle of Bévéziers (Beachy Head, 1690) was joined. These Western galleys were laid up at Rouen. Six of them were brought back into service until the end of the war of the League of Augsburg: the *Heureuse* and the *Palme* at Le Havre and then at Saint-Malo, the *Marquise* and the *Triomphante* at Brest, the *Martiale* and the *Emeraude* at La Rochelle and then Bordeaux. The crews and rowers who came from Marseille were supplemented by convicts recruited locally. Following the peace of Ryswick, these six galleys were kept at Rochefort. They were recommissioned in June 1701 at the start of the War of Spanish Succession. Their home port was Dunkirk. In July 1702, under the command of Charles Davy de la Pailleterie, they seized the *Licorne*, a Dutch warship armed with 46 guns. Jean Marteilhe, to whom we owe the *Mémoires d'un Protestant condamné aux galères de France pour cause de religion*, rowed on the *Palme*.

70. National archives, B⁶ 98, p173, 2 November 1705.

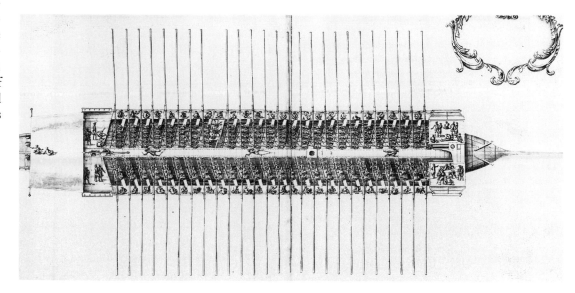

The late seventeenth-century French ordinaire *galley a* scaloccio *superbly demonstrated by this plan view from the* Album de Colbert *of 1670. They were rowed by five men per bench but it is interesting that in this view the oar crew on the port side all pull at their oars, while those on the starboard side are divided into three conventional 'pullers' and two – those outboard and mechanically least efficient – who push. (Service Historique de la Marine)*

Fitting out a Réale (*probably the 1692 vessel) at Marseille, the main French galley base, from an engraving by Jacques Régaud. By the standards of sailing ship navies, galleys were a relatively cheap form of sea power, particularly if the oar crew were criminals, prisoners of war or slaves, as was the case in the last centuries of galley warfare.*

port, stopping in harbour for four days and then sailing for a day. Was it necessary to rig out as many as forty working galleys (for this was the number of galleys in the fleet at its peak, in about 1690–1700)? About twenty would have been enough, but the king's desire for a show of strength dictated otherwise.

The re-emergence of the French galley fleet posed the immediate problem of recruiting rowers. A standard galley required 260 oarsmen, with about 450 for a *Réale* or *Patronne* (squadron flagship). As in Spain and Italy, the *chiourme* comprised three categories of men: slaves, who were also called Turks even though many of them came from North Africa; volunteers or *bonevoglies* and finally condemned men and convicts. The king of France, 'His Most Christian Majesty', bought his slaves at the human markets of the Mediterranean, Livorno, Malta, Alicante, Majorca or Cagliari, where the slave trade prospered until the end of the eighteenth century. Sometimes Barbary corsairs were captured by Christian galleys, and there were also fishermen, or pilgrims on their way to Mecca. There were various devices for acquiring these men, who then formed the pick of the *chiourme* and were given the most demanding jobs. 'Any man who has ever set foot in this kingdom is free,' an officer of the French royal navy wrote in 1694, 'and the only exceptions to this law are the Turks and Moors sent to Marseille to serve in galleys, because before their arrival they were bought in a for-

eign country which operates this type of business.'[71] Volunteers were used as well as slaves, recalling a time when teams of rowers were still entirely made up of free men. But these men were *bonevoglies* in name only. They led the lives of slaves or convicts rather than free men. They had to be 'shaved, wear the same clothes and pull on the oars, just like the convicts . . . and have their feet shackled.'[72] They were confined to the ship when they ran up gambling debts and drank too much at the local tavern. The job of the galley slave held fewer and fewer attractions. Towards the end of the 1670s, even the poorest landworkers and port labourers were not desperate enough to contemplate 'condemning themselves, even though they were not condemned men'.[73]

The use of men in galleys as a form of punishment became common towards the end of the fifteenth century, when those countries with a sailing navy found it more and more difficult to fill the benches with 'free men'. In France itself, Francois I, Henri II and Louis XIII drew heavily from the prisons, taking the men needed to 'man the galleys'. But after peace returned owing to a prolonged truce or civil war, the monarchy no longer armed the galleys and hence stopped sending convicts to war. The state under Louis XIV was not happy with the idea of rebuilding a fleet to use as a means of punishment again. So they built an impressive naval base at Marseille which operated, in times of war and peace, a 'city of galleys' whose penal population, towards 1690–1700, was about a fifth of the town's population: about 10,000 convicts and 2000 slaves kept in port, who were immediately available, out of a town of about 55,000 to 60,000 inhabitants.[74] The requirement to punish criminals, at a time when the absolute state was reasserting itself, fitted in perfectly with the require-

ments of the navy. Tens of thousands of convicts were needed to keep filling the benches of France's galleys: 38,000 during 1680 to 1715, and 22,000 during the Regency period and the reign of Louis XV, when the activities of the fleet had become more and more sporadic, right up to 1748, when convict prisons began to be built.

These figures are the result of quantitative research, with the aid of computers and the registry office and enrolment documents of the convicts. The officers of the '*chiourme bureaux*' took a scrupulous note on arrival of each convict or chaingang, detailing the 'particulars' of the prisoners. The enrolment statistics alone reveal a hitherto unrecognised fact relating to the justice system of the Ancien Regime, with its 'bureaucratic' magistrates who counted thieves, robbers, public nuisances, tramps, dissolutes, blasphemers, contrabands, deserters and rebels in the same lot, a strange mixture of scoundrels and poor devils who, together with the slaves bought or rounded up on the shores of the Mediterranean, made up the galley crews. Nearly two-thirds of the Sun King's convicts were not 'criminals' as we know them today, but soldiers without a regiment, contraband salt dealers, and protestants who maintained their allegiance to the new faith.[75] As well as information on the convicts, their crimes, and their social and geographical origins, the enrolment statistics provide some rather disconcerting information on the destiny of the penal population. The numbers of men lost at sea are inconseqential, well below the numbers for the crews of northern sailing ships during the same period. Deaths in home ports during the off-season are, on the contrary, amazing: one-third of convicts died in the *chiourme* hospitals within three years of their arrival in Marseille. One might think that

71. *Id.*, B⁶ 26, p431, 20 October 1694.

72. *Id.*, B⁶ 80, p227, sd (1672).

73. Sailor oarsmen replaced the *bonevoglies*. They were enlisted to row alongside criminals and slaves, but they unquestionably belonged to the free men and were primarily used as auxiliary or replacement rowers. They manned the skiff and the cutter and were in charge of taking on water and wood. During combat, they would be positioned along the walkway outboard of the benches and armed with a sabre to 'keep the oar crew in order'. Their numbers gradually decreased as the number of convicts increased. On a conventional galley, the number of sailor oarsmen went from 80 to 60 in 1683 and then decreased to 45 in 1688. From 1715 onwards, the number was set at 10.

74. See André Zysberg, 'L'arsenal des galères de France à Marseille (1660–1715)', *Neptunia* 59 (1985), pp20–31.

75. See André Zysberg, 'Les galères de France et la société des galériens (1660–1748)', doctoral thesis, EHESS, 1986.

this phenomenon was largely a result of the harshness of service, but the life expectancy of convicts did not improve even after the reign of Louis XIV, when the galleys did not leave port more than once a year and the men had long periods of inactivity. Whether they rowed or not, their death rates stayed the same, and the causes of death had the same symptoms, more those of 'concentration camps' than naval bases.

'Galley' conditions existed before the convicts actually reached the ships, in the 'stinking and insanitary dungeons' where they awaited their departure for Marseille. The journey itself was a terrible trial for men already weakened by imprisonment, 'fettered and desolate': the 'roughest punishment of the convicts' ac-

A plan of a Maltese galley from an eighteenth-century French encyclopaedia, although effectively copied from af Chapman's great work Architectura Navalis Mercatoria *of 1768. The vessel, rowing 30 benches a* scaloccio, *is typical of the last generation of galleys, although this example was a flagship of the Captain of the Order of St John of Malta. The armament was standard for the time: a 36pdr on the centreline, flanked by two 8pdrs and two 6pdrs, plus about eighteen small pierriers.*

cording to Nicolas Arnoul. The beginning of life as a galley slave was an enormous shock for the weakest, the most run-down and the most naive men. Stripped and beaten by the prison warders and by their fellow slaves, they did not survive the misery and oppression for long. Fated also were those to whom the captains took a dislike: confined to hospital or the supply ships, the majority would never be part of a working crew and never know life at sea. Those who survived three years and died in captivity never entered the 'professional' statistics; the same went for those who died of ordinary illness sustained as part of their daily lives in port. The lists of sick convicts give us an idea of the phyical wretchedness of the galley slaves. Many of them were 'worn out' before their time was up, 'exhausted', 'taken ill' or 'broken down'. The stinging salt water and rubbing chains gave them sores and blisters on their legs; the rowing broke their backs or tore their abdominal muscles.

The modern-age galley is thought of almost universally as a ship that more or less propelled itself; the amazing strength with which the men of that time rowed was alone what propelled the ship – and propelled it fast. In an

evocative essay on the subject, an author will not fail to contrast the splendour and allure of the galleys with the distress of the rowers, but without giving a basic explanation of how such a 'system' actually worked for several centuries and did not die out through its inhumanity, or quite simply because it did not change due to naval developments. Even though sophisticated ships succeeded the galleys, they did not actually replace them. As Jurien de la Gravière notes, the true successor to the galley was the steam-propelled ship.[76] There is a continuity here in the method of propulsion, the mechanical replacing the human engine. So how was it possible both to survive and row in the warships of the late eighteenth century? The following text, the result of a collaboration between an historian and an ergonomist, the latter interested in lateen rigging, the former coming to study the history of the galley via its connection with judicial repression, attempts to answer this question.

The standard galley had 52 oars arranged in

---

76. E Jurien de la Gravière, *Les derniers jours de la marine à rame* (Paris 1885). A small book, excellently researched, even if the author does not quote his sources.

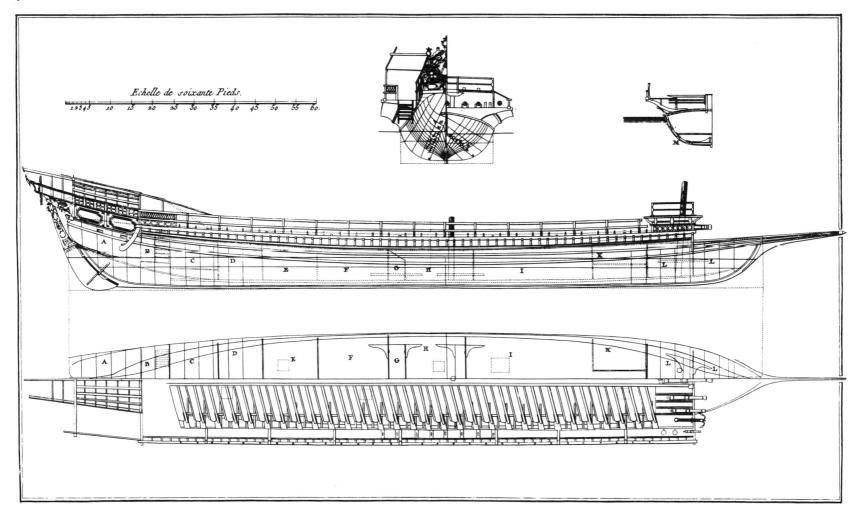

Echelle de soixante Pieds.

The internal arrangements of a galley from the manuscript known as 'La Science des Galères' by Barras de la Penne, Marseille 1697. The very limited internal capacity of these vessels is apparent; a high proportion of this was devoted to provisions, especially water.

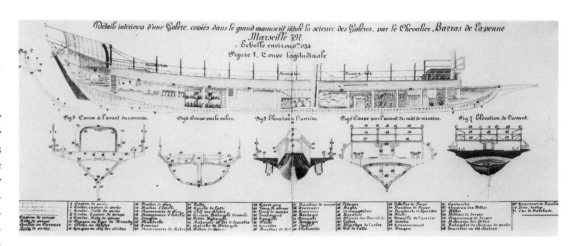

two straight rows, with five rowers per bench.[77] A *Réale* or *Patronne*, longer and wider but otherwise built the same, had 30 to 32 pairs of oars, with seven men on each bench. In the modern galley there was only one oar per bench, rather than three as in the medieval galley. This change took place during the sixteenth century as outlined above. It was probably the result of the development in recruitment of 'galley-rowers' (*galeotti*) when enrolment of volunteers became more and more difficult, and when they were gradually replaced by slaves and convicts. The medieval system required a good calibre of recruit, as each rower operated his own oar: at bench-level, the oar movements had to be perfectly synchronised, with three rowers of roughly equal strength and skill. But later on, by harnessing all of the convicts on one bench to a single oar, they could get away with using men of varying ability, both strong and weak, experienced and completely inexperienced in life at sea.[78]

The rowers were given positions which matched their physical capabilities, or conversely, each position or sailing post – the working men on board the galleys talked of 'sailing' rather than 'rowing' – required a well-placed rower, according to the progressive angle at which the oar touched the water. The men who manned the inboard end of the oar, near the gangway, worked much harder than those nearer the hull side or thole. If the man were young, strong and as tall as or taller than 1.65m, he would be considered a good 'sailor' and positioned at the end of the oar as a 'head' or 'lead' rower. The head of the bench controlled the other rowers. He was also put in charge of 'setting up' the new recruits. The

head rowers were the best of the bunch. They were chosen with care, usually from among the slaves, although with the influx of convicts the 'good' men among these were also made head rowers. Four of them were treated as sailors and were given the same treatment as the free men. Two were the head rowers from the benches nearest to the poop (one from each side), who were called the *espaliers* because of their proximity to the espale, the galley embarkation point on either side of the poop. They set the stroke: 'when they slowed down, everyone slowed down'. The other two were the head rowers at the prow, or *conillers*, who also held a key position in that they were responsible for positioning the anchors or 'irons'.

If a man did not have the qualities of a head rower, still less the stuff of an *espalier* or *coniller*, but was of medium stature with a good physique and still fairly young, he would probably be put in the position of *apostis*, next to the head rower. Anybody who looked rather grim and was on the small side but still young and strong would be given the place of of *tiercerol*, which was the middle position on the bench and possibly the least tiring because on the one hand there was no need to pull as hard as the head rower, and on the other hand it was not necessary to bend the spine to follow the course of the oar as the fourth and fifth rowers did. These last, the *quarterol* and *quinterol*, were among the weakest of the convicts.

The arrangement of the galley slaves was a delicate affair, because not only did each man have to be allocated the right position, but also the combined strength of each 'bench' had to be well balanced. Hence the advice of sieur Masse, a French galley master in the early eighteenth century. This expert writes:

The master always looks after the sailing arrangements. You have to know the strength and skills of each galley slave and spread them out, so that no bench is stronger than another

because a weak bench will undoubtedly hinder the movement of the galley . . . Another, bigger disadvantage is that when you have a weak bench it cannot work as effectively as the others; one weak bench affects the two or three benches behind it so the oar strokes are unbalanced and the men can even clash with those behind or in front. To prevent this you have to even out the men and when you have new recruits put one on each bench . . . if you have a good head rower put a weaker *apostis* next to him, or if you have a mediocre head rower, give him a good *apostis* so that, in the end, they balance themselves out. The same goes for the *quarterols* and *quinterols*.[79]

The wise management of the ship's resources did not discount poor conditions. It was a hard job. The rowers on the same bench were designated a *brancade*, or bench, the name given to the five-, six- or seven-branch chain with which the crew was shackled. Let us picture the living space given to a bench crew: five men had to work, eat and sleep in a rectangular space no bigger than 2.3m long by 1.25m wide. The author of a poem entitled 'The suffering and misery of the galley convicts'[80] describes the exigencies of the bench:

The galley is our home
In the open, whether it rains or snows
We have neither cover nor shelter . . .
We sleep four or five to a bench
Which is scarcely three sections wide,
And seems just made to the measure
Of a dead man's coffin.
In this *brancade* we all have to
Eat and work together . . .

Those who drudged the most were the the most undernourished. In 1665–70 the galley slave's ration at sea was 2lb of biscuit (980g), 4oz (120g) of beans minimally flavoured with oil and salt, 'and sometimes wine when they

77. There were in fact only 51 oars because one of the benches in the left-hand row, the 9th or 10th from the stern, was taken up by the *fougon*, the galley's stove.

78. For details on the development of fighting galleys and the recruitment of crews between the end of the Middle Ages and the start of the modern era, see: M Aymard, 'Oarsmen and galleys in the Mediterranean in the sixteenth century', *Mélanges en l'honneur de Fernand Braudel* (Paris 1973), pp49–64; J-C Hocquet, 'Sailors in Venice . . .', in *Le genti del mare Mediterraneo*, XVIIe International Symposium of Maritime History (Naples 1981), pp103–168; A Lutrell, 'Late-medieval oarsmen', in *Le genti del mare Mediterraneo*, pp87–101.

79. City Library, Marseille, MS 967, pp445–446.

80. Published in *Lou jardin deys musos prouvençalos* (Aix-en-Provence 1666), pp47–57 and kindly translated into French by Laurent Damonte.

were tired in action'. There was a big disproportion between the huge quantity of biscuit and the lack of other foods, apart from the traditional bowl of beans. The Secretary of State for the Navy, Seignelay, deigned to take an interest in this matter when writing in 1684 to the galley controllers, Delafont and d'Ortières, in reply to their curious request to evaluate the quantity of biscuit required by a galley slave:

> Most of the convicts cannot eat the amount of bread given to them, and keep it to sell, and by the time they return they have kept enough of it to sell in Marseille . . . You need to take two convicts from each galley, men who seem like big eaters, put them in the arsenal without telling them why, and feed them there for eight days on their usual ration to see what quantity of biscuit they eat.[81]

In 1685, at the initiative of the general administrator, Michel Begon, the indigestible and badly balanced diet of the working galley slave was changed. The ration of biscuit was reduced, to 26oz (790g). They were still given the same bean soup, but as well as the biscuit and beans they had, three times a week, on meat days, 3oz of bacon (90g) or 4oz of salt beef (120g) and 3oz (90g) of rice; on non-meat days they had two-thirds of a pint of wine (620cl).

One may wonder whether these changes in rations were actually applied. Jean-Francois Bion, almoner (purser) of the *Superbe* in 1700, mentions the wine but not the other foods; 'At sea,' he writes, 'they give out the biscuit at 8 in the morning. They have quite a lot of it and it is quite good. At 10 o'clock they are given a bowl of soup, made with a little oil, beans or peas, often half rotten, half mouldy . . . and when they are rowing they have a jug of wine in the evenings and mornings.'[82] There was a good hand-out of rice, but the galley slaves, like the sailors, preferred to keep it and sell it when they got back, as witnessed in the letter of the Secretary of State for the Navy to the customs controller in 1697:

> M de Roanes tells me that a galley slave under his command brought back 47 quintals (about 2.35 tons) of rice into Bordeaux and that you ordered your farm guards to seize it for payment of duties. You were right to do so and the seizure would be correct if the rice came from a fraudulent business run by the convicts; but if it came out of their rations saved during their time at sea, as seems to be the case . . . it is right to allow them the whole profit without duty payments as it was being brought back into Bordeaux, where it was taken from in the first place.[83]

The most wretched galley slaves had to content themselves with the king's rations, with probably the wrong quantity and quality of biscuit, wine, salt provisions and dry vegetables: they had no right to speak out.[84] Others, who may have had a bit of cash, bought foodstuffs from the ration officers and managed to get some fresh food, especially fruit and vegetables, at the ports. 'The 'sailor's lot is something of a nightmare', wrote a protestant galley slave:

> but it is better by half when you have something to eat and drink. A slave who has sailed all night can only expect for lunch some biscuit and a handful of badly seasoned beans; having eaten that and rowed for the rest of the day, he only has what is left of his bread for supper. He does get a measure of wine in the morning and another in the evening, but so much of it is ruined by the greedy supplies officer that it isn't much at all. Imagine what a relief it must be when you can buy some rations from the soldiers or sailors, or send out for something from the port of call.[85]

Wine was the greatest consolation. The galley slaves used it to soak or soften their biscuit. In addition to the king's ration of wine, given out four days a week, the crew would sometimes get an extra glassful when it had forced the pace in a chase or to get into a port. This bonus was called the 'banner wine' because the signal for its distribution was given by the galley commander, who then hoisted a flag or banner.

It was essential to drink water, and lots of it. It was like fuel, indispensable for the survival of the crew and the working of the galley. Just like the most arduous jobs done in a tropical cli-

81. National archives B⁶ 16, p16, 30 January 1684.

82. Jean-François Bion, *Relation des tourments qu'on fait souffrir aux protestants qui sont sur les galères de France*, ed P M Conlon (Geneva 1966), pp83–84 9.1 (original ed, London 1708).

83. National archives, B⁶ 29 p542, 4 December 1697.

84. Supplied by a contractor, the rations would be issued by a ship's purser hired by the contractor who would feather his own nest at the expense of the crew and the oarsmen. Some of the methods used are well known and documented. 'All the bread was weighed on the galleys using a steelyard', wrote Dumaitz de Giompy, 'but whether it was the wicked intention of the purser or whether it was simply the circumstances of the voyage, the one doling out the food always fared better than the one receiving it; this is why steelyards should not be used, only cup scales.' (National archives, B⁴ 9, p293, 1682). Sometimes the purser would sell the good-quality food when the ship was in port and replace it with damaged or more inferior produce.

85. Library of the Society of the History of French Protestantism, Court collection, No 11, volume 1, p741, 6 November 1692.

Galére Patrone à la Voile.

A Dutch engraving of 1701 showing a French patronne *galley under sail. In this mode the oars were secured by having their butt-ends lashed to a ringbolt. Although the lateen rig should have allowed them to point closer to the wind than a square rigged vessel, in practice their shallow hulls made them leewardly and the lack of freeboard prohibited the degree of heel associated with tacking close to the wind; as a result they rarely sailed with the wind anywhere but well aft of the beam.*

mate, such as cutting sugar cane, the galley slave's job required substantial and frequent drinks, at least a litre of water per working hour: 'If a man who is rowing in great heat does not drink now and again', wrote a galley master, 'he must stop rowing or die'.[86] So the galley carried huge quantities of water which were stowed away somewhere. As it was impossible to store it within the hull, under cover, because it was already full of equipment, it was kept on the deck, within reach of the rowers. The water was kept in barrels about 70cm by 35cm, with a capacity of 50 litres, and weighing about 60 kilos. The size, shape and capacity of these receptacles was very important. The contents of one barrel represented a week's ration for one slave, which was on average 7 litres a day per rower. The water was tapped with a small cane pump, 'so not a drop was spilled', and poured into a wooden or tin-plate *pinte* (about a quart) which, together with the *gavette* or bowl shared by the five convicts and slaves on the same bench, was the sum total of the crew's crockery. Each of these barrels was tucked away, either standing up in the space between two benches, or laid down on the deck under the benches, using a plank as a walkway to the rowers. The ship carried 500 of these water barrels, which when full weighed about 30 tons and contained a total of 25,000 litres. Before sailing, not only did each barrel have to be filled, but also the two cooking boilers had to be filled to the brim, as well as the convicts' *pintes*, 'this being the last item as the embarkation of as much water as possible was the priority'.[87] The slaves used up three-fifths of it, while the rest was needed for cooking and for the free men: officers, masters, seamen and soldiers, about 200 men. Even used sparingly and carefully measured out, this reserve of water lasted only a week: 'A galley can scarcely survive more than eight days before coming to a halt . . . it must never wait until the water runs out'.[88] As well as giving information on the sailing conditions and the hazards of war, this maximum period of eight days tells us the exact cruising time of a war galley at the end of the seventeenth century, and explains (partly) the need for the galley's frequent landings and 'stoppages', at least every five or six days.

Handling the oars demanded experience and application. 'First, they have to prepare their bodies', stated the almoner of the *Superbe*, and toughen up the inside of their hands to get a good grasp on the oar.'[89] To which Captain Barras de la Penne added: 'there is more to

rowing than you might think; the rower has to use his head'.[90] Restricting oneself to painting a grim picture of weary men, bombarded with blows from the master who stalks up and down from poop to prow, does not help to explain anything. We need to understand how the rowers, despite everything, adapted to the sailing conditions, and understood what was expected of them in human terms, for without strict economic use of essential items this man-machine system, which either strengthened or decimated the workforce within the first few weeks of sailing, would never have achieved anything, even the most modest of objectives. This is not to say that we have to forget the miseries of the galley or deflect from the constraints and atrocities that were the constant burden of these men.

The mechanics of rowing *a scaloccio*

The historian needs to be an ergonomist as well. It may seem absurd to try to explain how galleys of the classical period were sailed with the help of modern ergonomics. However, we are looking at what is effectively a professional job, with certain characteristics:
–a place of work, the bench, where five to seven men lived and toiled;
–a work tool, the oar;
–a basic method of working, relating to the position of the rowers' bodies in relation to the oar.

First-hand evidence is not wanting. It provides a reconstruction and a fairly precise and clear picture – proven drawings – of the galley slave's job. Rowing knowhow meant knowledge on several levels. Jean Marteilhe, author of *Memoirs of a Protestant Condemned to the French Galleys because of his Faith*, recalls the ten years he spent on a bench on the *Palme*, between the English Channel and the North Sea: he expresses the views of those who were there, the convicts.[91] Sieur Masse, a master during the first third of the eighteenth century, tells us in his articles how to 'set up' a galley: this is the voice of an officer.[92] The learned treatises of Barras de la Penne and de Fontette, two galley masters during 1680–1720, provide a perspective somewhat different from the man who, resting in his armchair on the galley poop, sees

86. City Library, Marseille, MS 967, pp220–221.

87. City Library, Marseille, MS 967, p444.

88. City Library, Marseille, MS 967, pp220–221.

89. Jean-François Bion, p81.

90. National Library, MF 9177, p187, sd.

91. Jean Marteilhe, *Mémoires d'un Protestant condamné aux galères de France pour cause de religion* (La Havre 1778). This is the edition quoted from here. A Zysberg re-edited Jean Marteilhe's text in full under the title *Mémoires d'un galérien du Roi-Soleil* (Paris 1982). The original edition was published in Rotterdam in 1757.

92. 'Mémoires du sieur Masse fils, comite réal, pour bien manoeuvrer une galère à la mer et la tenir dans sa véritable estive par de bons et justes arrimages', City Library of Marseille, MS 967, pp424–496.

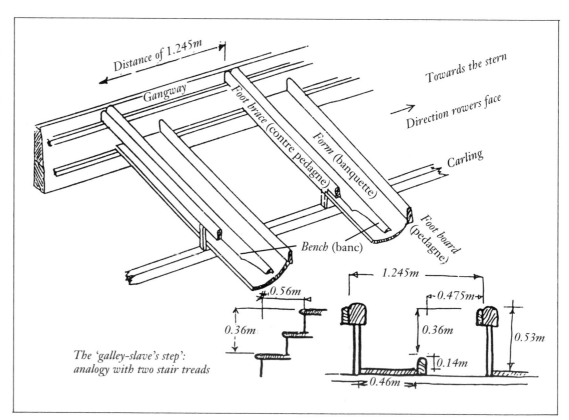

*The 'galley-slave's step':
analogy with two stair treads*

The bench of an ordinaire *galley.* (René Burlet)

The 'workplace' of an ordinaire *galley. Extreme positions of the oar:*
1. *Back in ordinary rowing mode*
2. *Forward in ordinary rowing mode*
3. *Forward in* passe-vogue *rowing mode.* (René Burlet)

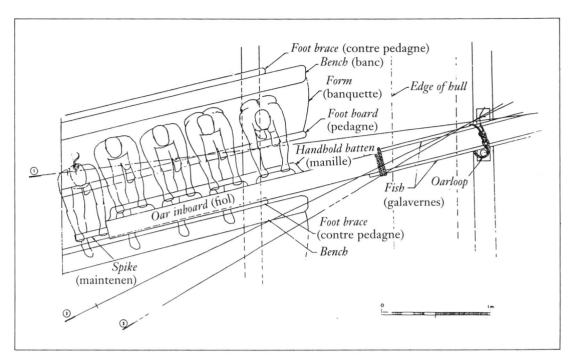

only a distant 'mechanical action' on which he acts indirectly, without dirtying his hands.[93]

What is here called the 'bench' comprises four parts: the bench itself, the form, the foot board and the foot brace. The bench is a strong length of pine, 7ft (2.28m) long, 6in (16cm) wide and 5in (14cm) thick (units are old French feet, *pieds*, and inches, *pouces*). It is curved at the edges 'so that the sharp edges do not hinder the master'. It is also slightly hollowed out on the underside 'to make the boat lighter', and because there was never any unused space aboard a galley, a musket was kept underneath. The rower did not sit on the bare wood. The plank that served as his seat was padded with old material tied up in a sort of small cushion; this was draped with a big piece of leather, which acted as a sort of apron to protect the rowers' legs from the spray. Their feet rested on the form, a fir plank as long as the bench, 17in (46cm) long, 50mm thick, which hung over the deck by about 50cm. Along the edge of the form was a pine board, of the same length, 14cm wide and 8cm thick, positioned about 15cm above it: the foot board. Beyond that the slaves had no immediate foot rest, and the convex structure of the deck lay bare before them. They had to make a forward lunge of about 50cm to reach the next rest, the foot brace, a pine bar 6ft (1.96m) long, 4in (10.8cm) wide and 2in thick, which was attached to the bench in front.[94]

Given the size and layout of this workspace, one has to ask how the slaves and convicts managed to row. Each one of them, whichever class of galley they were in, be it standard, *Patronne* or *Réale*, had only an amazingly narrow seat, about 45cm – the breadth of an average man (1.6m) is about 40cm. This means that the slaves could not bend their arms sideways, because this movement, which seems indispensable to anyone who has ever used an oar, required 85cm. The confines of the bench obliged the slaves to sail with their arms continually outstretched, pushing the oar towards the poop, which is quite possible, but also pulling it back towards the bow to push the blade through the water, and this seems almost impossible to imagine.

Profile of the rowing bench of an ordinaire *galley.* (René Burlet)

This position – arms constantly as straight as a plank – necessarily restricted breathing, and hence the ability to recuperate during a prolonged period of effort. The rower, a master noted, gets out of breath quickly. The sailing position meant yet another horror. When the boat was fully laden, the benches, *ie* the seating area, was only 1m from the surface of a flat-calm sea, and about 70cm from the scupper-holes, situated a foot above the waterline where deck water flowed out. So the slaves were permanently wet, their skin blistered and sore from the salt water. When the Mediterranean was a bit rough, they no doubt sailed with their feet in the water.

The tool used in rowing is the oar: '*pala-mente* is the term given to all the oars which, as everybody knows are really the galley's legs'. The oar in an ordinary galley, which was operated by five men, was 12m long and weighed at least 130kg; the oars in a large galley with seven oarsmen on each bench were anything up to 14m long and weighed nearly 160kg

93. Barras de la Penne, 'La science des galères', National Library, MF 9176–9179, sd; de Fontette, 'Traité des manoeuvres des galères et comment il faut remédier aux accidents qui arrivent dans un mauvais temps', City Library, Marseille, MS 967, pp343–420.

94. References to the dimensions of the rowing station differ slightly from one manuscript to another. We have generally adopted those given in a treatise on galley construction which is kept in the Navy's history department under classification No SH 134.

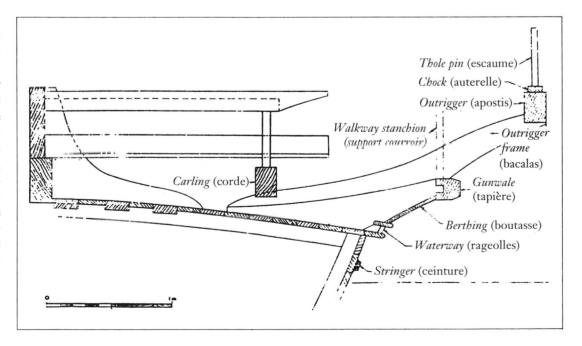

12/1: Dimensions of the Oars of French Ordinaire and Patronne galleys at the end of the seventeenth century

	Ordinaire	Patronne
Length overall (m)	12.25	14.31
Weight (estimated)	130 kg	160 kg
Length from blade end to thole (m)	8.49	10.06
Length from thole to 'maintenen' (loom or *fiol*) (m)	3.76	4.25
Minimum width of blade (cm)	12	?
Maximum width of blade (cm)	17.9	19.6
Diameter at loom or *fiol* (cm)	15.2	17.3

Based on: *'Traité de construction des galéres de Dabenat'* (Treatise on the construction of the Dabenat galleys), SHM, MS 408, pp525–533, and *'Traité de la palamente'* (Treatise on oars), Barras de la Penne, BN, MF 9177, p173 (for the blade). Another treatise dealing with the construction of galleys which is kept in the Navy's historical department (SH 134) gives very similar measurements.

(Table 12/1 gives the oar dimensions of a galley *ordinaire* set alongside those of a *Patronne*). Next to the suite of oars in a French galley in the seventeenth century, the oars which equipped the largest ship's boats of the nineteenth century, however long at 7.25m, cut a modest figure. Galley oars were hewn from beech, combining the qualities of strength and flexibility. The *rémolat réal*, the royal oar-maker, selected his wood from the forests of Dauphiné, Lyon, Languedoc, Lorraine and sometimes the Pyrenees. The oars were cut on site. Depending upon its diameter, a single trunk could provide from two to four 'blanks' which the oar-makers called *estelle*. They took the basic precaution of leaving the blanks to dry properly before working them. The *estelle* section, which was taken from the thickest part of the trunk closest to the roots, was made into the 'loom' or the fiol, or in other words the side gripped by the rowers, while the other end, taken from the top of the tree, was fashioned into the blade. The inboard part of the oar, which was some 3m long, had to be as heavy as its outboard part – almost three times larger so as to balance the oar perfectly on either side of its fulcrum. The oar's diameter increased from its 'wet' end towards the held end; it had a diameter of 3in at its blade (9.4cm), 5in (14.8 cm) where it was secured to the gunwale and almost 6in (15.2cm) at the *maintenen* (the

'spike' extension to the oar proper). Regardless of the skill of the craftsman, this balance was impossible to create naturally because that part of the oar which is closest to the water cannot be made too light. The balance was produced by embedding a lead plate into the fiol depth, the weight of this ballast being at most 5 kilos on an ordinary galley and 7 kilos on a *Réale*.

Once this work was completed, the oar-maker set about producing the optimum profile for the blade, and the oar then had to be 'fitted out'. Since it was impossible for the galley slaves to grip firmly a contraption which had a circumference of just over 50cm at its thickest end, the oar-maker made a beech *manille* or batten which he nailed to the loom or fiol. This was a multiple handhold comprising four handles on an ordinary galley and six on a *Réale*. There were four and six despite there being five and seven rowers respectively because the lead rower did not use the clevis but had his own special handhold called the *maintenen*, which was right at the end of the oar and which was simply the very rough end of the oar.

The oar-maker still had to protect that part of the oar which rested on the gunwale. Two twin 'fishes' made of holm oak, called *galavernes*, were nailed and secured to the oar at this spot. These fishes were about 6ft (1.90m) long, 9in (24cm) wide and 1⅔in (4.5 cm) thick and had a roughly tapered shape to match the profile of the oar; the *galavernes* were thicker towards the middle, with 'lugs' which would be used to lock the oar better on the apostis, or the galley's gunwale. To prevent the oar from cutting into the gunwale during operation, a piece of holm oak about 5cm thick called the *auterelle* was set into it. The oar was secured to the galley side by a long, slightly curved oak dowel driven into the side, like a stake. It was 73cm long and was called the *escaume* by Eastern sailors and the thole by Western sailors: it is the pivot point of the oar. The distance between two consecutive tholes is exactly the same as the distance separating two benches, ie 3ft 10¼in (1.25m). A rope or strop with an eyelet turned in to one end and the other terminating in a 'rat's tail', goes round the 'lugs' in the *galavernes* and holds the oar tight against the rowlock. It is held by an iron spike which is driven in between the rope strands.

The 'system' formed by the oar with its fixtures and its mode of articulation is not very complex, but the slightest imperfection can heighten fatigue among the rowers and more serious defects can eventually cause death. Each galley carried on board an oar-maker

with 'twelve spare oars, a few *galavernes* and *clevises*, marline for tying them together, nails for the *galavernes* and *clevises*, eighteen lead weights and associated tools'. The oar-maker was responsible for the on-board 'maintenance' of the oars. Small problems such as an oar being poorly balanced, a blade splitting or a *galaverne* breaking would be quickly and fairly easily repaired. When a blade was in danger of breaking it was 'fished' with an iron clamp, or if it was considered that the part could not be salvaged it was replaced by one of the spare oars. In other instances, the profile or 'tail' of the blade was poorly crafted and was too convex or, conversely, too flat like a badly trimmed quill pen which took too much or not enough ink when it was dipped into the ink-well. This fault would be felt immediately by the galley slaves, and the lead rower would respectfully inform the master, who would then instruct the oar-maker to bring his tools. But even the best tricks of the trade would not be able to repair a set of oars which were completely distorted because the wood used had been poorly selected or had been worked too soon, nor even worse increase the length of oars which had been cut too short by an oar-maker too fond of the bottle.[95]

With hands welded to the battens, the rowers formed one body with the oars, rowing with a monotonous backwards and forwards motion, prisoners of the squirrel cage which was the galley bench. The fate of the vessel and

A schematic rower showing distances between the major joints, as used in the following diagrams. (René Burlet)

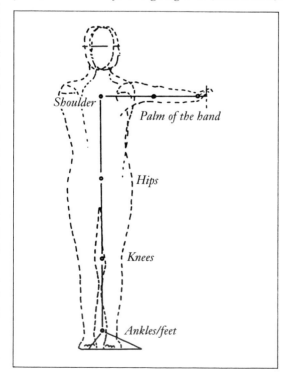

Shoulder · Palm of the hand · Hips · Knees · Ankles/feet

95. Nicolas Arnoul, Superintendent of Galleys, dismissed an oar-maker named Truc for this very reason: 'I dismissed him because he had failed to take due care on many occasions. He was more taken by the wine than by the wood I suspect; and the reason he was replaced . . . was because he did not apply himself to his work. This year he made the oars of the galley *Valeur* too short and I was therefore forced to return to port, exhausting the oarsmen.' (National archives, B⁶ 78, p259.)

its crew was at all times dependent upon the strength and also the skill of these men. Barras de la Penne wrote:

> There are three stages to the action of the rower. . . the first to stand up from the bench, the second to push the loom of the oar towards the stern of the galley; the lead rower then takes a step, puts his right foot on the foot board while the other stays resting against the form and stretches his body and arms towards the stern. The other rowers on his bench take the same step, to a greater or lesser extent depending upon how close they are to the lead rower . . . In the third stage, the rowers drop back on to the bench, leaning back sternwards, and still keeping their arms outstretched they describe a sort of circular line with the loom of the oar: it is during this third stage that they plunge the blade into the sea pushing it through the water, forcing it towards the stern as the rowers exert more force by pulling the loom towards the prow.[96]

The three stages described by Barras de la Penne clearly summarise the kinematics of a stroke. The captain did not, however, attempt to explain how the galley slaves managed to pull the oar towards the bow when they were forced to adopt a stance which was rather un-ergonomic: 'still keeping their arms outstretched' he said.

Taking the lead rower in the right-hand (starboard) row as an example, the accompanying series of drawings show the successive positions adopted by a schematised galley slave whose body is shown as a series of straight-line segments linking the main joints: wrist, shoulder, hips and ankles. The starting position (No 2) finds him standing up, his arms in front of him and slightly bent below his shoulders in order to keep the blade out of the water. His left foot – the one chained – is on the foot board while his free leg remains resting against the form. If it was a rower from the left-hand row his right leg would be the one chained, and it was always the shackled foot which rested on the foot board. This first step represents a movement of 30cm forwards and approximately 15cm in height, as though the rower were climbing a small step. Keeping his arms slightly below the horizontal – with the oar still out of the water – the head rower raises himself on the foot brace to adopt position No 3. He achieves this by bringing up his right leg, the free one, which he bends on the foot brace, and by supporting his weight on the left leg which is now braced against the foot board. With this second step, which would be like going up two steps of a 'standard' staircase at once, the head rower has completed his 'climb' towards the stern. At the start of the next phase – engagement – the lead rower gradually lifts his arms to lower the blade into the sea (Nos 3a and 4). Since he has only a very short space of time (about one second) to provide the power needed to pull the oar, the rower uses his right leg, which he presses against the foot brace. It is this straightening of the leg against the pine bar (acting as a kind of spring), and this movement alone, which enables him to return both his body and the oar to his bench (positions 5, 6 and 7) while still keeping his arms outstretched. At the end of the lead rower's physical exertions, having imparted the maximum angular speed possible to his oar, he appears to be almost off balance, with his trunk bent backwards and both legs braced, one against the foot brace and the other against the foot board. From then on the lead rower prepares his 'descent' (position No 8) by bending his left leg, which makes the return movement easier. The rower drops back on to his bench, his right foot returning to the form, whereas the left foot, which is shackled, remains on the foot board (positions 9 and 10). At the same time, the galley slave lowers his arms to lift the blade out of the water. He then returns to his original position seated on the bench. With one cycle completed, another can commence.

By joining the points matching the sequence of the positions of the oarsman's hold on the oar, we get a curve which represents the cycle of the lead rower. Its importance is fundamental because the trajectory of the blade can be deduced from it. It is a very short cycle: the angle swept by the oar reaches 18° in conventional rowing. This low clearance will be offset by high stroke rates exceeding 20 strokes per minute, or one stroke every three seconds. The other four galley slaves on the bench have no choice but to match the lead rower. The diagrams showing their respective hold points are again deduced because the distance separating each rower from the head of the bench is constant throughout the cycle and the arc made is identical.[97] The closer they are to the thole – the oar's fulcrum – the lower the grip on the battens and the working conditions become worse and worse. The *apostis* and the *tiercerol* are once again the best off: they remain standing for the best part of the cycle and they return to their starting position with their trunk slightly bent forwards. The *quarterol* adopts a much more curved position because he has to grip the oar in a position less than one metre from the form, *ie* the bench platform. Nevertheless, we have to assume that he is still

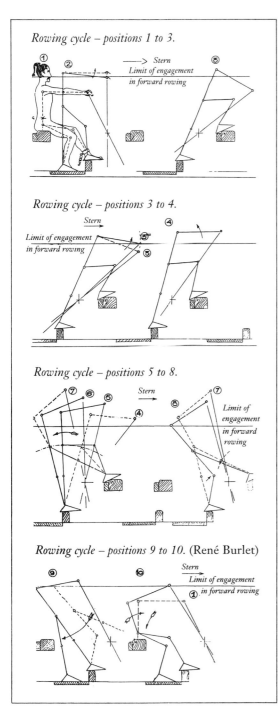

Rowing cycle – positions 1 to 3.

Rowing cycle – positions 3 to 4.

Rowing cycle – positions 5 to 8.

Rowing cycle – positions 9 to 10. (René Burlet)

---

96. National Library, MF 9177, p187.

97. The curves described by the wrists of these four oarsmen have all been offset horizontally by 17cm. This is the distance which would have separated the axis of the *manilles* from the axis of the *maintenen*, or the end of the oar held by the lead rower. This gap was without doubt just reason for the head of the bench to be called the 'lead rower', because he effectively rowed ahead of his four team members. When the oar was immersed in the water it would be he who would lunge furthest forward and get closest to the next bench. However, at the end of the rowing cycle, because he had moved furthest away from his bench, there would have been no fear of his missing it when he dropped backwards. If he received the order to lengthen his stroke he had to take care not to pull the oar too far back, because otherwise he would risk tipping up the rest of the *brancade* head over heels.

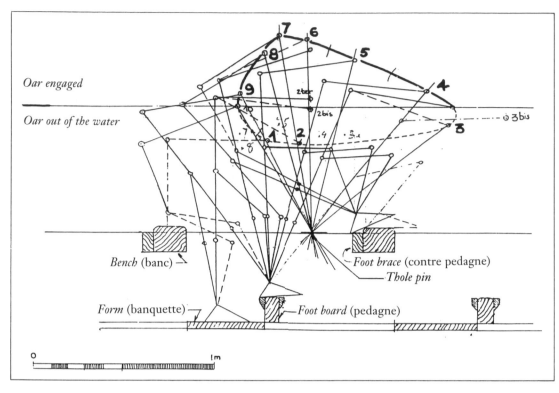

Oar engaged

Oar out of the water

Bench (banc)

Foot brace (contre pedagne)

Thole pin

Form (banquette)

Foot board (pedagne)

0   1m

The full cycle of the head rower in an ordinaire *galley*. (René Burlet)

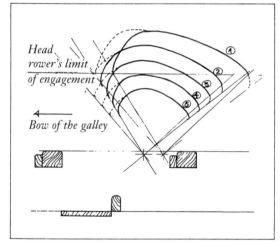

The hand positions for a brancade *of five rowers in an* ordinaire *galley. The solid lines represent the part of the cycle in which the oar blades are immersed; the pecked line is the zone in which the head rower can let his brancade 'fall towards the bow'.*
1. Head rower (vogue-avant); *necessarily followed by the other rowers*
2. Apostis
3. Tiercerol
4. Quarterol
5. Quinterol
(René Burlet)

Head rower's limit of engagement

Bow of the galley

Rowing cycle of the fifth rower (quinterol). (René Burlet)

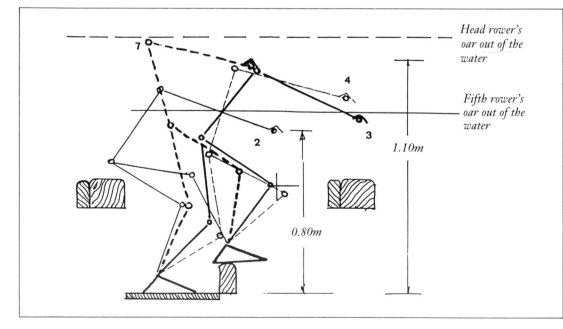

Head rower's oar out of the water

Fifth rower's oar out of the water

1.10m

0.80m

involved in powering the galley. This is not the case with the last rower, the *quinterol*, who is bent double during the stroke. His contribution to the forward movement of the vessel is practically nil: despite his discomfort, his role involves the least exertion and is reserved for the weediest rowers or for those who have to 'rest'.

The sequence of rowing shows that the oarsmen rowed with their legs and arms. Their arms, which were absolutely parallel throughout the stroke, outstretched on the battens, produced virtually no exertion apart from slight vertical movements of about 20 to 30cm which were used to lower or raise the blade from the water. It was the violent springing motion of the free leg bent against the foot brace which provided the vital work, and also the muscles of the back and the pelvic girdle which were also strained when the rowers leant forwards. They could not row any other way. Visual evidence is provided by the convicts depicted by Cornélius de Wael, one of the few painters and sculptors keen to show something other than the 'splendour' of the galleys. His galley slaves have scrawny chests but thighs like those of cyclists.

The fact that there is only one way of rowing suggests that the work of the oar has more than one variant. When the galley was required to chase a vessel or conversely take flight, the captain gave the command for *passe-vogue*, or bench crossing, rowing. This mode combined a tremendous acceleration of the stroke rate with a lengthening of the stroke because the galley slaves, instead of stepping on to the foot brace, had to place their unshackled foot on the bench in front. These bursts of speed were dreaded by the convicts. '*Passe-vogue* rowing is the most terrible punishment imaginable,' recalled Jean Marteilhe, 'because the timing or stroke rate has to be doubled and it is more tiring to row one hour like this than four hours of ordinary rowing, not to mention that in this type of rowing it is almost impossible not to miss a stroke, resulting in a hail of blows from the rope.'[98] Experienced masters did not much like the *passe-vogue* rowing which sometimes captains demanded for no reason at all, but just 'for show' to impress their distinguished guests. In his writings, Masse stated:

> I find this type of rowing is the least effective and the worst of all, and I never like to use it

98. Jean Marteilhe, p460.

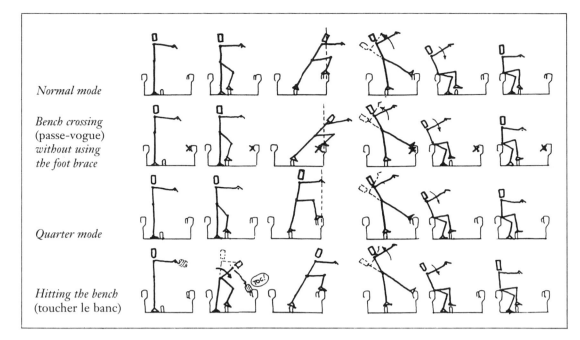

Normal mode

Bench crossing
(passe-vogue)
without using
the foot brace

Quarter mode

Hitting the bench
(toucher le banc)

The different modes of rowing. (René Burlet)

the same refreshment as the other quarter; and in this way the rowers can have a rest and take food.

Captains and masters mentioned two or three other types of rowing which had the same basic cycle. The most spectacular was 'hitting the bench' (*toucher le banc*) rowing. When the rowers 'climbed' towards the stern and before lowering the blade into the water, they hit the loom of the oar on the bench in front and 'the timing is so accurate that you can hear just one blow from all the rowers'.[102] With this mode of rowing, which was also called *picqu'a banc*, the multicoloured oars were raised in the form of a wing and then lowered into the sea. This was the display/parade mode of sailing used when entering and leaving port and most certainly a 'lovely mode of rowing', but was used sparingly because the violent jolt caused when the oar hit the bench shook the galley's hull and risked damaging it.

It was possible to row in the opposite direction to help the galley to go about. The captain gave the command: 'starboard team back water and port team row', when he wanted to turn to starboard, and vice versa if he wanted to turn to port. 'Back water' in rowing terminology means to row the wrong way. To go about, the 'back water' command was given for one side only: starboard to go right and port to move the left. To 'back water', the lead rower, the *apostis* and the *tiercerol* of each bench turned to face the bow and passed under the oar which was then grasped firmly; they then rowed 'backwards', one foot on the foot board and the other braced against their own bench. This change in rowing direction imposed quite a few additional constraints. The chained leg performed the hardest work, because it had to be lifted to bench level without the support of the foot brace; secondly, the three rowers who turned round were not able to use their batten because the oar did not turn round with them; finally they remained standing throughout the cycle. While they struggled to do this, the last two rowers, the *quarterol* and the *quinterol*, remained in the usual place seated on the bench, helping their companions to pull the oar: then, all together they 'back the oars'. If the order was given 'back water and row', the team which was not 'backing the oars' rowed in the conventional manner and turned the galley round.

The other methods of handling the oars were much less harsh than rowing and backing water. When quarter rowing in a flat sea, the team not working placed their oars *à la barbe*,

myself because it exhausts the rowers and is not the best method of propulsion for the galley . . . because for the little headway you might make in a short time you make your rowers out of breath and completely exhausted. So I would say that *passe-vogue* rowing is only effective for a short run of about an hour.[99]

The officers expressed a different point of view. Certainly,

the rowers have to be taken care of and are not to be put under strain except when the occasion demands it, such as when giving chase or when heading for port when time is short . . . It is, however, a good idea to make the rowers practise *passe-vogue* rowing for one hour every morning when at sea so that they are fit for it; this hardens them to the work; they feel better for the sweat caused by the effort which they are made to put into it; they are given wine afterwards.[100]

'Quarter' rowing was much better. The rowers were divided into two teams working in relay. On an ordinary galley the 'aft quarter' included the first twelve rows of benches starting from aft, and the forward quarter was made up of the next fourteen rows. Depending upon the voyage, each quarter would row for two to three *ampoulettes* – which was the name given to a half-hour sandglass – that is to say an hour or an hour and a half rowing in turns. This was

the best way of rowing in calm seas and over long distances when there was no requirement to row 'with all hands'. The galley master Masse wrote:

When leaving port, provided the sea is calm, the custom with the king's galleys is to row with all hands for four *orloges*, which is the same as two hours; afterwards we row in quarters, changing over each half-hour period for the first two occasions and then every hour, which is the normal rule in quarter rowing provided that the sea is calm and the weather good. If we are in a channel [this was what they called a crossing during which a squadron lost sight of the coast] the quarters might be three *orloges* or one and a half hours long, but this has to be set by the captain depending upon the weather at the time or what he considers the weather will be like and also depending upon the ship's course; everything is done to keep your rowers in good condition so that they can be of good use to you.[101]

This quarter rowing was by far and away the most economical way of rowing because it spared the rowers; the work period of the galley slaves never exceeded an hour and a half in each shift and was equalled by the rest and recuperation period. In this way the rowers could take refreshment in turns: according to Masse:

the breaks in quarter rowing give the rowers the opportunity to refresh themselves; in each rest period they are given wine, soup and beans; and at change-over those who have eaten row and the rowers now at rest are given

99. City Library, Marseille, MS 967, p447.
100. City Library, Marseille, MS 967, p399.
101. City Library, Marseille, MS 967, p452–453.
102. City Library, Marseille, MS 967, p319.

Positions of the oars at rest.

1. 'Rem à la barbe': butt secured with rope loop, parallel with water; used for the resting oars in quarter rowing when bringing them into action rapidly might be required
2. More permanently lashed (fournelée) to a ringbolt; used when under sail in calm weather
3. 'Sur les filarets': raised on stanchions in heavier weather.
(René Burlet)

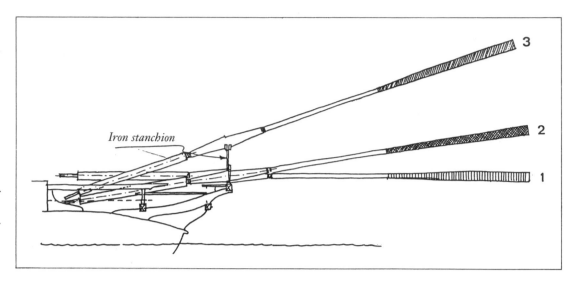

kept out of the water by passing the butt-end of the oar or *maintenen* through a loop of rope which was attached to the head of the bench. If 'raise oars' was general and the galley proceeded under sail only, this method of securing the oars was inadequate because the oars would not be high enough out of the water and could be damaged as soon as the vessel heeled to port or starboard and dipped the blades into the water. To prevent this type of accident, the oars were *fournelées*, in which the the *maintenen* was lashed down by a rope which was itself attached to an iron ring (the *fourneladou*). When the weather worsened and the sea became rough – which is no fanciful assumption – it was always possible to *paléger* by presenting the blades flat, parallel to the water surface so that they caught the wind as little as possible. And if, in spite of everything, this was not sufficient when a heavy squall got up, the captain would give the command 'raise oars on to the *filarets*'. It was done by setting iron bars called *batayolles* in the rails of the walkway and on the covering board at the deck edge. There were two rows of *filarets*, sited one above the other. These openwork railings were used by the soldiers stationed on the walkway as supports. They also had a much more mundane use: the oarsmen's washing and that of the soldiers would be dried on them. There again, on feast days or on ceremonial occasions, scarlet arming cloths bearing the *fleurs de lys* would be hung from them, as would the galley's good linen replacing the crew's clothes. During the feverish activity which occurred when leaving port they had to remember to 'double over' the *filarets*: the top barrier was then fastened on a level with the bottom barrier so that each strengthened the other as though they now formed only a single part. This measure would prove to be vital when the oars were raised on to these railings, because without it a single *filaret* could give way under the weight of the oars, which would then be lost overboard.

When the vessel was in the shelter of a harbour and at anchor, the oars were normally *fournelées*. However, where an anchorage proved to be too narrow to take the entire squad-

ron or if a crosswind caused the galleys to roll too much, the oars were *conillé*: the men on either side hoisted their oars inboard until they crossed either side of the gangway top to tail. According to Barras de la Penne, three galleys with their oars *conillées* did not take up any more room than a single galley with its oars *fournelées*. This manoeuvre would also be used in high seas when under sail to improve the vessel's stability. The captain would instruct his galley master as follows: 'The galley is having to be brailed up too much, order the men on the port side to *coniller* six oars'. This meant that six benches on the port side to which the galley was heeling – the lee-side team – had to slide their oars over to the other side. By doing this, the oars acted as a counterweight and in this way all or just some of the oars could be swung from either side as required. This also applied to the rowers: when the galley heeled over, at the signal '*fouerre*' or '*remble*', the convicts on the leeward side would press themselves against the middle line to help the galley right itself.

What was the performance of these vessels when they were propelled exclusively by oar power? With one or two exceptions, sources give no information on this subject, and it is pointless merely to quote the rare references to the speed of galleys without any verification.[103] Ships' logs give the approximate times of departure and arrival from one anchorage to another, but calculating average speeds sometimes gives ambiguous results, because during the course of a single voyage the galleys often combined different modes of propulsion: rowing and under sail, under sail only, rowing only, conventional rowing or pursuit rowing, all hands or quarter, without knowing exactly how such, and, such a part of the voyage was covered.

The authors have tried to obtain by experi-

mental means what records failed to document. This was not a question of reconstructing a galley and crewing it with 'volunteer' rowers,[104] but rather of using data obtained

103. The most critical assessment of the claimed speed of galleys under oar power is provided by Pierre Alexandre Forfait, the famous design engineer, who estimated that 'even in a flat calm the best equipped galley could make no more than four and a half miles in the first hour', quoted by P Masson, *Les Galères de France* (Aix-en-Provence 1938), p206.

104. In about 1930–1939, an American admiral, W L Rodgers, took an interest in the performance of galleys. Given the nature of his job, he was able to pay close attention to the force exerted by 12 men of the American Navy, all champion oarsmen, who rowed a cutter approximately 9m long at full stretch. These men managed to row like this for 3 miles at a speed of 7kts. After determining the hydrodynamic resistance of their boat, Rodgers calculated that each oarsman had supplied an effective power of a sixth of a horsepower (122 watts). The total power developed by the oarsmen was in fact much greater, because Rodgers did not take into account losses due to the travel of the oar through the water, nor the fact that they were working against inertia. With this initial estimate, he advanced the theory that a galley slave in medieval or modern times, who would have been less well nourished and punier than an athletic American sailor, would be capable of supplying an effective power of 92 watts over a relatively short period of time. He applied his theory to a vessel whose dimensions he knew: the Venetian trireme of the sixteenth century. He calculated the total resistance of the ship and, knowing the theoretical power requirement, he deduced the top speed of this galley with three oars per bench as being a little less than 7kts – a speed which, according to him, the galley slaves would not be able to maintain for more than 20 minutes – see W L Rodgers, *Naval Warfare under Oars, 4th to 16th Centuries* (Annapolis, Maryland 1939), pp231–232. Taking up this subject again in around the 1970s, another American historian, J F Guilmartin, assessed the cruising speed of the same Venetian trireme as 4kts – see *Gunpowder and Galleys* (Cambridge 1974), p197. These two results do not appear to be inconsistent: far from it, particularly with the second figure which agrees with the few observations of the people of the period and what can be gleaned from campaign reports. Our own calculations have produced very similar conclusions. However, the method used by Rodgers was questionable because it disregarded the possibility of an analysis of actual effort and only took into account the effective power needed to propel the vessel, whatever its mode of propulsion.

from ergonomic studies on the oar, the bench and the rowing motion. By making a distinction between the 'climbing' phase of the rowing cycle with the oar out of the water, and the 'engagement' phase, when the oar is in the water, an attempt was made to evaluate the work effectively provided by the head rower – the one who would produce the greatest effort, not only that needed to propel the ship, whatever its mode of propulsion, but also all the other work intrinsically linked to the operation of the oar in the environment in which the latter moved and with the actions of the rowers. Instead of concentrating simply on looking into the speed of the galley, which in itself has no significance, the authors decided that this was just one element in the problem, and that it was necessary to look at it in combination with all the other parameters such as condition of the hull (smooth or rough), wind speed (zero or headwind), the stroke speed and even the sailing mode (all hands or quarter). This study was conducted by engineer and physicist Jean Carrière, who is an expert in aircraft fuselage aerodynamics and who applied his knowledge and his processes to the problem of galleys under oar power.

By analysing the work involved at the most basic level, that of the rower, the authors gradually moved towards designing a 'model' which would work for all combinations of assumptions. This model was applied to an ordinary galley with five rowers per bench, propelled by a set of 51 oars (or 25 in the case of quarter rowing), as built in the Marseille shipyard in about 1680–1690. In the absence of any plans, this reference vessel was to be similar to those illustrated in an album of drawings at the end of the seventeenth century, showing the successive stages of galley construction. The rowing model used different categories of values: measurements, estimates, coefficients and numerical laws.[105] The term 'measurement' in this context means measurements in the strict sense of the word, taken from manuscripts or carried out from scale drawings of the era; estimates are deduced arithmetically or geometrically from these measurements.

Two examples will demonstrate the method. There is no first-hand written evidence giving the wetted surface of an ordinary galley. However, the main dimensions of the reference vessel, in particular its length on the waterline and its moulded beam, are known. The

wetted surface of a French *Réale* was calculated from the plan published by the Friends of the French Maritime Museum. Assuming that the form of the two hulls was identical, a proportionality rule gives the submerged surface of an ordinary galley as 253.37m². Similarly, sources give no indication of the travel of the blade during the oar stroke, but the ergonomic study was able to estimate, by means of linear projection, that the lead rower's wrist travelled a distance of 2.43m. As the rotation of the oar started and finished at the same point, it could be verified that the course of the oar through the water was the same as its course out of the water. Knowing the length of movement at the handhold, the distance between the end of the blade and the thole, and the distance between the butt-end and the thole, it was then possible to deduce the amplitude of movement of the blade.

Coefficients were used to calculate the various resistances to the ship's progress and the action of the oar in the water. These are 'dimensionless' numbers (having no unit of measurement). The following have been chosen for consideration:

1) Those affecting the resistance of the hull
a) The aerodynamic drag coefficient
This expresses the head resistance against the ship's top hamper; forecastle structure, masts and yards, ropes, awning and oars. It is estimated to be equal to the ratio of the front surface of these superstructures and the submerged surface of the hull, divided by 1000.
b) Viscosity resistance coefficient
This is one of the components of hydrodynamic resistance. It is called viscous resistance because, like all other fluids, water has a certain viscosity. First of all a coefficient is evaluated which expresses the friction drag. This depends upon a dimensionless number termed the Reynolds number, proportional to the product of the speed of the vessel multiplied by its length at waterline and another dimensionless number qualifying the roughness of the hull. The friction coefficient is not applied to one type of the vessel in particular,

12/2: Rowing Model – Assumptions and Results

	All hands rowing					Quarter rowing	
	Zero wind			Head wind		Zero wind	
Galley speed (in kts)	4	5	6	4	2	3.5	4
Galley speed (in m/s)	2.058	2.572	3.086	2.058	1.029	1.8	2.058
Stroke rate (strokes/minute)	23	21	26	21.8	20.5	23	
Head wind speed (in m/s)	0	0	0	3	5	0	0
Degree of roughness (in mm)	1	0.2	0.2	0.2	0.2	0.2	0.2
Length of rowing cycle (in s)	2.609	2.857	2.308	2.752	2.727	2.927	2.609
Length of build-up phase (in s)	1.366	1.807	1.403	1.549	0.907	1.857	1.649
Length of engagement phase (in s)	1.043	0.850	7.05	1.003	1.620	0.87	0.760
Work required per oarsmen (in joules)	83.9	109.1	164.1	118.5	122.6	78.4	104.1
Total work per oarsman during build-up (in joules)	264.8	247	262.7	255.5	317.5	235.8	239.3
Total work per oarsmen during engagement (in joules)	192.6	275.4	405	231.4	161.4	162.3	214
Total work during the cycle (in joules)	457.4	522.4	667.7	486.9	398.1	453.3	
Total power supplied per oarsman during build-up (in watts)	194	137	187	164.9	349.9	127	145
Total power supplied per oarsman during engagement (in watts)	185	324	574	230.7	99.6	187	282
Total power supplied per oarsman during the cycle (in watts)	175	183	289	176.9	175.6	136	174
Efficiency during engagement phase	0.44	0.4	0.41	0.51	0.76	0.48	0.49
Efficiency during the cycle	0.18	0.21	0.25	0.24	0.26	0.2	0.23

105. The full report of the method and all the results obtained appear in A Zysberg's doctoral thesis, Vol II, pp474–537. Those readers wishing to know more should refer to this work.

NB:The length of a rowing cycle of stroke is equal to the length of the buildup or 'climbing' phase added to that of the engagement phase, plus 0.2 seconds which corresponds to:
– the duration of the slight vertical movement needed to engage the oar in the water at the end of the 'climb'
– the length of time it takes to drop back on to the bench at the end of the engagement.

but to a 'flat plate'. To determine the coefficient of viscous resistance peculiar to the galley, the friction coefficient is weighted by a form factor.

c) Wave resistance factor

In this case what was investigated was the resistance caused by the undulating movement of the water when it is cleaved by the ship's bow. At low speeds, wave resistance is negligible; at high speeds it becomes the dominating component out of all the various hydrodynamic drag components. This factor was accounted for only at speed of 5.5kts.

2) Those affecting the resistance of the oar blade in the water

The hydrodynamic drag coefficient of the blade, or CX, is used to calculate the resistance created in the water as the oar moves through it. The blade CX is linked to its aspect ratio, or in other words the relation between the length (of necessity variable throughout the engagement phase) of the submerged part of the oar and the width (assumed constant) of the blade, or chord.

To calculate the work carried out by the oar during the engagement phase required a category of values which this study calls numerical laws:
– the law of blade length in the water;
– the law of angular velocity of the oar.

Since neither of these necessarily appeared in any documentation of the era, and they could not be deduced directly from the measurements gleaned from the archives, these two laws had to be constructed empirically. One of these is already familiar from the rowing diagram showing the movement of the lead rower's wrist, from which the diagram of blade movement at the other end of the oar was derived. Defining the law of angular velocity for the oar proved to be a much trickier business because the angular velocity curve of the oar could not be deduced from that of the blade's travel. In actual fact, the acceleration of the rotation of the oar has to precede the increase in immersion of the blade by some fractions of a second, although the angular velocity already reaches its maximum value when the galley

slaves with maximum effort immerse their oars full into the water. These two actions will therefore be shifted chronologically; their respective curves will not be homothetic and they will not have the same form. By trial and error, or by using successive approximations, a series of values was therefore sought which best matched how the speed of the stroke developed: very rapid acceleration of the oar's rotation at the start of the engagement phase, the maintenance of the maximum speed in the middle of this phase, slow falling off and then a sudden deceleration at the end of the cycle, the last value being zero.

The series of numbers which we obtained by doing this corresponds to an 'average' case of a galley making 5kts at 21 strokes per minute. However, since the angular velocity of the oar also depends upon the speed of the vessel and upon stroke rate, the series of values obtained does not apply to all of the hypotheses regarding the vessel's progress. Therefore the terms of the series relating to the angular velocity of the oar were to be adjusted by multiplying them by a weighting coefficient which was to vary according to each 'case' considered. This adjustment of assumptions relating to the vessel's speed and the law of angular velocity of the oar is the key to the rowing model. All of these cases have been processed by computer. On top of its computational ability, the computer simulated the actual creation of the model and also the methodical examination of its possibilities and limits.

This exercise began with the concept that there was a basic difference between the power needed to propel the galley and the power actually supplied by the rowers. The ratio between 'theoretical' power and 'actual' power is just the efficiency of the 'engine'. The computation of the work was carried out on three levels: ship, oar and rower. We started by using Froude's ratio to calculate the power needed to propel the galley. From this was deduced the work which had to be done by each oar. To this was added two other not inconsiderable amounts of work – that arising from the moment of inertia of the oar and that against the added mass of water. From the oar, it

was necessary to move on to the rower. The crudest and least acceptable solution was to divide the actual work carried out by the oar during the engagement phase by the number of rowers on the same bench, that is to say five men in the case of an ordinary galley. However, this would amount to suggesting that all of the galley slaves on a bench worked equally as hard, and this would contradict everything shown up by the ergonomic study. Therefore a different route was chosen. The effort required by each rower in order to move the oar only slightly is equal to the product of the force multiplied by the amount of this basic movement. By calling F the (supposed equal) force of each rower and d_1 d_2 d_3 d_4 and d_5 the respective movements of a lead rower, an *apostis*, a *tiercerol*, a *quarterol* and a *quinterol*, the total effort produced by a bench would be:

$$T = (F \times d_1) + (F \times d_2) + (F \times d_3) + (F \times d_4) + (F \times d_5).$$

The work of the fifth rower can be disregarded, because he had only a back-up role due to his position on the bench. By factorising F we obtain:

$$T = F (d_1 + d_2 + d_3 + d_4).$$

Bringing d_1 out of the expression between brackets leaves:

$$T = F \times d_1 \left(1 + \frac{d_2}{d_1} + \frac{d_3}{d_1} + \frac{d_4}{d_1}\right).$$

The length of the lever arm or the distance between the wrist of each rower and the fulcrum of the oar is known, which will be called l_1, l_2, l_3 and l_4. Given that the movement of the rower's wrist is proportional to the length of the lever arm, the following equation can be produced:

$$\frac{d_2}{d_1} = \frac{l_2}{l_1}; \frac{d_3}{d_1} = \frac{l_3}{l_1}; \frac{d_4}{d_1} = \frac{l_4}{l_1};$$

therefore

$$T = F \times d_1 \left(1 + \frac{l_2}{l_1} + \frac{l_3}{l_1} + \frac{l_4}{l_1}\right).$$

By replacing l_1, l_2, l_3 and l_4 with their respective values:

$$T = F \times d_1 \left(1 + \frac{3.28 + 2.84 + 2.40}{3.76}\right);$$

from which $T = F \times d_1 (1 + 2.27)$. However, the expression $F \times d_1$ is the work done by the lead

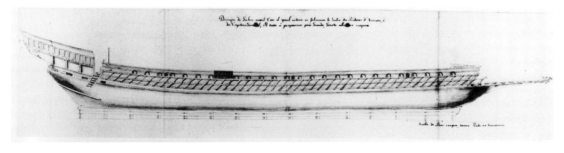

A draught of a Venetian 'narrow' (suttile) *galley from* Architettura Navale *of 1686 by Stefano di Zuane di Michiel.*

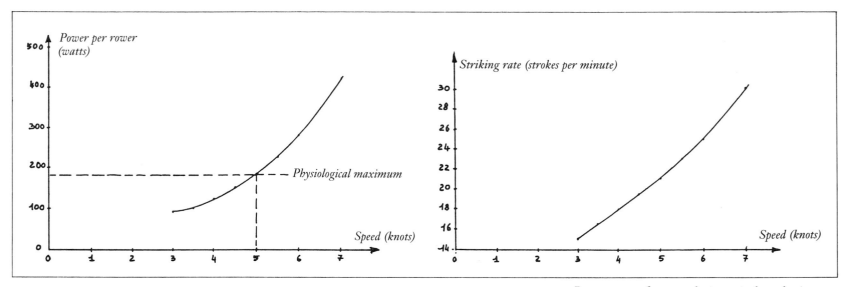

Power output of a rower during a single stroke, in relation to the speed of the galley (hull clean, normal rowing mode, zero wind).

rower (WLR), which means that the equation can be written T = 3.27 WLR. Taking the lead rower as a yardstick, the work applied to each oar is equivalent to that supplied by 3.27 theoretical lead rowers. The actual work done by the lead rower will therefore be equal to the actual work applied to each oar divided by 3.27. The oarsman is next for consideration. Apart from the effort required to push the oar through the water, and all the other effort needed to produce this movement, the lead rower also has to provide the force to accelerate his body in order to power the oar through the sea: this is work done against the mass-inertia of the rower's body.

After completing the computations for the engagement phase of the oar, it was then necessary to evaluate the work done by the lead rower during the 'climbing' phase when the blade is out of the water. In this way it was possible to calculate the work done owing to the inertia of the oar and that done against he inertia of the rower's body. The numerical results giving work and power are assembled in Table 12/2.

The lead rower of the galley at the end of the seventeenth century was expected to produce an average power of 183 watts during a rowing cycle of approximately 3 seconds, but what significance is to be attached to that first figure? A comparison with other data relating to the abilities of the rowers was essential, because without it the series of figures provided by the computer would have been worthless. The work performed by the galley slave was hard, and ranked alongside other hard, testing jobs such as cutting sugar cane or the manual extraction of coal from the bottom of a mine. In this context, specialists in labour physiology[106] estimated that the average man would be able to develop:

– 140 watts of power for ten hours,
– 170 watts of power for four hours,
– 200 watts of power for one hour.

These are maximum figures. Much lower limits would have to be assumed because, as we have seen, the cramped conditions of the bench would not allow the galley slaves to utilise their respiratory capacity to the full.

It is best to proceed by looking at an 'average' and 'best' case, with a galley proceeding with all hands with zero wind and clean hull at an average speed of 5kts and with a stroke rate of 21 strokes per minute. Masse wrote, 'Leaving port, assuming that the weather is calm, the King's galleys normally sail with all hands for four *orloges* which is two hours.' By applying this fact to our results it became apparent that our 'model' galley would perhaps be able to proceed at 5kts for the first hour, which even then would require each lead rower to supply 183 watts of power. There was no further reference to whether this speed was maintained for the second hour, but it probably fell to around 4kts. So much for 'cruising' speed: for maximum speed, the rowers pushed to their limits would perhaps manage to reach the 'wall' of 200 watts. With a tremendous increase in the stroke rate of at least 26 strokes per minute, *ie* a stroke every 2.3 seconds, a galley would reach 6kts (but certainly not 7kts), and at this speed 300 watts of power would have to be produced by each lead rower during each complete stroke cycle. This is half a horse-power! A speed as high as that would never be maintained for more than fifteen minutes. At that stroke rate a captain would be in danger of working his rowers to exhaustion within a quarter of an hour without having the assurance of achieving his goal.

The best mode of rowing to make full use of the ability of the rowers was quarter rowing.

Results show why experienced masters preferred this mode. Whilst with rowing 'with all hands' at 5kts the limit of endurance of the galley slaves would almost be reached after an hour, quarter rowing would ensure that a slightly lower speed could be sustained for ten hours or so and would not exhaust the rowers so much. With a striking rate of 23 strokes per minute and a speed of 4kts, quarter rowing would expend 174 watts of power per lead rower, and while this required some considerable exertion, it was less than the 200-watt barrier and also the rowers would be able to rest, eat and drink for an hour and a half to two hours before going back to the oars. When rowers were very tired, a sensible master would be content with quarter rowing at 20 strokes per minute which would require only an exertion of 136 watts from each lead rower.

Thus far, the argument has presupposed ideal rowing conditions: zero wind and little hull roughness. It is now time to look at less ideal cases, assuming firstly a headwind. Picture the following scenario: the squadron has weighed anchor to embark on quite a long voyage of about 30 miles. Halfway through the voyage, the rowers having rowed 'steadily' in quarter mode most of the time, the squadron is faced by a slight 2 metres per second (m/s) – 4kts – breeze coming directly head-on. The course demands that every attempt is made to hold the same heading, thus pointing too close to the wind to raise the sails. The masters have given the command 'all hands' because even this slight wind of little or no import has de-

106. J Scherrer, *et al, Précis de Physiologie du travail* (Paris 1981).

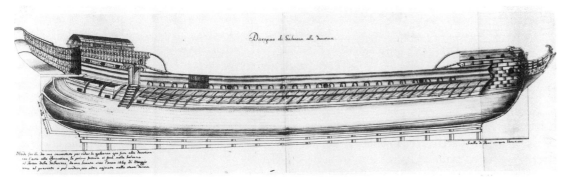

Draegene di Salanra alla Venetiana.

A draught of a Venetian galleasse from Architettura Navale *of 1686 by Stefano di Zuane di Michiel. The galleasse was a late attempt to combine the benefits of oared propulsion with a hull of improved capacity, firepower and seaworthiness to compete with sailing ships. Like most hybrids they combined the shortcomings of both types, being neither as handy under oars as a conventional galley nor as good under sail as a square-rigger.*

manded that all the oars are manned. There is no longer any question of quarter rowing. The rowers will be tired after an hour, perhaps less, without any chance of a rest period because the safe anchorage is more than three hours away. The breeze then becomes a moderate head-wind of 3m/s, then 4m/s, and finally 5m/s (10kts). Something which would be nothing of any consequence to any sailing vessel, and would not even merit a mention in the ship's log, becomes an unfortunate and disturbing event to the galley slaves. Maintaining the same effort and almost at the limit of the en-durance of the lead rower, *ie* approximately 180 watts, and with a headwind ranging between 3 and 5m/s, the average speed of the galley would fall to 4kts, 2.5kts and then 2kts. If this headwind freshened even more, reaching 6m/s, the vessel would not move at all. Then the only thing to do would be to go about. The basic lesson is that with a headwind in excess of 5m/s (18km/h), which could in no way be described as a hurricane, no modern galley could be rowed.

The condition of the hull would also have a not inconsiderable bearing on performance. At 5kts, if the level of roughness increased from 0.2mm (hull quite smooth and clean) to 0.5mm (dirty hull), the total power supplied by the rowers would increase 15 per cent. It is easy to understand why the galley crew insisted on the galley going into the graving dock at least once a month during a campaign. Nicolas Arnou wrote, 'When a galley has been fully graved, it goes much better and relieves the strain of the rowers like a well greased coach.'[107]

In examining the effect of the different row-ing theories, particular use has been made of the variation in overall power provided by the lead rower during one stroke. But it is also worth looking at the intermediate results. With a stroke rate of 21 strokes per minute and an average speed of 5kts (2.572m/s), each lead rower would have to supply an effective 109 joules in the course of each complete stroke cycle to overcome the hydrodynamic resistance of the hull. However, the total and actual work

expended by him in rowing the galley would be as much as 522 joules during each cycle. The gap, or rather the gulf, between these two fig-ures is the result of added force: essentially the battle against gravity and inertia of both the oar and the body of the rower. Just standing up from the seated position costs the galley slave 223 joules, that is to say twice that strictly re-quired to propel the ship; 80 per cent of the energy expended by the lead rower did not go into maintaining the galley's speed, but was used up by extra work. The result was par-ticularly poor efficiency. When fighting galleys at the end of the seventeenth century were pro-pelled by oar power alone they proved to be slow and cumbersome vessels which were never capable of exceeding a cruising speed of 4–5kts. This very fragile relationship between man and machine only worked in an ideal en-vironment: sea like glass, no headwind. Finally, it was the physiological capacities of the rowers, already weakened by poor treatment and the precariousness of the job, which were to blame for the vessel's poor endurance.

It is not surprising , therefore, that only 1–2 per cent of convicts in the time of Louis XIV, when the activities of the fleet were at their height, died in battle. They rarely lasted more than about sixty days and, bar one or two ex-ceptions, each galley only embarked on one voyage per year which was more or less testing depending upon destination. The length of time galleys spent at sea was very short com-pared with that of the typical Western sailing vessels, whose voyages normally lasted 200 to 300 days. Whilst a high-freeboard ship would spend several weeks at a stretch at sea, galleys spent frequent and prolonged periods in port. Out of a fifty-day campaign, a fleet of galleys in the Mediterranean would have spent at least thirty alongside or in the shelter of a port to take on water and wood, to rest the rowers and also so that the gentlemen officers could enjoy themselves with the local ladies. The leaders of the squadron did not take any risks. They pre-ferred to eat their rations and wait patiently and sensibly for the most favourable time to

leave. It is therefore hardly surprising that the mortality rate of the crews of sailing vessels was five to ten times higher than that of the con-victs on campaign.

As soon as a favourable wind arose, they raised the sails. Using a vessel designed for rowing as a sailing ship would appear surpris-ing or even paradoxical, and actually posed many problems. Galleys were equipped with a very full lateen rig which was constantly im-proved throughout the seventeenth and eight-eenth centuries. The logs of these galleys in the years 1720–1740 show that 20 per cent of the voyages were entirely under oar power, very often in quarter rowing mode, 20 per cent were entirely under sail, but the vast majority, 60 per cent, were under combined sail and oar power.[108] Masse wrote, 'we know from experi-ence that a galley under sail can only make good [a course] five compass points from the wind; even then the wind has to be moderate, the sea calm and the weather good; but when the wind is light and the galley is oar-assisted, it will make one point nearer the wind.'[109] Sail-ing 'by the wind' (close-hauled) – this is how they would proceed up to within four points of the wind – proved to the most sensible com-bination provided that the breeze was 'moder-ate', according to Masse, who knew what he was talking about. In calm seas and with a good breeze, the galley proved to be an excellent sailing ship with surprisingly good perfor-mance, making the best use of the now forgot-ten or unrecognised qualities of the large lateen sails. But in heavy weather, a vessel whose gunwale was 1.50m from the waterline, so shallow was its hull, proved to be a pitiful sea-boat with appalling sea-keeping qualities. The galley captain had no choice but to make for port and hole up there until the weather improved.

107. National Archives, B⁶ 78, p59, 1666. Remember that the graving operation consisted of coating the hull with one or more coats of molten tallow.

108. Compare these percentages with the very similar figures given in the study produced by E Fasano-Guarani, 'Au XVIe siècle, comment naviguent les galères', *Annals ESC* (1961), pp279–296.

109. City Library, Marseille, MS 967, p467.

Conclusions

For almost half a millennium man tried to improve the oar propulsion system of fighting ships, devoting effort, imagination and above all commendable perseverance to the task. This chapter has only looked at the two rowing systems for which there is a reasonable amount of information. *Alla zenzile* rowing, when the men were chained, and the problem of the quadriremes still has to be investigated, as do quite a number of projects and tests which were not followed up but which are no less worthy of interest.

At the beginning of this period, when galleys were rowed *alla zenzile* with two men to a bench, it was logical that someone would quickly have the idea to add a third rower to obtain an increase in speed under combat conditions. In Venice, this was applied to a narrow hull which was low in the water – the *galea sutile* or *sottile*, in which the placing of this third oarsman was tricky and difficult. The fifteenth-century galley investigated was a perfect example. Giving the newcomer the room, however slight, to row more or less properly, would quickly reach the limit of how many places this type of hull could accommodate. The *galea sutile* of the fifteenth century would never be able to carry a fourth rower.

To fit in this fourth rower, the hull had to be changed, but above all the apostis-to-apostis breadth had to be increased. Another type of vessel was therefore developed, the *bastardella* or bastard galley, stronger than the *sutile* galleys and wider. This allowed a fourth rower to be accommodated, and eventually a fifth. The modern galley was the direct descendant of this initial model. It was quickly realised (though this still has to be studied in depth) that in *alla zenzile* mode the efficiency of this fourth man was not as good as had been hoped. This is explained in detail in the account by Francesco Bressan, touched on earlier. The ideal, of course, was for the four men to be able to row like four *pianeros*, which was the reason for trying out a fourth man with just two oars, each operated by two men. In practical terms, the solution was attractive because it required few modifications and unquestionably brought about a better utilisation of the rowers.

Original research in this direction would be worth pursuing, as it is clear that *alla zenzile* rowing has in no way disclosed all its secrets.

A scaloccio rowing which followed it was supposed to resolve some of the problems, particularly the recruitment of oar crews, because it was difficult to row properly with the old system without a lot of experience: *alla zenzile* rowing was a real craft. They also tried to improve the efficiency of the men by removing some of the preoccupations: in a *scaloccio* rowing only the *pianero* was involved in 'setting the stroke' – all that the others had to do was to pull. The result was not completely as expected. This mode of rowing, which was a response to one particular problem, quickly demonstrated its limits. Surviving information on this type of oar system is of high quality and absolutely consistent. Most of the energy expended by the oarsmen was taken up in overcoming the mass inertia of the oar and the bodies of the men themselves, which successfully demonstrates the limits of a process: the greater part of the energy expended was not used to obtain the desired goal, but was dissipated in other ways.

Despite these improvements, the days of the galley were numbered by the advent of artillery. As soon as vessels were able to accommodate many guns firing through broadside ports, the die was cast. The smallest vessels of the early seventeenth century so armed were capable of sinking a galley with a well-aimed broadside, while the galleys could only respond with their few bow-chase guns. However, galleys did not disappear immediately. In France the *Généralat* and the *Régiment des Galères*, the country's oldest maritime organisation, was not dissolved until 1748. Spain followed suit in the same year but occasionally recommissioned a few vessels thereafter. Some new galleys were launched at even later dates: in France *L'Amazone* in 1751 and *La Bretonne* in 1756 – and at Brest which had never been associated with galleys like the Mediterranean ports. The country's last galley, *La Ferme*, although she had not sailed for many years, was not stricken until the beginning of the nineteenth century.

The small Italian states, which had always maintained several galleys, could not afford sailing battle fleets, so tended to keep their galley forces for as long as possible to preserve some vestiges of sea power. In 1804, for example, the King of the Two Sicilies ordered two half-galleys, named *La Ligurienne* and *La Béatrice*, of seventeen oars a side to be rowed by freemen. The latter was undoubtedly the last Mediterranean galley to take part in a naval battle when she participated in an attack on the island of Caprera in 1815.

In certain circumstances galleys could still be effective. For instance, at the beginning of the eighteenth century six galleys operated with some sucess from Dunkerque in a form of guerrilla war against Anglo-Dutch commerce. North Sea conditions could be favourable: fogs to allow surprise attacks, variable winds, and above all shallow water where a sailing ship could not following the escaping galley. Similar conditions existed in the Baltic, where the Swedes and the Russians fought over the Finnish archipelagoes. Each kept oared flotillas down to the nineteenth century (see Chapter 6 of *The Line of Battle*), and to the Russian navy went the distinction of fighting under oars for the last time, before Åbo in 1854. There is no little irony in the fact that a type born in the Mediterranean more than 2000 years earlier saw its final action in the Baltic, at a time when the steamship was already a practical proposition.

Mauro Bondioli
René Burlet
André Zysberg

Galleys lingered on in Mediterranean navies until the middle of the eighteenth century (and even later in the Baltic), one of the last forces using them actively being the Knights of St John, based after 1530 at Malta. This illustration shows the 'magistrale' galley, the flagship of the Grand Master of the Order in 1741. (National Library of Malta)

13

The Geographical Conditions of Galley Navigation in the Mediterranean

AS FOR ships of all types, navigation by galley in antiquity and the Middle Ages was governed primarily by the weather, in particular by prevailing winds and incidence of fog, rain, and storm. To the weather one can also add currents and tides in certain narrows and bights.

Because the climate of Europe has passed through various hotter and cooler phases over

Currents, prevailing winds (summer), and trunk routes. (From J H Pryor, Geography, Technology, and War [Cambridge 1988])

the past 2500 years,[1] we must question at the outset what weather conditions were like in various eras of the past, and whether climatic changes altered conditions of navigation in the Mediterranean at various times. Can modern meteorological and oceanographic observations be used with confidence to explore the geographical conditions of navigation in past centuries? How similar were the latter at various times to those of the modern era, for which meteorological and oceanographic observations are available in quantity?

Generally speaking, the European climate became cooler from *c*900 BC to around 300 BC, then warmed until the fourth century AD, cooled again from *c*AD 400, warmed from

1. See H H Lamb, *Climate: past, present and future, Vol 2: Climatic History and the Future* (London (1977), and 'Climate and the history of medieval Europe and its off-lying seas', in *Medieval Europe, 1992: a Conference on medieval archaeology in Europe, 21–24 September 1992, University of York. Pre-printed papers. Volume 2. Maritime studies, ports and ships* (York 1992), pp1–26; E Le Roy Ladurie, *Times of Feast, Times of Famine: a history of climate since the year 1000* (London 1971).

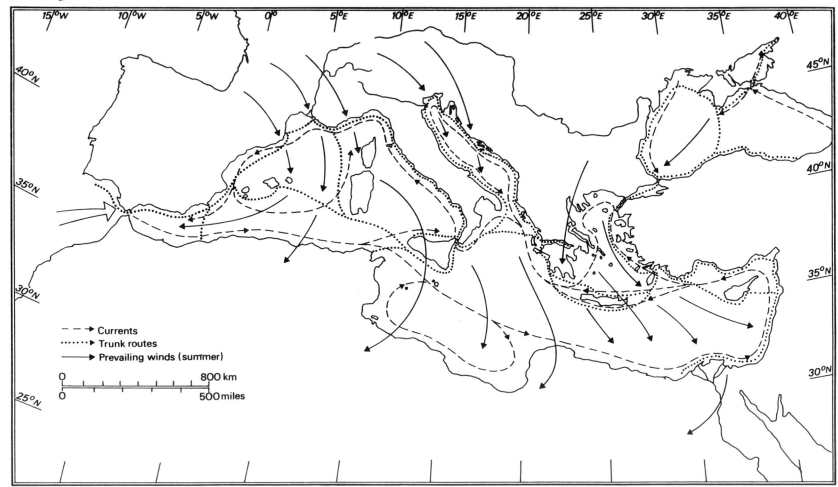

- – –► Currents
- ······► Trunk routes
- ——► Prevailing winds (summer)

0 ——— 800 km
0 ——— 500 miles

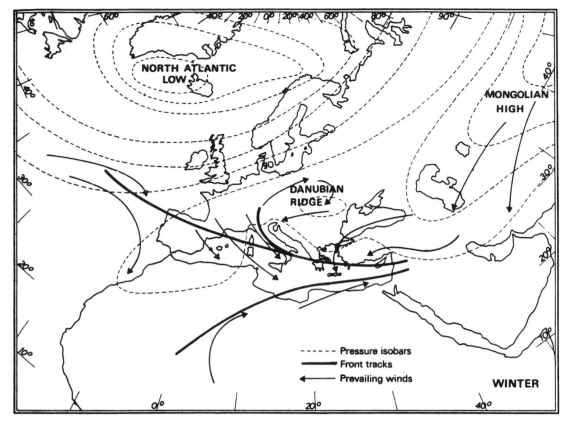

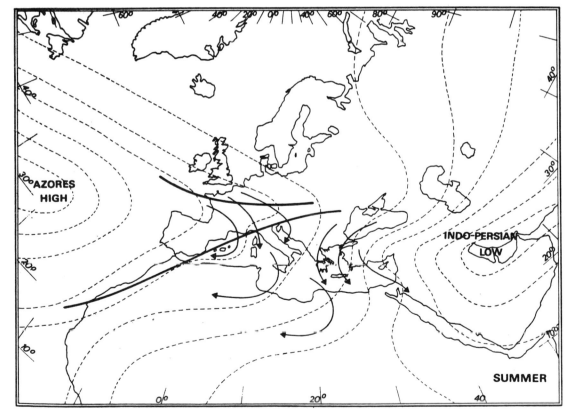

Normal Mediterranean sea-level pressure systems, front tracks, and prevailing winds – winter (top), summer (bottom). (From J H Pryor, Geography, Technology, and War [Cambridge 1988])

itime historians for purposes of elucidating the conditions of navigation in the Mediterranean over the centuries, the data compiled by historians of climate are also complicated by the fact that the evidence for the Mediterranean basin is far less extensive than that for trans-Alpine Europe. Since the same climatic changes may produce quite different effects in the Mediterranean basin to those they produce north of the Alps, the evidence of the climatic record from northern Europe must be used with caution.

The meteorology of the Mediterranean basin is fundamentally determined by the seasonal interactions of four great intercontinental air masses: the Azores high-pressure and Indo-Persian low-pressure systems in summer and the North Atlantic low-pressure and Mongolian high-pressure systems in winter. Climatic cooling should have the effect of weakening and shortening the influence of the two summer systems and strengthening and lengthening that of the two winter systems. One would expect shorter summers and longer winters, accompanied by increased cloud, rainfall, and fog, during such periods. The incidence of strong northwesterly to westerly winds and storms should also increase, as should wind velocities. The reverse should be the case in periods of climatic warming, although the historical record appears to show that climatic warming sometimes produced milder but wetter winters in the Mediterranean basin. A southerly movement of Arctic pressure systems in cooler periods may cause winds in the western basin of the sea to shift away from the northwest and more to the southwest in winter. So also, the incidence and strength of easterlies generated from northern low-pressure systems, such as the *levanter* in the Straits of Gibraltar and the *gregale* in the Ionian Sea, should increase in such periods. On the other hand, the occasional southerly and easterly winds experienced in the southern sectors of the sea, the various forms of the *scirocco*, which are normally generated by the influence of low-pressure systems in Saharan Africa and the Arabian Peninsula, should increase in frequency and strength in warmer periods and decrease in cooler ones. However, with possible minor variations such as these, because all four intercontinental systems reinforce each other to create prevailing northwesterly to northeasterly winds across the entire sea, climatic

around AD 900 to *c*1250 and then relapsed into a mini 'Ice Age' in the fourteenth and fifteenth centuries, warmed once again from around 1450 and then cooled again from *c*1525, and finally warmed from around 1800 to the present time.

The effects of these changes were extremely complex, and data from the historical record are frequently confusing since many short-term changes within the long-term patterns occurred in various regions of Europe. Moreover, when subjected to interpretation by mar-

variation should not cause great difference to the direction of the all-important prevailing winds.

As far as the current circulation in the sea is concerned, periods of cooler weather with higher rainfall should increase the influence of the current from the Black Sea through the Bosporus and Dardanelles and perhaps also increase the influence of outfall from rivers such as the Nile, Po, and Rhône. On the other hand, they should decrease the influence of the inflowing current through the Straits of Gibraltar since water gain from rainfall and river inflow should increase as a percentage of the loss of water from evaporation and the level of the Mediterranean should rise. Although the overall circulation of currents in the sea should not be affected by climatic change, current races in certain narrows may possibly vary in strength.

All this being said, the historical record provides no evidence whatsoever to suggest that in any period during the past 2500 years climatic variation causes changes in weather patterns which would invalidate any conclusions drawn from modern observations about the influence of meteorological conditions on navigation. Ancient and medieval observations of wind directions invariably coincide with the evidence of modern meteorological data.[2] The same is true of the current circulation in the Mediterranean and the tides experienced in certain narrows and bights. The currents of the Dardanelles, Bosporus, and Straits of Gibraltar, and the tides in the Evripos, Gulf of Sirte, and Straits of Messina are all mentioned in historical sources from antiquity and the Middle Ages.[3] There is no evidence that the conditions of navigation have ever changed significantly in historical times as a result of climatic changes. Those changes have certainly produced variations in mean average temperatures, the lengths of the seasons, and the incidence of snow, rain, storm, and fog. However, the fluctuations in mean average temperature of around 1–1.5°C in historical times have always been too small to produce discernible changes in the geographical and meteorological conditions of navigation which can be traced in the historical record.

The trireme reconstruction Olympias *under sail, heeling under the influence of a light quartering breeze. In some early trials the ship was sailed with the wind on the beam, and inclining trials have proved that the trireme has sufficient reserve of stability for safety in this condition, but clearly the acceptable maximum angle of heel is restricted by the low freeboard and outrigger. (Paul Lipke, by courtesy of the Trireme Trust)*

The limitations of galley navigation

Throughout all ages of galley navigation in the Mediterranean, from that of Greek aphract galleys of the eighth century BC to that of Renaissance galleys of the sixteenth century AD, war galleys of all varieties, no matter by what names they were known in their various civilizations, operated under limitations on their operational capabilities which made them extremely vulnerable to geographical conditions.[4] Lack of space in the hull for supplies, low cruising speed under oars, and limited sailing qualities lowered their range of operation, made it difficult for them to make way against contrary winds, and contributed to a need to follow coastal routes. Their low freeboard made it advisable for them to follow coastal routes of navigation except when military or political considerations overrode those of navigation. It also made it even more dangerous for them to navigate in winter than for sailing ships. In a metaphor, war galleys were thoroughbreds of the sea, bred for sprint races on level ground (in fine weather), and were ill-suited to other tasks, particularly cross-country races over uneven ground (in bad weather).

Their limitations were products of their fundamental design features: features which themselves were inescapable consequences of the primary purpose for which they were intended to be used. Ships which were designed essentially to be highly manoeuvrable and capable of being driven by oars at high speeds for short periods in battle, had of necessity to be built long and narrow in order to minimise water resistance and wavemaking by the hulls, to ride low in the water, and to have a shallow draught.

2. See William H. Murray, 'Do modern winds equal ancient winds', *Mediterranean Historical Review* 2 (1987), pp139–67.

3. See J H Pryor, *Geography, Technology, and War: Studies in the maritime history of the Mediterranean, 649–1571* (Cambridge 1988 reprinted 1992), pp xvii–xix.

4. In what follows immediately here, attention is focussed on the standard light war galleys of all the maritime powers. The degree to which the conclusions drawn about these galleys needs to be modified in the case of transport galleys and more unusual larger war galleys is addressed further below.

An oar is essentially a lever. Its stationary fulcrum is the blade in the water and the load that is moved is the hull of the ship at the thole/rowlock. The ship moves only because the blade does not, or as little as possible. The further out from the hull the blade can be placed in the water, the greater the distance the hull at the rowlock can be moved for each stroke of the oar. Consequently, it was always desirable to have oars as long as possible, with as a high a ratio as possible between the length of the shaft and blade outboard and that of the loom inboard, subject to the capability of men to handle them. That being the case, it was also necessary to mount the oars as close to parallel to the waterline as possible because the mechanical advantage enjoyed by the oarsmen over the load being moved (the mass of the galley) is the horizontal total length of the oar from the grip on the loom to the centre of pressure on the blade divided by the length from the thole to blade pressure centre. As long as the blade remains at the same maximum possible distance from the hull, this mechanical advantage becomes greater the more the oar is horizontal and lesser the closer it is to the vertical.

The mechanical advantage can be increased by using an outrigger to mount the thole, as on modern racing shells, thus allowing for a longer loom inboard. At various periods some powers did use outriggers for some of the oars on their galleys. But, in all periods they built galleys as low to the water as possible in order to maximise mechanical advantage.

The war galleys of Charles I of Sicily, the earliest for which any detailed specifications survive, had a total height amidships from keel to deck at the centre line of only 2.19m. The camber in the deck made their 'gunwales' only 1.92m above the keel, and it is unlikely that their freeboard amidships when normally laden was more than 0.55m or so; although it rose to about 1.50m and 2.11m at bow and stern respectively.[5] There is no reason to assume that Sicilian galleys were markedly different in this fundamental design feature from other war galleys throughout the Mediterranean in the thirteenth century nor, indeed, from galleys of the earlier Middle Ages or the later Renaissance. Figures of 0.55–0.75m for the freeboard of late-medieval and Renaissance galleys have been cited.[6] The light galleys specified by Marino Sanudo Torsello for a proposed Crusader squadron in the early fourteenth century were to have a depth amidships of 6.5 Venetian feet or 2.26m. A Venetian war galley designed by Pre Theodoro around 1550 had a depth amidship of only 5 Venetian feet or

1.74m. The standard Papal galley described by Bartolomeo Crescentio at the end of the sixteenth century had a height of 7.25 Neapolitan *palmi* or 1.98m to the 'gunwale'.[7]

Any ship with as little freeboard as medieval and Renaissance war galleys obviously was in grave danger of being swamped if caught out to sea in any sort of a swell, particularly so since galleys were designed not to ride with the waves but rather to slice through them. Their average length of around 33m and beam of around 3.65m amidships at the waterline made it impossible for them to ride the waves. It would require very little swell to produce waves capable of washing over the decks of galleys with a freeboard of 0.55m amidships. A study of tens of thousands of observations of wave heights at sea in the southeastern Mediterranean between Egypt, Israel, and Cyprus over the years 1948–80 produced conclusions of mean significant wave heights of ⩾1.2m in winter (December–March), and 0.5–1.0m in summer (June–September).[8] Medieval and Renaissance galleys would have found even these mean summer wave heights challenging and the winter ones beyond their capabilities. It is not at all surprising that the history of naval warfare throughout the Middle Ages and Renaissance is replete with examples of fleets of war galleys being virtually annihilated when caught at sea in heavy weather.[9] Roger of Hoveden, who went on the Third Crusade with Richard Coeur de Lion, declared: '. . . galleys cannot, nor dare not, go by that route [the open sea crossing from Marseilles to Acre] since, if a storm should arise, they may be swamped with ease. And therefore they ought always to proceed close to land'.[10]

Their oars were of limited use against the wind. Sea trials of the reconstructed Athenian trireme *Olympias* have show that rowing the galley into a wind gusting up to 25kts exhausted the oarsmen in 70 minutes and that the ship only made good 3kts. If this experience has extended application, a galley caught on a lee shore, such as the north coast of Crete or anywhere along the North African coast, in conditions any worse than the fresh breezes of Beaufort Force 5 would be in danger of being driven ashore. Except in emergencies, galleys were never rowed into a wind stronger than a zephyr. Even the great galleys of the later Middle Ages, which were designed to be sailed rather than rowed, had very limited upwind performance capabilities. Travelling on a Venetian great galley in 1395, Ogier VIII d'Anglure made Jaffa from Venice in 32 days, but took over five months for the return against the prevailing winds. Such a differential was quite

common. It simply reflected the inability of all ancient and medieval galleys to make their way against prevailing winds, and explains why routes closely hugging the coasts were favoured whenever a traverse against prevailing winds had to be made. Adverse winds of any strength forced galleys to stay in port until the weather changed.

Even their sails were of limited use when tacking, and this made it difficult and dangerous for them to undertake open-sea crossings against prevailing winds. Galleys were notoriously bad sailers. Their low freeboard meant that they could not heel very far before shipping water aboard in any case and, moreover, under sail galleys shipped their oars 'a-wing', with the shafts and blades raised as high as possible. A heel of more than 10 degrees would mean that wave crests would strike the leeward oars and either smash them or make a galley unmanageable.[11] Their sails were really only of much use in fair weather when navigating with the wind astern.

Problems of supplies also contributed to making open-sea crossings unusual for galleys. An Athenian *triērēs* carried 170 oarsmen, a Byzantine bireme *dromōn* 108, an Ayyūbid *shīnī* 140 (perhaps a trireme), the bireme galleys of Charles I of Sicily between 104 or 108, and Spanish and Venetian trireme galleys of the early sixteenth century around 150. In addition to these oarsmen, galleys also carried numbers of officers, marines and/or archers, deckhands, and specialists. The number of men in the crews packed into their slender hulls was very large but their stowage capacity for 'fuel', that is food and water, for these crews was very limited. Food was not perhaps such a great problem. The volume of food per day necessary to sustain an adult male's physical condition is not particularly large. However, that of

5. See Chapter 7.

6. J F Coates, 'The naval architecture of European oared ships', *Proceedings of The Royal Institution of Naval Architects* (Spring 1993), Paper No 9, p4.

7. Marino Sanudo Torsello, *Liber secretorum fidelium crucis super Terrae Sanctae recuperatione et conservatione* (Hanover 1611), II, iv.11 (p65); F C Lane, *Venetian Ships and Shipbulders of the Renaissance* (Baltimore, Maryland 1934), p236; B Crescentio, *Nautica Mediterranea* (Rome 1607), p15.

8. V Goldsmith and S. Sofer, 'Wave climatology of the Southeastern Mediterranean', *Israel Journal of Earth Sciences* 32 (1983), pp1–51.

9. Pryor, *Geography, Technology, and War*, p70.

10. Roger of Hoveden, *Chronica*, ed W Stubbs, Rerum Britannicarum medii aevi scriptores, 51 (London, 1870), Vol 3, p160.

11. See Chapter 7; also Coates, 'The naval architecture of European oared ships', p7.

water is. Considerable research has been devoted to this question, and an estimate of four pints of water per man per day during the Mediterranean summer is now regarded as a minimum. A war galley of the Kingdom of Sicily in the second half of the thirteenth century, with a total crew of 152, would require at least 76 gallons of water per day. A 20-day cruise would require that a galley stow aboard at least 1520 gallons (6.90 metric tonnes), or the equivalent of more than eleven of the 134-gallon *vegetes* used for the carriage of water at the time. This appears to have approached the limits of the stowage capacity of medieval and Renaissance galleys,[12] probably more because of the displacement problems caused by the weight of the water than because of the volume taken up in the hull for stowage (it would lower the hull in the water by around 8cm). For normal operations, galleys would not take aboard even as much water at this. As the Venetian propagandist of Crusade, Marino Sanudo Torsello, said in the early fourteenth century: 'in the summer time [galleys] are not able to stay at sea for many days without that they frequently put in to land to take on drinking water'.[13] In summer there was also a problem with water putrefying very quickly.

The galley sailing season

Until the development of the great galley in the later Middle Ages, galleys rarely sailed from late autumn to early spring because of the deterioration of weather conditions in the Mediterranean in winter, except when eco-

nomic, political, or military considerations overrode those of safe navigation. As Marino Sanudo Torsello wrote, when explaining why the galley fleet which he was proposing could not be expected to blockade the coast of Egypt: 'The reason for which is this: that armed galleys cannot stay out to sea in winter time, and even in calm weather they are ill advised to be found out of port at night time in winter.'[14] Even the summer sailing season was shorter for galleys than for sailing ships. Around the end of the fourth century AD, the Roman writer on military tactics, Vegetius, restricted the sailing season for galleys to 26 May to 14 September, whereas sailing ships might sail from 10 March to 10 November. The duration of the sailing season changed over time and was never a hard-and-fast rule; however, the general parameters of a more restricted season for galleys remained true to the end of the Middle Ages. When the Genoese developed winter sailing to the Holy Land in the thirteenth century, it was in large sailing ships, not galleys. With depressions entering the north of the Mediterranean basin in the winter, creating gales and strong prevailing northerly winds, particularly the *mistral* in the Gulf of the Lion, the *bora* in the Adriatic, and the *vardarac* in the Aegean, the winter was not sailing weather for galleys. Moreover, because much of the Mediterranean is quite shallow, particularly along the southern coasts, in the Sicilian Channel, and in the Adriatic and Aegean seas, even moderate gales can raise dangerous, short, breaking seas. For ancient and medieval shipping, and galleys in particular, which navigated by visual obser-

vation of coastal landmarks, the winter with its increased cloud, rain, fog in certain locations (*eg*, the Sea of Marmara and the Straits of Gibraltar), and generally reduced visibility also made navigation much more difficult. Their effective sailing season was confined to the months April through to September.

The summer in the Mediterranean was, however, an entirely different matter. From April to September, the Azores anti-cyclone system in the mid Atlantic and the Indo-Persian cyclone over Iran generate steady prevailing northerlies which provide ideal conditions for seafaring across the entire sea. Seas are generally slight and visibility good. Rain is infrequent. This was the season for naval warfare and for galley navigation. The main variation to the prevailing northerlies across the length and breadth of the sea is the various forms of the *scirocco: khamsin* in Egypt, *leveche* in Algeria, *ghibli* in Libya and *shlouq* in Palestine. These hot southerly winds from the Sahara can provide conditions which can facilitate east–west traffic along the southern coasts; however, they can also intensify into dangerous, dust-laden gales, which are extremely hazardous to shipping. The Crusader fleet of Louis IX was scattered all over the Eastern Mediterranean when caught by a *khamsin* off the south coast of Cyprus in 1249.

To a degree, the combination of design characteristics and performance capabilities which compelled war galleys to navigate by coastal routes, except in emergencies, were mitigated in the case of transport galleys and the few larger galleys designed for war. Certainly, the great galleys developed by Genoa and Venice in the late thirteenth and four-

12. See also J F Guilmartin, *Gunpowder and Galleys: Changing technology and Mediterranean warfare at sea in the sixteenth century* (Cambridge 1975), pp62–3; W L Rodgers, *Naval Warfare under Oars, Fourth to Sixteenth Centuries* (Annapolis, Maryland 1939), p232. See also Chapter 7, n.67.

13. Marino Sanudo Torsello, *Liber secretorum fidelium crucis*, I.4.2 (p28).

14. Sanudo, *Liber secretorum fidelium crucis*, I.4.2 (p28).

teenth centuries, which were essentially sailing ships with oars to assist in manoeuvring and in emergencies, were perfectly capable of open-sea crossings. Transport galleys, such as the *chelandion* of the Byzantines, the *tarrīda* of the Muslims, and the *tarida* of the West in the thirteenth century, which had lower length-to-beam ratios than war galleys and a higher freeboard, were probably also more capable of open-sea crossings. Yet there is precious little evidence of them actually making them.

The principal galley routes

The evidence of modern research into the naval architecture and navigational capabilities of war galleys is fully supported by analysis of the routes followed by galleys and galley fleets from antiquity to the Renaissance. Invariably, they followed coastal routes except in emergencies. The Athenian trireme fleet sent to Syracuse in 413 BC hugged the coasts all the way via Aegina, Lakonia, Elis, Zakinthos, Keffallinia, Akarnania, Corfu, Cape S Maria di Leuca, Metaponto, Crotone, and Reggio. When the Byzantine general Belisarios sailed from Constantinople to Tunisia in AD 533, the fleet, comprised of both galleys and sailing

Map of the Mediterranean showing localised winds. (Denys Baker after an original by the author)

ships, sailed by way of Eregli, Abydus, Sigeum in the Troad, Capes Malea and Tainaron, Methone, Zakinthos, presumably the coast of the foot of Italy, a deserted beach near Mt Etna, Porto Lombardo in Sicily, Gozo, and Malta. A Venetian galley fleet en route to the Holy Land in 1122–1123 sailed via Corfu, Methone, Rhodes, and Cyprus. The fleets of Philip Augustus and Richard the Lionheart, both of which contained many galleys, sailed from Messina for Acre via Crete, Rhodes, and Cyprus. Frederick II took his fleet from Messina to Acre in 1228 via Corfu, Keffallinia, Crete, Rhodes, and Cyprus. In 1351 the Genoese captain Simone Leccavello took his galley from Genoa to Khios via the west coast of Italy (stopping overnight at ports en route), the Straits of Messina, Crotone, Zakinthos, Attica, and Negropont (Khalkis).

In the late tenth century, the Byzantine admiral Nikephoros Ouranos wrote in his *Tactica* that:

> It is appropriate for a general [admiral] to have with him men with accurate experience of the sea in which he is sailing, which winds cause it to swell and which blow from the land, and who know the hidden rocks in the sea, the places which have no depth, the land along which one sails and the islands adjacent to it,

the harbours and the distance such harbours are from each other, and who know the area and its water; for many have perished from lack of knowledge of the sea and the surrounding areas, since winds frequently blow and scatter the ships in different directions.[15]

Nikephoros was paraphrasing the advice of an earlier, sixth-century Byzantine tactician, Syrianos Magistros. It is difficult to imagine a more direct testimonial to the fact that Byzantine fleets of the early and high Middle Ages navigated by the coasts and that the hazards which most concerned admirals were those of coastal meteorology, oceanography, and geography.

As a consequence, from antiquity to the Renaissance, almost all naval battles between galley fleets took place within sight of land, invariably along the major coastal routes of navigation for galleys. How many major battles took place along the southwest coast of the Balkans: Naupactus (431 BC), Rhium (429 BC), Sphacteria (425 BC), Actium (31 BC), Gulf of Corinth (AD 879), Durazzo (1081),

15. Nikephoros Ouranos, 'From the Tactica of Nikkephoros Duranos, chapters 119–123', 119.1.1–2 in A Dain (ed), *Naumachica partim adhuc inedita* (Paris 1943), p93 (in Greek). *Cf* 'Naumachiae of Syrianos Magistros', 5 in *ibid*, pp45–6.

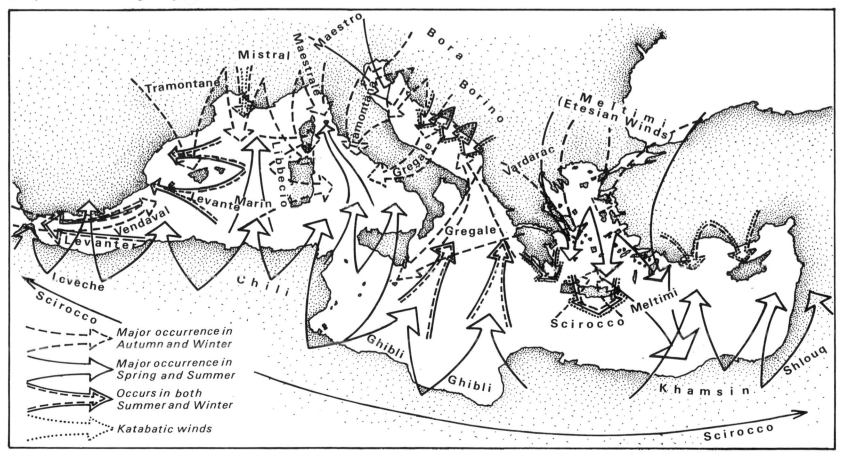

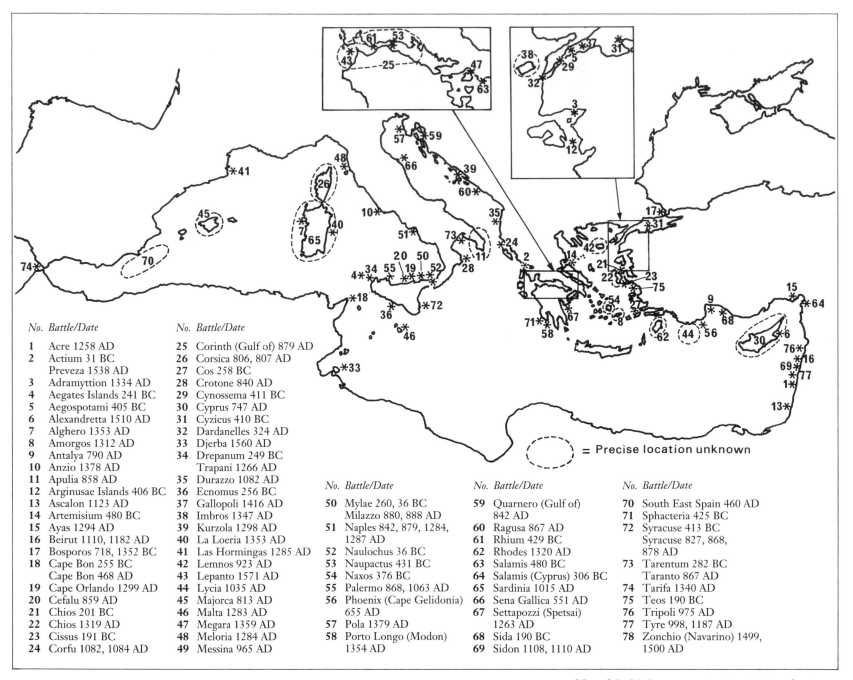

No.	Battle/Date
1	Acre 1258 AD
2	Actium 31 BC
	Preveza 1538 AD
3	Adramyttion 1334 AD
4	Aegates Islands 241 BC
5	Aegospotami 405 BC
6	Alexandretta 1510 AD
7	Alghero 1353 AD
8	Amorgos 1312 AD
9	Antalya 790 AD
10	Anzio 1378 AD
11	Apulia 858 AD
12	Arginusae Islands 406 BC
13	Ascalon 1123 AD
14	Artemisium 480 BC
15	Ayas 1294 AD
16	Beirut 1110, 1182 AD
17	Bosporos 718, 1352 BC
18	Cape Bon 255 BC
	Cape Bon 468 AD
19	Cape Orlando 1299 AD
20	Cefalu 859 AD
21	Chios 201 BC
22	Chios 1319 AD
23	Cissus 191 BC
24	Corfu 1082, 1084 AD

No.	Battle/Date
25	Corinth (Gulf of) 879 AD
26	Corsica 806, 807 AD
27	Cos 258 BC
28	Crotone 840 AD
29	Cynossema 411 BC
30	Cyprus 747 AD
31	Cyzicus 410 BC
32	Dardanelles 324 AD
33	Djerba 1560 AD
34	Drepanum 249 BC
	Trapani 1266 AD
35	Durazzo 1082 AD
36	Ecnomus 256 BC
37	Gallopoli 1416 AD
38	Imbros 1347 AD
39	Kurzola 1298 AD
40	La Loeria 1353 AD
41	Las Hormingas 1285 AD
42	Lemnos 923 AD
43	Lepanto 1571 AD
44	Lycia 1035 AD
45	Majorca 813 AD
46	Malta 1283 AD
47	Megara 1359 AD
48	Meloria 1284 AD
49	Messina 965 AD

No.	Battle/Date
50	Mylae 260, 36 BC
	Milazzo 880, 888 AD
51	Naples 842, 879, 1284, 1287 AD
52	Naulochus 36 BC
53	Naupactus 431 BC
54	Naxos 376 BC
55	Palermo 868, 1063 AD
56	Phoenix (Cape Gelidonia) 655 AD
57	Pola 1379 AD
58	Porto Longo (Modon) 1354 AD

No.	Battle/Date
59	Quarnero (Gulf of) 842 AD
60	Ragusa 867 AD
61	Rhium 429 BC
62	Rhodes 1320 AD
63	Salamis 480 BC
64	Salamis (Cyprus) 306 BC
65	Sardinia 1015 AD
66	Sena Gallica 551 AD
67	Settapozzi (Spetsai) 1263 AD
68	Sida 190 BC
69	Sidon 1108, 1110 AD

No.	Battle/Date
70	South East Spain 460 AD
71	Sphacteria 425 BC
72	Syracuse 413 BC
	Syracuse 827, 868, 878 AD
73	Tarentum 282 BC
	Taranto 867 AD
74	Tarifa 1340 AD
75	Teos 190 BC
76	Tripoli 975 AD
77	Tyre 998, 1187 AD
78	Zonchio (Navarino) 1499, 1500 AD

= Precise location unknown

Map of the Mediterranean showing the sites of major naval battles from Salamis (480 BC) to Lepanto (AD 1571). (Denys Baker after an original by the author)

Corfu (1082 and 1084), Korkula (1298), Porto Longo (1354), Zonchio (1499 and 1500), Prevesa (1538), Lepanto (1571)!

Coastal navigation allowed galleys to avoid prevailing winds out to sea and to reach along the coasts with the diurnal cycle of moderate land and sea breezes on either beam. Particularly in the summer, when the land heats and cools much more rapidly than the sea by day and night respectively, onshore and offshore breezes override prevailing wind systems around most of the coasts up to a dozen or so miles out to sea. These breezes were used from antiquity to the end of the days of sail by shipping attempting to make its way in any direction against prevailing winds. Because the sea breezes in particular frequently angle in to the coast rather than blow directly on to it, this effect could also be taken advantage of; for example, in the summer along the coast of Israel/Lebanon they frequently come in from the southwest, facilitating navigation to the north.

Since galleys could be beached easily, coastal navigation also offered them the great advantage of being able to simply run into port or ashore on to a beach if the wind turned contrary. It was far better to wait out a period of adverse weather than to be blown off course or even backwards, as freqenty happened to sailing ships.

The anti-clockwise current circulation in the sea could also be utilised to overcome the problems of voyages against prevailing winds. From the Straits of Gibraltar, this main Mediterranean current flows along the North African coast to Egypt, up the coasts of Palestine and Syria, west past Cilicia, Crete, and across the Ionian to the Straits of Messina, with eddies anti-clockwise around the Aegean and Adriatic seas, along the west coast of Italy, and west past Provence, the Languedoc, and Catalonia, to the approaches to Gibraltar. The current varies greatly in strength, but even when its strength is only of the order of a knot or so, as, for example, along the coast of Israel/

Lebanon, this could be of great use to ships whose average cruising speed was only two or three times that figure.

Navigation by coastal landmark was the order of the day. In the clear visibility of Mediterranean summers, shipping navigated from promontory to promontory. Navigation manuals, the ancient *periploi* and the medieval *portolans*, were constructed around passages from island to island and promontory to promontory.[16] Coasts with high profiles and clearly identifiable landmarks visible well out to sea provided the best conditions for navigation. Although other factors were involved, including the fact that the southern coasts were generally dangerous lee shores and that the east–west current drift along the northern coasts assisted navigation from east to west, it was at least partly as a consequence of the high-profile land of the northern coasts that these were favoured above the southern coasts for east–west and west–east navigation throughout antiquity and the Middle Ages whenever political conditions permitted.

At the same time, promontories thrusting south from the mainland on the northern coasts created some of the worst conditions for galley navigation in the entire sea. Cape Malea has a current sweeping around it from the Mirtoan Sea through Elafonisi Channel into the Ionian Sea. Its average strength is only about one knot, but that can be greatly increased by the wind. The Parnon range which forms the cape rises to 2600ft high and northeasterly and northwesterly winds bounce off it, producing katabatic winds colliding at the cape. Thus ships can experience sudden changes of wind direction and disturbed seas while rounding it. This was well known in antiquity, as Strabo wrote: 'And just as in early times the Strait of Sicily was not easy to navigate, so also the high seas, and particularly the sea beyond Maleae, were not, on account of the contrary winds; and hence the proverb, "But when you double Maleae, forget your home".'[17] Whole fleets could come to grief off Malea, as that of Korfu did in 480 BC, when it was unable to round the cape against the Etesian winds (*meltemi*) to join the Greek fleet at Salamis.[18] The two other promontories of the Peloponnesos, capes Tainaron (Matapan) and Akritas, were only marginally less dangerous than Malea. And to these one could add a whole range of capes which were notorious for navigation: Mount Athos (where the Persian fleet was destroyed in 492 BC), Baba Cape in the Troad, Cape Kapirevs on Evvoia, Cape Taşlik (Gelidonia) on the south coast of Turkey, Cape Sidheros at the easterly tip of Crete, Cape S Maria di Leuca,

Cape Bon in Tunisia, Cape Teulada in southwest Sardinia, Cape Passero at the southeast tip of Sicily and Mount Erice (San Giuliano) in the northwest, Cape de Palos and Cape de la Nao in Spain. Historical research has revealed a whole chain of ancient temples of Artemis and Poseidon and Christian chapels dedicated to St Nicholas and the Virgin on promontories and islands stretched out along the major trunk routes along the northern coasts of the sea.[19] These were built for good reasons!

But even with the inclement conditions which might be met rounding some of their promontories, the northern coasts were infinitely preferable to the southern. The low-lying coasts of the southern Mediterranean offered the worst conditions for navigation. Their lee shores, shoals, sandbanks, and lack of harbours and landmarks made them extremely treacherous for shipping dependent on human muscle and the wind for power, and on visual observation for navigation. As Diodorus Siculus wrote of the coast of Egypt:

The voyage along the coast of this sea [Egyptian Mediterranean coast] is exceedingly long, and any landing is especially difficult; for from Paraetonium in Libya as far as Jaffa in Coele-Syria, a voyage along the coast of some five thousand stades, there is not to be found a safe harbour except Pharos. And, apart from these considerations, a sandbank extends along practically the whole length of Egypt, not discernible to any who approach without previous experience of these waters. Consequently those who think that they have escaped the peril of the sea, and in their ignorance turn with gladness towards the shore, suffer unexpected shipwreck when their vessels suddenly run aground; and now and then mariners who cannot see land in time because the country lies so low are cast ashore before they realise it, some of them on marshy and swampy places and others on a desert region.[20]

The quicksands, low-lying land profile, and lee shores of the two Syrtes (Gulf of Gabes and Gulf of Sirte) were equally dangerous. Strabo wrote of them:

The difficulty with both this [Great] Syrtis and the Little Syrtis is that in many places their deep waters contain shallows, and the result is, at the ebb and flow of the tides, that sailors sometimes fall into the shallows and stick there, and that the safe escape of a boat is rare. On this account sailors keep at a distance when voyaging along the coast, taking precautions not to be caught off their guard and driven by winds into these gulfs.[21]

For galleys, low-lying coasts were even more dangerous than for sailing ships because their masts were much smaller and consequently the range of visibility of lookouts at their mastheads was much shorter. In the thirteenth century the height of the mastheads of galleys above the waterline was approximately 13.5m, whereas that of large sailing ships was approximately 32m. In comparable conditions this would mean that the range of visibility of a galley was only approximately 65 per cent of that of a large sailing ship.[22]

Because their cruising speeds under oars seem to have average out at around 3kts for daylight hours and 1.5kts when maintained continuously, galleys had great problems mounting narrows against currents or tides, unless they were lucky enough to have favourable winds. Consequently, the east to west passage of the Straits of Gibraltar, in which the east-flowing current averages around 4–6kts and where the prevailing winds in the summer navigation season are westerlies, presented a major obstacle to normal galleys. It was not until AD 1277–78 that Genoese and Majorcan, then Venetian, galleys, finally found a way out through the Straits to the Atlantic and the English Channel. They were able to do so because of a combination of factors: building larger galleys capable of sailing the Atlantic coasts, acquiring access to Muslim ports on either side of the approaches to the Straits where ships could lay over and wait for the occasional easterly winds, and utilising counter-current circulations close in to the shores of the Straits. There is also a possibility that the onset of the 'Little Ice Age' of the late thirteenth and fourteenth centuries increased the incidence of easterly Levanter winds in the Alboran Channel and the Straits and made the passage less difficult than it had been before.

16. See in particular, B R Motzo (ed), *Il compasso di navegare: opera italiana del metà di secolo XIII* (Cagliari 1947).

17. Strabo, *The Geography of Strabo*, 8 vols, trans H L Jones (London and Cambridge, Mass 1968), 8.6.20 (Vol 4, p189).

18. Herodotus, *Herodotus*, 4 vols, trans A D Godfrey (London and Cambridge, Mass 1957), VII.168 (Vol 3, p483).

19. E C Semple, *The Geography of the Mediterranean Region. Its relation to ancient history* (London 1932), Ch 21.

20. Diodorus Siculus, *Diodorus of Sicily*, 10 vols, trans C H Oldfather (London and Cambridge, Mass 1966), I.31 (Vol 1, pp101–3).

21. Strabo, *The Geography of Strabo*, trans H L Jones, 8 vols (London and Cambridge, Mass, 1949), Vol 8, p197.

22. Theoretically, the sailing ship would have a horizon of visibility from the crow's nest of approximately 20km and the galley one of approximately 13km. This, however, takes no account of atmospheric conditions.

Galleys must have experienced similar problems navigating in other narrows where currents or tides ran at more than their cruising speed under oars, unless they could count on favourable winds. For example, the currents in the Dardanelles and Bosporus can race at up to 6kts or 7kts from the Black Sea to the Aegean, and the prevailing winds from spring to autumn sweep down both straits from the northeast. Galleys attempting to mount these straits had to wait for occasional shifts to the west in the prevailing winds and had to make use of localised counter-currents close in to the shores.

In other narrows, such as the Straits of Messina and the Evripos between Evvoia (Negropont) and the Greek mainland, tidal races were the main difficulties. As Diodorus Siculus wrote of the Evripos:

Now it so happened that in former times also there had always been a current in that place [the Evripos] and that the sea frequently reversed its course [ie the tides], and at the time in question [410 BC] the force of the current was far greater because the sea had been confined into a very narrow channel; for passage was left for only a single ship [because of the construction of a causeway].[23]

In the Straits of Messina the tides at the north and south ends are those of the Tyrrhenian and Ionian Seas respectively. Thus, when it is high tide at Cape Peloro, it is low tide at San Giovanni only three miles to the south, and vice versa. The tide thus reaches maximum strength twice each lunar day in both directions, racing at up to 4kts, sometimes increased by the wind. Moreover, the stratigraphy of the seabed and upwelling waters of different densities and temperatures produce tidal rips, whirlpools (including the famous Scylla and Charybdis), and lines of breakers or *tagli* which race along the strait and which can reach up to 1.5m in height. These rips and whirlpools were worse before the stratigraphy of the seabed was changed by the Messina earthquake of 1783. For low-lying galleys these must have been very difficult conditions. In the Middle Ages all ships used local pilots to navigate the straits, and the critical few miles from Cape Peloro to San Giovanni must have been navigated at the slack of the tide. Similarly in the Evripos, where the tidal

Lepanto 1571, the last great battle between fleets of galleys, in which the forces of Christian Europe decisively defeated the Turks and stalled the Muslim advance westwards. Despite the advent of gunpowder artillery, such was the continuity of galley operations, that battles continued to be fought in similar locations to those of ancient times – and using similar tactics. (National Maritime Museum)

races can reach up to 6kts or 7kts and where a galley headed north would also have to battle the prevailing *meltemi* from the north. At Aulis, on the mainland shore of the Evripos opposite Khalkis, Agamemnon sacrificed his daughter Iphigenia to Artemis when his fleet was held up by contrary winds on its way to Troy.

By and large, the routes of galleys in antiquity and throughout the Middle Ages followed the northern coasts and islands of the sea. From Gibraltar to Marseilles via Cape de Gata, Cartagena, and Barcelona. From Genoa to the Straits of Otranto via Naples, Taranto, and the Straits of Messina. From Venice to the Holy Land via the coasts of Dalmatia and Albania, the Ionian islands, Crete, Rhodes, and Cyprus.

23. Diodorus Siculus, *Diodorus of Sicily*, XIII.47 (Vol 5, p251).

From Constantinople to Rhodes via the north coast of the Sea of Marmara, the Dardanelles, Mitilini, Khios, Samos, and Kos. From Alexandria to Rhodes or Crete via the coasts of Palestine, Syria, and Cilicia. When north–south voyages were required, or when it was necessary to make open-sea crossings, island-hopping routes involving the shortest open crossings possible would be chosen. From Algiers to Barcelona via the Balearics. From the Gulf of Genoa to Tunisia via the west coasts of Corsica and Sardinia. From the Sicilian Channel to Crete via the south and east coasts of Sicily, the Gulf of Taranto, and the Ionian islands. From Sicily to al-Andalus via Cape Spartivento (Sardinia), Majorca, Iviza, and Cape de la Nao (an unusual galley route this, but one sometimes taken by fleets in haste). The Aegean would be crossed at its narrowest, from Khios to Kafirevs Strait, Cape Sounion, Idhra, and Cape Malea. The route from Alexandria to Rome in Roman times ran via the coasts of Palestine, Syria, Cilicia, Rhodes, Crete, the Peloponnesos, the Straits of Otranto, the foot of Italy, and the Straits of Messina. This was the same route followed by the galleys of medieval Genoa, Pisa, Venice, and Florence, when regular navigation to Egypt was established from the twelfth century.

For Muslim shipping on the southern coasts of the sea, the state of the surviving sources do not permit definition of the major trunk routes for galley navigation. Although sailing ships might stand well out to sea or sail to the north and use the island-hopping routes along the northern axis of the sea when politico-military conditions permitted, this was rare. In most periods Muslim shipping of all types was forced to follow the southern coasts in spite of their dangers because of the menace of Christian corsairs and war fleets along the northern coasts. This is indicated strongly by the fact that coastal areas and islands such as Cyrenaica and Djerba became notorious haunts of Muslim corsairs. The records of the Cairo Geniza are replete with reports of ships lost or driven ashore along the coasts between Alexandria and Tunisia,[24] but in most cases it is not possible to know whether the ship was a sailing ship or a galley.

Navigational hazards

To enumerate all the dangers which lay across the routes within a few miles of the coasts habitually followed by galley traffic would be tedious. However, a few of the more salient dangers may be mentioned. From Gibraltar to Marseilles via the coasts of al-Andalus, Catalonia, and the Languedoc, there were few obstacles or dangers except for the rocks of Las Hormigas off Cape Palos, the islands in the approaches to Marseille, and the adverse currents and winds which would normally be experienced. However, from the Gulf of the Lion or Gulf of Genoa to the western tip of Sicily via the 'route of the islands', the west coasts of Corsica and Sardinia, there were many dangers, even though the prevailing winds were favourable: Cavallo bank, the Iles Sanguinaires (whose name betrays their role in maritime history), the inhospitable west coast of Asinara island, isolated rocks and islets, and the dangers in the channels between San Pietro and Sant' Antioco islands and the mainland of southwest Sardinia.

Shipping taking the open sea route from Spain to Sicily would leave the coast at Cape de la Nao and sail via Iviza, Majorca, and Cape Teulada in Sardinia to make landfull around Trapani. This route would be unusual for galleys because the crossing from Majorca to Sardinia is about 350 miles, and even with favourable winds would necessitate three or four nights at sea, something which galleys avoided whenever possible. And the prospect of making landfall on the rocky southwest coast of Sardinia at night would not be welcome. A galley in a hurry might brave the dangers of this route in high summer, but in spring or autumn the odds were not worth the risk. Roger of Lauria lost half the Sicilian fleet attempting the crossing in November 1285.

The west coast of Italy posed few dangers for shallow-draughted galleys. The trip from Genoa to the Straits of Messina could be made in easy daylight stages with favourable prevailing winds and lay-overs each night in the many ports. Offshore there were few hazards with the exception of the Meloria banks and some rocks and shoals off Montecristo and around the Pontine islands.

The Sicilian Channel between Sicily and Tunisia could be dangerous because of Sherki bank about 50 miles north of Cape Bon, which has Keith reef on it with only about 1.8m of water over the reef and strong currents and heavy seas around it. But galleys would keep close in to the Sicilian coast, staying well clear of such dangers. By doing so, they would also avoid the danger of being pushed south into

24. S D Goitein, *A Mediterranean Society: The Jewish communities of the Arab world as portrayed in the documents of the Cairo Geniza. Vol 1: Economic foundations* (Berkeley and Los Angeles 1967), Ch IV.8.

For the whole of its history the oared warship was effectively restricted to coastal navigation by the design compromises of its naval architecture. Although they could – and did – make open-water passages, these were understood to be fraught with danger. As here demonstrated by the trireme reconstruction Olympias, *galleys rarely sailed or fought out of sight of land. (Paul Lipke, by courtesy of the Trireme Trust)*

the Gulf of Gabes with its dangerous sand-banks by the prevailing northerly winds in the channel.

Even in summer the Ionian Sea can be unpredictable and its seas rough. Depressions moving east across the Mediterranean tend to come to a halt and linger in the Ionian. Galleys would normally take a coastal route from the Straits of Messina or Cape Passero, passing by Cape Spartivento, Crotone, across the Gulf of Taranto to Cape S Maria di Leuca, and across the Straits of Otranto to Kerkira (Corfu). Landfall at Kerkira was dangerous because of the Erikoúsa islets which guard its approaches to the north. We have today what amounts to the cargo manifest of a Pisan galley wrecked on Othonoí island in the Erikoúsa group while crossing the straits of Otranto shortly before 1273. The cargo was salvaged by officials of Charles I of Sicily.[25]

Thirty miles south of Zakinthos, in a direct line for Methone, lay the Strofádhes islands with their connecting reef including the notorious Arpia island, Harpy rock of the ancients. However, most galleys coming down from Corfu would pass through Zakinthos channel between the island and the mainland and hug the coast down the Gulf of Kiparissia to Methone, thus avoiding the Strofádhes. But, even for them, the approaches to Methone through the Oinoúsai islands with their surrounding islets and rocks were dangerous.

From Cape Malea the routes to the Levant and to Constantinople diverged. Crete was a problem. On the one hand, if a galley took the south coast to the Levant it had the advantage of having a windward shore and shelter from the prevailing *meltemi*. However, there were no major ports and few secure anchorages on the south coast and there was the obstacle of Gávdhos island and its offshore reefs. The south coast of Crete was also notorious for sudden katabatic squalls descending from the mountains. On the other hand, the north coast had much better ports (Khania and Iráklion in particular), but it was a dangerous lee shore on to which the *meltemi* could sweep an unwary ship. Nevertheless, when Crete was in Byzantine hands, and after 1211 when it was in Venetian hands, Byzantine and Venetian shipping respectively would invariably use the north coast, unless, perhaps, bound to or from Egypt or the Holy Land from or to the West.

The approaches to Rhodes could also be difficult. From Crete the course lay roughly northeast, whether a galley took the longer route south and east around Karpathos and Rhodes or the shorter one to the north and west of Karpathos through the Dodecanese.

The latter route involved negotiating the many shoals and rocks around the various islands and then battling the west-setting current in Rhodes Channel. But in the summer months the *meltemi* blows from west to northwest around Rhodes most of the time, so that at least made the run up from Crete relatively easy. The approaches to the main commercial port of Rhodes, Emborikos harbour, were, however, flanked by a sandbank. In 1395 the Venetian galley on which the pilgrim Ogier VIII, lord of Anglure, was travelling went aground on it.

Galleys bound for Egypt from the West would probably strike south from Crete to make landfall in Libya, a much shorter crossing of the open sea, and then follow the coast to Alexandria with a favourable current and the *meltemi* on the port quarter. But those which had gone on to Rhodes faced difficult choices of route to the Holy Land or Egypt. They could strike due south-southeast for Alexandria across the open sea. But this was a trip of some 375 miles and would necessitate three or four nights at sea, even with the *meltemi* astern. Nevertheless, for a ship bound for Egypt this route was almost unavoidable. The alternative, a much longer coastal voyage via Cilicia, Syria, and Palestine, involved a voyage against the current and exposure to the notorious katabatic winds sweeping into the Gulf of Antalya off the Taurus mountains.

For voyages from Rhodes to the Holy Land, the choice of route was easier. Galleys would follow the coast east to Cape Taşlik (medieval Cape Gelidonia). From Cape Taşlik, ships would avoid the Gulf of Antalya and strike south with the *meltemi* for Cyprus, making landfall at Cape Arnauti. From there the route lay via Paphos, the south coast of Cyprus, and across to the coast around Beirut, then coasting south to Acre or Jaffa.

From Egypt or Palestine back to the north or west, navigational conditions were much less favourable. The *meltemi* would virtually force galleys to hug the coasts north and west to Syria, Cilicia, and Rhodes. The route up the west coast of Asia Minor lay between the offshore islands and the mainland through narrow channels with currents generally setting north but against prevailing winds. Ruy Gonzalez de Clavijo commented in 1403 that: '. . . the voyage from Rhodes to Chios is dangerous, as the land of Turkey is very close on the right hand; and there are many islands, both inhabited and desert, on the other side; so that it is dangerous to sail over this route at night, or in bad weather'.[26] De Clavijo took 55 days to reach Constantinople from Rhodes and was con-

stantly held in port by contrary winds. In the early twelfth century the pilgrim Saewulf had reached Rhodes on 22 June 1103 but did not make Rodosto on the Sea of Marmara until 29 September. Both of these voyages were on sailing ships, but the oars of galleys would have mitigated the frustration caused by constantly adverse winds only to a limited degree. The same is true of the adverse currents and winds in the Dardanelles and Bosporus on the final haul up to Constantinople. These passages could best be made by staying close in to shore and using oars to take advantage of the counter-currents created when the main current leaves one shore to cross to the other. Cargoes and passengers from large sailing ships were frequently transferred to small boats with oars for this purpose.

Conclusions

From antiquity to the sixteenth century, galleys experienced many of the same difficulties navigating the Mediterranean as did sailing ships. The direction of prevailing winds, the incidence of storms, the closure of the seas in winter, the need for good visibility in order to navigate by landmark, the problems of low-lying coasts, the strength of currents and tides in narrows and bights, the dangers of lee shores, all these were conditions which affected all shipping. However, galleys had their own particular concerns. Any conditions which raised a sea of over a metre or so would imperil a galley. Winds of Beaufort force 4–5 would raise seas to the limits of their seaworthiness. For them the dangers of rounding promontories and of squalls descending suddenly from coastal highlands were more acute than for sailing ships. On the other hand, within the limitations of human muscle power, their oars gave them advantages when attempting to navigate against currents, tides, and winds in narrows and bights. They also had the advantage that they could be easily beached to wait out adverse conditions. Nevertheless, galleys always remained ships designed to perform a narrow range of functions extremely well, and their design characteristics meant that their ability to perform other functions was very limited.

John H Pryor

25. R Filangieri, *et al* (eds), *I registri della cancelleria angioina*, 33 vols (Naples 1950–81), Vol 25, pp35–9.

26. Ruy Gonzalez de Clavijo, *Narrative of the Embassy of Ruy Gonzalez de Clavijo to the Court of Timour, at Samarcand AD 1403–6*, trans C R Markham, Hakluyt Society Publications, First series, 26 (London 1859), p19.

14

Economics and Logistics of Galley Warfare

OAR POWERED warships fought the naval battles of the Mediterranean Sea for over two millennia. In whatever form they took over this great span of time – whether the Athenian *triērēs*, the Roman *liburna*, the *dromōn* of Byzantium, the *galea* of the maritime cities of medieval Italy, or any of the many variant and intermediate types – these vessels were fragile, of limited range, and expensive to operate. Nonetheless they were the dominant force in naval war because within the Mediterranean environment they had decided advantages to offset their weaknesses.

The main advantages of oared vessels in naval war were dash speed, manoeuvrability, and a certain degree of independence of wind. These advantages were conferred by an 'engine' consisting of a large crew of rowers who powered the low, slender vessels. Including officers, marines, and spare rowers, a fourteenth-century galley's crew was usually around 200 men and could sometimes reach almost 250. These men had to be equipped, paid, watered, and fed. From these considerations the basic parameters of the economics of galley warfare arise. Logistics cannot be completely separated from the economics of galley operation because the ships, supplies, manpower and so on had to be paid for. Logistics strictly defined is, however, usually thought of as primarily concerned with securing, storing, and delivering the supplies necessary to the functioning of a fighting unit. These actions are necessarily dependent upon the need to pay for such things.

It is impractical to cover the whole period, so this chapter will focus upon the wars fought between Venice and Genoa in the thirteenth and fourteenth centuries. However, the fundamental problems of 'naval warfare under oars'[1] were much the same in any age.

The strategic background

Objectives shape the military and naval efforts of states. To form a clear picture of the logistical requirements of galley fleets, it is necessary to understand what those forces were trying to achieve. The strategic goals of the Italian maritime powers in the thirteenth and fourteenth centuries were shaped by the commercial ambitions of their ruling élites. While the trade in imported oriental goods – silks, spices, and other fabled luxuries of the east – was only a small part of medieval commerce, the profit margins could be huge. The cargoes of only a few ships could have a significant impact on the fortunes of the influential and wealthy international merchants who dominated the governments of Venice, Genoa, and Pisa. Europe was at the western end of sea and caravan routes that knit together the Eurasian land mass and the islands of the western Pacific Ocean in a tenuous web of long-distance trade in goods that were so sought-after that they could bear the cost of transportation over vast distances. Mongol conquests in the thirteenth century greatly facilitated this trade by establishing relative peace and stability over most of the middle stretches of this trading net. This development had a very positive effect upon the economies of the Italian maritime cities who dominated trade in oriental goods within the Mediterranean/European trading sphere. The incomes of these Italian cities peaked in the late thirteenth century. The economic boom of the latter half of the thirteenth century both raised the stakes involved in the oriental trade

1. This is the title of the classic survey by William Ledyard Rodgers, *Naval Warfare under Oars: 4th to 16th Centuries* (Annapolis 1940; reprinted 1980).

The Bosporus separating Europe and Asia and giving access to the important Black Sea trade was one of the most strategically vital 'choke points' in Mediterranean commerce and warfare. This is one reason for the rise to prominence of Byzantium and its continuing influence as Constantinople and Istanbul. This late seventeenth-century painting by Jacob van Croos depicts shipping in the Bosporus, including examples of the galleys that were still the mainstay of Ottoman naval forces. (National Maritime Museum)

and provided increased resources for the conduct of war aimed at driving rivals out of the game.

Transportation over water is the least expensive way to move goods. At bottom this is a matter of simple physics: there is less friction to be overcome, so less energy is required. This helps to explain why Genoa and Venice became the premier middlemen in European trade. A glance at the map shows that these two cities occupy positions about as close to the centre of Europe as one can get by sea. The strong current which flows into the Mediterranean from the Atlantic through the Straits of Gibraltar, as well as Atlantic storms, made the all-sea route to northern Europe more difficult and less attractive than might otherwise be expected. Silks and spices from the East arrived in the Mediterranean in three areas: in the Black Sea, either at the mouth of the Don River or in the vicinity of Trebizond; along the eastern shores of the Mediterranean in the area dominated at one time by the crusading states (known in the Middle Ages as Outremer); and at Alexandria in Egypt. If a single city could dominate trade in any one of these areas it could reap great profits; if rivals could be eliminated from all of them the rewards would be immense. This, then, was the simple goal that dominated the strategic thinking of the Italian maritime cities. John Guilmartin has argued that control of the seas in the Mahanian sense was impossible for galley fleets.[2] His conclusion is largely based on the logistical limitations of the galley. He maintains that galley fleets did not have the range or seakeeping capabilities to drive opponents from the seas and maintain blockades of enemy ports in the way British fleets did during the Napoleonic wars that were the focus of Mahan's analysis. In this he is certainly correct. However, there are other ways that maritime commerce can be dominated, and commercial rivals eliminated.

Geography and climatology are of overwhelming importance to the understanding of navigation and maritime strategy in the medieval Mediterranean. The complex of basins along the northern shores of the Mediterranean is sharply indented and, especially in its eastern basins, profusely dotted with islands. The coasts often drop steeply into the deep basins of the inland sea. This provides many sheltered anchorages and harbours. The southern shores are less indented and there are fewer islands. There are also fewer good harbours. Along much of the southern coast shoals and reefs make navigation hazardous. The currents of the Mediterranean circulate counterclockwise, while winds are generally from the northwest.[3] The combined effect of winds, currents and geography was to channel maritime traffic along a few predictable routes. This practice, followed by ships that carried the most valuable eastern cargoes, of sailing along these routes only during a few weeks in spring and autumn, made interception of these fleets a relatively simple matter. These conditions created a relatively small number of 'strategic narrows' or 'focal zones' where shipping tended to concentrate.[4] The customary 'closing of the seas' in winter that continued until the late thirteenth century further accentuated the concentration of shipping in the early period.[5] Galleys could mount effective blockades by establishing bases of operations in these sensitive areas.

Nonetheless, we may say that the goal of domination of one or more of the entrepôt areas of the Mediterranean transportation sphere – the Black Sea, the eastern shores, or Alexandria – was a chimaera, beyond the naval or economic capabilities of any medieval sea power. Yet it must have seemed attainable to the Genoese and Venetians in the thirteenth and fourteenth centuries, because they tried to achieve it. Events and situations familiar to them would surely have appeared to hold out hope of at least the possibility of success. Constantinople, with its powerful fortifications and excellent harbour, is the best example of a base that allowed the control of straits, in this case the Bosporus, the narrowest of the strategic narrows. There are no alternative sea routes between the Black Sea and the Mediterranean and the Bosporus is so restricted that slipping past Constantinople unobserved would have been a highly unlikely possibility. As a consequence, Constantinople dominated trade between the Black Sea and the Mediterranean for

2. John F Guilmartin, Jr, *Gunpowder and Galleys: Changing Technology and Warfare at Sea in the Sixteenth Century* (Cambridge 1974), pp16ff.

3. For a detailed discussion of the geography and weather of the Mediterranean and their effects on navigation, see John H Pryor, *Geography, Technology, and War* (Cambridge 1988), pp12–24; and chapter 13 above. See also, John E Dotson, 'Naval Strategy in the First Genoese-Venetian War, 1257–1270', *The American Neptune* 46/2 (1986), pp84–90.

4. Dotson, 'Naval Strategy', pp85–6 and Pryor, *Geography, Technology and War*, p225 in the index at 'focal zones' and the extensive references given there. Pryor also calls these areas 'focal sectors' (p156) and 'strike zones' (figure 29, p184).

5. Frederic C Lane, 'The Economic Meaning of the Invention of the Compass', *American Historical Review* 68 (1963), pp605–17; reprinted in *Venice and History: The Collected Papers of Frederic C Lane* (Baltimore 1966), pp331–344.

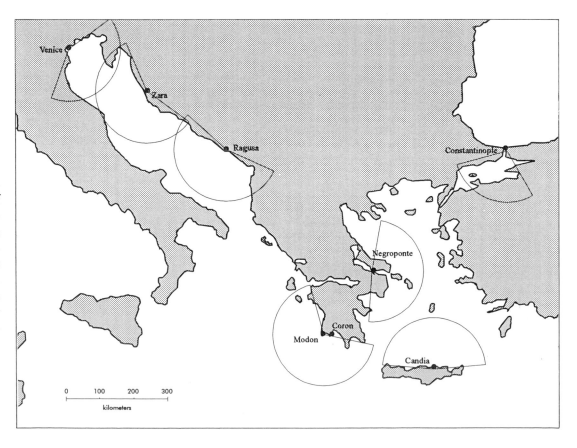

The main Venetian bases in the eastern Mediterranean, each with a radius of 150km – approximately two days' sailing for a galley, or half the typical extreme operational endurance. (Map by the author)

centuries. The Golden Bull of 1082 gave Venice an advantageous share of this dominance as a reward for naval assistance against the Norman invasion of Dalmatia. After the capture of Constantinople in 1204 by the forces of the Fourth Crusade, Venice gained control of the Black Sea trade by virtually exclusive use of that city as a naval and commercial base, and reinforced that control with a series of strategically located bases on the route between Constantinople and Venice. So Venice did wrest mastery of one of the three major entrepôt areas from a rival. Genoa, in turn, came to dominate the Black Sea trade as a result of the Treaty of Ninfeo in 1261, in which the Genoese promised to back the Greek emperor, Michael Paleologus, to regain Constantinople. Again control of this major strategic area changed hands. In addition to controlling strategic ports, maritime domination can be achieved by eliminating rivals. The collapse of Pisan naval power after the battle of Meloria in 1284 seemed to demonstrate that the complete elimination of a rival could be possible.[6] These examples, and others less spectacular, held out the possibility of victory that dominated the strategic thinking of the Italian maritime cities in the thirteenth and fourteenth centuries.

While Constantinople proved to be the key to domination of Black Sea commerce, the ports of Outremer were too numerous, providing too many alternatives, to allow a similar capture. Alexandria, on the other hand, in the possession of one or another powerful Islamic state, was, for that reason, out of reach of western attack. The islands and ports seized by Venice after the conquest of Constantinople in 1204 reflect expert thirteenth-century opinion on the bases that were needed to dominate the Black Sea trade. Constantinople itself was the linchpin, and the Venetian colony there was large and populous, capable of maintaining its own fleet that could, to a large extent, defend itself. To keep open communications between Venice and Constantinople other bases were necessary at key points along the route. Crete was worth fighting for since it lay not only on the route from Venice to Constantinople, but along the sea lane from Egypt and Outremer to Italy. An important support base between Crete and Constantinople was established at Negroponte on Euboea, so important to the Venetians that they eventually extended the name to the whole island. On the southwestern corner of the Peloponnese, or the Morea as it was known, the fortified twin ports of Modon and Coron guarded the passage between the Ionian Sea and the Aegean and eastern Medi-

terranean.[7] In the Adriatic Sea the current and the threat of the *bora* – a strong wind from the northeast that can arise without warning – combined to cause mariners to favour the Dalmatian coast in sailing to and from Venice.[8] Zara and Ragusa anchored this leg of the journey. The map opposite shows the major Venetian bases on the route to Constantinople. Galleys could, on average, cover approximately 75 to 80km in a day, whether by rowing or under sail. If one considers four days travel the outer limits of normal endurance, because of limited water stores and crowded conditions, the main Venetian bases are all within this distance of one another, except for two gaps along the northwestern coast of Greece and in the eastern Aegean. The map shows a radius of 150km (roughly two days, travel) centred on each base. These bases provided good mutual support and protection over most of the route.

Feeding and watering the crew

One may think of the logistical problem on two levels. On the first, the level of the individual galley, the chief difficulty was one of keeping the large crew supplied with food and water, especially water. The great limiting factor was the galley's ability to carry men and goods. Everything – officers, rowers, fighting men, water, food, and weapons as well as extra suits of sail, spare oars, and all the other gear of the galley – had to be contained in a vessel of severely restricted capacity. In the course of the fifteenth century artillery and ammunition came to be added to the load. Large crews, labouring intensively in a hot climate, required a great deal of water and a high-calorie diet to provide energy for the great physical exertion of rowing. This requirement for food and water, and the galley's inability to carry any considerable quantities of these vital supplies, compelled the practice of bringing the galleys ashore almost every night. This, in turn, shaped the amphibious nature of galley war. Fleets of galleys, unable to keep at sea for long periods, were unable to operate at great distances in the face of hostile forces. Galley fleets required bases in their operational areas.

Another factor, which is now difficult to assess, is the effect of the crowded and certainly uncomfortable conditions that prevailed on board a galley. The human density on the rowing benches approached levels that people presently experience only on public transport: six men abreast in a width of only about five metres. Deducting the *corsia*, or gangway, that ran down the centre of the vessel, there would be 1½–2m space on each side for the bench on

Venetian power in the eastern Mediterranean was based on a series of heavily fortified ports, one of the most important being Coron in the south of the Peloponnese. As depicted in this Turkish manuscript illustration, it was captured by the Ottomans in 1500, and along with the fall of other Venetian possessions in Greece transferred the balance of naval power in the area to the Muslim empire. (Topkapi Sarayi Muzesi, Istanbul)

which the three rowers sat. With perhaps a metre, or very little more, between benches it was very much like an airliner, or a bus, but the seating was on a backless bench, open to the elements – and with hard work thrown in. Medieval men were certainly much more inured to hardship than their modern descendants, but surely a chance to stretch one's legs every day or so would have been welcome.

Rowing is hard work; even moderate dehydration would have severely reduced a galley crew's ability to work efficiently. Modern studies have shown that dehydration sufficient to cause a loss of three per cent of body weight leads to observable decline in performance, including approximately a 30 per cent decrease in

6. Pisan merchants did not entirely disappear from eastern markets after 1284, but Pisa was no longer to intervene effectively in a military or political way. For a fuller discussion of the impact of the battle of Meloria on Pisa see Michel Balard, 'Génois et Pisans en orient (fin du XIIIᵉ- début du XIVᵉ siècle)', in *Genova, Pisa e il Mediterraneo tra due e trecento*, Atti della Società Ligure di Storia Patria, ns 24 (98), fasc 2, pp181ff.

7. Frederic C Lane, *Venice: a Maritime Republic* (Baltimore 1973), p43.

8. Dotson, 'Naval Strategy', p85.

endurance.[9] Even if those in command of the galley or fleet cared nothing for the comfort of their crews, this degradation in performance would have been noticeable and of some concern. In an individual weighing 70kg, this level of water loss would be 2.1 litres.[10] Extended heavy exertion can lead to water loss of up to 6.6 litres per day.[11] Not all of this loss would have to be made up by direct consumption of water, but – as we shall see – the diet of late medieval rowers did not provide a great amount of water contained in food, except in soups which would have to be made with water carried on board. Modern studies indicate that water intake should equal one millilitre for each kilocalorie expended. This suggests a water requirement of about four litres per individual.[12] For a crew of 200 men, such as might be expected on a trireme galley of the early fourteenth century, this would mean a water budget of some 800 litres per day.[13] John Pryor found that the water supplies carried by late medieval galleys varied widely, but were in the range of approximately 3000 to 5700 litres.[14] This would provide an endurance of something like four days to one week. Since galleys usually put in to shore every night, and rarely stayed at sea for more than three or four days, this limited water capacity would not have had a great practical effect on their range of action. The need for carefully spaced bases, or at least friendly ports, is underscored by the need for frequent resupply of water.[15]

A good illustration of the frequent stops by galleys, even when time was important, is found in the mid-fourteenth-century journey of the Genoese light galley of Simone Lecavello. In the autumn of 1351, during the Third Genoese-Venetian War, Lecavello was sent to find the main Genoese fleet in 'Romania' (the Byzantine Empire) with the urgent message that the Aragonese had allied with the Venetian enemy. There was, then, some pressure for this galley to make good time. The first leg of the voyage to Chios was completed in 34 days and was accomplished with only a single interruption when a Venetian galley was captured near Cape Santa Maria di Leuca and taken back to Crotone. There they remained for a day-and-a-half to rest and refit.[16] Lecavello found the main Genoese fleet under Paganino Doria engaged in the siege of the key Venetian base at Negroponte. On receiving Lecavello's news, Doria immediately lifted the siege and withdrew to the Genoese stronghold of Chios.[17] For Lecavello the voyage to Chios represents a continuous journey at what must have been almost the maximum practical effort. The accompanying map and chart indicate the approximate times and distances involved in the voyage to Chios. Frequent overnight rests gave ample opportunity to take on fresh water. The eight-day period from 24 September to 1 October appears to be one of continuous travel. The itinerary kept by the galley's notary indicates only arrival times at the places indicated, while elsewhere times of arrival and departure are recorded. This may mean simply that certain landmarks were passed, but it seems more likely that these were stops that lasted only a few hours, perhaps to take on water.

While water was probably the most critical consumable required by the galley crew, food – and enough of it to enable the rowers to maintain a high level of exertion – was also important. Types of activity and their frequency and pattern have an important impact on the amount of food needed to maintain fitness. Rowing a galley was undoubtedly hard work. The oars of a galley rowed *alla zenzile* were 9–10m long and weighed from 36 to 55kg.[18] Pulling these heavy oars against the resistance of water was exhausting; peak effort to give the galley its maximum speed could only be maintained for about twenty minutes before the crew would be completely blown.[19] A sprint of this kind might be used in an emergency – in battle, or in a last-ditch effort to avoid being hurled on to reef or rocks by a storm – but would not be a factor in the normal operational requirements of the vessel. Galleys typically operated under sail as much as possible. With a following wind they could make almost as much speed as their dash speed under oars and could maintain it for as long as the wind held. Unfortunately, this kind of performance under sail could be achieved only when the wind was almost dead astern. The ability of galleys to sail with a beam wind was very limited; because of their low freeboard (less than 0.75m) and projecting oars they could heel only to a maximum of about 12°.[20] They would then have to set the sails to a less efficient angle to avoid swamping or dragging the oars in the water with possibly disastrous results. As a consequence galley voyages were a combination of sailing and rowing according to conditions.

In 1595 the Venetian ambassador Leonardo Donà recorded details of his voyage from Venice to Constantinople. An analysis of this document shows that the two galleys that made this journey took 883 hours (25 August to 30 September) from Venice to Portolago in eastern Greece. Actual travel time was 340 hours. Rowing occupied 101 hours (29.7 per cent) of this travel time, sailing 136 hours (40 per cent), mixed rowing and sailing 40 hours (11.8 per cent), while the method of propulsion was not specified for 63 hours (18.5 per cent).[21] The proportion of the time spent rowing would

9. C Torranin, D P Smith, and R J Byrd, 'The effect of acute thermal dehydration and rapid rehydration on isometric and isotonic endurance', *The Journal of Sports Medicine and Physical Fitness* 19, pp1–9. The authors of this article studied dehydration as a result of sitting in a sauna, not from exercise, but the results may be extrapolated.

10. The 70kg (154lb) individual is a standard widely used in studies of nutrition. It is possible that the typical rower on a fourteenth-century galley was smaller than this.

11. A C Guyton, *Textbook of Medical Physiology* (Philadelphia 1981), p392.

12. The consumption of approximately 3900 kilocalories per day was probably approximately equal to, or a little less than, the energy expended by the rowers. It seems unlikely that galley rowers would gain weight in the course of a voyage. John F Guilmartin, Jr, *Gunpowder and Galleys*, p186, estimated that galley rowers would need at least two quarts of water per day. This seems a very conservative estimate. Rowers in the *Olympias*, a modern reconstruction of a Greek trireme, have needed approximately one litre of liquid per hour of sustained rowing (J T Shaw, 'Rowing in Ships and Boats', a paper given at the spring 1993 meeting of The Royal Institution of Naval Architects).

13. This level of water consumption is over twice what Guilmartin (*Gunpowder and Galleys*) and Pryor (*Geography, Technology, and War*) have assumed, but is, I believe, more realistic.

14. Pryor, *Geography, Technology, and War*, p77. Pryor gives the figures of 800 to 1500 gallons, which I have converted to approximate metric equivalents to maintain consistency with my other measurements.

15. For an extended discussion of the amounts of water carried by medieval galleys see Pryor, *Geography, Technology, and War*, pp75–86. Pryor is inclined to accept Guilmartin's estimates of the water needs of galley crews. My higher estimates would indicate even shorter unsupplied ranges than Pryor's estimates, further strengthening his argument regarding the limited endurance of galleys.

16. M Balard, 'A propos de la bataille du Bosphore. L'expedition génois de Paganino Doria à Constantinople (1351–1352)', in *Travaux et mémoires du Centre de recherches d'histoire et civilisation byzantine* IV (Paris 1970), p439 and J E Dotson, 'The Voyage of Simone Lecavello: A Genoese Naval Expedition of 1351', in *Saggi e documenti VI*, Civico Istituto Colombiano Studi e Testi 8 (Genoa 1985), p276. I will refer frequently to the activities of this galley and the others of the fleet of Paganino Doria. Account books and itineraries have survived which make this one of the best documented early naval expeditions. These records preserve information regarding not only the routes travelled, but manning, victualling, and expenses.

17. Balard, 'A propos de la bataille', p439.

18. John Coates, 'The Naval Architecture of European Oared Ships', a paper given at the spring 1993 meeting of The Royal Institution of Naval Architects.

19. Pryor, *Geography, Technology, and War*, p71, and sources cited there.

20. Coates, 'The Naval Architecture of European Oared Ships,' p7.

21. Elena Fasano-Guarini, 'Au XVIe siècle: Comment naviguent les galères', in *Annales: èconomies, sociètès, civilisations* 16 (1961), p285.

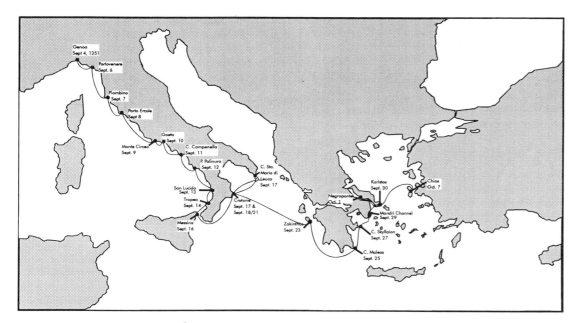

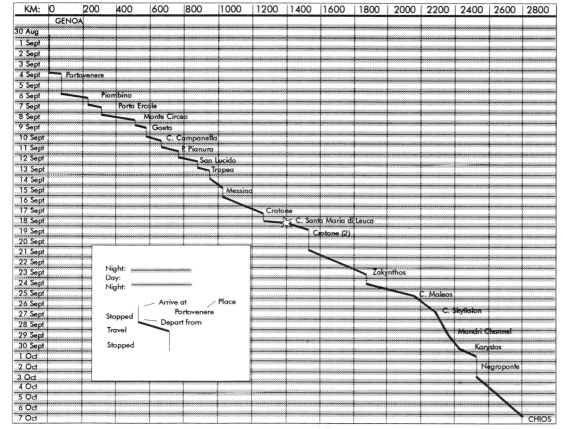

The voyage of Simone Lecavello from Genoa to Chios in 1351. The graph plots distance and time elapsed. (Map and graph by the author)

cient for prolonged heavy work, and even increase endurance over those that obtain most of their calories from fats.[25] The diet of hard, dry ship biscuit, a soup of beans and a little salt pork, accompanied by a couple of glasses of wine per day, would probably not appeal to refined tastes, but was well suited to the physiological needs of the galley crew.

The total weight of these rations was 1441 grams, of which 715 grams were biscuit. Assuming that the Genoese rations were roughly the same as the Venetian, we can make some estimates regarding the victualling needs of Paganino Doria's fleet. The rowing crew of Simone Lecavello's galley varied, but over the course of the voyage averaged around 175 men,[26] although there were also some 20 marines and officers. At 1441 grams per man Lecavello's crew would have needed rations weighing a little over 280kg per day, or around 9550kg for the 34-day voyage. Of this, about 4740kg would have been biscuit, the basic ration. Rowers in a single galley or small squadron might possibly have augmented their

22. Frederic C Lane, 'Diet and Wages of Seamen in the Early Fourteenth Century', in *Venice and History: The Collected Papers of Frederic C Lane* (Baltimore 1966; a translation of 'Salaires et régime alimentaire des marins au début du XIVᵉ siècle: Vie matérielle et comportements biologiques', *Annales: èconomies, sociètès, civilisations* [Jan–Feb 1963], pp133–38), p263.

23. Lane, 'Diet and Wages', p264.

24. R Passmore and J V G A Durnin, 'Human energy expenditure', *Physiological Review* 35 (1955), p801; reference and table in Jean Mayer and Beverly A Bullen, 'Nutrition, Weight Control, and Exercise', in Warren R Johnson and E R Buskirk (eds), *Structural and Physiological Aspects of Exercise and Sport* (Princeton, NJ 1980), pp260ff. The Food and Nutrition Board, Commission on Life Sciences of the National Research Council, *Recommended Dietary Allowances* (10th ed, Washington, DC 1989) considers that for a 'very active 23-year-old adult' male of 70kg a 'very active day' would consist of 8 hours resting, 8 hours very light work, 4 hours light work, 2 hours moderate work, and 2 hours heavy work. The energy requirement for this schedule is calculated to be 3938 kcal (p28, table 3–3). In this context heavy activity is defined as 'walking with load uphill, tree felling, heavy manual digging, basketball, climbing, football, soccer' (p27). Rowing a galley probably falls within this range.

25. David B Dill, 'Fatigue and Physical Fitness', in Johnson and Buskirk, *Structural and Physiological Aspects of Exercise and Sports*, p252 and Mayer and Bullen, 'Nutrition, Weight Control, and Exercise', p264f. Recently the British army, based on their experience in the Falklands, revised upwards their estimates of the caloric needs of combat soldiers from 3700 kilocalories per day to 4200 kilocalories and have increased the carbohydrate content of rations. [*The Times* (London), 6 August 1988, p3.]

26. Dotson, 'The Voyage of Simone Lecavello', p280.

have varied widely from voyage to voyage depending upon wind conditions, but it is probably safe to assume that the crew could expect to row about half the time a galley was at sea.

The Venetian Marino Sanuto, writing about 1320, calculated the provisioning needs for a projected crusade against Egypt. He based his estimates on rations distributed on Venetian galleys in his day.[22] The daily allowances, translated into modern measures were: 715 grams of ship biscuit, 536 millilitres of wine, 40 grams of cheese, 52 grams of salt pork, and 98 grams of beans. Frederic Lane estimated this to yield 3915 kilocalories, most of it (68.4 per cent) from the ship biscuit.[23] This is well within the range of caloric requirements one would expect from modern estimates. Modern studies have shown athletes engaged in high-intensity endurance contests such as cross-country running to have a daily caloric requirement of 4000 to 5000 kilocalories.[24] Furthermore, modern studies have indicated that diets that are high in carbohydrates, such as bread, pasta – or ship biscuit – are much more effi-

Although exaggerated for artistic effect, this picture does emphasise the crowding aboard galleys and the concomitant effect on endurance of the need to feed and water all these people. The painting by Cornelis Vroom (1591–1661), representing an engagement between Spanish sailing men of war and the galleys of a Barbary corsair squadron, also suggests the vulnerability of low-freeboard galleys when faced, from the sixteenth century onwards, with the massively superior firepower of sailing warships. (National Maritime Museum)

rations by purchase in ports of call; it is doubtful whether those in a large fleet could do so. Paganino Doria's fleet (of which Lecavello's galley was eventually a part) counted 60 galleys with about 190 men each, including marines, sailors, crossbowmen and officers for a total of approximately 11,400 men. This was equal to the population of a substantial town.[27]

Using the same calculations as for Lecavello's single galley, Doria's fleet would have required over 16,427kg of rations per day, including 8151kg of biscuit. Thus when Doria bought 116,000kg of biscuit in Chios, he acquired a biscuit ration of about two weeks for his fleet.[28] Acquiring biscuit in such quantities was a difficult undertaking. When Doria's fleet was established at the major Genoese base of Pera, opposite Constantinople, the resources of even that substantial settlement were insufficient to supply him with the victuals his crews needed. Constantinople itself, at this time allied with Genoa's enemies, was not available to him. Genoese merchant vessels were sent out from Pera to various ports along the west coast of the Black Sea as far as Caffa in the Crimea in search of grain. The quantities were so great, almost 800,000kg, that Doria had to turn to his Osmanli Turkish allies for mills to grind it. The establishments of twelve bakers were occupied in turning the flour into biscuit.[29] In addition to grain to make biscuit, Doria's agents purchased biscuit itself. Besides biscuit, the records of the expedition contain entries for wine and even figs. Clearly, keeping the men of a large fleet fed was a major undertaking.

Manning the fleets

The third major element required to keep a medieval galley fleet in operation was manpower. Venice – well organised as usual – used a system of conscription to provide rowers when war fleets were needed by the republic. These were not in any sense slaves, nor was the service considered demeaning; these were free men called upon to defend their city. Each of Venice's parishes kept registers of all their male residents between twenty and sixty years of age. These were organised into groups of twelve who, when duty called, drew lots among themselves to choose one of them to join the fleet. The draftee could buy his way out of service by hiring a substitute.[30] This system seems to have worked well enough until the Third Genoese-Venetian War. This was the war that saw Genoa send out Paganino Doria's fleet to Constantinople. Coming, as it did, immediately after the demographic disaster of the Black Death, it is not surprising that both cities found difficulty in manning their fleets. A half-century earlier, in 1294, the Venetians had no trouble manning a large war fleet using the traditional methods of conscription. In the following year the Genoese put to sea the largest fleet ever launched by any Italian city: 165 galleys with 35,000 men.

By the mid fourteenth century neither city could match its late-thirteenth-century efforts. Frederic Lane estimated that even by recruiting three out of every dozen eligible men the Venetians could man, at most, 25 galleys in 1350. Nearly a third of the first fleet of 35 galleys that they sent out that year came from Venetian colonies in Dalmatia and Greece.[31] To face Doria's fleet of over 60 galleys at the battle of the Bosporus, the Venetians had to rely on allies, Byzantium and Aragon, for the bulk of their fighting force. Doria's Genoese fleet may have been almost twice as large as the Venetian contingent, but neither could Genoa alone man such a large effort. In fact, Genoese proper made up an even smaller proportion of their fleet than did Venetians of theirs. Only some 13 per cent of Doria's men were Genoese; the rest came from towns along the Riviera, from Sicily, from Greece, and from Genoese settlements in the Levant.[32]

In addition to the original crews that put to sea with the fleets, galleys needed almost continual replacements. Men deserted, became ill, were dismissed for incompetence, executed for insubordination, and died in battle. Again, some of our best evidence of the day-to-day operation of a fourteenth-century galley fleet comes from the account books of Paganino Doria's expedition. On 3 September 1350, the day Simone Lecavello's galley sailed from Genoa, nine men deserted and two remained ashore after having repaid the advances they had received against their pay. Five men signed on that same day, so the net loss was six men. The pattern of desertion and recruitment continued as the galley moved east. Illness and wounds also brought losses to the galley. Some of the reasons for the continual attrition seem surprising; after Lecavello reached Chios he 'let go' seven men because they 'did not understand how to row'![33] Venetian and Genoese

27. Balard, 'A propos de la bataille', p433, n4.

28. Balard, 'A propos de la bataille', p440.

29. Balard, 'A propos de la bataille', p445.

30. Lane, *Venice*, p49.

31. Lane, *Venice*, p175.

32. Balard, 'A propos de la bataille', p437.

33. Dotson, 'The Voyage of Simone Lecavello', pp274ff.

populations in their overseas colonies played an important and continuing part in their war efforts. But increasingly from the mid fourteenth century both of them relied on foreigners, hired to man their galleys, or in allied fleets, to fill out their navies. Eventually galley fleets came to rely on prisoners, slaves and convicts to pull their oars.

Financing the fleets

On the strategic level, the level of navies and fleets, the problem was largely one of money. The ships, the men, the food and the water all had to be paid for. In this complex equation the galleys themselves may have been the cheapest element. Michel Balard, while noting that the accounts are incomplete and thus do not allow of a final balance, observed that provisioning accounted for 56 per cent of the expenditures of Paganino Doria's fleet while it was in eastern waters and, further, that even this amount appears to be underestimated because the patrons of individual galleys bought additional victuals.[34] Even though the accounts of Doria's expedition are remarkable for the information they provide, nonetheless they are incomplete and thus do not allow one to strike a final balance of the fleet's cost.

Balard's estimate of something over 1,000,000 Genoese *lire* as the cost of wages for the crossbowmen and seamen for the 13-month duration of the campaign is over half of the anticipated value of Genoa's maritime commerce in 1350, which has been calculated at 1,967,940 Genoese *lire*.[35] Even granting that much of this amount was not actually paid out – crewmen who did not return were not paid – and that the sale of slaves and booty to some extent offset expenses, the cost was still enor-

mous. Balard based his estimate on an average expenditure of 1300 Genoese *lire* per galley per month. The Venetians paid their Greek and Aragonese allies a subsidy of 1000 ducats per month per galley for the 40 per cent of their fleets that were subsidised.[36] Frederic Lane noted that over a million ducats were added to the Venetian public debt between 1345 and 1363, most of that amount the result of the war with Genoa.[37]

While it is impossible to reach a final accounting, even of Doria's well-documented expedition, certain general observations can be made. Victuals and wages made up, by far, the greatest expenses of medieval naval campaigns. The galleys themselves were usually merchant vessels pressed into service. They might be owned by wealthy individuals, or partnerships, as at Genoa, or by the state, as at Venice, but they did not exist solely for naval purposes. The very characteristics that made them the premier warships of their day also made them highly desirable for carrying the most expensive of cargoes. As a result, their design and construction was closely regulated at Genoa and controlled by the state at Venice.[38] Still, the expense of building and maintaining them was offset with income generated by their commercial use. There were many ways in which galley fleets could be made to subsidise their own activities. In fact, Doria's accounts reveal that much, though certainly not all, of the expenses of naval war could be offset by income generated by the sale of slaves, booty, and prizes.

In the First Venetian-Genoese War (1257–1270), the Genoese lost most of the battles and thereby sustained considerable losses of galleys. But, in the most celebrated commerce-raiding event of that war, the Genoese, in

1264, attacked a Venetian convoy organised around the great nef *Roccafortis*. Though *Roccafortis* herself escaped – her towering sides and castles proved too defensible for the attacking galleys – all the other ships were captured, with a loss to the Venetians that the Genoese estimated at 100,000 Genoese *lire*. When, in that same year, the Venetians captured the silk-laden *Oliva* in the harbour at Tyre and sold the ship and cargo for 11,000 hyperpers, Philip of Montfort, lord of Tyre and an ally of the Genoese, compensated them from his own treasury and from the sale of confiscated Venetian goods.[39] Naval operations could, then, often generate income to cover at least part of their expenses. Still, there is a rough correlation between the size of fleets and the prosperity of the cities launching them. It was no coincidence that the gargantuan fleet the Genoese sent out in 1295 was launched at the peak of the well-documented late-thirteenth-century economic boom.

John E Dotson

---

34. Balard, 'A propos de la bataille', p455.

35. Balard, 'A propos de la bataille', p459. For the estimate of Genoa's maritime commerce: Giuseppe Felloni, 'Struttura e movimenti dell'economia genovese tra due e trecento', *Genova, Pisa e il Mediterraneo tra due e trecento*, Atti della Società Ligure di Storia Patria, ns 24 (98), fasc 2 (Genoa 1984), p175.

36. Lane, *Venice*, p176.

37. Lane, *Venice*, p176. In 1350 the florin of Florence, virtually identical to the Venetian ducat, was worth 25 *soldi*, or 1¼ *lire* of Genoa [Peter Spufford, *Handbook of Medieval Exchange* (London 1986), p112]. 1000 ducats would, therefore, be equal to 1250 Genoese *lire*, very much in the same range as Balard's estimate.

38. John E Dotson, 'Merchant and Naval Influences on Galley Design at Venice and Genoa in the Fourteenth Century', in Craig L Symonds *et al*, *New Aspects of Naval History* (Annapolis 1981), pp20–32.

39. Dotson, 'Naval Strategy', p89, n24.

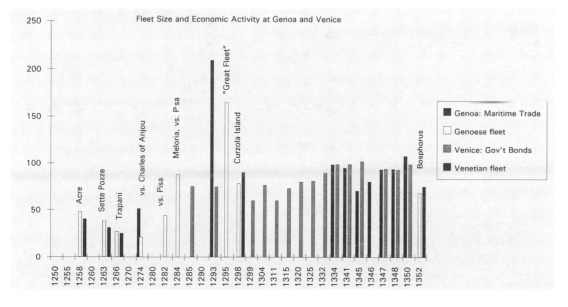

Bar chart relating fleet size to economic activity at Genoa and Venice. All the series are discontinuous, and the time line is distorted by the dates of available data, but fleet size does seem to move in roughly the same rhythm as the economy. This is perhaps not surprising, but there is a noticeably close synchronicity between the 'Great Fleet' sent out by Genoa in 1295 and the peak in anticipated harbour activity in 1293. The figures for the maritime trade of Genoa are drawn from bids for a tax farm on harbour dues presented as a percentage of the average (from Giuseppe Felloni); the Venetian Government Bonds are presented as a percentage of par value, as given by B J Kedar, Merchants in Crisis: Genoese and Venetian Men of Affairs and the Fourteenth Century Depression (New Haven 1986). The fleet sizes represent the number of galleys present at major sea battles between 1250 and 1352. (Graph by the author)

Naval Installations

THE EARLIEST harbour installations in the Mediterranean appear to date from the later second millennium BC, when the increasing size of merchant ships made it more convenient for them to be berthed against a quay for loading and unloading, rather than simply beached. Small boats, however, continued to be beached, and also warships when away from their home port (it is worth remembering that in the Mediterranean tides are so slight that they did not have to be taken into account). Already before that date harbourworks had been developed in the riverine civilisations of the Indus Valley and Mesopotamia, and then Egypt: since beaching boats and barges was often impracticable, river banks were reinforced to serve as quays; and then, to avoid the problems created by flood and current, docks were excavated in the river bank. Two such off-river harbour basins, which provided greater security and longer quay space, have been found in the northern Sudan (early second millennium) and Egypt (early fourteenth century BC). The existence of shipbuilding yards, and the storage of a sacred boat in a boathouse, in early fifteenth-century Egypt is confirmed by detailed surviving records, but no actual remains have been found.[1]

The technical knowledge of harbour construction, probably developed in rivers, was transferred to the sea coast and river mouths of the Levant (and perhaps Cyprus) by the late second millennium, probably just after a period of geological changes which had affected the Levantine coastline and created a number of good natural harbours in estuaries and behind offshore reefs and islands: for example, at Sidon, Tyre, Aradus and Dor. The earliest *built* harbourworks seem to date from the late second millennium (Dor, and possibly Kition) and the early first millennium (Tabbat-el-Hammam, Sidon, Athlit and Akko); they may be associated with the Phoenicians, who then developed trading posts and colonies all along the south coast of the Mediterranean as far as Gades (Cadiz).

Soon afterwards, probably in the late eighth/early seventh century, came the first major *built* harbourworks in the Aegean, probably in connection with the surge of Greek colonisation and the concomitant growth of maritime trade; also perhaps with the introduction of coinage which facilitated the financing of such large-scale public works. The earliest firmly datable harbourworks in the Aegean fall considerably later – those built by Polycrates in Samos in about 530 BC and singled out by Herodotus as a remarkable feat of engineering.

The availability of good natural harbours in the Aegean probably made the construction of harbourworks unnecessary before this time, except on a few more exposed coasts such as those of Crete, where a Bronze Age date has been argued for some remains, for example at Mallia, Nirou Khani, Amnisos and Mochlos on the north coast, and at Kommos on the south coast, where recent excavations have uncovered what may prove to be the earliest examples of shipsheds. A timber-framed masonry building of the Late Minoan IIIA2 period (c1370–1330 BC) consisted of six roofed galleries, each over 38m long, 5.20–5.60m wide and about 4m high, apparently not interconnecting. They opened on the seaward (west) side on to a large court, which was directly accessible from the sea, but lay some distance from the sea (probably about 130m) and about 5–6m above it; the reason for this was probably the exposed nature of the coast. The excavators compare similar shore-side galleries depicted on Aegean wall paintings of this period, and argue that these galleries were used to house ships, possibly warships, in the non-sailing months of winter.[2]

From the sixth century onwards the main developments in harbour engineering were due to the Greeks and then to the Romans, though the contribution of the Phoenicians may have been greater than we can now distinguish. We see the development of construction techniques from the Greeks' use of ashlar masonry

---

1. For early harbours see Blackman 1982, pp90–94; Shaw 1990; Raban 1991.

2. Maria C Shaw 1985; J W Shaw 1986, pp219–69, esp 255ff; J W and M C Shaw, forthcoming A; J W and M C Shaw, forthcoming B; J W and M C Shaw, forthcoming C. Raban 1991 also interprets as shipsheds the remains at Nirou Khani and Mallia. Shaw agrees on Nirou Khani, but not on Mallia.

A model of the trireme shipsheds of Zea, one of the military harbours of ancient Athens. The slipway angle is clear, as is the pitched roof covering a double 'hangar'. The model is in the maritime museum at Piraeus. (David Blackman)

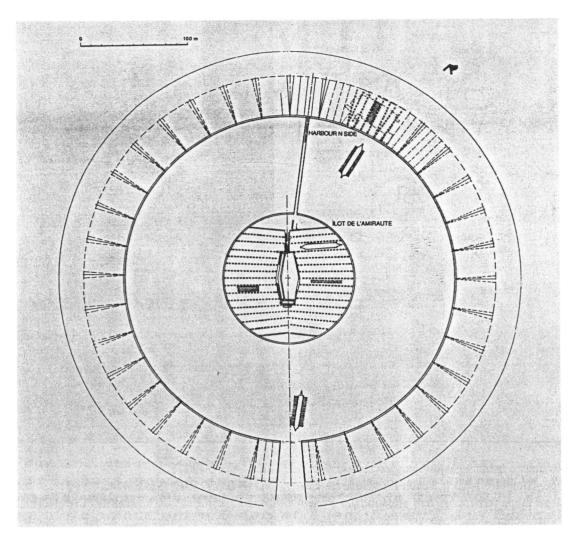

to the Romans' use of masonry bonded with mortar and then of solid concrete (with mortar which would set under water) for free-standing structures, which were no longer dependent on natural features. There is also a general increase in size, though this should not be exaggerated – small harbours are not necessarily early. Another feature of ancient harbours is that they were probably much shallower than modern harbours; ancient ships, and especially warships, were of shallower draught than modern ships, and in the Mediterranean there was no need to provide for large tidal ranges.

A major problem facing any archaeologist studying harbours which remained in use for long periods is that the surviving and visible features will reflect the last period of use; it may be very difficult to distinguish early features.

Military harbours

From the early fifth century onwards one sees at most Greek coastal cities or their outports the development of a separate military harbour, or a separate section for warships within the harbour, provided with greater security as befitted military installations. At Piraeus, the outport of Athens from the early fifth century onwards, the two smaller harbours and part of the larger harbour were reserved for warships. The dockyard was probably a restricted area, walled off on the landward side, though the famous naval storehouse (Philon's Arsenal) could be visited by citizens – and it is worth remembering that many of them would have had to enter the dockyard in the course of one of their principal civic duties – service as rowers in the fleet. There is plenty of evidence in Athenian literature of the fifth and fourth centuries that the dockyard was a matter of great civic pride, and in the fourth century construction of shipsheds was considered to be a model achievement for a great statesman. There was clearly public consciousness of the need for dockyard security, and arson in the dockyard was considered a serious crime. At Rhodes, a major naval power of the Hellenistic period, unlawful entry into the dockyard was a capital offence. At Carthage in the second century BC the dockyard was walled off with a double wall so that visiting voyagers could not see in, and they had direct access to the city from the commercial harbour. This is made clear in the famous description of the harbours by the historian Appian, drawing on the work of the earlier historian Polybius to describe the final siege and destruction of Carthage by the Romans. The passage is quoted in full here, but we shall return to it later:

The harbours communicated with each other, and there was an entrance to them from the sea, 70ft wide, which they closed with iron chains. The first harbour was given up to merchants, and contained all kinds of mooring-cables; in the middle of the inner harbour was an island, and both island and harbour were lined at intervals with large quays. The quays were full of slipways built for 220 ships and storerooms over the slipways for the triremes' gear. In front of every shipshed stood two Ionic columns, so that both harbour and island appeared to be lined with a colonnade. On the island had been built the Admiral's Headquarters; from here the trumpeter had to signal and the herald proclaim orders and the admiral supervise. The island lay opposite the entrance, and rose to a great height, so that the admiral could observe everything going on at sea, while approaching voyagers could not clearly see what was going on inside. The docks were not immediately visible even to merchants who had sailed in, for they were surrounded by a double wall, and there were gates which gave merchants access to the city directly from the first harbour without their going through the docks.[3]

Cnidus harbour has not been investigated in detail, but the smaller, west harbour was known as the 'trireme harbour'. Aegina, too, has a distinct military harbour.

However, one should probably not exagger-

---

3. Appian, *Punica* 96 (author's translation). The inner port at Carthage is the only certain Punic example of a *cothon*, a harbour type associated with the Phoenicians. But according to its recent excavator, Henry Hurst, it took its final form only in the second century BC; and some regard the layout as due to Greek engineers. It should be emphasised that *cothon* is not a synonym for 'military harbour': it means an inner, excavated harbour, probably originally of a particular shape (which may of course have served as a military harbour).

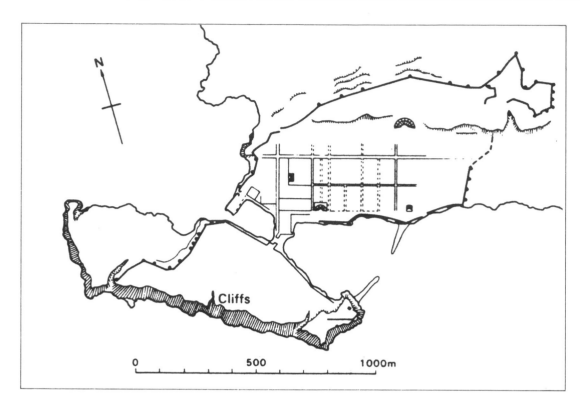

ate the separation of civil and military harbours: there was probably, for example, one pool of skilled labour for specialist tasks in the port area – rope- and sailmaking, caulking and repair of ships, shipbuilding, etc – and most of the population of the civil port would have also served as rowers, and probably the best rowers, in the warships of the Greek city states.

In cities ruled by monarchs there was a private harbour with security and seclusion as key features: Syracuse under Dionysius I, Halicarnassus under Artemisia, widow of Mausolus, and Alexandria under the Ptolemies; comparable are the harbours at Spalatum (Split) by Diocletian's palace, and at Constantinople in the Late Empire.

Major naval powers, such as Athens and Rhodes in their heyday, or later Rome, maintained naval bases at points on their own coasts, distant from the main naval base, or abroad. Some of Athens' bases simply served a few triremes or smaller guardships and probably had few harbour facilities: Boudoron on the island of Salamis; Rhamnous, Thoricus and Sunium on the coast of Attica; and Atalante Island off the coast of Locris in Central Greece; others were also commercial ports such as Naupactus, strategically situated in the Gulf of Corinth, and Samos in the eastern Aegean. Rhodes seems to have developed small

Remains of the slipways of the ancient Rhodian naval base of Eulimna, now Alimna. The bay offered natural protection on an island off Rhodes itself. (David Blackman)

naval bases on the coast of her territory on the mainland opposite (*peraea*) and on an offshore island off the west coast – Alimnia (ancient Eulimna, 'good-harboured').

In the Imperial Period Rome developed two exclusively military harbours as bases for the great imperial fleets: at Misenum near the commercial port of Puteoli in Campania, and at Ravenna, a lagoon harbour in the Po delta; neither has been studied as fully as they deserve. The 'overseas' bases of these two fleets in the Western Mediterranean and the Adriatic served also as commercial ports, as did the fleet bases of the provincial fleets of the East – the Syrian, Alexandrian and Pontic fleets.

In the Classical and Hellenistic periods coastal cities and the outports of inland cities

were normally fortified, and the actual harbour basin – one or more in the case of multiple harbours – was usually enclosed within the fortifications. The city walls were extended along the harbour moles, to end in towers as at any normal city gate. Entrances were kept narrow enough to be covered by artillery mounted on the towers (which meant up to about 100m in Classical times and up to about 300m later as a result of developments in artillery); and for chains or booms to be used to close the entrance. Use of these devices is attested by historians describing sieges, and by authors of technical handbooks on siege techniques and countermeasures.[4] Remains of towers and solid block buildings can still be identified at the entrance of many ancient harbours; in addition to housing artillery and the apparatus for hauling the entrance chains, they may also have served as lighthouses. At Thasos there were towers also along the course of the harbour walls. The improvement in artillery, which included shipborne artillery, led to more heavy fortifications in general in the fourth century and later.

There are some cases of harbour entrances being set back so that any enemy ship would be exposed to flanking fire from the shore if it tried to attack (*eg* Cantharus and Zea harbours in Piraeus). At one site, Halieis, the entrance was narrowed from 20m to 7m – an absolute minimum for ships to be able to enter – and traces were found of what seems to be the fix-

---

4. Blackman 1982, pp79, 194; 1988, p14.

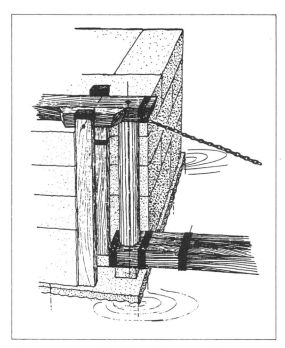

A reconstruction of the fixture for a moveable entrance boom from the site of the ancient harbour at Halieis. It was combined with a narrowing of the entrance itself to make an easily defensible harbour. (By courtesy of Michael H Jameson and the American School of Classical Studies)

ture for a lifting boom.[5] Ancient Greek geographers and coastal pilots refer to many cities as having a 'closable' (*kleistos*) harbour, which must refer to such arrangements. A harbour which was closable would presumably normally have been enclosed within fortification walls as well.

It is likely that military harbours would also have been walled off on the landward side;[6] so too major commercial harbours, where the authorities would have wanted to control the movement of people, particularly foreigners, and goods in and out of the city – in many cities the 'Emporion' was a clearly delimited area.

In military harbours the most distinctive feature was the shipsheds (see below), which must have taken up most of the available shoreline, leaving less space for quays than in commercial harbours. The two smaller and exclusively military harbours of Piraeus were probably an extreme example: when the Athenian fleet went to sea, the triremes launched from the shipsheds of Munychia and Zea had to sail round to the *choma*, a jetty in the largest harbour, Cantharus, for official inspection, and it was probably there that most of the crew embarked. In Rhodes the military harbour may well have had shipsheds along most of its landward shoreline, with quay space provided almost entirely along the inner side of the mole

which formed the eastern side of the harbour. Archaeologists studying the military harbour of Thasos assume a similar arrangement there.

Military harbours did need a lot of space for equipment, though not directly at the waterside. Oars and spars seem to have normally been stored in the shipsheds, and at least at Carthage there were storerooms for the gear above the shipsheds; at Oeniadae a storage chamber ran alongside the group of shipsheds. The Athenian naval lists refer to a number of storage buildings in the dockyard area, and an inscription survives containing the building specification for the great naval storehouse (for sails and rigging) built by Philon; its site has only recently been identified, on the west side of Zea harbour, and not on the north side as had been generally assumed. At Thasos a long colonnaded building or *stoa*, built in the fourth century, has been suggested as the naval storehouse.

The shipsheds

In antiquity warships were not kept in the water for long periods. To minimise rotting and the attacks of the *teredo navalis*, they were not only coated with pitch, and sometimes wax paint, but were kept out of the water and the weather when not in use (which was mainly in winter) in a position where they were rapidly available when needed. For this purpose a special type of covered slipway or 'shipshed' was developed in the sixth and fifth centuries BC, and was used until Roman times.[7]

Herodotus attests the construction of 'hauling-ways' (*holkoi*) in Egypt in the early sixth century: on the Red Sea by the Pharaoh Necho (died 593) for his triremes, and by the Greeks at a garrison in the Nile Delta at the same period – remains seen by Herodotus in the fifth century. He also refers to 'shipsheds' at Samos under Polycrates (*c*530).[8] Since we know that Polycrates developed a powerful navy and built the great mole in the harbour at Samos, he may well have built the first shipsheds in the Greek world. In the early fifth century the Athenians built shipsheds at Piraeus for their new fleet, and soon all the main harbours of Classical Greece must have had shipsheds along one section of the shoreline or in a separate military basin.

We must imagine a line of long narrow hangars sloping down into the water, roofed singly or in pairs or groups. Appian provided a vivid glimpse of the resulting effect in the passage quoted in full earlier: 'The quays were full of slipways built for 220 ships and storerooms over the slipways for the triremes' gear. In

front of every shipshed stood two Ionic columns, so that both harbour and island appeared to be lined with a colonnade.'

The most famous shipsheds in antiquity were those of Piraeus. By the second half of the fourth century BC they numbered 372, at a time when the total fleet size (triremes, joined by quadriremes and eventually quinqueremes) was slightly larger. They occupied almost completely the shoreline of the two smaller harbours (which were exclusively for military use): 196 in Zea and 82 in Munychia; and the southern end of the commercial harbour, Cantharus. Precisely how these numbers could have been fitted into the available shoreline in Zea and Munychia is still not fully clear, and deserves further study.[9]

The best-preserved remains are a group of ten studied in a rescue excavation by Dragatses and Dörpfeld in 1885 on the northeast side of Zea. They had a continuous back wall, with possibly a road behind. Rows of columns running down into the sea formed the partitions between the slips and supported a gable roof over each pair, and at intervals a solid wall divided the shipsheds into groups. The fairly open structure provided the ventilation necessary to dry out the ships, but security and fire-prevention also had to be considered, for the roof probably contained much timber and the triremes' timber gear (oars and spars) was stowed beside them.

The actual slips were low platforms 3m wide

5. M H Jameson, *Hesperia* 38 (1969), pp311–42; Jameson, in *Marine Archaeology*, ed D J Blackman, Colston Papers 23 (1973), pp219–31. His interpretation has, however, been contested by F J Frost, 'The "harbour" at Halieis', in *Harbour Archaeology*, ed A Raban, BAR Int Ser 257, pp63–5, who denies the existence of a harbour. The question seems still open, but later study has certainly shown that there has been a greater change in sea level than previously assumed, so that the cuttings for anchoring the timbers would have been 3–4m above, and not just above, the water: Jameson and others, *A Greek Countryside: The Southern Argolid from Prehistory to the Present Day* (Stanford 1994), p54 & n13.

6. Good examples are Piraeus, Thasos and Carthage (at least in the second century BC, which Hurst now regards as the date of the whole complex).

7. For earlier general accounts see especially Blackman 1968; 1982, pp204–6 (with full bibliography of earlier finds); 1987; 1991; 1993; and forthcoming; Coates 1993; and forthcoming; Mazarakis-Ainian 1992, pp49–70; Hurst 1979; 1993; and forthcoming; Shaw 1972; Simossi 1993; and forthcoming. Shipsheds seem to have been used only for warships, but this does not mean, as is often assumed (implicitly or explicitly), that merchant ships were never hauled ashore.

8. Herodotus 2.159.1; 2.154.5; 3.45.4.

9. Original report: Dragatses and Dörpfeld 1885. They reconstructed the gable roof with a sloping ridge; this has normally been accepted, but is not absolutely certain. For recent finds in Piraeus see Garland 1987; von Eickstedt 1991 (with full details).

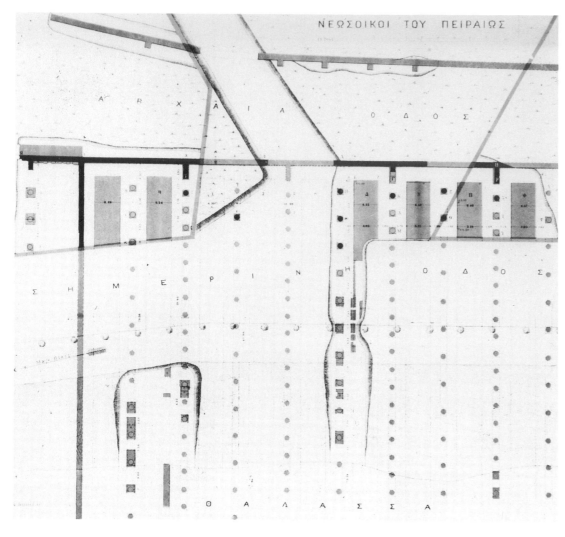

ΝΕΩΣΟΙΚΟΙ ΤΟΥ ΠΕΙΡΑΙΩΣ

Plan of the remains of the shipsheds at Zea produced as a result of the rescue excavation by Dragatses and Dörpfeld in 1885. It covered a range of ten slipways in the northeast of the harbour. (David Blackman)

At Oeniadae in western Greece investigations at the beginning of the century revealed a rock-cut chamber containing five shipsheds of the third century or earlier. The slips were not flat in cross-section, but were cut to fit the ship's sides, and they swung up at the inner end to fit the ship's stern (all warships had to be hauled up stern first because of the ram on the stem). The shipsheds have roughly the usual clear width (just over 6m), but are unusually long (47m), and have a steep gradient (1 in 6). Recesses at the head of each slip and at one side of the chamber will have been used to store gear.[10]

At Aegina the tops of walls of similar structures have been identified by Paul Knoblauch, 5.75–6.07m apart and 37–40m long, against the inner side of the north mole of the ancient military harbour; there is now the exciting prospect of detailed examination of these remains, which are just submerged and are free from overlying remains, which represent a considerable obstacle to the investigation of other sites, for example Rhodes (see below). There seems little room for access to the head of the slips from the mole. It is possible that the slips were only accessible from the water.

Impressive groups of shipsheds in the harbours of Syracuse and Carthage are mentioned by ancient authors. Of Syracuse we still know little, except that most of the 160 shipsheds built by Dionysius I took two ships;[11] no certain remains have been found. At Carthage, however, the large-scale excavations by Henry Hurst on the *Ilôt de l'Amirauté* and more limited investigation of the outer shore of the military harbour have added greatly to our knowledge of the shipsheds there, particularly as a result of the high standards of excavation.[12]

Hurst argues that the remains found belong to the last period of the harbour before the destruction by the Romans (146 BC); and that previously the harbour must have lain elsewhere, probably on the shore of the Lac de Tunis southwest of the city. The remains found consist of stone shipsheds, mostly 5.9m

cut in the bedrock, flat in cross-section and sloping seawards. There are no traces of 'keel-slots', and probably timber runners were laid on the slips, which have a gradient of 1 in 10. They average 37m long to the present waterline; the 'dry length' was perhaps somewhat longer originally, if we allow for a small rise in sea level since antiquity. They have a 'clear

width' between the rows of columns of just under 6m, which defines the maximum beam of ancient triremes. They have justifiably been regarded as the model of the ancient trireme shipshed. It has normally been accepted that they would also have housed the new warship types developed in the later fourth century – quadriremes and quinqueremes – but this is less certain.

Many of the other shipshed remains so far discovered fall into this category: for example, ten rock-cut slips at Apollonia in Cyrenaica, with a clear width of 6m and an apparent total length of 40m (this is the only site so far where the bottom ends of the slips seem to have been defined). With the top of the slips now just submerged, the original dry length would have been at most 28m, which is surprisingly short. The gradient is unusually shallow (1 in 14), so that ships could probably have been manhandled up these slips, whereas on slips with the more normal, steeper gradient (1 in 10 or steeper) pulleys or winches must have been used. Most of the slips at Apollonia had a central runner, and one – almost unique – had a 'keel-slot'.

Remains of an ancient shipshed in the basement of a building on the eastern side of Zea harbour. (David Blackman)

10. At Oeniadae each shipshed was separately roofed. There may have been bronze rings in the rock-cut piers at the head of each slip to make fast the ships.

11. Diodorus 14.42.45.

12. Hurst 1979; 1993; and forthcoming; Blackman 1987; 1989.

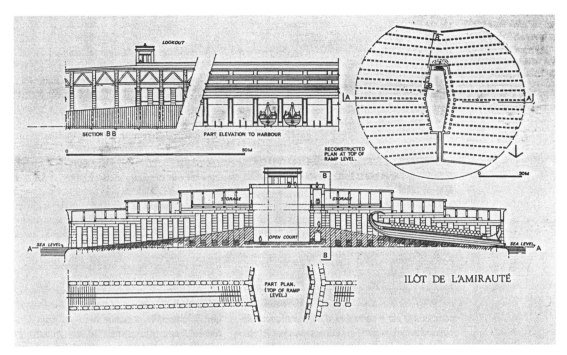

SECTION BB PART ELEVATION TO HARBOUR RECONSTRUCTED PLAN AT TOP OF RAMP LEVEL.

LOOKOUT

STORAGE STORAGE

OPEN COURT

SEA LEVEL SEA LEVEL

PART PLAN. (TOP OF RAMP LEVEL) ILÔT DE L'AMIRAUTÉ

Carthage: a reconstruction of Admiralty Island and its shipsheds by S Gibson based on the remains of ramp No 16. (S Gibson, by courtesy of Henry Hurst)

between the slips was by a cross-passage along the top of the slips inside an outer retaining wall, with three steps down to each slip. The back wall seems to have had fixtures for making fast the ships, and perhaps also for winches.[14]

In a second phase (early fourth century) the complex was considerably remodelled in poorer material; the ramps were widened to 3m and raised by 2.50–3.20m, and have been uncovered to a length of 15m. The reason why the ramps were raised so much was probably an abrupt relative rise in sea level. A third phase (later fourth century) has so far only been defined at one end of the row of shipsheds. The similarities to the Piraeus shipsheds are striking, except for the length which has not yet been determined.

Recent excavations in the military harbour of Thasos in the northern Aegean have defined part of a row of shipsheds along its northeast wall.[15] The one compartment whose dimensions are clear is 20m wide, over 40m long and open to the harbour. The structures seem to date from the mid fifth century, with traces of a late sixth-century phase below. It is assumed that each compartment contained three slipways, but the arrangement seems awkward. Twenty metres is too great a width to be spanned by a single roof without intermediate support, but no trace was found of any internal division in the one compartment so far investigated. This side of the harbour could have accommodated seven such units, with a total capacity of twenty-one ships of trireme dimensions; on the assumption of similar rows on the other two inner sides of the harbour, a total capacity of at most fifty shipsheds is suggested. These are at present the earliest known remains of shipsheds, though perhaps current work at Samos may lead to the discovery of remains of some of the famous sixth-century shipsheds. Other apparently very early evidence is appearing at Abdera, a Clazomenian colony on the Aegean coast of Thrace: a structure 9m wide and over 30m long, which seems to be a shipshed, was built in the later sixth and destroyed very early in the fifth century. There is evidence for a tile roof supported by unfluted stone columns, for wooden runners and a gradient of 1 in 12.[16]

The discovery of Hellenistic and earlier shipsheds at the Greek colony of Massalia (Marseille) was reported in 1993. During emergency excavations in the Place Jules Verne, before construction of an underground

wide and with a gradient similar to that at Piraeus (1 in 10), but there are a few wider shipsheds. The earth ramps seem to have been moulded lengthways as well as crossways to fit the profile of the ships' hulls. The longitudinal moulding (found on only one ramp) indicates a ship of 35m length, but most of the shipsheds were over 40m long. The roofs seem to have been of concrete, and flat.

Below these structures were found lines of timber post-holes and narrow trenches similar in appearance to prehistoric and early medieval post-built structures in northern Europe. Hurst argues that these could well be lines of upright timber staves or stocks which shipbuilders use to support the hulls of ships under construction or repair. There were many such post-hole lines in sequence, indicating that each had been used for only a short time. The shipbuilding interpretation is supported by evidence for metal smelting in the associated debris. The last phase before the stone shipsheds does contain a layout of regularly spaced lines which may be timber shipsheds, but again Hurst believes that they may reflect a mass shipbuilding operation. He argues that this shipbuilding area lay outside the harbour area of the time, which was not on the same site (see above).

A similar explanation may be appropriate for a pair of slips excavated at the seaward edge of the fifth-century city of Thurii in southern Italy. In the central part of a fine cobbled ramp is a grid of slots, clearly intended for a timber grid (or 'cradle') and shores supporting a ship. The very shallow gradient (1 in 20 – similar to that of a modern slip) and the amount of clear working space around the grid, indicate that this was an installation for repair or construction of ships.[13]

Important remains are now being excavated by Marguerite Yon at Kition in Cyprus. The kingdom of Kition was essentially Phoenician; the port was described by Strabo as 'closable' and has been identified with the small, filled-in basin at the foot of Bamboula hill, originally connected with the sea by a canal. The basin seems to have been lined with shipsheds; excavation has so far fully or partly uncovered seven shipsheds, in three phases of which the first (?second half of the fifth century) is the best preserved: ramps nearly 2m wide, with a gradient of 1 in 4.33, but only uncovered so far for a length of 11m; rabbets along them would probably have held longitudinal timbers to serve as groundways for some sort of stern poppets or a stern cradle about which the ship would have hinged as the bow rose under its own buoyancy during launching. Between the ramps ran longitudinal walls at intervals of 6m. These will have supported the roof, many tiles from which have been found. Communication

13. P Zancani Montuoro, 'Uno scalo navale di Thurii', in *Sibari, Thurii*, Atti e Memorie della Società Magna Grecia NS 13/14, (1972/73), pp75–9; reviewed by Blackman, *International Journal of Nautical Archaeology* 6 (1977), pp357–9; Blackman 1982, p205, fig 12. For a possible depiction of a timber cradle on an Attic black-figure vase see L Basch, *Le musée imaginaire de la marine antique* (Athens 1987), pp222–3, and figs 462–6.

14. Yon 1993; Yon *et al* 1991.

15. Simossi 1991; 1993; and forthcoming.

16. C Samiou-Lianou, 'Ancient cities-ports of Aegean Thrace: the case of Avdera', *Tropis V*, forthcoming.

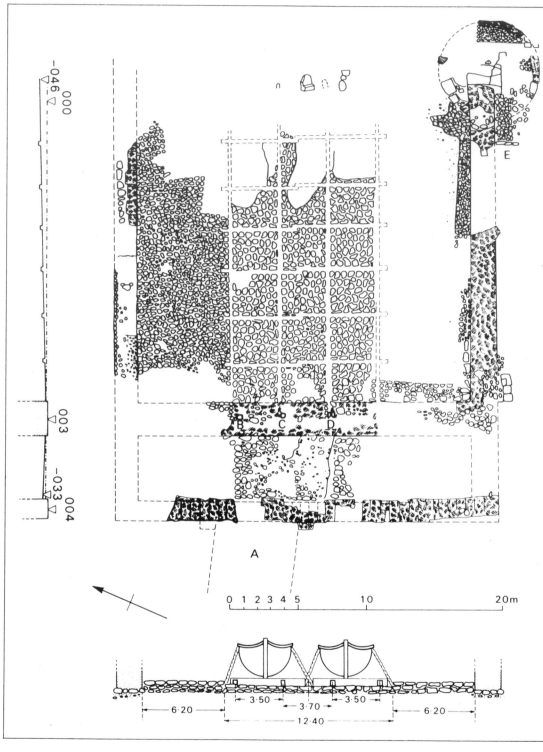

A plan of the excavation of a pair of slips from the fifth-century city of Thurii in southern Italy. Note the grid of slots which have been interpreted as intended for a cradle and shores to support a hull under either construction or repair. (David Blackman)

(5.5m) and longer (30m) than those at Sunium, and probably performed a similar function. Cuttings in the rock at its lower end may have held a timber construction to close the slip when the ship was hauled up. A single rock-cut slip has been found at Matala and a group of three at Rhethymno (both also in Crete), and three at Dor in Israel, 3.80–4.50m wide and 30m long. A rock cutting by the River Neda in the Peloponnese has also been interpreted as a shipshed.

To these examples of narrow *rock-cut* shipsheds we can now add examples of narrow *built* shipsheds, which cannot be explained away as due simply to the natural features of the site. A specific narrow type of shipshed can now be defined, with a clear width of just over 4m. The best example is provided by remains of shipsheds found at the south end of the little harbour (Mandraki), the ancient military harbour of Rhodes. Here excavations during the Second World War, which were not completed or published, revealed remains of seven north/south lines of piers or walls, which clearly belong to shipsheds. Removal of most of the levels between the piers and walls, and the presence of later buildings overlying the lower part of the slips, has made difficult the reconstruction of the original layout and building sequence, but re-examination of the site has provided evidence for at least two phases: (1) before the earthquake of 227/226; (2) second century BC; and there must have been at least one earlier phase, antedating phase 1. In both the identified construction phases there were three rows of piers on either side of a solid wall: those to the west had a clear width of 6–6.30m and those to the east a clear width of 4.20–4.40m in both phases. The dry length can be estimated at 40–45m in both phases and the gradient at 1 in 4.62 (phase 1) and 1 in 4.36 (phase 2). Clearly we are here dealing with the junction point of two sections of the dockyard of Rhodes: to the west of the wall – shipsheds for triremes or possibly quadriremes, which were the standard heavy unit in the navy of Hellenistic Rhodes; and east of the wall – shipsheds for smaller warships such as *hemioliae*

car park, remains of shipsheds of the third-second century BC were found stretching across the entire width of the site. The slips were of timber: either beams set in the beach or mobile timber rollers with ropes round them. The timbers showed traces of usage: the fixed timbers traces of ships' keels and the mobile timbers traces of ropes. The general purpose of this complex is clear; certain arrangements are particularly evocative, such as a slip cut in the sand with central keel blocks and the chocks of the shores still in place.[17]

A number of smaller shipsheds have been discovered, both shorter and narrower, mostly rock-cut and in groups of one to three. At Sunium a small rock-cut chamber just within the fortifications contains two short narrow slips to house small guard-ships at this strategic point. The slips are just over 21m long, 2.6m wide narrowing to 1.15m, cut deep into the rock as at Oeniadae, and very steep: 1 in 3.5 (at least partly due to the steep hillside). A single rock-cut slip has been found near the harbour of Siteia in Crete; it is similarly steep, but wider

17. A Hesnard, *Le Temps des Découvertes: Marsille, de Protis à la reine Jeanne* (Musée d'Histoire de Marseille, Dec 1993), p57. I am most grateful to Mme Hesnard for showing me the excavation records.

The remains of two small rock-cut slips at Sunium. The angle of the ways is very steep at about 1 in 3.5. (David Blackman)

dication of ships smaller than triremes in the fourth-century Athenian navy. Other possible examples of narrower shipsheds are some unpublished remains at Antikirrha (clear widths of 4.20–4.70m, apparently widening seawards); and some remains at Phalasarna which the excavator suggests may be of shipsheds (clear width 4m), though this is doubtful. Certainly the existence of a narrower category should not surprise us, since warships of narrower beam than the trireme remained in use in the Classical period and played a greater role again in the Hellenistic period.[19]

What must also have existed, though it is not yet clearly confirmed by archaeological evidence, is a third category of shipshed, for ships of wider beam than a trireme. Whether or not quadriremes and quinqueremes could be squeezed into 'trireme shipsheds' (and the wider shipsheds at Rhodes may have been built a little broader to house quadriremes as well as

or *trihemioliae*, the latter being particularly associated with Rhodes.[18]

There are some indications that similar

Plan of the shipsheds of the military port of Rhodes: those to the west are of a width suitable for larger triremes and quadriremes, but the eastern slips are narrower and presumably intended for lighter craft like trihemioliae with which Rhodes was closely associated. (By courtesy of Paul Knoblauch)

shipsheds may have existed in Zea and Munychia: Graser in 1872 claimed to have seen narrow shipsheds (10.37–13.81ft wide) as well as 'normal' trireme shipsheds (16–17.73ft wide), and also wider ones. In view of a find in Zea, reported in 1973–74, of slips with a clear width of 4.70m, his claims have perhaps been too quickly dismissed, though the evidence of the dockyard inventories gives almost no in-

18. D J Blackman, *Deltion* 27 (1972), pp686–7; Blackman and P Knoblauch, *Akten des XIII Internationalen Kongresses für Klassische Archaeologie, Berlin 1988* (1990) p499; Blackman 1987; 1989; final publication forthcoming. Supplementary investigation has led us to revise our dating of phase 1 to before the earthquake of 227/6 rather than immediately after.

19. Blackman 1989; 1991; B Graser, 'Meine Messungen in den alt-athenischen Kriegshaefen', *Philologus* 31 (1872), pp1–65; compare von Eickstedt 1991.

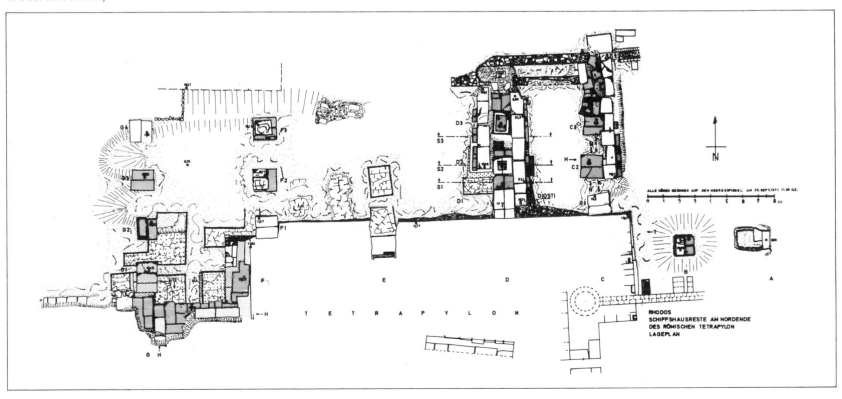

RHODOS
SCHIFFSHAUSRESTE AM NORDENDE
DES RÖMISCHEN TETRAPYLON
LAGEPLAN

triremes), naval developments in the Hellenistic period produced 'polyremes' of considerably wider beam.[20] The only firm indications in archaeological evidence so far are the two wider shipsheds (nos 25–26) among the thirty on the *Ilôt* at Carthage, with a minimum clear width of 7.1m at the upper end and 8m at the lower end, and the same length as the others (48m). Less reliable is Graser's claim (see above) to have seen 'quadrireme shipsheds' (17.96–19.62ft wide) and 'quinquereme shipsheds' (19.88–23.11ft wide) in Piraeus, but they cannot be dismissed *a priori* as impossible in the Athenian dockyard of the later fourth century BC. Evidence of even wider rock-cut slipways on Alimnia, an island off the west coast of Rhodes, is not yet fully investigated; most are between 8.50m and 11m wide, but have now a dry length of only 16–20m and a gradient of 1 in 7. It is possible that these may prove to be 'double shipsheds', taking two small warships, whose existence is attested by ancient authors, but no evidence of internal divisions has yet been found.[21]

Some recent studies have concentrated on the use of shipsheds and on methods of ship-hauling. Foley, Soedel and Doyle (1982) made an interesting study of the friction coefficients of wood and stone, in arguing against the use of timber on shipshed slipways; and they tried to use a fragmentary Greek inscription to argue for a very low displacement for the ancient trireme, which could therefore have been man-handled up the slips. Unfortunately, however, they were provided with an inaccurate version of the ancient Greek text, which vitiated their argument. Furthermore, the evidence for the use of timber on slipways is much stronger than they allow, while there is *some* evidence for the presence of equipment for ship-hauling in shipsheds.[22]

The best evidence for the use of timber on shipshed ramps comes from Hurst's excavations on the *Ilôt* at Carthage: in the surface of the earth ramps parallel timber cross-sleepers were set at regular intervals, and traces were found of one longitudinal timber runway – almost certainly one of a pair. This confirms our explanation of slots on the inner side of the stone side ramps of the Rhodes shipsheds (phase 2) as holding timber cross-sleepers. This seems more likely than that they were settings for timber shores, although shores would certainly also have been used. A recent find on the shore of the harbour of Kos has provided further confirmation: a shipshed of

A close-up of the remains of the shipsheds at Rhodes. (David Blackman)

the Hellenistic period, of the standard 'trireme type', has well cut slots in opposed pairs on the inner side of stone courses running down well inside the full width of the shipshed – clearly to hold timber sleepers, supported by stones midway. The full internal width is 5.50m and the inner stone courses are 2.90–3.0m apart (corresponding to the common width of rock-cut ramps, 3m) and have a gradient of 1 in 5.67; the slots are 0.80m apart. So far only a length of 20m has been confirmed, but it may have been as much as 45–50m.[23]

John Coates has recently been studying the question of hauling a trireme up a slipway or up a beach, as part of the report on the 1990 trials of the trireme reconstruction *Olympias*. After analysis of the practical problems involved he is convinced of the use of greased timber 'ground-ways' on the stone slips.[24]

Subjects which deserve further attention include: evidence for shipsheds which are wider or narrower than the standard 'trireme type'; more evidence for hauling gear in shipsheds, and for roofing methods; evidence for 'double shipsheds; launching and slipping calculations for the types of ship which are likely to have been housed in shipsheds; and the question of how such large numbers of shipsheds could have been accommodated on the harbour shorelines of Carthage (220) and Piraeus (372). For Carthage Hurst is forced to suggest that up to 50 shipsheds lay in the neighbouring Rectangular Harbour, which was mainly devoted to merchant shipping; he rejects the idea that in some sheds ships were doubled up, but Michael Clark has recently revived this idea as a solution for the similar problem at Piraeus.

Though we have ancient literary and pictorial evidence for the use of shipsheds by the Romans, no certain remains of shipsheds of the Roman period have yet been found.[25] The most likely are those identified at Minturnae on the River Garigliano, but they were never studied and have probably now been destroyed. There may also have been remains at Centumcellae, now lost; and possibly at Leptis Magna,

20. Reddé 1986, pp29–32; L Casson, *Ships and Seamanship in the Ancient World* (Princeton 1971), pp97–123.

21. Blackman 1991; and forthcoming; Coates forthcoming.

22. See Blackman 1987 for a detailed critique.

23. Ch Kantzia, *Deltion* 42 (1987), pp632–5. Remains of one or possibly two more shipsheds have been found, less well preserved. Rock-cut slipways at Rhethymno in Crete (unpublished) also have cuttings to hold timber cross-beams (and have 'keel-slots' in the floor of the slip).

24. Coates 1993. A number of other possible remains of shipsheds need to be further investigated: at Cnidus, A Raban reports that remains are now visible in the southeast corner of the larger harbour (*not* the 'trireme harbour') which may belong to slips; they were not visible to him in the 1970s, nor to the author in the 1960s (who only identified a rock-cut quay, and contested Iris Love's reference to 'cuttings for slips': Colston Papers 23 [see note 5] p122). Corcyra: doubtful remains, see Mazarakis-Ainian 1992, II pp45–6. Paros: The author remains unconvinced that any of the rock cuttings are from shipsheds; see Mazarakis-Ainian 1992, I, p63, II, pp67–72; D Auffray-Guillerm, *Archéologia* 269 (June 1991), pp66–75.

25. Le Gall 1953, pp103–11; Reddé 1986, pp161–2; Blackman 1988, p14 and note 32. New inscriptional evidence comes from the naval base at Moguntiacum (Mainz) on the Rhine at the confluence with the Main: three references to *navalia*, but so far no remains of them have been found: O Höckmann, *International Journal of Nautical Archeology* 22 (1993), p125 and references there (see below and note 27).

A reconstructed view of work being carried out on a trireme at the top of the slipway inside a shipshed. (Reconstruction by John Coates)

on the outer side of the southeast mole. We must certainly assume a different pattern of distribution: no longer did almost every harbour city need to accommodate warships and therefore need shipsheds – they must have been concentrated in the naval bases of the Roman fleet.

Dry docks and shipyards

A few small docks have been found, but none that could certainly be drained. However, the existence of dry docks at least in the Hellenistic period is confirmed by surviving fragments of the works of technical authors;[26] they may have been a response to the development of the gigantic 'polyremes'. The procedures would have been made more difficult by the lack of a tide. The entrance channel to the *cothon* at Motya may perhaps have served as a makeshift dry dock – if the *cothon* was ever a harbour at all.

A basic question which has still not been fully answered is: where were warships (and merchant ships, for that matter) built and repaired? There would have been space in the shipsheds to effect minor repairs, but not more; though at least one ramp on the island at Carthage seem to have been designed to allow easier access to the ship's hull. We cannot therefore project backwards in time the medieval *darsanas* (for example, at Venice, Barcelona, Khania in Crete, and Alanya in southern Turkey), which were used for shipbuilding and repair. It appears that in antiquity ships were beached for major repair, re-

caulking, etc. A late inscription from Athens refers to 'drying sites' which from the location which is given are clearly dockyard facilities.

As for shipbuilding, there is considerable literary, inscriptional and pictorial evidence, particularly from the Roman period, but the only structures that can plausibly be interpreted as shipbuilding facilities are those at Thurii, and some remains from the early, fourth-century, phase on the island at Carthage (for both see above).[27] It may well be that shipbuilding facilities were often less permanent than other harbour installations; that they were like the timber grids and cradles still seen on beaches today, and have disappeared leaving little or no trace. More remains are likely to have survived in wetter sites in northern Europe: it is now suggested that the Late Roman ships discovered in the river harbour of Moguntiacum (Mainz) may have been at the site of a breaker's yard, since associated finds included woodworking tools and countless oak wood shavings.[27]

David Blackman

26. Blackman 1989.

27. On shipyards in general see Blackman 1987, pp45–8; B Jordan, *The Athenian Navy in the Classical Period*, University of California Publications in Classical Studies 13 (1975), pp46–54. Athens at times had ships built near the timber sources in Macedonia: Blackman 1987. Other possible remains, at Apollonia: Blackman 1987.

28. Höckmann (note 24), p125f.

References and abbreviations used in the footnotes

D J Blackman (1968), 'The Ship-sheds', in J S Morrison and R T Williams, *Greek Oared Ships, 900–322 BC* (Cambridge), pp181–6.

D J Blackman (1982), 'Ancient Harbours in the Mediterranean', *International Journal of Nautical Archaeology* 11/2, pp79–104; 11/3, pp185–221, esp 204–6.

D J Blackman (1987), 'Triremes and shipsheds', *Tropis* II, pp35–52.

D J Blackman (1988), 'Bollards and Men', in *Mediterranean Cities: Historical Perspectives*, ed I Malkin and R C Hohlfelder (London 1988), pp7–20.

D J Blackman (1989), 'Some problems of ship operation in harbour', *Tropis* III, forthcoming.

D J Blackman (1991), 'New evidence for ancient ship dimensions', *Tropis* IV, forthcoming.

D J Blackman (1993), 'Les cales à bateaux', *Dossiers d'Archéologie* 183 (June 1993), pp32–39.

D J Blackman (forthcoming), 'Double ship-sheds?', *Tropis* V, forthcoming.

J F Coates (1993), 'Hauling a trireme up a slipway and up a beach', in J T Shaw (ed), *HN Ship Olympias: a reconstructed trireme* (Oxford).

J F Coates (forthcoming), 'Long ships, slipways and beaches', *Tropis* V, forthcoming.

I Ch Dragatses and W Dörpfeld (1885), 'Ekthesis peri ton en Peiraiei anaskaphon', *Praktika* (1885), pp63–8.

K-V von Eickstedt (1991), *Beiträge zur Topographie des antiken Piräus* (Athens).

V Foley, W Soedel and J Doyle (1982) 'A trireme displacement estimate', *International Journal of Nautical Archaeology*, 11/4, pp305–318.

R Garland (1987), *The Piraeus* (London).

J Guey and P-M Duval (1960), 'Les mosaïques de La Grange-du-Bief', *Gallia* 18, pp83–102.

H Hurst (1979), 'Excavations at Carthage 1977–8. Fourth interim report', *Antiquaries Journal* (1979), pp19ff (for the excavations on the *Îlot de l'Amirauté*).

H Hurst (1993), 'Le port militaire de Carthage', *Dossiers d'Archéologie* 183 (June 1993), pp42–51 (general survey).

H Hurst (forthcoming), *Excavations at Carthage: the British Mission*, Vol II: *The Circular Harbour North Side*, British Academy, forthcoming (for the excavations on the outer shore).

J Le Gall (1953), *Le Tibre, fleuve de Rome dans l'antiquité* (Paris).

Ph Mazarakis-Ainian (1992), *Les structures portuaires en Grèce antique*, Mémoire Univ Libre de Bruxelles, pp49–70.

A Raban (1991), 'Minoan and Canaanite Harbours', in R Laffineur and L Basch (eds), *Thalassa. L'Egée préhistorique et la mer*, *Aegaeum* 7 (Liège), pp129–46.

M Reddé (1986), *Mare Nostrum*, Bibl écoles françaises d'Athènes et de Rome, 260.

J W Shaw (1972), 'Greek and Roman Harbourworks', in G F Bass (ed), *A History of Seafaring* (London), pp87–112.

J W Shaw (1986), 'Excavations at Kommos (Crete) during 1984–1985', *Hesperia* 55, pp219–69.

J W Shaw (1990), 'Bronze Age Aegean Harboursides', in D A Hardy *et al* (eds), *Thera and the Aegean World III*, Vol I (Archaeology), pp420–36.

J W and M C Shaw (forthcoming A), 'Excavations at Kommos (Crete) during 1986–92', *Hesperia*, forthcoming.

J W and M C Shaw (forthcoming B), 'A proposal for LMIIIA Aegean Shipsheds at Kommos, Crete', *Tropis* V, forthcoming.

J W and M C Shaw (forthcoming C), 'Excavations at Kommos (Crete) 1993', *Hesperia*, forthcoming.

M C Shaw (1985), 'Late Minoan I Buildings J/T, and Late Minoan III Buildings N and P at Kommos', in J W and M C Shaw (eds), *Scripta Mediterranea VI* (Toronto), pp19–25.

A Simossi (1991), 'Underwater excavation research in the ancient harbour of Samos', *International Journal of Nautical Archaeology*, 20/4, pp281–98.

A Simossi (1993), 'Le port de guerre de Thasos', Dissertation, Aix-Marseille.

A Simossi (forthcoming), 'Le port de guerre de Thasos', *Tropis* V, forthcoming.

M Yon (1993), 'Le port de guerre de Kition', *Dossiers d'archéologie* 183 (June 1993), pp40–41.

M Yon, O Callot and J-F Salles (1991), 'Neosoikoi at Kition', *Tropis* IV, forthcoming.

The Athenian Navy in the Fourth Century BC

THE NAVAL greatness of Athens in the fifth century BC is indisputable. However, while our principal sources furnish much valuable detail about the skilful deployment of naval forces in battle, they shed little light, if any, on the workings, ships and gear of the Athenian navy. By contrast, these matters are richly documented by later inscriptions of the fourth century BC. Particularly illuminating is a series of official inventories that can be reasonably called the Navy's central archive. This material makes two cardinal points. First, in the course of the fourth century, Athens's fleet by far surpassed its fifth-century strength. Second, naval activity was sustained by a huge infrastructure, including an elaborate system of finance, which, except for (or rather in spite of) certain defects, functioned remarkably well.[1]

The naval infrastructure

In the early 350s, the board of Dockyard Commissioners received instructions to improve their book-keeping. Had those holding the office been professional bureaucrats, the requirement would have been fairly undemanding. But in fact they were simply ten laymen citizens chosen by lot, and for one year only, to carry a very heavy responsibility: to supervise an enormous amount of matériel stored in Piraeus' three naval harbours (Munychia, Zea, and Kantharos) and to issue ships and gear. In short, it was their duty to make sure that everything needed to run the Athenian navy was in place. Being the core of an extensive administration and a staff of technicians, the Commissioners co-operated directly with several financial officials, the ten generals, the board of Fleet Dispatchers, the naval architects and dockyard personnel, the Board of Trireme Construction, and, at the top of the pyramid, the Council of Five Hundred. Small wonder

that in certain years their board was subject to vacancies.[2]

At the expiry of their term, the Commissioners recorded on marble stelai the business conducted during their tenure as well as the hulls and gear in stock. Their accounts included a statement of what they had received from their predecessors and what they handed over to their successors. Thanks to the fortunate survival of a considerable part of that invaluable archive, we are now able to get an inside view of the Athenian navy at work.

The new instructions demanded that the stelai should not only be lengthier and more copious in detail, but also better organised through clear presentation of all naval matters in sections arranged in a more or less fixed order. A specific section in each record, reporting the total number of hulls, shows how Athens's naval potential grew in the course of several decades.

In 357/356, the fleet numbered 283 triremes, but four years later, in 353/352, it had been enlarged to 349 – an increase of 66 ships. In 330/329, the total had climbed to 410 units, of which 392 were triremes and 18 quadriremes (*tetrēreis*), a Carthaginian invention. In 326–325, there were 360 triremes and probably 50 quadriremes, while in the following year 7 quinqueremes (*pentēreis*) – a type of craft introduced early in the fourth century by the Syracusan ruler Dionysius I – had been added to that number. Finally, in 323/322, the last year for which a record exists, a total of 365 hulls consisted of 315 triremes and 50 quadriremes.

1. Inventories: *IG* 2².1604–32; E Schweigert, *Hesperia* 8 1939, pp17–25; D R Laing Jr, *Hesperia* 37 (1968), pp244–254. From the fifth century only a few fragments have survived: *IG* 1³.498–500.

2. Dockyard Commissioners: M H Jordan, *The Athenian Navy in the Classical Period* (Berkeley 1975), pp30–46. The instructions themselves have not survived but can be securely inferred from the marked changes distinguishing the records of the period after 357–356 from those of the preceding period.

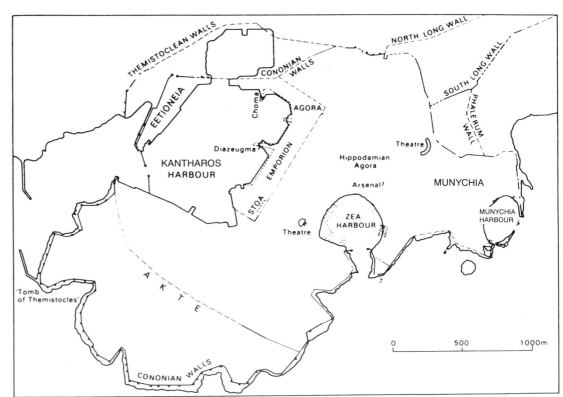

A map of the three ancient naval harbours of Piraeus and their defences. (David Blackman)

Triremes when not in commission were kept out of the water in hangar-like shipsheds, and Athens invested heavily in the construction of such buildings. This model from the maritime museum in Piraeus shows the basic structure, based on excavations of the military harbour of Zea.(David Blackman)

With a single exception, the figures for the period before 357/356 are not known, but the take-off to this steady rise goes back to at least the early 370s, when slightly over 100 units were at hand. These developments credibly reflect the extraordinarily great amount of planning, effort and determination invested in the build-up of a supreme navy worthy of its fifth-century imperial predecessor. In 404 BC, Athens had been forced to surrender all but twelve ships of her fleet to Sparta, the winner of the Peloponnesian War (431–404). Few people at the time would have predicted such a swift and steep upturn as the one that followed.[3]

The totals in the Commissioners' accounts, however, are misleading. One problem, about which more will be said later, is whether all hulls in a year could be fully equipped. Another is that the Commissioners listed seaworthy and unseaworthy or lost ships under one heading. For instance, the total of 410 units in 326/325 appears to include three useless horse-transports and hulls that had been lost in storms. Such ships were no longer part of the effective force but mere entries in the books; they went on being recorded until the legal issue of compensation had been settled. So the known totals are paper figures.[4]

This deficiency, however, is offset somewhat by the fact that there existed a number of light craft, especially the triacontors, which are never counted in the totals: in 325/324, a force was sent to establish a base somewhere in the Adriatic from which to protect the merchant shipping from Tyrrhenian pirates; even though the squadron included four triacontors, these are absent from the total of that year. On balance, therefore, the fleet's net potential was not significantly lower than that recorded. The number of shipsheds points in the same direction: in 330/329 (when the gross force numbered 410 units), the shipsheds were enlarged to accommodate 372 vessels; the capacity of Munychia, the smallest harbour, jumped from about 50 to 82 ships. Athens was abundantly supplied with hulls.[5]

Quality, however, ranks higher than sheer numbers, and the squadrons launched in the fourth century were in no way inferior to those that cruised up and down the Aegean in the days of the empire. Before 357/356, all triremes were quite crudely classed into 'new' (meaning 'as good as new'), 'old' (meaning 'relatively old'), and an intermediary category without a special label. With the improvement in the Commissioners' book-keeping came also a new way of classifying ships according to their age and performance abilities. The triremes stationed in each of the three naval harbours were divided into four ratings: 'firsts', 'seconds', 'thirds', and 'select'. The latter, also called *tachunautousai*, 'fast-sailing', were lightly built, especially agile craft used on special missions such as spearheading surprise attacks in formal battles, or running down the ravenous packs of pirates. Together with the 'firsts' they formed the cream of the fleet. Next to them came the amply serviceable 'seconds'. The Athenians were thoroughly mindful of keeping their ships properly maintained and repaired.[6]

In the years 357–355, determined to discipline her revolting allies Chios, Rhodes, Cos, and Byzantium, Athens launched two separate contingents, each of 60 ships. Coming down to the Piraeus to prepare their fleets, the admirals in charge of these expeditions found plenty of high quality hulls in the naval stations: in Zea, to take the largest harbour, there were about 30 'firsts', 46 'seconds', probably as many as 50 'select' (10, 16 and 17 per cent of the total of 283 triremes in 357/356), but only 8 'thirds'. An essentially similar situation prevailed in all naval stations in other years. The bulk of Athens's fleet consisted of craft distinguished by their outstanding performance in speed and manoeuvrability, qualities indispensable for ramming tactics. The lowest rating, the 'thirds', were numerically insignificant. When a fifth-century Athenian was asked of his place of birth, he proudly answered: 'From where the fine triremes come'; his fourth-century descendants had good reasons to be just as boastful.[7]

Some hulls were prizes towed home after a battle; after being repaired, equipped, and re-named, they became part of the fleet. But the majority were built in Athens's shipyards, the Telegoneia, where the hum of a substantial labour force could be heard almost all year around: shipwrights, joiners, fitters, specialists in the casting of bronze rams, makers of rope, sailcloth, and oars, each team of craftsmen aided by a team of assistants. All shipbuilding activity was supervised by the Council and its subcommittee, the Board of Trireme Construction. The Council, being directly responsible for the timely construction of all ships ordered by the People's Assembly in a year, inspected carefully every new hull and its gear.[8]

Outside the shipyards operated a vast and

3. Figures: V Gabrielsen, *Financing the Athenian Fleet: Public Taxation and Social Relations* (Baltimore and London 1994), pp127–128. Sections recording totals: N G Ashton, *BSA* 72 (1977), pp1–11. Quadriremes: Aristotle apud Pliny, *Natural History*, 7.207. Quinqueremes: Diodorus 14.41.3, 14.42.1–3, and J S Morrison, *C&M* 41 (1990), pp33–41. Surrender of fleet: Xenophon, *Hellenica*, 2.2.20.

4. Useless horse-transports, etc: *IG* 2².1628, lines 339–452, 483–96, to be seen together with Laing Jr (1968), pp246–47.

5. Triacontors: *IG* 2². 1969, lines 91–164, 217–32, to be compared with lines 783–812. Shipsheds: 1627, lines 398–405.

6. Before 357–356: *IG* 2².1604, and Gabrielsen, 1994, pp129–30. Four ratings: *IG* 2².1611, lines 73, 96, 147, 157. *Tachunautousai*: 1623, lines 276–308. Repairs: 1612, lines 96–261, and Gabrielsen, 1994, pp142–3.

7. Expeditions in 357–355: Diodorus, 16.7.3–4; 16.21.1–4. Hulls in Zea: Gabrielsen 1994, p130. Fifth-century Athenian: Aristophanes, *Birds*, 108.

8. Captures: *IG* 2².1606. Telegoneia: 1611, line 132. The Council: Pseudo-Xenophon, *Constitution of the Athenians*, 46.1; Demosthenes, 22.; the Strasbourg Papyrus (*Anonymus Argentinensis*), lines 9–11, see C W Fornara (ed), *Archaic Times to the End of the Peloponnesian War. Translated Documents of Greece and Rome*, volume 1 (Baltimore and London, 1977), pp94.

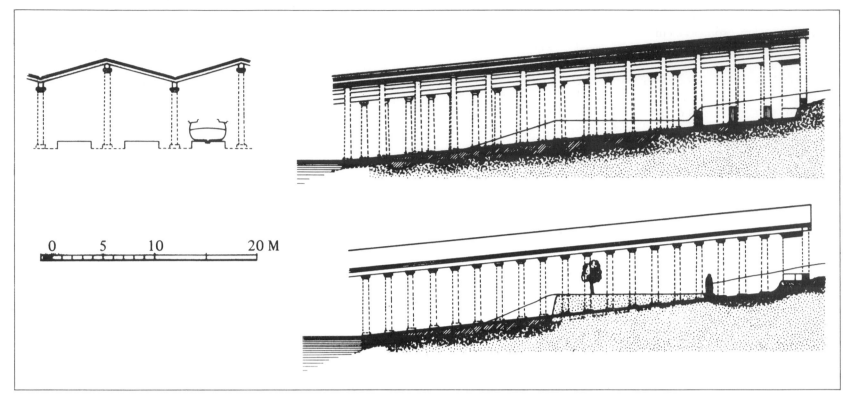

0   5   10   20 M

A drawing of the fifth-century Zea shipsheds. they were approximately 6m wide and 37m long.(David Blackman)

effective supply network, since virtually all materials had to come from abroad. The shippers and merchants who delivered naval supplies either directly to the dockyard administration or to the market of Piraeus formed only one part of that network; the state and its agents constituted the other. Access to timber, pitch, papyrus, hemp, flax, tin, and copper – all too immensely important to naval powers to be thrown freely into the market – required the permission of those controlling these resources. 'If some city is rich in ship-timber', wrote a fifth-century Athenian, 'where will it distribute it without the consent of the power controlling the sea? And if some city is rich in iron, copper, or flax, where will it distribute it without the consent of the power controlling the sea? In all these, however, I see the very materials of which also my ships are built: timber from one place, iron from another, copper from another, flax from another, wax from another.' Sails and papyrus for ropes came mainly from Egypt. Once at Piraeus, naval supplies were protected by an export ban; we only know, from a casual remark in 405, of a prohibition on the shipment overseas of leather bags (*askomata*, to keep water out of the lowest oarports), sailcloth, and pitch, but restrictions of this sort would have applied to all other items and at all other times.[9]

Diplomacy was a main key to foreign stores. A string of treaties with the Macedonian kings guaranteed Athens's right to import high-quality timber from Macedon or to send her

shipwrights there to build ships on the spot, thus saving the costly transport by sea. An alternative to diplomacy was forthright force. In a year before 350, the Athenians haughtily forbade the island of Ceos to export the ruddle (red ochre colouring) it produced to anywhere else but Athens. In this as well as in other periods, the cost of shipbuilding was not determined by economic factors alone.[10]

Alongside governmental agreements, materials were secured by middlemen, influential Athenians using their personal friendship with powerful suppliers: in the fifth century, Andocides, closely connected with the Macedonian royal house, arranged for the supply of oar timbers at the discount price of five drachmas apiece. Such people, acting within the corridors of power in a private capacity, rendered extremely valuable services, especially whenever the relations between supplier and consumer officially broke down. That was precisely what happened with Macedon and Athens in the latter part of the fourth century – a crisis, one might be led to suppose, that transmitted shock waves to the yards of the Piraeus. But if fifth-century Corinth could mint coins with silver from the Athenian mines during a time of open hostilities between the two states, there was really little to prevent fourth-century Athens from getting Macedonian timber also after she was enmeshed in a conflict with her main supplier. Anyhow, the force of 400 ships at that time tells us, if anything, that there was hardly a timber shortage.

On the whole, Athens's naval infrastructure was a solid one.[11]

The trierarch system

The system was not entirely flawless. At times, daunting defects threatened the smooth running of the navy, and the responsibility for that regrettable fact is attributable to the human factor.

Enraged by a recent naval defeat off Peparethos in 361/360, the Athenians fixed blame on their warship captains, the trierarchs. A trierarch was a wealthy citizen required by law to command and maintain a ship from his own means for a whole year. Originally, he was a warrior with financial obligations. Naval states, unable to meet the huge and unpredictable costs of fleets entirely from public funds, appointed captains capable of making payments on the spot and of taking on their shoulders a good part of the overall expenses of

9. 'If some city': Pseudo-Xenophon, 2.11–12. Egypt: Hermippos fr 63; Theophrastus, *Enquiry into Plants*, 4.8.4 Ban on exports: Aristophanes, *Frogs*, 364.

10. Treaties: *IG* 1³.89, 117 – and also 182. Ceos: M N Tod (ed), *A Selection of Greek Historical Inscriptions*, vol 2 (Oxford 1948), No 162.

11. Andocides: Andocides, 2.11. Corinth: C Kraay and V Emeleus, *The Composition of Greek Silver Coins: Analysis by Neutron Activation* (Oxford 1962), p34.

maintenance; governments simply allocated the pressures for resources to individuals ('privatisation' is not a recent invention). Indeed, the position brought honour. But it also entailed much trouble, risk of life, and often exorbitant financial demands, an aggregation felt to be particularly onerous during the distressing final years of the Peloponnesian War. To ease things for those eligible, in 408 BC the requirements were slackened by allowing two or more co-trierarchs to share a service on a ship. Yet many continued to find the burdens excessively heavy.[12]

On his return from a very long duty at sea, the trierarch Apollodoros enumerated a list of bitter complaints: he had been close to losing his life several times; his expenditure had been so high that he was compelled to raise a series of loans; his crew was constantly deserting; his co-trierarch refused to perform his half of the term of duty; at home, his farm had been neglected, his wife fell ill, while his mother breathed her last shortly after he reached harbour. These heartbreaking grievances were uttered in a law court and must be taken with a large pinch of salt – Apollodoros belonged to one of Athens's richest families. But they give an idea of what might prompt some men to shirk the duty. In 378/377, about fifty perfectly seaworthy triremes (half of Athens's force) lay inactive because of lack of captains.[13]

A shortage of men was bad enough, but a shortage of cash was intolerable. So the state, wisely preferring to start with incentives before exerting coercion, struck a new deal with its wealthy citizens: while they remained financially responsible for their ship, the trierarchs were permitted to have her captained at sea by a hired substitute. The measure had a happy side effect: it made it possible to mobilise for the navy also the cash of people who were too old to be able to serve personally on a trireme; the well-known orator Isocrates, for instance, was aged over eighty when he was saddled with the duty. The warrior turned taxpayer.[14]

The trierarchs blamed for the naval defeat off Peparethos in 361/360 were those who had transferred their active duty to a substitute. Not that the Athenians disapproved of the practice, but the failure had to be laid at somebody's door.

Men of Apollodoros's calibre preferred to equip their ships with their private gear. Most trierarchs, however, drew gear from the public stores. On the authorisation of the People's Assembly or the Council, the Dockyard Commissioners issued the hull and a complete set of equipment. For a trireme, they provided a set of 'wooden' gear – 170 working oars plus 30 spares, 2 rudders, 2 ladders, 3 poles, 2 mast partners, a main mast with yards, and a smaller mast (the so-called boat mast) with yards; and a set of 'hanging' gear – four *hypozomata*, two sails with their tackle, four different kinds of protective screens (three of canvas: *hypoblema*, *katablema*, and *pararrhumata leuka*, one of hair: *pararrhumata trichina*), ropes of varying thickness and length, two iron anchors, and *askomata* (leather bags protecting the lowest oarports). In the late 330s, the mast partners and the boat mast with its yards became obsolete. This change coincides with the introduction of the quadrireme, which – except for the number of its oars, which seem to have been fewer – carried the same equipment as a trireme.[15]

Before a trierarch put to sea, there was paperwork to be done. Since he was held directly accountable for the replacement of public property, the Commissioners noted meticulously in their ledger the hull and gear he received, with specification of the amounts to be paid in case of compensation; a copy was then handed over to the trierarch. On his return to the Piraeus, there was more red tape. Assisted by a professional 'tester', the Commissioners went carefully through the ship, drawing up a list of damages or losses. Rarely did captains manage to return their ships unscathed by the wear and tear of voyage and battle, and in consequence compensation was frequently claimed after the expiry of a term of service. Here the cause of damage or loss was crucial: if caused by enemy action, the state undertook financial responsibility; if caused by storms, the bill was payable by the trierarch, unless he proved able to convince a law court that his own negligence played no part in it. But it could take a long time before the state recovered its money. For even if the trierarch were convicted, a series of legal battles might ensue from his attempt to transfer responsibility to those previously in charge of the ship or to the naval officials; the Athenians were a litigious lot. Therefore, to avoid haggling with the Commissioners or ob-

12. Peparethos: [Demosthenes] 51.8–9; Diodorus, 15.95.1–2; see also G L Cawkwell, *CQ* ns 34 (1984), pp335–36, 339–40. Earliest attested co-trierarchs: Lysias, 32.24, 26; *IG* I².1951, lines 79–81.

13. Apollodoros: [Demosthenes] 50. Inactive ships: *IG* 2².1604 (those described as *anepiklêrôtoi*, 'unallotted').

14. Substitutes: Gabrielsen 1994, pp95–102. Isocrates: Isocrates, 15.4–5.

15. Trireme equipment: J S Morrison and R T Williams, *Greek Oared Ships* (Cambridge 1968), pp289–307; L Casson, *Ships and Seamanship in the Ancient World* (Princeton, N J 1971), pp82–92, 224–67. Obsolete items: *IG* 2².1624, lines 105–124; 1628, lines 369–95. Quadrireme equipment: 1629, lines 1068–85. Quadrireme oars: Morrison and Williams 1968, p291.

A reconstruction by John Coates of the naval port of Munychia in the fourth century. The breakwaters are defended by towers and crenellated walls, and the shipsheds are arranged around the interior of the harbour. The trireme on the left has just emerged from its shed and the main mast is being raised. (By courtesy of John Coates)

been due to difficulties in obtaining naval supplies, but on the other hand it is rather too large to be explained by that alone. Essentially, it was part of a preventive scheme.[19]

Throughout the fourth century, naval officials and captains were systematically draining the dockyards of equipment. The process can be traced to early in the century, and is reflected in the frequent need to cannibalise inactive (but seaworthy) ships in order to fit out those in commission. In 357/356, things had come to such a disheartening head that, as a trierarch observed in dismay, a fleet could not put to sea because the dockyards were depleted of gear and the market in the Piraeus, usually able to satisfy the demand for supplies, had dried up. His gloomy remark is confirmed by the Commissioners' accounts of that year. Barely 89 of the 283 triremes could be fully equipped. There were poles enough to fit out only 49 ships from Zea and 8 from Kantharos; in the latter harbour, a mere 16 ships could be provided with *hypozomata*; a total of 50 ships lacked oars. Again, in 353–352, 7 vessels from Munychia lacked oars, 19 lacked rudders, an equal number lacked masts, and 29 lacked sails – the force stationed there numbered more than 36 ships. And so forth. Most of the missing equipment was in the hands of officials and trierarchs.[20]

Disappearance of matériel is not unusual in such vast establishments, but in this case it had

noxious colleagues over public equipment, some men prudently chose to use their private sets of gear.[16]

The amounts involved were considerable. Replacement of a hull meant payment of 5000 drachmas. Moreover, provided that a severely damaged hull had managed the homeward trip, its captain was obliged to demolish it (probably at his own expense), and to return the ram to the dockyards. Good timbers and rams were reused. On the whole, wastage of materials was strictly avoided; battered rams were sold as scrap, broken pieces of *hypozomata* could be utilised for some other purpose, and even timbers no longer suitable for shipbuilding were put to some practical use: in one instance, 56 old masts, 406 teredo-damaged oars, and other useless wooden gear were given on loan to certain construction projects.[17]

For a complete set of equipment trierarchs were required to pay 2169 drachmas if it included an ordinary, 'heavy' sail, or 2299 drachmas if it included a finer, 'light' sail. Replacement of an entire ship amounted to 7169 or 7299 drachmas. Frequently the actual sums paid were much higher, since recalcitrant debtors could be ordered by a law court or the Council to pay double their original debt:

10,000 drachmas for a hull and 4338 or 4598 drachmas for gear. Such amounts, it should be noted, were additional to what the wealthy Apollodoros or other captains had spent during their active term. To appreciate fully the magnitude of economic demands, one ought to look at personal outlays through a series of years. For instance, Konon, son of the prominent general Timotheos and grandson of the victorious admiral in the battle of Knidos (394), is known to have captained eleven ships in a period of seventeen years. His total expenditure, including compensatory claims, amounted to the astronomical figure of 67,923 drachmas – at that time an unskilled workman made 1.5, a skilled 2 to 2.5 drachmas a day.[18]

The amounts paid for a hull and a complete set of gear do not represent market prices but nominal values fixed by the authorities. Even when the money worth of single items such as oars is given (in one case 2, in another 3 drachmas per oar), the figures reflect special bargains made in a juridical context, not real, purchase prices. Towards the end of our period, the value of gear had risen steeply: about 4100 drachmas for a trireme set and well over 6000 drachmas for a quadrireme set (the difference remains a puzzle). This increase might have

---

16. Accountability: *IG* 1³.236 (the Navy Law); Aeschylus, 3.19. 'Tester': *IG* 2².1604, line 56; 1612, line 220. Compensations: Gabrielsen 1994, pp136–9.

17. Value of a hull: *IG* 2².1628, lines 353–68. Obligations to demolish the hull and deliver the ram: 1623, lines 113–23. Sale of rams: 1629, lines 813–16. Broken *hypozomata*: 1610, lines 26–27. Useless timbers on loan: 1627, lines 374–95, see V Gabrielsen, *ZPE* 98 (1993), pp177–78.

18. Equipment valued at 2169 drachmas, *IG* 2².1629, lines 667–73 ('heavy' sail: 1631, lines 415–17), at 2299 drachmas, 1629, lines 577–84. Konon: Gabrielsen 1994, p222.

19. 2 drachmas per oar: *IG* 2².1622, lines 391–97. 3 drachmas per oar: 1631.371–72. Value of trireme gear, 1631, lines 446–48, 462–66, of quadrireme gear, 1629, lines 639–56.

20. Cannibalisation: *IG* 2².1607, 1609. Trierarch's observation: [Demosthenes] 47.20. Ships lacking gear: Gabrielsen 1994, pp146–9.

assumed unacceptable proportions. When a large-scale debt collection was carried out in the late 340s with a view to rectifying the situation, the list of defaulters included naval officials from the past forty years. One Euthynos, the treasurer of the Board of Trireme Construction in 346–345, was made to pay 3600 drachmas in compensation for 1800 oars – his colleague of an earlier year outclassed him by having absconded with 15,000 drachmas from the Trireme Fund. Another man withheld sets of hanging gear for 18 triremes, one-half of the force stationed in Munychia. But the prize goes to a certain Euthymachos, treasurer of the dockyards, who kept a formidable amount of equipment: *hypozomata* for 16 ships, sails for 35, tackle for 19, ropes for 30, anchors for 34 (that is, 68 anchors!), various screens for 114, and 510 oars; and this is only part of the story, for during the debt collection he paid a sum for additional items that he presumably kept for himself. A treasurer of a subsequent year (and his brother) stubbornly refused to surrender wooden equipment for 10 triremes.[21]

What these and many other people had managed to do was to misappropriate shamelessly costly public equipment; most of it did not lie idle in their backyard – in many cases it would have required a very large backyard – but presumably was unofficially transferred to captains willing to pay a generous gratuity in order to keep clear of cumbersome formal procedures, compensatory claims, and other inconveniences; the pickings were large and the temptation high. However odd it may sound, important transactions concerning the navy took place outside the official channels.

Lengthy retention of naval gear by trierarchs was habitual. In a certain year, one of the Dockyard Commissioners only exacted from defaulters 204,000 drachmas, the value of about 90 complete sets. If, as seems likely, not all these debts concerned complete sets, the number of debtors was huge. While some men might eventually return the gear itself, others simply opted for cash payments, thus keeping the material in their possession. Furthermore, not infrequently equipment or its monetary equivalent had to be wrenched from the withholder's firm grip.[22]

A captain of a squadron about to sail in 357/356 was required to recover gear for his ship from those owing it, the co-trierarchs Demochares and Theophemos. Since the defaulters declined, he took them to court, which established their liability and ordered them to surrender the gear to their successor. Demochares delivered the items in his possession, but Theophemos tenaciously still refused to do so. After several abortive appeals to Theophemos, the desperate captain approached the Council, which passed a decree authorising him (and other captains in the same plight) to recover the equipment in any way possible. Armed with the right of compulsory execution, the captain went to Theophemos's house to take part of his property in pledge, but all he achieved was to be beaten up by the impudent defaulter. When he reported the incident to the Council, the collector was instructed to bring the culprit for trial before that body – the offence now was against the Athenian people and its statutes. At the trial, Theophemos, who during all this had tried to transfer his liability to other colleagues, finally surrendered the equipment. Recounting his troubles, the captain explained that in all other ships previously in his charge he had used only his private gear in order to have as few dealings as possible with the authorities; that time, however, he had been forced by law to use public gear – and thus act as a debt-collector.[23]

Not all defaulters were tough customers like Theophemos, and towards the end of our period the situation at the dockyards had improved substantially. Systematic efforts to make naval officials and captains clear their debts, though not wholly effective, began slowly to yield results. Legislative innovations enlarged the number of captains needed in a year, tightened their responsibilities, and introduced more efficient methods of recovering matériel. Refinement of the Commissioners' book-keeping allowed better control. Wooden equipment continued to be kept together with the hulls in the shipsheds. But from a year after 347/346, most hanging gear was gathered together in a brand new and imposing storehouse at Zea, built by the architect Philon; its supervision was entrusted to a special treasurer. Besides, sets of hanging equipment for 100 triremes were placed on the Acropolis under the guardianship of the goddess Athena – misappropriation of this amounted to sacrilege. Lastly, the considerable rise in the value of public gear (about 4100 drachmas for a trireme set and over 6000 drachmas for a quadrireme set) was expected to have a preventive effect; the market prices were no doubt lower than these amounts.[24]

So the system had flaws. Yet the remarkable thing is that at all times, also when severe shortage crises hit the dockyards, Athenian squadrons managed to leave their home port fully equipped.

21. Naval officials: *IG* 2².1622, lines 379–437. Euthynos: 1622, lines 387–97. His colleague: Demosthenes, 22.17. Another man: 1622, lines 420–31. Euthymachos: 1622, lines 444–77. Treasurer and his brother: 1631, lines 350–60.

22. Dockyard Commissioner: Demosthenes, 22.63.

23. [Demosthenes] 47.19ff.

24. Legisative innovations: E Ruschenbusch, *ZPE* 31 (1978), pp275–284; P J Rhodes, *AJAH* 7 (1982), pp1–19; D M MacDowell, *CQ* ns 36 (1986), pp438–449; Gabrielsen 1994, pp182–99, 207–13. Philon's storehouse (*skeuotheke*): *IG* 2².505 and 1668; 1627, line 288. Treasurer of 'hanging equipment': *Hesperia* 37 (1968), p246, lines 241–44. Acropolis: 1627, lines 46–120.

An impression, seen from sea level, of a trireme emerging from the naval port of Munychia. (By courtesy of John Coates)

Manning the triremes

A fourth-century Athenian orator pinned on the triremes the epithet 'gluttonous'. Captains would have endorsed an ancient lexicographer's explanation that what the orator had in mind was the large costs involved in keeping triremes afloat, and particularly the fact that their complements, each numbering 200 men, demanded full pay. One of the signatories would have definitely been the trierarch Apollodoros.

In 362, he had to make his ship ready for an expedition to the northern Aegean. The Athenian people, nicknamed by Aristotle the 'trireme folk' or 'naval mob', were renowned for their skills as seamen, and on this occasion the state conscripted citizen oarsmen. But when those assigned to Apollodoros's ship came to Piraeus, he discovered that they were fewer than the prescribed number of 170. Normally, that was not a problem: before departure each ship was brought to the pier (choma) in the Kantharos harbour to undergo inspection and trials, and regulations stipulated that for that operation there should be no fewer than 100 men aboard – for launching the hull the minimum number of men was perhaps 140, for fitting it with hypozomata 50 or 90. Gaps in the complement could be filled just before the expedition set out, or else in the first port able to supply manpower.[25]

However, Apollodoros's problem was that those oarsmen who showed up were in pitiful shape, so he dismissed them and hired 170 professionals from the open market. Usually, the state provided the sixteen officers and ratings, the hyperesia – Athens was amply supplied with such specialists. But for Apollodoros the best was not good enough. He therefore engaged a crack team of his own; it appears that, although the state might be faced with recruitment crises among its citizens – sometimes met by scraping together all available manpower, including slaves – captains could cast their net wider and obtain experts from a well supplied market. All Apollodoros got from the state, then, were the marines, usually ten hoplites and four archers. It was to be an expensive undertaking.[26]

For only two of his fifteen months long service did he receive public funds to pay his complement; the rest had to come from his own pocket. We often hear of various rates of pay (commonly, a whole or one-half drachma) given to crews by the state, or of the practice of withholding part of their pay until disembarkation in order to prevent desertion. But as a rule public payments did not cover the whole duration of a voyage, nor did they represent the

entire sums received by crews. Captains, eager to have a model complement led by an expert helmsman, had to pay much more. A man bragged of having fought with distinction in the battle of Aigospotamoi (405) because he could afford to hire Phantias, the best helmsman in Greece, and a hyperesia worthy of him. No matter what naval planners at home decided, good oarsmen demanded to be paid in full (entelomisthoi) and promptly for their services; in addition, the top-level oarsmen, the thranites, who as leaders of a 'triad' had a greater responsibility for synchronised rowing, were provided with bonuses, while other oarsmen might demand advance payments. At the same time, these specialists had to be kept well fed and watered. If their requirements were not met, they defected. Finding fit crews was one thing; quite another was keeping them at the benches. As the employer of a large complement handling a special and expensive craft, the trierarch had an immensely difficult job.[27]

It was not mere ambition that induced Apollodoros or other captains to secure an excellent and complete crew, but two practical considerations as well. One was to turn their vessel into a first-rate performer under oar: 'Why is a trireme, fully manned, such a terror to the enemy and a joy to her friends', asks Xenophon, 'except by reason of her speed through the water?' The other was to ensure that it came back to the Piraeus in one piece – and thus avoid compensatory claims. Yet, as Apollodoros found out, even without such additional outlays, triremes remained very 'gluttonous' indeed. His highly-paid oarsmen deserted several times – and each time he had to hire new ones – while during an interim stop at the Piraeus they refused to re-embark unless they were given a pay rise. 'For the more ambitious I had been to man my ship with good rowers', Apollodoros complained,[28]

by so much was the desertion from me greater than from the other trierarchs. For the others had this advantage at any rate, that the oarsmen who had come to their ships from the lists of citizens stayed with them in order to make sure of their return home when the commanding admiral should discharge them; whereas mine, trusting in their skill as able rowers, went off wherever they were likely to be re-employed at the highest wages.

We do not know what the entire service cost him, but only that he had to borrow a sum well in excess of 5000 drachmas to meet some of his expenditure. Another man who had been captain for three consecutive years had spent 8000

drachmas (an annual average of 2666 drachmas). Still another had spent 36,000 in seven years (5142 drachmas a year). A single term's service had cost each of two co-trierarchs 2400 drachmas. It would not be wrong to say that the annual cost of running a ship averaged 3000 to 4000 drachmas. With compensations, often amounting to 7196 drachmas, a man's total outlays in a year could come up to 10,196 drachmas or even more. If sixty ships were commissioned in a year, the amount of private cash financing the fleet totalled over 600,000 drachmas – according to a recent estimate, this equalled the amount needed for running the Athenian democracy. At one point in the fourth century, the state coffers contained a mere 780,000 drachmas.[29]

All in all, defects left their imprint in other areas as well. But once again, regardless of whether the public finances were high or low, or whether the state had trouble with recruiting enough men who knew how to handle an oar, its fleets kept plying the seas with crack crews aboard, the hallmark of a superb navy. The credit for much of this goes to Athens's trierarchs.

The sad epilogue of Athenian sea power was written in 322 BC. In the battle off the island of Amorgos, the Athenian fleet suffered a crushing defeat by the numerically superior Macedonian forces. The eclipse was as sudden as it was dramatic. What the Macedonian admiral Kleitos really managed to accomplish was to strike a lethal blow not on a disintegrating giant, but on one of the most distinguished naval powers in the history of the Mediterranean.[30]

Vincent Gabrielsen

25. 'Gluttonous': Lysias fr 39 [Talheim], quoted by Harp. sv 'adephagous triereis'. Apollodoros: [Demosthenes] 50, especially 4–8. 'Trireme folk', 'naval mob': Aristotle, Politus, 1291b24, 1304a22. Regulations: IG 1³.153.

26. Hyperesia: M H Jameson, Historia 12 (1963), pp389–92; J S Morrison, JHS 104 (1984), pp48–59.

27. Rates of pay: Thucydides, 3.17.3; 8.45.2. Phantias: Lysias, 21.10. Entelomisthoi oarsmen: [Demosthenes] 50.18. Bonuses: Thucydides, 6.31.1–3. Desertions: Gabrielsen 1994, pp122–3.

28. 'Why is a trireme': Xenophon, Household Management, 8.8. Apollodoros's complaint: [Demosthenes] 50.15–16.

29. 8000 drachmas: Lysias, 19.29, 42. 36,000 dr.: Lysias, 21.2. Single term of service: Lysias, 32.26. Cost of democracy: M H Hansen, The Athenian Democracy in the Age of Demosthenes (Oxford 1991), pp315–16. State coffers: Demosthenes, 10.37.

30. Battle of Amorgos: Diodorus, 18.15.8–9; FGrH 239 B9 (Marmor Parium), see P Harding (ed), From the End of the Peloponnesian War to the Battle of Ipsus. Translated Documents of Greece and Rome, vol 2 (Cambridge 1985), p2.

Bibliography

Edited by Robert Gardiner from material supplied by the contributors.

INTRODUCTION

Because this volume covers such a long period of history there are few general books that relate to the whole subject, but some titles that cross many chapter divisions are quoted in this section.

R C ANDERSON, *Oared Fighting Ships from Classical Times to the Coming of Steam* (Kings Langley 1976).
A small outline survey, but the work of one of the foremost ship historians of his generation, so generally sound if outdated in places.

G F BASS (ed), *A History of Seafaring based on Underwater Archaeology* (London 1972).
An important popularising book in its day, with essays by the recognised experts, its main drawback was the uneven nature of the coverage, which emphasised recent archaeological work. The early chapters by Bass himself, Keith DeVries, Peter Throckmorton, J W Shaw, Peter Marsden, F van Doorninck and Enrico Scandurra are particularly relevant to this book.

Quand voguaient les galères, catalogue of an exhibition at the Musée de la Marine, 1990–91 (Paris 1990).
A series of well illustrated essays by leading scholars on various aspects of galley history, plus a catalogue of the Paris exhibition.

W L RODGERS, *Greek and Roman Naval Warfare* (Annapolis 1937).

———, *Naval Warfare under Oars: A Study of Strategy, Tactics, and Ship Design* (Annapolis 1940; reprinted 1980).
Two classic works summarising knowledge of galley warfare by a retired US admiral; now outdated in many respects.

PETER THROCKMORTON (ed), *History from the Sea* (London 1987).
Also published in New York as *The Sea Remembers*, this survey of underwater achaeology is a more modern version of Bass (see above). It is put together by an impressive array of scholars, but only a small percentage of the text is related to galleys.

COLIN THUBRON, *et al*, *The Venetians*, in 'The Seafarers' series by Time-Life (Amsterdam 1980).
Although popular and journalistic, this series is well researched and particularly strong on fresh illustrations from unusual sources.

PADDLED AND OARED SHIPS BEFORE THE IRON AGE

L BASCH, *Le musée imaginaire de la marine antique* (Athens 1987).

A comprehensive catalogue of ancient Mediterranean ship iconography, which the author treats as if it consisted almost wholly of technically correct representations. The lack of indexes is inexcusable in a work of this scale.

LIONEL CASSON, *Ships and Seamanship in the Ancient World* (Princeton 1971; new edition 1986).
This is the basic introductory textbook on ancient Mediterranean shipping in all its aspects. While Casson deals primarily with the classical period, his chapters on the pre-classical era are a valuable summary of the evidence. Full references to literary sources and adequate indexes.

J CHADWICK, 'The Muster of the Pylian Fleet', in P H Ilievski and L Crepajac (eds), *Tractata Mycenaea (Proceedings of the Eighth International Colloquium on Mycenaean Studies, Ohrid, 15–20 September 1985)*, (Skopje 1987), pp75–84.
This is the most detailed discussion to date on the Pylos Rower Tablets.

J F CHERRY, 'The First Colonization of the Mediterranean Islands: A review of Recent Research', *Journal of Mediterranean Archaeology* 3 (1990), pp145–221.
An important summary of the available evidence for the earliest voyages and colonisation of islands in the Mediterranean.

C G DOUMAS (trans A Doumas), *The Wall Paintings of Thera* (Athens 1992).
This de luxe colour edition is a must for anyone wishing to study the Thera wall paintings.

BJORN LANDSTRÖM, *Ships of the Pharaohs* (Garden City 1970).
A good collection of the evidence for Egyptian ships in the Bronze Age, but readers should beware the reconstructions, which are often based on insufficient evidence.

L MORGAN, *The Miniature Wall Paintings of Thera: A Study in Aegean Culture and Iconography* (Cambridge 1988).
This is the most in-depth study published to date on the Miniature Frieze in the West House at Thera.

T G PALAIMA, 'Maritime Matters in the Linear B Tablets', *Aegaeum* (Annals d'archéologie égéene de l'Université de Liège) 7 (1991), pp273–310, pl LXIII.
An up-to-date, and thoroughly comprehensive, study of all aspects of the Linear B tablets which have significance for Mycenaean seafaring.

T SÄVE-SÖDERBERGH, *The Navy of the Eighteenth Egyptian Dynasty* (Uppsala 1946).
A comprehensive study of Egyptian seafaring from a primarily textual viewpoint. Note that the author overemphasises the importance of Egyptian seafaring while denigrating the accomplishments of other maritime peoples, notably the Syro-Cannanites.

SHELLEY WACHSMANN, 'The Ships of the Sea

Peoples', *International Journal of Nautical Archaeology* 10 (1981), pp187–220.
A comprehensive study of the textual and iconographic evidence concerning the ships of the Sea Peoples and their relationship to Mycenaean ship types.

THE ANCESTRY OF THE TRIREME

L BASCH, *Le musée imaginaire de la marine antique*. See preceding section.

LIONEL CASSON, *Ships and Seamanship in the Ancient World*. See preceding section.

DOROTHEA GRAY, 'Seewesen', in F Matz and H-G Buchholz (eds), *Archaeologica Homerica I (ch G)* (Göttingen 1974).
Covers Homeric and other epic shipping and sea lore and presents the archaeological evidence in full, the whole of the Bronze Age included – far more, that is, than can possibly be considered relevant. The classification of the ships represented into 'galleys' and 'caïques' is misleading.

M C DE GRAEVE, *The Ships of the Ancient Near East*, Orientalia Lovanenia VII (Leuven 1981).
A meritorious collection of data.

J S MORRISON and R T WILLIAMS, *Greek Oared Ships 900–322 BC* (Cambridge 1968).
Full and systematic treatment of all data on galleys, the ship representations analysed by Williams, the literary evidence by Morrison. Not easy to consult: texts in Greek and Latin only (though often translated in the argument); no index locorum.

A SALONEN, *Die Wasserfahrzeuge in Babylonien*, Studia Orientalia VIII.4 (Helsinki 1939).
A very important pioneering study.

H T WALLINGA, *Ships and Sea-power before the Great Persian War. The Ancestry of the Trireme* (Leiden 1993).
The basis of the author's chapter in this book. The author endeavours to reconstruct the genesis of the early Greek sea powers, stressing the distinction between naval (state-owned) ships in the strict sense and auxiliary (armed merchant) galleys; and of the big-power navies of the Near East, including the Persian one.

THE TRIREME

A. ANCIENT SOURCES
Many of the Greek and Latin classics that form such an important body of evidence for ancient shipping have been translated and edited by Harvard University Press in the Loeb Classical Library and in the rather more accessible Penguin Classics paperback series. Some of the more important, with notes on modern editions, are listed below.

AESCHYLUS, *Persians*.
A play by a tragedian (525/4-456/5 BC) who fought the

Persians at Marathon in 490 BC and probably at the naval battle of Salamis in 480; the play contains a short description of the latter. Recent editions include that by H D Broadbent (Cambridge 1960), a translation of the play by A J Podlecki (Bristol 1991), and of all of the dramatist's work by K Mcleish and F Raphael (London 1991).

ARISTOPHANES, *Knights*, etc
Athenian comic dramatist (*c*448–385 BC); as a satirist, Aristophanes cannot always be taken at face value, but the references to naval matters in some of his plays provide direct, first-hand evidence of a unique kind. Numerous modern editions.

ARISTOTLE, *Parts of Animals* and *Constitution of Athens*.
Philosopher and scientist (384–322 BC), studied under Plato and was tutor to the young Alexander the Great. Recent edition of the former work by D M Balme (Oxford 1992).

Corpus Inscriptionum Graecarum, ed A Bockh (Berlin 1828–1877).
Usually abbreviated CIG by classical scholars; see *Inscriptiones Graecae*.

HERODOTUS, *History*.
Born in Halicarnassus in Asia Minor about 484 BC (died *c*425 BC), and the author of an early history of the wars between Greece and Persia. Translation by A D Godfrey, 4 vols (London and Cambridge, Mass 1957–61).

HOMER, *Odyssey*.
Thought to have been recited in its present form and subsequently written about 750 BC, the epic about the return of Odysseus from Troy is available in numerous editions.

Inscriptiones Graecae, ed A Kirchhoff (Berlin 1873ff); second edition, various editors (Berlin 1924ff).
Usually abbreviated to IG 1 for the first edition and IG 2¹ IG 2² and IG 2³ for the second. With *Corpus Inscriptionum Graecarum*, these volumes form an invaluable printed collection of Greek inscriptions, but since there is no translation and the commentary is in Latin, their use is confined to classical scholars.

THUCYDIDES, *History of the Peloponnesian War*.
Born *c*460–454 BC, died 399; Thucydides had practical experience commanding Athenian triremes during the war he later wrote about. Often regarded as the first real historian whose work has survived. Translated by C Forster Smith, in Loeb Classical Library, 4 vols (London and Cambridge, Mass 1919–23).

XENOPHON, *Anabasis* and *Greek History*.
Athenian-born soldier and historian (born *c*430 BC), with first-hand experience of much of the military history he wrote about. The former work covers the experiences of his band of Greek mercenaries in the Persian civil war, while the latter is the only contemporary account of the period 411–362 BC. Translated by Carleton L Brownson, 3 vols, Loeb Classical Library (London and Cambridge, Mass 1918–22).

B. MODERN WORKS

A ASSMANN, 'Seewesen' in Baumeister's *Denkmäler des Klassischen Altertums* III (Munich and Leipzig 1887).

J CARGILL, *The Second Athenian League* (London 1981).

A CARTAULT, *La triére Athenienne* (Paris 1881).
The first interpretation of the Lenormant relief as showing a three-level oared warship with the uppermost level of oars rowed through an outrigger.

A F B CREUZE, *Treatise on Naval Architecture* (Edinburgh 1841).
The first to point out that the trireme when holed would not sink since it had positive buoyancy.

J A DAVISON, 'The first Greek triremes', *Classical Quarterly* 41 (1947), pp18–24.
Used the switch by Polycrates of Samos (late sixth century BC) from pentecontors to triremes to date the latter's invention.

I X DRAGATZES, *Praktika* 1885 (published 1886).
Report on the excavation of the Zea shipsheds in Piraeus.

A HAACK, 'Uber attische Frieren', *Zeitschrift der Vereins deutscher ingenieure* (1895).
Good reconstruction of a three-level ship based on Lenormant relief.

J R HALE, 'Cushion and Oar', *The Oarsman* 5/2 and 5/3 (1973).
Analysed the rowing stroke exhibited on the Lenormant relief.

N G L HAMMOND, 'The Battle of Salamis', *Journal of Hellenic Studies* 76 (1956), pp26–37.

———, 'The narrative of Herodotus Bk VII and the Decree of Themistocles at Troezen', *The Journal of Hellenic Studies* 102 (1982), pp75–93.

A KÖSTER, *Das Antike Seewesen* (Berlin 1923).
Drew attention to the Ruvo vase but not as depicting a trireme.

J S MORRISON, 'The Greek Trireme', *The Mariner's Mirror* 27/1 (1941), pp14–44.
Argued against Tarn from a model of a three-level oar system based on the Lenormant relief and the Ruvo vase ship as representing triremes.

———, 'The first triremes', *The Mariner's Mirror* 65/1 (1979), pp14–44.
A reply to J A Davison's dating of the trireme's invention.

J S MORRISON and R T WILLIAMS, *Greek Oared Ships 900–322 BC* (Cambridge 1968; reprinted Oxford 1994).

J S MORRISON and J F COATES, *The Athenian Trireme* (Cambridge 1986).
Put the case for the reconstruction of a trireme by the Hellenic Navy subsequently named *Olympias*.

———, 'Sea Trials of the Reconstructed Athenian Trireme *Olympias*', *The Mariner's Mirror* 79/2 (1993), pp131–141.
A reply to criticisms of the reconstruction.

——— (eds), *An Athenian Trireme Reconstructed: the British Sea Trials of Olympias 1987*, BAR International Series 486, (Oxford 1989).

J B SALMON, *Wealthy Corinth* (Oxford 1984).
The city where a type of trireme was invented.

TIMOTHY SHAW (ed), *The Trireme Project: Operational Experience 1987–1990*, Oxbow Monograph 31 (Oxford 1993).

W W TARN, 'The Greek Warship', *The Journal of Hellenic Studies* 25 (1905), pp137–173.
Argued that a trireme with three levels of oars was impossible.

CECIL TORR, *Ancient Ships* (Cambridge 1984, reprinted Chicago 1964).
Ranks with A Assmann and A Cartault as a great pioneer of ancient nautical studies.

L WEBER, *Die Lösung der Trierenratsel* (Danzig 1896).
Argued that the solution lay in the Venetian *a scaloccio* oar system, the least likely solution of all that have been proposed.

HELLENISTIC OARED WARSHIPS
A. ANCIENT SOURCES

APPIAN, *Roman History*.
Roman citizen of Alexandria who wrote in Greek a history of various peoples down to the time of their incorporation into the Roman Empire. He lived in the first half of the second century AD. It is translated by H White in 4 vols of the Loeb Classical Library (London and Cambridge, Mass 1912).

ARRIAN, *Anabasis of Alexander and Indica*.
A Greek historian and philosopher, born about AD 96 in Nicomedia. He saw action against the Alani as Roman governor of Cappadocia. The life of Alexander the Great is his most important surviving work. It is translated with a number of useful Appendices by P A Brunt in 2 vols of the Loeb Classical Library (London and Cambridge, Mass 1976–1983).

ATHENAEUS, *Deipnosophistai* ('Professors at the Dinner Table').
He was born in Naucratis (Egypt) and lived between AD *c*160 and *c*230. His work of which about half (15 books) is preserved is important for the many, sometimes lengthy, citations from authors whose works have not otherwise survived. It is translated by C B Gulick in 7 vols of the Loeb Classical Library (London and Cambridge, Mass 1957–1967).

DIODORUS OF SICILY, *Bibliothēkē Historikē*.
Born at Argyrion in Sicily, he wrote in Greek between *c*60 and *c*30 BC his 'historical library' in 40 books covering the history of the entire world until his own times, of which the surviving texts are a fragment, valuable since clearly based on earlier historians whose work has not survived or has survived (*eg* Timaios also of Sicily) only in a few small fragments. The surviving work is translated in 12 vols (I–VI by C H Oldfather, VII by C L Sherman, VIII by C B Welles, IX and X by Russel M Geer, XI and XII by F R Walton, with a General Index by Russel M Geer) in the Loeb Classical Library (London and Cambridge, Mass 1946–1966).

GALEN, *On the Use of the Parts of the Body*.
A Greek physician and anatomist of Pergamum he lived between *c*AD 129 and AD 199, and practised in Rome. The work is translated with introduction and commentary by M T May in 2 vols of *Cornell Publications in the History of Science* (Ithaca, NY 1968).

TITUS LIVIUS, *History of Rome*.
Living between 59 (or 64) BC and AD 17 (or 12) Livy devoted his life to a monumental history of Rome from her earliest days; 35 of the 142 books survive, but some of the lost books are thought to have influenced later writers, *eg* Florus and Orosius. The surviving books are translated in 14 vols (I–V by B O Foster, VI–VIII by F G Moore, IX–XII (partly) by Evan T Sage, XII (partly) – XIV by A C Schelesinger with a General Index by Russel M Geer) in the Loeb Classical Library (London and Cambridge, Mass 1920–1967).

LUCAN, *The Civil War*.
Lucan's poem about the war between Julius Caesar and Pompey contains a vivid account of a naval battle off Massalia between the fleets of Decimus Brutus and the Massaliots in which current warship types are usefully if rather enigmatically described. He lived AD 39–65. The poem is translated by J D Duff in the Loeb Classical Library (London and Cambridge, Mass 1928).

GAIUS PLINIUS SECUNDUS, *Natural History*.
Pliny the Elder (*c*AD 23–29) served as a soldier and was in command of the Misenum fleet when he died observing too closely the eruption of Vesuvius. He wrote contemporary history but is known from his only surviving work the *Natural History* in 35 books. It is translated in 10 volumes (I–V and IX by H Rackham, VI–VIII by W H S Jones, and X by D E Eichholz) of the Loeb Classical Library (London and Cambridge, Mass 1940–1962).

PLUTARCH, *Lives*.
A philosopher and writer of historical biography, he was born (*c*AD 46) in Chaeronea in Boeotia, educated in Athens and lived some years in Rome. He died *c*AD 120. His *Lives* were written in pairs of Greeks and Romans of similar eminence (*eg* Demosthenes and Cicero, Alexander and Julius Caesar). They are translated by B Perrin in 11 vols of the Loeb Classical Library (London and Cambridge, Mass 1914–1926).

POLYBIUS, *The Histories*.
Born about 202 BC in Megalopolis, as a young man he was a soldier and statesman and was sent to Rome in 166 with the 1000 leading people of the Achaean League as hostages for Achaean good faith. He became a friend of the younger Scipio and developed the admiration of Rome as a future great power which was the subject of his 40–book *Histories* of which 5 survive. He died in 120 BC in his eighties after a fall from his horse. F W Walbank's *Historical Commentary on Polybius* (Oxford Vol I 1957, Vol II 1967, Vol III 1979) is an essential aid for study of the rise of Rome. The *Histories* are translated by W R Paton in six volumes of the Loeb Classical Library (London and Cambridge, Mass 1979–1980).

THE AUGUSTAN POETS
Virgil (born 70 BC), *Horace* (born 65 BC) and *Propertius* (born *c*50) make informative references to the battle of Actium. Virgil in Book 8 of the *Aeneid* describes the prophetic decoration of the shield of Aeneas (a Trojan hero who founded Rome) with scenes from the battle. Also in Book 5 he tells of a ship-race promoted by Aeneas in which the participating ships are recognisable as warship types of the first century BC. Virgil is translated by H R Fairclough in two volumes (1916 and 1918), Horace *Odes and Epodes* by C E Bennett (1914) and Propertius *Lyrical Poems* by G P Gooch (1990) in the Loeb Classical Library (London and Cambridge, Mass).

THEOPHRASTUS, *Enquiry into Plants* and *Characters*.
Philosopher and natural scientist, he was born about 372 BC in Lesbos, came to Athens and worked under Aristotle whom he succeeded as head of the Lyceum. The *Enquiry* is translated by A F Hort in two volumes (1916) and the *Characters* by J Rusten in one volume (1983) of the Loeb Classical Library (London and Cambridge, Mass).

VITRUVIUS POLLIO, *On Architecture*.
Vitruvius was a Roman engineer and architect who worked in Rome under Julius Caesar and then Augustus, to whom he dedicated his book written between 25 and 23 BC. It is translated by F Granger in two volumes of the Loeb Classical Library (London and Cambridge, Mass 1933 and 1934).

B. MODERN WORKS

R E ALLEN, *The Attalid Kingdom* (Oxford 1983).

N G ASHTON, 'The Naumachia near Amorgos in 322 BC', *Annual Report of the British School at Athens* 72 (1977), pp1–12.

R M BERTHOLD, 'Lade, Pergamon and Chios: Operations of Philip V in the Aegean', *Historia* 24 (1975), pp150–163.

A B BOSWORTH, 'The Death of Alexander the Great: Rumour and Propaganda', *Classical Quarterly* ns 21 (1971), pp112–136.

J BRISCOE, *A Commentary on Livy: 31–33* (Oxford 1973).

———, *A Commentary on Livy: 34–37* (Oxford 1981).

LIONEL CASSON, *Ships and Seamanship in the Ancient World* (Princeton 1971; reprint with addenda and corrigenda 1986).
See earlier section.

F DUNAND, *Le Culte d'Isis dans le basin oriental de la méditerranée* (Leiden 1973).

R M ERRINGTON, 'Diodorus Siculus and the Chronology of the Early Diadochoi 320–311 BC', *Hermes* 105 (1977), pp478–504.

E M FORSTER, *Alexandria* (New York 1971).

P GREEN, *Alexander to Actium* (London 1990).

H HAUBEN, 'Fleet Strength at the Battle of Salamis 306 BC', *Chiron* 6 (1976).

———, 'Antigonus's Invasion Plan for his attack on Egypt in 306 BC', *OLP* 6/7 (1975/6), pp267–271.

———, *Callicrates of Samos: A Contribution to the Study of the Ptolemaic Admiralty* (Louvain 1970).

A H McDONALD and F W WALBANK, 'Rhodian Quadriremes', *Journal of Roman Studies* 33 (1969).

R MEIGGS, *Roman Ostia* (second ed Oxford 1973).

I M MERTER, 'The Silver Coinage of Antigonus Gonatus and Antigonus Doson', ANS Mus. N9 (1960), pp39–52.

J S MORRISON, 'Hemiolia, trihemiolia', *International Journal of Nautical Archaeology* 9/2 (1980), pp121–126.

———, 'Hyperesia in Naval Contexts in the 5th and 4th Centuries BC', *Journal of Hellenic Studies* 104 (1984), pp48–59.

———, 'Athenian Sea-power in 323/2 BC: Dream and Reality', *Journal of Hellenic Studies* 107 (1987), pp88–97.

———, 'Tetrereis in the fleets of Dionysius I of Syracuse', *Classica et Mediaevalia* 41 (1990), pp33–41.

J S MORRISON and J F COATES, *Greek and Roman Oared Warships, 399–31 BC* (Oxford 1994).

E T NEWELL, *The Coinage of Demetrius Poliorcetes* (Oxford 1927).

H A ORMEROD, *Piracy in the Ancient World* (Liverpool 1924, second edition 1979).
Full treatment of an important aspect of the Hellenistic world.

E E RICE, *The Grand Procession of Ptolemy Philadelphus* (Oxford 1983).
New work on an interesting subject

W W TARN, *Hellenistic Military and Naval Developments* (Cambridge 1930, reprinted Chicago 1984).
An influential work in its time; the naval sections are now out of date.

———, *Antigonus Gonatas* (Oxford 1913).

W W TARN and G T GRIFFITH, *Hellenistic Civilisation* (third edition London 1958).
A useful short handbook of the subject covered more fully by P Green (above).

J H THIEL, *History of Roman Sea Power before the Second Punic War* (1951).

———, *Studies in the History of Roman Sea Power in Republican Times* (1946).

F W WALBANK, *Philip V of Macedon* (Cambridge 1940).

———, 'Sea Power and the Antigonids', in W L Adams and E N Borza (eds), *Philip II, Alexander the Great and the Macedonian Heritage* (Washington DC 1982), pp213–36.

———, *A Historical Commentary on Polybius* (Oxford: Vol I 1957, Vol II 1967, Vol III 1979).
See 'Ancient Sources'.

FLEETS OF THE EARLY ROMAN EMPIRE

LIONEL CASSON, *Ships and Seamanship in the Ancient World* (Princeton 1971; new edition 1986).
See earlier section.

———, *The Ancient Mariners* (Princeton, second edition 1991).
Chapters on the development of Roman sea power, Roman trade, and piracy in the Mediterranean.

D KIENAST, *Untersuchungen zu den Kriegsflotten der römischen Kaiserzeit*, Antiquitas Reihe 1 Band 13 (Bonn 1966).
Scholarly study of the personnel, role and history of the Roman fleets in the imperial period. In German.

F MEIJER, *A History of Seafaring in the Classical World* (London 1986).
Chapters on the development of Roman military and merchant seafaring.

M REDDÉ, *Mare Nostrum* (Rome 1986).
Exhaustive account of all aspects of the Roman military marine throughout its history. In French.

J ROUGÉ, (translated from the French by S Frazer), *Ships and Fleets of the Ancient Mediterranean* (Middletown, Connecticut 1975).
Contains chapters on the Roman navies.

C STARR, *The Roman Imperial Navy 31 BC–AD 324* (Cambridge second edition 1960).
Classic history of the Roman fleets of this period.

———, *The Influence of Sea Power on Ancient History* (Oxford 1989).
Excellent brief account of the importance and limitations of navies in the ancient world, with a chapter on the Roman imperial period.

H D L VIERECK, *Die römische Flotte* (Herford 1975).
A very full, if often speculative, account of Roman navies of all periods, with emphasis on the material aspects, including harbours, ships and armaments. In German.

LATE ROMAN, BYZANTINE AND ISLAMIC GALLEYS AND FLEETS

G F BASS and F H van DOORNINCK, Jr, *Yassi Ada I: A Seventh-Century Byzantine Shipwreck* (College Station, Texas 1982).

V CHRISTIDES, 'Naval warfare in the eastern Mediterranean. An Arabic translation of Leo VI's *Naumachica*', *Graeco-Arabica* 3 (1984), pp137–148.

R DOLLEY, 'Naval tactics in the heyday of the Byzantine thalassocracy', in *Atti dell' VIII Congresso di Studi Bizantini* (Rome 1953) pp324–339.

———, 'The warships of the Later Roman Empire', *Journal of Roman Studies* 38 (1948), pp47–53.

F H van DOORNINCK, Jr 'Did tenth-century dromons have a waterline ram? Another look at Leo, *Tactica*, XIX, 69', *The Mariner's Mirror* 79 (1993), pp387–392.

C J EISEMAN and B S RIDGWAY, *The Porticello Shipwreck: A Mediterranean Merchant Vessel of 415–385 BC* (College Station, Texas 1987).

A M FAHMY, *Muslim Sea-Power in the Eastern Mediterranean* (second edition Cairo 1966).

——, *Muslim Naval Organization in the Eastern Mediterranean from the Seventh to the Tenth Century AD* (Cairo 1966).

J HALDON and M BYRNE, 'A possible solution to the problem of Greek Fire', *Byzantinische Zeitschrift* 70 (1977), pp91–99.

J HAYWOOD, *Dark Age Naval Power: A Reassessment of Frankish and Anglo-Saxon Seafaring Activity* (London and New York 1991).

O HÖCKMANN, 'Darstellungen von Ruderschiffen auf zwei römischen Ziegelstampen aus Mainz', *Archäologisches Korrespondenzblatt* 14 (1984), pp319–324.

——, 'Römische Schiffsverbände auf dem Ober- und Mittelrhein und der Verteidigung der Rheingrenze in der Spätantike', *Jahrbuch des römisch-germanischen Zentralmuseums* 33 (1986), pp369–416.

——, 'Römische Schiffsfunde westlich des Kastells Oberstimm', *Bericht der römisch-germanischen Kommission* 70 (1990), pp321–347.

——, 'Late Roman Rhine vessels from Mainz, Germany', *International Journal of Nautical Archaeology* 22 (1993), pp125–135.

E HOLLSTEIN, 'Dendrochronologie der römerzeitlichen Schiffe von Mainz', in G Rupprecht, *Die Mainzer Römerschiffe: Berichte über Entdeckung, Ausgrabung und Bergung* (Mainz 1982), pp114–123.

A R LEWIS, *Naval Power and Trade in the Mediterranean AD 500–1100* (Princeton 1951).

P MARSDEN, 'The County Hall ship, London', *International Journal of Nautical Archaeology* 3 (1974), pp55–65.

FZ S MULLER, 'Verslag van de opgravingen van Romeinsche oudheden te Vechten . . .', in *Verslag van het verhandelde in de Algemeene Vergadering van het Provinciaal Utrechts Genootschap van Kunsten en Wetenschappen, Gehouden den 25 Juni 1895* (Utrecht, 1895), pp129–142 and 160–161.

W M MURRAY and PH H PETSAS, 'Octavian's Campsite Memorial for the Actium War', *Transactions of the American Philosophical Society* 79/4 (1988).

——, 'The spoils of Actium', *Archaeology* 41/4 (1989), pp27–35.

S PANCIERA, 'Liburna', *Epigraphica* 18 (1956), pp130–156.

E PÁSZTHORY, 'Über das "Griechische Feuer"', *Antike Welt* 17 (1986), pp27–37.

G RUPPRECHT, *Die Mainzer Römerschiffe: Berichte über Entdeckung, Ausgrabung und Bergung* (Mainz 1982).

J R STEFFY, 'The Reconstruction of the 11th century Serçe Liman vessel. A preliminary report', *International Journal of Nautical Archaeology* 11 (1982), pp13–34.

——, 'The Kyrenia ship: An interim report on its hull construction', *American Journal of Archaeology* 89 (1985), pp71–101.

——, 'The Mediterranean shell to skeleton transition: A northwest European parallel?' in H R Reinders and C Paul (eds), *Carvel Construction Technique: Fifth International Symposium on Boat and Ship Archaeology, Amsterdam 1988* (Oxford 1991), pp1–9.

M DE WEERD, *Schepen voor Zwammerdam* (Amsterdam 1988).

FROM DROMŌN TO GALEA

M A AGEIL, 'Naval policy and the use of the fleet of Ifriqiyyah from the 1st to 3rd centuries AH (7th to 9th centuries AD)', (PhD thesis, University of Michigan 1985).

HÉLÈNE AHRWEILER, *Byzance et la mer: la marine de guerre, la politique et les institutions maritimes de Byzance au VIIe-XVe siècles* (Paris 1966).
Concentrates on administration and more general aspects of Byzantine maritime affairs between the seventh and fifteenth centuries, but with short descriptions of ship types.

ALBERT OF AACHEN, *Historia Hierosolymitana*, in *Recueil des Historiens des Croisades: Historiens Occidentaux, Vol 4* (Paris 1879).

Annales Colonienses maximi, K Pertzed (ed), Monumenta Germaniae historica. Scriptores, Vol XVII (Hanover 1861).

H ANTONIADIS-BIBICOU, *Études d'histoire maritime de Byzance: à propos du 'Thème des Caravisiens'* (Paris 1966).

R B BANDINELLI, *Hellenistic-Byzantine Miniatures of the Iliad (Ilias Ambrosiana)* (Olten 1955).

L BASCH, 'Navires et bateaux coptes: état des questions en 1991', *Graeco-Arabica* 5 (1993), pp23–62.

C H BECKER, 'Arabische Papyri des Aphroditofundes', *Zeitschrift für Assyriologie und verwandte Gebiete* 20 (1907), pp68–104.

L T BELGRANO, *Documenti inediti riguardanti le due Crociate di San Ludovico IX, re di Francia* (Genoa 1859).

—— and C IMPERIALE (eds), *Annali Genovesi di Caffaro e de'suoi continuatori, Vol 2* (Genoa 1901).

E H BYRNE, *Genoese Shipping in the Twelfth and Thirteenth Centuries* (Cambridge, Mass 1930).

C CALISSE (ed), *Liber Maiolichinus de gestis Pisanorum* (Rome 1904).

V CHRISTIDES, 'Two parallel naval guides of the tenth century: Quda'ma's document and Leo VI's *Naumachica*: a study on Byzantine and Moslem naval preparedness', *Graeco-Arabica* 1 (1982), pp51–103.

——, 'Naval warfare in the Eastern Mediterranean (6th-14th centuries): an Arabic translation of Leo VI's *Naumachica*', *Graeco-Arabica* 3 (1984), pp137–48.

——, 'The naval engagement of Dha't as-Sawari AH 34/AD 655–656: a classical example of naval warfare incompetence', *Byzantina* 13 (1985), pp1331–1345.

A DAIN (ed), *Naumachica partim adhuc inedita* (Paris 1943).
Collection of original documents, particularly useful for Byzantine shipbuilding. Greek texts with brief Latin commentary.

R H DOLLEY, 'The warships of the later Roman Empire', *Journal of Roman Studies* 38 (1948), pp47–53.
At one time the dromōn reconstruction presented in this paper was widely accepted, but modern research has cast doubt on both its principles and details.

J E DOTSON, 'Merchant and naval influences on galley design at Venice and Genoa in the fourteenth century', in C L Symonds (ed), *New Aspects of Naval History: Selected Papers presented at the Fourth Naval History Symposium* (Annapolis 1981), pp20–32.

E EICKHOFF, *Seekrieg und Seepolitik zwischen Islam und Abendland: das Mittelmeer unter Byzantinischer und Arabischer Hegemonie (650–1040)* (Berlin 1966).
A history of Byzantine naval warfare, with some material on shipbuilding and ship types; presents an unconvincing reconstruction of a dromon.

A M FAHMY, *Muslim Naval Organisation in the Eastern Mediterranean from the Seventh to the Tenth Century AD* (Cairo 1966).

R FILANGIERI, *et al* (eds), *I registri della cancelleria angioina*, 33 vols (Naples 1950–81).

F FOERSTER, 'The warships of the kings of Aragón and their fighting tactics during the 13th and 14th centuries AD', *International Journal of Nautical Archaeology* 16 (1987), pp19–29.

J GILDEMEISTER, 'Über arabisches Schiffswesen', *Nachrichten der Königlichen Gesellschaft der Wissenschaften zu Göttingen. Philosophische-Historische Klasse* (1882), pp431–49.

A GRABAR and M MANOUSSACAS, *L'illustration du manuscrit de Skylitzes de la Bibliothèque Nationale de Madrid* (Venice 1979).

H KINDERMANN, *'Schiff' im Arabischen. Untersuchung über Vorkommen und Bedeutung der Termini* (Zwickau 1934).

F C LANE, 'Cotton cargoes and regulations against overloading', in his *Venice and History* (Baltimore 1966), pp253–68

A R LEWIS and T J RUNYAN, *European Naval and Maritime History, 300–1500* (Bloomington, Indiana 1985).
A general history of maritime affairs from late Antiquity to the Renaissance.

F MORALES BELDA, *La marina de Al-Andalus* (Barcelona 1970).

D NICOLLE, 'Shipping in Islamic art: seventh through sixteenth century AD', *American Neptune* 49 (1989), pp168–97.

G PARIS (ed), *L'estoire de la guerre sainte: histoire en vers de la troisième croisade (1190–1192) par Ambroise* (Paris 1897).

PETER OF EBOLI, *De rebus Siculis carmen*, ed E Rota (Muratori, *Rerum Italicarum scriptores*, nuova serie, t XXXI, pt 1, fasc 36–7), (Città di Castello 1905).

JULIUS POLLUX, *Pollucis Onomasticon*, ed E Bethe (Leipzig 1900–1937).

PROCOPIUS OF CAESAREA, *History of the Wars: Book III. The Vandalic War*, in H B Dewing (ed & trans), *Procopius, Vol 2* (London 1916).

J H PRYOR, 'The galleys of Charles I of Anjou, King of Sicily: ca. 1269–84', *Studies in Medieval and Renaissance History*, ns 14 (1993), pp34–103.

————, 'The Crusade of Emperor Frederick II, 1220–29: the implications of the maritime evidence', *American Neptune* 52 (1992), pp113–32.

ROBERT OF CLARI, *The Conquest of Constantinople*, trans E H McNeal (New York 1936).

MARINO TORSELLO SANUDO, *Liber secretorum fidelium crucis super Terrae Sanctae recuperatione et conservatione* (Hanover 1611).

W STUBBS (ed), *Chronicles and Memorials of the Reign of Richard I. Vol I: Itinerarium peregrinorum et gesta regis Ricardi*, Rerum Britannicarum medii aevi scriptores 38 (London 1864).

THUCYDIDES, *History of the Peloponnesian War*, in C Forster Smith (trans), *Thucydides* (London 1935).

VEGETIUS, *Epitoma rei militaris* (Stuttgart 1967).
Modern edition of an important late Roman compendium of military and naval science.

K M WOODY, 'Sagena piscatoris: Peter Damiani and the Papal election decree of 1059', *Viator* 1 (1970), pp33–54.

MERCHANT GALLEYS

Because this chapter covers most of the period of this book, many of the works cited earlier are relevant, but the following references furnish full documentation and further detail on the aspects noted.

LIONEL CASSON, *Ships and Seamanship in the Ancient World*, (Princeton 1971; new edition 1986).
Covers, among others Hatshepsut's ships, early Greek and Phoenician, and Greek and Roman.

F C LANE, *Venetian Ships and Shipbuilders of the Renaissance* (Baltimore 1934).
For 'great galleys'.

————, 'Merchant Galleys, 1300–34: Private and Communal Operation', *Speculum* 38 (1963), pp179–205.
Economic history background to the Venetian great galley voyages.

H G RAWLINSON, 'The Flanders Galleys: some notes on seaborne trade between Venice and England 1327–1532 AD', *The Mariner's Mirror* 12 (1926), pp145–68.

J SOTTAS, *Les messageries maritimes de Venise aux XIVe & XVe siècles* (Paris 1938).
Information on routes and cargoes, and pilgrim voyages.

NAVAL ARCHITECTURE AND OAR SYSTEMS OF ANCIENT GALLEYS

LIONEL CASSON and J R STEFFY, *The Athlit Ram* (College Station, Texas 1991).
A study of the only ancient galley ram so far discovered and its implications for oared warships.

J COATES, 'The naval architecture of European oared ships', The Royal Institution of Naval Architects, Spring Meeting 1993, Paper No 9.
An excellent survey of the current state of research on the hydrodynamics and oar systems of galleys from antiquity to the Renaissance.

V FOLEY and W SOEDEL, 'Ancient oared warships', *Scientific American* (Apr 1981), pp116–29.
Includes some information on the use of catapults at sea.

H FROST, 'The first season of excavation on the Punic wreck', *International Journal of Nautical Archaeology* 2/1 (1973), pp33–49.

————, 'The Punic wreck in Sicily', *International Journal of Nautical Archaeology* 3/1 (1974), pp33–54.
Two articles by the excavator reporting on a wreck of what is probably an oared auxiliary which sank in ballast.

W M MURRAY and P M PETSAS, 'Octavian's Campsite Memorial for the Actium Wars', *American Philosophical Society* 79 (1989).
Contains useful information on the rams of Hellenistic/Roman polyremes.

E R NADEL and S R BUSSOLARI, 'The *Daedalus* Project', *American Scientist* 76 (Jul–Aug 1988), pp351–60.
Report on the man-powered aircraft project, which has much on human ergonomics and endurance that is relevant to rowing.

J T SHAW (ed), *The Trireme Project*, Oxbow Monographs No 31 (Oxford 1993).
A series of studies of various technical aspects of the *Olympias*, edited by the project's rowing expert.

A W SLEESWYK, 'The prow of the "Nike of Samothrace" reconsidered', *International Journal of Nautical Archaeology* 11/3 (1982), pp233–43.
Detailed analysis of this important monument, arguing that it represents a *trihemiolia*.

F R WHIT and D G WILSON, *Bicycling Science – Ergonomics and Mechanics* (Cambridge, Mass 1976).

NAVAL ARCHITECTURE AND OAR SYSTEMS OF MEDIEVAL AND LATER GALLEYS

Many of the works quoted in the 'From Dromōn to Galea' section are also of relevance here, particularly Ahrweiler, Christides, Dain, Dolley, and Eickhoff.

ULRICH ALERTZ, *Vom Schiffbauhandwerk zur Schiffbautechnik* (Hamburg 1991).
A study of the transition from craft- to science-based shipbuilding in Italian galley design, 1400–1700.

————, 'Venezianischer Schiffbau: die Flandern-Galeere von 1410', *Das Logbuch* 27/4 (1991), pp140–7.
Reconstruction of a large merchant galley of the early fifteenth century.

R C ANDERSON, 'Italian Naval Architecture about 1445', *The Mariner's Mirror* XI (London 1925).
An analysis of the manuscript of Zorzi Trombetta da Modone (Timbotta).

————, 'The design of galleys in 1550', *The Mariner's Mirror* 20 (1934).

————, 'Jal's "Memoire No 5" and the manuscript "Fabrica di Galere",' *The Mariner's Mirror* 31 (1945).
Critical comparison between the 'Fabrica' of about 1410 and the Timbotta manuscript of around 1445.

ALDO BARADEL, 'The *paraschuxula* of the Venetian galleys of the fourteenth century', *The Mariner's Mirror* 70 (1984), pp411–4.

An attempt to explain this mysterious fitting as a hull reinforcement like the classical *hypozoma*.

A CHIGGIATO (ed), *Le ragioni antique dell' architettura navale in Fonti per la storia di Venezia* (Venice 1987).
Detailed edition of anonymous Venetian Shipbuilding manuscripts of the late fifteenth and early sixteenth centuries. Explains the underlying principles.

J COATES, 'The naval architecture of European oared ships', The Royal Institution of Naval Architects, Spring Meeting 1993, Paper No 9.
See previous section.

ENNIO CONCINA, *L'Arsenale della Repubblica di Venezia* (Milan 1988).
Examination of the development of shipbuilding since the twelfth century in the context of a history of the Venetian Arsenal.

B CRESCENTIO, *Nautica Mediterranea* (Rome 1607).
Published work by the Papal admiral on navigation, cartography and galley construction in western Italy.

RENEE DOEHAERD, 'Les galères genoises dans la Manche et la Mer du Nord a la fin du XIIIe et au debut de XIVe', *Bulletin de l'Institut Historique Belge de Rome* 19 (1938), pp5–76.
Collection of documents relating to Genoese merchant galley voyages to England.

BALDISSERA QUINTO DRACHIO, *Visione del Drachio*, translated and annotated by L Th Lehmann (Amsterdam 1992).
A complete edition of this important work with modern critical apparatus.

JAN FENNIS, *La 'Stolonomie', et son vocabulaire maritime marseillais* (Amsterdam 1978).
Critical edition of a French sixteenth-century manuscript on the building and employment of galleys.

JOSEPH FURTTENBACH, *Architectura Navalis* (Ulm 1629; reprinted in facsimile New York 1975).
Describes the art of galley building as practised in Genoa.

F C LANE, 'Venetian naval architecture about 1550', *The Mariner's Mirror* XX (1934), and *Venice and History* (Baltimore 1969; Italian edition *Le Navi di Venezia*, Turin 1983).
Excerpts and translation of Pre Theodoro's writings on Venetian shipbuilding of the fifteenth and sixteenth centuries.

————, 'From biremes to triremes', *The Mariner's Mirror* 49 (1963), pp48–50.
Short note on the development of the oar system of Venetian galleys around 1300.

G B RUBIN DE CERVIN, *La Flotta di Venezia* (Milan 1985).
A highly illustrated general history of Venetian shipping; concentrates on local types but some material on galleys.

ALBERTO SACERDOTI, 'Note sulla galera da mercato veneziano nel XV secolo', *Bollettino dell'Istituto di Storia della Societae dello Stato Veneziano* IV (1962), pp80–105.
Includes reconstruction drawings of the Venetian Great Galley.

J P SARSFIELD, 'The *Fabrica di Galere* ships', *The Mariner's Mirror* 75 (1989), pp51–2.

U TUCCI, 'Architettura navale veneziana. Misure di vascelli dela metà de Cinquecento', in *Bollettino dell'Atlante Linguistico Mediterraneo* 5/6 (1963–64).
Prints details of the anonymous sixteenth-century Venetian manuscript 'Misure di vascelle . . .' covering the dimensions and design principles of galleys.

OAR MECHANICS AND OAR POWER IN ANCIENT GALLEYS

T A COOK, *Rowing at Henley* (Oxford 1919).
A work primarily of historical interest in the development of rowing.

R MEIGGS, *Trees and Timber in the Ancient World* (Oxford 1982).
A wide-ranging book that contains many references to ancient ships and shipbuilding.

B RANKOV, 'Reconstructing the past: the operation of the trireme reconstruction *Olympias* in the light of historical sources', *The Mariner's Mirror* 80 (1994), pp131–46.

BILL SAYER, *Rowing and Sculling: The Complete Manual* (London 1991).
A clear and readable account of modern methods of sliding-seat rowing and sculling, and of coaching training and rigging, by a very successful rowing coach; includes good explanations of the underlying principles.

J T SHAW, 'Rowing in Ships and Boats', paper No 10, Spring Meeting of the Royal Institution of Naval Architects (1993).

—— (ed), *The Trireme Project: Operational Experience 1987–90*, Oxbow Monographs No 31 (Oxford 1993).
Particularly relevant chapters include Rankov's on rowing and Shaw's on steering to ram.

OAR MECHANICS AND OAR POWER IN MEDIEVAL AND LATER GALLEYS

Many of the works quoted above in the section 'Naval Architecture and Oar Systems of Medieval and Later Galleys' are also relevant to this chapter.

M AYMARD, 'Oarsmen and galleys in the Mediterranean in the sixteenth century', *Mélanges en l'honneur de Fernand Braudel* (Paris 1973), pp49–64.
For details on the development of fighting galleys and the recruitment of crews between the end of the Middle Ages and the start of the modern era.

R BURLET and A ZYSBERG, 'Le travail de la rame sur les galères de France vers la fin du XVIIe siècle', *Neptunia* 164 (Paris 1986).
Collaboration between an historian and an ergonomist; this article, in translation, was used as the basis for the section on *a scaloccio* rowing in Chapter 12 of this book.

E CONCINA, *Navis* (Turin 1990).
Includes analysis of 'A brief essential summary of all the things that had to be done for the defence of the State in the Venetian Republic', by Alesandro Zorzi, formerly Nicolò.

L FINCATI, *Le Triremi* (Rome 1881).
The culmination of Admiral Fincati's work into the rowing systems of medieval galleys.

NOËL FOURQUIN, 'Galères du Moyen-âge', in *Quand voguaient les galères*, catalogue of exhibition held at the Musée de la Marine in Paris from October 1990 to January 1991.

E JURIEN DE LA GRAVIÈRE, *Les derniers jours de la marine à rame'* (Paris 1885).
Small book, excellently researched, even if the author does not quote his sources.

J-C HOCQUET, 'Sailors in Venice. . . ', in *Le genti del mare Mediterraneo*, XVIIᵉ International Symposium of Maritime History (Naples 1981), pp103-168.

A JAL, *Archéologie Navale*, 2 vols (Paris 1840).
This early work of nautical archaeology contains much of relevance for the history of galleys; in particular Mémoire No 5 contains extracts from a work always subsequently referred to as 'Fabrica al galere', although its actual title given on the title page is 'Libro di marineria'.

A LUTRELL, 'Late-medieval oarsmen', in *Le genti del mare Mediterraneo*, XVII International Symposium of Maritime History (Naples 1981), pp87-101.

JEAN MARTEILHE, *Mémoires d'un Protestant condamné aux galères de France pour cause de religion* (Le Havre 1778).
This is the edition of this famous description of life in the galleys quoted from in this book. A Zysberg re-edited Jean Marteilhe's text in full under the title *Mémoires d'un galérien du Roi-Soleil* (Paris 1982). The original edition was published in Rotterdam in 1757.

P MASSON, *Les Galères de France* (Aix-en-Provence 1938).

PANTERO PANTERA, *L'Armata Navale* (Rome 1614).
Early printed work with much information on galleys, their armament and employment.

BARRAS DE LA PENNE, 'La science des galères', National Library, MF 9176–9179, sd.
A well-known manuscript exposition of the technicalities of galleys by a late-seventeenth-century galley master.

Rerum Italicarum Scriptores, ed L A Muratori, Vol XXXI (Città di Castello 1905).
Collection of Italian historians from the sixth to the sixteenth centuries.

ALBERTO TENENTI, *La marine venitienne avant Lépant* (Paris 1962).

ANDRÉ ZYSBERG, 'L'arsenal des galères de France à Marseille (1660–1715)', *Neptunia* 59 (1985), pp20–31.

——, 'Les galères de France et la société des galériens (1660–1748)', doctoral thesis, EHESS, 1986.
Two important pieces of work by an expert on the organisation and administration of the French galley fleets.

THE GEOGRAPHICAL CONDITIONS OF GALLEY NAVIGATION IN THE MEDITERRANEAN

B CRESCENTIO, *Nautica Mediterranea* (Rome 1607).
See earlier section.

RUY GONZALEZ DE CLAVIJO, *Narrative of the Embassy of Ruy Gonzalez de Clavijo to the Court of Timour, at Samarcand AD 1403–6*, trans C R Markham, Hakluyt Society Publications, First series 26 (London 1859).

DIODORUS OF SICILY.
See under 'Hellenistic Oared Warships'.

R FILANGERI, *et al.* (eds), *I registri della cancelleria angioina*, 33 vols (Naples 1950–81).

S D GOITEIN, *A Mediterranean Society: The Jewish Communities of the Arab world as Portrayed in the Documents of the Cairo Geniza. Vol. 1: Economic Foundations* (Berkeley and Los Angeles 1967).
The seminal study of the most important new body of source materials for medieval Mediterranean society to be discovered in the last hundred years.

V GOLDSMITH and S SOFER, 'Wave climatology of the Southeastern Mediterranean', *Israel Journal of Earth Sciences* 32 (1983), pp1–51.
An important study by oceanographers of sea conditions in the area bounded by Cyprus, Egypt and Israel.

H H LAMB, *Climate: Past, Present, and Future, Vol. 2: Climatic History and the Future* (London 1977).
Indispensable for any historian seeking to utilise geographical factors for explanation of historical events.

——, 'Climate and the history of medieval Europe and its offlying seas', in *Medieval Europe, 1992: a Conference on Medieval Archaeology in Europe, 21–24 September 1992, University of York. Pre-printed papers. Vol 2 Maritime studies, ports and ships* (York 1992), pp1–26.
Adds little to the author's previous work.

E LE ROY LADURIE, *Times of Feast, Times of Famine: A History of Climate since the Year 1000* (London 1971).
Useful for the history of climate and one of the few historical books which seek to interpret the work of climatologists for historians. However, it has little to say about maritime history.

B R MOTZO (ed), *Il compasso di navegare: opera italiana del metà di secolo XIII* (Cagliari 1947).

WILLIAM H MURRAY, 'Do modern winds equal ancient winds?', *Mediterranean Historical Review* 2 (1987), pp139–67.
A very important study which shows that, overall, the observations of ancient philosophers and scientists accord well with modern meteorological data.

NIKEPHOROS OURANOS, Ἐκ τῶν Τακτικῶν Νικηφορου Ουρανου, κεφαλαια ρια–ρκγ', 119.1.1–2, in A Dain (ed), *Naumachica partim adhuc* (Paris 1943), p93 (in Greek).

JOHN H PRYOR, *Geography, Technology and War: Studies in the Maritime History of the Mediterranean 649–1571* (Cambridge 1988).
A study of the effects of weather and geography on Mediterranean navigation, with particular reference to the limitations of galleys.

——, 'The galleys of Charles I of Anjou King of Sicily: ca. 1269–84', *Studies in Medieval and Renaissance History*, ns14 (1993), pp34–103.
The first study in any language of these galleys and the documents that record them, which provide the oldest surviving detailed data for the construction of galleys.

——, 'Winds, waves, and rocks: the routes and the perils along them', in K Friedland (ed), *Maritime Aspects of Migration* (Cologne 1989), pp71–85.
An attempt to reconstruct the navigational conditions and hazards along the medieval routes from the Latin West to the Levant.

ROGER OF HOVEDEN, *Chronica*, W Stubbs (ed), Rerum Britannicarum medii aevi scriptores 51, 4 vols (London 1870).

MARINO SANUDO TORSELLO, *Liber secretorum fidelium crucis super Terrae Sanctae Recuperatione et conservatione* (Hanover 1611).

E C SEMPLE, *The Geography of the Mediterranean Region. Its Relation to Ancient History* (London 1932).
Still the only work which has seriously attempted to interpret Mediterranean history in any period in the light of the

geography of the region. Many geographical observations are applicable to later periods of history also.

STRABO, *The Geography of Strabo*, trans H L Jones, 8 vols (London and Cambridge Mass 1968).

ECONOMICS AND LOGISTICS OF GALLEY WARFARE

JOHN E DOTSON, 'Merchant and naval influences on galley design at Venice and Genoa in the fourteenth century', in Craig L Symonds *et al*, *New Aspects of Naval History* (Annapolis 1981).

——, The voyage of Simon Lecavello: a Genoese naval expedition of 1351', in *Saggi e documenti VI*, Civico Istituto Columbiano Studi e Testi 8 Genoa 1985).
A study of one of the best documented early naval expeditions, with details of routes, manning, victualling and costs.

——, 'Naval strategy in the first Genoese-Venetian War, 1257–1270', *The American Neptune* (1986), pp84–90.

JOHN F GUILMARTIN, JR, *Gunpowder and Galleys: Changing Technology and Warfare at Sea in the Sixteenth Century* (Cambridge 1974).
An influential book that demonstrates the strengths and weaknesses of galleys when faced with the new technology of gunpowder artillery. These are also applicable to earlier periods.

F C LANE, 'The economic meaning of the invention of the compass', and 'Diet and wages of seamen in the early fourteenth century', in *Venice and History: The Collected Papers of Frederic C Lane* (Baltimore 1966).

——, *Venice: A Maritime Republic* (Baltimore 1973).

JOHN H PRYOR, *Geography, Technology and War: Studies in the Maritime History of the Mediterranean 649–1571* (Cambridge 1988).
See earlier section.

W L RODGERS, *Naval Warfare under Oars* (Annapolis 1940).
See 'Introduction'.

NAVAL INSTALLATIONS

D J BLACKMAN, 'The Ship-sheds', in J S Morrison and R T Williams, *Greek Oared Ships, 900–322 BC* (Cambridge 1968), pp181–6.

——, 'Ancient Harbours in the Mediterranean', *International Journal of Nautical Archaeology* 11/2 (1982), pp79–104; 11/3, pp185–221, esp 204–6.

——, 'Triremes and shipsheds', *Tropis* II (1987), pp35–52.

——, 'Bollards and Men', in *Mediterranean Cities: Historical Perspectives*, ed I Malkin and R C Hohlfelder (London 1988), pp7–20.

——, 'Les cales à bateaux', *Dossiers d'Archéologie* 183 (June 1993), pp32–39.

J F COATES, 'Hauling a trireme up a slipway and up a beach', in J T Shaw (ed), *The Trireme Project* (Oxford 1993).

I C DRAGATSES and W DÖRPFELD, 'Ekthesis peri ton en Peiraiei anaskaphon', *Praktika* (1885), pp63–8.

K-V VON EICKSTEDT, *Beiträge zur Topographie des antiken Piräus* (Athens 1991).

V FOLEY, W SOEDEL and J DOYLE, 'A trireme displacement estimate', *International Journal of Nautical Archaeology*, 11/4 (1982), pp305–318.

R GARLAND, *The Piraeus* (London 1987).

J GUEY and P-M DUVAL, 'Les mosaiques de La Grange-du-Bief', *Gallia* 18 (1960), pp83–102.

H HURST, 'Excavations at Carthage 1977–8. Fourth interim report', *Antiquaries Journal* (1979), pp19ff (for the excavations on the *Ilôt de l'Amirauté*).

——, 'Le port militaire de Carthage', *Dossiers d'Archéologie* 183 (June 1993), pp42–51 (general survey).

J LE GALL, *Le Tibre, fleuve de Rome dans l'antiquité* (Paris 1953).

P MAZARAKIS-AINIAN, *Les structures portuaires en Grèce antique*, Mémoire Univ Libre de Bruxelles (Brussells 1992), pp49–70.

A RABAN, 'Minoan and Canaanite Harbours', in R Laffineur and L Basch (eds), *Thalassa. L'Egée préhistorique et la mer*, *Aegaeum* 7 (Liège 1991), pp129–46.

M REDDÉ, *Mare Nostrum* (Rome 1986).

J W SHAW, 'Greek and Roman Harbourworks', in G F Bass (ed), *A History of Seafaring* (London 1977), pp87–112.

——, 'Excavations at Kommos (Crete) during 1984–1985', *Hesperia* 55 (1986), pp219–69.

——, 'Bronze Age Aegean Harboursides', in D A Hardy *et al* (eds), *Thera and the Aegean World III*, Vol I (Archaeology), (1990), pp420–36.

A SIMOSSI, 'Underwater excavation research in the ancient harbour of Samos', *International Journal of National Archaeology*, 20/4 (1991), pp281–98.

M YON, 'Le port de guerre de Kition', *Dossiers d'archéologie* 183 (June 1993), pp40–41.

THE ATHENIAN NAVY IN THE FOURTH CENTURY BC

G L CAWKWELL, 'Athenian Naval Power in the Fourth Century', *Classical Quarterly* ns 34 (1984), pp334–345.

V GABRIELSEN, *Financing the Athenian Fleet: Public Taxation and Social Relations* (Baltimore and London (1994).

M H JAMESON, 'The Provisions for Mobilization in the Decree of Themistokles', *Historia* 12 (1963), pp385–404.

B JORDAN, *The Athenian Navy in the Classical Period*. University of California Publications: Classical Studies Vol 13 (Berkeley 1975).

J S MORRISON, '*Hyperesia* in Nautical Contexts in the Fifth and Fourth Centuries BC', *Journal of Hellenic Studies* 104 (1984), pp48–59.

Glossary of Terms and Abbreviations

Complied by Robert Gardiner with the assistance of the contributors. This list assumes some knowledge of ships and does not include the most basic terminology. It also avoids those words which are defined on the only occasions in which they occur in this book.

'Abbasid. Relating to the second great Muslim ruling dynasty, the first 'Abbasid caliph being declared in AD 750.

actuaria [navis]. Latin general term for merchant galley but also used more specifically for a particular type of relatively large dimensions (30–50 oarsmen) with concave prow and projecting forefoot (*qv*); probably to be identified with the Greek *akatos*.

Aghlabid. Relating to the breakaway Muslim dynasty of North Africa that gained its independence in AD 799 and survived until defeated by the Fatimids in AD 909.

akatos, akation. See *actuaria*.

alla galozza. Synonymous with *a scaloccio* (*qv*).

alla sensile, alla zenzile. Medieval rowing system in which groups of rowers (usually no more than three but five is known) on the same bench pulled on individual oars. The thole pins (*qv*) for each bench were positioned in clusters on the outrigger (*qv*).

aphlaston. The fan-like ornament at the stern of ancient galleys in which the up-curving timbers of the hull terminated.

aphract. Uncovered, undecked, open; the opposite of cataphract (*qv*).

apostis. See *outrigger*. Also used in *a scaloccio* (*qv*) French galleys of the oarsman outboard of the lead rower.

Archaic. Term applied to Greek painted pottery of the period 700-480 BC.

archontes. Byzantine commander of a small squadron, usually three to five ships.

Arsenale. The Venetian state dockyard, which in its heyday was probably the greatest industrial complex in the West. The English term 'arsenal' for a military depot and armoury is derived from this institution, which itself was a particular form of the medieval *darsana* (ultimately from the Arabic *darsina-'a*).

artemon. The small, square foresail of ancient galleys.

a scaloccio. A system of rowing, replacing the earlier *alla zenzile* (*qv*), in which the oarsmen on each bench pulled in unison on a single large oar. On the largest galleys six or seven men per oar were employed but four or five was more usual.

askōma (plural askomata). Leather sleeve through which the lowest level of oars was worked in an ancient Greek three-level galley.

a strapada. The vigorous stand-and-sit rowing style employed by freemen oarsmen in medieval and later galleys. *See also la rancata.*

bacalas. The cantilevered frames supporting the outrigger structure of a French galley; known as *braccioli* in Italian.

backsplash. A spurt of water thrown upwards and forwards by the blade of an oar entering the water.

back water. In rowing or paddling, to reverse stroke so as to halt the craft or propel it backwards.

banquette. In French *a scaloccio* (*qv*) galleys the flat form on which rowers rested their feet when not rowing; the structural base of each bench.

bastarda, bastardella. An Italian development of the *sotile* (*qv*) galley to accommodate a fourth and eventually a fifth rower per bench, the 'bastard' galley was wider and more strongly built than its predecessor.

black figure pottery. An ancient Mediterranean style with black figures painted in black on an unglazed or slightly glazed red background.

bonavoglia. Oarsmen who were volunteers, rather than convicts, prisoners of war or slaves.

braccioli. See *bacalas*.

brails. Rigging lines used to reduce and control the area of sail catching the wind.

brancade. In late French galleys the multi-branched chain to which the rowers on each bench were shackled; the term became synonymous with each bench of rowers themselves.

brigantino, brigantin. In the Middle Ages a type of small, fast oared craft, decked and rigged with a single mast and sail; although the origin of the later English term 'brigantine', at this time the word did not refer to a particular rig.

butt. The end of the handle of an oar.

button. A projection or collar worked on an oar to help the oarsman maintain the correct gearing (*qv*). It bears on the thole pin (*qv*).

caltrop. Spiked device usually designed so that however it falls at least one barb points upwards; primarily used to impede the movement of cavalry but also useful against foot soldiers.

cant. In rowing a canted rig is one in which the oarsmen do not face directly towards the stern, as in most medieval galleys. In plan view, this gives what is sometimes called a herringbone rig.

cao [plural cavi] di sesto. In Venetian galley design, the end frames of the hull proper – the section determined by the *partisoni* (*qv*) process – beyond which was the bow or stern.

cataphract. From the Greek for 'covered', the term originally implied fully decked but later in the era of catapult-armed warships it was applied to vessels with screens and other defensive equipment, as opposed to the light and open craft. The term was used in a similar fashion of heavily armoured cavalry, where both horse and rider were protected.

catch. The beginning of the pull phase of an oar stroke.

cattus (plural catti). Large Muslim galley (eleventh–thirteenth centuries), possibly a trireme, protected by 'castles'.

caulk. To ram fibrous material (caulking) hard into a seam to make it watertight and to prevent the planks of the hull from sliding upon each other when the hull is subjected to longitudinal bending stresses.

celox. See *kelēs*.

centre of percussion. Of a pivoted body such as a solid wooden oar in its thole (*qv*), the centre of percussion is located and defined by the property that a blow received there creates no reaction at the pivot, *ie* the thole.

chelandion. A Byzantine warship, first mentioned around the beginning of the ninth century AD, possibly derived from *keles* (*qv*), a fast merchant galley of classical Greek times; the term later had the specific meaning of a transport galley, especially for horses. As *chelandium* or *chelandra* also applied to Muslim vessels.

chiourme. The collective term for the oar-crew of a French galley; they were recruited, whether slave, convict or nominal freemen, by state-run organisations called *chiourme bureaux*.

chord. The straight line joining two points on an arc.

Clazomenian. Of the ancient Greek city of Clazomenae in Ionia.

clench. To bend the protruding part of a spike or nail over to prevent it pulling out of timber; also, specifically, to rivet the end of a nail over a washer, or rove.

clevis. See *manille*.

columbaria. On medieval Italian bireme galleys the oarports through which the inner oarsmen worked their oars.

coniller. 1. As a noun: in French *a scaloccio* (*qv*) galleys the lead rowers of the foremost benches who were responsible for handling the anchors. 2. As a verb: the action of stowing the oars athwart the galley.

contre pedagne. The foot brace, at the height of the bench in front, used by the oarsmen in the stand-and-sit stroke of late French galleys.

corba de mezo. See *corba maistra*.

corba maistra. In a medieval Italian galley, the main frame or midship section defining the hull shape. Also called the *corba de mezo*.

corsia. The central gangway of a medieval or later galley; *coursie* in French.

corvus. Latin for 'raven'; a kind of hinged boarding bridge used by the Roman navy.

cothon. In ancient Greece an inner harbour, usually artificially made by excavation.

crank. Of ships, lacking in stability.

coursie. See *corsia*.

cubit. An ancient measure of length; 1 attic cubit = 0.444m; the older archaic cubit = 0.49m.

cutwater. The leading edge of the bow, sometimes a separate structural member, that cleaves the water when the craft is under way.

cybaea (Latin). See *kybaia*.

darsana. A medieval shipyard. *See also Arsenale.*

diekplous. In ancient Greek naval warfare a manoeuvre in which ships pushed through a gap in the enemy's line-abreast formation; more generally the gap in a line of ships through which it is possible for other ships to pass.

displacement. The mass of the volume of water occupied by the ship when afloat.

dowel. Round rod of wood, usually driven into holes drilled into timber as a fastening or filling.

dragon boats. Very long canoes paddled by large crews from southeast Asia, surviving today for ceremonial and racing purposes but originally used for war and piracy.

dromōn. Byzantine war galley, initially from the sixth century AD a fast single-level ship, but by the ninth century usually with two levels of oars and the standard ship of the battle line.

drungarios. A Byzantine admiral, particularly one commanding one of the fleets belonging to a maritime Theme, or administrative district. The *Drungarios of the Ploimen* was the commander of the Imperial fleet defending Constantinople.

elatē. Greek for silver fir; used in the manufacture of oars.

emporion. Market, or commercial harbour; ancient Greek.

epibatēs (plural epibatai). In ancient Greek usage, a fighting man in full armour carried on deck; also employed more generally for a passenger.

epōtis (plural epotides). 'Ear-timber', an athwartship beam at the bow of triremes and other ancient galleys that projected from the hull so protecting the outrigger (*qv*). Later applied also to a through-beam to which the quarter rudders were secured.

espalier. In French *a scaloccio* (*qv*) galleys the head rower of the aftermost benches who set the stroke; named from their proximity to the *espale* or embarkation ladders on each side of the poop.

Etesian winds. Certain Mediterranean winds that blow from the northwest for about forty days in the summer.

Fatimid. Relating to the Muslim dynasty in Africa that replaced the Aghlabids (*qv*) at the beginning of the tenth century. The dynasty was eventually to rule from Egypt until overthrown by Saladin in 1171.

fay. To fit together closely.

file. As used in this book the term refers to a line of oarsmen seen in plan. A trireme, for example, had three files of oarsmen per side, a quinquereme five, and so on; so the number of files, and not the number of levels at which the oars were worked, defined the type of galley.

finish. The end of the pull phase of an oar stroke.

fiol. The French term for the inboard length, or loom, of an oar; also called the *giron*, presumably from the Italian *zirone* (*qv*).

floor. In shipbuilding, transverse timbers across the keel and bottom planking.

foot. (Athenian) 0.296m; (Roman) 0.295m; (Venetian) 0.348m.

forefoot. The forward extremity of the keel; extended beyond the line of the stem in a ram bow.

fougon. The cooking apparatus or stove of a French galley.

fournelée. In French galleys the situation in which oars being rested were secured to a ringbolt (*fourneladou*) by a lashing taken around the *maintenen* (*qv*). In this mode the oars were raised somewhat above the horizontal and was used when the galley was at anchor. *See also rem à la barbe and sur les filarets.*

freeboard. The height of the top edge of the hull amidships, or the bottom edge of an opening in the ship's side, above the water when the ship is afloat.

fregata, fregada. In the Middle Ages a small galley.

furcata. On early medieval Italian galleys the single-piece 'forked' frames at bow and stern, rather than the full frames made up of floor timbers and futtocks.

fusta. A type of small galley.

galaverne. In *a scaloccio* galleys the strengthening piece, or fish, applied to the area of an oar around the thole pin (*qv*).

galea. Originally in late Roman times applied to a light, fast single-banked scouting vessel, and then more or less synonymous with dromōn (*qv*), but finally becoming a generic term for any oared vessel. It is not certain whether its etymology is Latin or Byzantine Greek.

galea grossa. See 'great galley'.

galee. Early medieval war galley; *see also galea.*

galeazza. A great galley (*qv*) performing the role of a warship; predecessor of the galleasse (*qv*).

galeotti. The oarsmen of galleys.

galia sotil. A 'narrow' galley of very fine lines; a warship rather than a merchantman.

galleasse. A sixteenth century Venetian innovation, a hybrid that attempted to combine the versatility of oared propulsion with the greater seaworthiness and broadside armament of the new full rigged ship. In effect they were a development of the great galley (*qv*) with a superimposed gundeck over the oars.

garboard. Strake of planking next to the keel, and by extension that general area of the hull.

gattus. *See cattus.*

gauloi. Phoenician sailing ships of rounded form; Greek version of the Phoenician for 'bowls'.

gearing. In rowing terms, roughly the ratio between the inboard and outboard lengths of an oar, but more accurately the ratio the distance between the centre of pressure of the blade and the thole bears to that between the effective point of application of the oarsman's pull and the thole (however, these distances are not known exactly).

Geometric. The term applied to Greek painted pottery with geometrical decoration of the period 900–700 BC.

Golden Bull. A charter whose high importance was marked by its decoration with a golden seal or *bulla*; a practice of Byzantine origin.

graffito. A rough drawing scratched on a wall or other suitable surface.

'great galley' [galea grossa]. Large medieval merchant galley first introduced by Venice at the end of the thirteenth century. More capacious than earlier galleys, they were usually sailed but they could be rowed *alla sensile* (*qv*) by at least 75 oarsmen per side.

Greek Fire. An incendiary material, probably composed of phosphorus and saltpetre (or possibly naphtha), that could be projected from flamethrowers or catapulted in pots. It could not be extinguished by water and possessed some of the attributes of napalm. Although incendiary compositions had been known since at least the fifth century BC, the development of Greek Fire with the above characteristics is conventionally attributed to one Callinicus in AD 673. For centuries it was a Byzantine monopoly, giving the Empire's dromōns a much-feared weapon in the bow-mounted 'siphons' that squirted Greek Fire.

ghurab. *See shīnī.*

handgrip. The extension of the loom (*qv*) of an oar.

harrāqa (plural harrāqāt). A Muslim ship type, first mentioned in the ninth century, whose principal feature was the fittings for Greek Fire.

hecatomb. A large-scale public sacrifice.

heel. Of a ship, angle of inclination from the upright.

Hellenistic. A term used by historians to denote the post-Classical Greek world, in the period roughly between the death of Alexander the Great in 323 BC and the hegemony of the Romans some three centuries later.

hemiolia (plural hemioliai). An ancient Greek galley with one and a half files of oars, the extra half-file being amidships at the greatest breadth of the hull. Probably the invention of Carian pirates, it was noted for its speed.

hendiadys. A figure of speech in which a single idea is conveyed by two linked words.

herringbone rig. *See cant.*

hippos (plural hippoi). A type of Phoenician merchantman.

histiokopos. Greek term for a merchant galley, literally translated as a ship that uses both sail and oars.

hogging. Bending or shearing of a ship's hull so that its ends drop relative to the middle; caused by wave action in a seaway.

hogging truss. A device stretching fore and aft on relatively long or weak vessels to prevent hogging (*qv*). In early craft it usually took the form of tensioned cables run over crutches amidships and fastened at the extremities of the hull.

holkas (plural holkades). An ancient Greek merchant ship (literally a 'towed ship' but merchant ships were often towed when not under sail).

hoplite. A heavily armed Greek infantryman.

hypēresia. The 'auxiliary group', 30-strong in a classical trireme, comprising 14 armed men and 16 specialist seamen who assist the captain.

hypozōma (plural hypozōmata). In ancient Greek galleys an undergirdling of tightened ropes pulling two points of a hull together to reduce tensile bending stresses.

ikria (plural). Platform decks at bow or stern; from Greek.

inboard. Generally, it is synonymous with inside the ship, but the inboard length of an oar is the distance between the fulcrum and the butt whereof the fulcrum may be placed.

interscalmium. The fore-and-aft distance between the centres of successive thole pins, the 'room' or spacing apart of oarsmen. Vitruvius gives the Greek equivalent as *dipēchiake*, which appears to suggest 'a space of two cubits', the space usually accepted for the 'room' of a Greek trireme.

karabos, karabion. In Byzantine sources a small oared warship; also occurs in Arabic sources.

katabatic winds. Those caused by cold air moving down the face of a mountain.

kataphrakta. *See cataphract.*

keel. Lowermost structural member of a ship's hull; in a frame-built vessel effectively the backbone, the frames forming the ribs.

keelson. Longitudinal member laid over and secured to floors inside a ship above the keel.

kelēs (plural keletes). A small merchant galley of the ancient Mediterranean noted for their speed (the term means 'racehorse'); sometimes applied to single-level galleys employed in naval service as scouts. Also occurs as the Roman *celox*.

kerkouros (plural kerkouroi). A type of ancient merchant galley, sometimes used as a supply ship to fighting fleets. It may have been derived from river craft and very large examples are known from ancient sources.

knot. Nautical measure of speed, 1 knot being one sea, or nautical, mile per hour. This equals 1 minute of latitude per hour or 1852 metres.

koumbarion (plural koumbaria). Byzantine description of a large and slow Muslim warship, probably a galley.

krater. A big, deep bowl for mixing wine; ancient Greek.

kybaia (Greek), cybaea (Latin). A capacious merchant galley of the ancient Mediterranean, noted for its box-like proportions.

la rancata. *See rancata.*

lee. The side or direction away from the wind or downwind (*leeward*); hence 'lee shore' is one onto which the wind is blowing.

lembos (plural lemboi). Used in a general sense for many types of oared small craft, but more specifically for a class of ancient Greek galley used in both peace and war between the third and first centuries BC; also occurs as the Latin *lembus*. It probably featured an extended forefoot, so could be converted into an auxiliary warship, and it was noted for its speed; bireme versions are recorded. *See also liburnian.*

lexica. Word books; dictionaries.

liburnian. A type of *lembos* supposedly invented by the Liburni, an Illyrian tribe noted for their piracy, it was originally single-banked but was later developed into a two-level galley. It was relatively light, fine-lined and associated with reconnaissance activities, and was much used by the Romans in the period of the Empire.

loom. The part of an oar between the thole (*qv*) or rowlock and the handle.

lusoria [navis]. Latin term for a small oared vessel, used for both trade and war; one of the late-Roman craft excavated at Mainz has been tentatively identified as of this type.

Mahanian. Concepts of sea power developed by the influential US naval historian Alfred Thayer Mahan (1840-1914), who emphasised the value of battle fleets and battlefleet actions, taking many of his examples from the rise of the Royal Navy in the age of sail.

manille. In *a scaloccio* (*qv*) rowing the hand-hold batten needed to grip the large diameter oars; also called the *clevis*.

maniskellion. Byzantine term for *askōma* (*qv*).

maintenen. In French *a scaloccio* (*qv*) galleys the spike extension of the oar gripped by the lead rower.

marqib. Generic Arabic term for ship but from the twelfth century often applied to a warship, although of of indeterminate characteristics.

metacentre. The point, usually designated M, in the middle plane of the ship through which the buoyancy force passes when the ship is inclined from the upright by a small angle.

metacentric height. The height of the metacentre (*qv*) above the ship's centre of gravity (usually designated G); it is, therefore, often designated GM.

moment of inertia (MoI). An entity relating to rotational motion analogous to mass in rectilinear motion. As force = mass x acceleration, so a couple (*ie* force x leverage) = MoI x angular acceleration. The MoI of a point mass M moving in a circle of radius r is Mr^2. The moment of inertia of an irregular body such as an oar, taken about the centre of gravity, can be expressed as Mk^2 where M is the mass of the oar and k, called the radius of gyration, is a characteristic distance that has usually to be determined by experiment.

moment of inertia about the thole (MIT). This is given by $M(k^2 +c^2)$ where M and k are as given in the moment of inertia definition and c is the distance between the centre of gravity and the oar and the thole.

monoxylon. A boat made from a single timber; a dugout.

mortise. In carpentry a recess cut to receive a tenon (*qv*).

musattah (plural musattahāt). Arab decked galley with rowers below and marines on deck; used from the twelfth century.

navis. A generic Latin term for ship.

navis cubiculata. Roman transport vessel with a cabin for passengers.

navis iudiciaria. Roman craft for ferrying high ranking officials and other important persons.

navis lusoria. *See lusoria.*

neck. The junction between the blade and the shaft of an oar.

newton. A unit of force, such that 1 newton is sufficient to accelerate a mass of 1 kilogram at a rate of 1 metre per second; 1 newton = 0.2248lbf.

oarbox. An outrigger (*qv*) boxed in to protect the oar crews, as employed in some Hellenistic and Roman warships.

oarloop. A strong band for attaching an oar to its thole pin. According to Homer, in ancient Greek ships it was made of leather, but in the trireme reconstruction *Olympias* rope grommets have proved to be better.

occulus. A device in the form of an eye, sometimes highly stylised, painted on the bows of ships since antiquity for reasons of religion or superstition.

Ommayid. *See Umayyad.*

ordinaire. The standard French galley of the seventeenth and eighteenth centuries, with four or five rowers per bench.

ossuary. A receptacle for the bones of the dead.

ousiakos. A large Byzantine warship but of unknown characteristics.

outboard. Generally synonymous with outside the ship, but in rowing the outboard

length of the the oar is the distance between the tip of the blade and the fulcrum, wherever the fulcrum may be in relation to the hull.

Outremer. The general medieval term for the crusading states, 'beyond the sea'.

outrigger. A structure built out from the hull proper to improve the efficiency of the oar system. In the trireme it provided a position for the third, uppermost, set of tholes and was called the *parexeiresia*. In medieval and later single-level galleys it allowed the use of longer, and hence more powerful, oars; it was then known as the *apostis* or *postizza*.

palamento. The rowing section of a galley's hull, and by extension the whole ensemble of rowers and their oars; the 'machinery' of a galley.

palmeta or palmetta. Fore or after deck platform of a medieval galley.

pamphylos. A large Byzantine warship associated with the province of Pamphylia; often used for transportation rather than battle.

papirella. A primitive reed raft; the type survives to this day on the Greek island of Corfu.

parados. The side gangway of an ancient Greek galley.

parexeiresia. *See outrigger.*

parrel. An assemblage of beads called trucks and wooden dividers called ribs strung onto a series of horizontal ropes. Forming a collar between yards and their masts, and designed to allow the yards to be raised and lowered easily, the parrel vaguely resembled a flexible abacus, with revolving beads intended to reduce friction while the ribs stopped them moving from side to side.

partisoni. In Venetian galley design, mathematically-based variations on the dimensions and shape of the midship section that determined the shape of the rest of the hull by establishing the rising and narrowing lines. Similar systems were in use through much of southern Europe in the Middle Ages and later; and known as 'whole moulding', the technique was employed for boats and small craft more widely and for even longer.

passe-vogue. In French *a scaloccio* (*qv*) galleys a mode of extremely strenuous rowing which required the rowers to push the oar beyond the bench in front of them (hence usually translated as 'bench crossing').

Patronne. Larger than usual French galley, with up to six rowers per bench; the flagship of a squadron commander.

pedagne. *See pontapiede.*

pentecontor. A Greek galley propelled by fifty oars; versions with both one and two levels of oars have been postulated.

pentērēs. A Greek galley with five files of oarsmen per side; otherwise known as a quinquereme, or a 'five'.

perineo. 'Spares', ancient Greek; used of both oars and supernumerary personnel.

periplous. In ancient Greek naval warfare the manoeuvre of outflanking the enemy's defensive line-abreast formation.

phaselos (Greek), phaselus (Latin). A slim, fast merchant galley varying greatly in size but principally associated with the carriage of passengers.

pianero. In *alla sensile* (*qv*) galleys the lead or head rower (nearest the gangway) who set the stroke. The outer oarsman continued to act as stroke when *a scaloccio* rowing was introduced.

picqu'a banc. *See toucher le banc.*

ploion (plural ploia). Greek generic term for ship or boat.

polis. Ancient greek for city, but by extension used of the government of a city; in modern terms, synonymous with 'state'.

polyreme. Generally, a galley with multiple files of oarsmen, but usually applied to those with more than three – *ie* those with more than triremes.

pontapiede. The foot board used in the stand-and-sit stroke of late medieval and Renaissance galleys. Called the *pedagne* in French.

postizza (plural postizze). Outrigger (*qv*) beams in medieval galleys into which the thole pins (*qv*) were inserted.

postizzo. In *alla sensile* (*qv*) galleys the second rower (from the gangway) on each bench.

power. Rate of doing work: eg, in rowing, mean pull x effective length x frequency of strokes. The effective power driving a hull is the resistance x the speed. Power in watts = newton metres per second.

proembolis, proembolion. A secondary ram mounted above the waterline in ancient galleys.

Punic. Relating to Carthage.

puntale in coverta. In Italian galley design literally the deck pillar or stanchion, but used to denote the depth in hold; often shortened to *puntale*.

pyxis. An ancient Greek casket.

qārib (plural qawārib). Arab ship type first mentioned in the ninth century AD; characteristics unknown.

qit'a (plural aqtā'). Muslim ship type mentioned from the twelfth century; characteristics indeterminate but usually a warship or military transport.

quarterol. In French *a scaloccio* (*qv*) galleys the fourth rower from the gangway on each bench.

quarter rowing. In French *a scaloccio* (*qv*) galleys the mode of rowing in which either the forward or the after half of the *chiourme* (*qv*) took turns at rowing while the other half rested.

quarter rudder. Steering device, usually in the form of an oar, situated not on the centreline as in modern boats but on the side of the hull aft (*ie* on the quarters). Steering oars might be positioned on one or both quarters and could be single or multiple according to the size and design of the craft.

quinquereme. *See pentērēs.*

quinterol. In French *a scaloccio* (*qv*) galleys the fifth rower from the gangway on each bench.

rancata. Short and fast stroke used by galley slaves when rowing *alla sensile* (*qv*); being restrained by foot manacles prevented the longer strokes of the *a strapada* (*qv*) style employed by free rowers.

rate of striking. The number of oar strokes per minute, or spm.

razzia. A raid in which destruction and plunder is the main object rather than permanent conquest; from the Algerian Arabic.

Réale. Extra large French galley, usually the prestige flagship of the galley fleet; could have up to seven rowers per bench.

red figure pottery. Ancient Mediterranean style characterised by figures left in the natural red of the pottery against a painted background of black.

rem à la barbe. Method of temporarily securing, when not in use, the oars of a French galley by looping a rope around the butt of each; the oar remained lashed to the thole and could be brought back into action very quickly. *See also fournelée* and *sur les filarets.*

return. The part of an oar stroke that separates successive pulls.

'room'. Of an oared ship or boat, a transverse section one *interscalmium* in length at any point in the fore-and-aft direction, and therefore accommodating the oarsmen working all the oars pivoted within it. *See also interscalmium.*

rhyton. A type of ancient stirrup cup, two-handled with a hole in the bottom through which wine was drunk.

saetia. *See sagitta.*

safīna (plural sufun). Generic Arabic term for ship, but sometimes used to denote warships or oared transports.

sagene. In ninth-twelfth century Byzantine sources a small fast galley used by pirates and raiders; probably developed by the Slavs of the Adriatic coast.

sagetia. *See sagitta.*

sagging. The opposite of hogging (*qv*).

sagitta. A fast galley, smaller than the usual warship, recorded from the eleventh century onwards; the type continued into the sixteenth century when the name had been modified into *sagetia* or *saetia*.

samaina. A type of war galley with a larger than usual hold capacity, associated with ancient Samos.

satoura, saktoura. A type of Muslim large warship mentioned in ninth-century Byzantine sources.

scholiast. An ancient commentator on Greek and Latin texts, usually from the Byzantine period.

shaft. Of an oar, the part extending from the thole (*qv*) to the blade.

shalandī (plural shalandiyyāt). Arab decked galley used from the tenth century; probably from the Greek *chelandion* (*qv*).

sheer. In the profile of a ship the upward curve towards the ends of the hull.

sheerstrake. The uppermost strake of the hull proper.

shīnī (plural shawānī). Used from the tenth century for both Byzantine and Muslim warships; in the twelfth century one source described it as a 140-oared galley, also described as a *ghurāb*.

shipshed. Building incorporating a slipway on which oared warships were normally hauled up when not at sea.

shroud. Heavy rope supporting a mast from behind and transversely.

siphon. A flamethrower for Greek Fire (*qv*) fitted in the bow of a Byzantine dromōn (*qv*).

slip. The movement of an oar blade through the water.

sotile, suttile (or other variant spellings). Of galleys, fine-lined or narrow, as distict from the great galley or *bastardella* (*qv*).

spm. Strokes per minute, rate of striking (*qv*) of oars.

stability. The strength of a ship's tendency to return to the upright, *ie* to right herself. The righting moment in tonne-metres = displacement in tonnes x metacentric height in metres x sine of the angle of heel.

stamnos. Ancient Greek jar.

stereobates. In architecture the solid mass of masonry forming the base of a wall or row of columns.

stopping. A setting composition brushed or trowelled into seams of planks to make them watertight.

strategos. The civil and military governor of a Byzantine Theme, or administrative district.

stretcher. Woodwork against which an oarsman presses his feet during the pull; also called the foot-stretcher.

stroke rate. *See rate of striking.*

sur les filarets. In French galleys the method of raising the oars on iron stanchions when not in use. The oars were more steeply angled than when *fournelées* (*qv*), so it was used in heavier weather conditions to prevent the oars being rolled under and damaged.

tarida (plural taride). Transport galley used by the Christian sea powers from the mid thirteenth century particulary for the carriage of horses; from the Arabic *tarrīda* (*qv*).

tarrīda (plural tarā'id). An Arab transport galley, especially one for carrying horses; twelfth-century examples could carry about 40 horses.

tachunautousai. In ancient Athens a category of selected 'fast-sailing' triremes, lightly built for agility and speed.

tenon. Rectangular block of hard wood, each half-length being fitted into opposing mortises (*qv*) to join two timbers side by side. Tenons may be locked into place by being drilled through and pegged.

tercerol. In French *a scaloccio* (*qv*) galleys the third rower from the gangway on each bench.

terzichio. The 'third' oarsman: the one nearest the thole in either *alla sensile* or *a scaloccio* rowing; also applied to his oar. Sometimes called the *terzarolo* in the West.

thalamos or thalamē. Ancient Greek for hold (of a ship).

thalamios. An oarsman in the lowest file of a three-level ancient Greek galley, usually translated into English as 'thalamian'; also descriptive of the equipment associated with such an oarsman. *Thalamites* was a Byzantine term for the same, and hence it is sometimes rendered in English as 'thalamite'.

thole, thole pin. A more-or-less vertical surface, particularly a pin, that takes the strain of the oar's pull. In ancient times the pin was used with an oarloop (*qv*), and later oars had a button (*qv*) to locate it correctly against the pin.

thranitēs (plural thranitai). Oarsman in a three-level ancient Greek galley who rowed through the outrigger (*qv*); probably derived from the architectural term for the top course of masonry.

Themes. Administrative districts of the Byzantine Empire and the basis of its military and naval organisation.

topwale. Used in this book of what was later to be called the gunwale – the thick longitudinal member that formed the top of the side of an open hull.

toucher le banc. In French *a scaloccio* (*qv*) galleys a ceremonial mode of rowing ('hitting the bench') in which the oar looms struck the benches in unison before the blades were lowered into the water; also called *picqu'a banc*.

triacontor. Ancient Greek galley rowed by thirty oarsmen.

trierarch. The captain of an ancient Greek galley (originally specifically commanding a *trièrēs*).

trièrēs. The Greek galley, better known as a trireme, whose characteristic feature was three files of oarsmen per side, rowing at three levels.

trihemiolia or trieremiolia. An ancient Greek galley with two full and one half file per side; probably invented in Rhodes and associated with light and fast naval craft.

trim. The fore and aft attitude of the ship; if the ship draws more water aft than forward, for example, she is said to 'trim by the stern'.

trireme. *See trièrēs.*

Umayyad or Ommayid. Relating to the first dynasty of the Muslim caliphate, which lasted from AD 661 until about 750 before being replaced by the 'Abbasids.

vangs. Braces from the peak of a gaff, sprit or lateen yard; led to the deck.

Varangians. Scandinavian rovers who penetrated the Byzantine Empire via the rivers of Russia. The Emperor later established a crack regiment recruited from these men, but the Varangian Guard eventually included other northerners, especially Anglo-Saxons.

wale. Thickened strakes of external hull planking acting as longitudinal strength members.

watt. The unit of power, equalling 1 newton-metre per second.

Ziridite. Relating to the eleventh-century Muslim dynasty established in Tunisia.

Zorzi's Principle. Advocated that for maximum leverage all the oarsmen on a bench should be positioned within half the distance between the gangway and the outrigger.

zirone. Inboard length of oar in Italian galleys. *See also fiol.*

zovo. In Italian galley design the deck beam at either end of the oared section of the hull which defined the beginning of the bow and stern sections.

zygios (plural zygioi). Oarsman in a three-level ancient Greek galley who sat on the thwarts (*zyga*), usually known in English as 'zygians'. At one time the upper level in two-level galleys, they became the middle level in triremes; in late-Greek (Byzantine) sources they are known as *zygités*.

Index